COOK'S SCIENCE

COOK'S SCIENCE

HOW TO UNLOCK FLAVOR IN 50 OF OUR FAVORITE INGREDIENTS

THE EDITORS AT AMERICA'S TEST KITCHEN
AND GUY CROSBY, PhD

BROOKLINE, MASSACHUSETTS

Copyright © 2016 by the Editors at America's Test Kitchen

America's Test Kitchen
17 Station Street, Brookline, MA 02445

Library of Congress Cataloging-in-Publication Data

Names: Crosby, Guy, editor. | America's Test Kitchen (Firm)
Title: Cook's science : how to unlock flavor in 50 of our favorite
   ingredients / the editors at America's Test Kitchen and Guy
   Crosby, PhD.
Description: Brookline, Massachusetts : America's Test Kitchen,
[2016] |
   Includes bibliographical references and index.
Identifiers: LCCN 2016020337 | ISBN 9781940352459
Subjects: LCSH: Cooking. | Food--Experiments. | Chemistry. |
Thermodynamics.
Classification: LCC TX651 .C6626 2016 | DDC 641.5--dc23
LC record available at https://lccn.loc.gov/2016020337

ISBN 978-1-940352-45-9
Hardcover: US $40.00 / $51.00 CAN

Manufactured in the United States of America
10 9 8 7 6 5 4 3 2 1

DISTRIBUTED BY
Penguin Random House Publisher Services
Tel: 800-733-3000

CHIEF CREATIVE OFFICER Jack Bishop
SCIENCE EDITOR Guy Crosby, PhD
EXECUTIVE EDITORS, COOK'S SCIENCE Molly Birnbaum
and Dan Souza
DESIGN DIRECTOR Greg Galvan
ASSOCIATE ART DIRECTOR Allison Boales
PHOTOGRAPHY DIRECTOR Julie Bozzo Cote
ASSOCIATE ART DIRECTOR, PHOTOGRAPHY Steve Klise
SENIOR STAFF PHOTOGRAPHER Daniel J. van Ackere
ADDITIONAL PHOTOGRAPHY Carl Tremblay and
Kevin White
ILLUSTRATORS John Burgoyne and MGMT. design, LLC
ASSISTANT PHOTOGRAPHY PRODUCER Mary Ball
PRODUCTION DIRECTOR Guy Rochford
SENIOR PRODUCTION MANAGER Jessica Lindheimer Quirk
PRODUCTION MANAGER Christine Walsh
IMAGING MANAGER Lauren Robbins
PRODUCTION AND IMAGING SPECIALISTS Heather Dube,
Sean MacDonald, Dennis Noble, and Jessica Voas
PROJECT MANAGERS Britt Dresser and Alyssa Langer
SCIENCE FELLOW/FACT CHECKER Carolyn Brotherton, PhD
TEST KITCHEN FELLOW Katherine Perry
COPYEDITOR Cheryl Redmond
PROOFREADER Ann-Marie Imbornoni
INDEXER Elizabeth Parson

Contents

Welcome to America's Test Kitchen

This book has been tested, written, and edited by the folks at America's Test Kitchen, a very real 2,500-square-foot kitchen located just outside of Boston. It is the home of *Cook's Illustrated* magazine and *Cook's Country* magazine and is the Monday-through-Friday destination for more than 60 test cooks, editors, and cookware specialists. Our mission is to test recipes over and over again until we understand how and why they work and until we arrive at the "best" version.

We start the process of testing a recipe with a complete lack of preconceptions, which means that we accept no claim, no technique, and no recipe at face value. We simply assemble as many variations as possible, test a half-dozen of the most promising, and taste the results blind. We then construct our own recipe and continue to test it, varying ingredients, techniques, and cooking times until we reach a consensus. As we like to say in the test kitchen, "We make the mistakes so you don't have to." The result, we hope, is the best version of a particular recipe, but we realize that only you can be the final judge of our success (or failure). We use the same rigorous approach when we test equipment and taste ingredients.

All of this would not be possible without a belief that good cooking, much like good music, is based on a foundation of objective technique. Some people like spicy foods and others don't, but there is a right way to sauté, there is a best way to cook a pot roast, and there are measurable scientific principles involved in producing perfectly beaten, stable egg whites. Our ultimate goal is to investigate the fundamental principles of cooking to give you the techniques, tools, and ingredients you need to become a better cook. It is as simple as that.

To see what goes on behind the scenes at America's Test Kitchen, check out our social media channels for kitchen snapshots, exclusive content, video tips, and much more. You can watch us work (in our actual test kitchen) by tuning in to *America's Test Kitchen* or *Cook's Country from America's Test Kitchen* on public television or on our websites. Listen in to *America's Test Kitchen Radio* (ATKradio.com) on public radio to hear insights that illuminate the truth about real home cooking. Want to hone your cooking skills or finally learn how to bake—with an America's Test Kitchen test cook? Enroll in one of our online cooking classes. If the big questions about the hows and whys of food science are your passion, join our Cook's Science experts for a deep dive. However you choose to visit us, we welcome you into our kitchen, where you can stand by our side as we test our way to the best recipes in America.

facebook.com/AmericasTestKitchen
twitter.com/TestKitchen
youtube.com/AmericasTestKitchen
instagram.com/TestKitchen
pinterest.com/TestKitchen
google.com/+AmericasTestKitchen

AmericasTestKitchen.com
CooksIllustrated.com
CooksCountry.com
CooksScience.com
OnlineCookingSchool.com

Recipes

Dressings, Sauces, Dips, and Salads

Soups, Stews, and Chilis

Pasta and Sauces

Rice, Grains, and Beans

Vegetables

Poultry

Meat

Fish and Shellfish

Tofu, Eggs, and Yogurt

Quick Breads, Pancakes, and Waffles

Cookies and Brownies

Yeast Breads, Rolls, and Pizza

Cakes

Pies, Tarts, Soufflés, and Fruit Desserts

DIY and Drinks

Introduction

How to Use This Book

For more than 20 years, we at America's Test Kitchen have worked to create foolproof recipes for the home cook. This is a carefully crafted process that hinges upon obsessively testing each variable, time and again. We get feedback from thousands of our readers every year (thank you!). Recipes are tested dozens and (in some cases) hundreds of times. The process involves a lot of trial and error. We learn from our failures as well as our triumphs.

But, perhaps most important, our recipe development process is successful because we take care to look at recipes through the lens of science. We use biology, chemistry, and physics to ask the big questions about how and why ingredients and cooking techniques work. These investigations help us to maneuver our way to a foolproof salt-and-pepper shrimp, supremely tender braised short ribs, or dense (but not too dense) almond cake. After all, we believe that knowledge, not experience, is what separates success from failure in the kitchen.

In the first volume in our series of *Cook's Illustrated* science books, *The Science of Good Cooking*, we explored 50 principles of cooking and how these ideas relate to basic kitchen techniques. In this new book, we examine the basic science of the ingredients themselves. Understanding how 50 favorite ingredients work—at the molecular level as well as at the stovetop—allows us to prepare them in ways that amplify their flavor and perfect their texture. How did we choose the ingredients? You will find items that crowd our pantry, produce we buy at the farmers' market, plus a few "special-occasion" options. There are many ways to prepare these ingredients, and many ways to make them taste much better, or much worse.

For every ingredient, we provide a science-based essay about where it comes from and the ways we use it in the kitchen. We conduct a test kitchen experiment to demonstrate its unique qualities and share the results; we include a full-page illustration; and we tie it all together with recipes that best showcase the ingredient.

You can use this volume as a traditional cookbook. The index of recipes starts on page xi. But you can also read it—front to back, or haphazardly, piece by piece. Read about individual ingredients when you plan to cook with them—or when you don't. The recipes in this book make great food, but their real purpose is to teach you how these key ingredients work.

Before we jump into the ingredients themselves, this introduction will cover our scientific process in the test kitchen, including the equipment we use, followed by an overview of the basic elements—the macronutrients—of all foods, and the way we perceive flavor.

One last note: This book is part of a larger project that we're very excited about. Check out our brand-new digital magazine (www.cooksscience.com), where we are exploring cutting-edge kitchen science and diving into the stories behind food and science. We've got cool new videos, plus all-new (and obsessively tested) recipes for the home cook. And it's free.

Our Process: The Test Kitchen

OUR PROCESS

Our magazines only publish a limited number of recipes in each issue, so each and every one gets serious, focused attention from a test cook. When they start work on a new recipe, the test cooks always begin without any preconceived ideas about what the "right" way to make it is. Thus, most of the magazine recipes begin with what's called a five-recipe test, in which the test cook prepares a set of diverse versions of the recipe. These may range from very old, traditional versions of a dish to cutting-edge takes on the same recipe. The test cook serves these to the other test cooks and editors on the team and together they critique the various recipes. In the weeks that follow, the test cook will pursue his or her own take on the recipe, experimenting broadly and informally with techniques, ingredients, and approaches before moving on to more controlled, scientific testing, tweaking individual variables one at a time. The other test cooks and editors on the team will taste all the different versions (sometimes as many as 130 different versions, as with our Old-Fashioned Chocolate Layer Cake recipe) and give feedback at each step in the process. This means that our recipes are always the product of many different palates and tastes working together, so it's not just one person's idea of spicy or salty or crispy that shapes the final product. But it's not finished there. The recipe goes through a lot of vetting before it's done, cooked by everyone from volunteer home cooks to in-house interns. We also do "abuse tests," making the recipe with the wrong equipment, or substituting out-there ingredients. We like to do it wrong, so you don't have to.

It takes months of research, testing and retesting, and writing and rewriting to develop a recipe at America's Test Kitchen. The test kitchen does tend to attract type A personalities, determined to find the best recipes, kitchenware, and grocery ingredients—no matter what. The endlessly curious team is always documenting and recording findings before, during, and after recipe development. We want to know exactly which ingredients and techniques are necessary to ensure perfect results every time, and why those ingredients and techniques are so essential. Extensive research goes into every recipe and story.

And, most important: The scientific method, which underpins everything we do in the test kitchen, is one of the most powerful tools for recipe development.

THE SCIENTIFIC METHOD

Every day we enter the kitchen with questions. Lots of questions. How do we make the best roast chicken? When should we add sugar to egg whites when making meringue? Where in the oven should we place a sheet pan of cookies to get crackled tops and browned bottoms? Who's making lunch?

Lunch making aside, these questions form the foundation of all the work we do in the test kitchen. We turn our inquisitive nature into answers and solutions through the scientific method. It may sound grand, but the scientific method isn't fancy; rather, it's a pragmatic way to get from point A to point B. From a question we form a hypothesis, or prediction, about how something works. We may hypothesize that it doesn't matter when you add sugar to egg whites when whipping up a meringue, for example. Then we design an experiment to test that hypothesis. We make three batches of meringue that are identical in every way except for when we add the sugar—the one variable we want to test. After we perform the test, we do a double-blind tasting, where neither the cook running the test nor the tasters know which sample is which. After we repeat the test a few more times we examine the results to determine whether our hypothesis was correct or not. If we conclude that we were indeed correct, we may use that knowledge to make better meringue cookies. If our hypothesis is wrong, we go back to the drawing board, revise our prediction, and start the testing process again. It's a slow process not especially well suited to the fast-paced world of food publishing, but it's something America's Test Kitchen values so highly that we take the time and resources to do it right.

WHERE LAB MEETS KITCHEN

TEXTURE ANALYZER

When it comes to food, there is no better way to measure and analyze than with our five senses. In the end, if a dish doesn't taste, look, smell, sound, and feel good we aren't interested. That being said, when we're trying to control variables in a well-designed experiment, quantitative instruments are invaluable tools. The CT3 Texture Analyzer from Brookfield Engineering is a sophisticated testing machine that can calculate a wide range of physical properties that are proven to correlate with human sensory evaluation of food. By pressing various probes into a piece of food (or pulling that food in opposite directions) it can quantify attributes like toughness, chewiness, stickiness, and gumminess. In this book we use it widely, from comparing the firmness of apple varieties before and after cooking to quantifying the difference in tenderness between steak cut with or across the grain.

MOISTURE ANALYZER

The Torbal ATS120 Moisture Analyzer is actually a very simple instrument. It combines a small oven compartment with a highly sensitive scale. The oven slowly evaporates moisture from the food and the scale tracks weight loss. If a food, such as a roast, contains both fat and water (which both contribute to our perception of juiciness), we can use this instrument to determine how much moisture is actually retained during cooking.

WHAT WE SEND TO THE LAB AND WHY

With a 2,500-square-foot kitchen and 50 test cooks and editors we can do a lot, but it's important to know when to delegate. For more sophisticated analysis we frequently turn to independent labs like Certified Labs. We send samples of cooked pasta to determine how much salt was absorbed during cooking, batches of strained yogurt to measure protein, fat, and sugar content compared to store-bought Greek yogurt, and samples of brewed tea to see which steeping method yields the most caffeine. We also partner with scientists at top universities, like Benjamin Wolfe at Tufts University, to analyze the types of bacteria growing in samples of homemade kimchi fermented at different temperatures.

HOW WE USE DATA TO MAKE GREAT FOOD

Who would have guessed that data analysis would be such a hot topic in 2016? The fact of the matter is we've been using data in the test kitchen to test equipment, rate supermarket staples, and inform our recipe development for more than two decades. In this book we gather both qualitative and quantitative data for a huge range of ingredients. We tracked moisture loss in pork shoulder roasts cooked at four different temperatures to find the ideal temperature for juicy, tender results. To find out if wild and farmed salmon need to be treated differently, we cooked samples to different internal temperatures and tasted them. And we compared the calcium content of dried cannellini beans to their final cooked texture to look for a correlation. Numbers themselves are meaningless out of context. But when we pair good data with rigorous testing and tasting we uncover hidden truths and surprising trends that push us forward in our pursuit of great home cooking.

The Basic Elements of Food

The key to good food lies in its composition. All food can be scientifically characterized by its composition of macro- and micronutrients. As the word implies, macronutrients take up a good deal of real estate, making up about 98 to 99 percent of the weight of a food, while the micronutrients make up the rest. Yet there are only four macronutrients: water, protein, carbohydrate, and fat.

WATER

In many foods, water is the most abundant component. Meat, poultry, fish, fruits, vegetables, and many dairy products all contain anywhere from 60 to 95 percent water by weight. Water is required for proteins and carbohydrates to function in food. Water also acts as a solvent for chemical and enzymatic reactions. Without water most molecules would be locked in place without the ability to move about and function.

HYDROGEN BONDS HOLD FOOD TOGETHER

Water is a very simple molecule and its properties depend entirely on its chemical structure. A single molecule of water contains two hydrogen atoms and an oxygen atom. Each hydrogen atom is bonded to the oxygen atom by two shared electrons, forming what is known as a covalent bond between the atoms.

The lone oxygen atom is said to be more "electronegative" than the hydrogen atoms, meaning the electrons in each covalent bond are held closer to the oxygen atom. This means that each water molecule holds both partial positive and partial negative electrostatic charges, charges that create electrostatic attraction between individual water molecules. And what form does that attraction take? Hydrogen bonds.

You may be asking, "Why are we talking about hydrogen bonds when all I want to do is cook good food?" But hydrogen bonds have a profound effect on the properties of water molecules—as well as their interactions with other molecules in food, especially proteins and carbohydrates. These interactions underlie many of the decisions we make in the kitchen.

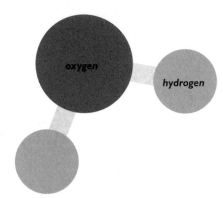

WATER CONTENT IN COMMON INGREDIENTS

FOOD	AVERAGE WATER CONTENT
Cucumber	96%
Silken Tofu	88%
Chicken Breast	76%
Soft/Fresh Goat Cheese	60%
Dried Apples	20%
Honey	16%
Dried Soybeans	12%

CLOSE UP: HYDROGEN BONDING

Water contains a partially negatively charged oxygen atom bound to two partially positively charged hydrogen atoms. This simple structure sets up the water molecule to interact with its neighboring water molecules through the formation of hydrogen bonds: weak electrostatic bonds between oppositely charged oxygen and hydrogen atoms. Water molecules in both liquid and ice phases are engaged in extensive hydrogen bonding, and these interactions lend water some of its special physical properties.

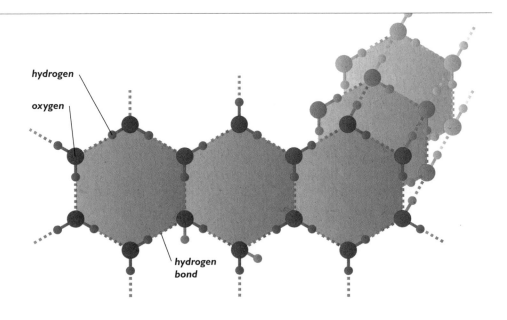

Hydrogen bonds are relatively weak electrostatic bonds, but because each molecule of water can form hydrogen bonds with at least three other molecules of water, it takes substantial energy to break these bonds. That's why water has such a high boiling point for such a small molecule: The water molecules must be wrenched apart in order to move faster as they are heated. Hydrogen bonds are the reason why water forms ice crystals when it freezes, and why water dissolves other molecules like sugars, acids, alcohols, and proteins (all capable of hydrogen bonding with water themselves). Hydrogen bonds between water molecules also explain why water and fat do not mix.

Any molecule containing what is called a hydroxy group (-OH) or an amino group (-N-H) is capable of forming hydrogen bonds with water. A molecule of sucrose (table sugar) contains eight hydroxy groups; this is why sugar is very soluble in water. In fact, sugar hydrogen bonds so well with water that it literally slows down the motion of the water molecules, which explains in part why concentrated sugar solutions like honey are so viscous. Because sugar forms so many hydrogen bonds, it is able to "bind" water molecules, which explains why sugar is hygroscopic, or able to absorb water from the air, especially in humid conditions.

Water also bonds strongly with proteins, which contain both amino and hydroxy groups. Proteins in the dry state, like the proteins in flour, for example, are completely immobile. But when water is added, it coats the surface of large protein molecules by forming many hydrogen bonds. The coating of water enables the dry proteins to change their shape. In flour, the two proteins, called gliadin and glutenin (see page 303), become flexible when wetted with water, just like a rigid piece of dry spaghetti becomes flexible when it is boiled in water. This enables the glutenin and gliadin to form chemical cross-links with each other. The result is the formation of stretchable, flexible gluten in flour. It would not be possible to make bread or pasta out of dough if it weren't for the water molecules hydrogen bonding with the proteins.

CRISP OR SOGGY? FREE, ADSORBED, AND BOUND WATER IS WHY

Water occurs in three forms in food: free, adsorbed, and bound. Free water is water that can literally be squeezed out of a food, like juice from an orange or the liquid that separates from yogurt. Adsorbed water is water that is attached to the surface of proteins, sugars, and large sugar molecules called polysaccharides (such as starch) through the formation of hydrogen bonds. It takes energy to separate the water molecules from the surface of proteins and polysaccharides, so it is not free flowing, and is more difficult to remove. The hydrated gluten proteins in bread dough are an example of adsorbed water. Finally, there is bound water. Bound water is locked inside of crystals, such as the crystalline forms of starch. Foods with little free and adsorbed water are dry and crispy, while foods with high levels are soft and soggy.

These three forms of water determine the texture of food—and its susceptibility to the growth of harmful microorganisms. Foods that contain high levels of free and adsorbed water will support the growth of bacteria, yeast, and mold, which cannot grow in a food that contains very little water, like dry pasta. (Food scientists have developed a method for measuring the amount of free and adsorbed water in food called the water activity of a food. Designated Aw, water activity is a dimensionless scale from 0–1. For more, see page 300.)

WHY DOES ICE FLOAT? (HYDROGEN BONDING)

The water molecule is particularly well set up to form hydrogen bonds, because it contains both a hydrogen bond acceptor (the partially negatively charged oxygen atom) and two hydrogen bond donors (the partially positively charged hydrogen atoms). The ideal arrangement of hydrogen bonding in water is one in which each water molecule is hydrogen-bonded to as many as four neighboring water molecules. And this highly ordered arrangement occurs in solid ice, in part because there is little thermal energy to disrupt the bonds. However, when the temperature rises, and the ice melts into a liquid, the increased thermal motion disrupts the bonds. This means that the hydrogen bonds in liquid water still exist, but are more transient, and less ordered. The result? Water molecules can pack more closely as a liquid, resulting in a liquid phase that is denser than its solid phase, and ice cubes that float in your glass of water.

HOW WATER LIVES IN FOOD

Like the water in fruit juices or yogurt, free water is free flowing and easily separated or removed from food.

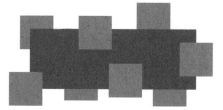

Adsorbed water is water attached to the surface of hydrophillic molecules, like proteins and carbohydrates. It is not free flowing and is difficult to remove.

Bound water is contained within a crystal structure, like water molecules in a starch granule, and is not removed from food with heat.

All of the foods we reach for in the pantry have a different pH level, ranging from acidic to alkaline. We charted a few.

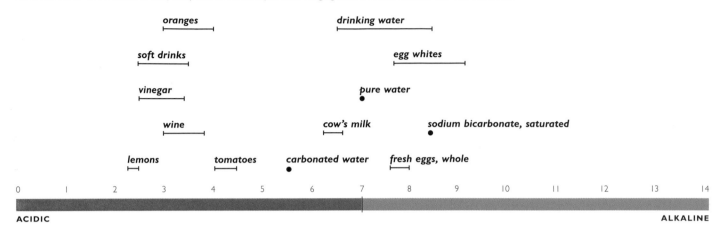

ACIDIC   ALKALINE

WHY DOES THIS TASTE SOUR? WHY IS MY MEAT MUSHY? WHY IS MY COOKIE SO PALE? PH AND WATER

Finally we come to the role of water, acids, and alkalis in food. The strength of acids and alkalis (or bases) is measured by the pH scale. This scale is something we refer to, and take into account, time and time again when cooking and developing recipes.

Water is a critical factor in determining the strength of acids and alkalis. When acids dissolve in water (H_2O) they form hydronium ions (H_3O^+), while alkalis form hydroxide ions (HO^-). The pH scale expresses the concentration of these ions in water. Stronger acids form higher concentrations of hydronium ions, while stronger alkalis form higher concentrations of hydroxide ions. The pH scale ranges from 0 to 14. Pure water has a pH of 7 and is completely neutral—neither acid nor alkaline. The pH of acids ranges from 0 to just a little below 7, while alkalis range from a little greater than 7 to 14.

The pH of a food affects many things. For example, most acids taste sour or tart. The pH of meat affects its tenderness and ability to hold water. Pork with a pH around 6.5 is more tender and moist than pork with a pH of 5.5 (see page 38). The Maillard reaction is responsible for forming the flavor and color of many delicious foods such as chocolate, roasted meat, coffee, and bread crust; the Maillard reaction proceeds almost 500 times faster at pH 9 than at pH 5. That's why cookies baked with alkaline baking soda (sodium bicarbonate) are a darker brown than cookies baked without. Enzymes play many important roles in food such as forming flavors and softer textures. The activity of an enzyme is dependent on the pH of the water surrounding the enzyme. Bacteria grow very slowly in foods with a pH lower than 4.6. That's why acidic tomato sauce and mayonnaise last longer in the refrigerator than baked goods, which are more alkaline. (For more on pH and fermentation, see page 214.)

PROTEIN

Proteins play many essential roles for both plants and animals, from providing structure in the form of muscle tissue to working as enzymes that are catalysts for the chemical reactions in photosynthesis; from hormones such as insulin, transporters of oxygen in the form of hemoglobin, to key components of the immune system such as the cytokines, and more.

Compared with water, proteins are very large, complex molecules. They are composed of dozens to many hundreds of amino acids, linked together in the form of a long chain. Some proteins, such as collagen, are composed of multiple extended chains of amino acids. These are fibrous proteins, and they are insoluble. Other proteins, called globular proteins, are folded into three-dimensional shapes—like those in egg whites or enzymes—and are soluble.

The human body derives only about 10 percent of its daily requirement of energy from protein in the diet. The bulk of the energy comes from carbohydrates and fat. That's because proteins are used to build essential components of the body rather than broken down and metabolized for energy. When proteins are consumed, they are broken down to individual amino acids, and then absorbed into the body, where they are reconstructed into new proteins, or smaller fragments of proteins called peptides.

The DNA in all living things determines when proteins are made, and how much is made. DNA encodes for 20 different amino acids. Some of these amino acids can be made in our body, while others, called essential amino acids, must be consumed in the diet because our body cannot make them. There are 10 essential amino acids we must obtain from our food. (Some sources cite nine essential amino acids. The 10th, tyrosine, which we include in our count, is essential only during periods of growth, which makes it very important for children.) Quinoa (page 335) is a good source, as is the combination of rice (page 313) and beans (page 341).

The protein content of foods varies quite widely. Raw flank steak and skin-on boneless chicken breasts both contain about 21 percent protein by weight, whole egg contains 13 percent protein, ripe tomatoes contain 1 percent, all-purpose flour contains between 10 and 12 percent protein (depending on the brand), and dry red kidney beans contain about 22 percent.

COMMON PROTEINS

The types of proteins we'll encounter in this book vary widely.

GLIADIN AND GLUTENIN

The proteins in flour that come together with water to form gluten in dough are called gliadin and glutenin.

RENNET

Rennet is the protein, traditionally from the stomachs of calves, that curdles the casein proteins in milk to form cheese.

MYOGLOBIN

Myoglobin is the red-pigmented protein responsible for the colors of raw and cooked meat.

ENZYMES

Important enzymes in foods we eat include alliinase, which forms the flavor of crushed garlic and chopped onion. Myrosinase creates the flavor of all cruciferous vegetables. Lipoxygenase forms many of the flavors in fresh fruits. Polyphenol oxidase causes potatoes, avocados, and apples to turn brown.

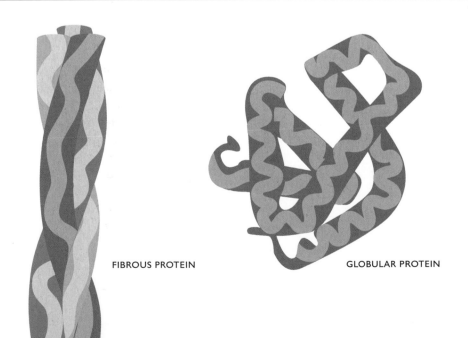

FIBROUS PROTEIN   GLOBULAR PROTEIN

THE STRUCTURE OF PROTEINS

Proteins are composed of amino acids (there are 20 different amino acids encoded by DNA) linked together through strong covalent bonds. Some proteins are composed of long, extended chains of amino acids—like those in collagen. Others, called globular proteins, are folded into three-dimensional shapes—like those in myoglobin in muscle tissue.

Simple carbohydrates are mono- and disaccharides, such as glucose and lactose, and are
found in high concentrations in fruits, dairy
products, and sugar-added foods like desserts
and soft drinks. Complex carbohydrates are any
longer polymers of sugars, including starch and
fructo-oligosaccharides. While we often think
of complex carbohydrates as healthier for us
than simple ones, the most important detail in
carbohydrate nutrition comes in how the sugars
are packaged. Complex carbohydrates that are
components of whole grains, vegetables, and
legumes are good for us because our body
metabolizes the sugars more slowly when
they're bound up with fiber. In contrast, our
body quickly digests and absorbs the sugars that
make up complex carbohydrates when they're
eaten in the form of refined grains. Refined
grains, like white flour and white rice, have been
milled to remove the bran and germ. These
outer coatings of the grain contain fiber, which
slows the digestion of sugar, as well as many
nutrients, like B vitamins.

Amino acids themselves are small molecules composed of carbon, hydrogen, oxygen, and
nitrogen atoms. A few also contain sulfur atoms. The sequence of the amino acids in a protein determines its three-dimensional structure and function.

There are a number of ways to change proteins. When foods are cooked, proteins
undergo a change in their 3-D structure called denaturation, which irreversibly changes
their function. When enzymes are heated above their denaturation temperature they lose all
activity. The same thing happens to muscle proteins in meat when cooked. Once it's denatured, it is impossible to restore cooked meat back to its raw state. When eggs are cooked
their proteins are denatured and turn into a solid. The water in the egg does not evaporate
but becomes trapped inside the denatured protein matrix. In addition to heat, proteins can
also be denatured by acids and alcohol. For example, marinating raw fish in lime juice or sake
to make ceviche gives the fish a cooked appearance.

CARBOHYDRATE

The word "carbohydrate" is based on the general formula for this family of molecules:
$C_n(H_2O)_m$. That is, for every carbon atom (C) there is one molecule of water (H_2O), so
carbohydrates are a form of "hydrated carbon." Carbohydrates in their simplest form, such
as glucose and fructose, are called monosaccharides. Monosaccharides contain a single ring
of atoms composed of carbon, hydrogen, and oxygen. Carbohydrates that contain two
rings of atoms bonded together are called disaccharides. These include common table sugar
(sucrose) and the milk sugar called lactose.

Sucrose is formed by bonding one molecule of glucose with one molecule of fructose,
along with the loss of one molecule of water. When sucrose is heated to very high temperatures (500 degrees and higher), all of the water molecules are driven off, leaving nothing but
atoms of black carbon (charcoal). If the sucrose is not heated so high (around 340 degrees),
only some of the molecules of water are lost, resulting in the formation of delicious-
smelling caramel.

After the simple mono- and disaccharides come more complex oligosaccharides. These
are larger molecules, containing three to 10 monosaccharides bonded together in a single
chain. The most common examples in food are called fructo-oligosaccharides (FOS),

CLOSE UP ON CARBOHYDRATES

Carbohydrates come in a number of forms.
Monosaccharides are the simplest, containing
a single ring of atoms. Disaccharides contain two rings of atoms bonded together.
Oligosaccharides are larger, with between three
and 10 monosaccharides bonded together. And
polysaccharides are very large, with thousands
of sugar molecules bonded together.

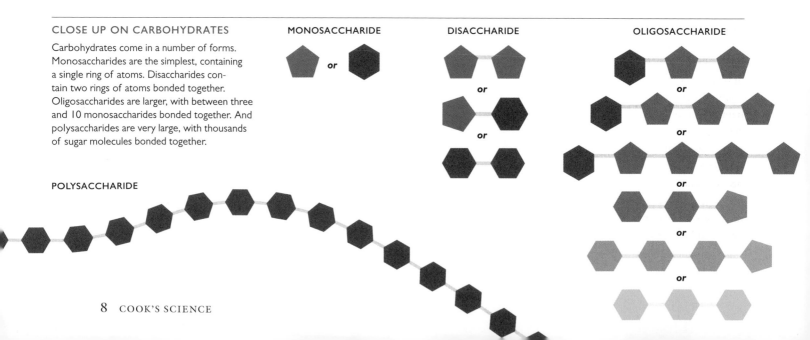

MONOSACCHARIDE · DISACCHARIDE · OLIGOSACCHARIDE · POLYSACCHARIDE

AMYLOPECTIN

AMYLOSE

TWO STARCHES: AMYLOPECTIN AND AMYLOSE

Starch is composed of amylopectin and amylose molecules, both of which are giant polymers of glucose molecules linked end to end. To put the size in perspective, a potato starch granule is about 60 microns wide, or 30 times wider than the length of a whole *E. coli* cell. Amylopectin is highly branched. In contrast, amylose is dense, lacking branching points, and actually folds into a tightly wound helix.

composed of a glucose unit plus two to 10 fructose molecules linked together in short chains, and occuring in many vegetables, including Jerusalem artichokes, leeks, onions, and asparagus. The oligosaccharides are a good source of food for the trillions of bacteria living in our gut. But sometimes they cause the formation of too much uncomfortable gas.

Finally, there are polysaccharides. These are very large molecules composed of thousands of sugar molecules linked together in very long straight chains, and in highly branched structures. The most common examples in food are starch, pectin, and cellulose. Starch contains two very large molecules called amylose and amylopectin. Amylose is a long chain of several thousand glucose molecules linked together end to end. Amylopectin is much larger, containing 5,000 to 20,000 glucose molecules bonded together in a highly branched structure that resembles a tree, with many long and short branches attached to a central trunk. An immense number of amylose and amylopectin molecules come together in starch granules, which, despite the large number of molecules, are still too small to be seen by the eye. Cornstarch (page 323) is a good example; it appears as a very fine powder, made of agglomerated starch granules. The ratio of amylose to amylopectin is also important. In potato starch, this ratio changes depending on the variety of potato, and will greatly affect the final texture of your mashed potatoes.

There are three other important types of complex polysaccharides: pectin, cellulose, and hemicellulose. Pectin is composed of a number of different sugar molecules linked together in very long chains with numerous short branches of sugar molecules. Hemicelluloses contain many of the same sugars found in pectin, but arranged in different sequences. Pectin and hemicellulose are important components of plant cell walls. Both act as a glue to hold the cellulose fibrils together in cell walls (see page 177). Pectin also acts as the glue that holds plant cells together, and is wildly important when making jams and jellies (see page 276 for Classic Strawberry Jam). Calcium ions are very important in determining the strength of pectin. When vegetables are boiled in water, the calcium ions are removed and the pectin network is weakened and breaks down, causing the vegetables to soften. This explains why most canned tomatoes contain calcium chloride as an added ingredient to strengthen the pectin and keep the tomatoes from becoming soft and mushy.

FAT

The final macronutrient is fat. Fat occurs in food in two forms: solid and liquid.

A solid fat, like butter, is a solid at room temperature but melts slightly above. A liquid fat, such as vegetable oil, is liquid at room temperature but may solidify in the refrigerator. The difference is the temperature at which they melt. And this difference has everything to do with their chemical structure.

Chemically, both solid fats and oils are classified as triglycerides. A triglyceride is composed of three fatty acids bonded to a single molecule of glycerol, which is a polyol, or sugar alcohol. Triglycerides contain many carbon and hydrogen atoms and a much smaller number of oxygen atoms. There are two types of fatty acids: saturated and unsaturated. Fatty acids containing one or more carbon-carbon double bonds are said to be "unsaturated." A saturated fatty acid contains no carbon-carbon double bonds. Saturated fatty acids are straight linear molecules like a pencil. And, just like pencils packed in a box, triglycerides containing lots of saturated fatty acids can pack together and form crystalline structures that are solid at room temperature. So triglycerides that are high in saturated fatty acids like butter are solids at room temperature. The presence of carbon-carbon double bonds produces a bend in the structure of unsaturated fatty acids. Triglycerides high in unsaturated fatty acids, like vegetable oils, cannot form crystalline structures at room temperature, so they are liquids. The fat in fish is highly unsaturated and will not solidify in very cold water. Cocoa butter, the fat in chocolate, is high in saturated fatty acids, which gives chocolate the special property of melting in your mouth but not in your hand. Most of the fat in beef is solid at room temperature because it is high in saturated fatty acids.

Because triglycerides contain many carbon and hydrogen atoms and few oxygen atoms, they cannot participate in hydrogen bonding with water molecules. Therefore, they are insoluble in water. In fact, the high number of carbon and hydrogen atoms makes triglycerides repel water molecules. That's why oil and water don't mix.

SATURATED OR UNSATURATED FATTY ACIDS? THAT CAN MEAN SOLID OR LIQUID FATS

Triglycerides are composed of three fatty acids linked to a glycerol backbone. The presence of double bonds within the fatty acid chains affects how efficiently fats can pack together. Saturated fats do not have double bonds, and can therefore pack together closely. Unsaturated fatty acids have one or more double bonds, and their bent or kinked structure prevents the long carbon chains from packing closely together. While food fats that contain mostly saturated fats are solids, those with a significant amount of unsaturated fatty acids are liquids at room temperature. This is why butterfat, which is made up of primarily saturated fatty acids, is a solid, and olive oil, composed mostly of a mono-unsaturated fat, is a liquid.

SATURATED FATTY ACID

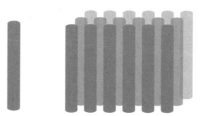

Saturated fat has no double bonds and a linear shape. Saturated fatty acids pack tight and are likely to be solid at room temperature.
Example: Butterfat

UNSATURATED FATTY ACID

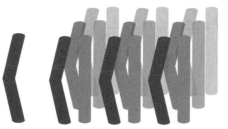

Unsaturated fat has one or more double bonds, lending a bent shape to the fatty acid. Unsaturated fatty acids pack more loosely, and the resulting oil will be liquid at room temperature.
Example: Olive oil

Finally we come to the smoke point of oils. Highly refined oils have very high smoke points. This is because the presence of small amounts of impurities, such as particulate matter and free fatty acids (or, fatty acids not attached to any other molecules), greatly depress the smoke point of oils. Extra-virgin olive oil (EVOO) has a lower smoke point than refined soybean oil because unrefined EVOO contains lots of particulate matter. As oil is used for cooking and frying the level of free fatty acids increases so the smoke point decreases.

MICRONUTRIENTS

Finally, micronutrients, which occur in very small amounts in most foods, include trace minerals and vitamins. Humans need very small amounts of these in the diet—but they are indeed essential. Micronutrients have an effect on more than human health, however. It is well-established that the more abundant micronutrients such as calcium and phosphorus affect the texture of certain foods such as legumes. Other micronutrients such as zinc, copper, and selenium are required for the activity of certain enzymes in food. Micronutrients such as magnesium and iron are key parts of the colored pigments chlorophyll and myoglobin, respectively. Certain minerals, such as iron and aluminum, act as catalysts for oxidation reactions that can cause rancidity of fats and oils, as well as a "warmed-over flavor."

SOURCES OF COMMON MICRONUTRIENTS

MICRONUTRIENT	BEST SOURCES*	NATURAL ROLES IN FOOD SOURCES
Iron (Fe)	Oysters, beef, white beans, spinach	Iron is a component of hemoglobin, which transports oxygen in the blood. Iron is also a required cofactor of many enzymes.
Selenium (Se)	Brazil nuts, tuna	Selenium is an element in the rare amino acid selenocysteine, a building block of enzymes called selenoproteins.
Vitamin A (beta-carotene, retinol)	Cod liver oil, sweet potatoes, carrots	In plants, vitamin A serves as a membrane-bound antioxidant.
Vitamin C (ascorbic acid)	Guava, broccoli, oranges	Vitamin C is the most abundant cellular antioxidant in plants.
Vitamin B12 (cobalamin)	Clams, beef liver, fortified cereals	Vitamin B12 is biosynthesized only by bacteria and archaea microbes and is required for the production of the amino acid methionine.

*These are the sources with the highest concentrations on a weight basis, not necessarily the most delicious sources.

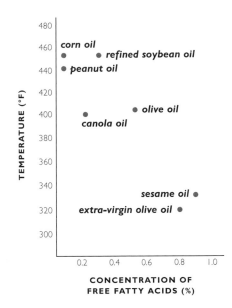

SMOKE POINT—AND FLAVOR

The greater the concentration of free fatty acids in oil, the lower its smoke point. More refined oils, which have undergone more processing steps to remove solids, tend to have higher smoke points as a result. Extra-virgin olive oil has around 0.8 percent free fatty acids, and a smoke point of 320 degrees, whereas refined canola oil has free fatty acids closer to 0.2 percent and a smoke point of 400 degrees. However problematic the free fatty acids may be when cooking with oils, these compounds are often the major source of flavor in our favorite fats. For instance, the green apple or fruity notes of extra-virgin olive oil come from volatile aldehydes such as hexanal and Z-3-hexenal. These aroma compounds are derived from the enzymatic breakdown of linoleic and linolenic acids, which are long-chain fatty acids abundant in olives.

Elements of Flavor Perception

When it comes to deciding what foods we like, and what we choose to eat, flavor is by far the most important factor. But what is flavor? Much of flavor comes from taste and smell, but flavor is not something we sense with our mouth or our nose alone. Instead, our perception of flavor begins as a combination of senses—including smell, taste, touch, and sound. Where flavor is ultimately perceived, however, is in our brain. Electrical signals from the taste cells in our mouth and olfactory cells in our nose are sent to the brain where they are processed and interpreted as the flavor of what we are eating.

TASTE

TASTE DETECTION THRESHOLDS

We have the ability to taste salty, sweet, bitter, sour, and umami (and, some scientists say, fat) with the taste receptors on our tongue and in our mouth. Here is a chart listing three different compounds, and the threshold at which we can detect their taste. Note: 1% is the same as 1 part per hundred, which can be written as 1 part/10^2. (For smell detection thresholds, see page 14.)

COMPOUND	DETECTION THRESHOLD	FLAVOR, SOURCE
Sucrose	0.3%	Sweet, Sugar
Salt	0.02%	Salty, Sodium chloride
Quinine	0.0002%	Bitter, Tonic water

Many people automatically assume that "taste" is synonymous with "flavor." This is not true. Taste is the sense that comes straight from the receptors on our tongue and in our mouth. It is hardwired into our brain—our chromosomes contain genes that code for the production of receptor proteins located on the surface of taste cells. These receptors detect the presence of molecules in our mouth, and trigger the taste cells to send electrical signals to the brain. There are proven receptors for at least five different tastes, and possibly a sixth: sweet, salty, sour, bitter, umami—and fat. The presence of sweet, salt, sour, and bitter has been known for a long time, while umami, which means meaty or savory, was only discovered in the early part of the 20th century by a Japanese chemist. It was accepted as the fifth taste when the receptor for the amino acid glutamate was identified in 2000.

Anthropologists believe our sense of taste evolved as a means of survival. We need sweet-tasting sugars for energy, and salt to maintain the fluid level in our body. The taste of sour suggests spoilage, while bitter is a warning against eating potentially toxic substances such as alkaloids in plants. Its not surprising that we are about a thousand times more sensitive to bitter taste than sweet. Umami signals the presence of essential amino acids required to build important new proteins in our body. Initial evidence that fat, or "oleogustus," is the sixth basic taste was presented in the journal *Chemical Senses* in 2015. It makes sense that humans evolved the ability to taste fat, as fat is a source of energy, like sugars.

SMELL

While the tastes we can sense are limited to only five or six basic types, the number of odors we can smell is enormous. It is estimated that humans possess about 350 to 400 different receptors for smell and can differentiate more than 10,000 different odors. The odors that we can recognize are learned based on experience rather than hardwired into our brain at birth. Odors from food enter our nose by two different routes. Orthonasal smell is what we smell by sniffing in through our nose. Retronasal smell is caused by odors that enter from the back of the mouth when food is chewed and swallowed and that we perceive on the exhale. Studies show that retronasal smell is the most important contributor not just for smell but also for the flavor of food. (Try holding your nose and see how much flavor you can detect when eating. A fresh tomato will taste somewhat sweet and sour, and perhaps even a little salty, but without smelling the aroma we would not be able to recognize it as a tomato.) Molecules that we can taste, like sweet sugars and sour acids, are not volatile, so we cannot

CLOSE UP: TASTE AND SMELL

Our systems for smell and taste are complicated and interconnected. Smell begins, of course, in the nose, where scent molecules trigger a system that begins with smell receptors and ends with signals sent to the brain. Taste begins in the mouth, where receptors for salty, sweet, bitter, sour, and umami likewise send signals. These nerve impulses are interpreted by the brain to create the larger sense of flavor.

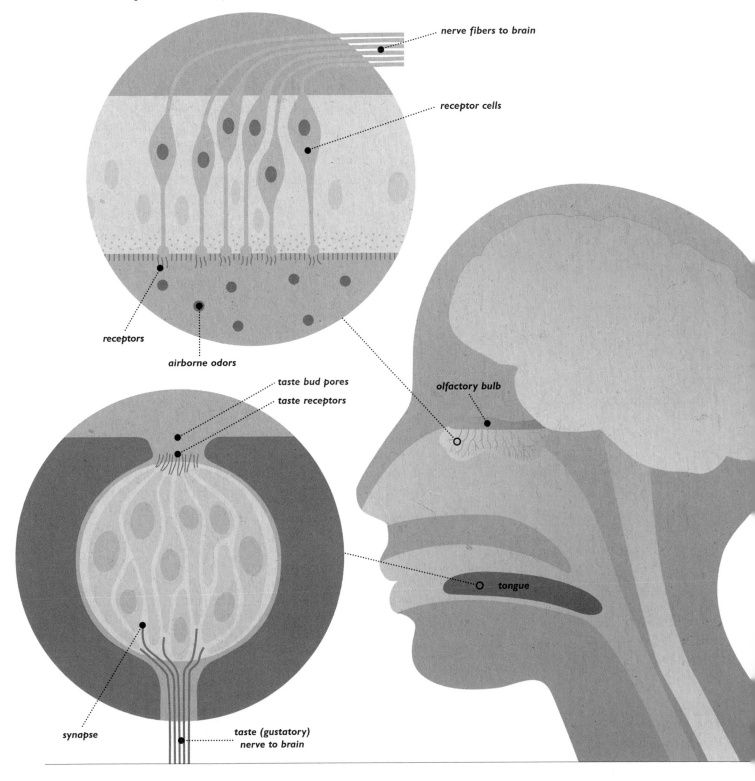

nerve fibers to brain

receptor cells

receptors

airborne odors

taste bud pores

taste receptors

olfactory bulb

tongue

synapse

taste (gustatory) nerve to brain

It's amazing how sensitive our noses can be. Here is a chart listing different compounds, and the threshold at which we can detect their smell. Note: 1% is the same as 1 part per hundred, which can be written as 1 part/10^2. One ppt (part per trillion) is 1 part/10^{12}, and one ppb (part per billion) is 1 part/10^9. For context, 1mg/L is equal to 1 ppm (part per million), which is the same as 1,000 ppb. Thus, the amount of salt required for taste detection is about a trillion times higher than the amount of 2,4,6-nonatrienal that can be picked up by our smell receptors. (For more on taste detection, see page 12.)

COMPOUND	DETECTION THRESHOLD	AROMA, SOURCE
Acetaldehyde	25,000 ppt	Fresh, Yogurt
2-furfurylthiol	36 ppt	Sulfur, Cooked beef
2-methoxy-3-hexylpyrazine	1 ppt	Green pepper, White wine
2,4,6-nonatrienal	0.0002 ppt	Sweet, Oat flakes

SULFUR COMPOUNDS AND FOOD AROMA

Some of the most smelly and easily detected aroma compounds in foods contain sulfur atoms. These sulfur compounds can arise from the action of food-derived enzymes or from chemical reactions that occur upon cooking, and often provide the unique flavors that define the taste of a given food. For instance, when garlic and mustard are chopped, enzymes produce the sulfur-containing compounds allicin and allyl isothiocyanate, which lend these foods their pungent odors. The sulfur compound 2-furfurylthiol lends coffee its signature roasted aroma. In general, sulfur volatiles are naturally present at very low concentrations. However, differing concentrations of the same aroma compound can lead to very different aroma perceptions by the human brain. At low concentrations, dimethyl sulfide gives the impression of canned corn, but at high concentrations, the same sulfide smells like cooked cabbage.

smell them. Cells for taste and smell turn over about every 10 to 30 days because of their harsh environment. As we age, fewer cells are produced to replace the ones lost so our sense of taste and smell declines with age.

The amazing difference between taste and smell is apparent in our level of sensitivity. In order to taste sweet, salty, sour, bitter, and umami substances, they must be present in food at about a fraction of 1 percent by weight. But humans can smell many compounds at the level of 1 part per trillion, and some even thousands of times lower than this. (One part per trillion is equivalent to 1 second in 32,000 years.) The record for smell-ability is reported to be held by a sulfur-containing compound called pyrrolidino[1,2-*e*]-4*H*-2,4-dimethyl-1,3,5-dithiazine that occurs in boiled seafood (detectable at one hundred-thousandth of a part per trillion or 1 part per quadrillion). This is closely followed by 2,4,6-nonatrienal, detectable at two ten-thousandths of a part per trillion, which is responsible for the sweet aroma of oat flakes. The pyrazine compound 2-methoxy-3-hexylpyrazine, which has the aroma of green bell pepper, is detectable at 1 part per trillion and is found in many white wines. One drop of this compound in a 30,000-gallon swimming pool would make the entire pool smell like green bell pepper.

There are genetic differences in our ability to taste and smell. The most thoroughly studied are differences in the taste of bitter compounds. Professor Linda Bartoshuk, at the Univeristy of Florida, has pioneered the study of supertasters, tasters, and nontasters of bitter tasting compounds such as PROP (6-propylthiouracil).

Supertasters cringe when tasting an extremely dilute solution of PROP dissolved in water or soaked into a small piece of filter paper, while nontasters can't taste anything. For tasters the bitter taste of PROP is very subtle. The proportion of supertasters and nontasters is about 25 to 30 percent of the population for each, with the rest (40 to 50 percent) being regular tasters. Supertasters tend to be very picky eaters, do not like hot spicy foods, and find bitter-tasting cruciferous vegetables to be unpleasant. They tend to eat fewer vegetables than others and do not especially enjoy wine or coffee, as they are too bitter. Nontasters actually prefer less salt on food than supertasters. That's because the intense bitter taste perceived by super-tasters reduces their ability to taste salt, and supertasters therefore add more salt to their food to compensate. Supertasters also appear to be more sensitive to sweet and sour than tasters and nontasters, but the effect is not as pronounced as it is with bitter.

Why are some people supertasters and others are not? It comes down to genetics, and the number of taste cells. Taste buds on the tongue and in the back of the throat are composed of 50 to 100 taste cells each, in structures called papillae. Simply put, supertasters have many more taste papillae than tasters, who have more than nontasters. Supertasters are genetically programmed to produce more taste receptors.

CHAPTER 1

Short Loin

This cut is wildly tender and mild in flavor. Treat it with care.

HOW THE SCIENCE WORKS

Let's begin with the anatomy of a cow. There are eight different cuts of beef sold at the wholesale level (see illustration, page 17). From this first series of cuts, known in the industry as primal cuts, a butcher (usually at a meat-packing plant in the Midwest but sometimes on-site at your local market) will make the retail cuts that you bring home. How you choose to cook a particular piece of beef depends on where the meat comes from on the cow and how it's butchered.

The short loin, a primal cut that extends from the last rib through the midsection of the animal to the hip area, is the Cadillac of beef. It contains two major muscles—the tenderloin and the shell. While the shell is large, with a robust beef flavor, the tenderloin is extremely tender with a milder flavor (and a hefty price tag). Many of our favorite cuts come from the short loin, including strip steak, T-bone, and porterhouse. The strip is cut from the shell, while the T-bone and porterhouse include both the flavorful shell and buttery tenderloin, split by a T-shaped bone.

The primal cut called the short loin is the Cadillac of beef.

We'll begin with the tenderloin. You can buy it whole. It is a long and relatively thin muscle that weighs roughly 6 pounds. You can also buy the cylindrical center-cut portion of the tenderloin, sometimes called the Chateaubriand, on its own. (This cut is named after the 19th century French writer, politician, and diplomat François-René de Chateaubriand, who was also an avid food lover.) This center-cut portion weighs in at 2 pounds. Tenderloin can be sliced crosswise into steaks, called filets mignons. Unpeeled tenderloins come with a very thick layer of exterior fat and connective tissue still attached, which needs to be removed before cooking. Peeled roasts have scattered patches of fat that are fine to leave on.

Because the tenderloin is positioned right below the spine, this muscle sees little movement and does not contain much intramuscular fat or tough connective tissue. It's the most tender cut of beef, but the near absence of intramuscular fat also means it has very mild flavor. The flavor compounds we describe as "beefy" come mostly from the fat in the muscle. As a result, when it comes to cooking tenderloin, we often add flavorful crusts, like the ones on our Pepper-Crusted Beef Tenderloin Roast (page 18) or Roast Beef Tenderloin with Onion and Mushroom Stuffing (page 19), and we take care not to overcook the roast to maintain optimal tenderness.

The shell muscle is larger than the tenderloin, and has a more robust beef flavor and more fat. From the shell muscle comes the strip steak, a test kitchen favorite, one that comes bone-in or boneless, and—just to make it confusing—is also called the top loin, sirloin strip steak, Kansas City strip steak, or New York strip steak.

And splitting the difference? The T-bone and porterhouse steaks, which both boast a T-shaped bone that runs through the meat separating the two muscles: the flavorful shell and the buttery tenderloin. Because the tenderloin is small and will cook more quickly than the shell, these steaks are often positioned over the cooler side of the fire when grilling, like for our Grilled Tuscan Steaks with Olive Oil and Lemon (page 21). The porterhouse is really just a huge T-bone steak, with a larger tenderloin section, cut farther back on the animal. (For more on porterhouse steaks, see Practical Science, page 22.)

TEST KITCHEN EXPERIMENT

Conventional wisdom holds that frozen steaks should be thawed before cooking, but we wondered if steaks could be cooked straight from the freezer. We cut a strip loin, which comes from the shell, right next to the tenderloin, into eight steaks, cut each steak in half crosswise, and froze them. We then thawed half of each steak in the refrigerator overnight and kept the other half frozen. Using our preferred method, we seared both sets of steaks in a hot skillet for 90 seconds per side and then transferred them to a 275-degree oven until they reached 125 degrees, or medium-rare. To track moisture loss, we weighed each steak before and after cooking.

RESULTS

Not surprisingly, the frozen steaks took longer to finish cooking through in the oven (18 to 22 minutes versus 10 to 15 minutes for the thawed steaks). What was surprising was that the frozen steaks actually browned in the skillet just as well as, and in the same amount of time as, the thawed steaks. Furthermore, they had thinner bands of gray, overcooked meat directly under the crust than the thawed steaks had. We also found that these steaks lost on average 9 percent less moisture during cooking than the thawed steaks did. Sampling the steaks side by side, tasters unanimously preferred the cooked-from-frozen steaks to their thawed counterparts.

TAKEAWAY

A fully frozen steak is extremely cold, which prevents overcooking while the surface reaches the very high temperatures necessary for browning reactions. As for the difference in moisture loss, we know that when meat is cooked to temperatures higher than 140 degrees, its muscle fibers begin to squeeze out a significant amount of moisture. As its slightly thicker gray band indicated, the steak that had been thawed had more overcooking around the edge, so it made sense that it also had greater moisture loss.

While we prefer to start with steak that's never been frozen for the best texture, if we do have frozen steaks on hand, from now on we'll cook them straight from the freezer. For best results, freeze steaks, uncovered, overnight on a baking sheet (this dries them out to prevent excess splattering during cooking) and then wrap them tightly in plastic wrap, place in a zipper-lock bag, and return to the freezer. To ensure that the steaks brown evenly, add oil to the skillet until it measures ⅛ inch deep. And because frozen steaks will splatter more during searing, be sure to use a large skillet. Once browned, place the steaks on a rack set in a rimmed baking sheet, transfer them to a 275-degree oven, and cook them to the desired internal temperature.

YES, YOU CAN COOK YOUR STEAKS STRAIGHT FROM THE FREEZER

While we will always prefer to cook steaks that have never been frozen, if we are cooking frozen steaks, we've found that steaks cooked straight from the freezer brown just as well; have thinner bands of gray, overcooked meat; and lose less moisture than thawed steaks.

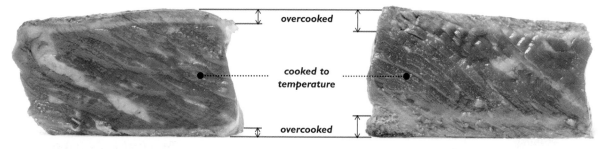

COOKED STRAIGHT FROM FREEZER
A frozen steak is less prone to overcook around its perimeter during searing.

FROZEN, THAWED, THEN COOKED
A steak that goes into the pan warmer (after thawing) will overcook more around its perimeter.

FOCUS ON: BEEF

To pick a particular cut of beef, it helps to understand more about the anatomy of a cow. There are eight different primal cuts. How you choose to cook a particular cut of beef depends on where it comes from and how it's butchered. Here, we take a look at them all, and focus on the short loin.

CHUCK (OR SHOULDER)

The chuck (or shoulder) runs from the neck down to the fifth rib. There are four major muscles in this region, and meat from the chuck tends to be flavorful and fairly fatty, which is why ground chuck makes great hamburgers. Chuck also contains significant connective tissue, so when the meat is not ground it requires a long cooking time to become tender.

RIB

The rib section extends along the back of the animal from the sixth to the twelfth rib. The prime rib comes from this area, as do rib-eye steaks. Rib cuts have excellent beefy flavor and are quite tender.

SIRLOIN

The sirloin contains relatively inexpensive cuts that are sold as both steaks and roasts. We find that sirloin cuts are fairly lean and tough. In general, we prefer other parts of the animal, although top sirloin is our favorite inexpensive holiday roast.

ROUND

Roasts and steaks cut from the round are usually sold boneless and are quite lean and can be tough. Again, we generally prefer cuts from other parts of the cow, although top round has good flavor and can be tender if sliced thin.

BRISKET/PLATE

Moderately thick boneless cuts are removed from primal cuts that run along the underside of the animal. The brisket is rather tough and contains a lot of connective tissue. The plate is rarely sold at the retail level (it is used to make pastrami).

FLANK

The flank (see page 23) contains both the flank steak and the skirt steak. Flank steak contains a good amount of fat and connective tissue, and has wide muscle fibers. Skirt steak is thin and fatty with exceptional beef flavor.

SHORT LOIN

The short loin extends from the last rib back through the midsection of the animal to the hip area. It contains two major muscles—the tenderloin and the shell. The tenderloin is extremely tender (it is positioned right under the spine) and has a quite mild flavor. This muscle may be sold whole as a roast or sliced crosswise into steaks, called filets mignons. The shell is a much larger muscle and has a more robust beef flavor as well as more fat. Strip steaks come from this muscle. Two steaks from the short loin area, called the T-bone and the porterhouse, contain portions of both the tenderloin and shell muscles, separated by a piece of lumbar vertebra.

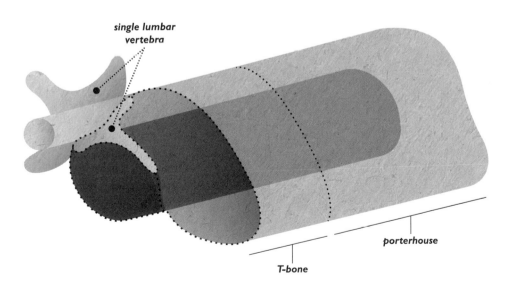

single lumbar vertebra

porterhouse

T-bone

■ **Tenderloin Muscle**
■ **Shell Muscle**

Pepper-Crusted Beef Tenderloin Roast

✓ WHY THIS RECIPE WORKS

When it comes to special-occasion entrees, it's hard to beat beef tenderloin. It's easy to make and, as the most tender cut of beef, it's luxurious to eat. But that tenderness comes at a cost (beyond the hefty price tag): Tenderloin is not known for its beefy flavor. To give it a boost, we wanted to give ours a crunchy peppercorn crust that would stick to the roast without being punishingly spicy.

GLUE ON THE PEPPERCORNS To make sure we ended up with a full peppercorn crust and not just a measly scattering of pepper, we rubbed the roast with a mixture of coarse kosher salt and baking soda, which roughed up the surface and made it slightly tacky. We then pressed the cracked peppercorns onto the sticky surface. We also sprayed the twine with vegetable oil, so that it wouldn't stick to the roast when we removed it and take our peppercorns with it.

MANIPULATE THE PEPPER'S HEAT For a crust that was satisfyingly crunchy we needed to use so much cracked pepper that its spiciness overwhelmed the mild flavor of the meat. To tame the heat, we first added sugar to the salt and baking soda rub. Sucrose, or table sugar, has been proven to temper spiciness. Next, we simmered the peppercorns in oil before applying them to the roast, which tamed their heat by pulling out an oil-soluble compound known as piperine.

AMP UP THE PEPPER FLAVOR Unfortunately, simmering the peppercorns also dulled their flavor by drawing out the three other oil-soluble compounds—limonene, sabinene, and pinene—that together are largely responsible for creating the citrusy, piney notes that give pepper its depth. To restore complexity to our lackluster pepper, we scanned databases used by perfumists and flavorists to identify aromatic ingredients that might share those dominant flavor compounds. We zeroed in on two: orange zest (the oil of which contains about 95 percent limonene) and nutmeg (the oil of which contains about 58 percent pinene and sabinene). By adding these ingredients to the oil-simmered peppercorns, we created a crust that was not too spicy but still full of distinct pepper flavor.

FINISH WITH SAUCE To give an extra boost of flavor, we created a sauce that mirrored and enhanced the flavors we had used to prepare the beef.

PEPPER-CRUSTED BEEF TENDERLOIN ROAST
SERVES 10 TO 12

Not all pepper mills produce a coarse enough grind for this recipe. For alternative methods for cracking peppercorns, see "Cracking Down on Peppercorns." Serve with Red Wine–Orange Sauce (recipe follows), if desired.

1½	tablespoons kosher salt
1½	teaspoons sugar
¼	teaspoon baking soda
½	cup plus 1 tablespoon olive oil
½	cup coarsely cracked black peppercorns
1	tablespoon finely grated orange zest
½	teaspoon ground nutmeg
1	(6-pound) whole beef tenderloin, trimmed

1. Adjust oven rack to middle position and heat oven to 300 degrees. Set wire rack in rimmed baking sheet. Combine salt, sugar, and baking soda in bowl; set aside. Heat 6 tablespoons oil and peppercorns in small saucepan over low heat until faint bubbles appear. Continue to cook

---

PRACTICAL SCIENCE
CRACKING DOWN ON PEPPERCORNS

Here are two other ways to achieve coarsely cracked peppercorns, each about the size of a halved whole one.

With a good pepper mill (such as our favorite model, from Cole & Mason, the Derwent Gourmet Precision Pepper Mill), grinding peppercorns to the perfect size for coating steaks or our Pepper-Crusted Beef Tenderloin Roast is easy. But even on their largest settings, many pepper mills create a grind size that's too small, resulting in a crust that isn't crunchy. Here are two other ways to achieve coarsely cracked peppercorns, each about the size of a halved whole one. Be sure to sift the cracked peppercorns before measuring to remove the finely ground particles (save them for another use).

BLENDER
Process 1 cup peppercorns (a smaller amount doesn't work as well) in blender on any speed until no whole ones remain.
PROS Fast and painless
CONS Low yield, with about half of peppercorns turning to dust

SKILLET/POT
On cutting board, rock bottom edge of skillet over 2 tablespoons peppercorns until they crack. Repeat with more peppercorns.
PROS Minimal waste
CONS Slow and arduous

at bare simmer, swirling pan occasionally, until pepper is fragrant, 7 to 10 minutes. Drain peppercorn mixture in fine-mesh strainer and discard cooking oil. Mix peppercorns with orange zest, nutmeg, and remaining 3 tablespoons oil.

2. Set tenderloin on sheet of plastic wrap. Sprinkle salt mixture evenly over surface of tenderloin and rub into tenderloin until surface is tacky. Tuck tail end of tenderloin under about 6 inches to create more even shape. Rub top and side of tenderloin with peppercorn mixture, pressing to make sure peppercorns adhere. Spray three 12-inch lengths kitchen twine with vegetable oil spray; tie head of tenderloin to maintain even shape, spacing twine at 2-inch intervals.

3. Transfer prepared tenderloin to prepared rack, keeping tail end tucked under. Roast until thickest part of meat registers about 120 degrees (for rare) or about 125 degrees (for medium-rare) (thinner parts of tenderloin will be slightly more done), 1 hour to 1 hour 10 minutes. Transfer to carving board and let rest for 30 minutes.

4. Remove twine and slice meat into ½-inch-thick slices. Serve.

RED WINE–ORANGE SAUCE

MAKES 1 CUP

2	tablespoons unsalted butter, plus 4 tablespoons cut into 4 pieces and chilled
2	shallots, minced
1	tablespoon tomato paste
2	teaspoons sugar
3	garlic cloves, minced
2	cups beef broth
1	cup red wine
¼	cup orange juice
2	tablespoons balsamic vinegar
1	tablespoon Worcestershire sauce
1	sprig fresh thyme
	Salt and pepper

1. Melt 2 tablespoons butter in medium saucepan over medium-high heat. Add shallots, tomato paste, and sugar; cook, stirring frequently, until deep brown, about 5 minutes. Add garlic and cook until fragrant, about 1 minute. Add broth, wine, orange juice, vinegar, Worcestershire, and thyme sprig, scraping up any browned bits. Bring to simmer and cook until reduced to 1 cup, 35 to 40 minutes.

2. Strain sauce through fine-mesh strainer and return to saucepan. Return saucepan to medium heat and whisk in remaining 4 tablespoons butter, 1 piece at a time. Season with salt and pepper to taste.

Roast Beef Tenderloin with Onion and Mushroom Stuffing

✔ WHY THIS RECIPE WORKS

For a recipe for stuffed beef tenderloin with a deeply charred crust, a tender, rosy-pink interior, and an intensely flavored stuffing that stayed neatly rolled in the meat, we chose the almost perfectly cylindrical Chateaubriand and used a "double-butterfly" procedure—making two cuts so the roast opened up into three parts (like a business letter). In this way the roast accommodated 50 percent more filling than a conventionally butterflied roast.

CREATE A GOOD CRUST We created a suitable crust for our tenderloin recipe in a shortened cooking time by coating the exterior of the roast with a layer of kosher salt an hour before searing. This allowed the salt to pull out moisture from the meat, which was then reabsorbed during the hour rest, to ensure a dry surface for quick browning.

STUFF IT WELL In our initial tests, we learned a couple of things about what not to do when stuffing tenderloin. First, don't use bread crumbs; they turn into absorbent little sponges saturated with blood-red juices. Second, no bulky ingredients; they'll just fall out. To get the most flavor mileage out of a small amount of stuffing, we used earthy cremini mushrooms and caramelized onions, which contributed sweetness and bound the mushrooms into a thick, slightly sticky jam that was easy to spread. We added minced garlic, a splash of Madeira, and a compound butter for full, well-rounded flavors.

ROAST BEEF TENDERLOIN WITH ONION AND MUSHROOM STUFFING

SERVES 6 TO 8

Center-cut beef tenderloin roasts are sometimes sold as Chateaubriand. This recipe can be doubled to make two roasts. Sear the roasts one after the other, wiping out the pan and adding new oil after searing the first roast. Both pieces of meat can be roasted on the same rack.

The cattle's diet can greatly influence the flavor—and nutrition—of beef.

While specific cuts have specific flavor profiles, there are a few factors that influence the flavor of beef. They include cattle breed and age, the amount the cattle exercise, slaughter and storage conditions, and aging. And then there's diet.

While most American beef is grain-fed for the last 120 days before slaughter, many supermarkets are starting to carry grass-fed options as well. In 2007, the USDA defined the term: "Grass and forage shall be the feed source consumed for the lifetime of the ruminant animal, with the exception of milk consumed prior to weaning." Grain-fed beef has long been promoted as richer and fattier, while grass-fed beef has gotten a bad rap as lean and chewy with an overly gamy taste. But there's more to this story.

"There are a lot of desirable attributes to grass-fed beef," says Dr. Susan Duckett, Professor of Animal Sciences at Clemson University—including added nutrition. Grass-fed beef is leaner (like lean chicken breast, she says), and higher in certain vitamins, minerals, antioxidants, and omega-3 fatty acids.

Finally, grass-fed beef also contains twice the amount of conjugated linoleic acid (CLA) isomers, a small family of fatty acids that purportedly fight cancer and lower the risk of diabetes. Why? Microorganisms that live in the gut of ruminants like cows restructure dietary fats, says Duckett. In particular, they transform linoleic acid into CLA—but only if the conditions are right. When a cow's diet is high in grain, the pH of its gut is lowered, making it a less friendly environment for these microorganisms. "Not so much with a foraged diet," says Duckett. Cows that eat foraged grass have a gut with a higher pH. The microorganisms are happier. More CLA is created. "It's how it was meant to be."

In terms of palatability, the incredibly lean tenderloin does not exhibit much difference in flavor between grain- and grass-fed. For fattier cuts, we tasted grain- and grass-fed strip steaks and rib-eye steaks. While tasters could not tell the difference between the strip steaks, they did find flavor differences between the fattier rib eyes. Interestingly, preferences were evenly split as to which option was better.

What accounts for the apparent turnaround in meat that's often maligned? The answer may lie in new measures introduced in recent years that have made grass-fed beef taste more appealing, including "finishing" the beef on forage like clover that imparts a sweeter profile.

Journalist Jo Robinson spent years studying grass-fed beef for her book *Pasture Perfect*. We spoke to her about what to look for when buying grass-fed beef to cook at home. First, says Robinson, it's important to understand that all grass-fed beef is not created equal. Some is very lean, and should be treated more like chicken than beef when cooking. To get optimal flavor, however, that means some fat. Look for marbling. And if you're purchasing at a farmers' market, or direct from a ranch, "ask your producer how much of a fat cover was on the meat—it should be between a half and a full inch, closer to a full inch," she says. Finally, look to buy from producers who boast "rotational grazing" or "management intensive grazing." This, says Robinson, means that the farmers are working to produce lush, nutritious grass for their cattle to graze on—and therefore will be producing lush, nutritious, and tender beef, too.

STUFFING

- 8 ounces cremini mushrooms, trimmed and broken into rough pieces
- ½ tablespoon unsalted butter
- 1½ teaspoons olive oil
- 1 onion, halved and sliced ¼ inch thick
- ¼ teaspoon salt
- ⅛ teaspoon pepper
- 1 garlic clove, minced
- ½ cup Madeira or sweet Marsala

BEEF ROAST

- 1 (2- to 3-pound) center-cut beef tenderloin roast, trimmed
  Kosher salt and pepper
- ½ cup baby spinach
- 3 tablespoons olive oil

HERB BUTTER

- 4 tablespoons unsalted butter, softened
- 1 tablespoon whole-grain mustard
- 1 tablespoon chopped fresh parsley
- 1 garlic clove, minced
- ¾ teaspoon chopped fresh thyme
- ⅛ teaspoon salt
- ⅛ teaspoon pepper

1. FOR THE STUFFING: Pulse mushrooms in food processor until coarsely chopped, about 6 pulses. Heat butter and oil in 12-inch nonstick skillet over medium-high heat. Add onion, salt, and pepper; cook, stirring occasionally, until onion begins to soften, about 5 minutes. Add mushrooms and cook, stirring occasionally, until all moisture has evaporated, 5 to 7 minutes. Reduce heat to medium and continue to cook, stirring frequently, until vegetables are deeply browned and sticky, about 10 minutes. Stir in garlic and cook until fragrant, 30 seconds. Slowly stir in Madeira and cook, scraping bottom of skillet with wooden spoon to loosen any browned bits, until liquid has evaporated, 2 to 3 minutes. Transfer mushroom mixture to plate and let cool completely.

2. FOR THE BEEF ROAST: Insert chef's knife about 1 inch from bottom of roast and cut horizontally, stopping just before edge. Open meat like book. Make another cut diagonally into thicker portion of roast. Open up this flap, smoothing out butterflied rectangle of meat. Season cut side of roast with kosher salt and pepper. Spread cooled mushroom mixture over interior of roast, leaving ½-inch border on all sides; lay spinach on top of stuffing. Roll roast lengthwise and tie with 8 pieces kitchen twine, evenly spaced.

3. Stir 1 tablespoon oil, 1½ teaspoons kosher salt, and 1½ teaspoons pepper together in small bowl. Rub roast with oil mixture and let stand at room temperature for 1 hour.

4. Adjust oven rack to middle position and heat oven to 450 degrees. Heat remaining 2 tablespoons oil in 12-inch skillet over medium-high heat until just smoking. Add beef and cook until browned on all sides, 8 to 10 minutes. Transfer beef to wire rack set in rimmed baking sheet and place in oven. Roast until thickest part registers 120 degrees (for rare), 16 to 18 minutes, or 125 degrees (for medium-rare), 20 to 22 minutes.

5. FOR THE HERB BUTTER: While meat roasts, combine butter ingredients in bowl. Transfer roast to carving board; spread half of butter evenly over top of roast. Tent roast with aluminum foil; let rest for 15 minutes. Cut roast between pieces of twine into thick slices. Remove twine and serve with remaining butter.

Grilled Tuscan Steaks with Olive Oil and Lemon

✔ WHY THIS RECIPE WORKS

This Italian-style preparation is deceivingly simple: a thick, juicy steak, grilled rare and drizzled with high-quality olive oil and a squeeze of lemon. We wanted the flavor of the steak to be complemented by the lemon and oil, without these delicate flavors getting lost in the process.

COOK IT RIGHT T-bone and porterhouse steaks are most commonly called for in the recipes for Tuscan-style grilling we tried, and we found no reason to veer from this tradition. Both feature meat from the shell (or strip) on one side and the tenderloin on the other, which is larger on the porterhouse. For these hefty, expensive steaks, we used our go-to grilling method: a two-level fire. We achieved a browned crust over the hot side of the grill, then moved the steaks to the cooler side to evenly cook them through.

CHOOSE GOOD OIL Since the oil is an essential component of this dish, we recommend using extra-virgin

olive oil, which has a more distinctive character and bolder flavor than pure olive oil (for more on extra-virgin olive oil, see page 357). We also discovered differences among brands, and found that we preferred a fuller-bodied oil for this recipe.

REST, SLICE, AND GARNISH We evaluated steaks treated with oil in five different ways: marinated before grilling, brushed on the meat before grilling, brushed on the meat during grilling, drizzled on the whole cooked steaks before slicing, and drizzled over the sliced steak at serving time. In the end, we preferred the oil over the sliced steak for a few reasons. It was the easiest, least fussy method; it flavored the meat more effectively, bringing the full fruity, peppery impact of the raw oil to the fore; and it guaranteed a hit of oil with each bite of steak. Drizzling the steaks with the olive oil after slicing and serving the steaks with wedges of lemon also ensured that the flavor nuances of the oil remained intact and the lemon stayed bright and fresh.

GRILLED TUSCAN STEAKS WITH OLIVE OIL AND LEMON
SERVES 4 TO 6

Be sure to buy steaks that are at least 1 inch thick.

- 2 (1¾-pound) porterhouse or T-bone steaks, 1 to 1½ inches thick, trimmed
  Salt and pepper
- 3 tablespoons extra-virgin olive oil
  Lemon wedges

1A. FOR A CHARCOAL GRILL: Open bottom vent completely. Light large chimney starter three-quarters filled with charcoal briquettes (4½ quarts). When top coals are partially covered with ash, pour evenly over half of grill. Set cooking grate in place, cover, and open lid vent completely. Heat grill until hot, about 5 minutes.

1B. FOR A GAS GRILL: Turn all burners to high, cover, and heat grill until hot, about 15 minutes. Leave primary burner on high and turn other burner(s) to low.

2. Clean and oil cooking grate. Pat steaks dry with paper towels and season with salt and pepper. Place steaks on hotter side of grill with tenderloin sides (smaller side of T-bone) facing cooler side of grill. Cook (covered if using gas) until dark crust forms, 6 to 8 minutes. (If steaks start to flame, move them briefly to cooler side of grill.) Flip steaks and turn so that tenderloin sides are facing cooler side of grill. Continue to cook (covered if using gas) until dark brown crust forms on second side, 6 to 8 minutes longer.

3. Transfer steaks to cooler side of grill with bone side facing hotter side of grill. Cover grill and continue to cook until meat registers 115 to 120 degrees (for rare) or 120 to 125 degrees (for medium-rare), 2 to 4 minutes longer, flipping halfway through cooking.

4. Transfer steaks to carving board, tent with aluminum foil, and let rest for 10 minutes. Cut shell and tenderloin pieces off bones, then slice each piece crosswise into ½-inch-thick slices. Transfer to serving platter, drizzle with oil, and serve with lemon wedges.

GRILLED TUSCAN STEAKS WITH GARLIC ESSENCE

Rub halved garlic cloves over bone and meat on each side of steaks before seasoning with salt and pepper.

PRACTICAL SCIENCE WHEN BUYING A PORTERHOUSE, STEAK BUYER BEWARE

The porterhouse steak with the largest tenderloin section is, surprisingly, not the best.

In the beef world, it doesn't get much more impressive (or expensive) than a porterhouse steak, a cross-cut, bone-in slice of the short loin. This cut features a large section of buttery tenderloin (by definition it must be at least 1¼ inches in diameter—anything smaller is labeled a T-bone) on one side of the bone and a section of the beefy shell muscle (see illustration, page 17) on the other.

When shopping for a porterhouse, many cooks make the mistake of looking for the steak with largest tenderloin portion possible. Why is that a problem? Well, it turns out that where the tenderloin is largest (roughly the last 6 inches of the short loin before it meets up with the sirloin), the accompanying shell portion is divided by a line of tough sinew. On the outside of that line sits a portion of top sirloin, a much more heavily used muscle. Steaks cut from this section are colloquially known as vein-end porterhouses, and while they may look impressive at the supermarket, they are supposedly tougher on the plate.

To see and taste the difference ourselves we visited Kinnealey Quality Meats in Brockton, Massachusetts, where butchers cut us vein-end and center-cut (where there is no section of top sirloin) porterhouses from three different short loins. Back in the kitchen we vacuum-sealed the steaks, cooked them in a water bath to an internal temperature of 125 degrees, and tasted.

Sure enough, once tasters crossed the vein of sinew, they were met with a significantly chewier piece of meat. The section of top sirloin was not only tougher, but it was also streaked with chewy connective tissue and rubbery fat. So if you don't wish to pay porterhouse prices for sirloin quality, look for a porterhouse where the shell muscle isn't marked by a vein of sinew.

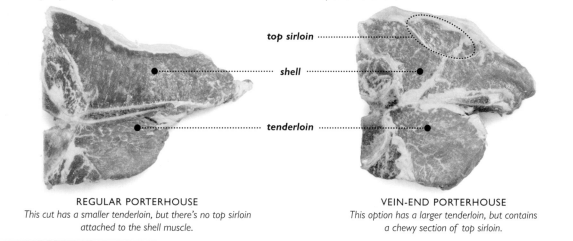

top sirloin ········

shell ········

tenderloin ········

REGULAR PORTERHOUSE
This cut has a smaller tenderloin, but there's no top sirloin attached to the shell muscle.

VEIN-END PORTERHOUSE
This option has a larger tenderloin, but contains a chewy section of top sirloin.

CHAPTER 2

Flank

This flavorful cut of meat is—surprisingly—best cooked to medium.

HOW THE SCIENCE WORKS

A few cuts are made from the primal flank. They include (the aptly named) flank steak, a flat cut with a distinct longitudinal grain, as well as skirt steak, which is a thinner, fattier steak with an exceptionally beefy flavor. In this chapter, we will focus on both. Cuts from the flank are flavorful and juicy but need special care to make them tender and not tough.

Some of the biggest differences among primal cuts are, of course, the amount of fat and the presence of bones, but perhaps most important is the basic characteristics of their muscles. Muscle tissue is composed of muscle fibers, connective tissue, fat, and water. In every muscle, there are thousands of muscle fibers, each of which contains very long individual muscle cells. The fibers are packed into bundles, surrounded by connective tissue (see illustration, page 25).

Flank steak contains a good amount of collagen, the major protein in tough connective tissue (30 percent more than rib eye, for example, according to data from the U.S. Department of Agriculture). The other major impediment to tenderness, however, is the size of its muscle fibers. Cuts from the flank are unique in the size of their muscle fibers, which are about 30 percent thicker than those in rib eye, and 60 percent thicker than those in the very tender tenderloin. In fact, they are so big that you can see bundles of them with the naked eye. The thicker the muscle fibers, the more force it takes to bite through them.

How does cooking help? When subjected to heat, muscle fibers begin to shrink in diameter, which makes them

> **The muscle fibers in the flank are uniquely large in size.**

easier to chew—this process starts at temperatures as low as 104 degrees. When the meat reaches 120 degrees shrinking increases significantly, maxing out around 140 degrees. Because the meat fibers are so large in the flank, we have found that these cuts benefit from a bit more cooking than usual. Even if you generally like steak rare, we recommend cooking steaks from the flank to medium-rare or medium. The additional heat shrinks muscle fibers enough to decrease chewiness. This means that we cook flank steaks to 130 degrees after resting (so remove them from the heat when the steaks are about 125), and skirt steaks to 135 degrees after resting (so remove them from the heat when the steaks are about 130 degrees). There's an additional benefit to cooking flank cuts a bit more than usual: As the very thick muscle fibers shrink in diameter they separate from each other, creating gaps between fibers that make the fibers easier to bite through, and the meat better able to absorb maximum flavor from post-cooking marinades and sauces.

Because of the tendency for chewiness, it's important, when serving cooked flank cuts, to take great care to cut across the grain, to shorten the muscle fibers and create a more tender bite (see Test Kitchen Experiment, page 24). Flank and skirt steaks are relatively thin and therefore cook quickly, making them ideal for the grill, which we use for our Thai Grilled Beef Salad (page 26). No grill? No worries. Our Philly Cheesesteaks (page 32) are cooked in a skillet, and our Bistro-Style Flank Steaks (page 26) are seared in a skillet and then finished in the oven.

TEST KITCHEN EXPERIMENT

Cooks have a bad habit of categorizing raw cuts of beef as either tender or tough, when in reality the nature of the cut itself is only a part of the picture. How a steak is cooked (and to what final internal temperature) will greatly influence tenderness, as will how you slice it. Cutting matters not only at the butcher shop but also at home and especially when it comes time to carve meat before serving. The most important consideration? Whether you cut with or against the grain, or orientation, of the muscle fibers. Cutting with the grain means slicing parallel to the muscle fibers, and against means slicing perpendicular to the fibers. This is crucial with flank steak, with its wide muscle fibers, relatively high proportion of connective tissue, and clear longitudinal grain. To quantify how much of an influence carving direction has on tenderness, we ran the following experiment.

EXPERIMENT

We cooked a flank steak and (for comparison purposes) a section of strip loin (which comes from the shell section of the short loin—see page 17), which features thin muscle fibers and little connective tissue, in a temperature-controlled water bath to an internal temperature of 130 degrees. We then used an ultrasensitive piece of equipment called a CT3 Texture Analyzer from Brookfield Engineering (see page 3) to test how much force was required to "bite" into the meat. We tested this both when the meat was carved with the grain and when it was carved against the grain. We repeated the experiment three times, analyzed the data, and compared it to our own tasters' remarks.

RESULTS

We found that it took, on average, 383 grams of force for the probe to "bite" 5 millimeters into a piece of flank steak cut against the grain, while flank steak cut with the grain required an average of 1729 grams of force for the probe to travel the same distance. In other words, it took more than four times as much force for this machine to bite steak sliced with the grain as it did steak sliced against the grain. No one wants to work that hard when chewing!

TAKEAWAY

All cuts benefit from slicing against the grain, but it really pays to execute this step correctly when dealing with cuts from the flank. And while most cooks would argue that flank is a much less tender cut than the expensive strip, that's not necessarily true. When we compared both steaks sliced with the grain we found that flank was indeed 193 percent tougher than strip. However, when we compared the two steaks sliced against the grain, that number dropped to just 16 percent. Our tasters' comments closely mirrored this data. That's why flank—when properly prepared—can rival premium steaks that cost significantly more.

TESTING THE TEXTURE OF MEAT CUT WITH AND AGAINST THE GRAIN

We used the CT3 Texture Analyzer from Brookfield Engineering to record the force it took to "bite" into pieces of meat cut with, and against, the grain. The results? Very clear. Cut against the grain for a more tender piece of meat.

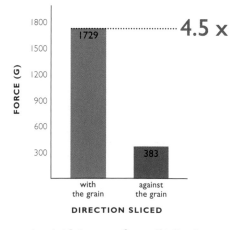

It took 4.5 times more force to "bite" a piece of meat sliced with the grain.

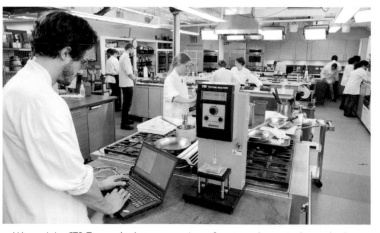

We used the CT3 Texture Analyzer to test piece after piece of meat in the test kitchen.

FOCUS ON: MEAT MUSCLES

Meat is made up of muscle. Whether the meat comes from a cow, pig, chicken, or lamb, the makeup of the muscle fibers, water, connective tissue, and fat is quite similar. The muscle structure of fish is quite different (see page 81).

FAT

Fat is produced and stored in a specialized form of connective tissue called adipose cells; these cells store energy. There are two types of fat in most animals—the thick layer of fat that surrounds the muscles and the thin filaments that run through the muscles. The thick layer is generally removed during butchering. The thin filaments are called marbling and are key to flavor and perceived juiciness.

MUSCLE FIBER

Each muscle contains thousands and thousands of individual muscle fibers that are thinner than a human hair and often several inches long. Each fiber is composed of smaller units called myofibrils. Each myofibril is divided into thousands of sarcomeres, the basic unit of measure, like a foot to a mile. The primary proteins in muscle fibers are called actin and myosin. Individual fibers are bundled together and wrapped in connective tissue—these are the thin strands visible as the "grain" in many cuts of meat.

WATER

Muscle fibers are saturated with water molecules. Lean meat has a high water content and is often a tender cut. (Most cuts contain about 75 percent water.) Most of the water is contained within the myofibrils that make up a single muscle cell. The remaining water is found in the spaces between individual muscle fibers. This water is especially prone to being lost when meat is cooked.

myofibril

CONNECTIVE TISSUE

Connective tissue is the "wrapping" that encases bundles of long muscle fibers and holds them together creating structural stability in mammals and birds. It also acts as the link between muscles and bones in the form of tendons enabling muscle action to move the skeletal system and produce motion. The parts of these animals involved with motion, such as legs, rump, and shoulders, therefore have more connective tissue to help reinforce the muscles required for strenuous movement. Connective tissue is very tough, so the parts of an animal that are used for motion are tougher cuts of meat than the parts used for maintaining posture, like the belly, back, and ribs. As an animal ages, its connective tissue becomes more abundant and stronger, and its meat becomes tougher.

There are three types of connective tissue: the epimysium, the perimysium, and the endomysium. The epimysium surrounds a whole muscle; the perimysium surrounds each bundle of muscle fibers; the endomysium surrounds each individual muscle fiber.

Connective tissue is composed largely of four proteins called collagen, elastin, reticulin, and a glycoprotein called "ground substance." Collagen is the dominant protein, comprising about 60 percent or more of the proteins found in connective tissue.

ELASTIN

Compared to collagen, elastin is a much smaller, loosely wound protein, and is the major protein in what is known on meat as "silverskin." Elastin is not broken down by heat, which is why silverskin is usually removed before cooking meat such as pork ribs.

COLLAGEN

Collagen is unique in that it occurs as very long fibers composed of three identical protein molecules wound together in the form of a triple helix. The three proteins are held together by numerous weak attractive forces known as hydrogen bonds (see page 4). Heating collagen above 140 degrees begins to break those bonds, allowing the three proteins to slowly unwind to form the protein known as gelatin, which can hold up to 10 times its weight in water. Therefore, the conversion of collagen to gelatin tenderizes tough cuts of meat.

Bistro-Style Flank Steaks

✔ WHY THIS RECIPE WORKS

This rustic French restaurant dish is typically made with hanger steak, which can be hard to find in the United States. We wanted to get juicy bistro-style steaks without breaking the bank—or hunting down obscure cuts of meat. We immediately turned to flank steak, which is both common and affordable. But flank steak is not designed to sear as individual steaks in a sauté pan. Our solution? By cutting a 2-pound piece of meat into four portions, we create thick steaks perfect for pan searing.

BROWN THOSE STEAKS We browned the steaks in a skillet to create a crust and then finished them in the oven to prevent the fond (the browned bits on the bottom of the pan) from burning. Later, we used the pan drippings to create a simple sauce of shallot, white wine, and butter.

LET THEM REST When the steaks were medium-rare, we let them rest. In the test kitchen, we rest most meat and poultry after cooking. The theory is that resting—or allowing the meat to sit undisturbed for a time before serving—allows the juices to redistribute themselves more evenly throughout the meat. As a result, meat that has rested will shed much less juice than meat sliced straight from the grill or the oven. To test this theory, we grilled four steaks and let two rest while slicing into the other two immediately. The steaks that had rested for 10 minutes shed 40 percent less juice than the steaks sliced right after cooking. Here, the steaks rested while we made a pan sauce. Be sure to cut the steaks against the grain (see Test Kitchen Experiment, page 24).

BISTRO-STYLE FLANK STEAKS
SERVES 4

After cutting the meat into pieces, you should have four steaks with the grain (the long striations) running parallel to the long side. The amount of time that the steaks need in the oven will depend on the thickness of the meat—use an instant-read thermometer to check. Be careful when making the pan sauce, as the skillet handle will be hot.

- 1 (2-pound) flank steak, trimmed
   Salt and pepper
- 2 teaspoons vegetable oil
- 3 tablespoons unsalted butter
- 1 large shallot, minced
- ¾ cup dry white wine

1. Adjust oven rack to middle position and heat oven to 400 degrees. Cut steak in half lengthwise with grain, then cut each piece in half crosswise against grain to make 4 equal-size steaks. Pat steaks dry with paper towels and season with salt and pepper.

2. Heat oil in 12-inch skillet over medium-high heat until just smoking. Add 1 tablespoon butter and swirl to melt. Lay steaks in pan and cook until well browned, 3 to 5 minutes per side. Move skillet to oven and cook until steaks register 125 degrees (for medium-rare), 3 to 5 minutes. Transfer steaks to plate and tent with aluminum foil.

3. Return skillet with drippings to medium-high heat (skillet handle will be hot). Add 1 tablespoon butter and shallot and cook until shallot is browned, about 2 minutes. Add wine and any accumulated beef juices from plate and bring to boil, scraping up any browned bits. Continue to boil until slightly thickened and reduced to about ½ cup, about 5 minutes.

4. Remove sauce from heat and swirl in remaining 1 tablespoon butter until melted. Season with salt and pepper to taste. Slice steaks thin against grain on bias and serve with sauce.

Thai Grilled Beef Salad

✔ WHY THIS RECIPE WORKS

In the best versions of this Thai grilled beef salad, known as nam tok, *the cuisine's five signature flavor elements—hot, sour, salty, sweet, and bitter—come into balance, making for a light but satisfying dish that's traditionally served with steamed jasmine rice. When we set out to re-create it, the recipes that we found were all over the map in terms of the beef that they called for, not to mention the method for preparing it. We tested a wide variety of cuts, from lean tenderloin to heavily marbled New York strip steak. We landed on flank steak for its uniform shape, moderate price, and decent tenderness when grilled.*

FLIP YOUR STEAK THAI STYLE This salad's Thai name, nam tok (literally "water falling"), refers to the beads of moisture that form on the surface of the steak as it cooks—an age-old Thai cookery clue that the meat is ready to be flipped. While this method sounded imprecise, during testing we found it to be a surprisingly accurate gauge of when the flank steak was halfway done. Here's why: As the steak's interior gets hotter, its tightly packed fibers contract and release some of their interior moisture, which pushes to the meat's surface. When turned at this point and cooked for an equal amount of time on the second side, the steak emerged deeply charred on the outside and medium-rare within. (Note: We do not recommend this technique across the board for steaks; since the thickness and density of the meat fibers vary from cut to cut, the time it takes for heat to penetrate and for beads of moisture to be pushed to the meat's surface differs.)

BALANCING ACT The dressing for this dish should have a good balance among hot, sour, salty, and sweet to provide a counterpoint to the subtle bitter char of the meat. Fish sauce, lime juice, and sugar provided three of these elements, but the fourth, spicy element needed some extra attention. A fresh Thai chile added a fruity, fiery hit to each bite, but on its own it lacked depth. To remedy this, we toasted a bit of cayenne pepper and sweet paprika for a deeper, more complex spicy flavor. The final element of the dressing—toasted rice powder—was called for in most of the recipes we found, and was simple to make with a spice grinder. We found it added extra body to the dressing, and could work as a slightly crunchy element when sprinkled on at the table.

THAI GRILLED BEEF SALAD
SERVES 4 TO 6

Serve with rice, if desired. If fresh Thai chiles are unavailable, substitute ½ serrano chile. Don't skip the toasted rice; it's integral to the texture and flavor of the dish. Any variety of white rice can be used. Toasted rice powder (kao kua) can also be found in many Asian markets; substitute 1 tablespoon rice powder for the white rice.

1	teaspoon paprika
1	teaspoon cayenne pepper
1	tablespoon white rice
3	tablespoons lime juice (2 limes)
2	tablespoons fish sauce
2	tablespoons water
½	teaspoon sugar
1	(1½-pound) flank steak, trimmed
	Salt and coarsely ground white pepper
1	seedless English cucumber, sliced ¼-inch-thick on bias
4	shallots, sliced thin
1½	cups fresh mint leaves, torn
1½	cups fresh cilantro leaves
1	Thai chile, stemmed, seeded, and sliced thin into rounds

1. Heat paprika and cayenne in 8-inch skillet over medium heat; cook, shaking pan, until fragrant, about 1 minute. Transfer to small bowl. Return skillet to medium-high heat, add rice and toast, stirring constantly, until deep golden brown, about 5 minutes. Transfer to small bowl and let cool for 5 minutes. Grind rice with spice grinder, mini food processor, or mortar and pestle until it resembles fine meal, 10 to 30 seconds (you should have about 1 tablespoon rice powder).

2. Whisk lime juice, fish sauce, water, sugar, and ¼ teaspoon toasted paprika mixture in large bowl and set aside.

3A. FOR A CHARCOAL GRILL: Open bottom vent completely. Light large chimney starter filled with charcoal briquettes (6 quarts). When top coals are partially covered with ash, pour in even layer over half of grill. Set cooking grate in place, cover, and open lid vent completely. Heat grill until hot, about 5 minutes.

3B. FOR A GAS GRILL: Turn all burners to high, cover, and heat grill until hot, about 15 minutes. Leave primary burner on high and turn off other burner(s).

4. Clean and oil cooking grate. Season steak with salt and white pepper. Place steak on hotter side of grill and cook until beginning to char and beads of moisture appear on outer edges of meat, 5 to 6 minutes. Flip steak and continue to cook until meat registers 125 degrees, about 5 minutes longer. Transfer to cutting board, tent with aluminum foil, and let rest for 10 minutes (or allow to cool to room temperature, about 1 hour).

5. Line large platter with cucumber slices. Slice steak ¼ inch thick against grain on bias. Transfer sliced steak to bowl with fish sauce mixture. Add shallots, mint, cilantro, chile, and half of rice powder, and toss to combine. Arrange steak over cucumber-lined platter. Serve, passing remaining rice powder and remaining toasted paprika mixture separately.

Grilled Beef Satay

✔ WHY THIS RECIPE WORKS

Beef satay, a well-known Thai street food, should consist of tender strips of assertively flavored meat grilled to lightly burnished perfection. But at some point in its journey from the streets of Bangkok to American restaurants, satay lost something—and we wanted it back. The first step was to pick the right meat. Thanks to its evenly distributed fat, flank steak had good flavor and, as an added benefit, its symmetrical shape made slicing easier.

COOK THAI-STYLE Flipping individual skewers over a very hot flame was a difficult task. Instead, we created a setup that mimicked those of the Thai street vendors. The vendors use trough-shaped grills, which suspend the meat inches above the hot coals. For our version, on a charcoal grill, we filled a disposable aluminum roasting pan with charcoal and lined up the skewers over the pan.

MARINATE AND BASTE For maximum flavor, we kept the marinade simple, using only fish sauce (for a savory flavor boost), oil, and sugar (to aid with browning). During grilling, we basted the meat heavily with a sauce made of coconut milk redolent with ginger, lemon grass, and spices. This provided a boost in flavor but didn't make the meat mushy (see Practical Science, opposite page).

GET SAUCY The peanut sauce is a key element of satay. Using chunky peanut butter as a base, we spiced things up with Thai red curry paste and garlic. Coconut milk contributed body, and chopped roasted peanuts offered additional texture. A final hit of lime juice, coupled with soy and fish sauce, lent brightness.

GRILLED BEEF SATAY
SERVES 6

You will need ten to twelve 12-inch metal skewers for this recipe, or you can substitute bamboo skewers, soaked in water for 30 minutes. The disposable aluminum roasting pan used for charcoal grilling should be at least 2¾ inches deep; you will not need the pan for a gas grill. Kitchen shears work well for poking the holes in the pan. Unless you have a very high-powered gas grill, these skewers will not be as well seared as they would be with charcoal. Serve with Peanut Sauce (recipe follows). To make it a meal, serve this dish with white rice.

PRACTICAL SCIENCE THE USDA MEAT GRADING SYSTEM

The meat grading system put in place by the USDA will help you choose what to buy. Prime is best.

The USDA assigns eight different quality grades to beef, but most of the meat available to consumers is confined to just three: prime, choice, and select. Grading is strictly voluntary on the part of the meat packer. If meat is graded, the meat should bear a USDA stamp indicating the grade, though it may not be visible to the consumer. To grade meat, inspectors—or, more often today, Video Imaging Analysis (VIA) machines—evaluate color, grain, surface texture, and fat content and its distribution. Prime meat (often available only at butcher shops) has a deep maroon color, fine-grained muscle tissue, and a smooth surface that is silky to the touch. It also contains fat that is evenly distributed and creamy white instead of yellow, which indicates an older animal that may have tougher meat. Choice beef has less marbling than prime, and select beef is leaner still.

Our blind tasting of all three grades of rib-eye steaks produced predictable results: Prime ranked first for its tender, buttery texture and rich, beefy flavor. Next came choice, with good meaty flavor and a little more chew. The tough and stringy select steak followed, with flavor that was barely acceptable. We've found the same to be true for other cuts, including flank. Our advice: When you're willing to splurge, go for prime steak, but a choice steak that exhibits a moderate amount of marbling is a fine, affordable option. Just steer clear of select-grade steak.

PRIME
Prime meat is heavily marbled with intramuscular fat. About 2 percent of graded beef is considered prime.

CHOICE
The majority of graded beef is choice. It is generally moderately marbled with intramuscular fat.

SELECT
Select beef has little marbling, which can make it drier, tougher, and less flavorful than the two higher grades.

BASTING SAUCE

- ¾ cup canned regular or light coconut milk
- 3 tablespoons packed dark brown sugar
- 3 tablespoons fish sauce
- 2 tablespoons vegetable oil
- 3 shallots, minced
- 2 lemon grass stalks, trimmed to bottom 6 inches and minced
- 2 tablespoons grated fresh ginger
- 1½ teaspoons ground coriander
- ¾ teaspoon red pepper flakes
- ½ teaspoon ground cumin
- ½ teaspoon salt

BEEF

- 2 tablespoons vegetable oil
- 2 tablespoons packed dark brown sugar
- 1 tablespoon fish sauce
- 1 (1½- to 1¾-pound) flank steak, trimmed, halved lengthwise, and sliced on slight bias against grain into ¼-inch-thick slices
- 1 (13 by 9-inch) disposable aluminum roasting pan (if using charcoal)

1. FOR THE BASTING SAUCE: Whisk all ingredients together in medium bowl. Transfer one-third of sauce to small bowl and set both bowls aside.

2. FOR THE BEEF: Whisk oil, sugar, and fish sauce together in medium bowl. Toss beef with marinade and let stand at room temperature for 30 minutes. Weave beef onto 12-inch metal skewers, 2 to 4 pieces per skewer, leaving 1½ inches at top and bottom of skewer exposed. You should have 10 to 12 skewers.

3A. FOR A CHARCOAL GRILL: Poke twelve ½-inch holes in bottom of disposable roasting pan. Open bottom vent completely and place roasting pan in center of grill. Light large chimney starter mounded with charcoal briquettes (7 quarts). When top coals are partially covered with ash, pour into roasting pan. Set cooking grate over coals with bars parallel to long side of roasting pan, cover, and open lid vent completely. Heat grill until hot, about 5 minutes.

3B. FOR A GAS GRILL: Turn all burners to high, cover, and heat grill until hot, about 15 minutes. Leave all burners on high.

4. Clean and oil cooking grate. Place beef skewers on grill (directly over coals if using charcoal) perpendicular to grate bars. Brush meat with basting sauce in small bowl and cook (covered if using gas) until browned, about 3 minutes. Flip skewers, brush with half of basting sauce in medium bowl, and cook until browned on second side, about 3 minutes. Brush meat with remaining basting sauce and cook 1 minute longer. Transfer to large platter and serve.

PEANUT SAUCE
MAKES ABOUT 1½ CUPS

- 1 tablespoon vegetable oil
- 1 tablespoon Thai red curry paste
- 1 tablespoon packed dark brown sugar
- 2 garlic cloves, minced
- 1 cup canned regular or light coconut milk
- ⅓ cup chunky peanut butter
- ¼ cup roasted unsalted peanuts, chopped
- 1 tablespoon lime juice
- 1 tablespoon fish sauce
- 1 teaspoon soy sauce

Heat oil in small saucepan over medium heat until shimmering. Add curry paste, sugar, and garlic; cook, stirring constantly, until fragrant, about 1 minute. Add coconut milk and bring to simmer. Whisk in peanut butter until smooth. Remove from heat and stir in peanuts, lime juice, fish sauce, and soy sauce. Let cool to room temperature.

PRACTICAL SCIENCE ROOTING OUT MUSHINESS

Ginger in a marinade will make beef mushy.

We find that acidic ingredients and certain juices, like papaya and pineapple, which are often added to marinades to tenderize meat, actually turn the exterior mushy. We avoided these in our marinade for beef satay, but the meat still turned mushy. Could fresh ginger be the culprit?

To find out, we soaked beef in three different marinades for 30 minutes and then grilled each sample. The first marinade contained 2 tablespoons of ginger, the second contained 4 tablespoons, and the third contained no ginger at all.

The beef marinated in 2 tablespoons of ginger was markedly mushy; 4 tablespoons was even worse. Only the beef without ginger in its marinade had the proper tender—but not mushy—texture. What was going on? Fresh ginger contains an enzyme known as zingibain that, if left too long on meat, breaks down collagen on the meat's surface, producing the same mushy effect as acids and some juices. We expunged ginger from the marinade, saving it for the basting sauce instead. (For more on ginger, and ginger marinades, see page 243.)

Mexican-Style Grilled Steak (Carne Asada)

✓ WHY THIS RECIPE WORKS

To create a recipe for a carne asada platter, we started with skirt steak. Since it's most tender and juicy when cooked to medium, we were able to create plenty of char on its exterior without overcooking it. Couple that with an inventive way to corral the coals in the grill, a flavorful dry rub, and some salsa with fruity, smoky red chile and we had a take on carne asada that satisfied like the original.

GO WITH SKIRT Mexican cookbooks are divided on the best cut of meat for carne asada. Some go the thriftier route, calling for chuck roast, but pricier tenderloin and strip steak appear, too. We tested them all, sliced or pounded to ¼ inch thick, marinated in salt and lime juice, and grilled until charred. Inexpensive chuck's tough connective tissue and pockets of sinew and fat made it a flop. Super tender steaks didn't fare much better. While we didn't cook any of the steaks to well-done as a number of traditional recipes suggest, to get good charring on a thin steak, medium was the most realistic goal. Cooked to this degree, both tenderloin and strip were inevitably dry and mealy. Flank steak was better, but hard to pound thin. This left us with skirt steak and sirloin steak tips. Not only do these cuts have a beefier flavor, but because of their muscle structure (see page 25), they were tender when grilled to medium. Skirt steak, in the end, won out for both flavor and texture, and since it's inherently thin, all we needed to do was give it a few good whacks with a meat pounder.

USE A DRY RUB While many carne asada recipes call for a marinade, we found that this soaking step introduced too much extra moisture, making it impossible to get the kind of flavor-producing browning we wanted on the steaks when grilled. Therefore, we ditched the marinade and instead treated the steaks to a dry rub of salt and cumin. To work in the traditional lime flavor, we added a squeeze of citrus before serving. Garlic was also an added flavor bonus. To prevent it from burning in the rub, we smashed cloves and rubbed them over the steaks' charred crusts after they came off the grill. This simple step brought a burst of fresh garlic flavor and aroma to the meat.

CORRAL THE COALS For a charcoal grill, concentrating the charcoal directly under the steaks using a disposable aluminum roasting pan was our first step toward getting a really hot fire. And since greater availability of oxygen translates into a fire that burns hotter, instead of poking a few holes in the pan, we maximized the airflow by cutting the bottom out of the pan completely.

SERVE WITH SALSA AND BEANS Many carne asada recipes call for a tomatillo salsa, but it was the versions that had a red chile salsa that really stuck with us. The chiles' fruity, slightly smoky flavor added incredible depth to the steak. We toasted dried guajillo chiles and used fire-roasted diced tomatoes for a punchy and intense salsa. And, of course, no carne asada platter would be complete without beans. We opted for creamy refried beans over the brothy boiled kind. A quick homemade version with canned pinto beans, onion, garlic, and rich meaty depth from bacon was easy to prepare and tasted far superior to the canned stuff.

MEXICAN-STYLE GRILLED STEAK (CARNE ASADA)

SERVES 4 TO 6

Two pounds of sirloin steak tips, also sold as flap meat, may be substituted for the skirt steak. After cutting the meat into pieces, you should have four steaks with the grain (the long striations) running parallel to the long side. Serve with Red Chile Salsa and Simple Refried Beans (recipes follow).

- 1 (2-pound) skirt steak, trimmed
- 2 teaspoons kosher salt
- ¾ teaspoon ground cumin
- 1 (13 by 9-inch) disposable aluminum roasting pan (if using charcoal)
- 1 garlic clove, peeled and smashed
   Lime wedges

1. Pound steak to ¼ inch thick. Cut steak in half lengthwise with grain, then cut each piece in half crosswise against grain to make 4 equal-size steaks. Combine salt and cumin in small bowl. Sprinkle salt mixture evenly over both sides of steaks. Transfer steaks to wire rack set in rimmed baking sheet and refrigerate, uncovered, for at least 45 minutes or up to 24 hours. Meanwhile, if using charcoal, use kitchen shears to remove bottom of disposable pan and discard, reserving pan collar.

2A. FOR A CHARCOAL GRILL: Open bottom vent completely. Light large chimney starter filled with charcoal briquettes (6 quarts). When top coals are partially covered with ash, place disposable pan collar in center of grill over bottom vent and pour coals into even layer in collar. Set cooking grate in place, cover, and open lid vent completely. Heat grill until hot, about 5 minutes.

2B. FOR A GAS GRILL: Turn all burners to high, cover, and heat grill until hot, about 15 minutes. Leave all burners on high.

3. Clean and oil cooking grate. Place steaks on grill (if using charcoal, arrange steaks over coals in collar) and cook, uncovered, until well browned on first side, 2 to 4 minutes. Flip steaks and continue to cook until well browned on second side and meat registers 130 degrees, 2 to 4 minutes longer. Transfer steaks to cutting board, tent loosely with aluminum foil, and let rest for 5 minutes.

4. Rub garlic thoroughly over 1 side of steaks. Slice steaks against grain into ¼-inch-thick slices and serve with lime wedges.

RED CHILE SALSA
MAKES 2 CUPS

Guajillo chiles are fruity with just a bit of heat. (For more on chiles, see page 251.) Our favorite brand of fire-roasted tomatoes is DeLallo. Serve the salsa alongside the steak.

1¼	ounces dried guajillo chiles, wiped clean
1	(14.5-ounce) can fire-roasted diced tomatoes
¾	cup water
¾	teaspoon salt
1	garlic clove, peeled and smashed
½	teaspoon distilled white vinegar
¼	teaspoon dried oregano
⅛	teaspoon pepper
	Pinch ground cloves
	Pinch ground cumin

Toast guajillos in 10-inch nonstick skillet over medium-high heat until softened and fragrant, 1 to 2 minutes per side. Transfer to large plate and, when cool enough to handle, remove stems and seeds. Place guajillos in blender and process until finely ground, 60 to 90 seconds, scraping down sides of blender jar as needed. Add tomatoes and their juice, water, salt, garlic, vinegar, oregano, pepper, cloves, and cumin to blender and process until very smooth, 60 to 90 seconds, scraping down sides of blender jar as needed. (Salsa can be stored in refrigerator for up to 5 days or frozen for up to 1 month.)

SIMPLE REFRIED BEANS
MAKES ABOUT 1½ CUPS

2	slices bacon
1	small onion, chopped fine
2	garlic cloves, minced
1	(15-ounce) can pinto beans (do not rinse)
¼	cup water
	Kosher salt

Heat bacon in 10-inch nonstick skillet over medium-low heat until fat renders and bacon crisps, 7 to 10 minutes, flipping bacon halfway through. Remove bacon and reserve for another use. Increase heat to medium, add onion to fat in skillet, and cook until lightly browned, 5 to 7 minutes. Add garlic and cook until fragrant, about 30 seconds. Add beans and their liquid and water and bring to simmer. Cook, mashing beans with potato masher, until mixture is mostly smooth, 5 to 7 minutes. Season with salt to taste, and serve.

PRACTICAL SCIENCE
DOES POKING MEAT CAUSE MOISTURE LOSS?

Nope, another factor causes moisture loss.

A widespread belief holds that piercing meat with a fork during cooking should be avoided since it allegedly allows precious juices to escape. To put this theory to the test, we cooked two sets of five steaks to medium-rare. We gently turned one set with a pair of tongs, the other by jabbing the steaks with a sharp fork. We then compared the raw and cooked weights of each steak. Both sets of steaks lost the same amount of moisture during cooking—an average of 19.6 percent of their weight. The reason: Virtually all moisture that is lost when meat is cooked is a result of muscle fibers contracting in the heat and squeezing out their juices. Piercing does not damage the fibers enough to cause additional juices to leak out (any more than poking a wet sponge with a fork would expel its moisture). When it comes to moisture loss in meat, internal temperature is the most important factor. We like tongs because they keep our hands away from the heat source, but a fork will do no harm, at least to the meat.

Philly Cheesesteaks

✔ WHY THIS RECIPE WORKS

To get a real Philly cheesesteak, you have to go to Philadelphia. Or do you? In restaurants, these sandwiches are made using a meat slicer, a flat-top griddle, and pricey rib eye—all three of which, as far as we were concerned, were out of the question for a sandwich made at home. Bringing cheesesteaks home required coming up with a simple and economical way to mimic the thinly shaved slivers of rib eye usually obtained with a meat slicer. We found that when partially frozen, skirt steak's thin profile and open-grained texture made for easy slicing, and its flavor was nearest to rib eye but without the sticker shock.

FREEZE, THEN SLICE To re-create the thin-sliced meat that is essential to the classic sandwich, we tried a number of short-cut methods (including buying presliced deli roast beef and using a food processor to slice the meat), but slicing by hand gave us the best results by far. A quick stint in the freezer made the meat easier to slice thinly and cleanly. Then we coarsely chopped the steak before cooking it to imitate the restaurant method of hashing the steak with metal spatulas.

BROWN IN BATCHES On a restaurant's flat-top griddle, moisture evaporates almost instantly, allowing the meat to crisp up nicely. Using a 12-inch nonstick skillet and cooking the meat in batches proved to be a reasonable alternative. We let each batch drain in a colander before returning it to the pan to mix with the cheese, further cutting down on extra moisture—and greasiness.

PRACTICAL SCIENCE
PREVENTING A STICKY SITUATION

Keep steaks from sticking to the pan by not moving them until a crust has formed.

Steak sticks during cooking through the adhesion of dissolved proteins to the cooking surface in a process known as adsorption. While the mechanisms by which proteins adsorb onto a skillet are complicated and not fully understood, we do know that once the pan becomes hot enough, the link between the proteins and the pan will loosen, and the bond will eventually break.

To prevent steak from sticking, follow these steps: Heat oil in a heavy-bottomed skillet over high heat until it is just smoking (on most stovetops, this takes 2 to 3 minutes). Sear the meat without moving it, using tongs to flip it only when a substantial browned crust forms around the edges. If the meat doesn't lift easily, continue searing until it does.

GO ALL-AMERICAN Provolone cheese is the typical crowning touch to classic Philly cheesesteak. We, however, loved melty, gooey American cheese on top instead. We amped up the complexity of the cheese flavor with a little bit of nutty Parmesan.

PHILLY CHEESESTEAKS
SERVES 4

Top these sandwiches with chopped pickled hot peppers, sautéed onions or bell peppers, sweet relish, or hot sauce.

- 2 pounds skirt steak, trimmed and sliced with grain into 3-inch-wide strips
- 4 (8-inch) Italian sub rolls, split lengthwise
- 2 tablespoons vegetable oil
- ½ teaspoon salt
- ⅛ teaspoon pepper
- ¼ cup grated Parmesan cheese
- 8 slices white American cheese (8 ounces)

1. Place steak pieces on large plate or baking sheet and freeze until very firm, about 1 hour.

2. Meanwhile, adjust oven rack to middle position and heat oven to 400 degrees. Spread split rolls on baking sheet and toast until lightly browned, 5 to 10 minutes.

3. Using sharp knife, shave steak pieces as thin as possible against grain. Mound meat on cutting board and chop coarsely with knife 10 to 20 times.

4. Heat 1 tablespoon oil in 12-inch nonstick skillet over high heat until just smoking. Add half of meat in even layer and cook without stirring until well browned on 1 side, 4 to 5 minutes. Stir and continue to cook until meat is no longer pink, 1 to 2 minutes. Transfer meat to colander set in large bowl. Wipe out skillet with paper towel. Repeat with remaining 1 tablespoon oil and remaining sliced meat.

5. Return now-empty skillet to medium heat. Drain excess moisture from meat. Return meat to skillet (discard any liquid in bowl) and add salt and pepper. Heat, stirring constantly, until meat is warmed through, 1 to 2 minutes. Reduce heat to low, sprinkle with Parmesan, and shingle slices of American cheese over meat. Allow cheeses to melt, about 2 minutes. Using heatproof spatula or wooden spoon, fold melted cheese into meat thoroughly. Divide mixture evenly among toasted rolls. Serve immediately.

CHAPTER 3

Pork Loin

This extra-lean cut must be treated more like chicken than beef.

HOW THE SCIENCE WORKS

Pork is one of the most widely consumed meats outside of the United States (in China, the word for "pork" also means "meat") and also one of the most controversial (it is outlawed in many religions). In the last few decades, pigs have been bred to be leaner—and therefore they cook up to be drier and less flavorful without the right treatment.

There are a few factors that influence the quality of your pork. The first is the pH level of the raw meat, which is influenced by how the pig is treated immediately before slaughter. The second includes the fat content, structure, and type of muscle. And, finally, there's cooking technique.

The pH level of raw pork can tell you a lot about how the cooked meat will turn out: tender and juicy or tough and dry. A pH level below 7 is acidic, while over 7 is alkaline. The reason the pH is important is that it directly affects the electrical charge of the muscle proteins. If the muscle fibers' charges are equally positive and negative—a state known as the "isoelectric point," which for pork is at pH 5.2—there is a lack of electrical repulsion between them, causing the fibers to bind tightly together when heated, pushing out moisture and making the cooked pork tough and dry. The ideal pH for pork is between 6.5 and 6.8, where there is just enough repulsion between muscle fibers for them to remain separate and cook up tender and moist. Unfortunately, much of the pork sold in your supermarket has a pH closer to 5.5. (We tested three samples from three different markets, plus one wholesale butcher, and ended up with an average pH of 5.52.)

Also, enzymes called calpains, which break down muscle proteins and help make the meat tender, are more active the closer the meat is to pH 7. This means that pork with a pH of 6.0 will be much more tender than pork with a pH of 5.5.

The pH of raw pork will tell you a lot about how it will turn out when cooked.

What changes the pH level? It all comes down to the amount of glycogen, or the storage form of glucose for mammals, in the muscle at the time of slaughter, which is largely dependent on the amount of stress experienced by the animal immediately before. Acute stress lowers the level of glycogen, and a lack of glycogen builds up lactic acid, which lowers the pH, and ultimately has a negative effect on the cooked meat (see page 38).

The second factor influencing the quality of the pork you serve is the cut you choose. In this chapter we concentrate on the loin, which comes from the top of the pig, running from the shoulder to the leg.

This primal cut is the leanest, most tender part of the pig—mainly because the muscles are not worked much. Rib and loin chops are cut from this area, as well as pork loin roasts and tenderloin roasts. The amount of fat and collagen varies depending on the exact cut. But all cuts from the loin can become dry if overcooked. The tenderloin is exceptionally delicate and lean; it cannot be overcooked without ruining its texture and flavor.

The final factor affecting the quality of any cut, including pork loin, is cooking technique. Because this cut possesses so little fat, it needs to be treated differently, more like chicken than beef. We generally brine pork tenderloin, a salt-water soaking technique that both seasons the meat and helps restructure the meat proteins to better hold on to water while cooking. As with many lean meats, we cook pork loin either low and relatively slow to retain moisture (see Milk-Braised Pork Loin, page 36, or Slow-Roasted Bone-In Pork Rib Roast, page 41) or hot and fast on the grill for color and flavor (Grilled Pork Tenderloin Steaks, page 40).

TEST KITCHEN EXPERIMENT

Throughout years of cooking in the test kitchen, we've noticed that we tend to season lean meat much less generously than fatty meat. But anecdotal evidence alone wasn't enough to convince us that we need to treat pork loin differently than, say, a strip steak or even ground beef. To bolster our anecdotal evidence with real data, we set up the following experiment.

EXPERIMENT

We rounded up five meats ranging in fat content: turkey breast, pork loin, strip steak (beef), and both 80 percent and 90 percent lean ground beef. We cooked the meat and chopped it into pieces. We then tossed 10-gram portions of each meat with increasing amounts of salt (0.1 percent, 0.25 percent, 0.5 percent, 0.75 percent, 1 percent, and 1.5 percent by weight of each sample). We had tasters try the samples blind in order, starting with an unsalted control, and had them record at what percentage the meat tasted properly seasoned. We also sent cooked samples of each type of meat to a lab to determine fat content.

RESULTS

Sure enough, the fattier the meat the more salt it needed to taste properly seasoned. Tasters preferred the lean turkey breast (0.7 percent fat) and pork loin (2.6 percent fat) seasoned with 0.5 percent salt by weight. The strip steak (6 percent fat) and 90 percent lean ground beef (10 percent fat) required about 0.75 percent salt by weight to taste seasoned. And finally, the 80 percent lean ground beef (20 percent fat) tasted seasoned to a majority of tasters only when it reached 1 percent salt by weight.

TAKEAWAY

In 2012, a study published in the science journal *Chemosensory Perception* showed that fats in food may activate certain regions of the brain, thereby influencing how tastes are perceived. More specifically, fat has a dulling effect on taste. Our test lends credence to this. So when you season meat, remember to use a heavier hand on fatty burgers than you would on only moderately fatty meats like strip steak and 90 percent lean ground beef. Use a lighter hand on lean meats like turkey breast and pork loin.

FATTIER MEAT NEEDS MORE SALT

We tasted 6 samples each of ground turkey breast, pork loin, strip steak, 90 percent lean ground beef, and 80 percent lean ground beef, with increasing amounts of salt, and determined which sample tasted best. The results? The fattier the meat, the more salt it needed to taste properly seasoned. Why? Fat, it has been shown, has a dulling effect on our sense of taste.

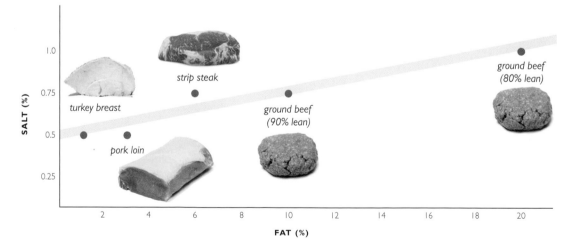

FOCUS ON: PORK

There are four different primal cuts of pork available on the wholesale level. Here, we focus on the loin, which can be cut in many different ways.

SHOULDER

Cuts from the shoulder are well marbled with fat and have a lot of connective tissue (see page 43). They are ideal candidates for slow-cooking techniques like braising, stewing, or barbecuing. Cuts from the front leg are less pricey, but otherwise quite similar.

SIDE/BELLY

The underside is the fattiest part of the animal and is the source of both bacon and spareribs (see page 51).

LEG

The rear legs are often referred to as "ham." This primal cut is sold as large roasts and is available fresh or cured.

LOIN

The area between the shoulder and back legs is the leanest, most tender part of the animal. A whole pork loin weighs 14 to 17 pounds, runs the entire length of the backbone, and can be split into a number of different cuts. The rib roast and loin roast form the "center-cut loin."

BLADE-END ROAST This is our favorite boneless roast for roasting. It is cut from the shoulder end of the loin and has more fat and flavor than the boneless center-cut loin roast.

BLADE CHOP Cut from the shoulder end of the loin, these chops can be difficult to find at the market. They are fatty, with good flavor and juiciness.

RIB ROAST Often referred to as the pork equivalent of prime rib or rack of lamb, this mild, fairly lean roast consists of a single muscle with a protective fat cap. It may include from five to eight ribs.

RIB CHOP Cut from the rib section of the loin, these chops have a relatively high fat content, making them flavorful and unlikely to dry out during cooking. They are a favorite in the test kitchen. Note: Rib chops are also sold boneless. In fact, most boneless pork chops you'll find are cut from the rib chop.

LOIN ROAST This popular boneless roast is juicy, tender, and evenly shaped, with somewhat less fat than the rib roast.

LOIN CHOP These chops are identified by the bone that divides the loin meat from the tenderloin muscle. The lean tenderloin section cooks more quickly than the loin section, making it a challenge to keep these chops moist.

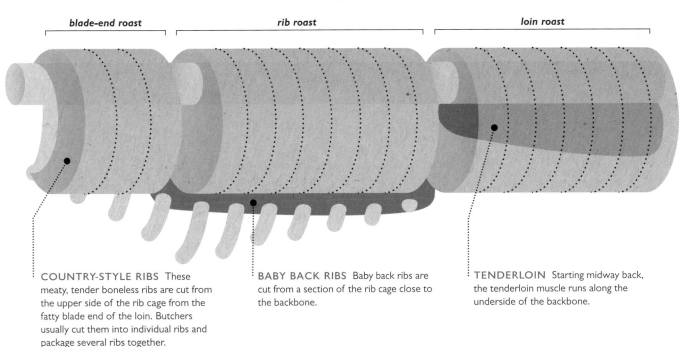

blade-end roast   *rib roast*   *loin roast*

COUNTRY-STYLE RIBS These meaty, tender boneless ribs are cut from the upper side of the rib cage from the fatty blade end of the loin. Butchers usually cut them into individual ribs and package several ribs together.

BABY BACK RIBS Baby back ribs are cut from a section of the rib cage close to the backbone.

TENDERLOIN Starting midway back, the tenderloin muscle runs along the underside of the backbone.

Milk-Braised Pork Loin

✔ WHY THIS RECIPE WORKS

This Italian classic involves braising a pork loin in a large quantity of milk. Oven braising at a low temperature yields a juicy and tender roast. As the roast cooks, the milk curdles and reduces into an intensely flavorful but unattractive sauce. We minimized curdling and amped up the flavor by adding a touch of fat from rendered salt pork. Then, while the roast rested, we stirred in wine, mustard, and herbs to finish the sauce.

BRINE YOUR PORK   There are two cuts traditionally used for this dish: a fat- and collagen-streaked shoulder roast or a lean pork loin. Tasters found that the shoulder roast made the already rich dish overwhelming. But the lean loin needed some help to keep it from becoming dry. In the test kitchen, we typically fix potentially dry roasts with a brine. The salt solution helps the meat to take on water weight during the soak. And the salt has the added benefit of reshaping the protein molecules in the meat so that the proteins can hold on to the added water, even after the meat is cooked. Submerging the loin in a salt and sugar solution for 90 minutes or so (our usual pretreatment for this cut) helped it to stay moist during cooking and gave it a nice seasoning boost, too.

ADD FAT   At first, the milky sauce for this dish was turning into a liquid strewn with unattractive curdled bits. That wouldn't work. This was happening because the slightly acidic juices shed by the pork caused the milk's casein proteins to bind together into curd-like clusters, a reaction that sped up when the milk was heated. We tried whisking the sauce to break up the clumps, and whisking the milk as it cooked to prevent the formation of clumps. Both techniques worked—kind of. The real fix, however, came when we added fat. This made the milk less likely to curdle in acidic conditions, since the fat molecules wedged themselves between the casein proteins, literally preventing them from bonding. We tried adding heavy cream and rendered bacon fat, but settled on salt pork for its clean-tasting meatiness.

AND BAKING SODA   Baking soda may sound like an odd addition to a braising sauce, but we've discovered that this alkaline ingredient has considerable powers beyond leavening. A small amount of baking soda raised the pH of the sauce to create conditions more favorable for Maillard browning, a series of reactions that produce flavorful aromatic compounds. The addition of baking soda also neutralized the slightly acidic juices from the pork and thus reduced the likelihood of the milk curdling.

MILK-BRAISED PORK LOIN
SERVES 4 TO 6

The milk will bubble up when added to the pot. If necessary, remove the pot from the heat and stir to break up the foam before returning it to the heat. We prefer natural pork, but if your pork is enhanced (injected with a salt solution—see "Enhanced or Not?") do not brine. Instead, skip to step 2.

	Salt and pepper
¼	cup sugar
1	(2- to 2½-pound) boneless pork loin roast, trimmed
2	ounces salt pork, chopped coarse
3	cups whole milk
5	garlic cloves, peeled
1	teaspoon minced fresh sage
¼	teaspoon baking soda
½	cup dry white wine
3	tablespoons chopped fresh parsley
1	teaspoon Dijon mustard

1. Dissolve ¼ cup salt and sugar in 2 quarts cold water in large container. Submerge roast in brine, cover, and refrigerate for 1½ to 2 hours. Remove roast from brine and pat dry with paper towels.

PRACTICAL SCIENCE ENHANCED OR NOT?

Enhanced pork is injected with a sodium solution—and is far from our first choice at the supermarket.

Because modern pork is so lean and therefore somewhat bland and prone to dryness if overcooked, many producers now inject their fresh pork products with a sodium solution. So-called enhanced pork is now the only option at many supermarkets, especially when buying lean cuts like the tenderloin. (To be sure, read the label; if the pork has been enhanced it will have an ingredient label.)

Enhanced pork is injected with a solution of water, salt, and one or more of the following: sodium phosphate, sodium lactate, potassium lactate, sodium diacetate, and varying flavor agents, generally adding 7 to 15 percent extra weight. While enhanced pork does cook up juicier (it has been pumped full of water), we find the texture almost spongy and the flavor is often unpleasantly salty. We prefer the genuine pork flavor of natural pork and prefer to brine lean cuts to keep them juicy. Note that enhanced pork loses six times more moisture when frozen and thawed compared to natural pork—yet another reason to avoid it.

2. Adjust oven rack to middle position and heat oven to 275 degrees. Bring salt pork and ½ cup water to simmer in Dutch oven over medium heat. Simmer until water evaporates and salt pork begins to sizzle, 5 to 6 minutes. Continue to cook, stirring frequently, until salt pork is lightly browned and fat has rendered, 2 to 3 minutes. Using slotted spoon, discard salt pork, leaving fat in pot.

3. Increase heat to medium-high, add roast to pot, and brown on all sides, 8 to 10 minutes. Transfer roast to large plate. Add milk, garlic, sage, and baking soda to pot and bring to simmer, scraping up any browned bits. Cook, stirring frequently, until milk is lightly browned and has consistency of heavy cream, 14 to 16 minutes. Reduce heat to medium-low and continue to cook, stirring and scraping bottom of pot constantly, until milk thickens to consistency of thin batter, 1 to 3 minutes longer. Remove pot from heat.

4. Return roast to pot, cover, and transfer to oven. Cook until meat registers 140 degrees, 40 to 50 minutes, flipping roast once halfway through cooking. Transfer roast to carving board, tent with aluminum foil, and let rest for 20 to 25 minutes.

5. Once roast has rested, pour any accumulated juices into pot. Add wine and return sauce to simmer over medium-high heat, whisking vigorously to smooth out sauce. Simmer until sauce has consistency of thin gravy, 2 to 3 minutes. Off heat, stir in 2 tablespoons parsley and mustard and season with salt and pepper to taste. Slice roast into ¼-inch-thick slices. Transfer slices to serving platter. Spoon sauce over slices, sprinkle with remaining 1 tablespoon parsley, and serve.

Grilled Glazed Pork Tenderloin Roast

✓ WHY THIS RECIPE WORKS

On top of lean pork tenderloin's susceptibility to dryness, another problem to solve when cooking is its ungainly tapered shape. By the time the large end hits a perfect medium (140 degrees), the skinnier tail is guaranteed to be overdone. For this recipe, we solved the problem—and also created a more presentation-worthy cut—by tying two tenderloins together, making a larger roast.

BRINE IT Keeping meat of any kind juicy on the grill is a perennial challenge. In the test kitchen, we have a couple of tricks for addressing the problem, namely salting and brining. Both techniques introduce salt into the flesh, where it tenderizes the meat and increases water retention. Using our preferred type of pork, unenhanced (or natural)—meaning that it had not been injected with a solution of water, salt, and sodium phosphate—we ran side-by-side tests in which we salted and brined a few tenderloins, slicked them with oil, and grilled them. Tasters reported that while both options proved juicier and more evenly seasoned than an untreated control, the brined samples were the most succulent.

BIND IT Tying two pork tenderloins together solved the problem of uneven cooking by creating, in effect, one large roast. This large roast could also stay on the grill longer without the center overcooking, giving us more time to develop a really browned crust. But when we carved it, each slice flopped apart into two pieces. The next step was to find a way to bind them together more permanently. Trying to get meat to stick together might sound unorthodox, but it's something that happens naturally all the time, at least with ground meat. When sausages, burgers, meatballs, and meatloaf are prepared, soluble sticky proteins are released, which fuse together to form a cohesive whole. We used that as inspiration. Anytime meat is damaged (during grinding, slicing, or even pounding), sticky proteins are released. The proteins' gluey texture is what makes it possible to form a cohesive burger from nothing but ground beef. We tried roughing up the surfaces of the tenderloins in a variety of ways, but, in the end, we found that a few simple scrapes of a fork along the length of each one before brining, followed by a very thorough drying after brining, was the key.

COOK HIGH AND LOW Many pork tenderloin recipes call for grilling the meat directly over a hot fire the entire time. The result? A well-browned exterior with a thick band of dry, overcooked meat below its surface—no thanks. A better approach, we've found, is to employ a combination high-low method: High heat provides great browning—which means great flavor—and low heat cooks meat evenly. We began the pork over low heat and followed by searing over high. During its initial stay on the cooler side of the grill, the meat's surface warmed and dried, making for fast, efficient browning (and therefore precluding overcooking) when it hit the hotter part of the grate.

USE UMAMI-RICH GLAZES Finally, we wanted a burnished, bold glaze. Most glazes contain sugar, which caramelizes when exposed to heat, deepening flavor. But we wanted to add still more complexity—even meatiness. We did this by including glutamate-rich ingredients that enhance savory flavor, like miso and hoisin sauce. In addition, pork has a high concentration of nucleotides. When glutamates and nucleotides are combined, these compounds have a synergistic effect that magnifies meaty, savory flavor significantly more than glutamates alone do.

PRACTICAL SCIENCE HOW SLAUGHTER AFFECTS FLAVOR AND JUICINESS

Mail-ordered Berkshire pork has better flavor and juiciness than regular supermarket pork—and this has everything to do with pH.

After years of advertising pork as "the other white meat," pork producers have started to change their tune. Nowadays, fat, flavor, and even deeper color are making a comeback, with chefs and consumers paying top dollar for specialty breeds touted as being fattier, juicier, and far more flavorful. But we were skeptical: Are those pedigreed labels like Berkshire (known as Kurobuta in Japan) and Duroc a true indication of quality—or just a premium price tag? (Once mail-order shipping is factored in, specialty pork can cost at least twice as much as supermarket meat.)

When we tasted a sampling of mail-ordered Berkshire pork, however, we were sold. And we wondered if its better flavor and juiciness were related to anything more than just the specific breed. As it turned out, the meat's deep pink tint was more significant than we thought. According to Kenneth Prusa, professor of food science at Iowa State University, that color really is an indication of quality.

The color reflects the meat's pH, which Prusa pinpoints as the "overall driver of quality" in pork. In mammals, normal pH is around 7. But Prusa told us even small differences in pH can have a significant impact on pork's flavor and texture. Berkshire pigs are bred to have a slightly higher pH than normal (due in part to a higher percentage of slow-twitch endurance muscles), which in turn makes their meat darker, firmer, and more flavorful. In fact, a high pH can be even more important than fat in determining flavor. Conversely, pork with low pH is paler, softer, and relatively bland. In addition to genetics, pH is influenced by husbandry conditions, along with slaughtering and processing methods. Berkshire pigs are raised in low-stress environments that keep them calm. And the calmer the animal, the more evenly blood flows through its system, distributing flavorful juices throughout. Berkshire pigs are also slaughtered with methods that minimize stress, which causes a buildup of lactic acid in the muscles and lowers pH. Chilling the meat very rapidly after slaughter is yet another factor that affects pH, which begins to decline immediately once blood flow stops. Increasingly, commercial producers are adopting similar measures in slaughtering and processing in an effort to keep the pH of their pork as high as possible. We tested three samples of Berkshire pork and found the pH to average out to 6.02, as compared to an average pH of 5.52 for supermarket pork.

Bottom line: Berkshire pork won't become a regular purchase for most of us, but we think it is worth the occasional splurge. In the meantime, we'll be picking out the pinkest pork at the supermarket.

GRILLED GLAZED PORK TENDERLOIN ROAST
SERVES 6

Since brining is a key step in having the two tenderloins stick together, we don't recommend using enhanced pork in this recipe.

2   (1-pound) pork tenderloins, trimmed
     Salt and pepper
     Vegetable oil
1   recipe glaze (recipes follow)

1. Lay tenderloins on cutting board, flat side (side opposite where silverskin was) up. Holding thick end of 1 tenderloin with paper towels and using dinner fork, scrape flat side lengthwise from end to end 5 times, until surface is completely covered with shallow grooves. Repeat with second tenderloin. Dissolve 3 tablespoons salt in 1½ quarts cold water in large container. Submerge tenderloins in brine and let stand at room temperature for 1 hour.

2. Remove tenderloins from brine and pat completely dry with paper towels. Lay 1 tenderloin, scraped side up, on cutting board and lay second tenderloin, scraped side down, on top so that thick end of 1 tenderloin matches up with thin end of other. Spray five 14-inch lengths of kitchen twine thoroughly with vegetable oil spray; evenly space twine underneath tenderloins and tie. Brush roast with vegetable oil and season with pepper. Transfer ⅓ cup glaze to bowl for grilling; reserve remaining glaze for serving.

3A. FOR A CHARCOAL GRILL: Open bottom vent completely. Light large chimney starter filled with charcoal briquettes (6 quarts). When top coals are partially covered with ash, pour into steeply banked pile against side of grill. Set cooking grate in place, cover, and open lid vent completely. Heat grill until hot, about 5 minutes.

3B. FOR A GAS GRILL: Turn all burners to high, cover, and heat grill until hot, about 15 minutes. Leave primary burner on high and turn off other burner(s).

4. Clean and oil cooking grate. Place roast on cooler side of grill, cover, and cook until meat registers 115 degrees, 22 to 28 minutes, flipping and rotating halfway through cooking.

5. Slide roast to hotter part of grill and cook until lightly browned on all sides, 4 to 6 minutes. Brush top of roast with about 1 tablespoon glaze and grill, glaze side down,

until glaze begins to char, 2 to 3 minutes; repeat glazing and grilling with remaining 3 sides of roast, until meat registers 140 degrees.

6. Transfer roast to cutting board, tent with aluminum foil, and let rest for 10 minutes. Carefully remove twine and slice roast into ½-inch-thick slices. Serve with remaining glaze.

MISO GLAZE
MAKES ABOUT ¾ CUP

3   tablespoons sake
3   tablespoons mirin
⅓   cup white miso paste
¼   cup sugar
2   teaspoons Dijon mustard
1   teaspoon rice vinegar
¼   teaspoon grated fresh ginger
¼   teaspoon toasted sesame oil

Bring sake and mirin to boil in small saucepan over medium heat. Whisk in miso and sugar until smooth, about 30 seconds. Remove pan from heat and continue to whisk until sugar is dissolved, about 1 minute. Whisk in mustard, vinegar, ginger, and sesame oil until smooth.

SWEET AND SPICY HOISIN GLAZE
MAKES ABOUT ¾ CUP

1   teaspoon vegetable oil
3   garlic cloves, minced
1   teaspoon grated fresh ginger
½   teaspoon red pepper flakes
½   cup hoisin sauce
2   tablespoons soy sauce
1   tablespoon rice vinegar

Heat oil in small saucepan over medium heat until shimmering. Add garlic, ginger, and pepper flakes; cook until fragrant, about 30 seconds. Whisk in hoisin and soy sauce until smooth. Remove pan from heat and stir in vinegar.

Garlic-Lime Grilled Pork Tenderloin Steaks

✔ WHY THIS RECIPE WORKS

One of the most common ways to grill pork tenderloin is to turn it into medallions. But this often means that instead of an easy-to-manage roast you end up with small coins that demand constant attention—or slip through the grill grate. Despite those pitfalls, the extra surface area provided by cutting does allow for more flavor. We just had to figure out another way to achieve this. We did it by cutting the tenderloin into "steaks" rather than medallions, and by using a bold marinade and finishing sauce.

CUT DIFFERENTLY We decided that if more surface area—for a better ratio of browned exterior to tender interior—was our goal, perhaps slicing the tenderloin was not the best way to go. Instead, we cut each tenderloin in half to create two shorter cylinders and then pounded the halves into "steaks" that were ¾ inch thick. The cutting and pounding steps took just minutes, but created 30 percent more surface area.

MARINATE BOLDLY We started our marinade with salt. In addition to seasoning the meat, salt dissolves proteins within the meat, which helps it trap moisture and become more tender. We also included oil, as most of the aromatics, herbs, and spices that we add to marinades are soluble in fat; plus, oil helped the marinade evenly coat the meat. For flavor, we added minced garlic, lime juice and zest for acidity and extra lime flavor, and honey (which adds complexity and encourages browning). Finally, we included umami-rich fish sauce to heighten the savory flavor without making the pork taste distinctly Asian or fishy. We cut thin slashes in the steaks to promote better penetration of the marinade, and we let the excess marinade stay on the steaks to help keep their exteriors from drying out on the grill.

GET SAUCY Setting aside some extra marinade to use as a sauce didn't work. The raw garlic and lime juice tasted too harsh. But we found an easy fix: Just a few teaspoons of mayonnaise gave the reinvigorated sauce lightly creamy body and balanced its flavors.

GARLIC-LIME GRILLED PORK TENDERLOIN STEAKS
SERVES 4 TO 6

Since marinating is a key step in this recipe, we don't recommend using enhanced pork.

2	(1-pound) pork tenderloins, trimmed
1	tablespoon grated lime zest plus ¼ cup juice (2 limes)
4	garlic cloves, minced
4	teaspoons honey
2	teaspoons fish sauce
¾	teaspoon salt
½	teaspoon pepper
½	cup vegetable oil
4	teaspoons mayonnaise
1	tablespoon chopped fresh cilantro
	Flake sea salt (optional)

1. Slice each tenderloin in half crosswise to create 4 steaks total. Pound each half to ¾-inch thickness. Using sharp knife, cut ⅛-inch-deep slits spaced ½ inch apart in crosshatch pattern on both sides of steaks.

2. Whisk lime zest and juice, garlic, honey, fish sauce, salt, and pepper together in large bowl. Whisking constantly, slowly drizzle oil into lime mixture until smooth and slightly thickened. Transfer ½ cup lime mixture to small bowl and whisk in mayonnaise; set aside sauce. Add steaks to bowl with remaining marinade and toss thoroughly to coat; transfer steaks and marinade to large zipper-lock bag, press out as much air as possible, and seal bag. Let steaks sit at room temperature for 45 minutes.

3A. FOR A CHARCOAL GRILL: Open bottom vent completely. Light large chimney starter filled with charcoal briquettes (6 quarts). When top coals are partially covered with ash, pour evenly over half of grill. Set cooking grate in place, cover, and open lid vent completely. Heat grill until hot, about 5 minutes.

3B. FOR A GAS GRILL: Turn all burners to high, cover, and heat grill until hot, about 15 minutes. Leave primary burner on high and turn off other burner(s).

4. Clean and oil cooking grate. Remove steaks from marinade (do not pat dry) and place over hotter side of grill. Cook, uncovered, until well browned on first side,

3 to 4 minutes. Flip steaks and cook until well browned on second side, 3 to 4 minutes. Transfer steaks to cooler side of grill, with wider end of each steak facing hotter side of grill. Cover and cook until meat registers 140 degrees, 3 to 8 minutes longer (remove steaks as they come to temperature). Transfer steaks to cutting board and let rest for 5 minutes.

5. While steaks rest, microwave reserved sauce until warm, 15 to 30 seconds; stir in cilantro. Slice steaks against grain into ½-inch-thick slices. Drizzle with half of sauce; sprinkle with sea salt, if using; and serve, passing remaining sauce separately.

Slow-Roasted Bone-In Pork Rib Roast

✔ WHY THIS RECIPE WORKS

Often referred to as the pork equivalent of prime rib or rack of lamb, this part of the loin is a mild, fairly lean roast consisting of a single muscle with a protective fat cap. It is basically a bone-in loin roast, but with more of the fat cap attached. Treated the right way, it can be truly impressive: moist, tender, and full of rich, meaty taste. All this—and for less money than a prime rib costs. But why can't you cook it like prime rib? We were determined to find out.

GIVE IT A RUB Salting the meat and letting it rest for 6 hours ensured that the pork was well seasoned and helped it hold on to just the right amount of moisture. We removed the bones from the pork so that we could salt the meat on all sides; we then nestled the meat back up against the bones and secured it with kitchen twine. Cooking the roast with the bones attached ensured that even the interior of the meat stayed moist.

ADD SOME SUGAR The addition of some brown sugar to the salt rub provided pleasing molasses notes that paired nicely with the pork. As a bonus, it also contributed a gorgeous mahogany color, which allowed us to skip the tedious task of searing the meat. Without searing, the fat cap didn't render, but this was easily fixed by scoring deep crosshatch marks into the fat to help it melt and baste the meat during roasting.

COOK IT LOW AND SLOW Cooking the roast in a 250-degree oven for 3 to 4 hours prevented the exterior from overcooking before the interior had a chance to reach the proper temperature, resulting in evenly cooked meat.

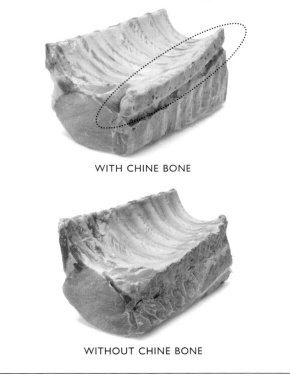

PRACTICAL SCIENCE
HOW TO BUY BONE-IN PORK RIB ROAST

If you plan to make our Slow-Roasted Bone-In Pork Rib Roast, here's what to look for when you visit the butcher.

When making our Slow-Roasted Bone-In Pork Rib Roast, you'll want a 4- to 5-pound center-cut roast with a fat cap that's ¼- to ½-inch-thick. But you might have to go one step further at the butcher counter, as some roasts come with the chine bone, or part of the back bone, attached. Ask the butcher to remove as much of this bone as possible to facilitate carving.

WITH CHINE BONE

WITHOUT CHINE BONE

Blasting the roast under the broiler for a couple of minutes just prior to serving ensured the fat had a chance to crisp up.

SLOW-ROASTED BONE-IN PORK RIB ROAST
SERVES 6 TO 8

This recipe requires refrigerating the salted meat for at least 6 hours before cooking. For easier carving, ask the butcher to remove the chine bone. Monitoring the roast with an oven probe thermometer is best. If you use an instant-read thermometer, open the oven door as infrequently as possible and remove the roast from the oven while taking its temperature. The sauce may be prepared in advance or while the roast rests in step 3.

1 (4- to 5-pound) center-cut bone-in pork rib roast, chine bone removed
2 tablespoons packed dark brown sugar
1 tablespoon kosher salt
1½ teaspoons pepper
1 recipe Port Wine–Cherry Sauce (recipe follows)

1. Using sharp knife, remove roast from bones, running knife down length of bones and following contours as closely as possible. Reserve bones. Combine sugar and salt in small bowl. Pat roast dry with paper towels. If necessary, trim thick spots of surface fat layer to about ¼-inch thickness. Using sharp knife, cut slits, spaced 1 inch apart, in crosshatch pattern in surface fat layer, being careful not to cut into meat. Rub roast evenly with sugar mixture. Wrap roast and ribs in plastic wrap and refrigerate for at least 6 hours or up to 24 hours.

2. Adjust oven rack to lower-middle position and heat oven to 250 degrees. Sprinkle roast evenly with pepper.

PRACTICAL SCIENCE
WHY ADD CREAM TO A BUTTER SAUCE?

Cream stabilizes the butterfat.

To dress up our pork, we turned to a classic French preparation: *beurre rouge*. The beauty of this sauce, which translates as "red butter," is that at its most basic it requires just two components: butter and an acidic liquid. (Red wine and red vinegar for beurre rouge and white for beurre blanc are traditional.) The preparation is equally simple: Just whisk cold butter into the reduced acidic liquid.

The problem is that butter sauces, like any mixture of fat and water, don't always stay emulsified. That's because the butter is highly temperature-sensitive: If the sauce gets too hot (above around 135 degrees), the butter—itself an emulsion of fat and water—will "break" and the butterfat will separate. If it gets too cold (below 85 degrees), the butterfat solidifies and forms crystals that clump together and separate when the sauce is reheated.

The key to foolproofing a butter sauce is thus stabilizing the butterfat so that it doesn't separate. We do this by whisking in the butter a little bit at a time, which keeps the temperature of the sauce relatively stable. Even more important, we also add cream. Cream contains a relatively high proportion of casein proteins that surround and stabilize the butterfat droplets so that they don't separate from the emulsion. It also contains lecithin, an emulsifier. Cream is such an effective stabilizer that our sauce can be made ahead, chilled, and gently reheated before serving.

Place roast back on ribs so bones fit where they were cut; tie roast to bones with lengths of kitchen twine between ribs. Transfer roast, fat side up, to wire rack set in rimmed baking sheet. Roast until meat registers 145 degrees, 3 to 4 hours.

3. Remove roast from oven (leave roast on sheet), tent with aluminum foil, and let rest for 30 minutes.

4. Adjust oven rack 8 inches from broiler element and heat broiler. Return roast to oven and broil until top of roast is well browned and crispy, 2 to 6 minutes.

5. Transfer roast to carving board; cut twine and remove meat from ribs. Slice meat into ¾-inch-thick slices and serve, passing sauce separately.

PORT WINE–CHERRY SAUCE
MAKES ABOUT 1 ¾ CUPS

2 cups tawny port
1 cup dried cherries
½ cup balsamic vinegar
2 shallots, minced
4 sprigs fresh thyme, plus 2 teaspoons minced
¼ cup heavy cream
16 tablespoons unsalted butter, cut into ½-inch pieces and chilled
1 teaspoon salt
½ teaspoon pepper

1. Combine port and cherries in bowl and microwave until steaming, 1 to 2 minutes. Cover and let stand until plump, about 10 minutes. Strain port through fine-mesh strainer into medium saucepan, reserving cherries.

2. Add vinegar, shallots, and thyme sprigs to port and bring to boil over high heat. Reduce heat to medium-high and reduce mixture until it measures ¾ cup, 14 to 16 minutes. Add cream and reduce again to ¾ cup, about 5 minutes. Discard thyme sprigs. Off heat, whisk in butter, few pieces at a time, until fully incorporated. Stir in cherries, minced thyme, salt, and pepper. Cover pan and hold, off heat, until serving. Alternatively, let sauce cool completely and refrigerate for up to 2 days. Reheat in small saucepan over medium-low heat, stirring frequently, until warm.

CHAPTER 4

Pork Shoulder

This tough cut turns meltingly tender due to the power of gelatin.

HOW THE SCIENCE WORKS

While pork loin may be one of the leanest cuts, the shoulder is marbled with fat and laced with connective tissue. It's a primal cut made for low and slow heat, one that with extended cooking time will transform from tough to fall-apart tender.

Two cuts come from the shoulder. One, from the lower region of the arm, is called, simply, the pork shoulder, also known as a picnic roast. The other, less logically named cut from the upper section of the shoulder is the pork butt roast. It is also known as the Boston shoulder or the Boston butt, though it comes from neither Boston nor the rump. (Rumor has it that in Revolutionary New England, particularly in Boston, this cut was stored in specialty barrels called "butts.")

Cuts from the shoulder are known for their intense flavor, due to a high amount of intramuscular fat, which renders when cooked, and a fat cap, which can turn into a bronzed, bacon-like crust. Its meat is dark in color, darker than pale pork loin, because the shoulder muscle provides motion for the pig, therefore producing much energy and requiring oxygen. The abundance of a red, oxygen-storing pigment known as myoglobin gives pork shoulder its deep color.

Other factors distinguish the shoulder, especially in comparison to the loin. One is the length of the basic muscle unit known as the sarcomere (see illustration, page 25). A shoulder-muscle sarcomere is almost 40 percent longer than that of a loin muscle. And the longer the sarcomere, the tougher the meat, due to the fact that longer fibers have fewer intersections between them, and are therefore harder to bite through.

Another difference is the amount of connective tissue. As we've learned (see illustration, page 25), meat is made up of muscle fibers, connective tissue, fat, and water.

"Boston butt" comes from neither Boston nor the rump.

Connective tissue, which is a membranous, translucent mix of cells and protein filaments, surrounds the bundles of muscle fibers, providing structure and support. When a muscle gets a lot of exercise, like the shoulder muscle of a pig does, it needs more connective tissue to reinforce its structure and its connection to bones. Connective tissue is made predominantly of a protein called collagen.

Collagen consists of three individual protein chains, tightly wound together in a triple helix strand. It is tough—so tough that it is nearly impossible to chew when raw. Pork from the shoulder contains about 50 percent more collagen than pork from the loin. But temperature changes that. When meat reaches 140 degrees that triple protein strand begins to unwind. When held ideally between 160 and 180 degrees for an extended period of time, the protein strands that make up collagen unwind further and convert to gelatin, which is a single strand of protein and important because it is incredibly soft and able to retain up to 10 times its weight in water. Gelatin is a powerful substance, allowing tough cuts like pork shoulder to become juicy and tender.

It's important to note that it takes several hours at this temperature for most of the collagen in a Boston butt to convert to gelatin—a process dependent on both time and temperature (see Test Kitchen Experiment, page 44). To keep the meat at prime collagen-melting temperature without losing too much moisture, we cook it low and slow. We smoke our Smoky Pulled Pork (page 46) for an hour and a half, and then continue to grill it at a low temperature for a couple more hours. Cut into strips, the lacquered pork butt in our Chinese Barbecued Pork (page 49) is cooked in a low oven. And we simmer the pork for our French-Style Pork Stew (page 50) to make a flavorful broth.

TEST KITCHEN EXPERIMENT

We prize cuts like pork rib chops and pork tenderloin for their inherent tenderness, but we love pork shoulder for just the opposite reason: It's tough. Though counterintuitive, initial toughness can result in meltingly tender, juicy meat, thanks to the conversion of the connective tissue protein collagen to gelatin. This transformation feels like true kitchen alchemy, but we know it's grounded in hard science. At temperatures starting around 140 degrees, collagen, a triple helix made of three protein chains, unwinds to form three strands of supple gelatin. Traditional cooking methods like braising and slow roasting bring the temperature of the meat well over the 140-degree threshold into the 190- to 200-degree range, where the collagen is converted in a couple of hours. Modern low-temperature cooking in a water bath, often done sous vide (in a vacuum-sealed bag), has shown us that the same process takes place at lower temperatures, but requires longer cooking times. We set up an experiment to explore this relationship between temperature and time on both collagen breakdown and moisture loss.

EXPERIMENT

We sealed multiple 40-gram portions of boneless pork shoulder in vacuum-sealed bags and placed them in temperature-controlled water baths at four different temperatures: 140 degrees, 158 degrees, 176 degrees, and 194 degrees (these temperatures correspond to 60, 70, 80, and 90 degrees, respectively, on the centigrade temperature scale). We cooked the samples until the meat transitioned from having the firm texture of a pork chop to the point where we could just shred it. After establishing a cook time for each temperature, we tested additional samples to determine moisture loss for each combination of time and temperature.

RESULTS

We discovered a clear inverse time-temperature relationship for the conversion of collagen to gelatin. At 140, 158, 176, and 194 degrees it took 31, 16, 7, and 2 hours, respectively, for the pork shoulder to turn just shreddable. When we looked at moisture loss we found just the opposite: as the temperature increased so too did the amount of moisture squeezed from the meat. At 140, 158, 176, and 194 degrees, the meat lost 29.8, 33.1, 35.9, and 37.5 percent moisture, respectively.

TAKEAWAY

We can see from this experiment that seemingly small changes in temperature have a huge impact on both how long it takes for collagen to convert to gelatin and how much moisture the meat retains. The major reason it can take so long for this conversion to take place is that in order for the gelatin to unwind from the triple helix, hundreds of electrostatic hydrogen bonds (see page 4) holding the gelatin chains together must be broken. The upshot is that increasing the cooking temperature from, say, 140 to 158 degrees has a dramatic effect on cooking time—in this case 31 hours versus just 16 hours. But that time savings comes at the cost of juiciness—in this case about 11 percent more moisture loss. Dropping from 194 degrees all the way down to 140 degrees saves over 25 percent more moisture. And these are differences that we could taste. This also goes to show that internal temperature, not cooking time, determines how juicy a piece of meat stays.

FAST VS. SLOW: MOISTURE LOSS

During the process of collagen breakdown while samples of pork shoulder cook, the temperature makes a big difference in terms of both time and moisture loss.

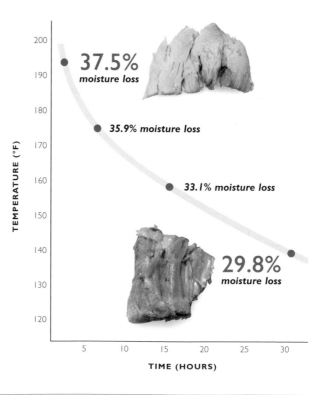

37.5% *moisture loss*

35.9% *moisture loss*

33.1% *moisture loss*

29.8% *moisture loss*

TEMPERATURE (°F)

200
190
180
170
160
150
140
130
120

5   10   15   20   25   30

TIME (HOURS)

Technique 101: Grilling

Despite today's fancy grills and gear, grilling remains a basic—primitive, even—cooking technique: Go outside, put food over hot coals or an open flame, and cook until it's done. Grilling is much less precise than stovetop cooking because of the differences among various grills, the vagaries of live flames, and environmental conditions (yes, weather can have a significant impact). Understanding how your grill works will reduce these variables. A charcoal grill offers some advantages over gas, including more options for creating custom fires and a better ability to impart smoke flavor.

COOKING GRATE

Hinged or removable grates are most manufacturers' answer to dropping in new coals without disturbing the cooking food. We find hinged grates more user-friendly than the removable grates that come with other grills; lifting a section of the cooking surface often forced us to relocate food and, more annoyingly, the searing-hot grate to the ground.

CHARCOAL

Many grill aficionados are fans of hardwood charcoal, but we find that it can be inconsistent in its heat output and it burns too quickly. For consistently great results, we prefer to use regular charcoal briquettes.

CHIMNEY STARTER

For igniting charcoal briquettes, nothing is safer or more effective than a chimney starter. You place briquettes in the top chamber, then you crumple a sheet of newspaper, place it in the smaller chamber under the coals, and light it. In about 20 minutes, the coals are covered in a fine, gray ash and are ready to be poured into the grill.

CHARCOAL GRATE

Make sure to arrange lit coals carefully (see below) on this grate.

ASH CATCHER

Helps keep cleanup to a minimum.

VENTS

The openings on the vessel's base and lid that draw in (or shut out, or let escape) and direct air inside the grill make it possible to cook a larger variety of foods with greater precision.

TOP VENT

Smartly designed lids wear their top vents off center, which encourages heat and smoke to be pulled from the coals across the cooking surface and around the indirectly cooking food.

BOTTOM VENT

Bottom vents, meanwhile, draw air into the coals. Fully open, they make the fire burn hotter and faster; partially closed, they cool the temperature and slow coal consumption; fully closed, they put out the fire.

OUR FAVORITE GRILL

Weber Performer Platinum Deluxe Charcoal Grill
The convenience of gas plus the heat output of charcoal make this grill a worthwhile (albeit pricey) upgrade from the basic model. Built around our favorite 22.5-inch Weber kettle is a roomy, easy-to-roll cart (much sturdier than the kettle's legs) with a pullout charcoal storage bin; a lid holder; a grill grate with removable center; and, most significant, a gas ignition system that lights coals with the push of a button—no chimney starter needed.

DIFFERENCE BETWEEN GRILLING AND BARBECUE

It helps to think of grilling, grill roasting, and barbecuing along a cooking-time continuum. Grilling is the fastest cooking method, generally performed with high heat directly over coals. Grill roasting involves longer cooking times and more-moderate heat. In addition, food is often positioned away from coals and cooked via indirect heat. Barbecuing takes the longest, uses gentle indirect heat, and involves the slow breakdown of connective tissue into gelatin in beef, pork, or poultry.

CUSTOM GRILL FIRES

The best way to control the temperature of your charcoal grill? Custom grill fires. Depending on the recipe, you can arrange coals in a single-level fire, two-level fire, half-grill fire, banked fire, or double-banked fire.

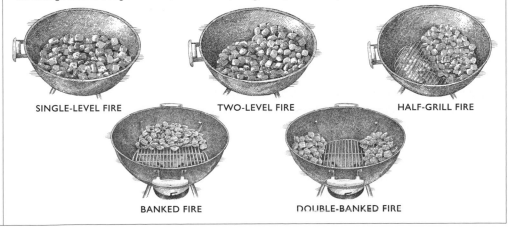

SINGLE-LEVEL FIRE TWO-LEVEL FIRE HALF-GRILL FIRE

BANKED FIRE DOUBLE-BANKED FIRE

Smoky Pulled Pork on a Gas Grill

✓ WHY THIS RECIPE WORKS

Pulled pork is traditionally best made on a charcoal grill. But the reality is that most home cooks rely on a gas grill. And simply using a charcoal recipe on a gas grill—a solution that often works for other dishes—is a total failure in this case. That's because it is so difficult to imbue pulled pork with rich, smoky flavor when cooking on a gas grill. We cut our pork butt into three pieces to increase the surface area that the smoke could cling to. After salting the pork overnight, we take it directly from the fridge to the grill: The meat's cool temperature allows more smoke to condense onto its surface. As we developed this recipe, the only thing that wasn't up for debate was what cut of pork to use. Pork butt is ideal because it's collagen rich and has the right amount of intramuscular fat. During cooking, that fat renders while the collagen transforms into water-retaining gelatin, together giving pulled pork its tender texture.

USE CHIPS In our quest to get the richest smoke flavor possible into pulled pork made on a gas grill, we experimented with other sources of smoke beyond the traditional wood chips. Our conclusion? Getting things like cinnamon sticks to smolder on the grill is fun and quirky, but wood chips still provide the best smoke flavor (for more on smoking, see page 91). When wood smolders, the cellulose, hemicellulose, and lignin compounds that it contains break down and flavor food. So we looked for pantry items with a similar makeup to see if they would work any better. Cinnamon sticks, dried garbanzo beans, and walnut shells all produced smoke, but it was weak—almost sweet—rather than bold, as you'd expect with wood-smoked barbecue. Made by compressing wood chips and sawdust, smoker pucks and bricks were hard to arrange on the gas grill, and they usually caught fire. Wood pellets and sawdust-type products, sealed in a foil packet according to their instructions, required frequent refueling for pulled pork—they would be fine for a quickly smoked pork chop but were not worth the effort here.

MAKE A PACKET Instead of inundating the meat with smoke at the beginning, we get the most out of the wood chips by soaking half of them in water to delay when they begin to smoke. Our foil packets are the right size and shape to sit on the grill, and they have just the right size and number of openings to allow in enough oxygen so that the chips smolder, but not so much that they catch fire.

SAUCE IT Finally, we stir together a bright and spicy vinegar sauce that highlights the pungent smoke flavors of our pulled pork. A combination of cider vinegar, ketchup, brown sugar, and red pepper flakes cut cleanly through the pork's richness and, like the rub, helped amplify the smoky flavor.

SMOKY PULLED PORK ON A GAS GRILL
SERVES 8 TO 10

Pork butt roast is often labeled Boston butt in the supermarket. We developed this recipe with hickory chips, though other varieties of hardwood can be used. (We do not recommend mesquite chips.) Before beginning, check your propane tank to make sure that you have at least a half-tank of fuel. If you happen to run out of fuel, you can move the pork to a preheated 300-degree oven to finish cooking. Serve the pulled pork on white bread or hamburger buns with pickles and coleslaw.

PORK

	Kosher salt and pepper
2	teaspoons paprika
2	teaspoons packed light brown sugar
1	(5-pound) boneless pork butt roast, trimmed
9½	ounces wood chips (4 cups)
2	(9-inch) disposable aluminum pie plates
1	(13 by 9-inch) disposable aluminum roasting pan

VINEGAR SAUCE

2	cups cider vinegar
2	tablespoons ketchup
2	teaspoons packed light brown sugar
1	teaspoon red pepper flakes
1	teaspoon kosher salt

1. FOR THE PORK: Combine 5 teaspoons salt, 2½ teaspoons pepper, paprika, and sugar in small bowl. Cut pork against grain into 3 equal slabs. Rub salt mixture into pork, making sure meat is evenly coated. Wrap pork tightly in plastic wrap and refrigerate for at least 6 hours or up to 24 hours.

2. Just before grilling, soak 2 cups wood chips in water for 15 minutes, then drain. Using large piece of heavy-duty aluminum foil, wrap soaked chips in 8 by 4½-inch foil packet. (Make sure chips do not poke holes in sides or bottom of packet.) Repeat with remaining 2 cups unsoaked chips. Cut 2 evenly spaced 2-inch slits in top of each packet.

3. Remove cooking grate and place wood chip packets directly on primary burner. Place disposable pie plates, each filled with 3 cups water, directly on other burner(s). Set grate in place, turn all burners to high, cover, and heat grill until hot and wood chips are smoking, about 15 minutes. Turn primary burner to medium and turn off other burner(s). (Adjust primary burner as needed to maintain grill temperature of 300 degrees.)

4. Clean and oil cooking grate. Place pork on cooler side of grill, directly over water pans; cover; and smoke for 1½ hours.

5. Transfer pork to disposable pan. Return disposable pan to cooler side of grill and continue to cook until meat registers 200 degrees, 2½ to 3 hours.

6. Transfer pork to carving board and let rest for 20 minutes. Pour juices from disposable pan into fat separator and let stand for 5 minutes.

7. FOR THE VINEGAR SAUCE: While pork rests, whisk all ingredients together in bowl. Using 2 forks, shred pork into bite-size pieces. Stir ⅓ cup defatted juices and ½ cup sauce into pork. Serve, passing remaining sauce separately.

Indoor Pulled Pork with Sweet and Tangy Barbecue Sauce

✓ WHY THIS RECIPE WORKS

Grilling, whether on charcoal or gas, isn't possible during the winter in much of the country. We wanted to find a way to bring the operation indoors. Boneless pork butt has a lot of connective tissue, which needs to break down in order for the meat to become tender. For this to happen, it needs to hold an internal temperature of around 200 degrees for at least an hour. The dry heat of the oven caused the pork to heat too slowly, which resulted in a leathery exterior. Covering the meat with aluminum foil was an easy solution; the foil trapped steam and moisture, and the temperature of the pork rose into the ideal zone much more quickly.

STRIKE A BALANCE At 325 degrees, three hours of covered cooking rendered the meat meltingly tender, while an additional hour and a half uncovered helped a nice crust to form. Splitting the pork butt in half horizontally created more surface area, which translated into even more thick crust (or bark).

ADD SMOKE Adding a few tablespoons of liquid smoke to the brine infused the meat with authentic smoky flavor. We incorporated even more smokiness by adding a dry rub (which we fortified with smoked paprika) and a wet rub (mustard combined with a little more liquid smoke).

INDOOR PULLED PORK WITH SWEET AND TANGY BARBECUE SAUCE
SERVES 6 TO 8

Pork butt roast is also called Boston shoulder or Boston butt. If the pork is enhanced (injected with a salt solution), do not brine in step 1. Sweet paprika may be substituted for the smoked paprika. Covering the pork with parchment paper and then aluminum foil prevents the acidic mustard from eating holes in the foil. Lexington Vinegar Barbecue Sauce or South Carolina Mustard Barbecue Sauce (recipes follow) can be substituted for the Sweet and Tangy Barbecue Sauce. Alternatively, use 2 cups of your favorite barbecue sauce thinned with ½ cup of the defatted pork cooking liquid in step 5. Serve the pork on hamburger buns with pickle chips and thinly sliced onion.

PORK

	Salt and pepper
½	cup plus 2 tablespoons sugar
3	tablespoons plus 2 teaspoons liquid smoke
1	(5-pound) boneless pork butt roast, trimmed and halved lengthwise
¼	cup yellow mustard
2	tablespoons smoked paprika
1	teaspoon cayenne pepper

SWEET AND TANGY BARBECUE SAUCE

1½	cups ketchup
¼	cup molasses
2	tablespoons Worcestershire sauce
1	tablespoon hot sauce
½	teaspoon salt
½	teaspoon pepper

1. FOR THE PORK: Dissolve 1 cup salt, ½ cup sugar, and 3 tablespoons liquid smoke in 4 quarts cold water in large container. Submerge pork in brine, cover, and refrigerate for 1½ to 2 hours.

2. While pork brines, combine mustard and remaining 2 teaspoons liquid smoke in bowl; set aside. Combine paprika, cayenne, 2 teaspoons salt, 2 tablespoons pepper, and remaining 2 tablespoons sugar in second bowl; set aside.

3. Adjust oven rack to lower-middle position and heat oven to 325 degrees. Set wire rack in rimmed baking sheet lined with aluminum foil. Remove pork from brine and pat dry with paper towels. Rub mustard mixture over entire surface of each piece of pork. Sprinkle entire surface of each piece with paprika mixture. Place pork on prepared wire rack. Place piece of parchment paper over pork, then cover with sheet of foil, sealing edges to prevent moisture from escaping. Roast pork for 3 hours.

4. Remove pork from oven; remove and discard foil and parchment. Carefully pour off liquid in bottom of sheet into fat separator and reserve for sauce. Return pork to oven and cook, uncovered, until well browned and tender and

meat registers 200 degrees, about 1½ hours. Transfer pork to serving dish, tent with foil, and let rest for 20 minutes.

5. **FOR THE BARBECUE SAUCE:** While pork rests, pour ½ cup defatted cooking liquid from fat separator into medium bowl; whisk in all sauce ingredients.

6. Using 2 forks, shred pork into bite-size pieces. (Shredded and sauced pork can be cooled, tightly covered, and refrigerated for up to 2 days. Reheat gently before serving.) Toss with 1 cup sauce and season with salt and pepper to taste. Serve, passing remaining sauce separately.

LEXINGTON VINEGAR BARBECUE SAUCE
MAKES ABOUT 2½ CUPS

1	cup cider vinegar
½	cup ketchup
½	cup water
1	tablespoon sugar
¾	teaspoon salt
¾	teaspoon red pepper flakes
½	teaspoon pepper

Place all ingredients in medium bowl, add ½ cup defatted cooking liquid reserved from step 5, and whisk to combine.

SOUTH CAROLINA MUSTARD BARBECUE SAUCE
MAKES ABOUT 2½ CUPS

1	cup yellow mustard
½	cup distilled white vinegar
¼	cup packed light brown sugar
¼	cup Worcestershire sauce
2	tablespoons hot sauce
1	teaspoon salt
1	teaspoon pepper

Place all ingredients in medium bowl, add ½ cup defatted cooking liquid reserved from step 5, and whisk to combine.

PRACTICAL SCIENCE LIQUID SMOKE

Liquid smoke can be just fine—as long as you know what to avoid when selecting a brand.

We were among the many people who assume that there must be some kind of synthetic chemical chicanery going on in the making of "liquid smoke" flavoring. But according to the Colgin Company (which has been bottling liquid smoke since the 19th century), that's not the case. Liquid smoke is made by channeling smoke from smoldering wood chips through a condenser, which quickly cools the vapors, causing them to liquefy (just like the drops that form when you breathe on a piece of cold glass). The water-soluble flavor compounds in the smoke are trapped within this liquid, while the nonsoluble, carcinogenic tars and resins are removed by a series of filters, resulting in a clean, smoke-flavored liquid.

Curious about the manufacturing process for this product, we wondered if we could bottle up some smoke for ourselves. To do this, we created a small-scale mock-up of the commercial method, involving a kettle grill, a duct fan, a siphon, and an ice-chilled glass coil condenser.

In a comparison of homemade and store-bought liquid smoke, homemade was praised for its clean, intense, smoky flavor. But we spent an entire day and $50 on materials to produce 3 tablespoons of homemade liquid smoke. Commercial liquid smoke is just fine, especially if you avoid brands with additives such as salt, vinegar, and molasses. Our top-rated brand, Wright's Liquid Smoke, contains nothing but smoke and water.

Chinese Barbecued Pork

✓ WHY THIS RECIPE WORKS

Chinese barbecued pork (aka char siu) is ruby-red in color, deeply browned with crusty edges and a sticky glazed exterior. In other words? Irresistible. These lacquered strips of pork are "barbecued" not on a grill but in the oven. To replicate this classic Chinese dish at home, we used pork butt for its flavor and fat but cooked it in strips at a low temperature so that the fat rendered and collagen melted into gelatin before we cranked up the temperature to create that burnished crust.

MARINATE THE MEAT After tinkering with traditional marinade ingredients, we settled on a combination of soy sauce, dry sherry, hoisin sauce, and five-spice powder. We eliminated hard-to-find ingredients such as red bean curd, and instead boosted the flavor of the marinade with ginger, garlic, toasted sesame oil, and white pepper. Pricking the pork butt with a fork before marinating enhanced the penetration of the marinade so much that just 30 minutes was sufficient.

COVER WITH FOIL, THEN BROIL Traditional recipes call for cutting the meat into thin strips and hanging the strips on metal rods that go inside refrigerator-size ovens, which allows the heat to hit the meat from all sides and create a thick crust. To achieve similar results in a home oven, we started by cooking the strips of pork on a rack set in a baking sheet and covered with foil. We then let them cook for a while longer, uncovered, before cranking up the heat and broiling them to crisp, chewy perfection.

GET THE LACQUERED LOOK To achieve a lacquered appearance, a honey glaze is applied to char siu during the last few minutes of cooking. To mimic the traditional red color, we supplemented the honey with ketchup.

CHINESE BARBECUED PORK
SERVES 6

Pork butt roast is often labeled Boston butt in the supermarket. The pork will release liquid and fat during the cooking process, so be careful when removing the pan from the oven. If you don't have a wire rack that fits in a rimmed baking sheet, you can substitute a broiler pan, although the meat may not darken as much. Pay close attention to the meat when broiling—you are looking for it to darken and caramelize, not blacken. Do not use a drawer broiler—the heat source will be too close to the meat. Instead, increase the oven temperature in step 5 to 500 degrees and cook for 8 to 12 minutes before glazing and 6 to 8 minutes once the glaze has

been applied; flip the meat and repeat on the second side. This dish is best served with rice and a vegetable side dish. Leftover pork makes an excellent addition to fried rice or an Asian noodle soup.

1	(4-pound) boneless pork butt roast, halved lengthwise, each half turned on its side, cut into 8 strips, and trimmed
½	cup sugar
½	cup soy sauce
6	tablespoons hoisin sauce
¼	cup dry sherry
2	tablespoons grated fresh ginger
1	tablespoon toasted sesame oil
2	garlic cloves, minced
1	teaspoon five-spice powder
¼	teaspoon ground white pepper
⅓	cup honey
¼	cup ketchup

1. Using fork, prick pork 10 to 12 times on each side. Place pork in 2-gallon plastic zipper-lock bag. Combine sugar, soy sauce, hoisin, sherry, ginger, oil, garlic, five-spice powder, and pepper in medium bowl. Measure out ½ cup marinade and set aside. Pour remaining marinade into bag with pork. Press out as much air as possible; seal bag. Refrigerate for at least 30 minutes or up to 4 hours.

2. While meat marinates, combine honey and ketchup with reserved marinade in small saucepan. Cook glaze over medium heat until syrupy and reduced to 1 cup, 4 to 6 minutes.

3. Adjust oven rack to middle position and heat oven to 300 degrees. Set wire rack in aluminum foil–lined rimmed baking sheet and spray with vegetable oil spray.

4. Remove pork from marinade, letting any excess drip off, and place on prepared wire rack. Pour ¼ cup water into bottom of sheet. Cover roast with heavy-duty foil, crimping edges tightly to seal. Cook pork for 20 minutes. Remove foil and continue to cook until edges of pork begin to brown, 40 to 45 minutes longer.

5. Turn on broiler. Broil pork until evenly caramelized, 7 to 9 minutes. Remove sheet from oven and brush pork with half of glaze; broil until deep mahogany color, 3 to 5 minutes. Using tongs, flip meat and broil until other side caramelizes, 7 to 9 minutes. Brush meat with remaining glaze and continue to broil until second side is deep mahogany, 3 to 5 minutes. Let cool for at least 10 minutes, then cut into thin strips and serve.

French-Style Pork Stew

✔ WHY THIS RECIPE WORKS

The French boiled dinner known as potée *inspired our rustic pork stew. Traditional recipes for* potée *are somewhat laissez-faire, calling for simmering any number of fresh and smoked cuts of pork in water with sausages and whatever sturdy vegetables are on hand. Once cooked, the meat is sliced and served on a platter with a small amount of broth. Our adaptation features a more thoughtful selection of bite-size chunks of pork, sausage, and vegetables in lots of flavorful broth.*

CHOOSE YOUR PORK   To begin: pork butt. With its mix of lean and fat, the butt contributed solid pork flavor to the broth, making the 2 hours it takes to become succulent and tender well worth it. Add to that two other types of pork: kielbasa and smoked ham shank. The kielbasa has a firm bite and straightforward pork flavor. The smoked shank was a great choice because of its size and meatiness—just one yielded well over a cup of shredded pork that was a nice supplement to the butt—and it infused the broth with a delicate smokiness.

ADD DEPTH   To give depth to the cooking liquid, we used a mixture of chicken broth and water. Aromatics, herbs, and spices season the broth, and a careful selection of vegetables—savoy cabbage, carrots, and potatoes—complete the meaty yet light dish.

FRENCH-STYLE PORK STEW
SERVES 8 TO 10

Pork butt roast, often labeled Boston butt in the supermarket, is a very fatty cut, so don't be surprised if you lose a pound or even a little more in the trimming process (the weight called for in the recipe takes this loss into account). Serve with crusty bread.

- 6   sprigs fresh parsley, plus ¼ cup chopped
- 3   large sprigs fresh thyme
- 5   garlic cloves, unpeeled
- 2   bay leaves
- 1   tablespoon black peppercorns
- 2   whole cloves
- 5   cups water
- 4   cups chicken broth
- 3   pounds boneless pork butt roast, trimmed and cut into 1- to 1½-inch pieces
- 1   meaty smoked ham shank or 2 to 3 smoked ham hocks (1¼ pounds)
- 2   onions, halved through root end, root end left intact
- 4   carrots, peeled, narrow end cut crosswise into ½-inch pieces, wide end halved lengthwise and cut into ½-inch pieces
- 1   pound Yukon Gold potatoes, unpeeled, cut into ¾-inch pieces
- 12 ounces kielbasa sausage, halved lengthwise and sliced ½ inch thick
- ½   head savoy cabbage, shredded (8 cups)

1. Adjust oven rack to middle position and heat oven to 325 degrees. Cut 10-inch square of triple-thickness cheesecloth. Place parsley sprigs (fold or break to fit), thyme sprigs, garlic, bay leaves, peppercorns, and cloves in center of cheesecloth and tie into bundle with kitchen twine.

2. Bring water, broth, pork, ham, onions, and herb bundle to simmer in large Dutch oven over medium-high heat, skimming off scum that rises to surface. Cover pot and place in oven. Cook until pork chunks are tender and skewer inserted in meat meets little resistance, 1¼ to 1½ hours.

3. Using slotted spoon, discard onions and herb bundle. Transfer ham to plate. Add carrots and potatoes to pot and stir to combine. Cover pot and return to oven. Cook until vegetables are almost tender, 20 to 25 minutes. When ham is cool enough to handle, using 2 forks, remove meat and shred into bite-size pieces; discard skin and bones.

4. Add shredded ham, kielbasa, and cabbage to pot. Stir to combine, cover, and return to oven. Cook until kielbasa is heated through and cabbage is wilted and tender, 15 to 20 minutes. Season with salt and pepper to taste, then stir in chopped parsley. Ladle into bowls and serve. (Stew can be made up to 3 days in advance.)

CHAPTER 5

Pork Belly

Bacon may be a simple breakfast staple, but the science of its appeal—and the best way to cook it—deserve a deeper dive.

HOW THE SCIENCE WORKS

The primal cut subject to the greatest amount of popular-culture obsession? Hands down, it's the fatty, meaty underside of a pig, the source of pork belly and the resulting modern-day darling, bacon. Long a staple in Asian and Latin cuisines, pork belly has become increasingly popular in upscale restaurants of all kinds and, more recently, has started showing up in supermarkets, too. Fresh pork belly is simply unsliced, uncured, unsmoked bacon.

When cooking pork belly on its own, most home cooks tend to either braise or slow roast. Extended cooking encourages tough collagen in the meat to break down into softer gelatin that makes the meat seem supple (see page 25). Most pork belly—and bacon—sold today contains about 60 percent fat.

American bacon begins with pork belly—and a cure. Curing, or the act of preserving food, has been in practice since ancient times. It involves the addition of table salt, which helps to deprive bacteria and mold of water as well as tenderize meat; sugar, which alleviates the heavy salt flavor; and the curing salts sodium nitrite and/or sodium nitrate, which add flavor, slow rancidity and bacteria growth, and help maintain a bright red-pink color.

To make bacon at home, we cure fresh pork belly for 7 to 10 days in a rub of maple sugar and pink salt (a combination of table salt and sodium nitrite; see page 53). Most supermarket products use the modern wet-cure method, injecting bellies with a brine composed of salt, sugar, sodium nitrite (to set color and act as a preservative), sodium phosphate (to retain moisture), and, in some cases, liquid smoke. Next comes smoking. At home, we cook bacon in an outdoor smoker, while most supermarket bacons are dry-smoked with smoke derived from wood or sawdust.

Bacon is so appealing in part because of its 150 unique aroma compounds.

What exactly makes bacon so appealing? Much of it comes down to its smell. Scent, after all, constitutes the majority of how we perceive flavor. One hundred and fifty aroma compounds have been identified in cooked bacon, its unique flavor created by a combination of compounds from the cured pork belly and the smoke, the most important of which are produced during the cooking process. Among them are compounds called furans, created by the oxidative degradation of bacon's fatty acids, which impart sweet, nutty, caramel-like flavors. The Maillard reaction, a chemical reaction between amino acids and sugars that takes place during cooking, creates heterocyclic compounds, which impart both roasted nut-like flavors and green, vegetable-like aromas. And 98 aroma compounds have been identified in smoke alone, mainly the smoky-flavored compounds called phenols and a compound called cyclotene, which has a burnt sugar odor. This smoke flavor is absorbed into the cured pork belly to give bacon its true flavor. (Most of the aroma compounds in smoke are water-soluble, so they readily dissolve within the moisture in pork belly.) Couple the appealing scent of cooked bacon with its high percentage of fat and salt and its crisp crunch, and it's no wonder we're obsessed.

Here in the test kitchen, we make our own bacon (page 54), and we've developed two techniques for cooking already-cured bacon. A skillet and a bit of water will help create crisp-tender bacon that doesn't shrivel as it cooks (page 56). An oven and a sheet pan will help you cook bacon for a crowd (page 55). And don't forget fresh pork belly, which we roast until it's supple and tender, and then quickly fry so that its skin is bronzed and crisp (page 56).

TEST KITCHEN EXPERIMENT

Bacon's production and labeling are confusing. Traditionally, super-market bacon is cured with table salt and sodium nitrite. Over the past 10 years, however, bacon producers have added to the confusion with products labeled "uncured." A closer look leads to fine print that reads: "no nitrates or nitrites added except those naturally occurring in celery juice." We wondered what was up.

First, it's important to understand a bit about nitrite and nitrate. Nitrite is the compound responsible for slowing rancidity in fat, providing the characteristic flavor and color of bacon, and preventing the paralytic illness botulism, whose salt-tolerant bacterium thrives in the anaerobic conditions of the meat curing process. Nitrate can convert into nitrite during cured-meat production but does not itself provide any of the benefits of nitrite. Nowadays, nitrate is only used for dry-cured sausages that benefit from the continued conversion of nitrate into protective nitrite during the slow drying process. This is why we focused on nitrite here.

Take a look at a package of bacon with an "uncured" label and you'll see the same reddish hue of the cured bacon you grew up eating. Fry up a slice and you may be hard pressed to tell any difference at all. Curious about how a product can be labeled uncured and yet look and taste cured, we set up the following experiment.

EXPERIMENT

We prepared two raw 4-pound skinless pork bellies using our recipe for bacon (page 54), which calls for ¾ teaspoon pink salt, as our control. Pink salt contains sodium nitrite, and most closely mimics a supermarket-cured bacon. We then prepared two bellies each for three variations. For one we substituted 3 teaspoons of cultured celery powder from a natural-curing agent manufacturer (the ratio 3 teaspoons to 4 pounds of belly was provided by the manufacturer) for the pink salt. For the second set we substituted 3 teaspoons of uncultured celery powder (to determine the impact that culturing has on the ingredient) purchased from a nutrition store. For the final set of bellies we omitted the curing agent entirely. After marinating the bellies for 10 days, we smoked them to 150 degrees, sliced them into strips, and tasted them lightly fried. We also sent samples of each to an independent lab for analysis of both nitrate and nitrite content.

RESULTS

The samples with no cure added averaged 13 parts per million (ppm) nitrate and less than 10 ppm (the low end threshold for analysis) of nitrite. The samples treated with uncultured celery powder contained more nitrate at 23 ppm but also registered less than 10 ppm sodium nitrite. Tasters found neither set of samples to taste, look, or smell like bacon. Each had a gray appearance and was compared to a smoked pork roast.

The samples treated with pink salt or cultured celery powder provided a very different story, both in the numbers and in their appearance. The samples treated with pink salt averaged 47 ppm nitrate and 27 ppm nitrite, while the cultured celery powder samples averaged 38.5 ppm nitrate and 15 ppm nitrite. Tasters considered both sets of samples to be "bacon-y" in appearance, aroma, and flavor. Tasters showed a slight but insignificant preference for the bacon cured with pink salt.

TAKEAWAY

Nitrite (not nitrate) is the key compound in preserving and adding color and flavor to bacon. Based on the lab data, our tasting notes, and our observations, we can conclude that the samples with no curing agent and those prepared with uncultured celery powder were technically uncured.

Based on their pink coloring, bacon-like flavor, and significant quantities of residual nitrite, the pink salt and cultured celery powder samples were indeed cured. The disparity in nitrite content between bacons cured with pink salt and cultured celery powder is a direct result of the quantities of each curing agent used, not a reflection of the agents themselves. (In previous lab tests, we found that Farmland Hickory Smoked Bacon, which uses pink salt, registered an average of 9.7 ppm nitrite, while Farmland's cultured celery powder counterpart averaged 16.3 ppm nitrite.) The bottom line is that if it looks and tastes like bacon, it contains nitrite, no matter what the label states. Producers who cure their bacon with cultured celery powder are permitted by the USDA to use the label "uncured" because it is considered a natural source of nitrite.

BACON: NITRITES AND METHODS OF CURING

CURE TYPE	NITRATE (PPM)	NITRITE (PPM)
None	13	<10
Celery Powder	23	<10
Cultured Celery Powder	38.5	15
Pink Salt	47	27

JOURNEY: FROM PIG TO PACKAGE

Many steps need to take place before that strip of hot, crispy bacon hits your plate.

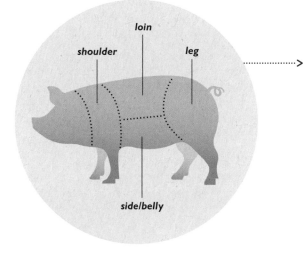

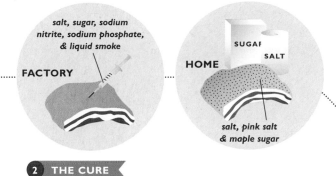

FACTORY

salt, sugar, sodium nitrite, sodium phosphate, & liquid smoke

HOME

SUGAR
SALT

salt, pink salt & maple sugar

❶ BELLY UP

In America, bacon is made from pork belly. Slab bacon is unsliced bacon. Canadian bacon is made from the pork loin. Middle bacon, popular in Australia and New Zealand, comes from the side of a pig rather than the belly.

❷ THE CURE

The first step is curing. At home, we cure pork belly in a rub of salt, maple sugar, and pink salt (sodium chloride and sodium nitrite) before smoking it over hardwood chunks. Most supermarket products use the modern wet-cure method, injecting the bellies with a brine composed of salt, sugar, sodium nitrite, sodium phosphate, and, sometimes, liquid smoke. These slabs are then tumbled in drums and hung to distribute the cure throughout the meat.

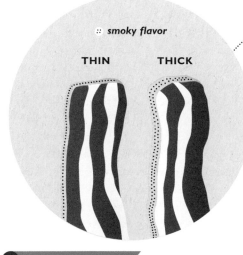

smoky flavor

THIN   THICK

❸ THANK YOU FOR SMOKING

Most bacon is smoked, or goes through thermal processing, bringing the temperature of the meat to 130 degrees. Supermarket varieties include hickory- or applewood-smoked bacon. Artisanal producers leave the bacon to cure for anywhere from a day to a month, then slow-smoke it over wood fires, generally from one to three days. For many supermarket varieties, if the bacon is not smoked, liquid smoke is added to the cure.

❹ THICK AND THIN

For smoked bacon, the thickness of the slices makes a difference in final flavor. In our own tasting of 10 supermarket varieties, we found that brawnier strips, which ranged from ⅛ inch to ⅕ inch, were the smokiest strips. Why? When we spoke to an expert on meat processing, Iowa State University Distinguished Professor Joe Sebranek, we found out. "Smoke is applied to intact, unsliced bellies," Sebranek told us. "A thicker slice has more of the surface area where smoke is deposited included with the slice."

DIET BACON

Pigs destined for bacon are usually slaughtered around 8 to 10 months of age. Over the last 30 years, pigs have been bred to be leaner. This has resulted in the production of bacon with a fat content that has declined from about 80 percent to as low as 50 percent. Today, most bacon sold averages around 60 percent fat.

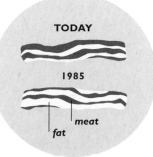

TODAY

1985

meat

fat

Home-Cured Bacon

✓ WHY THIS RECIPE WORKS

We love bacon. Maybe it's the smoky maple scent that wafts from the skillet. Or the crispy bits of fat intertwined with the chewy streaks of meat. Or the irresistible flavor it imparts to everything it comes into contact with. Bacon is just plain good. And what's better than the store-bought stuff? Making your own. We aimed to start with a relatively inexpensive slab of pork belly and create our own blend of salt, sugar, and seasonings to flavor it, for home-made bacon that would easily surpass anything we'd find at the grocery store.

REMOVE THE SKIN While it's important to remove the skin from your pork belly, we found it essential to take time with this step to ensure that we left as much of the thick layer of fat intact as possible. Fat absorbs flavor, so once you've cured and smoked the belly, you'll be glad you left it all on there.

RUB IT DOWN Curing the pork belly—a process that took 7 to 10 days—added flavor and firmed it up. We used maple sugar as our rub's base; it gave the bacon a sweetness that perfectly complemented the meatiness. Pink salt was key as well; it contains sodium nitrite, prevents bacterial growth, boosts flavor, and preserves the meat's red color. Flipping the pork every other day ensured the cure was evenly distributed, and a rinse under cold water at the end prevented the bacon from being excessively salty.

USE A SMOKER A smoker produced the best results because it was the ideal source for moderate, indirect heat that allowed the bacon to cook slowly and evenly. (But we also found a way to make bacon using a charcoal grill—a great option if you own a charcoal grill and aren't ready to make the leap toward buying a smoker.) Placing lit coals on top of unlit charcoal allowed us to achieve the proper temperature without having to replenish the coals halfway through cooking. The water pan in the smoker also helped even out the heat.

ADD SOME SMOKE A few wood chunks placed on top of the charcoal imparted the requisite smoky flavor, and placing the pork belly fat side up allowed the rendered fat to baste the meat.

HOME-CURED BACON
MAKES ABOUT 3½ POUNDS

Note that it takes one week for the bacon to cure. Do not use iodized salt—we developed this recipe using Diamond Crystal kosher salt. Measurement varies among brands of kosher salt. If you use Morton kosher salt, which has denser crystals, measure out ⅓ cup for this recipe.

1	cup maple sugar
½	cup Diamond Crystal kosher salt
1	tablespoon peppercorns, cracked
2	teaspoons minced fresh thyme
¾	teaspoon pink salt
1	bay leaf, crumbled
1	(4-pound) pork belly, skin removed
4	medium hickory wood chunks

1. Combine sugar, kosher salt, peppercorns, thyme, pink salt, and bay leaf in small bowl. Place pork belly in 13 by 9-inch glass baking dish and rub all sides and edges of pork belly with dry cure mixture. Cover dish tightly with plastic wrap and refrigerate until pork feels firm yet still pliable, 7 to 10 days, flipping meat every other day.

2. Soak wood chunks in water for 1 hour, then drain. Thoroughly rinse pork with cold water and pat dry with paper towels.

3. Open bottom vent of smoker completely. Arrange 1½ quarts unlit charcoal briquettes in center of smoker in even layer. Light large chimney starter three-quarters filled with charcoal briquettes (4½ quarts). When top coals are partially covered with ash, pour evenly over unlit coals. Place wood chunks on coals. Assemble smoker and fill water pan with water according to manufacturer's instructions. Cover smoker and open lid vent completely. Heat

---

PRACTICAL SCIENCE SALT PORK

Salt pork is another cured product made from pork belly, but it is fattier, and, unlike bacon, it isn't smoked.

Many stew, soup, chowder, and baked bean recipes call for salt pork, which is made from the same cuts as bacon: the sides and belly of the pig. Salt pork is salt cured (in either dry salt or a salt brine), but it's not smoked, while bacon is. Another difference? It's fattier than bacon. We like salt pork in several of our stews and frequently use its plentiful rendered fat to brown and flavor the meat and vegetables. If you can't find salt pork, use bacon, but remember that it will add a smoky undertone. Don't confuse salt pork with fat back, which is unsalted and uncured and comes from the layer of fat running along the pig's back. Looking for a project? Use fat back to make your own lard and cracklings (and please invite us over to snack on the latter). You can find both salt pork and fat back in the meat section of the supermarket, usually next to packaged hot dogs.

smoker until hot and wood chunks are smoking, about 5 minutes.

4. Clean and oil smoking grate. Place pork belly meat side down in center of smoker. Cover (positioning lid vent over pork) and smoke until pork registers 150 degrees, 1½ to 2 hours.

5. Remove bacon from smoker and let cool to room temperature before slicing. Bacon can be wrapped tightly with plastic and refrigerated for up to 1 month or frozen for up to 2 months.

HOME CURED BACON ON A CHARCOAL GRILL

For step 3, open bottom vent of charcoal grill halfway and place one 13 by 9-inch disposable aluminum roasting pan filled with 2 cups water on 1 side of grill. Arrange 1 quart unlit charcoal briquettes evenly over half of grill opposite roasting pan. Light large chimney starter one-third filled with charcoal briquettes (2 quarts). When top coals are partially covered with ash, pour evenly over unlit coals. Place wood chunks on coals. Set cooking grate in place, cover, and open lid vent halfway. Heat grill until hot and wood chunks are smoking, about 5 minutes. Clean and oil cooking grate. Place pork belly meat side down on cooler side of grill over water-filled pan and smoke as directed in step 4.

Oven-Fried Bacon

✔ WHY THIS RECIPE WORKS

A couple strips of bacon are always a welcome accompaniment to a plate of eggs, but bacon requires frequent monitoring when cooked on the stovetop, and the grease can be messy. And microwaving isn't any better, producing unevenly cooked and flavorless strips. We were looking for an easier way, using the oven.

USE A BAKING SHEET Bacon renders a lot of fat while cooking. This means we needed to use a pan that could contain it. The best bet? A rimmed baking sheet. It also enabled us to cook more strips at the same time. Rotating the baking sheet front to back halfway through the cooking time ensured even cooking.

FIND THE RIGHT TEMPERATURE After testing higher and lower temperatures, we ultimately determined that 400 degrees was ideal: The bacon was medium-well-done after 9 to 10 minutes and crisp after 11 to 12 minutes. The oven-fried strips were consistently cooked throughout, showing no raw spots and requiring no turning or flipping during cooking (which is a must with pan frying). With a texture that was more like a seared piece of meat than a brittle cracker, color that was a nice brick red, and smoky meaty flavor, this bacon had everything we were looking for—without the mess.

A large rimmed baking sheet is important here to contain the rendered bacon fat. This recipe is easy to double for a crowd: Simply double the amount of bacon and use two rimmed baking sheets. However, if you're cooking more than one sheet of bacon at a time, be sure to rotate the sheets and switch their oven positions once about halfway through cooking. You can use thin- or thick-cut bacon here, though the cooking times will vary.

12   slices bacon

Adjust oven rack to middle position and heat oven to 400 degrees. Arrange bacon on rimmed baking sheet. Cook until fat begins to render, 5 to 6 minutes; rotate sheet. Continue cooking until bacon is crisp and brown, 5 to 6 minutes for thin-cut bacon or 8 to 10 minutes for thick-cut bacon. Transfer bacon to paper towel–lined plate, drain, and serve.

OVEN–FRIED MAPLE-FLAVORED BACON

After roasting, pour off most of grease and drizzle maple syrup over each strip (¼ cup total). Return sheet to oven and continue cooking for 2 to 3 minutes, or until maple syrup begins to bubble. Transfer with tongs to paper towel–lined plate, drain, and serve.

Stovetop Bacon

✔ WHY THIS RECIPE WORKS

Our oven-baked method allows you to cook up lots of bacon slices at once because you use a large baking sheet. But if you're just cooking a handful of slices, try this stovetop method. We use—surprise!—water in the skillet to guarantee that the bacon ends up both crisp and tender, not shriveled.

ADD WATER   The addition of water to the skillet keeps the initial cooking temperature low and gentle, so the meat retains its moisture and stays tender. By the time the water reaches its boiling point (212 degrees), the bacon fat is almost completely rendered, so you're also much less likely to burn the meat while waiting for the fat to cook off.

You can use thin- or thick-cut bacon here, whole or cut into pieces, though the cooking times will vary.

6   slices bacon

Place bacon in 12-inch skillet, add just enough water to cover (½ cup), and bring to boil over high heat. Lower heat to medium and simmer until water has evaporated, about 8 minutes. Lower heat to medium-low and cook bacon until crisp and well browned, 5 to 8 minutes longer. Transfer bacon to paper towel–lined plate, drain, and serve.

Crispy Slow-Roasted Pork Belly

✔ WHY THIS RECIPE WORKS

For tender, flavorful pork belly with a crisp crown of skin, we started by scoring the skin and rubbing it with salt. To help tenderize and season the meat, we rubbed it with a mixture of salt and brown sugar. We then air-dried the belly overnight in the refrigerator to start to dry the skin. Roasting the pork belly low and slow helped further dry the skin and turn tough collagen to gelatin while keeping the meat juicy. Finally, we fried the skin and added a few quick, bracing sauces for an impressive holiday or party centerpiece.

ADD SALT AND DRY   We wanted to help the skin lose moisture so that it could cook up crisp and puffy. A salt rub, which we typically apply to the surface of meat to draw out moisture and thus encourage browning and crisping, was an obvious step. Combining salt and sugar in a rub to apply to the meat (not the skin; the sugar burns under high heat) took care of seasoning, too. Air-drying overnight helped to wick away the excess moisture.

COOK LOW AND SLOW   Gentle cooking encourages tough collagen in the meat of pork belly to break down into soft, moisture-holding gelatin, helping the belly to seem moist and supple. We cooked the belly in a 250-degree oven for 3 to 3½ hours to do just that.

FRY THE SKIN   We wanted to end up with skin that was puffy and crispy, similar to the texture of the popular pork-skin snack pork rinds. Using the oven didn't work—it only succeeded in giving the skin a tacky, tough surface.

Even the broiler only gave us a spottily crunchy surface. The solution? Frying. Deep frying was unnecessary, as we only needed about ½ inch of oil to submerge the skin. Combining the rendered fat from the roasted pork with vegetable oil gave us the fat that we needed. Ten minutes in the hot fat gave us skin that was both crispy and golden.

CRISPY SLOW-ROASTED PORK BELLY
SERVES 8 TO 10

This recipe requires seasoning and refrigerating the pork belly for at least 12 hours before cooking. Be sure to ask for a flat, rectangular center-cut section of skin-on pork belly that's 1½ inches thick with roughly equal amounts of meat and fat. Serve the meat in small portions with our Spicy Mustard Sauce (recipe follows), plus white rice and steamed greens or boiled potatoes and salad.

1	(3-pound) skin-on center-cut fresh pork belly, about 1½ inches thick
	Kosher salt
2	tablespoons packed dark brown sugar
	Vegetable oil

1. Using sharp chef's knife, slice pork belly lengthwise into 3 strips about 2 inches wide, then make ¼-inch-deep crosswise cuts through skin and into fat spaced ½ inch apart. Combine 2 tablespoons salt and brown sugar in small bowl. Rub salt mixture into bottom and sides of pork belly (do not rub into skin). Season skin of each strip evenly with ½ teaspoon salt. Place pork belly, skin side up, in 13 by 9-inch baking dish and refrigerate, uncovered, for at least 12 hours or up to 24 hours.

2. Adjust oven rack to middle position and heat oven to 250 degrees. Set wire rack in rimmed baking sheet and spray with vegetable oil spray. Transfer pork belly, skin side up, to prepared rack and roast until meat registers 195 degrees and paring knife inserted in meat meets little resistance, 3 to 3½ hours, rotating sheet halfway through roasting.

3. Transfer pork belly, skin side up, to large plate. (Pork belly can be held at room temperature for up to 1 hour.) Pour fat from sheet into 1-cup liquid measuring cup. Add vegetable oil as needed to equal 1 cup and transfer to 12-inch skillet. Arrange pork belly, skin side down, in skillet (strips can be sliced in half crosswise if skillet won't fit strips whole) and place over medium heat until bubbles form around pork belly. Continue to fry, tilting skillet occasionally to even out hot spots, until skin puffs, crisps, and turns golden, 6 to 10 minutes. Transfer pork belly, skin side up, to carving board and let rest for 5 minutes. Flip pork belly on its side and slice ½ inch thick (being sure to slice through original score marks). Reinvert slices and serve.

SPICY MUSTARD SAUCE
MAKES ABOUT 1 CUP

⅔	cup Dijon mustard
⅓	cup cider vinegar
¼	cup packed dark brown sugar
1	tablespoon hot sauce
1	teaspoon Worcestershire sauce

Whisk all ingredients together in bowl.

Spaghetti Carbonara

✔ WHY THIS RECIPE WORKS

Most carbonara pastas are so rich that it's hard to eat a whole bowlful. We lightened the usual recipe by dismissing additions like cream and butter, cutting any oil, and including only a tablespoon of the rendered bacon fat (but still keeping that porky flavor). The challenge? To make a sauce that didn't break or clump.

REDUCE THE WATER   Having done away with additions like cream and butter, we had to find other ways to make our sauce smooth and prevent the eggs from setting into curds and the cheese from melting into lumps. Reducing by half the amount of water typically used to boil pasta gave us a concentrated starchy liquid that we reserved for our sauce. The starch in the water coated the proteins in the cheese and prevented them from clumping together. The starch also worked in concert with the egg proteins to lend viscosity to the sauce.

USE THE RIGHT RATIO OF WHITES TO YOLKS
Egg yolks introduce a pleasant custardy richness, but they also have a powerful thickening ability that can turn the sauce into glue just minutes after serving if too many are used. Three egg whites and four yolks gave us a sauce with the custard flavor that we were after and an ideal thickness that did not change significantly as it cooled during a 15-minute serving window.

PRACTICAL SCIENCE
WHY ANIMAL FATS TASTE SO GOOD

It's all about the fatty acids.

The bacon fat in our Spaghetti Carbonara adds undeniable flavor and got us thinking: Why does animal fat taste so much better than plant-based fats in certain cooking applications? It has to do with the fatty acids that give any fat its particular flavor profile. In refined oils such as pure olive oil, many of the volatile fatty acids and aroma compounds have been stripped away to make a neutral-tasting oil that will work in a variety of applications. Meanwhile, unrefined oils like extra-virgin olive oil have plenty of flavor, but because some of their volatile fatty acids and aroma compounds evaporate when exposed to heat, they lose most of it after a few minutes of cooking. But when the fatty acids in an unrefined animal fat are exposed to heat, they oxidize to form new flavor compounds that actually improve flavor and make it taste more complex. Try bacon fat instead of butter on the bread for a grilled cheese sandwich, or use it to sauté greens like kale or collards. Substitute the animal fat of your choice for the oil for fried eggs or roasted Brussels sprouts. Chicken fat is a great substitute for the butter in rice pilaf.

MIX WARM   Mixing the spaghetti with the sauce in a warm serving bowl rather than a hot skillet or pot allowed the residual heat of the pasta to "cook" the sauce without any chance of overcooking the eggs.

SPAGHETTI CARBONARA
SERVES 4

It's important to work quickly in steps 2 and 3. The heat from the cooking water and the hot spaghetti will thicken the sauce only if used immediately. Warming the mixing and serving bowls helps the sauce stay creamy. Use a high-quality bacon for this dish; our favorites are Farmland Hickory Smoked Bacon and Vande Rose Farms Artisan Dry Cured Bacon, Applewood Smoked.

8	slices bacon, cut into ½-inch pieces
3	garlic cloves, minced
2½	ounces Pecorino Romano cheese, grated (1¼ cups)
3	large eggs plus 1 large yolk
1	teaspoon pepper
1	pound spaghetti
1	teaspoon salt

1. Bring bacon and ½ cup water to simmer in 10-inch nonstick skillet over medium heat; cook until water evaporates and bacon begins to sizzle, about 8 minutes. Reduce heat to medium-low and continue to cook until fat has rendered and bacon browns, 5 to 8 minutes longer. Add garlic and cook, stirring constantly, until fragrant, about 30 seconds. Drain bacon mixture in fine-mesh strainer set in bowl. Set aside bacon mixture. Measure out 1 tablespoon fat and place in medium bowl. Whisk Pecorino, eggs and yolk, and pepper into fat until combined.

2. Meanwhile, bring 2 quarts water to boil in large pot. Set colander in large bowl. Add pasta and salt to pot; cook, stirring frequently, until al dente. Drain pasta in colander set in bowl, reserving cooking water. Pour 1 cup cooking water into liquid measuring cup and discard remainder. Return pasta to now-empty bowl.

3. Slowly whisk ½ cup reserved cooking water into Pecorino mixture. Gradually pour Pecorino mixture over pasta, tossing to coat. Add bacon mixture and toss to combine. Let pasta rest, tossing frequently, until sauce has thickened slightly and coats pasta, 2 to 4 minutes, adding remaining reserved cooking water as needed to adjusting consistency. Serve immediately.

CHAPTER 6

Chicken Breasts

Chicken breasts can so easily cook up dry and tough. But not when you choose the right technique.

HOW THE SCIENCE WORKS

Americans eat a lot of chicken. In 1992, in fact, the amount of chicken consumed in the United States surpassed that of beef, according to the USDA. The average American now eats about 82 pounds of chicken per year versus about 50 pounds of beef. We eat some whole birds, yes. Wings, too (see page 67). But lean white chicken breasts account for 60 percent of the chicken sold in stores, and the vast majority of those are boneless and skinless.

Boneless, skinless chicken breasts are tricky to cook for a number of reasons. First: They are lean. And the lack of flavorful fat means that they can taste bland. They need major help coaxing out their delicate flavor, and they often benefit from being served alongside punchy sauces. Fat also helps to give the perception of moistness when eating, and a lack of fat makes any dryness in the meat highly noticeable. Compound this with the fact that chicken breasts need to be cooked to a high internal temperature, and trouble abounds.

First off, why the high temperature? Beef, of course, can be eaten rare. But not chicken. This is in part because many factory-farmed chickens are raised in relatively unsanitary conditions, and therefore they can be contaminated with pathogenic microorganisms such as *Salmonella enterica* and *Campylobacter jejuni*, which are responsible for many instances of food-borne illness. Chickens ingest the bacteria, which can then contaminate their intestines, migrate to the hens' ovaries, and contaminate their eggs. (The incidence of contaminated eggs is now quite low, according to USDA surveys, occurring in one of every 20,000 eggs.) But Salmonella can also migrate into the muscle tissue of chickens, meaning processed whole broiler chickens and chicken parts can be contaminated with Salmonella, not just on the surface, but inside the meat. Routine USDA surveys have found

on average about 25 percent of all broiler chickens to be contaminated with Salmonella. For this reason, the USDA recommends that chicken be cooked to an internal temperature of 165 degrees. (We often cook chicken to 160 degrees. It rises to 165 degrees off the heat.)

But virtually all bacteria are killed at 140 degrees, so why heat to 165? Salmonella are hardy bacteria, not rapidly killed at the lower temperature. Only when held at 140 degrees for 35 minutes will the population of Salmonella decline to a safe level. The USDA chose 165 because at this temperature all Salmonella will be killed within seconds, removing the risk of any bacteria left to make us sick.

So, given that chicken breasts need to be cooked to 165 degrees, how do we do that without driving out all the moisture and leaving them chalky and dry? Well, first, there are a few things we don't do: We don't throw our chicken breasts on a white-hot grill without caution; we don't sear them hard in a skillet without careful planning; and we certainly don't just toss them under the broiler—all are recipes for leathery flesh. Instead, we start by brining—or salting—our chicken breasts so that they are well seasoned and retain moisture during cooking (for more on brining, see page 351). We often use gentle-heat cooking methods to deliver tender, moist chicken breasts, including poaching (like in our Perfect Poached Chicken Breasts, page 62). When we grill or pan-sear, we are sure to move quickly so as to not overcook the breasts. Surprise ingredients like milk powder help to achieve grill marks with speed in our Grilled Glazed Boneless, Skinless Chicken Breasts (page 63). Starting with a cold pan helps in our only skin-on recipe, the shatteringly crisp Crispy-Skinned Chicken Breasts with Vinegar-Pepper Pan Sauce (page 65).

Beef can be eaten rare. But not chicken.

TEST KITCHEN EXPERIMENT

A pan sauce takes advantage of the flavorful browned bits, or fond, left in a pan after searing food. Pan sauces are an excellent way to enliven otherwise dull chicken breasts. To maximize browning, cooking school students are taught the following techniques: Blot food dry before browning, use enough oil to prevent sticking, and make sure that the oil is smoking before the protein is added to the pan. But are there cases when these rules actually limit the amount of fond that is created? To find out, we decided to test these rules.

EXPERIMENT

We browned four bone-in, skin-on chicken breasts following our usual protocol: patting the chicken dry, heating 1 tablespoon of vegetable oil over medium-high until smoking, and then searing the chicken, starting skin side down, until both sides were deeply browned. We repeated the test three more times, skipping the step of patting the chicken dry for one, reducing the oil to ¼ teaspoon for the second, and adding the chicken to the pan when the oil was only shimmering for the third. We also tested a batch for which we made all three of these changes at once.

RESULTS

While each change resulted in a bit more sticking and greater fond development, the batch in which we made all three changes at once delivered the best results. It took this batch 1 to 2 minutes longer on each side to reach the same level of browning as the batch cooked the standard way, but the fond it produced covered about 25 percent more of the skillet's surface.

TAKEAWAY

The adhesion of dissolved molecules or particles, such as the proteins in chicken, to a surface is known as adsorption. While the mechanisms by which proteins adsorb onto a skillet are complicated and not fully understood, one thing is very clear: The more the protein is able to bond to the pan, the more fond is left behind. The bonds will be limited if there's a significant barrier of oil, and they will break when exposed to high heat. Both of these factors detracted from fond development in our first batch.

In contrast, using less oil encourages bonding. A cooler pan also encourages bonding because it allows the bonds to remain intact longer. Placing wet skin in the pan causes the pan's temperature to drop because water removes heat from the pan during evaporation. Adding the chicken when the oil is shimmering rather than smoking also means a cooler pan and more sticking. Combining these three factors makes the biggest difference.

For a really chicken-y pan sauce, don't pat skin-on chicken dry, use just ¼ teaspoon oil in a 12-inch skillet, and add the chicken when the oil starts to shimmer. Note: This method is best for skin-on poultry; without a protective layer of skin, steaks, chops, and skinless chicken will develop a band of overcooked meat.

BETTER PAN SAUCE? IGNORE THE RULES

LESS FOND
Lots of oil and high heat limit sticking and, thus, fond development.

MORE FOND
Less oil, wet skin, and lower heat encourage fond development.

Technique 101: Sous Vide

For sous vide cooking, vacuum-sealed food (the name literally means "under vacuum") is immersed in a water bath that is typically heated to the food's final serving temperature (for example, 165 for chicken breasts or 125 degrees for medium-rare steak). When cooking meat, this method works better than using boiling water, a hot pan, or the oven, because the meat is cooked precisely and evenly. Since the water temperature never exceeds the meat's ideal doneness temperature, there is no risk that the outer layers of meat will overcook. Sous vide is great not only for foods that can easily dry out or overcook, like chicken, but also for those that need tenderizing, like tough cuts of meat.

SOUS VIDE AT HOME

Sous vide is a technique that has been used in high-end restaurants for decades (short ribs cooked for 72 hours straight, anyone?). But there are also options for home cooks, including two styles of sous vide machines: self-contained insulated boxes called water ovens and stick-like circulators, which attach to the inside of any cooking pot and continuously heat and circulate water (no stove required). Stick machines take less space in the home kitchen; our favorite is the Anova One.

HOLD AT TEMP

Because the temperature is so stable in sous vide, the food can be held in the bath for hours without the risk of overcooking.

USE ANY POT, ANYWHERE

You do not need to use the stove when cooking sous vide with a stick machine (or a water oven). As long as your pot (or cooler or bin) has a depth of 8 inches so that it can hold enough water to properly circulate, and you place it near a power outlet, you are good to go.

NO HOT SPOTS

Circulators actively pull water to the heating element and disperse it, continually doing this to bring the water up to, and maintain, temperature. To illustrate for ourselves how this principle works, we attached stick-style circulators to identical vessels each filled with 6 quarts of water, started their motors, and placed one drop each of blue and yellow food dye in opposite corners of each container. Within 15 seconds, the water in all the containers was evenly green.

VACUUM-SEALED BAG

When sealed in an airtight, vacuum-sealed bag, the food cooks extremely evenly and there is no evaporation. (Food can also be put in a sealed zipper-lock bag.) It's important to note that just because moisture is trapped within the bag, this doesn't mean that the meat still contains all this moisture. The amount of moisture squeezed out of the muscle tissue is directly dependent on the internal temperature of the meat. (You wouldn't want to cook chicken breast meat any higher than 165 degrees. In fact, you could cook it lower, for longer—see page 64.)

LOOK AT THE DIFFERENCE

Sous vide cooking keeps the outer edges of a piece of meat from overcooking—because the water never exceeds the target temperature, neither will the meat. Searing cold meat in a pan, however, runs the risk of overcooking the outside of the meat before the inside reaches the correct temperature. (You can, and we often do, sear sous vide meat after it's finished cooking. Once patted dry, the steak will undergo the Maillard reaction and brown quickly.)

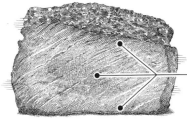

SOUS VIDE
Evenly cooked throughout

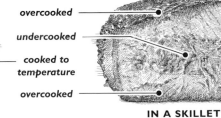

overcooked

undercooked

cooked to temperature

overcooked

IN A SKILLET
Uneven and overcooked on the edges

Perfect Poached Chicken Breasts

✔ WHY THIS RECIPE WORKS

All too often, boneless, skinless chicken breasts are dry and stringy. Sure, they're lean and mild, but the way we treat them doesn't help: searing, grilling, throwing them under the broiler—all paths toward dry and leathery flesh. Poaching is one way to ensure tender, moist chicken, but this finicky technique rarely gets any attention these days. We wanted to take away some of the fussiness and figure out how to use this method to boost flavor, for meat that's exceptionally moist, succulent, and anything but bland.

BRINE FIRST Brining ensures well-seasoned breast meat, and we found that this held true even when poaching. To our typical saltwater brine we added a little sugar as well as a couple of unusual ingredients: soy sauce, which contributed meatiness and depth, and several smashed garlic cloves, for a complex, sweet background flavor.

POACH IN THE BRINE LIQUID Rather than toss out our flavor-packed brine, we used it as our poaching liquid as well. And with the chicken breasts and poaching liquid combined from the beginning, we had a much more hands-free poaching method: We simply heated the pot over medium heat until the water temperature reached 175 degrees; we then removed the pot from the heat and allowed it to sit, covered, until the breasts were cooked through.

USE LOTS OF WATER Using 4 quarts of water meant we had a larger reserve of heat and thus better assurance that the breasts would hit the desired internal temperature of 165 degrees.

AND A STEAMER BASKET (AND MALLET) Raising the breasts off of the bottom of the pot with a steamer basket eliminated the risk of one side cooking faster, and lightly pounding the thicker end of the breasts further promoted more even cooking.

PERFECT POACHED CHICKEN BREASTS
SERVES 4

To ensure that the chicken cooks through, don't use breasts that weigh more than 8 ounces each. If desired, serve the chicken with our Warm Tomato-Ginger Vinaigrette (recipe follows) or in a salad or sandwiches.

- 4 (6- to 8-ounce) boneless, skinless chicken breasts, trimmed
- ½ cup soy sauce
- ¼ cup salt
- 2 tablespoons sugar
- 6 garlic cloves, peeled and smashed

1. Cover chicken breasts with plastic wrap and pound thick ends gently with meat pounder until ¾ inch thick. Whisk 4 quarts water, soy sauce, salt, sugar, and garlic in Dutch oven until salt and sugar are dissolved. Arrange breasts, skinned side up, in steamer basket, making sure not to overlap them. Submerge steamer basket in brine and let sit at room temperature for 30 minutes.

2. Heat pot over medium heat, stirring liquid occasionally to even out hot spots, until water registers 175 degrees, 15 to 20 minutes. Turn off heat, cover pot, remove from burner, and let stand until meat registers 165 degrees, 17 to 22 minutes.

3. Transfer breasts to carving board, cover tightly with aluminum foil, and let rest for 5 minutes. Slice each breast on bias into ¼-inch-thick slices, transfer to serving platter or individual plates, and serve.

WARM TOMATO-GINGER VINAIGRETTE
MAKES ABOUT 2 CUPS

Parsley may be substituted for the cilantro.

- ¼ cup extra-virgin olive oil
- 1 shallot, minced
- 1½ teaspoons grated fresh ginger
- ⅛ teaspoon ground cumin
- ⅛ teaspoon ground fennel
- 12 ounces cherry tomatoes, halved
  Salt and pepper
- 1 tablespoon red wine vinegar
- 1 teaspoon packed light brown sugar
- 2 tablespoons chopped fresh cilantro

Heat 2 tablespoons oil in 10-inch nonstick skillet over medium heat until shimmering. Add shallot, ginger, cumin, and fennel and cook until fragrant, about 15 seconds. Stir in tomatoes and ¼ teaspoon salt and cook, stirring frequently, until tomatoes have softened, 3 to 5 minutes. Off heat, stir in vinegar and sugar and season with salt and pepper to taste; cover to keep warm. Stir in cilantro and remaining 2 tablespoons oil just before serving.

Grilled Glazed Boneless, Skinless Chicken Breasts

✓ WHY THIS RECIPE WORKS

Throwing a few boneless, skinless chicken breasts on the grill and painting them with a barbecue sauce always sounds like a good idea. These lean chicken parts are available everywhere, they cook fast, and they make a light, simple meal. But because they cook so quickly, it's hard to get chicken that not only tastes grilled but also has a good glaze without overcooking it. We used a brine, corn syrup, and a surprise ingredient—milk powder—to help solve these problems.

BRINE AWAY To produce great grilled flavor and glaze the meat in a relatively short period of time, we brined the meat while the grill heated up, to season it and keep it moist during cooking.

USE MILK POWDER To hasten the Maillard, or browning, reaction, we sprinkled the chicken breasts with dry milk powder. Why? The Maillard reaction takes place only after large proteins break down into amino acids and react with so-called reducing sugars like glucose, fructose, and lactose. Dry milk powder contains about 36 percent protein and about 50 percent lactose—the two components that we needed to speed up the browning reaction. In addition, the milk powder created a thin, tacky surface, perfect for holding the glaze.

ADD CORN SYRUP We wanted to limit the amount of sweetness in the glaze so as not to overpower the mild flavor of the chicken. For a savory glaze with balanced flavor, we used a small amount of corn syrup, which is less sweet than other sweeteners, to provide viscosity but not a lot of sweetness.

GRILLED GLAZED BONELESS, SKINLESS CHICKEN BREASTS

SERVES 4

Don't skip the milk powder—it's essential to this recipe.

- ¼ cup salt
- ¼ cup sugar
- 4 (6- to 8-ounce) boneless, skinless chicken breasts, trimmed
- 2 teaspoons nonfat dry milk powder
- ¼ teaspoon pepper
  Vegetable oil spray
- 1 recipe Miso Sesame Glaze (recipe follows)

When it comes to choosing which boneless, skinless chicken breasts to buy, options abound. We tasted eight different brands, and found that our favorite is Bell & Evans Air-Chilled Boneless Skinless Chicken Breasts. The interesting thing: The flavor for all the breasts we tasted was pretty much the same across the board. The winner came out on top because of texture. And why were there textural differences? We discovered it all came down to processing.

It was only when we asked the manufacturer of our winner to walk us through its methods that we uncovered a good, albeit peculiar, lead for our findings: Once a whole chicken is broken down into parts, the breasts are "aged" on the bone in chilled containers for as long as 12 hours before the bones (and skin) are removed. This aging period, it turns out, actually improves tenderness. Why? For one, enzymes present in the meat are at work during the aging period. The natural protease enzymes break down the contracted muscle fibers making them more tender.

In addition: "When you bone [too soon], the meat will be tough because there is still energy in the muscle," said Casey Owens, associate professor of poultry processing at the University of Arkansas. "Cutting it can cause the muscle to contract, and a shorter, contracted muscle is related to tougher meat." Owens also explained that while 4 to 6 hours of chilling before boning is effective—and 12 hours is ideal—many companies skip the aging process altogether. Why? Building time into the process costs money. Instead, some opt for shortcut tenderizing methods like electrical stimulation of the carcass, which forces the breast muscle to contract and relax, releasing its energy.

1. Dissolve salt and sugar in 1½ quarts cold water. Submerge chicken in brine, cover, and refrigerate for at least 30 minutes or up to 1 hour. Remove chicken from brine and pat dry with paper towels. Combine milk powder and pepper in bowl.

2A. FOR A CHARCOAL GRILL: Open bottom vent completely. Light large chimney starter mounded with charcoal briquettes (7 quarts). When top coals are partially covered with ash, pour two-thirds evenly over half of grill, then pour remaining coals over other half of grill. Set cooking grate in place, cover, and open lid vent completely. Heat grill until hot, about 5 minutes.

2B. FOR A GAS GRILL: Turn all burners to high, cover, and heat grill until hot, about 15 minutes. Leave primary burner on high and turn other burner(s) to medium-high.

3. Clean and oil cooking grate. Sprinkle half of milk powder mixture over 1 side of breasts. Lightly spray coated side of breasts with oil spray until milk powder is

moistened. Flip breasts and sprinkle remaining milk powder mixture over second side. Lightly spray with oil spray.

4. Place chicken, skinned side down, over hotter part of grill and cook until browned on first side, 2 to 2½ minutes. Flip chicken, brush with 2 tablespoons glaze, and cook until browned on second side, 2 to 2½ minutes. Flip chicken, move to cooler side of grill, brush with 2 tablespoons glaze, and cook for 2 minutes. Repeat flipping and brushing 2 more times, cooking for 2 minutes on each side. Flip chicken, brush with remaining glaze, and cook until chicken registers 160 degrees, 1 to 3 minutes. Transfer chicken to plate and let rest for 5 minutes before serving.

MISO SESAME GLAZE
MAKES ABOUT ⅔ CUP

---

3 tablespoons rice vinegar
1 teaspoon cornstarch
3 tablespoons white miso
2 tablespoons corn syrup
1 tablespoon toasted sesame oil
2 teaspoons grated fresh ginger
¼ teaspoon ground coriander

Whisk vinegar and cornstarch together in small saucepan until cornstarch has dissolved. Whisk in miso, corn syrup, oil, ginger, and coriander. Bring mixture to boil over high heat. Cook, stirring constantly, until thickened, about 1 minute. Transfer glaze to bowl.

Pan-Seared Chicken Breasts

✔ WHY THIS RECIPE WORKS

What cook desperate for a quick dinner hasn't thrown a boneless, skinless chicken breast into a hot pan, keeping fingers crossed for edible results? The fact is, pan searing alone is a surefire way to ruin this cut. For a chicken breast recipe with flavorful, moist, and tender meat, we gently parcooked boneless, skinless breasts in the oven and then seared them on the stovetop. Salting the chicken breasts helped keep them moist, as did cooking them covered in the oven. To get a crisp, even crust, and to keep the meat moist and tender, we turned to a Chinese technique called velveting.

SALT IT   Like brining, salting changes the structure of meat proteins, helping them to retain more moisture as they cook. Ideally, chicken should be salted for 6 hours to ensure full penetration and juiciness. But boneless, skinless breasts are supposed to be quick and easy, so we didn't want to commit more than 30 minutes to the cause. We found that poking holes into the meat with a fork created channels for the salt to penetrate further into the chicken, maximizing the short salting time—a time that could overlap with the parcooking.

PARCOOK IT   Parcooking the chicken before searing means the breasts would cook gently and evenly, and the parcooked, warm chicken would take much less time to develop a flavorful brown crust when seared than straight-from-the-fridge meat. Less time in the hot skillet equals less moisture loss. We achieved this by placing the breasts in a baking dish that we wrapped tightly in foil before heating. In this enclosed environment, any moisture released by the chicken stayed trapped under the foil, keeping the

---

PRACTICAL SCIENCE SALMONELLA

It's possible to kill all Salmonella without bringing chicken to 165 degrees.

The USDA has done a good job of educating consumers that poultry needs to be cooked to an internal temperature of 165 degrees in order to ensure that no viable Salmonella remains in the meat. So, does that mean 165 degrees is the magic temperature at which Salmonella dies? Not exactly. It turns out that reduction of Salmonella is a function of both time and temperature. For a piece of chicken with 5 percent fat (the higher the fat content, the slower Salmonella is killed), it takes less than 10 seconds at 165 degrees to kill essentially 100 percent of the Salmonella. Drop that temperature to 160 degrees and the same kill-rate of Salmonella (and therefore level of safety) can be achieved by holding the chicken there for around 14 seconds. At 155 degrees it takes 50 seconds; at 150 degrees we get the same effect after 3 minutes. In fact, the USDA commissioned a study that tested down to 136 degrees internal temperature, where it would take 69 minutes to render Salmonella benign.

Why does this curve matter? Well as anyone who's eaten a dry piece of chicken breast knows, a large quantity of moisture is expelled from chicken breast cooked to 165 degrees. In the test kitchen we frequently brine chicken and cook at low temperatures to help mitigate this effect, but with the introduction of affordable sous vide equipment for the home cook there's now another option. Chicken breast can be vacuum-sealed and cooked at 155 degrees (the test kitchen's favorite temperature for juiciness and tenderness) until the internal temperature matches that of the water, and then held there for at least 50 seconds (longer is fine as the meat can't overcook in the temperature-controlled water bath) to ensure complete safety.

exterior from drying out without becoming so wet that it couldn't brown quickly.

VELVET IT To end up with moist exteriors, our pan-seared boneless chicken breasts needed light protection. But slurries made with melted butter and the usual suspects—cornstarch and flour—each had issues. Cornstarch is a pure starch prone to forming a gel that left pasty spots on the meat. The proteins in flour, on the other hand, link together to form gluten, leading to an overly tough, bready coating. Using a combination of cornstarch and flour, however, created the perfect light, crisp, evenly browned coating.

PAN-SEARED CHICKEN BREASTS WITH LEMON AND CHIVE PAN SAUCE
SERVES 4

For the best results, buy similarly sized chicken breasts. If the breasts have the tenderloin attached, leave it in place and follow the upper range of baking time in step 1. For optimal texture, sear the chicken immediately after removing it from the oven. We prefer kosher salt in this recipe. If using table salt, reduce salt amounts by half. The chicken can be prepared without the pan sauce; if not making pan sauce, let the chicken rest for 5 minutes before serving in step 2.

CHICKEN

- 4   (6- to 8-ounce) boneless, skinless chicken breasts, trimmed
- 2   teaspoons kosher salt
- 1   tablespoon vegetable oil
- 2   tablespoons unsalted butter, melted
- 1   tablespoon all-purpose flour
- 1   teaspoon cornstarch
- ½   teaspoon pepper

PAN SAUCE

- 1   shallot, minced
- 1   teaspoon all-purpose flour
- 1   cup chicken broth
- 1   tablespoon lemon juice
- 1   tablespoon minced fresh chives
- 1   tablespoon unsalted butter, chilled
      Salt and pepper

1. FOR THE CHICKEN: Adjust oven rack to lower-middle position and heat oven to 275 degrees. Using fork, poke thickest half of breasts 5 or 6 times and sprinkle with ½ teaspoon salt. Transfer breasts, skinned side down, to 13 by 9-inch baking dish and cover tightly with aluminum foil. Bake until chicken registers 145 to 150 degrees, 30 to 40 minutes.

2. Remove chicken from oven and transfer, skinned side up, to paper towel–lined plate; pat dry with paper towels. Heat oil in 12-inch skillet over medium-high heat until just smoking. While skillet is heating, whisk melted butter, flour, cornstarch, and pepper together in bowl. Lightly brush top of chicken breasts with half of butter mixture. Place chicken in skillet, coated side down, and cook until browned, about 4 minutes. While chicken browns, brush with remaining butter mixture. Flip chicken, reduce heat to medium, and cook until second side is browned and chicken registers 160 degrees, 3 to 4 minutes. Transfer chicken to large plate and let rest while preparing sauce (if not making pan sauce, let chicken rest for 5 minutes before serving).

3. FOR THE PAN SAUCE: Add shallot to now-empty skillet and cook over medium heat until softened, about 2 minutes. Add flour and cook, stirring constantly, for 30 seconds. Slowly whisk in broth, scraping up any browned bits. Bring to vigorous simmer and cook until reduced to ¾ cup, 3 to 5 minutes. Stir in any accumulated chicken juices; return to simmer and cook for 30 seconds. Off heat, whisk in lemon juice, chives, and butter. Season with salt and pepper to taste. Pour sauce over chicken and serve immediately.

Crispy-Skinned Chicken Breasts with Vinegar-Pepper Pan Sauce

✔ WHY THIS RECIPE WORKS

To create a pan-seared chicken breast with shatteringly crispy skin and moist, tender meat, we started the breasts skin side down in a cold pan and weighed them down briefly with a pot to ensure good contact. (For more on the science of chicken skin, see page 69.) Once the skin started to brown, we removed the weight to promote evaporation and let the skin continue to crisp. Then we flipped the breasts to finish cooking the meat. Finally, we created a silky, flavorful sauce with a bright, acidic finish, as a foil for the skin's richness.

SALT FOR MOISTER MEAT Salting the chicken breasts prior to searing them not only seasoned the meat and helped it retain moisture as it cooked, but also assisted in drying out the skin, an important step toward crispness. Poking holes in both the skin and meat with a sharp knife prior to salting further encouraged these results.

POUND AND WEIGH Pounding the chicken created breasts of even thickness, which promoted evenly cooked meat, while weighing down the breasts with a Dutch oven for a portion of the cooking time ensured that more of the skin would remain in contact with the pan for consistent, even browning.

START WITH A COLD PAN While pounding the chicken and weighing it down promoted more even cooking, it wasn't enough; the lean meat was still drying out in the time it took for the skin to crisp. The solution was to start the breasts in a cold pan. Putting the meat skin side down in the oiled pan before turning on the heat allowed more time for the skin to render its fat before the temperature of the meat reached its doneness point.

CRISPY-SKINNED CHICKEN BREASTS WITH VINEGAR-PEPPER PAN SAUCE
SERVES 2

This recipe requires refrigerating the salted meat for at least 1 hour before cooking. Two 10- to 12-ounce chicken breasts are ideal, but three smaller ones can fit in the same pan; the skin will be slightly less crispy. A boning knife or sharp paring knife works best to remove the bones from the breasts. To maintain the crispy skin, spoon the sauce around, not over, the breasts when serving.

CHICKEN
- 2   (10- to 12-ounce) bone-in split chicken breasts
  Kosher salt and pepper
- 2   tablespoons vegetable oil

PAN SAUCE
- 1   shallot, minced
- 1   teaspoon all-purpose flour
- ½   cup chicken broth
- ¼   cup chopped jarred hot cherry peppers, plus ¼ cup brine
- 1   tablespoon unsalted butter, chilled
- 1   teaspoon minced fresh thyme
  Salt and pepper

1. FOR THE CHICKEN: Place 1 chicken breast, skin side down, on cutting board, with ribs facing away from knife hand. Run tip of knife between breastbone and meat, working from thick end of breast toward thin end. Angling blade slightly and following rib cage, repeat cutting motion several times to remove ribs and breastbone from breast. Find short remnant of wishbone along top edge of breast and run tip of knife along both sides of bone to separate it from meat. Remove tenderloin (reserve for another use) and trim excess fat, taking care not to cut into skin. Repeat with second breast.

2. Using tip of paring knife, poke skin on each breast evenly 30 to 40 times. Turn breasts over and poke thickest half of each breast 5 or 6 times. Cover breasts with plastic wrap and pound thick ends gently with meat pounder until ½ inch thick. Evenly sprinkle each breast with ½ teaspoon kosher salt. Place chicken, skin side up, on wire rack set in rimmed baking sheet, cover loosely with plastic, and refrigerate for 1 hour or up to 8 hours.

3. Pat chicken dry with paper towels and sprinkle each breast with ¼ teaspoon pepper. Pour oil in 12-inch skillet and swirl to coat. Place chicken, skin side down, in oil and set skillet over medium heat. Place heavy skillet or Dutch oven on top of breasts. Cook chicken until skin is beginning to brown and meat is beginning to turn opaque along edges, 7 to 9 minutes.

4. Remove weight and continue to cook until skin is well browned and very crispy, 6 to 8 minutes. Flip chicken, reduce heat to medium-low, and cook until second side is lightly browned and meat registers 160 degrees, 2 to 3 minutes. Transfer breasts to individual plates and let rest while preparing pan sauce.

5. FOR THE PAN SAUCE: Pour off all but 2 teaspoons fat from skillet. Return skillet to medium heat and add shallot; cook, stirring occasionally, until shallot is softened, about 2 minutes. Add flour and cook, stirring constantly, for 30 seconds. Increase heat to medium-high, add broth and cherry pepper brine, and bring to simmer, scraping up any browned bits. Simmer until thickened, 2 to 3 minutes. Stir in any accumulated chicken juices; return to simmer and cook for 30 seconds. Off heat, whisk in cherry peppers, butter, and thyme; season with salt and pepper to taste. Spoon sauce around breasts and serve.

CRISPY-SKINNED CHICKEN BREASTS WITH LEMON-ROSEMARY PAN SAUCE

In step 5, increase broth to ¾ cup and substitute 2 tablespoons lemon juice for brine. Omit peppers and substitute rosemary for thyme.

CHAPTER 7

Chicken Wings

Want the best chicken wings? Treat them like breasts.

HOW THE SCIENCE WORKS

On Super Bowl Sunday 2016, Americans ate more than 1.3 billion chicken wings, according to the National Chicken Council. Wings may be small, but they're not simple. To cook them, it's important to understand how the wings' combination of meat and skin actually works.

First off? Meat. In general, there are two types of muscle fibers in chicken: red fibers and white fibers. The red color is due to the protein myoglobin, which helps to store oxygen in muscle cells. This means that muscle fibers that require a lot of oxygen—mainly muscles used for prolonged effort, like walking or flying—contain more myoglobin and appear darker, while muscle fibers that do not require much oxygen appear as white. Dark meat also contains more fat and connective tissue, and needs to be cooked to a higher temperature, for longer, than white meat.

A popular misconception is that chicken wings contain mainly dark meat and can be thrown into the same category as chicken thighs or legs. But, in fact, chicken wings are white meat, closer in this way to chicken breasts than any other cut. Why? Chickens do not use their wings for endurance movement (have you ever seen a chicken on a long flight?), and therefore, according to the Department of Agriculture at the University of Kentucky, they contain little of the red pigment myoglobin. While the white meat of chicken breasts (page 59) should be carefully monitored so that it is not overcooked, wings do have more flexibility, mainly because of the presence of bones and the amount of skin.

Which brings us to just that: skin. Wings have a lot. Skin accounts for 22 percent by weight of chicken wings, which is twice the amount found in thighs or drumsticks.

Contrary to popular belief, chicken wings contain white—not dark—meat.

Chicken skin contains 53 percent moisture, 37 percent fat, and between 9 and 13 percent protein, of which 60 to 80 percent is collagen. And the amount—and nature—of this collagen greatly affects how chicken wings cook.

A few things happen when collagen hits heat. First, the collagen fibers swell, which weakens the attraction between the three proteins that make up its triple-helix structure. Next, these collagen fibers undergo shrinkage—up to 75 percent of their length. And, finally, the collagen begins to unwind into gelatin, the gel-like substance that provides tenderness and moisture-holding capacity in many meats. This conversion to gelatin begins at temperatures as low as 135 degrees in chicken wings, which is as much as 20 degrees lower than the conversion point of connective tissue in chicken muscle. All that melting collagen helps retain moisture in the meat as it cooks, keeping the wings more juicy and tender.

When cooking, we treat chicken wings a little like chicken breasts: Because the meat is white meat and not dark meat, we treat it gently, careful not to dry it out, as in our Crispy Fried Chicken Wings (page 70). But of course chicken wings are not meat alone. Treatment of the skin is key. When cooking them on their own—grilling, frying, or roasting—it's important to dehydrate the skin and render the fat so that the skin can become crispy, not soggy. We help the skin to dry out in our Grilled Chicken Wings (page 71) with cornstarch, before searing them. And we take advantage of the thickening collagen-to-gelatin conversion as well as the rich chicken flavor when using chicken wings in our Best Chicken Stew (page 72).

TEST KITCHEN EXPERIMENT

We recently took an informal poll of our test cooks, asking whether they thought chicken wings were white or dark meat. The majority of the cooks said dark meat, while a small, but vocal, minority claimed they were white meat. We decided the only way to get consensus was to run an experiment.

EXPERIMENT

We excised the meat from 1 pound of chicken wings (from the drumette and flat sections), vacuum-sealed it in a uniform shape, and cooked it to 170 degrees (a temperature at which it is easy to identify the difference between dried-out white meat and juicy dark meat) in a temperature-controlled water bath. We followed the same procedure with meat cut from both chicken thighs (dark meat) and breasts (white meat). We had tasters try all three samples blind and asked them to note the juiciness and fibrousness of each. We then asked tasters to indicate, still blindly, whether the wing meat sample was more similar to the thigh meat or breast meat. Finally, we sent samples of wing, breast, and thigh meat to an independent lab to analyze for fat and protein. We repeated the test three times.

RESULTS

Our initial observations of the wing meat were that it appeared just as light colored as breast meat, both raw and when cooked. Our tasters' feedback on juiciness and fibrousness for the breast meat and wing meat were very closely matched to one another, while both were significantly different than that for thigh meat. When asked directly, tasters unanimously found wing meat to be more similar to breast meat than to thigh meat. Finally, the lab results supported our tastings. The breast and wing meat averaged 0.7 percent and 1.1 percent fat, respectively, while the thigh meat averaged more than double that at 2.5 percent. Protein averages corresponded to these differences: Breast meat contained 23 percent; wing meat, 22 percent; thigh meat, 20 percent.

TAKEAWAY

The way in which a muscle is used while an animal is alive has a great impact on how it reacts to cooking. The dark meat of chicken legs (the thigh and drumstick) are composed of slow-twitch muscle fibers, which have access to a steady supply of oxygen thanks to their high proportion of the oxygen-storing protein myoglobin (also responsible for the darker color of the meat). This allows the legs to perform the constant, steady work of moving the chicken around. Dark meat in chicken is also abundant in both collagen and fat, two elements that lend richness and juiciness to the cooked meat. Chicken breast meat, on the other hand, is low in oxygen-providing myoglobin, collagen, and fat. The low level of myoglobin not only gives breast muscle its white appearance but also impacts its function. The fast-twitch muscles of a chicken's breast provide rapid bursts of movement but tire quickly. Breast meat, due to its lack of collagen and fat, dries out very quickly if overcooked.

Modern chickens, as opposed to, say, ducks, are not flying birds. They spend the majority of their time walking on their legs, with the occasional burst of flight to avoid a threat. So their wings are in fact made of fast-twitch white muscle, just like chicken breasts. Surprised? So were many of our cooks. But don't feel too bad; it's easy to think of wings as dark meat—after all they are wrapped in skin and divided with bone in much the same way as thighs and drumsticks. These findings help explain why so many fried chicken wings, even when coated in a butter-based sauce and dipped in blue cheese dressing, still feature dry, overcooked meat.

SEE THE DIFFERENCE

We tested the amount of fat and protein in breast meat, wing meat, and leg meat. The result? Wing meat is much closer to white breast meat than dark leg meat—a result that you can see when all were cooked to 170 degrees.

DRY AND CHALKY: BREAST MEAT
Fat: 0.7%, Protein: 23%

DRY AND CHALKY: WING MEAT
Fat: 1.1%, Protein: 22%

TENDER AND JUICY: LEG MEAT
Fat: 2.5%, Protein: 20%

FOCUS ON: CHICKEN WINGS

Americans may not eat as many chicken wings as chicken breasts, but when it comes to certain holidays—say, Super Bowl Sunday—wings are the top choice. And they deserve special attention, as wings are unique among poultry cuts in their ratio of meat to skin and bone. Interestingly, chicken wings are white, not dark, meat. But because they contain a good deal of collagen, when cooking they do not easily fall into either category.

SKIN

Chicken wings have the highest proportion of skin compared to other chicken parts—22 percent by weight, or twice the amount found in thighs. The skin itself is about 53 percent moisture, 37 percent fat, and 10 percent protein, of which around 70 percent is collagen.

MEAT

Contrary to popular belief, the meat in chicken wings is white meat, not dark meat, containing far less of the oxygen-holding protein myoglobin (for more, see page 68).

White Meat
Dark Meat

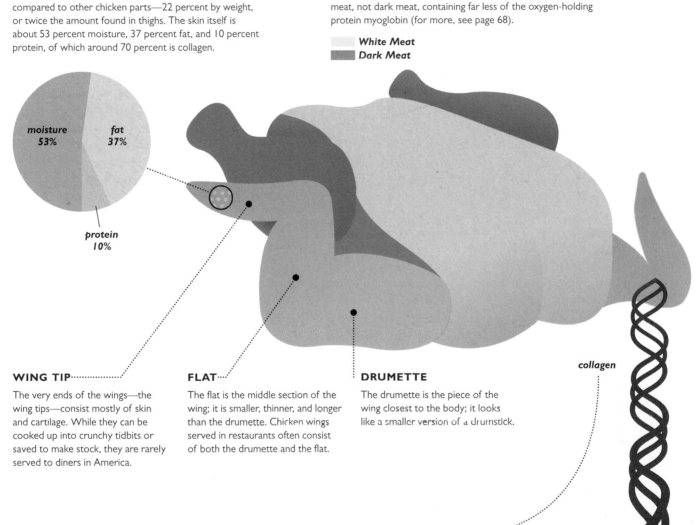

moisture
53%

fat
37%

protein
10%

collagen

gelatin

WING TIP

The very ends of the wings—the wing tips—consist mostly of skin and cartilage. While they can be cooked up into crunchy tidbits or saved to make stock, they are rarely served to diners in America.

FLAT

The flat is the middle section of the wing; it is smaller, thinner, and longer than the drumette. Chicken wings served in restaurants often consist of both the drumette and the flat.

DRUMETTE

The drumette is the piece of the wing closest to the body; it looks like a smaller version of a drumstick.

THE POWER OF COLLAGEN

The robust amount of collagen in chicken-wing skin unwinds into moisture-holding gelatin at temperatures as low as 135 degrees—20 degrees lower than the temperature at which collagen found in chicken muscle unwinds. Since the meat in chicken wings is lean and delicate white meat, the extra gelatin from the skin is extremely helpful when cooking because it provides the perception of juiciness thanks to its moisture-holding capacity. Interestingly, researchers found that marinating chicken wings in marinades containing both acid (lemon juice) and salt for 20 hours significantly lowered the denaturation temperature of the chicken-wing skin collagen even further—to as low as 122 degrees.

WITH HEAT

When collagen is heated, its triple helix structure unwinds into gelatin, which can hold up to 10 times its weight in water.

Crispy Fried Chicken Wings

✓ WHY THIS RECIPE WORKS

The best fried chicken wings feature a crispy, well-browned crust and superjuicy meat. All too often wings are served with soggy or leathery skin wrapped around dried-out meat—their buttery or sugary sauce their only saving grace.

SALT AND AIR-DRY   Despite what many cooks think, chicken wings are actually composed of white meat, more similar to muscle from the breast than the thighs (see page 68). Like breast meat, chicken wings can easily turn dry in the heat of the fryer. We found that they greatly benefit from a pretreatment such as brining or salting. While brining was effective at increasing moisture retention in the meat, it also introduced unwanted moisture in the skin. Salting provided much of the same benefit without water gain. To further dry the skin and help the batter cling, we air-dried the wings on a wire rack set in a rimmed baking sheet for up to 24 hours. This long stay in the refrigerator also gave the salt extra time to penetrate the meat.

USE CORNSTARCH AND MILK   Cornstarch, a pure starch, forms an incredibly crisp crust when fried. We found it crisped up faster than bare chicken skin, allowing us to fry the wings for less time and retain more moisture in the meat. We substituted skim milk for water in our batter because its protein and lactose quickly undergo the Maillard reaction, producing deep browning in record time.

DIP, DON'T SAUCE   To keep the wings crispy from the first bite to the last, we ditched the traditional method of saucing the entire wing in favor of serving them with a dip.

CRISPY FRIED CHICKEN WINGS
SERVES 6 TO 8

After step 1, the wings can be frozen for up to one month; thaw at room temperature for 30 minutes before proceeding. Use a Dutch oven that holds 6 quarts or more for this recipe.

- 3 pounds chicken wings, cut at joints, wingtips discarded
  Kosher salt
- 2 quarts vegetable oil
- 1 cup cornstarch
- ½ teaspoon baking powder
- ¾ cup skim milk
- 1 recipe Buffalo Dip, Ranch Dip, or Honey-Mustard Dip (recipes follow)

1. Toss wings with 2 teaspoons salt and spread into even layer on wire rack set in rimmed baking sheet. Refrigerate wings, uncovered, for at least 8 hours or up to 24 hours.

2. Add oil to large Dutch oven until it measures about 1½ inches deep and heat over medium-high heat to 375 degrees. In large bowl, whisk together cornstarch and baking powder; whisk in milk until smooth. Working with up to 8 wings at a time, dip wings into batter and carefully add to oil. Fry wings, adjusting burner as necessary to maintain oil temperature between 325 and 330 degrees, stirring occasionally until wings turn deep brown and crispy, 7 to 10 minutes. Drain wings on paper towel–lined plate, transfer to serving platter, and serve immediately with dip. Return oil to 375 degrees and repeat with remaining wings in batches of up to 8.

BUFFALO DIP
MAKES ABOUT 1 CUP

- 4 tablespoons unsalted butter
- ½ cup hot sauce, preferably Frank's Louisiana Hot Sauce
- 2 tablespoons Tabasco sauce or other hot sauce, plus more to taste
- 2 teaspoons cider vinegar
- 1 teaspoon cornstarch

Melt butter in small saucepan over low heat. Whisk hot sauces, vinegar, and cornstarch in small bowl until combined. Whisk hot sauce mixture into butter and bring to rapid simmer over medium heat. Remove from heat and cover to keep warm.

RANCH DIP
MAKES ABOUT 1 CUP

- ⅔ cup mayonnaise
- ¼ cup buttermilk
- 2 tablespoons minced fresh dill
- 1 tablespoon minced shallot
- 2 teaspoons white wine vinegar

1 small garlic clove, minced
¼ teaspoon salt
¼ teaspoon pepper
¼ teaspoon sugar

Whisk all ingredients together and let sit until flavors blend, about 15 minutes. (Dip can be refrigerated for up to 3 days.)

HONEY-MUSTARD DIP
MAKES ABOUT ¾ CUP

½ cup yellow mustard
⅓ cup honey
Salt and pepper

Whisk all ingredients together and let sit until flavors blend, about 15 minutes. (Dip can be refrigerated for up to 1 day.)

Grilled Chicken Wings

✔ WHY THIS RECIPE WORKS

There are quite a few challenges with grilling chicken wings: The fat drips away over the fire (and fat mixed with fire means flare-ups), and by the time the outside is properly charred and crisped, the meat is overcooked. Our solution? We grilled them over moderate heat. We began grilling with the thicker skin side facing up so that the fat could render, and then we flipped the wings at the end of cooking to crisp the skin. We decided to brine these wings, rather than salt them overnight as in our Crispy Fried Chicken Wings (page 70). We often brine breasts (see page 59), though not thighs or drumsticks—further proof that wings are closer to breasts than anything else.

BRINE AWAY Brining helps meat retain moisture, even if it's slightly overcooked. Most recipes call for brining chicken parts for 30 minutes to an hour, and we decided to go with the shorter amount of time here, in part because wings are so small.

DRY THAT SKIN The brining approach had one downside: The moisture from the brine made the wings steam and stick to the grill. While the problem of excess moisture was insurmountable in our fried chicken wings, we solved the problem here by tossing the wings with cornstarch before grilling. The high heat of the grill, plus the thin layer of cornstarch, worked like a charm—no sticking.

GRILLED CHICKEN WINGS
MAKES 2 DOZEN WINGS

If you buy whole wings, cut off wingtips before brining. Don't brine the wings for more than 30 minutes or they'll be too salty.

½ cup salt
2 pounds chicken wings, wingtips discarded
1½ teaspoons cornstarch
1 teaspoon pepper

1. Dissolve salt in 2 quarts cold water in large container. Prick chicken wings all over with fork. Submerge chicken in brine, cover, and refrigerate for 30 minutes.

2. Combine cornstarch and pepper in bowl. Remove chicken from brine and pat dry with paper towels. Transfer wings to large bowl and sprinkle with cornstarch mixture, tossing until evenly coated.

3A. FOR A CHARCOAL GRILL: Open bottom vent completely. Light large chimney starter filled with charcoal briquettes (6 quarts). When top coals are partially covered with ash, pour evenly over grill. Set cooking grate in place, cover, and open lid vent completely. Heat grill until hot, about 5 minutes.

3B. FOR A GAS GRILL: Turn all burners to high, cover, and heat grill until hot, about 15 minutes. Turn all burners to medium.

4. Clean and oil cooking grate. Grill wings (covered if using gas), thicker skin side up, until browned on bottom, 4 to 6 minutes. Flip chicken and grill until skin is crisp and lightly charred and meat registers 165 degrees, about 3 to 5 minutes. Transfer chicken to platter, tent loosely with aluminum foil, and let rest for 5 to 10 minutes. Serve.

CREOLE GRILLED CHICKEN WINGS

Add ¾ teaspoon dried oregano, ½ teaspoon garlic powder, ½ teaspoon onion powder, ½ teaspoon white pepper, and ¼ teaspoon cayenne pepper to cornstarch mixture in step 2.

TANDOORI GRILLED CHICKEN WINGS

Reduce pepper to ½ teaspoon. Add 1 teaspoon garam masala, ½ teaspoon ground cumin, ¼ teaspoon garlic powder, ¼ teaspoon ground ginger, and ⅛ teaspoon cayenne pepper to cornstarch mixture in step 2.

Best Chicken Stew

✔ WHY THIS RECIPE WORKS

In working to make a chicken stew that could satisfy like its beef brethren, we looked to two different chicken parts: We seared wings to provide rich chicken flavor and plenty of thickening gelatin (thanks to the skin), and then we gently simmered bite-size pieces of boneless chicken thighs for tender bites throughout the stew.

START WITH WINGS Because boneless, skinless thighs have very little connective tissue compared to, say, beef chuck, chicken stew tends to lack richness and body. For a full-flavored gravy, we seared and simmered (and then discarded) a pound of wings; the collagen and flavor they contributed to the stew resulted in velvety texture and rich flavor. We discarded the wings because we discovered that we had to sacrifice some kind of chicken meat in order to get good flavor—by the time the broth tastes good and has some body, the meat is pretty dried out no matter where it came from on the bird.

ADD UMAMI Some bacon, crisped in the pot before we browned the wings in the rendered fat, added pork flavor and a hint of smoke. Soy sauce and anchovy paste may sound like strange additions to an all-American stew, but they add essential umami taste.

REDUCE TWO WAYS Finally, we took full advantage of the concentrating effect of reduction by cooking down wine, broth, and aromatics at the start and simmering the stew uncovered during its stay in the oven.

BEST CHICKEN STEW
SERVES 6 TO 8

Mashed anchovy fillets (rinsed and dried before mashing) can be used instead of anchovy paste. Use small red potatoes measuring 1 ½ inches in diameter.

- 2 pounds boneless, skinless chicken thighs, halved crosswise and trimmed
  Kosher salt and pepper
- 3 slices bacon, chopped
- 1 pound chicken wings, cut at joints
- 1 onion, chopped fine
- 1 celery rib, minced
- 2 garlic cloves, minced
- 2 teaspoons anchovy paste
- 1 teaspoon minced fresh thyme
- 5 cups chicken broth
- 1 cup dry white wine, plus extra for seasoning
- 1 tablespoon soy sauce
- 3 tablespoons unsalted butter, cut into 3 pieces
- ⅓ cup all-purpose flour
- 1 pound small red potatoes, unpeeled, quartered
- 4 carrots, peeled and cut into ½-inch pieces
- 2 tablespoons chopped fresh parsley

1. Adjust oven rack to lower-middle position and heat oven to 325 degrees. Arrange chicken thighs on baking sheet and lightly season both sides with salt and pepper; cover with plastic wrap and set aside.

2. Cook bacon in Dutch oven over medium-low heat, stirring occasionally, until fat renders and bacon browns, 6 to 8 minutes. Using slotted spoon, transfer bacon to medium bowl. Add chicken wings to pot, increase heat to medium, and cook until well browned on both sides, 10 to 12 minutes; transfer wings to bowl with bacon.

3. Add onion, celery, garlic, anchovy paste, and thyme to pot; cook, stirring occasionally, until dark fond forms on pan bottom, 2 to 4 minutes. Increase heat to high; stir in 1 cup broth, wine, and soy sauce, scraping up any browned bits; and bring to boil. Cook, stirring occasionally, until liquid evaporates and vegetables begin to sizzle again, 12 to 15 minutes. Add butter and stir to melt; sprinkle flour over vegetables and stir to combine. Gradually whisk in remaining 4 cups broth until smooth. Stir in wings and bacon, potatoes, and carrots; bring to simmer. Transfer to oven and cook, uncovered, for 30 minutes, stirring once halfway through cooking.

4. Remove pot from oven. Use wooden spoon to draw gravy up sides of pot and scrape browned fond into stew. Place over high heat, add thighs, and bring to simmer. Return pot to oven, uncovered, and continue to cook, stirring occasionally, until chicken offers no resistance when poked with fork and vegetables are tender, about 45 minutes longer. (Stew can be refrigerated for up to 2 days.)

5. Discard wings and season stew with up to 2 tablespoons wine. Season with salt and pepper to taste, sprinkle with parsley, and serve.

CHAPTER 8

Lamb

This young meat has a unique, gamy flavor—for better or worse, depending on your preference. Luckily, it's easily controlled.

HOW THE SCIENCE WORKS

Sheep are the oldest domesticated animals, raised starting around 9,000 years ago in the Middle East. Today some breeds are kept for their milk or wool, but many are slaughtered for meat. Lamb comes from sheep under 14 months old, while meat from older animals is called mutton.

In the United States, most lamb is slaughtered between four and eight months, though milk-fed, or "hothouse," lamb is slaughtered at six to eight weeks. The younger the lamb, the more tender the meat. Why? The tenderness of cooked lamb is directly related to the number of chemical cross-links holding the collagen proteins together. The number of cross-links increases with the age of the animal, and as the number increases, the process of breaking down the collagen to soluble gelatin becomes more difficult, requiring longer cooking times and higher temperature.

Despite its tenderness, Americans don't eat a lot of lamb. While the world's per capita consumption has increased (from 3.95 pounds per year in 1965 to 4.17 pounds in 2007, according to the USDA), in the United States it has only gone down. Way down. Today, Americans eat just 0.88 pounds of lamb per year, compared with close to 82 pounds of chicken. By contrast, annual consumption per capita of lamb in Australia is 26 pounds. In 1995, researchers conducted a survey of 600 homes in Tulsa, Oklahoma, and asked families to rank seven proteins (beef, chicken, fish, lamb, pork, turkey, and veal) on variables including taste, preference, and health. Lamb came in dead last.

This is in part because lamb has a strong and distinctive flavor. It's a flavor that comes mainly from its fat—in particular, branched-chain fatty acids (BCFAs) produced by bacteria in the lamb's rumen. (Research published in the journal *Meat Science* in 1997 proved that these BCFAs, which are found in a far higher concentration in lamb meat than any other meat, are responsible for this characteristic "gamy" flavor.) The concentration and resulting pungency of these BCFAs depend in part on the breed of lamb, but mainly on the lambs' diet. Lambs raised on a diet of grass tend to have a more intense flavor than those raised on a diet of grain. The grassy, gamy flavors, known as "pastoral flavors," that occur in pasture-finished lamb come from an increased amount of compounds called indoles, primarily one called skatole, found in the fat tissues. The amount of BCFAs and indoles increases with age.

The lamb that you buy in the store comes from a few different places. Domestic lamb is distinguished by its larger size and milder flavor, while lamb imported from Australia or New Zealand features a gamier taste. This flavor change is largely due to chemistry: Imported lamb is pasture-fed on mixed grasses, while lamb raised in the United States begins on a diet of grass but finishes with grain. The switch to grain has a direct impact on the composition of the animal's fat, reducing the concentration of the BCFAs, and ultimately leading to sweeter-tasting meat.

The most tender cuts of lamb are often from the ribs or loin, and we slowly and carefully cook them to a precise temperature (see Roast Butterflied Leg of Lamb, page 76, or Roast Rack of Lamb, page 77). For cuts with more fat and collagen, like the shank and leg, we trim the fat and then braise the meat to break down the collagen into moisture-holding gelatin (see Braised Lamb Shanks, page 79). We grill Grilled Lamb Kofte (page 79) in order to render as much fat as possible from the ground meat.

Lamb's unique flavor comes from its fat.

TEST KITCHEN EXPERIMENT

When we cook a rib-eye steak or roast a rack of lamb, it's the muscle itself (rather than the fat or water contained in and around it) that most grabs our attention. This makes sense, given that the muscle fibers provide much of the characteristic color and texture of a given cut. And yet, when it comes to flavor, we might just be better off focusing on the fat, especially when dealing with lamb. Research has shown that unique branched-chain fatty acids are responsible for much of the "grassy" and "gamy" flavor we associate with lamb (see page 75). To find out just how important these fatty acids are, we ran the following experiment.

EXPERIMENT

We separately ground lean domestic lamb from the loin and domestic lamb fat trim from the rib section and then combined them in varying ratios to create three different blends. The first consisted of 100 percent lean meat. The second contained 90 percent lean meat and 10 percent fat, and the third contained 80 percent lean meat and 20 percent fat. We made 20-gram burger patties out of each blend and cooked them in a hot skillet until well browned on both sides (at which point the thin patties were fully cooked). We had tasters try all three samples and note the intensity of the lamb flavor for each.

RESULTS

Tasters unanimously found the 90:10 and 80:20 blends to have more characteristic lamb flavor than the 100 percent lean patties. While the responses were more split for the meat and fat blends, a slight majority of tasters marked the 80:20 blend has having more lamb flavor than the 90:10 patties.

TAKEAWAY

We find it intriguing that even though they technically contained less lamb meat, both the 90:10 and 80:20 blends tasted more like lamb. This test provides further support to the old adage that fat equals flavor. We would argue that when it comes to lamb, that correlation cannot be overstated.

With this knowledge we have a greater ability to cook lamb to our particular tastes. Beyond choosing between grass-fed and grain-fed lamb (page 75) and selecting a particular cut at the supermarket, lamb flavor can be controlled in the kitchen by adjusting fat content through trimming. Removing some, or all, of the fat cap on a rack of lamb will create a milder end product, while leaving it intact will boost lamb flavor.

THE FLAVOR OF LAMB IS IN THE FAT

We ran a taste test containing three samples of lamb—one containing 100 percent meat, another with 90 percent meat and 10 percent fat, and a third with 80 percent meat and 20 percent fat. The results? Tasters unanimously found the samples containing fat far more "lamby" than the pure meat sample. When it comes to lamb, fat really does equal flavor.

FAT	0%	10%	20%
MEAT	100%	90%	80%

MORE MEAT LESS FLAVOR
Tasters found the sample containing 100 percent meat less flavorful.

MORE FAT MORE FLAVOR
Tasters found the samples containing both meat and fat to have more lamb flavor.

FOCUS ON: LAMB

Lamb, which is less popular than beef (or, really, any other meat in America), has been staging somewhat of a comeback, at least in restaurants—and for good reason. Lamb can be relatively inexpensive; it takes well to a variety of cooking methods, such as roasting, stewing, and grilling; and its flavor is grassy and rich. Note that most markets contain just a few of our favorite cuts, and you may need to special order lamb.

RIB

The rib area is directly behind the shoulder and extends from the fifth to the 12th rib. The rack (all eight ribs form this section) is cut from the rib. When cut into individual chops, the meat is called rib chops. Meat from this area has a fine, tender grain and a mild flavor.

LOIN

The loin extends from the last rib down to the hip area. The loin chop is the most familiar cut from this part of the lamb. Like the rib chop, it is tender and has a mild, sweet flavor. But while the rib chop has meat all on one side of the bone, the loin chop has a T-shaped bone running through its center, separating two muscles.

SHOULDER

This area extends from the neck through the fourth rib. Meat from this area is flavorful, although it contains a fair amount of connective tissue and can be tough if not cooked long enough to tenderize. Chops, roasts, and boneless stew meat all come from the shoulder.

LEG

The leg area runs from the hip down to the hoof. It may be sold whole or broken into smaller roasts and shanks (one comes from each hind leg). These roasts may be sold with the bones in, or they may be butter-flied and sold boneless.

FORESHANK/BREAST

This primal cut is from the underside of the animal and is called the foreshank and breast. This area includes the two front legs (each yields a shank) as well as the breast, which is rarely sold in supermarkets.

GRASS-FED VS. GRAIN-FED

Grass-fed and grain-fed lamb taste different. This is because when lambs eat grain—even just for a short period before slaughter—it impacts the composition of the animal's fat, where most of its unique flavor resides. A grain-based diet reduces the concentration of the medium-length branched fatty acids, the ones that give lamb its distinctive flavor. This means that grain-fed lamb has a less intense "lamb" flavor, and can taste slightly sweeter.

THIS FAT IS NOT LIKE THE OTHERS

Lamb's unique flavor comes, for the most part, from its fat. Beef and lamb each contain both saturated and unsaturated fatty acids. But lamb also has smaller, branched-chain fatty acids, produced by bacteria in their rumen. These medium-length branched-chain fatty acids make up a small percentage of the total fat, but because they are fairly volatile and have a very low odor threshold, humans can detect them at low concentrations. They give lamb its particular "gamy" flavor.

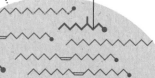

branched–chain fatty acid

lamb

beef

saturated fat

unsaturated fat

TYPES OF FAT IN MEAT

Roast Butterflied Leg of Lamb

✔ WHY THIS RECIPE WORKS

Lamb has a richness of flavor unmatched by beef or pork, with a meaty texture that can be as supple as that of tenderloin. It pairs well with a wide range of robust spices—especially one of our favorite cuts, the leg, which is great to serve to a crowd. But roasting a bone-in leg of lamb can be difficult; it cooks unevenly and is hard both to flavor and to carve. Choosing the boneless version alleviates some of these issues—the meat cooks more evenly and carving is simplified—but it has its own problems: a poor ratio of well-browned crust to tender meat and pockets of sinew and fat that hide among the mosaic of muscles. We wanted a roast leg of lamb with a good ratio of crispy crust to evenly cooked meat and one that was dead simple to carve and serve, as well as provided us with a ready-made sauce.

BUTTERFLIED IS BEST We decided to forgo bone-in and tied boneless roasts in favor of a butterflied leg of lamb. Essentially a boneless leg in which the thicker portions have been sliced and opened up, this cut has several benefits: a uniform thickness for even cooking and the ability to be seasoned thoroughly. And most important: easy access to big pockets of chewy intramuscular fat and connective tissue (making removal of these portions easy), which helps to control the heady lamb flavor.

SALT INSTEAD OF BRINE While many people brine lamb, we found that generously seasoning the leg with salt worked better; as with a brine, salting the lamb resulted in well-seasoned, juicy, and tender meat. Unlike brining, however, salting left the lamb with a relatively dry surface—one that browned and crisped far better during roasting. Scoring the fat cap in a crosshatch pattern ensured that the salt penetrated the meat thoroughly.

START LOW, FINISH HIGH With a roast too large for stovetop searing, we knew we'd have to sear it in the oven. Finishing with the sear (rather than the typical approach of starting with it) produced the best results. After slowly roasting our lamb at 250 degrees, we finished it under the broiler for juicy, tender roasted lamb with a burnished, crisp crust.

SPICE INFUSION We tried a standard spice rub to flavor our lamb, but it scorched under the intense heat of the broiler, so we ditched it in favor of a spice-infused oil. The oil seasoned the lamb during cooking and then became a quick sauce for serving alongside the juicy, boldly spiced lamb.

ROAST BUTTERFLIED LEG OF LAMB WITH CORIANDER, FENNEL, AND BLACK PEPPER
SERVES 8 TO 10

We prefer the subtler flavor and larger size of lamb labeled "domestic" or "American" for this recipe. The amount of salt (2 tablespoons) in step 1 is for a 6-pound leg. If using a larger leg (7 to 8 pounds), add an additional teaspoon of salt for every pound.

LAMB

1	(6- to 8-pound) butterflied leg of lamb
	Kosher salt
⅓	cup vegetable oil
3	shallots, sliced thin
4	garlic cloves, peeled and smashed
1	(1-inch) piece ginger, sliced into ½-inch-thick rounds and smashed
1	tablespoon coriander seeds
1	tablespoon fennel seeds
1	tablespoon black peppercorns
3	bay leaves
2	(2-inch) strips lemon zest

SAUCE

⅓	cup chopped fresh parsley
⅓	cup chopped fresh cilantro
1	shallot, minced
2	tablespoons lemon juice
	Salt and pepper

1. FOR THE LAMB: Place lamb on cutting board with fat cap facing down. Using sharp knife, trim any pockets of fat and connective tissue from underside of lamb. Flip lamb over, trim fat cap so it's between ⅛ and ¼ inch thick, and pound roast to even 1-inch thickness. Score fat cap in ½-inch crosshatch pattern, being careful to cut down to, but not into, meat. Rub 2 tablespoons salt over entire roast and into slits. Let stand, uncovered, at room temperature for 1 hour.

2. Meanwhile, adjust 1 oven rack to lower-middle position and second rack 4 to 5 inches from broiler element. Heat oven to 250 degrees. Stir together oil, shallots, garlic, ginger, coriander seeds, fennel seeds, peppercorns, bay leaves, and lemon zest on rimmed baking sheet and bake on lower rack until spices are softened and fragrant and shallots and garlic turn golden, about 1 hour. Remove sheet from oven and discard bay leaves.

3. Thoroughly pat lamb dry with paper towels and transfer, fat side up, to sheet (directly on top of spices). Roast on lower rack until lamb registers 120 degrees, 30 to 40 minutes. Remove sheet from oven and heat broiler. Broil lamb on upper rack until surface is well browned and charred in spots and lamb registers 125 degrees (for medium-rare), 3 to 8 minutes.

4. Remove sheet from oven and, using 2 pairs of tongs, transfer lamb to carving board (some spices will cling to bottom of roast); tent with aluminum foil and let rest for 20 minutes.

5. FOR THE SAUCE: Meanwhile, carefully pour pan juices through fine-mesh strainer into medium bowl, pressing on solids to extract as much liquid as possible; discard solids. Stir in parsley, cilantro, shallot, and lemon juice. Add any accumulated lamb juices to sauce and season with salt and pepper to taste.

6. With long side facing you, slice lamb with grain into 3 equal pieces. Turn each piece and slice across grain into ¼-inch-thick slices. Serve with sauce. (Briefly warm sauce in microwave if it has cooled and thickened.)

Roast Rack of Lamb

✔ WHY THIS RECIPE WORKS

For many, hosting company for dinner means pulling out all the stops to present a centerpiece-worthy entree. Old standbys like turkey or prime rib are great choices, except that they eat up precious time and energy: From salting and trussing to roasting and resting, it can take hours or even days to get them from supermarket to table. Enter rack of lamb. With dramatically curved rib bones attached to a long, lean loin, it is as grand as any beef roast or whole bird. What's more, its tenderness and delicate but distinctive flavor make it approachable for those who have not tried lamb: Because the loin muscle of the animal gets little exercise, the meat doesn't develop any overly strong, gamy flavors.

REMOVE SOME FAT The key to lamb's unique flavor is its high proportion of fat, most of which covers one side of the rack like a cap. We know from experience that leaving the fat on leads to a very strong lamby flavor (see page 74). But we didn't want to remove all the fat, because this would leave us with a dry rack and little flavor.

Therefore, we left a thin layer of fat over the loin and had the butcher remove most of the fat between the bones.

SLOW ROAST To end up with meat that's juicy and a rosy medium-rare from center to edge, we had to think about our technique. Simple rack of lamb recipes just have the cook roast the lamb in a hot oven for a half-hour. But these racks come out pink only in the very center, a dusty gray elsewhere. Just slow roasting, however, didn't give us the flavorful browning on the exterior. Searing and then roasting was better, but the ends of the lamb were overcooked. What if we reversed it? Slow-roasting the meat in a 250-degree oven until it reached the target serving temperature of 125 degrees was the first step. This took between 65 and 85 minutes. Searing would come next. But first we paused to figure out the seasoning.

SEASON BEFORE COOKING There is no need to salt your rack of lamb ahead of time, a treatment which changes the meat's structure to help it hold on to more juices. We discovered this by salting two racks and letting them sit for 1 hour before cooking and then asking tasters to compare their flavor and texture to racks that were seasoned and then immediately cooked. They were both equally juicy. That's because salt's ability to help meat retain juices is most apparent when meat is exposed to high temperatures, and our lamb was being cooked at a low temperature. That meant that it never got hot enough for moisture to be squeezed out.

SEAR LAST Searing the fat caps in a hot skillet after the racks come out of the oven worked wonders. And it happened fast. This was because the slow roasting time warmed up and dried out the fat cap, allowing it to immediately jump to the temperature necessary for browning. Because the rack browned in just 2 minutes, none of the meat overcooked during this step.

ROAST RACK OF LAMB WITH ROASTED RED PEPPER RELISH
SERVES 4 TO 6

We prefer the milder taste and bigger size of domestic lamb, but you may substitute imported lamb from New Zealand or Australia. Since imported racks are generally smaller, in step 1 season each rack with ½ teaspoon of salt and reduce the cooking time to 50 minutes to 1 hour 10 minutes. A rasp-style grater makes quick work of turning the garlic into a paste.

LAMB

2 (1¾- to 2-pound) racks of lamb, fat trimmed
to ⅛ to ¼ inch, rib bones frenched
Kosher salt and pepper

1 teaspoon ground cumin

1 teaspoon vegetable oil

RELISH

½ cup jarred roasted red pepper, rinsed,
patted dry, and chopped fine

½ cup minced fresh parsley

¼ cup extra-virgin olive oil

¼ teaspoon lemon juice

⅛ teaspoon garlic, minced to paste
Kosher salt and pepper

1. FOR THE LAMB: Adjust oven rack to middle position and heat oven to 250 degrees. Score fat layer in ½-inch crosshatch pattern, being careful to cut down to, but not into, meat. Combine 2 tablespoons salt and cumin in bowl. Rub ¾ teaspoon salt mixture over entire surface of each rack and into slits. Reserve remaining salt mixture for serving. Place racks, bone side down, on wire rack set in rimmed baking sheet. Roast until meat registers 125 degrees (for medium-rare) or 130 degrees (for medium), 1 hour 5 minutes to 1 hour 25 minutes.

2. FOR THE RELISH: While lamb roasts, combine red pepper, parsley, olive oil, lemon juice, and garlic in bowl. Season with salt and pepper. Let stand at room temperature for at least 1 hour before serving.

3. Heat vegetable oil in 12-inch skillet over high heat until just smoking. Place 1 rack, bone side up, in skillet and cook until well browned, 1 to 2 minutes. Transfer to carving board. Pour off all but 1 teaspoon fat from skillet and repeat browning second rack. Tent racks with aluminum foil and let rest for 20 minutes. Cut between ribs to separate chops, then sprinkle cut side of chops with ½ teaspoon salt mixture. Serve, passing relish and remaining salt mixture separately.

ROAST RACK OF LAMB WITH SWEET MINT-ALMOND RELISH

Substitute ground anise for cumin in salt mixture. Omit Red Pepper Relish. While lamb roasts, combine ½ cup minced fresh mint, ¼ cup sliced almonds, toasted and chopped fine, ¼ cup extra-virgin olive oil, 2 tablespoons red currant jelly, 4 teaspoons red wine vinegar, and 2 teaspoons Dijon mustard in bowl. Season with salt and pepper. Let stand at room temperature for at least 1 hour before serving.

PRACTICAL SCIENCE WHY PAIR LAMB AND MINT?

Because lamb and mint are a scientific flavor match.

In 2011, researchers published an article in *Scientific Reports* called "Flavor Network and the Principles of Food Pairings," introducing a complicated, graphic flavor network that "captures the flavor compounds shared by culinary ingredients." The theory goes that foods that share similar flavor compounds complement each other, tasting better together (even seemingly incongruous ingredients—think blue cheese and chocolate). This theory can expand to include not only ingredients that share the same flavor compounds, but also those that share compounds that have similar chemical structures. Many science-minded chefs, including Heston Blumenthal at the Fat Duck in London, are on board. There are even companies—like the well-named FoodPairing.com—that exist to help bartenders and chefs discover "unseen pairings based on science."

That's all well and good, but what does this tell us about lamb? Lamb is traditionally served with fresh mint in recipes originating in places like England and the Middle East. (We include mint in our Grilled Lamb Kofte recipe, page 79.) Does science explain why these two ingredients pair so well?

Let's start with the unique flavor of lamb. Roasted and grilled lamb has a flavor unlike any other cooked meat, distinguished by the release of volatile aroma compounds in the fat during cooking. The majority of these compounds are branched-chain fatty acids (BCFAs)—for more on this, see page 75.

And mint? Mint is rich with branched-chain ketones, which are chemically related to lamb's BCFAs and have similar, though not identical, aromas. This means, according to the theory of food pairing, that lamb and mint are a scientific match. (The dominant flavor compounds in mint are not found in other herbs, like tarragon or basil. But it's important to note that this doesn't mean other herbs taste bad with lamb. See Roast Butterflied Leg of Lamb, page 76.)

In addition, researchers have found another interesting compound in lamb that originates from the animal's diet. This compound, called 2,3-octanedione, is formed when the lamb consumes fresh clover and ryegrass. It is stored in the lamb's fat and, according to this theory, chemically bridges the gap between the BCFAs and the branched-chain ketones, with a similar sweet, fruity aroma that complements the aroma of mint.

Braised Lamb Shanks

✓ WHY THIS RECIPE WORKS

The lamb shank is a richly flavored, tough cut of meat, easily turned meltingly tender through long cooking. Braising is the ideal cooking method; this long, slow, moist cooking method causes the connective tissue to disintegrate and renders the fat without drying out the meat. But lamb shanks have a high fat content, and all too often the sauce is greasy. We wanted to find a way to lose the fat without sacrificing the flavor.

TRIM WELL Even a long, slow braise will not successfully render all the exterior fat on a lamb shank. If your butcher has not already done so, it is essential to take the time to carefully trim the lamb shanks of the excess fat that encases the meat.

BROWN THE SHANKS We found that browning the shanks served two important functions: It provided a great deal of flavor to the dish, due to the Maillard reaction, and it helped render some of the exterior fat. (Be sure to drain the fat from the pan after browning.)

DEFAT THE LIQUID The final step to avoiding a greasy finished product was to defat the braising liquid after the shanks had cooked—either by skimming it from the surface using a ladle, or by refrigerating the braising liquid and then lifting off the solidified fat from the top.

USE PLENTY OF LIQUID A combination of wine and chicken broth provided a well-balanced braising liquid, which complemented the lamb rather than overpowering it, as beef stock did. We found that using a generous amount of liquid—more than is called for in most braises—guaranteed that plenty would remain in the pot, resulting in the perfect sauce.

BRAISED LAMB SHANKS IN RED WINE WITH HERBES DE PROVENCE
SERVES 6

If you're using smaller shanks than the ones called for in this recipe, reduce the braising time by up to 30 minutes. Côtes du Rhône works particularly well here.

6	(12- to 16-ounce) lamb shanks, trimmed
	Salt and pepper
2	tablespoons vegetable oil
3	carrots, peeled and cut into 2-inch pieces
2	onions, sliced thick
2	celery ribs, cut into 2-inch pieces
2	tablespoons tomato paste
4	garlic cloves, minced
1	tablespoon herbes de Provence
2	cups dry red wine
3	cups chicken broth

1. Adjust oven rack to middle position and heat oven to 350 degrees. Pat lamb shanks dry and season with salt. Heat 1 tablespoon oil in Dutch oven over medium-high heat until just smoking. Brown 3 shanks on all sides, 7 to 10 minutes. Transfer shanks to large plate and repeat with remaining 1 tablespoon oil and remaining 3 lamb shanks.

2. Drain all but 2 tablespoons fat from pot. Add carrots, onions, celery, tomato paste, garlic, herbes de Provence, and pinch salt and cook until vegetables are just starting to soften, 3 to 4 minutes. Stir in wine, then broth, scraping up browned bits on bottom of pan, and bring to simmer. Nestle shanks, along with any accumulated juices, into pot.

3. Return to simmer, cover pot, transfer to oven, and cook for 1½ hours. Uncover and continue to cook until tops of shanks are browned, about 30 minutes. Flip shanks and continue to cook until remaining sides are browned and fork slips easily in and out of shanks, 15 to 30 minutes longer.

4. Remove pot from oven and let rest for 15 minutes. Using tongs, transfer shanks and vegetables to large plate and tent with aluminum foil. Skim fat from braising liquid and season with salt and pepper to taste. Return shanks to braising liquid to warm through before serving.

Grilled Lamb Kofte

✓ WHY THIS RECIPE WORKS

In the Middle East, kebabs called kofte *feature ground meat, not chunks, mixed with lots of spices and fresh herbs. These ground lamb patties are typically grilled over high heat on long metal skewers, making them tender and juicy on the inside and encasing them in a smoky, crunchy coating of char. We wanted to get their sausage-like texture just right. To do this, we skipped the traditional bread panade in favor of a little gelatin to keep our kofte moist after grilling. And we added ground pine nuts for richness and to keep the kofte from being too springy.*

BUY GROUND LAMB While kofte is traditionally made by mincing the meat by hand with a cleaver, we wanted to make our recipe as streamlined as possible, so we decided to use ground lamb from the grocery store.

USE GELATIN Just a little. We typically use a panade made from soaked bread or bread crumbs to keep ground meat patties moist when cooked through, since the bread's starches help hold on to moisture released by the meat as it cooks. But a panade gave our kofte an unwelcome pastiness. Instead we found that a small amount of gelatin resulted in tender, juicy kofte.

GRILL HACK To mimic the concentrated heat of a traditional kofte grill, when using a charcoal grill for this recipe, we piled charcoal into a disposable aluminum roasting pan and set it in the center of the grill.

GRILLED LAMB KOFTE
SERVES 4 TO 6

You will need eight 12-inch metal skewers for the kofte. Serve with rice pilaf or make sandwiches with warm pita bread, sliced red onion, and chopped fresh mint. Grate the onion on the large holes of a box grater.

YOGURT-GARLIC SAUCE

1	cup plain whole-milk yogurt
2	tablespoons lemon juice
2	tablespoons tahini
1	garlic clove, minced
½	teaspoon salt

KOFTE

½	cup pine nuts
4	garlic cloves, peeled
1½	teaspoons hot smoked paprika
1	teaspoon salt
1	teaspoon ground cumin
½	teaspoon pepper
¼	teaspoon ground coriander
¼	teaspoon ground cloves
⅛	teaspoon ground nutmeg
⅛	teaspoon ground cinnamon
1½	pounds ground lamb
½	cup grated onion, drained
⅓	cup minced fresh parsley
⅓	cup minced fresh mint
1½	teaspoons unflavored gelatin
1	large disposable aluminum roasting pan (if using charcoal)

1. FOR THE YOGURT-GARLIC SAUCE: Whisk all ingredients together in bowl. Set aside.

2. FOR THE KOFTE: Process pine nuts, garlic, paprika, salt, cumin, pepper, coriander, cloves, nutmeg, and cinnamon in food processor until coarse paste forms, 30 to 45 seconds. Transfer mixture to large bowl. Add lamb, onion, parsley, mint, and gelatin; knead with your hands until thoroughly combined and mixture feels slightly sticky, about 2 minutes. Divide mixture into 8 equal portions. Shape each portion into 5-inch-long cylinder about 1 inch in diameter. Using eight 12-inch metal skewers, thread 1 cylinder onto each skewer, pressing gently to adhere. Transfer skewers to lightly greased baking sheet, cover with plastic wrap, and refrigerate for at least 1 hour or up to 24 hours.

3A. FOR A CHARCOAL GRILL: Using skewer, poke 12 holes in bottom of disposable pan. Open bottom vent completely and place pan in center of grill. Light large chimney starter two-thirds filled with charcoal briquettes (4 quarts). When top coals are partially covered with ash, pour into pan. Set cooking grate in place, cover, and open lid vent completely. Heat grill until hot, about 5 minutes.

3B. FOR A GAS GRILL: Turn all burners to high, cover, and heat grill until hot, about 15 minutes. Leave all burners on high.

4. Clean and oil cooking grate. Place skewers on grill (directly over coals if using charcoal) at 45-degree angle to grate. Cook (covered if using gas) until browned and meat easily releases from grill, 4 to 7 minutes. Flip skewers and continue to cook until browned on second side and meat registers 160 degrees, about 6 minutes longer. Transfer skewers to platter and serve, passing yogurt-garlic sauce separately.

CHAPTER 9

White Fish

White fish comes in many varieties—and all are fragile. How do you keep your fillet intact?

HOW THE SCIENCE WORKS

Most fish varieties have a similar shape: bullet-like, slightly bulbous, primed to move in the water. Fish consist of muscle tissue, laced with connective tissue, a backbone, and a rib cage. Some have fins. Others also have unattached tiny pin bones. Most have skin, which is quite fatty, and scales, which are made of the same material as human teeth.

Fish are delicate, in part, because water is denser than air. This means that fish are buoyant, not fighting against gravity, and therefore do not need thick bones and tough connective tissue to support their bodies. Because moving through water is comparatively easy, most fish do not need the fat for fuel or dark meat muscles used by mammals for endurance.

In general, the muscle structure of fish differs from that of land animals. In beef the muscle fibers are long, sometimes very long, bound together in bundles by connective tissue (page 25). In fish, the muscle fibers are quite short, sometimes a small fraction of an inch, and are arranged in sheets, nested among folded layers of very thin connective tissue. This is why, when fish is cooked, the flesh flakes. The heat of cooking softens the collagen sheets, permitting the short sections of muscle fibers to separate. These shorter sections of muscle fibers are much easier to bite through, contributing to the tenderness of fish (see page 83).

The muscle structure of fish is different than that of land animals.

The connective tissue in fish is likewise different from that in beef or poultry. It's weaker, in part because the collagen in fish connective tissue contains far fewer chemical cross-links than animal collagen. In addition, fish collagen begins to shrink, and then break down into tenderizing gelatin, at much lower temperatures: 113 degrees, and 120 degrees, respectively—compared to 140 degrees (when collagen breakdown starts) or 160 or 180 degrees (when the process really moves) for beef. This means that fish can be cooked to a lower temperature, and still finish tender.

Here, we focus on white fish. These are mostly fish that swim close to the ocean bottom, and not very much. Because they swim only intermittently, when they do swim, they need the ability to accelerate quickly. This is why most fish muscles are "fast twitch" muscles, primed for short bursts of speed. Fast twitch muscles are composed of white fibers—hence, white fish's, well, white color.

"White fish" is a term that encompasses many species of deepwater saltwater fish, all of which are mild flavored and white fleshed. It's a big group that includes cod, flounder, haddock, hake, halibut, pollock, and sole, among others. At the market, you will most often see flounder and sole (which are delicate and flaky); cod, haddock, and sea bass (which are medium-flaky); and grouper, halibut, and monkfish (which are more firm and meaty). An important side note: In restaurants and stores, white fish are frequently mislabeled. In 2011 the *Boston Globe* reported that 48 percent of fish collected from 134 restaurants, grocery stores, and fish markets in Massachusetts and DNA-tested by a laboratory in Canada were sold with the incorrect species name.

We take utmost care to cook these delicate fish gently. We braise halibut in a low oven (page 84). Even when we serve white fish as part of a larger dish, like New England Fish Chowder, page 86, and California Fish Tacos, page 87, we cook white fish gently—lightly poaching cod in water flavored with salt pork to make a flavorful broth, and coating cod in batter and fast-frying the fish to make sure it does not overcook.

TEST KITCHEN EXPERIMENT

When cooked, white fish have a tendency to stick to the pan; coupled with their delicate structure, this makes moving them from skillet to plate a challenge. Many home cooks turn to nonstick skillets. But the nonstick coating wears off with time and normal cooking. We wondered if we could make a stainless-steel skillet nonstick enough to cook fish. We ran an experiment to find out.

EXPERIMENT

We patted three 6-ounce skinless cod fillets dry with paper towels. For the first sample we sprayed the fillet on all sides with vegetable oil spray. We also sprayed a 10-inch stainless-steel skillet. We heated the pan over medium heat until shimmering (325 degrees) before adding the fish and cooking it until golden brown on the first side, about 3 minutes. We then flipped the fish and cooked until golden on the second side. Next, we heated 1 tablespoon of vegetable oil in a 10-inch stainless-steel skillet over medium-high heat until just smoking (425 degrees). We dragged the fish across the bottom of the pan to ensure we had an even layer of oil underneath the entire fillet. After 90 seconds, we flipped the fish and cooked it until the second side had browned. For the third sample we heated an empty 10-inch stainless-steel skillet for 2 minutes over medium-high heat and then added the fish. We cooked the fillet until browned on the first side but were unable to flip it due to sticking. We repeated the test three times with cod and then again with halibut and snapper fillets.

RESULTS

For all three fish species we achieved the most consistent nonstick performance using vegetable oil and a smoking-hot pan. The samples coated in vegetable oil spray tended to stick about a third of the time. The fish in the uncoated stainless-steel pan stuck every time.

TAKEAWAY

Lean white fish has a tendency toward sticking. The adhesion of dissolved solids, such as the proteins in fish, to a surface is known as adsorption. While the mechanisms by which proteins adsorb onto a skillet are complicated and not fully understood, one thing is very clear: Most white fish species store fat primarily in their livers, leaving very little fat within the muscle tissue itself to render and lubricate the flesh touching the pan during cooking. The keys to preventing sticking are using a release agent (most often a form of fat) to create a barrier between the fish and pan, and to break any bonds that do form as rapidly as possible. High heat breaks these bonds more quickly than low heat.

The vegetable oil spray performed moderately well because it contains more than just oil—it also has lecithin, an emulsifier, which helps form a stable film of oil, creating an even barrier. The downside is that the spray loses its efficacy, browns, and forms a sticky film at high temperatures, meaning we are forced to cook at a lower temperature and wait longer for the exterior to develop browning, in the meantime overcooking more flesh below the surface.

As oil heats up it tends to form an uneven layer because the surface of the pan heats unevenly–the oil moves away from hotter areas of the pan and pools in cooler spots. We use a generous amount of vegetable oil to eliminate the pooling effect. By gently dragging the fillet across the pan we ensure the entire surface of the fish is in contact with oil. And, because refined vegetable oil has a high smoke point, we can sear at a high temperature to ensure that the bonds between fish and pan are quickly broken, and to get flavorful browning before the interior overcooks. For the sample in the dry skillet, the entire surface of the fish bonded directly to the pan, making a clean release nearly impossible. We don't recommend trying this at home.

SEAR IN VEGETABLE OIL

We tried searing white fish in a stainless-steel skillet using vegetable spray oil, vegetable oil, and nothing at all. If you want your fish not to stick, stick with vegetable oil. Or, use a nonstick skillet for maximum protection against sticking.

**NOTHING ADDED:
TOTALLY STUCK**

**VEGETABLE OIL SPRAY:
A LITTLE STUCK**

**VEGETABLE OIL:
A CLEAN BREAK**

FOCUS ON: FISH MUSCLE

Fish, like mammals, are made up of skin and bones, connective tissue, and muscle fiber. The structure of fish muscle differs from land animals (see page 25), however. Let's take a look.

epidermis   derma

SKIN

The fish body is fully covered by muscle tissue, under two layers of fish skin (the outer epidermis and inner derma, which contains the scales).

MUSCLE FIBER

Fish muscle is made of muscle fibers composed of the same muscle proteins (actin and myosin) as land animals, but in fish the muscle fibers are much shorter (less than an inch in length). The muscle fibers are arranged in sections called myotomes, which are separated by very thin sheets of connective tissue called myocommata.

The muscle proteins also exhibit a gel-forming ability that contributes to a soft, tender, gel-like texture when cooked. These proteins, plus the gelatin released by heating collagen, bind water. This is why cooked fish loses only about 15 percent water by weight (significantly less than beef, with 20 to 25 percent water loss), which helps keep it moist.

CONNECTIVE TISSUE

In fish, connective tissue is arranged in very thin sheets separating short sections of muscle fibers, rather than thicker casings wrapped around bundles of long muscle fibers as in land animals. Fish contain much less connective tissue (about 3 percent by weight) than land animals (about 10 to 15 percent by weight on average).

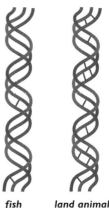

fish   land animals

LESS COLLAGEN BUT EASIER TO PRODUCE GELATIN

The collagen in fish contains far fewer chemical cross-links than the collagen in land animals. More cross-links in collagen means tougher connective tissue. The collagen molecules in fish contain only about one chemical cross-link for every 100 amino acids in collagen, which is about 10 times less than in land animals. As a result, collagen in fish is easily broken down to gelatin with heat at lower temperatures than in pork and beef.

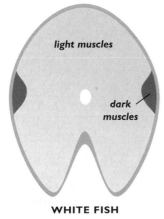

light muscles

dark muscles

WHITE FISH

LIGHT MUSCLES AND DARK MUSCLES

There are two types of muscles in fish flesh: light muscles and dark muscles. The light muscles are classified as "fast" muscles for short bursts of high-speed swimming, and constitute about 90 percent of the muscle in white fish. The dark muscles are "slow" muscles used for persistent slow-speed swimming, and constitute the remaining 10 percent of the muscle. (Salmon, on the other hand, contains up to 40 percent dark muscles so they can swim upstream for long durations during spawning season.)

Braised Halibut with Leeks and Mustard

✓ WHY THIS RECIPE WORKS

When it comes to methods for cooking fish, braising is often overlooked. But this approach, which requires cooking the fish in a small amount of liquid so that it gently simmers and steams, has a lot going for it: Braising is gentle and thus forgiving, all but guaranteeing moist, succulent fish. Plus, it makes a one-pot meal since the cooking liquid becomes a sauce, and it's easy to add vegetables to the pan to cook at the same time. To get started, we chose halibut for its sweet, delicate flavor and firm texture that made for easier handling.

SAUTÉ BEFORE BRAISING   While braising fish offers a lot of appeal, it does have a downside: Because the fish is partially submerged in a small amount of cooking liquid, you are essentially half-steaming, half-simmering it. In tests comparing steaming halibut to completely submerging it in water and simmering it, we found that steaming took 57 percent longer. Why? For the fish to cook, molecules have to transfer their energy to the food through direct contact. Not only does simmering water generate only a small amount of steam, but many of those steam molecules condense on the lid rather than hitting, and transferring their energy to, the fish. Thus, far more molecules come in contact with the food in the simmering water than they do in the steam, making simmered food cook faster. So it's no surprise that in our early tests for braised fish fillets, by the time the steamed portion had cooked through, the simmered portion had overcooked. To address this discrepancy, we parcooked one side of the fillets by sautéing them briefly, and then we arranged them atop a bed of wine and vegetables, raw side down, for the braise. This gave the upper portion that cooked through more slowly by steam a jump start. The result: perfectly moist, evenly cooked fillets.

ADD WINE   For the cooking liquid, wine supplemented by the juices released by the fish and vegetables during cooking delivered a sauce with balanced flavor and just the right amount of brightness. Butter gave it some much-needed richness and the right velvety texture.

PRACTICAL SCIENCE   REHEATING FISH

Fish is easy to overcook, which makes the prospect of reheating leftovers even more daunting. Here's how to do it.

Fish is notoriously susceptible to overcooking, so reheating previously cooked fillets is something that makes nearly all cooks balk. But since almost everyone has leftover fish from time to time, we decided to figure out the best approach to warming it up.

As we suspected, we had far more success reheating thick fillets and steaks than thin ones. Both swordfish and halibut steaks reheated nicely, retaining their moisture well and with no detectable change in flavor. Likewise, salmon reheated well, but thanks to the oxidation of its abundant fatty acids into strong-smelling aldehydes, reheating brought out a bit more of the fish's pungent aroma. There was little we could do to prevent trout from drying out and overcooking when heated a second time.

To reheat thicker fish fillets, use this gentle approach: Place the fillets on a wire rack set in a rimmed baking sheet, cover them with foil (to prevent the exterior of the fish from drying out), and heat them in a 275-degree oven until they register 125 to 130 degrees, about 15 minutes for 1-inch-thick fillets (timing varies according to fillet size). We recommend serving leftover cooked thin fish in cold applications like salads.

BRAISED HALIBUT WITH LEEKS AND MUSTARD
SERVES 4

We prefer to prepare this recipe with halibut, but a similar firm-fleshed white fish such as striped bass or sea bass that is between ¾ and 1 inch thick can be substituted. To ensure that your fish cooks evenly, purchase fillets that are similarly shaped and uniformly thick.

4	(6- to 8-ounce) skinless halibut fillets, ¾- to 1-inch-thick
	Salt and pepper
6	tablespoons unsalted butter
1	pound leeks, white and light green parts only, halved lengthwise, sliced thin, and washed thoroughly
1	teaspoon Dijon mustard
¾	cup dry white wine
1	teaspoon lemon juice, plus lemon wedges for serving
1	tablespoon minced fresh parsley

1. Sprinkle halibut fillets with ½ teaspoon salt. Melt butter in 12-inch skillet over low heat. Place fillets in skillet, skinned side up, increase heat to medium, and cook, shaking pan occasionally, until butter begins to brown (fish should not brown), 3 to 4 minutes. Using spatula, carefully transfer fillets to large plate, raw side down.

2. Add leeks, mustard, and ½ teaspoon salt to skillet and cook, stirring frequently, until leeks begin to soften, 2 to 4 minutes. Add wine and bring to gentle simmer. Place halibut, raw side down, on top of leeks. Cover skillet and cook, adjusting heat to maintain gentle simmer, until fish registers 135 to 140 degrees, 10 to 14 minutes. Remove skillet from heat and, using 2 spatulas, transfer halibut and leeks to serving platter or individual plates. Tent with aluminum foil.

3. Return skillet to high heat and simmer briskly until sauce is thickened, 2 to 3 minutes. Remove pan from heat, stir in lemon juice, and season with salt and pepper to taste. Spoon sauce over halibut and sprinkle with parsley. Serve immediately with lemon wedges.

Cod Baked in Foil with Leeks and Carrots

✔ WHY THIS RECIPE WORKS

Cooking en papillote—*where the food is baked in a tightly sealed, artfully folded parchment package to essentially steam in its own juices—may seem as outdated as beef Wellington and pheasant under glass. But there's a reason this technique has held its own: It's an easy, mess-free way to enhance delicate flavor, particularly that of fish, leaving no odors to linger in the kitchen. The fish cooks quickly in such a moist environment, and because there's no water added to dilute flavors, it's a more flavorful method than ordinary poaching. When done correctly, that is. We started off by picking mild haddock or cod over more assertive salmon or tuna, which can overpower vegetables. And then we went from there.*

USE FOIL All of the classic recipes call for cutting parchment paper into attractive shapes such as teardrops, hearts, and butterflies and then creasing the seams into painstakingly precise little folds. But just looking at the illustrations made our thumbs throb. We went directly to aluminum foil, sandwiching the fish between two 12-inch squares, and then crimping the edges to create a seal.

CHOOSE WISELY Vegetable selection was important (potatoes failed to cook evenly in the packets, and eggplant turned to mush), as was preparation (carrots and leeks could be added raw, but fennel had to be wilted slightly in the microwave). Adding a final flavoring touch—a compound butter—contributed to a full-flavored sauce that perfectly complemented the fish.

COD BAKED IN FOIL WITH LEEKS AND CARROTS
SERVES 4

Haddock, red snapper, halibut, and sea bass also work well in this recipe as long as the fillets are 1 to 1¼ inches thick. The packets may be assembled several hours ahead of time and refrigerated until ready to cook. If the packets have been refrigerated for more than 30 minutes, increase the cooking time by 2 minutes. Open each packet promptly after baking to prevent overcooking, and make sure to open packets away from you to avoid steam burns.

- 4 tablespoons unsalted butter, softened
- 2 garlic cloves, minced
- 1¼ teaspoons finely grated lemon zest, plus lemon wedges for serving
- 1 teaspoon minced fresh thyme
- Salt and pepper
- 2 tablespoons minced fresh parsley
- 2 carrots, peeled and cut into 2-inch-long matchsticks
- 2 leeks, white and light green parts only, halved lengthwise, washed thoroughly, and cut into 2-inch-long matchsticks
- ¼ cup dry vermouth or dry white wine
- 4 (6-ounce) skinless cod fillets, 1 to 1¼ inches thick

1. Combine butter, 1 teaspoon garlic, ¼ teaspoon lemon zest, thyme, ¼ teaspoon salt, and ⅛ teaspoon pepper in small bowl. Combine parsley, remaining lemon zest, and remaining garlic in another small bowl and set aside. Place carrots and leeks in medium bowl, season with salt and pepper, and toss to combine.

2. Adjust oven rack to lower-middle position and heat oven to 450 degrees. Cut eight 12-inch-long sheets of aluminum foil; arrange 4 pieces flat on counter. Divide carrot-leek mixture among arranged foil sheets, mounding vegetables in center of each piece. Pour 1 tablespoon vermouth over each mound of vegetables. Pat cod fillets dry with paper towels, season with salt and pepper, and place 1 fillet on top of each vegetable mound. Divide butter mixture among fillets, spreading over top of each piece. Place second square of foil on top of fish, crimp edges together in ½-inch fold, then fold over 3 more times to create packet about 7 inches square. Place packets on rimmed baking sheet, overlapping slightly if necessary.

3. Bake packets 15 minutes, then carefully open foil, allowing steam to escape away from you. Using thin metal spatula, gently slide cod and vegetables onto plate, along with any accumulated juices, and sprinkle with parsley mixture. Serve immediately, passing lemon wedges separately.

New England Fish Chowder

✔ WHY THIS RECIPE WORKS

New England fish chowder got its start on the fishing vessels that plied the Newfoundland coast in the 18th century. Sailors would throw a piece of their catch (typically cod or haddock) into a pot with water, salt pork, and bulky crackers known as ship's biscuits or hardtack, which helped thicken the stock. When chowder hit the New England mainland at the turn of the 19th century, cooks took to bulking up the broth with potatoes instead of crackers, and milk—especially canned evaporated milk—became a regular addition. Today, the richness quotient has been upped even further, with chowders often featuring a base consisting almost entirely of cream. The trouble is, many modern chowders are so rich that they mask the flavor of the fish altogether. We wanted to honor the soup's simple roots by showcasing moist, tender morsels of fish in a delicate, clean-tasting broth.

GENTLY POACH We experimented with using clam juice and chicken broth as a base for this chowder, but found them both too potent. When we cooked up a water-based chowder, we were encouraged to find that the broth had a clean, light flavor. But the fish itself got mixed reviews: After just 10 minutes of cooking, some pieces were moist and tender while others were dry and overdone. A simple solution: We slipped cod fillets into the water flavored with salt pork, onion, and seasonings; covered the pot; turned off the heat; and let the fish poach for 5 minutes. We then transferred the fillets to a bowl and set them aside. Tasting this speedy stock, we were happy to discover that it had developed a significant amount of flavor in just 5 minutes. Plus, this gentle approach eliminated any chance of overcooking the fragile fillets.

PICK MILK For tradition's sake, we experimented with replacing 2 cups of the water with evaporated milk, added once the potatoes were tender. The resulting chowder was panned for its sweetness, as was one made with equal parts evaporated and regular milk. Half-and-half was too rich: It masked the delicate flavors that we were working hard to protect. In the end, tasters applauded the light,

fresh taste of chowder made with whole milk. A tablespoon of cornstarch whisked into the milk before adding it to the pot coated its proteins, preventing it from curdling as the soup simmered.

NEW ENGLAND FISH CHOWDER
SERVES 6 TO 8

Haddock, or other flaky white fish, may be substituted for the cod. Garnish the chowder with minced fresh chives, crisp bacon bits, or oyster crackers.

2	tablespoons unsalted butter
2	onions, cut into ½-inch dice
4	ounces salt pork, rind removed, pork rinsed and cut into 2 pieces
1½	teaspoons minced fresh thyme
	Salt and pepper
1	bay leaf
5	cups water
2	pounds skinless cod fillets, sliced crosswise into 6 equal pieces
1½	pounds Yukon Gold potatoes, peeled and cut into ½-inch dice
2	cups whole milk
1	tablespoon cornstarch

1. Melt butter in Dutch oven over medium heat. Add onions, salt pork, thyme, ¾ teaspoon salt, and bay leaf; cook, stirring occasionally, until onions are softened but not browned, 3 to 5 minutes. Add water and bring to simmer. Remove pot from heat, gently place cod fillets in water, cover, and let stand until opaque and nearly cooked through, about 5 minutes. Using metal spatula, transfer cod to bowl.

2. Return pot to medium-high heat, add potatoes, and bring to simmer. Cook until potatoes are tender and beginning to break apart, about 20 minutes.

3. Meanwhile, whisk milk, cornstarch, and ½ teaspoon pepper together in bowl. Stir milk mixture into chowder and return to simmer. Return cod and any accumulated juices to pot. Remove pot from heat, cover, and let stand for 5 minutes. Remove and discard salt pork and bay leaf. Stir gently with wooden spoon to break cod into large pieces. Season with salt and pepper to taste. Serve immediately.

Fish sauce is rich in glutamates, a type of amino acid (the same molecules that make up proteins). Glutamates are tastebud stimulators that give food the meaty, savory flavor known as umami. Glutamates are often found in animal proteins, and in the case of fish sauce, they come from fermented fish.

Knowing that seaweed is a potent (and vegetarian) source of glutamates, we optimistically tried subbing a strong salted kelp broth for fish sauce in a Thai dipping sauce. When it failed to contribute sufficient depth, we turned to another source of savory flavor: nucleotides.

Nucleotides are naturally occurring substances; they include inosinate and guanylate, which are found in meat, seafood, and dried mushrooms. When flavor-boosting nucleotides are paired with glutamates, the perception of umami is significantly increased. Sure enough, a salty broth made with dried shiitake mushrooms (rich in nucleotides) and soy sauce (glutamates) provided just the right meaty punch as a 1:1 substitute for fish sauce. Here's how to make it: In a saucepan, simmer 3 cups of water, ¼ ounce of sliced dried shiitake mushrooms, 3 tablespoons of salt, and 2 tablespoons of soy sauce over medium heat until reduced by half. Strain, cool, and store in the fridge for up to three weeks.

California Fish Tacos

✓ WHY THIS RECIPE WORKS

Simple, satisfying fresh fish tacos from the West Coast combine fried fish, sliced cabbage, and a creamy white sauce in a corn tortilla. We chose mild but sturdy white fish for our tacos—we liked cod, in particular, for its clean taste, and its easy availability.

THINK TEMPURA We started with a batter of flour, beer, and salt, and after cutting our fish into 4 by 1-inch strips (the perfect size to fit in a corn tortilla) and seasoning them, we dipped and fried the strips. At first the coating was thick and cumbersome. But taking a cue from Japanese tempura batter—a superthin batter that creates a crispy coating—we increased the ratio of beer to flour, thinning out the batter until it was just thick enough to coat the fish. Substituting a bit of cornstarch for some of the flour gave the now-crispy coating good crunch. One more trick: baking powder. Many batters use baking powder because when the powder is activated, it produces carbon dioxide, which makes for a light coating. It worked.

FRY FAST It's important not to overcook this delicate fish. It helps that the tempura-like coating acts as a protective barrier. We paid extra attention to how long we let the fish fry—not that long! We found that keeping the oil between 325 and 350 degrees allowed us to fry the fish for only 2 minutes per side, so it emerged from the pot golden brown and optimally tender.

TALK TOPPINGS A quick pickle of red onions and jalapeños added color and spice to the tacos, and we used a portion of the vinegary pickling liquid to dress shredded cabbage. Our creamy white sauce got tang from lime juice and sour cream, and fresh cilantro leaves provided the finishing touch.

CALIFORNIA FISH TACOS
SERVES 6

Although this recipe looks involved, all the components are easy to execute and most can be made in advance. Use a Dutch oven that holds 6 quarts or more to fry the fish. Fillets of meaty white fish like cod, haddock, or halibut work best in this recipe. Cut the fish on a slight bias if your fillets aren't quite 4 inches wide. You should end up with about 24 pieces of fish. Light-bodied American lagers, such as Budweiser, work best here. Serve with green salsa, if desired.

PICKLED ONIONS

1	small red onion, halved and sliced thin
2	jalapeño chiles, stemmed and sliced into thin rings
1	cup white wine vinegar
2	tablespoons lime juice
1	tablespoon sugar
1	teaspoon salt

CABBAGE

3	cups shredded green cabbage
¼	cup pickling liquid from pickled onions
½	teaspoon salt
½	teaspoon pepper

WHITE SAUCE

½	cup mayonnaise
½	cup sour cream
2	tablespoons lime juice
2	tablespoons milk

FISH

- 2 pounds skinless white fish fillets, cut crosswise into 4 by 1-inch strips
  Salt and pepper
- ¾ cup all-purpose flour
- ¼ cup cornstarch
- 1 teaspoon baking powder
- 1 cup beer
- 1 quart peanut or vegetable oil
- 24 (6-inch) corn tortillas, warmed
- 1 cup fresh cilantro leaves

1. FOR THE PICKLED ONIONS: Combine onion and jalapeños in medium bowl. Bring vinegar, lime juice, sugar, and salt to boil in small saucepan. Pour vinegar mixture over onion mixture and let sit for at least 30 minutes. (Pickled onions can be made and refrigerated up to 2 days in advance.)

2. FOR THE CABBAGE: Toss all ingredients together in bowl.

3. FOR THE WHITE SAUCE: Whisk all ingredients together in bowl. (Sauce can be made and refrigerated up to 2 days in advance.)

4. FOR THE FISH: Adjust oven rack to middle position and heat oven to 200 degrees. Set wire rack in rimmed baking sheet. Pat fish dry with paper towels and season with salt and pepper. Whisk flour, cornstarch, baking powder, and 1 teaspoon salt together in large bowl. Add beer and whisk until smooth. Transfer fish to batter and toss until evenly coated.

5. Add oil to large Dutch oven until it measures about ¾ inch deep and heat over medium-high heat to 350 degrees. Working with 5 or 6 pieces at a time, remove fish from batter, allowing excess to drip back into bowl, and add to hot oil, briefly dragging fish along surface of oil to prevent sticking. Adjust burner, if necessary, to maintain oil temperature between 325 and 350 degrees. Fry fish, stirring gently to prevent pieces from sticking together, until golden brown and crispy, about 2 minutes per side. Transfer fish to prepared wire rack and place in oven to keep warm. Return oil to 350 degrees and repeat with remaining fish.

6. Divide fish evenly among tortillas. Top with pickled onions, cabbage, white sauce, and cilantro. Serve.

PRACTICAL SCIENCE FIX FOR "FISHY" SEAFOOD

Fish that smells or tastes a little "fishy" isn't necessarily bad; there's an easy solution if you find it unpleasant.

Fish begins to spoil faster than meat, because the pH of fish flesh is close to neutral, or around 6.2 to 7. This is because fish don't produce lactic acid following death like land animals and birds do. And this higher pH creates a very favorable environment for the growth of bacteria—of which there is a lot. In fact, the "slime coat" on the skin of all fish is rich with bacteria. When fish are processed and filleted, the bacteria from the skin reaches the fillets, and then grows rapidly within a few days—even when refrigerated. (The type of bacteria on fish thrives at cold temperatures, in part because the natural habitat of fish is so cold.)

But this doesn't mean you have to eat fish the day it was caught. Unless the fish or seafood you've bought is literally the catch of the day, chances are it will smell and taste at least a little fishy, thanks to a compound found in nearly all seafood called trimethylamine oxide, or TMAO. This compound is odorless when fish and shellfish are alive, but once they're killed, the bacteria slowly transforms TMAO into TMA (trimethylamine), which has a fishy odor. But that doesn't mean that the seafood has gone bad or is unusable. We've found an easy way to eliminate the smell: Soak the fish or the shellfish meat in milk for 20 minutes and then drain and pat dry. The casein in milk binds to the TMA, and when drained away, it takes the culprit that causes fishy odor with it. The result is seafood that's sweet smelling and clean flavored. Another option is to squeeze lemon juice on fish. TMA is an "amine," meaning it is a weak alkali. The citric acid in lemon juice neutralizes the TMA to form a nonvolatile, nonsmelling salt called trimethylammonium citrate (TMAC). This explains why lemon slices are frequently served with fish, and why most recipes add lemon.

CHAPTER 10

Salmon

Salmon is a unique fish. It's pink and flavorful and can cook up to be silky and fine—if you treat it right.

HOW THE SCIENCE WORKS

Salmon is a unique fish for a number of reasons. Salmon are born in fresh water and then travel to the sea. When mature, they typically return to freshwater streams to spawn. To help fuel their upriver swim, salmon are relatively high in fat. Unlike the fat in white fish, which is generally stored mostly in the liver, the fat in salmon is spread throughout the flesh.

Salmon have pink flesh thanks to a compound called astaxanthin, which comes from the crustaceans found in their diet. Salmon, unlike other varieties of fish, store the astaxanthin in their muscles, rather than in their skin or ovaries. (Farmed salmon are fed a diet enriched with both synthetic astaxanthin and a related carotenoid pigment called canthaxanthin, so their color can differ from that of wild salmon.) This compound also gives salmon its unique flavor: When heated, it forms volatile aromas.

> **Salmon have pink flesh due to astaxanthin, which comes from the crustaceans found in their diet.**

There are many varieties of salmon, both wild and farmed. Most Atlantic salmon is farmed (the number of wild Atlantic salmon declined in the 1960s with overfishing), while wild salmon comes from the Pacific. Eating wild versus farmed salmon is a controversial subject, igniting conversation about environmental concerns, contamination, and levels of omega-3 fats. Studies conducted with wild salmon and farmed Atlantic salmon show there are significant differences resulting in different textures, flavors, and appearance when cooked. Because farmed Atlantic salmon has been selected to provide, among other things, faster growth, its genetic makeup differs from wild salmon.

This doesn't mean there is a difference in muscle structure or composition—the size and number of muscle fibers are virtually the same for wild salmon and farmed Atlantic salmon. The difference comes down to the structure of the collagen protein that makes up about 90 percent of the connective tissue in salmon. Wild salmon has a higher amount of collagen (and thus connective tissue) and, more importantly, a significantly greater number of chemical cross-links between collagen molecules. The flesh of wild salmon therefore turns noticeably firmer when cooked than farmed salmon does. Farmed salmon also contains more fat, as much as twice the amount in wild salmon. The higher fat content contributes not only to greater lubricity, but also to flavor. (See Test Kitchen Experiment, page 90.)

We love salmon because it's rich without being aggressively fishy, and, unlike a lot of white fish, it needs no dressing up to taste good. Because salmon has a greater water-holding capacity and more fat than white fish, it reacts differently to heat, and we prefer to cook it to a lower temperature.

We use a number of techniques to make sure that the salmon flesh remains tender and silky (i.e., not overcooked), including roasting it in an oven that begins very hot and then is immediately lowered (page 93), or quickly broiling it (see Miso-Glazed Salmon, page 95). Salmon goes well with smoke, and emerges tender and smoky after cooking on a low-heat grill for our Grill-Smoked Salmon (page 92)—for more on the technique of smoking, see page 91. Occasionally we even brine it (see Sesame-Crusted Salmon, page 94).

Even relatively fatty fish like salmon can go from tender and moist to chalky and dry in a flash. In the test kitchen we use an instant-read digital thermometer to tell when salmon is done, and we prefer it cooked to 125 degrees for flesh that has the ideal balance of firm and silky. The majority of the salmon we cook in the test kitchen is farmed Atlantic, but as we've cooked more wild varieties, such as king, coho, sockeye, and chum, we started to wonder if this catchall temperature was appropriate across the board. We set up the following test to find out.

EXPERIMENT

We cooked multiple samples of four species of wild Pacific salmon—king (Chinook), sockeye (red), coho (silver), and chum—along with farmed Atlantic salmon to both 120 degrees and 125 degrees internal temperature in temperature-controlled water baths. We asked tasters, blind to the differences in internal temperature, to pick which sample offered the ideal firm yet silky texture for each type of salmon.

RESULTS

Tasters unanimously preferred the coho, sockeye, and chum samples cooked to 120 degrees and the farmed Atlantic cooked to 125 degrees. While a few tasters preferred the king sample at 125 degrees, the majority preferred it at 120 degrees.

TAKEAWAY

Farmed Atlantic salmon differs significantly from the half-dozen commercial wild varieties caught in the Pacific Ocean from the coast of northern California to Alaska. Chief among these differences: The collagen protein in farmed Atlantic salmon contains fewer chemical cross-links than that in wild varieties, which translates into softer flesh; and farmed Atlantic salmon contains more fat than any wild variety (up to four times as much fat as the leanest wild variety), providing the perception of juiciness when cooked. Interestingly, tasters' preferences closely correlated with fat content. The wild variety that a few tasters preferred at 125 degrees is also one of fattiest (see the chart), while the leaner wild species were all at their best at 120 degrees.

With naturally firmer flesh, and less fat to provide lubrication, wild salmon can have the texture of overcooked fish even at 125 degrees. By cooking the wild varieties to just 120 degrees, their muscle fibers contract less and therefore retain more moisture.

NOT ALL SALMON IS THE SAME

The difference between farmed and wild salmon is clear at first glance. You can see the fat lacing the farmed Atlantic salmon, while the wild silver (coho) salmon is far leaner.

SPECIES	WILD VS. FARMED	FAT (GRAMS PER 100G FLESH)	IDEAL INTERNAL TEMP (F)
Atlantic	Farmed	13.42	125
King (Chinook)	Wild	11.73	120
Sockeye (Red)	Wild	7.28	120
Coho (Silver)	Wild	5.57	120
Chum	Wild	3.67	120

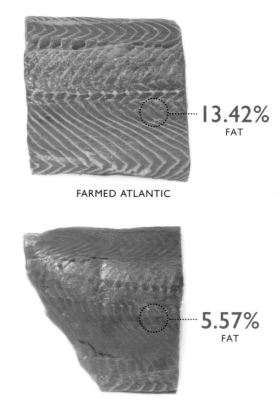

13.42% FAT

FARMED ATLANTIC

5.57% FAT

WILD SILVER (COHO)

Technique 101: Smoking

Though plenty of rib and brisket enthusiasts convert their grills into makeshift smokers—we've made do with an indirect fire, a pan of water, and soaked wood chips—proper lower-temperature smoking is best achieved with a designated appliance.

HOLD LOW HEAT

Other than introducing wood to the fire, smoking is all about holding the heat at a low, steady temperature for a long time—a full day, in some cases—a process that not only bathes the meat in smoke flavor, but also helps tenderize it by breaking down its tough connective tissue.

LONG-BURNING FIRE

Home smokers typically have the advantage of a larger fuel capacity for a longer-burning fire, as well as a water reservoir and vents. According to manufacturers, these features keep the ambient temperature in the necessary 225- to 250-degree range for up to 24 hours with little tending of the fire.

HOW DO YOU GET SMOKE FLAVOR?

Most organic materials—everything from tea leaves to grass—will burn. But the smoke flavor we associate with foods as diverse as smoked salmon or barbecued ribs comes from the unique smoke created by hardwood. Each type of wood creates subtly different smokes, but the basics are the same.

Ninety-eight aroma compounds have been identified in smoke. The majority of smoke-flavored compounds are created by the pyrolysis (burning in the absence of air) of lignin, a major constituent of wood, along with cellulose. Burning the lignin in wood produces compounds called "phenols." A fairly large group of smoky flavored phenols are produced from lignin, including guaiacol, vinyl-guaiacol, syringol, and others. But the aroma of smoke is also due to other classes of compounds, especially those formed by the pyrolysis of related polymers cellulose and hemicellulose, including a compound with the odor of burnt sugar called cyclotene. Only when combined do the compounds generated from lignin and cellulose produce the flavors characteristic of smoke.

THERMOMETER

OUR FAVORITE SMOKER

We conducted a 12-hour temperature test, recording the temperature of each model every hour while smoking turkey breasts, ribs, brisket, and pork shoulder on three stand-alone smokers. Our favorite smoker, the Weber Smoky Mountain Cooker, included twin 18.5-inch grates, which provided ample room for four pork butts, two whole turkeys, or four rib racks; a water pan; and many vents. Our only complaint? A lack of handles made transport and cleanup difficult.

WATER RESERVOIR

The water reservoir—really, a built-in water pan in most stand-alone smokers—absorbs and retains heat and produces moister results.

VENTILATION

The best smokers come with a multitude of vents, which you can open and close at will, for excellent temperature control.

GRATE

The charcoal (or wood) sits here.

DOOR

The door allows you to add more fuel without taking the whole smoker apart.

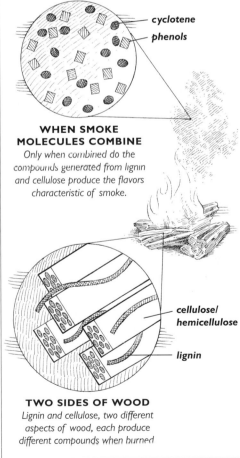

cyclotene

phenols

WHEN SMOKE MOLECULES COMBINE

Only when combined do the compounds generated from lignin and cellulose produce the flavors characteristic of smoke.

cellulose/ hemicellulose

lignin

TWO SIDES OF WOOD

Lignin and cellulose, two different aspects of wood, each produce different compounds when burned

Grill-Smoked Salmon

✓ WHY THIS RECIPE WORKS

The process of smoking fish over hardwood to preserve its delicate flesh has a long tradition. But smoked salmon's unique taste and texture don't come easy: The translucent, mildly smoky slices are produced by ever-so-slowly smoking (but not fully cooking) salt-cured fillets at roughly 60 to 90 degrees, a project that requires specialized equipment and loads of time (at least 24 hours and as long as five days). Then there is hot smoking, a procedure in which cured fillets are fully cooked at higher temperatures (100 to 250 degrees) for 1 to 8 hours. The higher heat results in a drier texture and a more potent smokiness, so the fish is often flaked and mixed into dips and spreads. In our recipe, we wanted to combine the best elements of cold-smoked salmon and hot-smoked salmon.

CURE IT To prepare the salmon for smoking, we quick-cured the fish with a mixture of salt and sugar to draw moisture from the flesh, which firmed it up. Salt is important to get the correct texture, but with salt alone the finished dish would be too salty. Sugar, like salt, is hygroscopic, meaning it attracts water, and can help firm up salmon. But because individual molecules of sucrose are much larger than sodium and chloride ions, sugar is, pound for pound, about 12 times less effective than salt at attracting moisture. Using both together was a workable option: The ratio of 2 parts sugar to 1 part salt produced well-balanced taste and texture in the finished salmon.

COOK IT We cooked the fish indirectly over a gentle fire with ample smoke to produce salmon that was sweet, smoky, and tender. We smoked individual fillets, rather than a whole side of salmon, because this ensured more thorough smoke exposure in the same amount of time by creating more surface area. Serving the fish alongside a "smoked salmon platter" sauce was the perfect pairing.

GRILL-SMOKED SALMON
SERVES 6

Use center-cut salmon fillets of similar thickness so that they cook at the same rate. If using wild salmon, cook until thickest part of fillet registers 120 degrees. The best way to ensure uniformity is to buy a 2½- to 3-pound whole center-cut fillet and cut it into six pieces. If you'd like to use wood chunks instead of wood chips when using a charcoal grill, substitute two wood chunks, soaked in water for 1 hour, for the wood chip packet. Avoid mesquite wood chunks for this recipe. Serve the salmon with lemon wedges or our "Smoked Salmon Platter" Sauce.

2 tablespoons sugar
1 tablespoon kosher salt
6 (6- to 8-ounce) center-cut skin-on salmon fillets
2 cups wood chips

1. Combine sugar and salt in bowl. Set wire rack in rimmed baking sheet, set salmon on rack, and sprinkle flesh side evenly with sugar mixture. Refrigerate, uncovered, for 1 hour. With paper towels, brush any excess salt and sugar from salmon and blot dry. Return salmon on wire rack to refrigerator, uncovered, while preparing grill.

2. Just before grilling, soak 1 cup wood chips in water for 15 minutes, then drain. Using large piece of heavy-duty aluminum foil, wrap soaked and unsoaked chips together in 8 by 4½-inch foil packet. (Make sure chips do not poke holes in sides or bottom of packet.) Cut 2 evenly spaced 2-inch slits in top of packet.

3A. FOR A CHARCOAL GRILL: Open bottom vent halfway. Light large chimney starter one-third filled with charcoal briquettes (2 quarts). When top coals are partially covered with ash, pour into steeply banked pile against side of grill. Place wood chip packet on coals. Set cooking grate in place, cover, and open lid vent halfway. Heat grill until hot and wood chunks are smoking, about 5 minutes.

3B. FOR A GAS GRILL: Remove cooking grate and place wood chip packet directly on primary burner. Set grate in place, turn primary burner to high (leave other burners off), cover, and heat grill until hot and wood chips are smoking, 15 to 25 minutes. Turn primary burner to medium. (Adjust primary burner as needed to maintain grill temperature of 275 to 300 degrees.)

4. Fold piece of heavy-duty foil into 18 by 6-inch rectangle. Place foil rectangle on cooler side of grill and place

---

PRACTICAL SCIENCE GRAY AREA

There is only a minor flavor difference in the gray area.

The gray portion of tissue one can often see in salmon is a fatty deposit rich in omega-3 fatty acids and low in the natural pink pigments found in the rest of the fish. To get a handle on how the gray area affects flavor, we oven-roasted several fillets of salmon, then removed the gray portion from half of them and left it intact on the others. Only a few discerning tasters noted that the samples with the gray substance had an ever-so-slightly fishier flavor; most couldn't tell the difference. It's easy enough to remove the gray stuff by peeling off the skin of the cooked salmon and then scraping it away with the back of a knife, but the flavor difference is so minor that we don't think it's worth the hassle.

salmon fillets on foil, spaced at least ½ inch apart. Cover (position lid vent over salmon if using charcoal) and cook until center of thickest part of fillet is still translucent when checked with tip of paring knife and registers 125 degrees, 30 to 40 minutes. Transfer to platter and serve warm or at room temperature.

"SMOKED SALMON PLATTER" SAUCE
MAKES 1½ CUPS

1	large egg yolk, plus 1 hard-cooked large egg, chopped fine
2	teaspoons Dijon mustard
2	teaspoons sherry vinegar
½	cup vegetable oil
2	tablespoons capers, rinsed, plus 1 teaspoon brine
2	tablespoons minced shallot
2	tablespoons minced fresh dill

Whisk egg yolk, mustard, and vinegar together in medium bowl. Whisking constantly, slowly drizzle in oil until emulsified, about 1 minute. Gently fold in capers and brine, shallot, dill, and hard-cooked egg.

Oven-Roasted Salmon

WHY THIS RECIPE WORKS

For an oven-roasted salmon recipe that would give us a nicely browned exterior and a silky, moist interior, we developed a hybrid roasting method, preheating the oven to 500 degrees but then turning down the heat to 275 just before placing the fish in the oven.

PREHEAT THE BAKING SHEET To prevent the oven temperature from dropping too rapidly when adding the fish to the oven, we preheated the baking sheet. This necessitated cooking the fish with its skin on, so the fillets could be placed skin side down in the pan to protect the flesh. The first time we tried this, the fish tasted a little too fatty. We solved the problem by cutting slits through the skin before placing the fillets on the sheet to allow most of the fat directly beneath the skin to be rendered.

HIGH THEN LOW Because we started high, and then immediately turned down the oven, the initial blast of high heat firmed the exterior and helped render some fat. The fish then gently cooked in the oven and stayed moist as the temperature slowly dropped.

RELISH IT Our oven-roasted salmon recipe was complete when we added an easy relish. After testing dozens of combinations, we found that one with an acidic element worked best. Tasters especially liked a tomato-basil relish and a spicy cucumber relish.

PRACTICAL SCIENCE WOOD SMOKE TASTE TEST

How much difference does the choice of wood really make?

Hickory and mesquite are the most readily available types of smoking wood, but some grilling pros swear by more exotic woods. To see for ourselves how much difference the choice of wood really makes, we used eight types to smoke chicken, salmon, baby back ribs, and pork chops.

Our old standby, hickory, though acceptable across the board, was deemed "generic." Mesquite's distinctive "barbecue potato chip" flavor was universally disliked, while "sweet," "subtle" apple and cherry wood were big hits in every application.

WOOD	CHICKEN	FISH	BEEF/ PORK	COMMENTS
Apple	Great	Great	Great	An all-around hit, with "sweet," "fruity," "subtly complex" flavor.
Cherry	Great	Great	Great	Well liked for "mild," "fruity" sweetness.
Hickory	Good	Good	Good	Overall, "generic but good," with "balanced" flavor.
Oak	Good	Good	Good	"Mild," "nutty," and "herbal," with hints of "vanilla."
Maple	Good	Fair	Good	Evoked pleasant memories of "bacon" for some but was "resin-y" on salmon.
Alder	Fair	Good	Good	"Delicate" flavor with notes of "coriander" and "juniper," though some found it "bitter" with chicken.
Pecan	Fair	Fair	Good	"Intense" and "spicy" with pork but brought "cigarette-like" off-flavors to chicken and fish.
Mesquite	Fair	Fair	Fair	In general, "harsh" and "acrid," reminding some of "burnt rubber."

To ensure uniform pieces of fish that cook at the same rate, buy a whole center-cut fillet and cut it into four pieces. If using wild salmon, cook until thickest part of fillet registers 120 degrees. If your knife is not sharp enough to easily cut through the skin, try a serrated knife. It is important to keep the skin on during cooking to protect the flesh; remove it afterward if you choose not to serve it.

- 1 (1¾- to 2-pound) skin-on salmon fillet, about 1½ inches thick
- 2 teaspoons olive oil
  Salt and pepper
- 1 recipe relish (recipes follow)

1. Adjust oven rack to lowest position, place rimmed baking sheet on rack, and heat oven to 500 degrees. Use sharp knife to remove any whitish fat from belly of salmon and cut fillet into 4 equal pieces. Make 4 or 5 shallow slashes about an inch apart along skin side of each piece of salmon, being careful not to cut into flesh.

2. Pat salmon dry with paper towels. Rub fillets evenly with oil and season with salt and pepper. Reduce oven temperature to 275 degrees and remove baking sheet. Carefully place salmon, skin side down, on baking sheet. Roast until centers of thickest part of fillets are still translucent when cut into with paring knife and thickest part of fillets registers 125 degrees, 9 to 13 minutes. Transfer fillets to serving platter or individual plates, top with relish, and serve.

- 12 ounces ripe tomatoes, cored, seeded, and cut into ¼-inch dice (about 1½ cups)
- ½ small shallot, minced (about 1 tablespoon)
- 1 small garlic clove, minced
- 1 tablespoon extra-virgin olive oil
- 1 teaspoon red wine vinegar
- 2 tablespoons chopped fresh basil
  Salt and pepper

Combine all ingredients in medium bowl. Season with salt and pepper to taste.

- 1 cucumber, peeled, seeded, and cut into ¼-inch dice (about 2 cups)
- ½ small shallot, minced (about 1 tablespoon)
- 1 serrano chile, stemmed, seeded, and minced (about 1 tablespoon)
- 2 tablespoons chopped fresh mint
- 1–2 tablespoons lime juice
  Salt

Combine cucumber, shallot, chile, mint, 1 tablespoon lime juice, and ¼ teaspoon salt in medium bowl. Let stand at room temperature to blend flavors, 15 minutes. Season with additional lime juice and salt to taste.

Sesame-Crusted Salmon

✔ WHY THIS RECIPE WORKS

Most sesame-crusted salmon recipes are one-note affairs. But we set out to liven things up. First, we brined our fillets to ensure that each piece was seasoned and remained moist after cooking. The sesame seeds themselves were brined and toasted to bring out their flavor. Finally, we used a tahini paste that we thickened with citrus juice to glue the citrus zest, scallions, ginger, and spice to the fillets (see opposite).

BRINE THE SALMON It may seem odd to brine something that basically lived in a brine, but the saltwater soak played a double role: It seasoned the salmon's flesh and subtly changed its protein structure, helping it retain moisture. And it took just 15 minutes.

AND THE SEEDS We wanted a way to liven up the dull sesame flavor. While brainstorming possible solutions, we discovered Japanese *gomashio*. The term translates as "sesame salt" and at its most basic is just those two ingredients. To make the savory blend, you toast the seeds and then mix or grind them with salt. Instead of grinding the seeds with salt after toasting them, we just submerged them in some of the brine for the fish, drained them, and toasted them whole in a skillet. The brine woke up the nutty flavor of the seeds by infusing each one with salt. What's more, because the starch in the seeds absorbed water from the brine and then gelatinized during toasting, the seeds were now crispier than ever.

SESAME-CRUSTED SALMON WITH LEMON AND GINGER
SERVES 4

Purchase fillets that are about the same size and shape. If any have a thin belly flap, fold it over for a more even thickness. If using wild salmon, cook until thickest part of fillet registers 120 degrees.

	Salt
¾	cup sesame seeds
4	(6- to 8-ounce) skinless salmon fillets
2	scallions, white parts minced, green parts sliced thin
1	tablespoon grated lemon zest plus 2 teaspoons juice
4	teaspoons tahini
2	teaspoons grated fresh ginger
⅛	teaspoon cayenne pepper
1	teaspoon vegetable oil

1. Adjust oven rack to middle position and heat oven to 325 degrees. Dissolve 5 tablespoons salt in 2 quarts water. Transfer 1 cup brine to bowl, stir in sesame seeds, and let stand at room temperature for 5 minutes. Submerge salmon fillets in remaining brine and let stand at room temperature for 15 minutes.

2. Drain seeds and place in 12-inch nonstick skillet. Cook seeds over medium heat, stirring constantly, until golden brown, 2 to 4 minutes. Transfer seeds to pie plate and wipe out skillet with paper towels. Remove salmon from brine and pat dry.

3. Place scallion whites and lemon zest on cutting board and chop until whites and zest are finely minced and well combined. Transfer scallion-zest mixture to bowl and stir in lemon juice, tahini, ginger, cayenne, and ⅛ teaspoon salt.

4. Evenly distribute half of paste over bottoms (skinned sides) of fillets. Press coated sides of fillets in seeds and transfer, seed side down, to plate. Evenly distribute remaining paste over tops of fillets and coat with remaining seeds.

5. Heat oil in now-empty skillet over medium heat until shimmering. Place fillets in skillet, skinned side up, and reduce heat to medium-low. Cook until seeds begin to brown, 1 to 2 minutes. Remove skillet from heat and, using 2 spatulas, carefully flip fillets over. Transfer skillet to oven. Bake until center of fillets is translucent when checked with tip of paring knife and registers 125 degrees, 10 to 15 minutes. Transfer to serving platter and let rest for 5 minutes. Sprinkle with scallion greens and serve.

PRACTICAL SCIENCE
SURPRISING TAHINI THICKENER

You can thicken tahini by adding liquid.

For our sesame-crusted salmon recipe, a smear of tahini on each fillet helps boost the sesame flavor. But tahini has a thin consistency, which means that it won't stay put on the moist, slick surface of a fish fillet. To thicken the tahini and give it some holding power, the solution is a bit surprising: Stir in 2 teaspoons of juice.

You'd think that adding a liquid would thin tahini rather than thicken it. Why the opposite? Tahini is simply sesame-seed butter, made by grinding hulled sesame seeds into a paste. Much of its makeup is carbohydrates, and when a small amount of juice (or any water-containing liquid) is added to tahini, a portion of each carbohydrate molecule is drawn to the water. As a result, clumps of carbohydrates appear. As the amount of water is increased, more clumps develop, causing the tahini to thicken overall. If you keep adding water, eventually you'll cross over the threshold of thickening it; enough water in the system will cause the tahini to loosen and thin out. This is similar to what happens when chocolate seizes. A small amount of added water acts like a glue, wetting particles just enough to get them to stick together, but eventually if you add too much water, the mixture turns into an evenly thinned-out liquid.

This same process also occurs with peanut butter (both all-natural and commercial varieties of the stuff): For example, if you make satay sauce for grilled meat, peanut dipping sauce for spring rolls, or dan dan noodles, you will notice that clumps appear when you first add liquid to the peanut butter. But as you keep adding liquid to reach the required consistency for these sauces, the lumps disappear.

Miso-Glazed Salmon

✓ WHY THIS RECIPE WORKS

The Japanese technique of marinating fish in miso started as a way to preserve a fresh catch without refrigeration during its long journey inland. In the last few years, however, after its introduction by chef Nobu Matsuhisa at his namesake restaurant, it has become a popular restaurant preparation in this country. The technique itself is quite simple. Miso is combined with sugar, sake, and mirin (sweet Japanese rice wine) to make a marinade that is typically applied to oily fish like salmon or black cod and left to sit for about three days; during that time, the marinade seasons the fish and draws moisture out of its flesh so that it becomes quite firm and dense. The fish is then scraped clean and broiled, producing meaty-textured, well-seasoned fillets with a lacquered savory-sweet glaze. But three days is just too long to wait for such a simple dish. We wondered if we could tweak the traditional technique to produce miso-marinated salmon just to our liking: moist, well-seasoned fillets that were slightly firmer than usual and evenly burnished on the surface.

MARINATE IT The question was how long to let the fish marinate. To find out, we made several more batches of a marinade, coated four skin-on salmon fillets with each, and let the fish sit for 30 minutes, 1 hour, 6 hours, and 24 hours. After wiping off the excess paste, we placed the fillets on a wire rack set in a foil-lined baking sheet and broiled them 6 inches from the element. The results were convincing: The batches that had been marinated for 6 and 24 hours delivered deep, complex seasoning throughout. There was a textural bonus to marinating, too; the salmon had firmed up just a bit at the surface, which made for a nice contrast to its silky interior.

PRACTICAL SCIENCE MISO PRIMER

The different types of miso available in the grocery store can be confusing. Here is a rundown on what to buy.

An essential ingredient in the Japanese kitchen, miso paste is made by fermenting soybeans and sometimes grains (such as rice, barley, or rye) with a mold called *koji*. Packed with savory flavor, miso is used to season everything from soups and braises to dressings and sauces. Although countless variations of the salty, deep-flavored ingredient are available, three common types are white *shiro* (despite its name, this miso is light golden in color), red *aka*, and brownish-black *hatcho*. Flavor profiles are altered by changing the type of grain in the mix, adjusting the ratio of grain to soybeans, tweaking the amounts of salt and mold, and extending or decreasing the fermentation time, which can range from a few weeks to a few years.

We tasted the South River brand of white and red miso (available in some grocery stores, Asian markets, and online) along with an Asian brand of harder-to-find dark brown miso plain, in miso soup, and in miso-glazed salmon. The white miso was mild and sweet, the red miso nicely balanced salty and sweet, and the black miso was strong, complex, and prune-like. Though flavor nuances will vary from brand to brand, if you're looking to keep just one type of miso on hand, moderately salty-sweet red miso is a good all-purpose choice. Miso will easily keep for up to a year in the refrigerator (some sources say it keeps indefinitely).

RED MISO

GLAZE IT The only remaining problem was that the glaze was overbrowning before the interior was cooked. Reducing the sugar to ¼ cup helped (and nobody missed the extra sweetness), but the real fix was lowering the oven rack. By moving the rack 8 inches from the element, the fillets cooked up tender and silky just as the glaze took on an attractively deep bronze color—and if the edges started to burn, we simply pulled up the foil underneath to act as a shield. It was just the result we wanted in a fraction of the time.

MISO-GLAZED SALMON
SERVES 4

Note that the fish needs to marinate for at least 6 or up to 24 hours before cooking. Use center-cut salmon fillets of similar thickness. If using wild salmon, cook until thickest part of fillet registers 120 degrees. Yellow, red, or brown miso paste can be used instead of white.

½	cup white miso paste
¼	cup sugar
3	tablespoons sake
3	tablespoons mirin
4	(6- to 8-ounce) skin-on salmon fillets
	Lemon wedges

1. Whisk miso, sugar, sake, and mirin together in medium bowl until sugar and miso are dissolved (mixture will be thick). Dip each fillet into miso mixture to evenly coat all flesh sides. Place fish skin side down in baking dish and pour any remaining miso mixture over fillets. Cover with plastic wrap and refrigerate for at least 6 hours or up to 24 hours.

2. Adjust oven rack 8 inches from broiler element and heat broiler. Place wire rack in rimmed baking sheet and cover with aluminum foil. Using your fingers, scrape miso mixture from fillets (do not rinse) and place fish skin side down on foil, leaving 1 inch between each fillet.

3. Broil salmon until deeply browned and centers of fillets register 125 degrees, 8 to 12 minutes, rotating sheet halfway through cooking and shielding edges of fillets with foil if necessary. Transfer to platter and serve with lemon wedges.

CHAPTER 11

Shrimp

Part of the flavor of this wildly popular shellfish comes from the shell.

HOW THE SCIENCE WORKS

Shrimp are crustaceans, one of tens of thousands of arthropod species with an exoskeleton, which they molt in order to grow. There are just about 2,000 species of shrimp, around 300 of which are marketed worldwide—both wild and farmed shrimp. In America, most shrimp comes already frozen and defrosted at the market, with a few exceptions.

And Americans love shrimp. In fact, it is the most popular seafood in the United States, the most consumed per capita. It overtook the former king of seafood—canned tuna—in 2002. In 2012, Americans ate, on average, 3.8 pounds of shrimp per year, a number that has doubled since the 1980s, according to the National Oceanic and Atmospheric Administration.

But how shrimp gets to the plate is controversial, due to both the impact on the environment and to other marine life. There are both wild and farmed shrimp available at most markets. The Monterey Bay Aquarium Seafood Watch recommends buying wild-caught shrimp (minus those from shrimp fisheries in Mexico or Louisiana, which have run into trouble with labor laws and management), or farmed shrimp from the United States, and avoiding imported farmed shrimp. We've found that wild shrimp have a sweeter flavor and firmer texture than farm-raised. So the best option for the average shopper? Wild-caught, domestic, frozen shrimp.

All shrimp is composed of around 80 percent water, 17 percent protein, 2 percent carbohydrate, and 1.2 percent fat, mostly from the shell. The muscle structure of shrimp (and lobster, page 113) is closer to that of mammals (page 25) than fish (page 83). In shrimp, connective tissue surrounds longer individual muscle fibers and bundles of muscle fibers rather than separating the short muscle fibers like the connective tissue in white fish. This is why

Your best option? Wild, domestic, frozen shrimp.

shrimp meat, like beef, does not flake when cooked. During cooking, shrimp change color (from gray-black to pink) because when the proteins denature (starting at around 120 degrees), the pigment astaxanthin (also found in salmon, page 89) is released, free to develop its pink color. We prefer shrimp cooked to 140 degrees.

Shrimp are extremely perishable because their pH (around 6.6 to 7.9) is ideal for microbial growth. This is why most shrimp are frozen before sale—even though freezing and thawing releases enzymes (when the ice crystals pierce the cells) that degrade the muscle protein, making it mushy. Freezing and thawing also releases water inside the shrimp muscle, which can cause dryness. Shrimp that are not immediately frozen are also occasionally subject to a condition called melanosis, in which phenols inside the shell surface are oxidized, causing harmless black discoloration.

One of the most flavorful parts of shrimp? The shell. The main structural element in shells is a polysaccharide called chitin. Chitin does not break down when heated, so it doesn't soften or fall apart when cooked, though it is flexible. The shell contains proteins, sugars, and umami-rich glutamates and nucleotides, many of which are water-soluble and are absorbed into the flesh when cooked. The shell also easily undergoes the flavor-inducing Maillard reaction.

Shrimp shells can be used to add flavor to a dish on their own—in our Shrimp Fra Diavolo recipe (page 102), we brown them alone to begin building a briny, flavorful broth. They also add flavor directly to the meat in our roasted shrimp recipe (page 103)—not to mention protect the meat from overcooking. Yes, you can even eat them: The thin shells in our Salt and Pepper Shrimp (page 100) are rendered perfectly crisp.

TEST KITCHEN EXPERIMENT

When cooking with shrimp it's easy to view the shell as simply an impediment to accessing the sweet, briny flesh inside. The wide availability of peeled shrimp suggests many cooks avoid dealing with it altogether. But to overlook these crustaceans' exoskeletons is to take a pass on a considerable amount of flavor. Restaurant chefs have long saved shrimp shells for stock in much the same way they do beef and chicken bones. Calling for shell-on shrimp allows us to pull a range of enticing flavor compounds into a dish—but we wanted to know the ideal length of time to cook shrimp shells for the best flavor and aroma. We designed an experiment for simmering shrimp shells to determine just that.

EXPERIMENT

We simmered batches of shrimp shells (each batch contained the shells from 1½ pounds of large shrimp, or 4 ounces of shells) in 1½ cups of water, covered, for 5, 10, 15, and 30 minutes. After simmering, we strained the shell broth off of the shells. To eliminate the chance that any flavor concentration resulted from evaporation, we added water back into the longer-cooked samples so that all samples were the same volume. Samples were tasted warm (160 degrees) and tasters were asked to comment on the intensity of the shrimp flavor of each sample. We repeated the test three times, each time with a different set of tasters.

RESULTS

To our surprise, tasters almost unanimously chose the 5- and 10-minute simmered samples as "more potent," "shrimpier," and "more aromatic" than the 15- and 30-minute simmered samples. By analyzing the rankings from each round of testing we found an inverse relationship between cooking time and shrimp flavor intensity.

TAKEAWAY

While it may seem counterintuitive that a shorter simmering time produces a more intensely flavored stock, a closer look provides a clear explanation. While some savory compounds found in shrimp shells, such as glutamic acid and the free nucleotide inosine monophosphate (IMP), are nonvolatile (they stay in the stock, rather than release into the atmosphere), our experiment shows that the compounds that we associate with shrimp flavor are highly volatile. Shrimp shells contain about 10 percent by weight polyunsaturated fatty acids that quickly oxidize during cooking into low-molecular-weight aldehydes, alcohols, and ketones. These low-molecular-weight molecules rapidly release into the air, providing a pleasant aroma during cooking, but leaving behind a bland broth. So to get the most out of your shrimp shells, remember that longer isn't better: Keep your simmering time to 5 minutes for the best shrimp flavor.

SHRIMP SHELLS: WHEN IS THEIR FLAVOR BEST?

You might think that simmering shrimp shells for longer would make a more flavorful stock, but that is incorrect. The compounds associated with shrimp flavor are very volatile, so a shorter simmer is in fact better. The best time? Only 5 minutes.

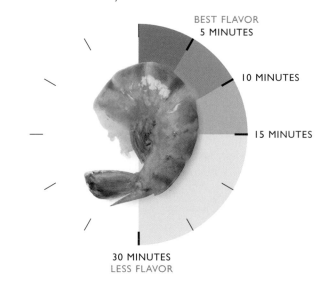

BEST FLAVOR
5 MINUTES

10 MINUTES

15 MINUTES

30 MINUTES
LESS FLAVOR

FOCUS ON: SHRIMP

Shrimp come in all sizes and from all over the world. Some things remain constant.

HEAD

The shrimp head is rarely eaten in the U.S., though it does contain a good deal of flavor. The head of shrimp contains the hepatopancreas, which releases digestive enzymes after the shrimp is killed. These enzymes can render the shrimp's meat mushy, which is why the head is often removed right after death.

EYES

Most varieties of shrimp have two compound eyes, which are capable of detecting movement. (Mantis shrimp, a related breed of shrimp rarely eaten, however, have one of the most complex visual systems ever discovered, containing 16 photoreceptor pigments, compared to human eyes, which have only three.)

ANTENNAE

Shrimp have two sets of antennae—one long, one short—to help them maneuver in their surroundings, and sample chemicals in the water.

SHELL

Shrimp shells are made of a substance called chitin, which does not break down when heated. The shells contain proteins and sugars as well as nucleotides and glutamates, which contribute umami flavors and can aid in instigating the Maillard reaction. The shells are also used to protect the more-fragile meat during cooking.

VEIN

The "vein" running down the length of the shrimp's back is the digestive tract. We tend to remove it before cooking. (Leaving the tract in place doesn't affect the flavor of shrimp, but it's not terribly appealing. To remove it and peel the shrimp in one easy step, snip along the crustacean's back with scissors.)

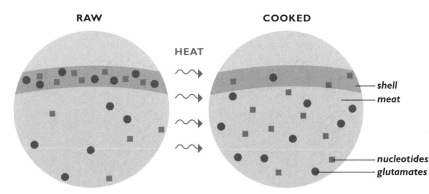

RAW   HEAT   COOKED

shell
meat

nucleotides
glutamates

COOKING WITH THE SHELL

The shell does more than protect the meat. Shrimp shells contain healthy amounts of glutamates and nucleotides, water-soluble compounds that dramatically enhance savory umami flavor when present together. These compounds are absorbed by the shrimp meat during cooking, amplifying the effect of its own glutamates and nucleotides.

MEAT

The muscle structure of shrimp is closer to that of mammals than white fish. Connective tissue surrounds the longer individual muscle fibers and bundles of muscle fibers, as opposed to separate short fish muscle fibers. This is why shrimp meat, unlike white fish, does not flake when cooked. Shrimp also contain many volatile aroma compounds, which are easily lost during cooking.

Salt and Pepper Shrimp

✔ WHY THIS RECIPE WORKS

Shrimp that are dipped in a batter and fried until golden and crisp are undeniably good, but we'd argue that the Chinese take on frying these crustaceans—salt and pepper shrimp—boasts an exterior that's even more tempting. The key ingredient to that texture might surprise you. It's not a batter but simply the shrimp shells. To keep our shell-on deep-fried salt and pepper shrimp shells crispy and crunchy rather than tough, we employed several tricks: medium-sized shrimp, cornstarch, hot oil, and a bit of a brine.

KEEP THEM SMALL AND DRY First, we chose medium-large shrimp (31 to 40 per pound). The shells of this size shrimp are thinner relative to those on more jumbo specimens, and therefore it's easier to get them crisp. Next, we coated them in a thin layer of cornstarch to dry out their shells, which helped make them brittle upon frying.

USE HOT OIL Getting—and keeping—the oil as hot as possible helped to thoroughly dry out the shrimp shells, which aided in browning and crisping. It also dried them out quickly so that they wouldn't have a chance to over-cook. We cooked them in small batches in very hot oil, which helped keep the temperature of the oil from dipping too low.

PRACTICAL SCIENCE DO NOT PEEL THESE SHRIMP

Yes, you can eat the shells.

Most of us peel shrimp before eating it—and for good reason. Made of an elastic substance known as chitin, the shell can be tough. But great salt and pepper shrimp feature a fried shell as crispy—and appealing to eat—as the skin on fried chicken.

Interestingly, the process by which poultry skin and shrimp shells become crisp and edible is somewhat different. Raw chicken skin is flabby because its fat molecules (which make up 50 percent of its weight) coat its proteins, preventing them from cross-linking and crisping up the texture when cooked; it also contains a lot of water. The high heat of frying takes care of both issues: It causes the fat to render, allowing the proteins to cross-link and become more rigid, and it drives off water, turning the cross-linked proteins brittle.

Chitin, on the other hand, does not break down when exposed to heat. Furthermore, its rubbery texture is entirely caused by moisture. To crisp the shells, it is necessary to dehydrate them as much as possible—something that can be accomplished only by a very dry heat method like frying. (Most methods will leave the shells chewy and flexible; think shrimp boil.) For this reason, we eschew a wet batter and instead toss the shrimp in seasoned cornstarch. This light, dry coating helps pull moisture from the shells, which evaporates in the hot oil, leaving them brittle and crisp.

SEASON WELL To season the shrimp and keep them moist, we tossed them with salt and a little rice wine and let them sit briefly before dredging and frying. For an extra jolt of spiciness, after frying the shrimp, we also dredged and fried a couple of thinly sliced jalapeños. And to give the dish lots of depth, we added black peppercorns, Sichuan peppercorns, cayenne, and sugar to the coating and fried more of the same with ginger and garlic to make a flavorful paste. Finally, we tossed the shrimp in this aromatic paste to unify the dish and keep the flavorings well distributed.

SALT AND PEPPER SHRIMP
SERVES 4 TO 6

In this recipe the shrimp are meant to be eaten shell and all. To ensure that the shells fry up crisp, avoid using shrimp that are extra large or jumbo. We prefer medium-large (31- to 40-count) shrimp, but large (26- to 30-count) may be substituted. Serve with steamed rice. We prefer frozen shrimp; thaw them overnight in the fridge or under running cold water and blot them dry before proceeding with this recipe.

1½	pounds shell-on medium-large shrimp (31 to 40 per pound)
2	tablespoons Chinese rice wine or dry sherry
	Kosher salt
2½	teaspoons black peppercorns
2	teaspoons Sichuan peppercorns
2	teaspoons sugar
¼	teaspoon cayenne pepper
4	cups vegetable oil
5	tablespoons cornstarch
2	jalapeño chiles, stemmed, seeded, and sliced into ⅛-inch-thick rings
3	garlic cloves, minced
1	tablespoon grated fresh ginger
2	scallions, sliced thin on bias
¼	head iceberg lettuce, shredded (1½ cups)

1. Adjust oven rack to upper-middle position and heat oven to 225 degrees. Set wire rack in rimmed baking sheet and set aside. Toss shrimp, rice wine, and 1 teaspoon salt together in large bowl and set aside for 10 to 15 minutes.

2. Grind black peppercorns and Sichuan peppercorns in spice grinder or mortar and pestle until coarsely ground. Transfer peppercorns to small bowl and stir in sugar and cayenne.

3. Heat oil in large Dutch oven over medium heat until oil registers 385 degrees. While oil is heating, drain shrimp and pat dry with paper towels. Transfer shrimp to bowl, add 3 tablespoons cornstarch and 1 tablespoon peppercorn mixture, and toss until well combined.

4. Carefully add one-third of shrimp to oil and fry, stirring occasionally to keep shrimp from sticking together, until light brown, 2 to 3 minutes. Using wire skimmer or slotted spoon, transfer shrimp to paper towel–lined plate. Once paper towels absorb any excess oil, transfer shrimp to prepared rack and place in oven. Return oil to 385 degrees and repeat in 2 more batches, tossing each batch thoroughly with coating mixture before frying.

5. Toss jalapeño rings and remaining 2 tablespoons cornstarch in medium bowl. Shaking off excess cornstarch, carefully add jalapeño rings to oil and fry until crispy, 1 to 2 minutes. Using wire skimmer or slotted spoon, transfer jalapeño rings to paper towel–lined plate. After frying, reserve 2 tablespoons frying oil.

6. Heat reserved oil in 12-inch skillet over medium-high heat until shimmering. Add garlic, ginger, and remaining peppercorn mixture and cook, stirring occasionally, until mixture is fragrant and just beginning to brown, about 45 seconds. Add shrimp, scallions, and ½ teaspoon salt and toss to coat. Line platter with lettuce. Transfer shrimp to platter, sprinkle with jalapeño rings, and serve immediately.

Shrimp Cocktail

✔ WHY THIS RECIPE WORKS

Shrimp cocktail is a classic at parties, but it rarely does justice to the festive occasion: The shrimp are overcooked, rubbery, and flavorless, and they're served with a sugary-sweet cocktail sauce. Starting them in cold water and leaving their shells on during cooking gave us a tender, flavorful cocktail.

START FROZEN Once shrimp are harvested, their bodies are immediately flash-frozen. So (with few exceptions) the "fresh" shrimp we see at the seafood counter are actually frozen shrimp that the grocer thawed. Far better, then, to start with frozen shrimp so we could control the thawing. We chose whole shell-on shrimp and snipped the shells and deveined them. Shrimp prepared this way didn't curl when cooked; plus, the shells added flavor.

COOK GENTLY Boiling shrimp was too harsh. After some experimentation, we came up with a solution: Add shrimp—and herbs, to help season the shrimp as

---

---

they cook—to cold water in a large pot, turn the burner on, bring the liquid to 170 degrees (hot but still a good 42 degrees away from boiling), and then pull the pot off the heat and let it sit, covered, for about 5 minutes, with the addition of flavorful lemon. When the shrimp were pink and tender, we added ice to stop the cooking process. The slow cooking process gave the shrimp more time to take on the flavor of the shell.

SAUCE IT Finally, we developed a traditional ketchup- and horseradish-based cocktail sauce that was balanced enough to complement the sweet shrimp instead of hiding their flavor.

SHRIMP COCKTAIL

SERVES 6 TO 8

Buy refrigerated prepared horseradish, not the shelf-stable kind, which contains preservatives and additives. (Refrigerated products are simply grated horseradish, vinegar, and salt. Shelf-stable ones add a laundry list of other ingredients, including sugar, eggs, citric acid, high-fructose corn syrup, soybean oil, artificial flavorings, and preservatives.) We prefer frozen shrimp; thaw them overnight in the fridge or under running cold water and blot them dry before proceeding with this recipe.

SHRIMP

2	pounds shell-on jumbo shrimp (16 to 20 per pound)
2½	tablespoons salt
10	sprigs fresh thyme
3	bay leaves
2	teaspoons peppercorns
½	teaspoon celery seeds
8	(2-inch) strips lemon zest plus ¼ cup juice, spent halves reserved (2 lemons)
8	cups ice

COCKTAIL SAUCE

1	cup ketchup
¼	cup prepared horseradish
1	teaspoon Worcestershire sauce
1	teaspoon lemon juice
½	teaspoon Old Bay seasoning
⅛	teaspoon cayenne pepper

1. FOR THE SHRIMP: Using kitchen shears or sharp paring knife, cut through shell and meat of shrimp and devein but do not remove shell. Combine shrimp, 4 cups cold water, salt, thyme sprigs, bay leaves, peppercorns, and celery seeds in Dutch oven. Set pot over medium-high heat and cook, stirring occasionally, until water registers 170 degrees and shrimp are just beginning to turn pink, 5 to 7 minutes.

2. Off heat, add lemon zest and juice and spent halves. Cover and let sit until shrimp are completely pink and firm, 5 to 7 minutes. Stir ice into pot and let shrimp cool completely, about 5 minutes. Drain shrimp in colander and peel, leaving tails intact. Refrigerate shrimp until ready to use.

3. FOR THE COCKTAIL SAUCE: Whisk all ingredients in bowl until combined. Serve cocktail sauce with shrimp. (Sauce can be refrigerated for up to 24 hours.)

Shrimp Fra Diavolo

✓ WHY THIS RECIPE WORKS

Ideally, shrimp fra diavolo is a lively and piquant dish, with tangy tomatoes countering briny, plump shrimp, and pepper flakes and garlic providing a spirited kick. But too often the seared shrimp are overcooked and chewy, and the spice obliterates all the other flavors, leaving the dish hot but disappointingly one-dimensional. In this version, we boosted the flavor of the sauce by first browning the shrimp shells and using them to make stock. This stock formed the basis of our sauce, in which we poached our shrimp, leaving them plump and succulent.

USE THE SHELLS Crustacean shells contain loads of proteins and sugars that are ideal for building the flavorful browning known as the Maillard reaction, plus flavor-boosting compounds called glutamates and nucleotides. The sauce in shrimp fra diavolo often tastes largely of cooked tomato and chile, but not really of seafood. To amp up savory shrimp flavor and brightness, we took a cue from classic seafood bisques and eked out a shrimp stock by browning the shells (an ingredient we would have otherwise discarded), deglazing the pan with white wine, and simmering the mixture with the juice from the canned tomatoes. In just minutes (see Test Kitchen Experiment, page 98), the shells gave up remarkably rich flavor, which the wine and tomato juice balanced with acidity.

PRACTICAL SCIENCE SHRIMP VS. PRAWN

Is there really any difference between shrimp and prawns?

Biologically speaking, there is a difference between shrimp and prawns, and it's mainly about gill structure—a distinguishing feature that is hard for the consumer to spot and is typically lost during processing and cooking. This simple fact may be why the terms are often used interchangeably or can vary depending on factors as random as custom and geography. "Prawn" is a term often used in the southern United States, for example, while northerners might refer to the same specimen as "shrimp." In Britain and in many Asian countries, it's all about size: Small crustaceans are called shrimp; larger ones, prawns. Size is actually not a good indication of a true shrimp or a true prawn, as each comes in a wide range of sizes, depending on the species. Taste won't provide a clue either: As we found in our shrimp and prawn boil here in the test kitchen, each type can sometimes taste more or less sweet, again depending on the species.

The bottom line: We found no problem substituting one for the other in any recipe. The most important thing is to make sure that the count per pound (which indicates the size) is correct so that the same cooking times will apply.

POACH THE SHRIMP In many traditional dishes, the shrimp are flambéed. We, however, found that this technique produced overcooked, rubbery shrimp. Poaching, with its gentle cooking, was the answer. It produced the tender shrimp we were after.

ADD HEAT AND GARNISH In honor of the dish's "devilish" reputation, we added a bit more heat in the form of minced *pepperoncini* peppers. Generous amounts of chopped parsley and basil contributed freshness, and a drizzle of extra-virgin olive oil provided a fruity, peppery finish.

SHRIMP FRA DIAVOLO
SERVES 4

If the shrimp you are using have been treated with salt (check the bag's ingredient list), skip the salting in step 1 and add ¼ teaspoon of salt to the sauce in step 3. Adjust the amount of pepper flakes depending on how spicy you want the dish. Serve the shrimp with a salad and crusty bread or over spaghetti. If serving with spaghetti, adjust the consistency of the sauce with some reserved pasta cooking water. We prefer frozen shrimp; thaw them overnight in the fridge or under running cold water and blot them dry before proceeding with this recipe.

1½	pounds large shrimp (26 to 30 per pound), peeled and deveined, shells reserved
	Salt
1	(28-ounce) can whole peeled tomatoes
3	tablespoons vegetable oil
1	cup dry white wine
4	garlic cloves, minced
½–1	teaspoon red pepper flakes
½	teaspoon dried oregano
2	anchovy fillets, rinsed, patted dry, and minced
¼	cup chopped fresh basil
¼	cup chopped fresh parsley
1½	teaspoons minced pepperoncini, plus 1 teaspoon brine
2	tablespoons extra-virgin olive oil

1. Toss shrimp with ½ teaspoon salt and set aside. Pour tomatoes into colander set over large bowl. Pierce tomatoes with edge of rubber spatula and stir briefly to release juice. Transfer drained tomatoes to small bowl and reserve juice. Do not wash colander.

2. Heat 1 tablespoon vegetable oil in 12-inch skillet over high heat until shimmering. Add shrimp shells and cook, stirring frequently, until they begin to turn spotty brown and skillet starts to brown, 2 to 4 minutes. Remove skillet from heat and carefully add wine. When bubbling subsides, return skillet to heat and simmer until wine is reduced to about 2 tablespoons, 2 to 4 minutes. Add reserved tomato juice and simmer to meld flavors, 5 minutes. Pour contents of skillet into colander set over bowl. Discard shells and reserve liquid. Wipe out skillet with paper towels.

3. Heat remaining 2 tablespoons vegetable oil, garlic, pepper flakes, and oregano in now-empty skillet over medium heat, stirring occasionally, until garlic is straw-colored and fragrant, 1 to 2 minutes. Add anchovies and stir until fragrant, about 30 seconds. Remove from heat. Add drained tomatoes and mash with potato masher until coarsely pureed. Return to heat and stir in reserved tomato juice mixture. Increase heat to medium-high and simmer until mixture has thickened, about 5 minutes.

4. Add shrimp to skillet and simmer gently, stirring and turning shrimp frequently, until they are just cooked through, 4 to 5 minutes. Remove pan from heat. Stir in basil, parsley, and pepperoncini and brine and season with salt to taste. Drizzle with olive oil and serve.

Roasted Shrimp

✔ WHY THIS RECIPE WORKS
To keep our "roasted" shrimp (they're actually broiled) plump and moist, we brined them briefly. To further protect them as they cooked and to produce a more roasted flavor, we left their shells on—though, unlike with our Salt and Pepper Shrimp (page 100), we don't expect you to eat the shells later. (Frying gets the shells crisper than roasting can.) The shells browned quickly in the heat of the oven and transferred flavor to the shrimp itself. To get tons of flavor onto the shrimp, we tossed them in a potent mixture of aromatic spices and herbs, along with butter and olive oil.

USE JUMBOS Bigger shrimp can spend more time browning and developing flavor under the broiler before overcooking and drying out. Plus, there are fewer pieces to crowd the baking sheet and thwart browning.

LEAVE THE SHELLS ON We found that cooking shrimp in their shells kept them juicier, but our shell-on roasted shrimp boasted such savory depth that we wondered if there wasn't more to this outer layer than we thought. Our science editor confirmed our suspicions.

First, shrimp shells contain water-soluble flavor compounds that are absorbed by the shrimp flesh during cooking. Second, the shells are loaded with proteins and sugars—almost as much as the flesh itself. When they brown, they undergo the flavor-enhancing Maillard reaction just as roasted meats do, which gives the shells even more flavor to pass along to the flesh. Third, like the flesh, the shells contain healthy amounts of glutamates and nucleotides, compounds that dramatically enhance savory umami taste when present together in food. These compounds also get transferred to the meat during cooking, amplifying the effect of its own glutamates and nucleotides.

BRINE BRIEFLY AND BROIL Plumping up the shrimp with a quick saltwater soak further buffered them from the oven's heat and also seasoned them throughout. Broiling the shrimp on a wire rack set in a baking sheet allowed the hot air to circulate around them for deep, even color.

PRACTICAL SCIENCE SHRIMP SIZE

When buying shrimp, use this "count per pound" chart.

Shrimp are sorted by size. But the names for the different shrimp sizes vary from vendor to vendor, so that one company's large is another company's extra-large. The best way to eliminate ambiguity is to disregard the name and select shrimp based on the actual count per pound, which is clearly labeled on the packaging. The letter U (for "under") means that there should be fewer than that number of shrimp in a pound; two numbers separated by a slash indicates the range of shrimp per pound in that particular size. Most important: The smaller the number per pound, the bigger the shrimp.

TEST KITCHEN NAME	COUNT PER POUND (U = UNDER)
Colossal	U/12 (under 12 per pound)
Extra-Jumbo	U/15
Jumbo	16/20 (16 to 20 per pound)
Extra-Large	21/25
Large	26/30
Medium-Large	31/40
Medium	41/50
Small	51/60
Extra-Small	61/70

GARLICKY ROASTED SHRIMP WITH PARSLEY AND ANISE
SERVES 4 TO 6

Don't be tempted to use smaller shrimp with this cooking technique; they will be overseasoned and prone to overcook. We prefer frozen shrimp; thaw them overnight in the fridge or under running cold water and blot them dry before proceeding with this recipe.

¼   cup salt
2   pounds shell-on jumbo shrimp (16 to 20 per pound)
4   tablespoons unsalted butter, melted
¼   cup vegetable oil
6   garlic cloves, minced
1   teaspoon anise seeds
½   teaspoon red pepper flakes
¼   teaspoon pepper
2   tablespoons minced fresh parsley
    Lemon wedges

1. Dissolve salt in 1 quart cold water in large container. Using kitchen shears or sharp paring knife, cut through shell of shrimp and devein but do not remove shell. Using paring knife, continue to cut shrimp ½ inch deep, taking care not to cut in half completely. Submerge shrimp in brine, cover, and refrigerate for 15 minutes.

2. Adjust oven rack 4 inches from broiler element and heat broiler. Combine melted butter, oil, garlic, anise seeds, pepper flakes, and pepper in large bowl. Remove shrimp from brine and pat dry with paper towels. Add shrimp and parsley to butter mixture; toss well, making sure butter mixture gets into interior of shrimp. Arrange shrimp in single layer on wire rack set in rimmed baking sheet.

3. Broil shrimp until opaque and shells are beginning to brown, 2 to 4 minutes, rotating sheet halfway through broiling. Flip shrimp and continue to broil until second side is opaque and shells are beginning to brown, 2 to 4 minutes longer, rotating sheet halfway through broiling. Transfer shrimp to serving platter and serve immediately, passing lemon wedges separately.

CHAPTER 12

Scallops

The key to great scallops is first finding scallops that haven't been chemically treated.

HOW THE SCIENCE WORKS

Live scallops are bivalves, animals sandwiched between two "valves," or shells. They are found in all oceans, but not in fresh water. They can live up to 20 years and usually grow no larger than 6 inches in length. Rings form on scallop shells with time (similar to those found within the trunks of old trees), a result of annual water temperature change. Scallops feed on phytoplankton in the water, and are capable of swimming short distances, mainly to escape from predators, like starfish.

The scallops we buy in the market do not bear much resemblance to a live scallop. Within their shells, which can snap open and shut to propel the scallops through the water, is an adductor muscle. This is the muscle we typically cook and eat, and the only one we see in the store: It's small and round and sweetly flavored. There are additional elements within the scallop shell that we don't see in the store: the reproductive glands or roe (popular for consumption in Europe), the fleshy mantle, and gills. Scallops, unlike other shellfish such as oysters or mussels, have eyes—up to 100 of them, spread around the edge of the mantle, each with its own lens, retina, and optical nerve. Because scallops are filter feeders, toxins present in seawater can build up inside some of their tissues—though not in the adductor muscle—and so there are restrictions in the United States against selling these other parts.

The sweet taste of scallops is due to two things: a significant amount of the simplest amino acid called glycine, which is moderately sweet, and glycogen, which is a polymer of glucose and is used as a source of energy. Tests have shown that little glycogen is broken down during cooking, so most of the sweetness of scallops comes from glycine. Glycine, which is 70 percent as sweet as sucrose, is present at fairly high levels because it helps to regulate the salt content of the cells. Scallops also contain a fair amount of free amino acids, such as glutamic acid, which contribute umami taste.

Three kinds of scallops are often found in the market: Bay, sea, and calico scallops. Bay scallops, harvested from North Carolina to Maine, are small and cork-shaped, with a limited season—fall through midwinter. The larger sea scallops are shucked at sea, and are available in markets year-round. Calico scallops are the smallest of the three varieties, and are usually sold frozen.

A big thing to watch for when buying scallops, especially sea scallops, is whether they are "wet" or "dry." What's the difference? Wet scallops are treated with a solution of water and sodium tripolyphosphate to preserve them as soon as they are harvested at sea, and are often frozen. This means that they contain more moisture, and are therefore heavier—but also shed more water when cooked (page 106). They also can have a soapy taste. Dry scallops have a sweet, fresh flavor and are easier to brown because they release less water in the pan.

So the key to cooking great scallops is to start with dry scallops. (But if wet is all you can find, soak them in 1 quart of cold water, ¼ cup of lemon juice, and 2 tablespoons of salt for 30 minutes to mask any chemical flavors.) Next? Get them nice and brown. We do this in our Pan-Seared Scallops recipe (page 108) by heating oil until it smokes before searing the scallops on one side and then butter-basting them. For our Grilled Sea Scallops (page 109), we use a hot, well-oiled grill. It's also important to deal with excess moisture. When building a pan sauce for our Garlicky Scallops with Bread Crumbs (page 110), we let the seared scallops sit in a strainer over a bowl. This way, we capture the excess moisture, and use just as much as we need.

> *We only eat one small part of the scallop.*

TEST KITCHEN EXPERIMENT

A large percentage of the scallops available to consumers in this country have been soaked in a solution containing sodium tripolyphosphate (STPP), which causes the scallops to absorb and retain moisture, before being frozen for sale. For this reason, scallops containing STPP are known in the industry as "wet" while those without additives (and the extra water weight) are marketed as "dry." To find out exactly what STPP does to scallops, we decided to purchase dry scallops and treat them with STPP ourselves. Following commercial protocols for STPP treatment, we'd be able to track how much moisture they absorbed and how their texture and flavor changed. And by comparing them to both frozen and fresh scallops, we hoped to figure out which type is best.

EXPERIMENT

We soaked 24 fresh (never frozen) dry sea scallops in solutions containing increasing concentrations of STPP. We tested 1, 2, 3, 4, 5, 6, 7, and 8 percent solutions of STPP (each also with 1 percent table salt). The soaked scallops were drained, patted dry, sealed in airtight bags, and frozen for two weeks. After thawing them in the refrigerator, we patted them dry, sealed them in bags, and cooked them to 130 degrees in a temperature-controlled water bath. We tasted the treated scallops next to two controls: unsoaked scallops that had been frozen, thawed, and cooked; and unsoaked scallops that were just cooked. We repeatedly weighed the scallops to determine moisture gain and loss.

RESULTS

We found very similar results among samples treated with between 2 and 8 percent STPP, and therefore averaged the results from those samples. The scallops soaked in the STPP solutions picked up an average of 14 percent moisture before freezing and cooking. These scallops lost considerable moisture during thawing and cooking, but started with enough additional water that they ended with a net gain of 1.9 percent. During cooking, the scallops that were frozen without treatment and those that were never frozen lost 4.2 and 5.3 percent moisture, respectively. The scallops treated with STPP lost 6.7 percent moisture, and were very hard to sear because there was so much liquid in the pan.

Tasters showed a clear and strong preference for scallops without STPP. At the low end of the STPP range, tasters noted a "soapy" off-flavor; anything above 2 to 3 percent was described as "bitter" and "unpleasant." The texture of the STPP scallops was "bouncy" and "unnatural."

TAKEAWAY

We learned a few important lessons. First, buying wet scallops means paying for a significant amount of additional water weight (14 percent in our test) at the price of scallop meat. Second, even though the scallops treated with STPP lost moisture during both thawing and cooking, they still ended up with a net gain in moisture. This resulted in washed-out flavor and a bouncy texture. Finally, we learned why it's difficult to get a good sear on STPP scallops—they shed about 25 percent more moisture during cooking than fresh, dry scallops. The liquid releases into the skillet, dropping the temperature and preventing browning. It's clear that whereas the producer benefits from the use of STPP, the home cook pays.

HEAVY-WEIGHT LOSERS: STPP SCALLOPS

We compared the weight of scallops frozen without treatment, and soaked in STPP, before we froze and after we cooked them.

UNTREATED: LOST 5.3% MOISTURE
The scallops that were never treated and never frozen lost 5.3% of their precooked weight, and retained their sweet, briny flavor.

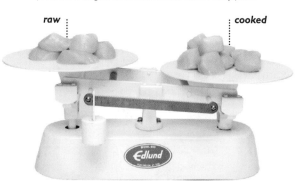

SOAKED IN STPP SOLUTION: GAINED 1.9% MOISTURE
These "soapy" tasting scallops took on so much water they finished with a net gain of 1.9% (despite having lost a lot of moisture during cooking).

FOCUS ON: SCALLOPS

We only eat one small part of the whole scallop, which is the only bivalve that swims. Here, we take a look at the large sea scallop.

ADDUCTOR MUSCLE

This is the one part of the scallop that we eat in the U.S. This muscle connects the two shells together, allowing the scallop to swim. The muscle itself is composed of bundles of very short fibers made of proteins called myosin and actin (the same proteins that are in land animal muscle fibers), which are separated within thin sheets of connective tissue. The adductor has a good deal of the amino acid glycine, and tastes sweet as a result.

CATCH MUSCLE

The catch muscle next to the adductor keeps the shell closed; we remove this tough muscle before cooking, if it is still attached.

GILLS

Scallops open their shells when breathing, using their gills to pull in oxygen from the water.

MANTLE

This fleshy layer forms the outer wall of the scallop's body, enclosing its internal organs. It is made up of proteins including collagen, and secretes calcium carbonate to form the scallop's shell. It also contains the scallop's eyes.

EYES

Yes, scallops have eyes. Each scallop has up to 100 eyes, along the edge of the mantle, each with a separate socket, and its own lens, retina, cornea, and optic nerve. The eyes are capable of seeing shadow and movement.

REPRODUCTIVE GLANDS (ROE)

These glands lie next to the adductor muscle, and give that muscle its color (see sidebar, page 110). These organs are consumed in Europe, though not typically in the U.S.

MOVE LIKE A SCALLOP

It's not often that you see a scallop swim—but swim they do. The adductor muscle connects the two shells, opening and closing them to move forward in the water.

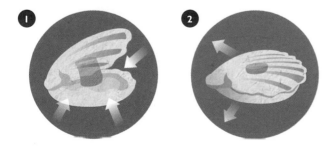

TAKING THE TEMPERATURE OF SCALLOPS

We typically recommend cooking scallops until their sides are firm and their centers are slightly translucent. Since determining whether the scallop's interior is done requires cutting into it, we decided that it would be useful to have a more precise (and less destructive) way of assessing doneness. After searing a few batches, we determined that scallops are perfectly cooked when their centers reached 115 degrees. Because scallops are usually cooked over high heat, carryover cooking will add another 10 to 15 degrees, for an ideal final temperature of 125 to 130 degrees.

Pan-Seared Scallops

✓ WHY THIS RECIPE WORKS

For a restaurant chef, pan-seared scallops are as easy as it gets: Slick a superhot pan with oil, add the shellfish, flip them once, and serve. The whole process takes no more than a couple of minutes and produces golden-crusted beauties with tender, medium-rare interiors. But try the same technique at home and you're likely to run into trouble. The problem? Most home stovetops don't get nearly as hot as professional ranges, so it's difficult to get properly browned scallops without overcooking them. And restaurant chefs pay top dollar for scallops without chemical additives, which are known in the industry as dry scallops. The remainders—called wet scallops—are treated with a solution of water and sodium tripolyphosphate (STPP) to increase shelf life and retain moisture. Unfortunately STPP lends a soapy off-flavor to the scallops, and the extra water makes it even harder to achieve good browning. Our solution? Heat that skillet more than usual. And baste with butter.

HOT SKILLET We decided to work with wet scallops first. If we could develop a good recipe for finicky wet scallops, it would surely work with premium dry (untreated) scallops. We found that waiting to add the scallops to the skillet until the oil was beginning to smoke, cooking the scallops in two batches instead of one, and switching to a nonstick skillet were all steps in the right direction.

BUTTER BASTE But it wasn't until we tried a common restaurant technique—butter basting—that our scallops really improved. We seared the scallops in oil on one side and added butter to the skillet before flipping. (Butter contains milk proteins and sugars that brown rapidly when heated.) We then used a large spoon to ladle the foaming butter over the scallops. Waiting to add the butter ensured that it had just enough time to work its browning magic on the scallops, but not enough time to burn.

SOAK 'EM Finally, we addressed the lingering flavor of STPP. We soaked a batch of wet scallops in a quart of water for 30 minutes, soaked a second batch for an hour, and left a third batch untreated. We then cooked each batch according to our recipe and sent them to a lab to be analyzed for STPP.

The scallops soaked for 30 minutes only had about 10 percent less STPP than the untreated batch, and soaking for a full hour wasn't much better: Only about 11 percent of the STPP was removed. Tasters were still able to clearly identify an unpleasant chemical flavor in both soaked samples. Why? The phosphates in STPP form a chemical bond with the proteins in scallops. The bonds are so strong that they prevent the STPP from being washed away, no matter how long the scallops are soaked.

The solution: Rather than try to remove the chemical taste from STPP-treated scallops, we masked it by soaking them in a solution of water, lemon juice, and salt. For dry scallops, we simply skipped the soaking step and proceeded with the recipe.

PAN-SEARED SCALLOPS
SERVES 4

We recommend buying "dry" scallops, which don't have chemical additives and taste better than "wet." Dry scallops will look ivory or pinkish; wet scallops are bright white. If using wet scallops, soak them in a solution of 1 quart cold water, ¼ cup lemon juice, and 2 tablespoons salt for 30 minutes before proceeding with step 1, and do not season with salt in step 2. To remove the tendons from the scallops, simply peel away the small, rough-textured crescent-shaped tendon and discard.

1½	pounds large sea scallops, tendons removed
	Salt and pepper
2	tablespoons vegetable oil
2	tablespoons unsalted butter
	Lemon wedges or Orange-Lime Vinaigrette (recipe follows)

1. Place scallops on rimmed baking sheet lined with clean dish towel. Place second clean dish towel on top of scallops and press gently on towel to blot liquid. Let scallops sit at room temperature for 10 minutes while towels absorb moisture.

2. Sprinkle scallops on both sides with salt and pepper. Heat 1 tablespoon oil in 12-inch nonstick skillet over high heat until just smoking. Add half of scallops in single layer, flat side down, and cook, without moving, until well browned, 1½ to 2 minutes.

3. Add 1 tablespoon butter to skillet. Using tongs, flip scallops and continue to cook, using large spoon to baste scallops with melted butter (tilt skillet so butter runs to 1 side) until sides of scallops are firm and centers are opaque, 30 to 90 seconds longer (remove smaller scallops as they finish cooking). Transfer scallops to large plate and tent loosely with aluminum foil. Wipe out skillet with wad of paper towels and repeat cooking with remaining oil, scallops, and butter. Serve immediately with lemon wedges or vinaigrette.

ORANGE-LIME VINAIGRETTE
MAKES ABOUT ½ CUP

2   tablespoons orange juice
2   tablespoons lime juice
1   small shallot, minced
1   tablespoon minced fresh cilantro
⅛   teaspoon red pepper flakes
2   tablespoons vegetable oil
2   tablespoons extra-virgin olive oil
    Salt

Combine orange juice, lime juice, shallot, cilantro, and pepper flakes in medium bowl. Slowly whisk in vegetable and olive oils. Season with salt to taste.

Grilled Sea Scallops

✔ WHY THIS RECIPE WORKS

Using large dry scallops kept our grilled scallops from falling through the cooking grate and avoided the soapy flavor that afflicts wet scallops. To make flipping easier, we incorporated a couple of techniques into our recipe: We lightly coated the scallops with a slurry of vegetable oil, flour, cornstarch, and sugar and threaded them onto doubled metal skewers. Superheating the grates and then painting them with numerous layers of oil also helped get our grilled scallops off the grill in one piece.

NONSTICK THOSE SCALLOPS Like fish (see page 82), scallops exude a protein that fuses with the metal grate when they hit the grill bare. To create a barrier between the flesh and the cooking surface, we lightly coat the scallops with a mixture of oil, flour, and cornstarch, along with just a touch of sugar to promote browning.

WET OR DRY We strongly recommend purchasing dry scallops (those without chemical additives), but if the only scallops you can find are wet, there is an option: Soak the scallops in a solution of 1 quart cold water, ¼ cup lemon juice, and 2 tablespoons table salt for 30 minutes to help disguise any chemical taste before proceeding with step 1, and season only with pepper in step 3.

GRILLED SEA SCALLOPS
SERVES 4

We recommend buying "dry" scallops, which don't have chemical additives and taste better than "wet." Dry scallops will look ivory or pinkish; wet scallops are bright white. You will need eight to twelve 12-inch metal skewers for this recipe. Double-skewering the scallops makes flipping easier. Serve with vinaigrette (recipes follow), if desired.

1½ pounds large sea scallops, tendons removed
1   (13 by 9-inch) disposable aluminum roasting pan
2   tablespoons vegetable oil
1   tablespoon all-purpose flour
1   teaspoon cornstarch
1   teaspoon sugar
    Salt and pepper
    Lemon wedges

1. Place scallops on rimmed baking sheet lined with clean dish towel. Place second clean dish towel on top of scallops and press gently on towel to blot liquid. Let scallops sit at room temperature, covered with towel, for 10 minutes. To double-skewer scallops, thread 4 to 6 scallops, 1 flat side down, onto 1 skewer and then place second skewer through scallops parallel to and about ¼ inch from first. Return skewered scallops to towel-lined baking sheet; refrigerate, covered with second towel, while preparing grill.

2A. FOR A CHARCOAL GRILL: Open bottom vent completely. Light large chimney starter mounded with charcoal briquettes (7 quarts). Meanwhile, poke twelve ½-inch holes in bottom of disposable pan and place in center of grill. When top coals are partially covered with ash, empty coals into pan. Set cooking grate in place, cover, and open lid vent completely. Heat grill until hot, about 5 minutes.

2B. FOR A GAS GRILL: Turn all burners to high, cover, and heat grill until hot, about 15 minutes.

3. While grill heats, whisk oil, flour, cornstarch, and sugar together in small bowl. Remove towels from scallops. Brush both sides of skewered scallops with oil mixture and season with salt and pepper.

4. Clean cooking grate, then repeatedly brush grate with well-oiled paper towels until grate is black and glossy, 5 to 10 times.

5. Place skewered scallops on grill (over hot coals if using charcoal). Cook (covered if using gas) without

moving scallops until lightly browned, 2½ to 4 minutes. Carefully flip skewers and continue to cook until second side of scallops is browned, sides are firm, and centers are opaque, 2 to 4 minutes longer. Serve immediately with lemon wedges.

CHILE-LIME VINAIGRETTE
MAKES ABOUT 1 CUP

---

1   teaspoon finely grated lime zest
    plus 3 tablespoons juice (2 limes)
1   tablespoon Sriracha sauce
2   tablespoons honey
2   teaspoons fish sauce
½   cup vegetable oil

Whisk lime zest and juice, Sriracha sauce, honey, and fish sauce until combined. Whisking constantly, slowly drizzle in oil until emulsified.

BASIL VINAIGRETTE
MAKES ABOUT 1 CUP

---

2   tablespoons champagne vinegar
1   cup packed fresh basil leaves
3   tablespoons minced fresh chives
2   garlic cloves, minced
2   teaspoons sugar
1   teaspoon salt
½   teaspoon pepper
⅔   cup vegetable oil

Pulse vinegar, basil, chives, garlic, sugar, salt, and pepper in blender or food processor until roughly chopped. With blender or processor running, slowly drizzle in oil until emulsified, scraping down sides as necessary.

Garlicky Scallops with Bread Crumbs

✓ WHY THIS RECIPE WORKS

Saucy scallops blanketed with toasted crumbs represents the best of old-fashioned American cooking, but not when the seafood is waterlogged and tough. To avoid the potential pitfalls of this dish, we turned to a stovetop skillet when making our garlicky scallop recipe. We seared the scallops on one side, removed them from the pan, built the sauce in the empty pan, and returned the scallops to finish cooking in the sauce. To eliminate any raw alcohol flavor, we cut the sherry with bottled clam juice, letting the mixture simmer for several minutes to concentrate the flavors and cook off excess alcohol.

DEAL WITH WATER   Scallops, especially wet scallops, have a lot of water, and, even so, the amount of water varies from scallop to scallop. To build a pan sauce that wasn't too watery—or too dry—we placed the seared scallops in a strainer set over a bowl to collect the juice, then poured it into a measuring cup and added enough clam juice to equal ⅔ cup.

TOP IT OFF   The crumb topping was toasted in the empty skillet before the scallops were cooked. Japanese-style panko was too finely textured, while crumbs made from white sandwich bread became sandy on top and soggy underneath. Crumbs from a chewy supermarket baguette were sturdy enough to retain a crisp texture even after sitting on top of the saucy scallops.

PRACTICAL SCIENCE PINK VS. WHITE SCALLOPS

Female scallops turn pink when spawning.

The part of the scallop that's sold at the fish counter is the large adductor muscle that opens and closes its shell. This muscle takes its color from the reproductive gland that lies next to it inside the shell. In male scallops, the gland is grayish white and hence the muscle remains white, or ivory. Female scallops turn pink only when they're spawning; during this period, their glands fill with orange roe and turn bright coral, giving the adductor muscle a rosy hue.

   To see if there were any differences besides color, we pan-seared and tasted white male scallops alongside peachy female scallops. They cooked in the same amount of time and had identical textures, although tasters did note that the pink scallops—which retained their tint even after cooking—had a somewhat sweeter, richer flavor. Both colors, however, are absolutely normal and do not indicate anything about the freshness, done-ness, or edibility of a scallop. Note: In general, "wet" scallops are bright white in color, while "dry" scallops (our preferred choice) vary in color from white to coral, and everything in between.

GARLICKY SCALLOPS WITH BREAD CRUMBS
SERVES 4

We recommend buying "dry" scallops, which don't have chemical additives and taste better than "wet." Dry scallops will look ivory or pinkish; wet scallops are bright white. Vermouth can be substituted for the sherry. If using vermouth, increase the amount to ½ cup and reduce the amount of clam juice to ½ cup. To prepare this recipe in a 10-inch skillet, brown the scallops in 3 batches for about 4 minutes each, using 2 teaspoons oil per batch.

1	(3-inch) piece baguette, cut into small pieces
5	tablespoons unsalted butter, cut into 5 pieces
1	small shallot, minced
	Salt and pepper
2	tablespoons minced fresh parsley
2	pounds large sea scallops, tendons removed
4	teaspoons vegetable oil
4	garlic cloves, minced
⅛	teaspoon red pepper flakes
2	teaspoons all-purpose flour
⅓–⅔	cup bottled clam juice
⅓	cup dry sherry
2	teaspoons lemon juice, plus lemon wedges for serving

1. Pulse bread in food processor until coarsely ground; you should have about 1 cup crumbs. Melt 1 tablespoon butter in 12-inch nonstick skillet over medium heat. Add crumbs, shallot, ⅛ teaspoon salt, and ⅛ teaspoon pepper. Cook, stirring occasionally, until golden brown, 7 to 10 minutes. Stir in 1 tablespoon parsley and transfer to plate to cool. Wipe out skillet with paper towels.

2. Thoroughly dry scallops with paper towels; toss with ¼ teaspoon salt and ¼ teaspoon pepper in bowl. Return skillet to high heat, add 2 teaspoons oil, and heat until shimmering. Add half of scallops in single layer and cook until well browned, about 5 minutes (do not flip scallops). Remove pan from heat and transfer scallops to large strainer set over bowl to catch any accumulated juices. Wipe out skillet with paper towels. Repeat with remaining 2 teaspoons oil and scallops; transfer scallops to strainer.

3. Return skillet to medium heat and add 1 tablespoon butter. When melted, add garlic and pepper flakes; cook, stirring frequently, until garlic just begins to color, about 1 minute. Add flour and cook, stirring frequently, for 1 minute. Pour accumulated scallop juices into measuring cup and add enough clam juice to measure ⅔ cup. Increase heat to medium-high and slowly whisk in clam juice mixture and sherry. Bring to simmer and cook until mixture reduces to ¾ cup, 3 to 4 minutes. Whisk in remaining 3 tablespoons butter, 1 tablespoon at a time. Stir in lemon juice and remaining tablespoon parsley.

4. Reduce heat to medium-low, return scallops to pan, and toss to combine. Cook, covered, until scallops are pink and cooked through, 2 to 3 minutes. Uncover and sprinkle with toasted bread crumbs. Serve with lemon wedges.

Broiled Scallops with Creamy Mushroom Sauce

✔ WHY THIS RECIPE WORKS

Bonne femme is French for "good wife" or "good woman" and refers to dishes that are prepared simply and served family style, often in the casserole dish or pan in which they are cooked. For scallops, this usually means that they are topped with a simple white wine or cream sauce with mushrooms, and then placed under the broiler to brown. For our modern take, we chose dry sea scallops, broiled them separately, and added a few extras for both flavor and texture to the sauce.

BROIL FIRST In many traditional recipes, the scallops and sauce are broiled together. We found that this broke the sauce, and overcooked our scallops. Instead, we broiled the scallops first, before adding the sauce. To preserve the creamy, delicate texture of the sea scallops, we cooked them to medium-rare, which meant the scallops were hot all the way through, but the centers still retained some translucence. The process took just between 4 and 7 minutes.

WHIP CREAM For the sauce, many traditional recipes use fish fumet (homemade fish stock) but that was too time-consuming for us, so we instead added a bit of chicken broth to round out the flavor. Fresh thyme added herbal notes, and lemon juice brightened the sauce. Our crowning touch came from an old French cookbook, which reserved some heavy cream and whipped it to stiff peaks. Once the rest of the sauce reduced, we let it cool to room temperature and gently folded in the whipped cream. This way, when we spooned the sauce over the scallops, it didn't run down the sides and onto the plate; rather, it clung to the scallops, giving the overall dish a luxurious feel.

BROILED SCALLOPS WITH CREAMY
MUSHROOM SAUCE
SERVES 4

We recommend buying "dry" scallops, which don't have chemical additives and taste better than "wet." Dry scallops will look ivory or pinkish; wet scallops are bright white. The cooking time of scallops will depend on the strength of your broiler and the size of the scallops; we found that extra large scallops (about 2 inches in diameter and 1 inch thick) take about 7 minutes while smaller scallops (about 1 inch in diameter and ½ inch thick) take only 4 minutes. These scallops can also be cooked in individual baking dishes; adjust the oven rack so that the rims are 6 inches from the heating element.

2	cups heavy cream
1	cup dry white wine
½	cup chicken broth
1	pound white mushrooms, trimmed and sliced thin
1	large shallot, minced
1	teaspoon minced fresh thyme
	Salt and pepper
1	teaspoon lemon juice
	Unsalted butter, for baking dish
1¼	pounds large sea scallops (about 16 scallops), tendons removed

1. Bring 1½ cups heavy cream, wine, broth, mushrooms, shallot, thyme, ½ teaspoon salt, and pepper to taste to boil in 12-inch nonstick skillet over high heat. Reduce to simmer and cook until mixture has thickened and measures between 2 and 2½ cups, 20 to 25 minutes; add lemon juice off heat. Transfer to large bowl and let cool slightly.

2. Meanwhile, adjust oven rack 6 inches from broiler element and heat broiler. Thoroughly butter inside of a 2-quart broiler-safe baking dish; set aside. Using stand mixer, whip remaining ½ cup heavy cream on medium-low speed until small bubbles form, about 30 seconds. Increase speed to medium-high and continue to whip mixture until it thickens and forms stiff peaks, about 1 minute longer; set aside.

3. Pat scallops dry with paper towels, season with salt and pepper, and arrange in single layer in prepared dish. Broil scallops until exterior looks opaque but interior remains translucent, 4 to 7 minutes.

4. While scallops cook, gently fold whipped cream into cooled mushroom sauce until almost no white streaks remain (a few streaks are okay). Spoon sauce over broiled scallops and continue to broil until sauce is nicely browned and scallops are cooked through, about 1 minute. Serve immediately.

CHAPTER 13

Lobster

Lobster is the only animal we eat that we regularly kill in the kitchen ourselves. Here's how to do it right.

HOW THE SCIENCE WORKS

Lobsters are crustaceans, part of the family *Homaridae*, green-brown insect-like animals with exoskeletons that they molt in order to grow. There are many species of lobster found in oceans around the world, but the most common in the United States is *Homarus americanus*, or the American lobster.

Lobsters didn't start out as a delicacy. Until the mid-19th century, in the coastal states, lobsters were considered the lowest of foods (and eating them a sign of poverty) in part because they were so plentiful. Lobsters were so commonplace, in fact, that they were used as bait and fertilizer.

Today, wild American lobsters are caught from Maine down to North Carolina and often held in tanks, selling for upwards of $10 per pound and eaten at high-end restaurants or with vats of melted butter by vacationers. We eat the tail as well as the claws and sometimes the legs. The soft green mass in the body of a cooked lobster is a digestive gland, sort of like a liver

Yes, you can hypnotize a lobster.

and a pancreas combined. It's known to marine biologists as the hepatopancreas and to lobster fans as the tomalley, and it has a creamy texture and intense flavor (see page 118).

The muscle structure of lobster meat is different than that of white fish (page 81). The muscle fibers in lobsters are longer, especially in the tail section, and, as in mammals, connective tissue surrounds the individual muscle fibers and bundles of muscle fibers. This is why lobster meat, unlike white fish, does not flake when cooked. The structure of lobster and shrimp are similar, and we've found that we prefer them both cooked to 140 degrees (see page 97).

The quality of lobster meat depends to a large extent on where the crustacean is in its molting cycle, during which the old, hard shell is replaced with a soft, new one. During the molting stage the lobster's muscle fibers grow in length—about 14 percent with each molt—and they increase in width with age. This means that the older, larger lobsters do tend to be tougher when cooked. (Hard-shell lobsters taste better and are meatier.)

The most distinctive thing about lobsters, however, is that they are the only animals we regularly kill ourselves in the kitchen. Lobsters are cooked alive for two reasons, related to both flavor and health: First, the instant a lobster dies, enzymes within its body begin to break down the flesh and cause it to turn mushy. Second, like other shellfish, deceased lobsters are vulnerable to bacterial contamination that can cause food poisoning.

The most common method of cooking lobsters is plunging them into boiling water, where they will continue to move about for a short time. Though there's no way to know the extent to which the lobster suffers during this time, most scientists agree that the lobster's primitive nervous system, more like that of an insect than a human, prevents it from processing pain the way we do. Still, most cooks find putting live lobsters into a pot unpleasant. We tried to figure out a way to sedate the lobster before cooking—and therefore minimize the time it spent moving in the pot. We tried a number of techniques, including a knife through its head, a soak in clove-scented water, and hypnotization, but landed upon a simple approach: a 30-minute stay in the freezer, which rendered the lobster motionless before it went into the pot (see page 116).

We use this freezing technique in all three lobster recipes, beginning with the simple Boiled Lobster (page 116), the meat of which can be used for the New England Lobster Roll (page 117). For our Grilled Lobsters (page 117), we split the lobsters in half before placing them on the grill.

TEST KITCHEN EXPERIMENT

One seemingly undisputed lobster factoid is that the leggy crusta-ceans must be cooked either alive or immediately after being killed so that the meat doesn't turn mushy. And yet, high-end restau-rants will often kill a number of lobsters at the beginning of an evening's dinner service, separate their claws and tails, store them raw, and then cook them to order throughout the night. Their lob-ster meat never gets mushy, even if it's the last dish to go out that night. To get to the bottom of when to cook a lobster, we ran the following experiment.

EXPERIMENT

We purchased a number of 1¼-pound live lobsters and killed them all with a knife through the carapace, or hard upper shell where the head is located. For 12 of the lob-sters we separated the tails and claws from the bodies and kept them raw under refrigeration for 30 minutes, 1, 2, 4, 6, and 12 hours. To cook the lobsters, we quickly blanched the tails and claws to separate the meat from the shell and then sealed the shelled meat individually in vacuum-sealed bags and cooked it in a temperature-controlled water bath to 140 degrees. We iced all samples and tasted them blind at the same chilled temperature. We sampled the meat from two lobsters for each time interval and compared its texture to the meat of two lobsters we cooked immediately after death. We also repeated the test with 12 more lobsters that we killed but left completely intact before cooking.

RESULTS

Tasters noted slight differences in flavor between samples, but they were not consistent within a given time sample. More notable was the fact that tasters found no consis-tent differences in texture across samples that were broken down immediately after death and stored for anywhere from 30 minutes up to 12 hours. On the other hand, for the lobsters that we stored intact after death, the tail meat had turned mushy by the 30-minute mark.

TAKEAWAY

Differences in flavor were attributable to natural varia-tions from lobster to lobster. The stark difference between the texture of lobster meat immediately separated from the body and meat left intact during storage, however, was due to the presence of digestive enzymes found in the hepato-pancreas. In vertebrates, an acidic stomach is responsible for the initial breakdown of ingested food. It is believed that because lobsters (like all crustaceans) lack an acidic stomach for this purpose, their digestive enzymes work more effec-tively, rapidly breaking down muscle tissue if left intact after death. The bottom line is that if you want to prep lobster ahead of time for grilling or sautéing, you can—just make sure to separate the tail and claws before storage.

HERE'S WHY, IF COOKING LOBSTER AHEAD OF TIME, YOU MUST SEPARATE THE TAIL FROM THE BODY

When a dead lobster is left to sit intact, the digestive enzymes found in the body quickly break down proteins in the tail, leaving us with mushy meat that collapses under a 2-pound weight. Lobster tail meat that is separated from the body immediately, however, remains tender yet firm.

NOT SEPARATED
The digestive enzymes rendered this tail meat sample mushy.

IMMEDIATELY SEPARATED
This tail meat sample remained tender yet firm.

FOCUS ON: LOBSTER

Lobsters are the only animal that we kill ourselves during the cooking process.

HEAD

A lobster's nervous system is distributed throughout the body, not centered in the head. (This is why knifing a lobster through the head before cooking does not always kill it instantly.)

CLAW

Lobsters have two types of claws: the "crusher" claw, which is larger and heavier; and the "cutter" claw, which is far thinner.

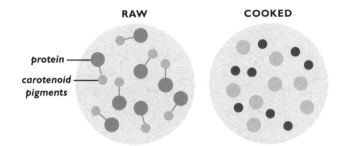

protein

carotenoid pigments

RAW   COOKED

WHY COOKED LOBSTERS ARE RED

The muscles in lobster, especially the tail muscles, are classified as fast-twitch muscles, meaning they are used only during sudden movement. Fast-twitch muscles contain very little of the red protein pigment myoglobin (the compound that makes beef or pork red), so the tail muscles of lobster contain very little color in their raw state. The reddish color we see in cooked lobster meat is due to carotenoid pigments that in the raw state, are bound together with proteins. But when cooked, the proteins denature and release the carotenoids, allowing them to assume their natural red. This also happens in lobster's shells, turning them from brownish-green in live lobsters to bright red when cooked.

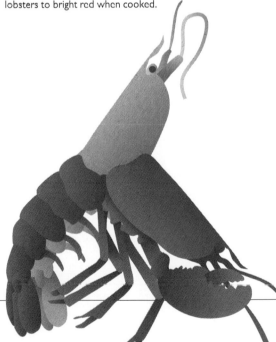

TAIL

The tail muscle is predominantly what we eat. The tail, which is used to quickly escape from predators, is capable of bending quickly and a lot. The large flexor and extensor muscles there are made for rapid swimming, composed of fast-acting, short muscle fibers. Lobster tail muscle contains little fat, but a bit more collagen than in other crustaceans.

MEAT

Lobster meat is composed of muscle proteins, bundled into muscle fibers that are more similar to mammal muscle fibers than white fish's. Lobster muscle fibers are much shorter than those in land animals, though they are longer than those in white fish—long enough that lobster meat does not flake when cooked.

MOLTING

Lobsters molt about once a year, shedding their shell in order to grow. Take care not to cook a lobster just before or just after molting. Before, the lobster loses a significant amount of muscle mass in order to slip out of its shell. After, the lobster absorbs water to swell into the new shell, making its meat mushy. Hard-shell lobsters taste better and are meatier. (Squeeze the shell before purchasing—a soft-shell lobster will give, slightly, to the pressure.)

Boiled Lobster

✔ WHY THIS RECIPE WORKS

Cooking lobster at home can be a daunting process: How do you deal with that thrashing tail, and how do you know it's done? We sedated our lobsters by placing them in the freezer for 30 minutes, and we determined doneness by taking the tails' temperature.

CHOOSE BOILING Our first decision was whether to boil, steam, or roast the lobsters. Roasted lobster can be difficult to prepare because the slow heat of the oven causes proteins in the meat to adhere to the shell. Steaming requires a steamer or a rack, and can leave the lobsters slightly underseasoned. Boiling in salt water, therefore, was the way to go. We just had to figure out a way to do so without the lobsters thrashing around in the pot.

FREEZE BRIEFLY Many cooks advocate anesthetizing lobsters before cooking them. Some believe it is more humane, while others argue that gently handled lobsters are tastier and more tender. Mostly we hoped it would make the little guys more manageable. We tested several methods of desensitizing lobsters, and tasted each supposedly desensitized lobster against one that was summarily tossed into boiling water. The first few methods ranged from grisly to quirky, and since they didn't sedate the lobster, didn't produce better flavor or texture, were too labor-intensive, or all of the above, we quickly moved on. In Harold McGee's *On Food and Cooking* we discovered the most successful technique for sedating a lobster yet: immersing the lobster in an ice bath for 30 minutes before cooking. We found it easier and simpler to put the lobsters in the freezer.

TEMP THE TAIL Most lobster recipes are accompanied by intimidating charts that tell you how long to boil based on your lobster's weight, whether it has a hard or soft shell, and how many are being cooked in the same pot. But what if your lobsters are difference sizes? What if you're unsure about the comparative firmness of their shells? Why can't you simply take the temperature of a lobster the way you do with other kinds of meats? We did just that, and found that the target temperature turned out to be just a bit higher than the temperature to which we cook white fish: 140 degrees.

BOILED LOBSTER
SERVES 4 OR YIELDS I POUND MEAT

To cook four lobsters at once, you will need a pot with a capacity of at least 3 gallons. If your pot is smaller, boil the lobsters in batches. Start timing the lobsters from the moment they go into the pot.

4   (1¼-pound) live lobsters
⅓   cup salt

1. Place lobsters in large bowl and freeze for 30 minutes. Meanwhile, bring 2 gallons water to boil in large pot over high heat.

2. Add lobsters and salt to pot, arranging with tongs so that all lobsters are submerged. Cover pot, leaving lid slightly ajar, and adjust heat to maintain gentle boil. Cook for 12 minutes, then, holding lobster with tongs, insert thermometer through underside of tail into thickest part; meat should register 140 degrees. If necessary,

---

PRACTICAL SCIENCE THE BEST WAY TO GET A LIVE LOBSTER INTO THE POT

Freezing is the best method to calm a lobster before it hits the pot.

To ensure food safety and firmer flesh, lobsters should be cooked alive. The most common method is to put them head first into boiling water, where they will continue to move about for a little while. There's no way to know how much the lobster suffers during this time. But most scientists do agree that the lobster's primitive, insect-like nervous system prevents it from processing pain the way humans do. That doesn't take away from the fact that most cooks find putting live lobsters into a pot unpleasant. If we could figure out how to sedate the lobster before cooking—and minimize the time it spent moving in the pot—these could be only positive developments.

First we tried the popular restaurant technique of slicing through the lobster's head. However, Win Watson of the University of New Hampshire's Department of Biological Sciences informed us that because a lobster's nervous system is distributed throughout its body, this method does not always instantly kill the crustacean. Sure enough, lobsters dispatched this way continued to thrash vigorously before we put them in the pot, and we continued to see movement for another 2 minutes once they were in the water.

Next, we "hypnotized" a lobster by rubbing its shell and standing it on its head, where it remained stock-still for a full hour. Unfortunately, it perked right up once in the pot. Then we tried soaking a lobster in a cold saltwater bath scented with clove oil, a technique recommended by the food science website cookingissues.com. This made the lobster's movements more languid—but those movements still continued for about 2 minutes in the pot. In the end, the simplest approach worked best: a 30-minute stay in the freezer, which rendered the lobster motionless before it went into the pot. After a few flutters, all motion stopped.

return lobster to pot for 2 minutes longer, until tail registers 140 degrees.

3. Serve immediately or transfer lobsters to rimmed baking sheet and set aside until cool enough to remove meat, about 10 minutes. (Lobster meat can be refrigerated in airtight container for up to 24 hours.)

New England Lobster Roll

✔ WHY THIS RECIPE WORKS

For our lobster roll, we mostly adhered to tradition—top-loading supermarket hotdog bun, mayonnaise, and lots of lobster—but we added a hint of crunch in the form of small amounts of lettuce and celery (a contentious addition), and we added complementary brightness with lemon juice, cayenne, and chives.

SIZE IT UP Traditionalists like to leave lobster meat in generous hunks, and the effect is one of impressive opulence, but it's darn hard to eat. Chunks are fine for the claws and knuckles because they're tender and, being smaller, well seasoned by the salted cooking water. But the tail is so meaty and dense that large pieces can seem undersalted and tough. So we bucked tradition and cut the tail into smaller pieces, making it easier to eat and giving it more surface area for the seasoned dressing to cling to.

ADD EXTRAS As for the contentious vegetable additions, we opted for a single soft lettuce leaf to line each roll and a couple of tablespoons of minced celery for unobtrusive crunch. Chopped onions and even milder shallots were nixed as too overwhelming, but a mere teaspoon of chives gave our salad a hint of bright herb flavor. A splash of lemon juice and a tiny pinch of cayenne pepper made a perfect counterpoint to the richly flavored meat and the buttery bun.

NEW ENGLAND LOBSTER ROLL
SERVES 6

This recipe is best when made with lobster you've cooked yourself. Use a very small pinch of cayenne pepper, as it should not make the dressing spicy. We prefer New England–style top-loading hot dog buns because they provide maximum surface on the sides for toasting. If using other buns, butter, salt, and toast the interior of each bun instead of the exterior.

2	tablespoons mayonnaise
2	tablespoons minced celery
1½	teaspoons lemon juice
1	teaspoon minced fresh chives
	Salt
	Pinch cayenne pepper
1	pound lobster meat, tail meat cut into ½-inch pieces and claw meat cut into 1-inch pieces
6	New England–style hot dog buns
2	tablespoons unsalted butter, softened
6	leaves Boston lettuce

1. Whisk mayonnaise, celery, lemon juice, chives, ⅛ teaspoon salt, and cayenne together in large bowl. Add lobster and gently toss to combine.

2. Place 12-inch nonstick skillet over low heat. Butter both sides of hot dog buns and sprinkle lightly with salt. Place buns in skillet, with 1 buttered side down; increase heat to medium-low; and cook until crisp and brown, 2 to 3 minutes. Flip and cook second side until crisp and brown, 2 to 3 minutes longer. Transfer buns to large platter. Line each bun with lettuce leaf. Spoon lobster salad into buns and serve immediately.

Grilled Lobsters

✔ WHY THIS RECIPE WORKS

For a lobster recipe in which the smoky grilled flavors would penetrate the meat, we found that simply splitting the lobsters in half was the way to go. Starting them cut side down and then flipping them after 2 minutes kept moisture loss to a minimum. To allow the claws to finish cooking at the same time as the tail meat, we cracked one side of each claw and cooked them covered with an aluminum pie plate.

PREP THE LOBSTERS We discovered that freezing the lobsters for 30 minutes helped to sedate them. Then we perfected our technique for preparing them for this recipe: First, with the blade of a chef's knife facing the head, kill the lobster by plunging the knife into the body at the point where the shell forms a "T." Move the blade down straight through the head. Holding the upper body with one hand and positioning the knife blade so that it faces the tail end, cut through the body toward the tail, making sure to cut all the way through the shell. You should have two halves now. Use a spoon to remove and discard the stomach sac. Remove and discard the intestinal tract. Scoop out the green tomalley and transfer to a medium bowl.

CONCENTRATE ON THE CLAWS In our testing, we discovered that the claws of the lobster cooked more slowly than the rest, because they were the only part still encased completely in the shell. To accelerate the cooking of the claws, we used the back of a chef's knife to whack one side of each claw to make a small opening. Covering them with an aluminum plate while on the grill also helped.

GRILLED LOBSTERS
SERVES 2 AS A MAIN DISH OR 4 AS AN APPETIZER

The lobsters are done when the tail registers 140 degrees. When grilling the lobsters, have a rimmed baking sheet ready by the grill.

2   (1½- to 2-pound) live lobsters
6   tablespoons unsalted butter, melted
2   garlic cloves, minced
1   slice hearty white sandwich bread, torn into 1-inch pieces
2   tablespoons minced fresh parsley
2   9-inch disposable pie plates or small roasting pans
    Lemon wedges

1. Place lobsters in large bowl and freeze for 30 minutes. Meanwhile, mix melted butter and garlic together in small bowl. Pulse bread in food processor until finely ground, 10 to 15 pulses. Measure out ¼ cup and place in medium bowl (discard remainder or reserve for another use). Split lobsters in half lengthwise, removing stomach sac and intestinal tract. Scoop out green tomalley and add to bowl with crumbs. Add parsley and 2 tablespoons melted garlic butter to tomalley and crumbs and mix with fork. Using back of chef's knife, whack 1 side of each claw, just to make opening (this will help accelerate cooking). Season tomalley mixture with salt and pepper. Season tail meat with salt and pepper. Brush cut side of lobster halves with half of remaining garlic butter.

2A. FOR A CHARCOAL GRILL: Open bottom vent completely. Light large chimney starter filled with charcoal briquettes (6 quarts). When top coals are partially covered with ash, pour evenly over grill. Set cooking grate in place, cover, and open lid vent completely. Heat grill until hot, about 5 minutes.

2B. FOR A GAS GRILL: Turn all burners to high, cover, and heat grill until hot, about 15 minutes. Leave all burners on high.

3. Clean and oil cooking grate. Place lobsters on grill flesh side down. Cook, uncovered, for 2 minutes. Transfer lobsters to rimmed baking sheet, turning shell side down. Spoon tomalley mixture evenly into open cavities of all 4 lobster halves. Place lobsters back on grill, shell side down. Brush lobsters with remaining garlic butter and cover claws with disposable pie plates or roasting pans. Cook until tail meat registers 140 degrees and turns opaque creamy white color, 4 to 6 minutes.

4. Serve lobsters immediately with lemon wedges.

GRILLED LOBSTERS WITH TARRAGON CHIVE BUTTER

In step 1, add 2 teaspoons minced fresh chives and 1 teaspoon minced fresh tarragon to garlic butter. Replace parsley in bread-crumb mixture with 2 tablespoons minced fresh chives and 2 teaspoons minced fresh tarragon leaves.

GRILLED LOBSTERS WITH CHILI BUTTER

In step 1, add 1½ teaspoons chili powder and ¼ teaspoon cayenne to garlic butter. Serve lobsters with lime wedges rather than lemon wedges.

PRACTICAL SCIENCE
TO EAT OR NOT TO EAT LOBSTER TOMALLEY

During red tide, avoid the tomalley.

In recent years there has been concern that eating the soft green mass called tomalley can lead to the contraction of paralytic shellfish poisoning (PSP), the illness caused by red tide. Red tide refers to a naturally occurring population explosion of particular types of poison-producing plankton that are ingested by filter feeders like clams and scallops. People who eat infected shellfish may experience dizziness and nausea. Lobsters do not filter-feed, but they do consume clams and scallops. If a lobster eats infected bivalves, the PSP toxin could accumulate in its tomalley, though not in the meat. So it's fine to eat lobster meat during red tide occurrences, when the sale of clams and mussels is prohibited, but it's a good idea to forgo the tomalley when there's a shellfish ban in place.

CHAPTER 14

Tofu

There are very few ingredients you want to make dry. This is one of them.

HOW THE SCIENCE WORKS

Tofu is an ancient food. Legend says it has been produced in China since the Han Dynasty, more than 2,000 years ago. But it wasn't until the 10th century that it began to catch on, the art of making and cooking tofu crossing the borders to Japan and Korea and elsewhere in Asia.

Tofu is made from soybeans, which are known for their ability to grow in poor soil and produce a high yield, not to mention being a complete source of dietary protein. Tofu is one of the most important sources of protein in Asia. But while soybeans have been grown in America since the early 19th century, they were first used mainly for animal feed. It took the health food movement of the 1970s to give soy—and tofu—any heft as a food for human consumption, but the reality is tofu is an incredibly versatile ingredient.

There are two basic types of tofu: Momen tofu, which comes as soft, firm, and extra firm; and Kinugoshi tofu, or silken tofu. To make tofu, manufacturers begin with soybeans, which are cleaned and soaked and then ground with water to make soy milk. The soy milk is heated in order to inactivate enzymes, and the leftover insoluble solids are removed from the soy milk before coagulation (see illustration, page 121).

To turn soy milk into tofu, one of four coagulants is added: nigari, sulfates, glucono-delta-lactone (GDL), or acids like lemon juice. These coagulants all act to link the soy proteins together and form a gel-like structure. Nigari-type coagulants, which are extracted from salt water, react rapidly with soymilk and create the most flavorful tofu, with a subtle sweet taste and aroma, but because they react so quickly they must be added with control, therefore requiring more skill. Sulfate-type coagulants, such as calcium

Tofu has been produced for 2,000 years. But it took the health food movement of the 1970s to bring it to America.

sulfate, react slowly and are the most widely used. GDL, a naturally occuring food additive, entered the world of tofu production in the 1960s, and today it's most commonly used to make silken tofu. Traditional acidic coagulants such as lemon juice will work for the home tofu-maker but are rarely used in the industry.

After the curds are formed via coagulation, the firmer momen tofus are pressed, while silken is not. Tofu is usually packed in containers with water, pasteurized, and kept refrigerated for retail sale, with a shelf life of about three weeks. There are a host of varieties to buy at supermarkets, but you can also make it at home (page 125).

Tofu can have a sweet soy flavor that we accentuate with marinades and sauces. We prefer extra-firm or firm tofu for stir-fries, as both have been pressed enough for much water to be removed, therefore holding their shape during high-heat cooking. Medium and soft tofu boast a creamy texture; we pan-fry them to achieve a crisp outside and silky interior. Silken tofu has a soft, ultracreamy texture and is often used as a base for smoothies and dips.

Because tofu is relatively delicate, high in protein and water, but with none of the confounding factors found in meats like insulating bones or fat, it cooks quickly. Because tofu is moist, and packed in water, one of the most important steps in preparing cooked tofu is drying out its exterior. This doesn't mean so dry it's crumbly, but with just enough moisture removed that it can quickly and easily achieve a nicely browned crust when heated (see Caramel Tofu, page 123). Drying, which we accomplish by letting the tofu drain on paper towels, also improves the texture of tofu that is served uncooked (see Chilled Marinated Tofu, page 122).

TEST KITCHEN EXPERIMENT

In The Science of Good Cooking *(2012) we proved that, contrary to popular belief, marinades do most of their work on the very surface of meat and poultry, not deep into the tissue. (Oil-soluble flavors, like most in our marinades, are incapable of deeply penetrating water-filled meat. Only the salt in salty marinades traveled far enough for our tasters to discern a difference in chicken breasts.) We wondered whether the same was true for tofu, so we ran a similar experiment.*

EXPERIMENT

We marinated blocks of firm and extra-firm tofu in four different marinades (based on soy sauce, red wine, yogurt, and lemon and garlic) for 15, 30, 60, and 120 minutes. We used zipper-lock bags and pressed out as much as air as possible to ensure full contact between the tofu and marinade. Afterwards, we wiped off the excess marinade and baked the tofu in a 300-degree oven until hot throughout, along with an unmarinated control. We then trimmed the outer 3 millimeters off of each block and had tasters sample the interior blind and choose which marinade correlated with each sample.

RESULTS

We found a slight, but insignificant, difference between tasters' responses for the firm and extra-firm tofu. The following results are therefore an average for the two types.

Tasters were relatively unsuccessful at correctly matching the sample to the marinade at the 15-minute mark, but improved dramatically at it by the 30-minute mark, with slightly increasing accuracy at 60 and 120 minutes. At 30 minutes (the minimum threshold for accurate responses) every taster correctly identified the unmarinated control, suggesting that each type of marinade imparted at least some flavor to the interior of the tofu. Every taster correctly identified the sample soaked in the soy-based marinade, 80 percent of tasters did the same for tofu from the lemon-garlic marinade, and 60 percent were accurate for the red wine and yogurt marinades.

TAKEAWAY

While tofu, which is high in protein, is a common substitute for meat and poultry, its structure is significantly different than animal muscle. Meat is made up of individual muscle fibers that are bundled together into tight packages by connective tissue (see page 25), which translates to a dense, resilient texture. By comparison, firm tofus are composed of coagulated curds of soy protein that are pressed into block form. While these blocks may look smooth and homogenous, they are anything but. As we can see in the photographs below (and as we found in our blind tasting), marinades are able to seep in between curd clumps and migrate toward the center of the block. The strong, water-soluble flavor compounds in soy sauce and garlic are better at moving through high-moisture tofu than those found in red wine or yogurt. These results stand in sharp contrast to our previous findings on chicken breasts, where we discovered that tasters couldn't tell the difference between marinated and unmarinated samples once the exterior portions had been trimmed away.

Considering that we often cut tofu into bite-size pieces with greater surface area (and thus more points of entry for marinade), marinating can have a profound impact—seasoning it not only at the surface, but also deep inside.

MARINATING TOFU VS. CHICKEN: A DIFFERENCE YOU CAN SEE

We soaked firm and extra-firm tofus in a handful of different marinades, for different amounts of time, and found that marinating can have a profound effect on tofu, with flavor seeping to its core. Contrast that with chicken breast (of the same size), on which, we've found, marinating has little effect except on the outermost layer.

TOFU
Our soy marinade reached the center of the tofu square.

CHICKEN
*Our dark-colored marinade did not move past
the outer edge of the chicken breast.*

JOURNEY: FROM SOY BEAN TO TOFU

Tofu has been made by hand for 2,000 years. Today, the process of manufacturing the tofu that you find in the market has been turned into a science. Here are the steps that every package of tofu takes before making it to your fridge.

1 START WITH BEANS

Tofu starts with soybeans, soaked for 8 to 10 hours at 60 to 68 degrees. Next they are ground, during which new water is added to make a bean slurry—a rough version of soy milk. Both the amount of added water and the temperature at which the beans are ground are carefully controlled; they vary depending on the type of tofu to be made. Enough water is added so that the finished tofu will contain 88 to 90 percent water.

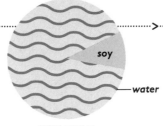

soy

water

SOY BEAN SLURRY

212°

2 HEAT THE SOY MILK

Next, this soy milk is heated for around 5 minutes at 212 degrees in order to inactivate enzymes. (One particular enzyme—lipoxygenase—is responsible for producing the undesirable "beany" flavor that can be present in soy milk.)

GOOD   **BAD**

3 ADD A COAGULANT

The next step in the process is to coagulate the soy milk while it is hot. This is done by adding coagulants, which help to link the soy proteins together in order to form a gel-like structure. There are four types: nigari, calcium and magnesium sulfate salts, GDL, and acids like lemon juice. Each type of coagulant reacts at a different speed, and is used to make a different type of tofu (see page 119.)

4 FORM THE CURDS

With time, and the proper amount of coagulant, the soy milk forms curds, which have a smooth and cohesive texture. When too much coagulant is used, the texture will become coarse and crumbly.

5 PRESS IT DOWN

Depending on the type of tofu, the curd may or may not be cut or broken before pressing to expel the whey. (It's necessary for soft, firm, and extra-firm tofu.) Longer pressing times and pressures are required for firmer tofus, and pressing is usually done in molds of various sizes. As a general guideline, tofu manufacturers apply light initial pressure for 5 to 10 minutes, followed by a stronger pressure for 10 to 15 minutes to make soft tofu. For firmer tofu, a higher pressure is applied for 20 to 30 minutes. Silken tofu is not pressed. All tofu is then packed in containers filled with water to keep it moist. It is then pasteurized and kept refrigerated for retail sale.

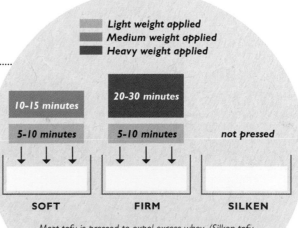

Light weight applied
Medium weight applied
Heavy weight applied

10-15 minutes   20-30 minutes

5-10 minutes   5-10 minutes   *not pressed*

SOFT   **FIRM**   **SILKEN**

Most tofu is pressed to expel excess whey. (Silken tofu is not.) Soft and firm tofus are pressed lightly for 5 to 10 minutes. Soft gets medium pressure for another 10 to 15 minutes, while firm tofu gets a firm pressure for up to 30 minutes.

Chilled Marinated Tofu

✅ WHY THIS RECIPE WORKS

Marinated raw tofu is served throughout Japan during the sticky summer months as a cool and refreshing appetizer or snack. In the best renditions, a flavorful marinade and a few choice garnishes amplify the tofu's delicate sweet soy flavor. We achieved this by gently letting the tofu drain on a towel-lined baking sheet, and making an umami-rich broth that complemented the delicate flavor of the tofu.

MAKE DASHI   The marinade for this dish is typically a soy sauce–enhanced dashi, the ubiquitous Japanese broth prepared from kombu seaweed and bonito (skipjack tuna) flakes. We replaced the bonito with a glutamate-rich combination of wakame seaweed, fish sauce, mirin, and sugar. Don't be intimidated by the seaweeds—you can find seaweed in the international aisle of well-stocked supermarkets, in Asian and natural foods markets, and online. Wakame is a traditional garnish in miso soup and many Japanese salads. It is available dried in thin sheets, shreds (or flakes), or fresh-salted. Both dried and fresh varieties are used to flavor soups and can be made into salads. (Note that dried wakame must be rehydrated in water for at least 3 to 5 minutes before using, while fresh-salted wakame should be rinsed briefly to remove the excess salt and then soaked in water for 1 to 2 minutes.) Our homemade dashi served as a well-rounded marinade: sweet, salty, and robust—almost meaty in its intensity. A splash of rice wine vinegar, added off the heat after the broth had steeped, provided a bit of balance.

GARNISH WELL   For the garnishes, we liked a sprinkle of crumbled nori, sliced scallions, and a drizzle of toasted sesame oil.

CHILLED MARINATED TOFU
SERVES 4 TO 6

For an accurate measurement of boiling water, bring a full kettle of water to a boil and then measure out the desired amount.

14	ounces firm tofu, halved lengthwise, then cut crosswise into ½-inch-thick squares
	Salt and pepper
2	cups boiling water
¼	cup fish sauce
¼	cup mirin
4	teaspoons sugar
¼	ounce wakame
¼	ounce kombu
4	teaspoons rice vinegar
2	sheets toasted nori, crumbled
2	scallions, sliced thin on bias
	Toasted sesame oil

1. Spread tofu over paper towel–lined baking sheet, let drain for 20 minutes, then gently press dry with paper towels. Season with salt and pepper.

2. Meanwhile, combine boiling water, fish sauce, mirin, sugar, wakame, and kombu in bowl. Cover and let sit for 15 minutes. Strain liquid through fine-mesh strainer, discarding solids, then return broth to now-empty bowl.

3. Add tofu and vinegar, cover, and refrigerate until cool, at least 2 hours or up to 2 days. To serve, use slotted spoon to transfer tofu to platter, top with nori and scallions, and drizzle with sesame oil to taste.

Tofu and Vegetable Salad

✅ WHY THIS RECIPE WORKS

Our goal for this recipe was a light and easy Asian-inspired salad that boasted plenty of vegetables in a fresh, bright vinaigrette. Draining and then lightly browning the tofu before adding the vinaigrette provided a good contrast of texture and flavor, especially alongside this collection of hearty vegetables.

PICK THE VEG   First we sought out a mix of vegetables that, along with the tofu, would give our salad enough heft to make it a main course. We settled on napa cabbage, snow peas, red bell pepper, bean sprouts, and carrots.

AND THE TOFU   Next we considered the tofu. We preferred soft tofu here for its creamy, custard-like texture, and we pan-fried it to give it a slightly crispy surface. Draining the tofu on a paper towel–lined baking sheet before cooking helped to give it the light golden crust we were after. Tofu is around 88 percent water, so this step also kept the tofu's liquid from watering down the dressing.

VIN IT UP   For a vinaigrette with plenty of punch, we combined mild rice vinegar and lime juice with honey, fish sauce, fresh ginger, nutty toasted sesame oil, and spicy, garlicky Sriracha sauce. A sprinkling of cilantro and toasted sesame seeds provided the perfect accents.

TOFU AND VEGETABLE SALAD

SERVES 4 TO 6

We prefer soft tofu for this recipe. Firm or extra-firm tofu will also work here, but it will taste drier.

1 ¾	pounds soft tofu, cut into ¾-inch cubes
	Salt and pepper
3	tablespoons lime juice (2 limes)
3	tablespoons honey
2	tablespoons rice vinegar
2	tablespoons fish sauce, plus extra as needed
1	tablespoon grated fresh ginger
1 ½	teaspoons Sriracha sauce
6	tablespoons vegetable oil
3	tablespoons toasted sesame oil
4	cups shredded napa cabbage
6	ounces snow peas, strings removed, cut in half lengthwise
2	carrots, peeled and shredded
1	red bell pepper, stemmed, seeded, and cut into ½-inch pieces
1	cup bean sprouts
2	scallions, sliced thin on bias
3	tablespoons minced fresh cilantro
1	tablespoon sesame seeds, toasted

1. Spread tofu over paper towel–lined baking sheet, let drain for 20 minutes, then gently press dry with paper towels. Season with salt and pepper. Meanwhile, whisk lime juice, honey, vinegar, fish sauce, ginger, and Sriracha together in medium bowl. Slowly whisk in ¼ cup vegetable oil and sesame oil until incorporated. Measure out ¼ cup vinaigrette and set aside for salad.

2. Heat 1 tablespoon vegetable oil in 12-inch nonstick skillet over medium-high heat until shimmering. Add half of tofu and brown lightly on all sides, about 5 minutes; transfer to bowl with remaining vinaigrette. Repeat with remaining 1 tablespoon vegetable oil and remaining tofu. Gently toss tofu to coat with vinaigrette, then let cool to room temperature, about 10 minutes.

3. Combine cabbage, snow peas, carrots, bell pepper, bean sprouts, and scallions in large bowl. Drizzle with reserved vinaigrette and toss to combine. Add tofu mixture and toss gently to combine. Season with fish sauce to taste. Sprinkle with cilantro and sesame seeds and serve.

PRACTICAL SCIENCE FREEZING TOFU

Freezing tofu will give it a spongy consistency that is highly absorbent.

We've often wondered why some tofu in Chinese restaurants has a distinctive spongy texture that allows it to soak up more of the sauce in a dish. This texture is produced by freezing the tofu solid before thawing and cooking it—a method that was originally used in China (and Japan) to preserve tofu during the winter months. Tofu is about 88 percent water; as it freezes, the ice crystals expand, pushing apart the protein network. When thawed, the water drains away, leaving the tofu with a spongy consistency that is highly absorbent. We experimented with freezing tofu in the test kitchen and quite liked the results. When stir-fried, the slabs did absorb sauce readily and had a resilient, slightly chewy texture that was far more meat-like than fresh tofu. And because the thawed tofu contained less water, it formed a nice crust when deep-fried. To freeze, slice extra-firm tofu into ½- to ¾-inch-thick slabs, spread them in a single layer on a baking sheet or plate, and place them in the freezer overnight. (At this point, the tofu can be placed in zipper-lock bags and stored in the freezer for up to a month.) To use, thaw to room temperature and press each slab gently over a colander to expel any remaining water before cooking.

Caramel Tofu

✔ WHY THIS RECIPE WORKS

For a tofu recipe that would convince even the most reluctant diner, we tossed cubes of tofu with cornstarch, lightly pan-fried them, and served them with a traditional Vietnamese salty-sweet caramel sauce. The combination was satisfying, surprisingly savory, and addictive.

FIND BALANCE To achieve the tricky balance of sweet and savory in our sauce, we kept our caramel base simple and added a healthy dose of savory garlic, fish sauce, and pepper. To ensure that our caramel sauce was sweet but still had depth, we added a thinly sliced onion to caramelize in the sauce. The caramel can go from amber-colored to burnt quickly, so it's important to have some water at the ready to stop the caramelization.

CARAMEL FLAVOR Most of us think of caramel as a sweet sauce. But if cooked long enough, caramel will become less sweet and more complex. Here's what happens: When table sugar is heated, a cascade of chemical reactions occurs that transforms some—and eventually all—of its single type of molecule into literally hundreds of different compounds that bring new flavors, aromas, and colors. At first these compounds are mild and buttery in flavor, and the caramel still tastes very sweet. With continued cooking, even more sugar molecules break down, and the caramel begins to taste markedly less sweet; meanwhile bitter, potent-tasting molecules also begin to form (along with those that bring a darker color). We found that cooking sugar to between 350 and 400 degrees produced a caramel with subtle sweetness and an appealingly bitter edge. Any additional cooking, though, made the caramel taste acrid and burnt.

DRY AND PAN-FRY As with most of our tofu recipes, we first dried the tofu on a towel-lined baking sheet. Tossing the tofu with cornstarch further helped dry it out, and added a little extra crust. Pan-frying it gave it an appealing crisp, browned exterior. Finally, we drizzled it with the caramel sauce and topped it with some chopped peanuts for textural contrast and a sprinkling of cilantro and scallions for a fresh finish.

CARAMEL TOFU
SERVES 4

Firm or extra-firm tofu can be used. Serve over rice.

21	ounces firm tofu, cut into ¾-inch cubes
	Salt and pepper
1¾	cups water
⅓	cup sugar
6	tablespoons vegetable oil
5	garlic cloves, minced
1	onion, halved and sliced thin
3	tablespoons fish sauce
½	cup plus 2 teaspoons cornstarch
½	cup fresh cilantro leaves
¼	cup dry-roasted peanuts, chopped
3	scallions, green parts only, sliced thin on bias

1. Spread tofu over paper towel–lined baking sheet, let drain for 20 minutes, then gently press dry with paper towels. Season with salt and pepper.

2. Meanwhile, pour ¼ cup water into medium saucepan, then sprinkle sugar evenly over top. Cook over medium heat, gently swirling pan occasionally (do not stir), until sugar melts and mixture turns color of maple syrup, 7 to 10 minutes.

3. Stir in 3 tablespoons oil and garlic and cook until fragrant, about 30 seconds. Off heat, slowly whisk in remaining 1½ cups water (sauce will sizzle). Stir in onion, fish sauce, 2 teaspoons cornstarch, and 1 teaspoon pepper. Return pan to medium-low heat and simmer vigorously until onion is softened and sauce has thickened, 10 to 15 minutes. Remove from heat and cover to keep warm.

4. Spread remaining ½ cup cornstarch in shallow dish. Working with several tofu pieces at a time, coat thoroughly with cornstarch, pressing gently to adhere; transfer to plate.

5. Heat remaining 3 tablespoons oil in 12-inch nonstick skillet over high heat until just smoking. Add tofu and cook, turning as needed, until all sides are crisp and well browned, 10 to 15 minutes; transfer to paper towel–lined plate to drain. Transfer tofu to platter, drizzle with sauce, and sprinkle with cilantro, peanuts, and scallions. Serve.

Tofu Banh Mi

✔ WHY THIS RECIPE WORKS

In Vietnam, banh mi is simply a term for all kinds of bread, but in the United States most people recognize it as a Vietnamese-style sandwich featuring chicken, pork, or tofu and crunchy pickled vegetables. For our own version, we started by making crispy, flavorful tofu.

DRAIN AND DREDGE We sliced the tofu into sandwich-size slabs and drained them on paper towels to make it easier to get a crispy crust. Then we dredged the slabs in cornstarch and seared them in a hot skillet until they were nicely browned. Cornstarch does a number of things here: It absorbs surface moisture, helping the coated tofu to brown faster; it breaks down to glucose, which enhances browning; and the cornstarch releases amylose, which forms a more crispy crust on the surface.

ADD ACCOUTREMENTS For the vegetables, we quick-pickled cucumber slices and shredded carrot in lime juice and fish sauce. Sriracha-spiked mayonnaise gave the sandwich a spicy kick, while a sprinkling of fresh cilantro added an authentic garnish.

TOFU BANH MI
SERVES 4

14	ounces firm tofu, sliced crosswise into ½-inch-thick slabs
	Salt and pepper
⅓	cup cornstarch

2	carrots, peeled and shredded
½	cucumber, peeled, halved lengthwise, seeded, and sliced thin
1	teaspoon grated lime zest plus 1 tablespoon juice
1	tablespoon fish sauce
¼	cup mayonnaise
1	tablespoon Sriracha sauce
3	tablespoons vegetable oil
4	(8-inch) Italian sub rolls, split lengthwise and toasted
⅓	cup fresh cilantro leaves

1. Spread tofu over paper towel–lined baking sheet, let drain for 20 minutes, then gently press dry with paper towels and season with salt and pepper. Spread cornstarch in shallow dish. Dredge tofu in cornstarch and transfer to plate.

2. Meanwhile, combine carrots, cucumber, lime juice, and fish sauce in bowl and let sit for 15 minutes. Whisk mayonnaise, Sriracha, and lime zest together in separate bowl.

3. Heat oil in 12-inch nonstick skillet over medium-high heat until just smoking. Add tofu and cook until both sides are crisp and browned, about 4 minutes per side. Transfer to paper towel–lined plate.

4. Spread mayonnaise mixture evenly over cut sides of each roll. Assemble 4 sandwiches by layering ingredients as follows between prepared rolls: tofu, pickled vegetables (leaving liquid in bowl), and cilantro. Press gently on sandwiches to set. Serve.

Homemade Tofu

✔ WHY THIS RECIPE WORKS

In Japan, tofu is made at dawn, like bread, for early morning distribution, and it boasts a silky-smooth texture and a clean, delicate taste. Unfortunately, truly fresh tofu is hard to come by in American grocery stores. Happily, tofu is no harder to make than yogurt. We make it happen in a few relatively easy steps: making soy milk from soy beans, curdling the hot soy milk with the mineral salt nigari, and then pressing the resulting curds.

START WITH BEANS We found it best to start with dried beans and make our own soy milk. Using processed soy milk from the market often meant that the tofu would not coagulate properly. To make the milk, we soaked soybeans until they split apart easily—anywhere

from 12 to 18 hours—and then blended them with water until smooth. We used a bean-to-water ratio of 1 to 3 so that the tofu would contain around 86 percent water when finished.

STRAIN AND COAGULATE Next, we brought this mixture to a boil in a Dutch oven, simmered it until thickened, and then drained it through cheesecloth. (You can discard the remaining soy bean pulp or save it for another use.) To make the tofu, we brought our soy milk back to a boil and then added the nigari in two stages.

PRESS WELL Once the milk started to form curds, we transferred the curds to a tofu mold (which you can find online or make yourself out of a quart-size berry container; see the recipe headnote) and pressed them until the tofu reached our desired firmness. The amount of pressing time changes the tofu's texture: 20 minutes for soft, 30 minutes for medium, and 40 to 50 minutes for firm.

HOMEMADE TOFU
MAKES 14 OUNCES

Dried soybeans are available at Asian markets and some supermarkets, and online. Liquid nigari can be found online at culturesforhealth.com and at Asian supermarkets. You can find tofu molds online, but if you don't want to invest in one, poke three even holes in the bottom of a quart-size plastic berry container and then cut off the lid and trim it down to fit just inside the container. Line the container with muslin or cheesecloth and scoop the curds into the container just as you would with a mold. Cover the curds with the muslin/cheesecloth and place the trimmed plastic lid on top.

| 8 | ounces (1¼ cups) dried soybeans, picked over and rinsed |
| 2 | teaspoons liquid nigari |

1. Place beans in large container, cover with 2 inches water, and soak until beans are pale yellow and split apart when rubbed between your fingertips, 12 to 18 hours.

2. Drain and rinse beans; you should have about 3 cups. Working in 3 batches, process 1 cup soaked soybeans with 3 cups water in blender until mostly smooth, about 3 minutes; transfer to Dutch oven. (You will use 9 cups water total.)

3. Bring soybean mixture to boil over medium-high heat, stirring often with rubber spatula to prevent scorching

and boiling over. Reduce heat to medium-low and simmer, stirring often, until slightly thickened, about 10 minutes. Meanwhile, line colander with butter muslin or triple layer of cheesecloth and set over large bowl.

4. Pour soybean mixture into prepared colander. Being careful of hot liquid, pull edges of muslin together and twist to form tight pouch, then firmly squeeze with tongs to help extract as much liquid as possible. You should have about 8 cups of soy milk; discard soybean pulp or reserve for another use.

5. Transfer strained milk to clean Dutch oven and bring to boil over medium-high heat, stirring often; remove from heat. Combine ½ cup water and nigari in measuring cup.

6. While stirring soy milk in fast figure-8 motion with rubber spatula, add ¼ cup nigari mixture, about 6 stirs. Cover pot and let sit undisturbed for 2 minutes. Uncover, sprinkle remaining ¼ cup nigari mixture over top and gently stir using figure-8 motion, about 6 stirs. Cover pot and let sit undisturbed until curds form and whey is pooling on top and around sides of pot, about 20 minutes.

7. Line tofu mold with butter muslin or triple layer of cheesecloth and place in colander set over large bowl. Using skimmer or large slotted spoon, gently transfer soy milk curds to prepared mold, trying not to break up curds. Cover with excess muslin, add top of mold, and weight with 2-pound weight until desired firmness is reached: 20 minutes for soft, 30 minutes for medium, or 40 to 50 minutes for firm.

8. Gently remove tofu from mold and place in baking dish. Fill with cold water to cover and let sit until tofu is slightly firmer, about 10 minutes. (Tofu can be refrigerated in airtight container filled with water for up to 10 days.)

PRACTICAL SCIENCE HOW TO STORE TOFU

Store your tofu in plain tap water for up to 10 days.

We've always stored leftover tofu in water, unchanged. But we spoke to an artisanal tofu maker who recommended changing the water daily (which we like to do for our more delicate, home-made tofu). We also read that storing it in lightly salted water is the best method. To find out which approach kept store-bought tofu tasting fresh the longest, we tried each using extra-firm, firm, and silken tofu, storing the samples in plastic containers. As a control, we also placed a sample of each style in a zipper-lock bag with as much air pressed out as possible.

The samples without any liquid lasted only four to six days. We don't recommend storing leftover tofu in salted water: Although these samples stayed fresh for two weeks, they also picked up a noticeable salty flavor almost immediately. The samples stored in water that we changed daily were edible for 10 days, after which they began losing flavor. However, in the end, our preferred method was our old standard: Submerging the tofu in plain tap water (and not changing it) kept the tofu as fresh tasting as straight-from-the-package tofu for 10 days and didn't require any maintenance. Just make sure that the water is clear; cloudy water can be a sign of bacterial growth, and the tofu should be discarded.

CHAPTER 15

Eggs

Just a few degrees makes a difference when it comes to the texture of a cooked egg.

HOW THE SCIENCE WORKS

Eggs come in many forms, from different animals, in different sizes and shades and ratios of white to yolk. Here, we concentrate on chicken eggs, but that doesn't stop the litany of choice. There are natural eggs, free-range eggs, certified organic eggs, and eggs enriched with omega-3 fatty acids. Egg color can change—the shell due to breed, the yolk due to diet. We cook eggs on their own, in or out of the shell, mixed with other ingredients, scrambled or baked or fried. Eggs are incredibly common, but not simple.

The fundamental challenge in egg cookery is that an egg is not just one ingredient but two: the white and the yolk. Each contains different types and ratios of proteins, fats, and water, which means that each reacts differently to heat, coagulating at different temperatures. Plus the white, often being on the outside and in closer contact with the heat source, cooks faster than the yolk. The goal of basic forms of egg cookery is to prevent the white from turning rubbery before the yolk has a chance to reach the desired consistency.

The white itself is 88 percent water, 11 percent protein, and 1 percent minerals and carbohydrates. The white is fully set at 180 degrees, although it begins to thicken at around 145 degrees. The yolk, on the other hand, is 50 percent water, 34 percent lipids, and 16 percent protein. It begins to thicken at 150 degrees and is fully set at 158 degrees. Thus the temperature range for cooking the yolk is much narrower than for the white, which presents a challenge when making, for example, soft-boiled eggs.

The proteins in yolks are very different from those in whites. The former exist as "spheres within spheres," like little Russian dolls, the subparticles of egg yolk proteins nested within larger particles of proteins. When cooked, the larger particles, containing the smaller particles, cross-link

Eggs are two ingredients in one: the white and the yolk.

together into coagulated spheres, which do not come apart when heated, and produce a granular texture when fully cooked. (Cooking the egg yolks until they only just begin to set produces a smooth, runny texture.) The proteins in egg whites, however, are globular and unwind when heated, forming a network that traps water and sets to a smooth, solid gel. The types of proteins found in egg whites are numerous; the most abundant is called ovalbumin.

Yolks also contain an enzyme called amylase. When cooked, the amylase deactivates. When raw, it digests starch. This means that if raw yolks are left too long in, say, a pudding or pie filling, the still-active amylase can digest the starch, turning the dish into something akin to soup.

Finally, the pH of egg white protein increases with age, from slightly alkaline when fresh to as high as pH 9 when a month or more old. This is due to release of carbon dioxide through the pores in the shell. Carbon dioxide dissolves in water and forms carbonic acid, so when this carbon dioxide escapes from the egg white, the pH increases. As a result, older eggs are easier to whip because of the higher pH and its effect on the electrical charge of the proteins.

Here, we cook eggs simply, using tricks of time and temperature to maintain the optimal textures of white and yolk. For our soft-cooked eggs, we achieve a set white and runny yolk every time by steaming rather than boiling (page 130). Our fried eggs (page 131) call for a hot pan to crisp the edges of the white, and a lid to finish solidifying the white before the yolk becomes granular. We beat egg whites on their own to create a wildly fluffy omelet (page 131) and a delicate—but not too delicate—cheese soufflé (page 132), and use whole eggs to create the sturdy structure we need to bake a cherry clafouti (page 134).

TEST KITCHEN EXPERIMENT

Different cooks favor different motions when using a whisk. Some prefer side-to-side strokes, others use circular stirring, and others like the looping action of beating that takes the whisk up and out of the bowl. Is any one of these motions more effective?

EXPERIMENT

We compared stirring, beating, and side-to-side motions in three core whisking applications: emulsifying vinaigrette and whipping small amounts of cream and egg whites. We timed how long the dressing stayed emulsified and how long it took us to whip cream and egg whites to stiff peaks.

RESULTS

In all cases, side-to-side whisking was highly effective. It kept the vinaigrette (made of oil and vinegar) fully emulsified for 15 minutes, and it whipped cream to stiff peaks in 4 minutes and egg whites in 5 minutes. Circular stirring never fully emulsified the dressing, and it took more than twice as long as side-to-side whisking to whip cream and egg whites (10 and 12 minutes, respectively). Beating was even less effective for emulsifying, and whipping cream dragged on with minimal effect for 8 minutes before we threw in the towel. Beating was only effective at whipping egg whites, creating stiff peaks in a record 4 minutes.

TAKEAWAY

So why does a side-to-side motion work so well—and the other actions so poorly? The first reason is that side-to-side whisking is simply an easier motion to execute quickly and aggressively. Second, this action causes more of what scientists call "shear force" to be applied to the liquid. As the whisk moves in one direction across the bowl, the liquid starts to move with it. But then the whisk is dragged in the opposite direction, exerting force against the rest of the liquid still moving toward it. Because stirring and beating take the liquid in the same direction of the whisk, they produce less shear force.

In vinaigrette, the greater shear force of side-to-side whisking helps break oil into tinier droplets that stay suspended in vinegar, keeping the dressing emulsified longer. To create stiff peaks in cream and egg whites, shear force and efficiency are both key. As the tines are dragged through the liquid, they create channels that trap air. Since the faster the channels are created, the faster the cream or whites gain volume, rapid side-to-side strokes are very effective.

Their greater shear force is also better at keeping each type of foam stable. In cream, shear force disrupts the proteins surrounding the fat molecules, freeing them to form a protective coating around the air bubbles; in egg whites, shear force performs a similar function, unfolding proteins that then create a protective film around the bubbles.

In whipping egg whites, however, beating had an advantage even over side-to-side strokes. Because egg whites are very viscous, more of them will cling to the tines than cream, even at the beginning of whipping. This allows the whisk to create wider channels that trap more air. With side-to-side strokes, the reverse motion will disrupt some of the channels that were just created, slowing the process of trapping air and building volume. Since beating takes the whisk out of the liquid during some of its action, these larger channels can stay open longer, trapping more air. In this case, the effect is more important than shear force in quickly creating volume.

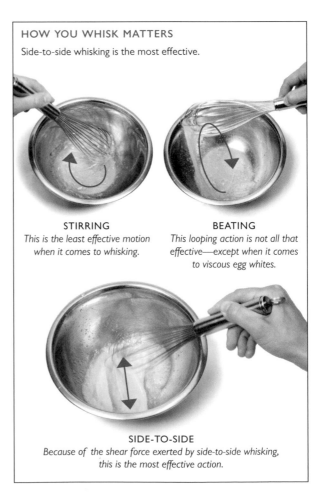

HOW YOU WHISK MATTERS
Side-to-side whisking is the most effective.

STIRRING
This is the least effective motion when it comes to whisking.

BEATING
This looping action is not all that effective—except when it comes to viscous egg whites.

SIDE-TO-SIDE
Because of the shear force exerted by side-to-side whisking, this is the most effective action.

FOCUS ON: EGGS

Eggs may seem simple—the basis of many basic recipes (scrambled eggs, fried eggs) which need little more than eggs, a pan, and some butter—but they are actually quite complex, the yolk and the white behaving as two separate ingredients, combined. Let's take a closer look.

SHELL

The shell and inner membrane keep the contents in place and keep out bacteria. The shell is permeable and over time the contents of an egg can evaporate. Each egg shell contains about 10,000 tiny pores to let gases in and out. To prevent bacteria from entering through these pores there is an antibacterial membrane on the inside of the shell. It is this same membrane that often makes it hard to peel the shells off hard-boiled eggs.

WHITE

Egg white is also called albumin. It is made up of protein and water and is divided into thick and thin layers, with the thickest layer closest to the yolk. A slight cloudiness indicates extreme freshness. As eggs age, the white becomes thinner and clearer. The white is 88 percent water, 11 percent protein, and 1 percent minerals and carbohydrates.

EGG WHITE PROTEINS

The proteins in whites are globular and unwind when heated, forming a network that traps water and sets to a smooth, solid gel. The proteins in whites are numerous, with the most abundant being the ovalbumins, which set at 180 degrees. Less abundant are ovotransferrins, which set when heated to 140 degrees or are whipped, and globulins, which likewise set when foamed.

UNCOOKED

egg white proteins

COOKED

egg white proteins at 180°

egg yolk proteins

egg yolk proteins at 158°

YOLK

Most of the egg's vitamins and minerals, as well as all of the fat and some of the protein, are found in the yolk. It also contains lecithin, a powerful emulsifier. When making mayonnaise, for example, the lecithin from egg yolk coats the surface of oil droplets, preventing them from merging with one another and helping them remain suspended in water. The yolk is 50 percent water, 34 percent lipids, and 16 percent protein. It begins to thicken at 150 degrees and is fully set at 158 degrees.

EGG YOLK PROTEINS

Egg yolk proteins are "spheres within spheres," meaning that the subparticles of egg yolk proteins are nested within larger particles of proteins. When cooked, the larger particles, containing the smaller particles, cross-link together into coagulated spheres, which do not come apart when heated, and produce a granular texture when fully cooked. (Cooking the egg yolks until they only just begin to set produces a smooth, runny texture.)

egg yolk solidifies

egg white solidifies

refrigerator temperature

| 41° | 145° | 150° | 158° | 180° |

Not only do the egg yolk and egg white proteins act inherently differently, they solidify at different temperatures.

Soft-Cooked Eggs

✔ WHY THIS RECIPE WORKS

Traditional methods for making soft-cooked eggs are hit or miss. We wanted one that delivered a set white and a fluid yolk every time. To figure out a method, we tested temperature, and cooking methods. The result? Foolproof, but far from traditional.

USE COLD EGGS AND HIGH HEAT Temperature extremes deliver the steepest temperature gradient, ensuring that yolks stay fluid while whites cook through. Using refrigerator-cold eggs and boiling water—consistent temperatures—also makes the recipe more foolproof.

STEAM, DON'T BOIL The biggest problem with the most widely used soft-cooked egg technique—dropping cold eggs into boiling water—is that you can perfect the cooking time for a set number of eggs, but every time you add or subtract an egg (or even use a different pan), that timing is thrown off. That's because the number of eggs added to the pot (and how well that pot can hold heat) affects how little—or how much—the water temperature drops from the boiling point of 212 degrees. Even a 1- or 2-degree drop significantly influences the cooking time. We tried adding one egg, four eggs, and six eggs to a quart of boiling water and took note: With the addition of one egg, the water temperature (212 degrees) was unchanged, but with four eggs, the water dropped to 210 degrees and took

a full minute to return to a boil; with six eggs, the water dropped to 202 degrees and took 2 minutes to get back to 212 degrees. Steaming eggs over ½ inch of boiling water, however, removes the big problem with the boiling technique: Because steaming involves so little liquid, the water returns to a boil within seconds, no matter how many eggs you add to the pot. By steaming your eggs, you can cook up one, two—even six—perfect soft-cooked eggs every time.

SHOCK WITH COLD WATER Transferring the pot of eggs to the sink and placing it under cold water halts carryover cooking. This way, the yolks stay runny and the whites stay tender.

YES, YOU CAN PEEL A SOFT-COOKED EGG Though it seemed unlikely to us, soft-cooked eggs are actually easier to peel than are hard-cooked eggs. This is because the soft-cooked white is more yielding. Start by cracking the broad end of the egg against a hard surface and then peel away both the shell and the inner membrane. A quick rinse in warm water removes any remaining wisps of membrane and shards of eggshell. Split the egg in half and serve it over toast, or have it your usual way.

SOFT-COOKED EGGS
MAKES 4

Be sure to use large eggs that have no cracks and are cold from the refrigerator. Because precise timing is vital to the success of this recipe, we strongly recommend using a digital timer. You can use this method for one to six large, extra-large, or jumbo eggs without altering the timing. If you have one, a steamer basket does make lowering the eggs into the boiling water easier. We recommend serving these eggs in eggcups and with buttered toast for dipping, or you may simply use the dull side of a butter knife to crack the egg along the equator, break the egg in half, and scoop out the insides with a teaspoon.

4   large eggs
       Salt and pepper

1. Bring ½ inch water to boil in medium saucepan over medium-high heat. Using tongs, gently place eggs in boiling water (eggs will not be submerged). Cover saucepan and cook eggs for 6½ minutes.

2. Remove cover, transfer saucepan to sink, and place under cold running water for 30 seconds. Remove eggs from saucepan and serve, seasoning with salt and pepper to taste.

PRACTICAL SCIENCE
WHAT DOES PERFECTLY COOKED MEAN?

A perfect soft-cooked egg has whites at 180 degrees and yolks at less than 158.

The proteins in egg whites and egg yolks solidify at different temperatures, making the perfect soft-cooked egg an exercise in precision. Whites that are firm yet tender must reach 180 degrees, while the yolk must stay below 158 degrees to remain runny. To achieve this temperature differential, it's essential to start cooking your eggs in hot water so that the whites will be blasted with enough heat to solidify before the heat has time to penetrate to the yolks.

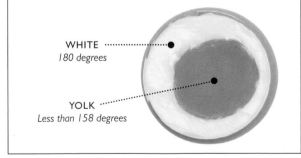

WHITE
180 degrees

YOLK
Less than 158 degrees

Perfect Fried Eggs

☑ WHY THIS RECIPE WORKS

A perfect fried egg is the sort that you find at the best diners: sunny-side up and crisp on its underside and edges, with a tender and opaque white and a perfectly runny yolk. We used a hot nonstick skillet, a touch of butter, and a lid to produce perfectly cooked fried eggs—with crisp edges, tender whites, and runny yolks—in just a few minutes.

PREHEAT THE PAN A quick blast of high heat can cause hot spots to form on the pan, and, thus, cook the eggs at different rates. We preheated our pan on low heat for 5 full minutes, which guaranteed that there would be no hot spots in the skillet that could lead to unevenly cooked eggs.

USE TWO FATS We used vegetable oil, with its high smoke point, while preheating the pan. Adding a couple pats of butter to the pan right before slipping in the eggs resulted in great flavor and browning due to the butter's milk proteins—it gave the eggs a real diner-style richness.

ADD THE EGGS ALL AT ONCE It's difficult to get the eggs to cook evenly if you break them into the pan one by one. Instead, we cracked the eggs into small bowls so we could add them to the skillet simultaneously; they cooked at the same rate.

COVER IT UP Adding a lid to the skillet trapped heat and steam so the eggs cooked from above as well as below, firming up the whites before the yolks overcooked. Moving the pan off the heat after 1 minute of cooking allowed the whites to finish cooking—gently—while keeping the yolks liquid.

PERFECT FRIED EGGS
SERVES 2

When checking the eggs for doneness, lift the lid just a crack to prevent loss of steam should they need further cooking. When cooked, the thin layer of white surrounding the yolk will turn opaque, but the yolk should remain runny. To cook two eggs, use an 8- or 9-inch nonstick skillet and halve the amounts of oil and butter. You can use this method with extra-large or jumbo eggs without altering the timing.

- 2   teaspoons vegetable oil
- 4   large eggs
       Salt and pepper
- 2   teaspoons unsalted butter, cut into 4 pieces and chilled

1. Heat oil in 12- or 14-inch nonstick skillet over low heat for 5 minutes. Meanwhile, crack 2 eggs into small bowl and season with salt and pepper. Repeat with remaining 2 eggs and second small bowl.

2. Increase heat to medium-high and heat until oil is shimmering. Add butter to skillet and quickly swirl to coat pan. Working quickly, pour 1 bowl of eggs in 1 side of pan and second bowl of eggs in other side. Cover and cook for 1 minute. Remove skillet from burner and let stand, covered, 15 to 45 seconds for runny yolks (white around edge of yolk will be barely opaque), 45 to 60 seconds for soft but set yolks, and about 2 minutes for medium-set yolks. Slide eggs onto plates and serve.

Fluffy Omelets

☑ WHY THIS RECIPE WORKS

We love the impressive height and delicate texture of a fluffy omelet. It's like a soufflé in a skillet—or would be if we could figure out how to keep it from collapsing before it got to the plate. To make sure that the eggs were cooked through but moist and tender, we folded butter-enriched yolks into stiffly whipped whites. We filled our omelets with light but boldly flavored fillings.

USE SEPARATED EGGS To create an omelet that was fluffy but didn't taste like Styrofoam, we first needed to separate the whites from the yolks and treat them as distinct entities. This is because each component contributes a different—and competing—quality to the results: Whites build structure, while the rich-tasting fat in yolks weakens it. Next steps: We whipped the whites with cream of tartar, an acid that can alter the electric charge on the proteins of egg whites, allowing the proteins to help form a more stable foam. We also stirred melted butter into the yolks to enhance their taste. We then recombined the two components. The extra fat kept the omelet from tasting too lean, while the cream of tartar allowed the omelet to stand tall and sturdy, despite the weakening effects of butter and yolks.

FILL 'ER UP The delicate nature of this omelet meant that we couldn't put just anything in there—and not in large quantities. The trick was figuring out when, exactly, to add the fillings. Sprinkling them on after the omelet had baked meant that the filling rested on—but did not mesh with—the puffy bed of eggs. Filling the omelets before they went into the oven was a better solution. A light sprinkling of Parmesan made for a nice minimalist option, but we also worked up a few more substantial variations.

FLUFFY OMELETS
SERVES 2

A teaspoon of white vinegar or lemon juice can be used in place of the cream of tartar, and a handheld mixer or a whisk can be used in place of a stand mixer. We recommend using the fillings that accompany this recipe; they are designed not to interfere with the cooking of the omelet.

4	large eggs, separated
1	tablespoon unsalted butter, melted, plus 1 tablespoon unsalted butter
¼	teaspoon salt
¼	teaspoon cream of tartar
1	recipe filling (recipes follow)
1	ounce Parmesan cheese, grated (½ cup)

1. Adjust oven rack to middle position and heat oven to 375 degrees. Whisk egg yolks, melted butter, and salt together in bowl. Place egg whites in bowl of stand mixer and sprinkle cream of tartar over surface. Fit stand mixer with whisk and whip egg whites on medium-low speed until foamy, 2 to 2½ minutes. Increase speed to medium-high and whip until stiff peaks just start to form, 2 to 3 minutes. Fold egg yolk mixture into egg whites until no white streaks remain.

2. Heat remaining 1 tablespoon butter in 12-inch oven-safe nonstick skillet over medium-high heat, swirling to coat bottom of pan. When butter foams, quickly add egg mixture, spreading into even layer with spatula. Remove pan from heat and gently sprinkle filling and Parmesan evenly over top of omelet. Transfer to oven and cook until center of omelet springs back when lightly pressed, 4½ minutes for slightly wet omelet or 5 minutes for dry omelet.

3. Run spatula around edges of omelet to loosen, shaking gently to release. Slide omelet onto cutting board and let stand for 30 seconds. Using spatula, fold omelet in half. Cut omelet in half crosswise and serve immediately.

ASPARAGUS AND SMOKED SALMON FILLING
MAKES ¾ CUP

1	teaspoon olive oil
1	shallot, sliced thin
5	ounces asparagus, trimmed and cut on bias into ¼-inch lengths
	Salt and pepper
1	ounce smoked salmon, chopped
½	teaspoon lemon juice

Heat oil in 12-inch nonstick skillet over medium-high heat until shimmering. Add shallot and cook until softened and starting to brown, about 2 minutes. Add asparagus, pinch salt, and pepper to taste, and cook, stirring frequently, until crisp-tender, 5 to 7 minutes. Transfer asparagus mixture to bowl and stir in salmon and lemon juice.

MUSHROOM FILLING
MAKES ¾ CUP

1	teaspoon olive oil
1	shallot, sliced thin
4	ounces white or cremini mushrooms, trimmed and chopped
	Salt and pepper
1	teaspoon balsamic vinegar

Heat oil in 12-inch nonstick skillet over medium-high heat until shimmering. Add shallot and cook until softened and starting to brown, about 2 minutes. Add mushrooms and ⅛ teaspoon salt and season with pepper to taste. Cook until liquid has evaporated and mushrooms begin to brown, 6 to 8 minutes. Transfer mixture to bowl and stir in vinegar.

Cheese Soufflé

✓ WHY THIS RECIPE WORKS

We wanted a cheese soufflé with bold cheese flavor, good stature, and a light, but not-too-airy, texture, without the fussiness of most recipes. To bump up the cheese flavor without weighing the soufflé down, we added light-but-potent Parmesan cheese to the traditional Gruyère. To get the texture just right while keeping the preparation simple, we beat the egg whites to stiff peaks, and then—rather than carefully fold them into the cheese-béchamel—added the sauce right to the mixer, and beat everything until uniform.

CHEESE CHOICE At first, our trial soufflés didn't have enough cheese flavor, and we wondered if it was the fault of the béchamel. Flour, after all, has a tendency to mute flavors, and its thickening power, while essential to providing the soufflé with stability, can also weigh things down. We dialed back on the amounts of butter and flour, and the flavor of the cheese came through. We added feathery Parmesan in addition to the traditional Gruyère to get the cheese flavor we wanted, without the extra weight.

BEAT IT We started by whipping the egg whites to stiff peaks, as is soufflé convention, in order to create maximum volume. But the soufflé was ending up too light, and we wondered if we could dial that back and not work the eggs so hard. Whipping them to soft peaks instead gave the soufflé a dense, squat consistency. Was there a middle ground? There is no good visual indicator of egg whites whipped to "medium peaks," so instead of folding egg whites beaten to stiff peaks into the cheese-béchamel mixture, we beat these two components together, thus slightly deflating the whipped egg whites. This soufflé rose beautifully in the oven, and its consistency was perfect: light but not too light.

CHEESE SOUFFLÉ
SERVES 4 TO 6

Serve this soufflé with a green salad for a light dinner. Comté, sharp cheddar, or gouda cheese can be substituted for the Gruyère. To prevent the soufflé from overflowing the soufflé dish, leave at least 1 inch of space between the top of the batter and the rim of the dish; any excess batter should be discarded. The most foolproof way to test for doneness is with an instant-read thermometer. To judge doneness without an instant-read thermometer, use two large spoons to pry open the soufflé so that you can peer inside it; the center should appear thick and creamy but not soupy.

1	ounce Parmesan cheese, grated (½ cup)
¼	cup (1¼ ounces) all-purpose flour
¼	teaspoon paprika
¼	teaspoon salt
⅛	teaspoon cayenne pepper
⅛	teaspoon white pepper
	Pinch ground nutmeg
4	tablespoons unsalted butter
1⅓	cups whole milk
6	ounces Gruyère cheese, shredded (1½ cups)
6	large eggs, separated
2	teaspoons minced fresh parsley
¼	teaspoon cream of tartar

1. Adjust oven rack to middle position and heat oven to 350 degrees. Spray 8-inch round (2-quart) soufflé dish with vegetable oil spray, then sprinkle with 2 tablespoons Parmesan.

2. Combine flour, paprika, salt, cayenne, white pepper, and nutmeg in bowl. Melt butter in small saucepan over medium heat. Stir in flour mixture and cook for 1 minute. Slowly whisk in milk and bring to simmer. Cook, whisking constantly, until mixture is thickened and smooth, about 1 minute. Remove pan from heat and whisk in Gruyère and 5 tablespoons Parmesan until melted and smooth. Let cool for 10 minutes, then whisk in egg yolks and 1½ teaspoons parsley.

3. Using stand mixer fitted with whisk, whip egg whites and cream of tartar on medium-low speed until foamy, about 1 minute. Increase speed to medium-high and whip until stiff peaks form, 3 to 4 minutes. Add cheese mixture and continue to whip until fully combined, about 15 seconds.

4. Pour mixture into prepared dish and sprinkle with remaining 1 tablespoon Parmesan. Bake until risen above rim, top is deep golden brown, and interior registers 170 degrees, 30 to 35 minutes. Sprinkle with remaining ½ teaspoon parsley and serve immediately.

PRACTICAL SCIENCE BUSTING SOUFFLÉ MYTHS

There are many myths about soufflés—and all the ways they can be destroyed. We set them right.

MYTH The soufflé will collapse from loud noises or sudden movements.
REALITY Steam will keep a hot soufflé fully inflated. No loud noise or slamming of the oven door can change that.

MYTH The egg whites must be gently folded into the base.
REALITY Egg whites whipped to stiff peaks will have ample structure to handle aggressive beating, even in a stand mixer.

MYTH Prodding to check doneness will make it collapse.
REALITY A soufflé is not a balloon; it's a matrix of very fine bubbles. No tool can pop enough of them to cause it to fall.

MYTH You can't make a fallen soufflé rise again.
REALITY Yes, your soufflé will fall after it's been out of the oven for about 5 minutes. But returning it to a 350-degree oven will convert the water back into steam and reinflate it (it will lose about ½ inch of height).

Cherry Clafouti

✔ WHY THIS RECIPE WORKS

When we have a surplus of summer fruit and not much time to make dessert, we usually throw together a crisp or cobbler. Easy, satisfying, and crowd-pleasing. But we've often admired France's answer to those simple desserts: clafouti, a rustic yet graceful baked custard that is studded with fresh fruit such as apricots, plums, or, most classic, cherries. To make it, you mix up a batter without any chemical leaveners using flour, sugar, eggs, milk and/or heavy cream, and a touch of vanilla or almond extract; pour it into a buttered baking dish; scatter cherries (usually unpitted) on top; and bake it for a half hour. When finished, the custard should be rich and tender but resilient enough to be neatly sliced and the fruit plump enough to disrupt the custard with bright, sweet-tart flavor.

PIT AND SPICE THE CHERRIES Cherry clafouti is traditionally made with unpitted cherries because the stones lend the dessert a fragrant spice flavor—but they also make it tricky to slice and eat. Our solution? We used pitted cherries and tossed them with a little cinnamon. If that sounds like an odd solution, it's not; both cherry pits and cinnamon contain a compound called linalool that lends the dessert a similarly warm, floral complexity.

AND THEN ROAST THEM Briefly roasting halved and pitted cherries for our clafouti added a little time to traditional approaches that call for tossing whole raw cherries into the batter—but it was worth the effort. Instead of bursting and leaking juices into the custard, leaving it soggy and stained red, the fruit added bright, sweet-tart flavor that complemented the rich custard.

JUST ENOUGH FLOUR Custards can range from soft and creamy, like pastry cream, to more resilient and bready, like a crêpe. The textural difference largely depends on the ratio of three key ingredients: eggs, dairy, and flour. The proteins in the eggs provide the structure, linking together into a network as the custard heats, while both fat from the dairy and starch from the flour dilute that structure by interrupting the egg proteins and preventing them from knitting together too tightly. So when we set out to achieve the tender-but-set texture of our Cherry Clafouti, we conducted more than a dozen tests, fiddling with the amounts of each component. Not surprisingly, too much flour made the custard too bready, whereas an excess of dairy yielded custard that was too loose. Ultimately, we settled on a relatively moderate amount of each: 1⅔ cups dairy, four eggs, and ½ cup of flour, which yielded a clafouti that was soft but sliceable.

CHERRY CLAFOUTI
SERVES 6 TO 8

We prefer whole milk, but 1 or 2 percent low-fat milk may be substituted. Do not substitute frozen cherries for the fresh cherries.

1½	pounds fresh sweet cherries, pitted and halved
1	teaspoon lemon juice
2	teaspoons all-purpose flour, plus ½ cup (2½ ounces)
⅛	teaspoon ground cinnamon
4	large eggs
⅔	cup (4⅔ ounces) plus 2 teaspoons sugar
2½	teaspoons vanilla extract
¼	teaspoon salt
1	cup heavy cream
⅔	cup whole milk
1	tablespoon unsalted butter

1. Adjust oven racks to lowest and upper-middle positions; place 12-inch ovensafe skillet on lower rack and heat oven to 425 degrees. Line rimmed baking sheet with aluminum foil and place cherries, cut side up, on sheet. Roast cherries on upper rack until just tender and cut sides look dry, about 15 minutes. Transfer cherries to medium bowl, toss with lemon juice, and let cool for 5 minutes. Combine 2 teaspoons flour and cinnamon in small bowl; dust flour mixture evenly over cherries and toss to coat thoroughly.

2. Meanwhile, whisk eggs, ⅔ cup sugar, vanilla, and salt in large bowl until smooth and pale, about 1 minute. Whisk in remaining ½ cup flour until smooth. Whisk in cream and milk until incorporated.

3. Remove skillet (skillet handle will be hot) from oven and set on wire rack. Add butter and swirl to coat bottom and sides of skillet (butter will melt and brown quickly). Pour batter into skillet and arrange cherries evenly on top (some will sink). Transfer skillet to lower rack and bake until clafouti puffs and turns golden brown (edges will be dark brown) and center registers 195 degrees, 18 to 22 minutes, rotating skillet halfway through baking. Transfer skillet to wire rack and let cool for 25 minutes. Sprinkle clafouti evenly with remaining 2 teaspoons sugar. Slice into wedges and serve.

CHAPTER 16

Cream

This fatty, flavorful dairy product can be whipped into a soft cloud.

HOW THE SCIENCE WORKS

Humans have been drinking animal milk for thousands of years, since the first dairy animals were domesticated. The game changed in 1863 when Louis Pasteur invented pasteurization, a process that has altered over time but that today commonly involves heating milk to 161 degrees for 15 seconds in order to kill microbes.

Today, we use milk mainly from cows, but also sheep, goats, and buffalo. According to the FDA standard of identity for milk, whole cow's milk has a minimum of 3.25 percent fat and 8.25 percent milk solids-not-fat, a category that includes protein, sugar (lactose), and minerals. But milk is only a starting point. Milk can be left to sit and cream will rise to the top. Cream can be churned into butter; the leftover liquid is called buttermilk. Milk can be cultured and turned into cheese.

Here, we concentrate on cream. Cream was once made by allowing fresh whole milk to sit; as it cooled, the less-dense fat globules would rise to the top. Today, cream is made through a process of centrifuging, which forces the fat-rich, less-dense cream to separate. Four types of cream are produced, each according to standards set by the U.S. government. Half-and-half contains 10.5 to 18 percent fat, while light cream contains 18 to 30 percent. Light whipping cream has 30 to 36 percent fat, and heavy whipping cream (or heavy cream) contains a minimum of 36 percent fat. Government regulations require that all forms of cream be pasteurized, while some manufacturers stabilize cream by ultra-high temperature (UHT) pasteurization, which prolongs shelf-life but slightly compromises flavor and whipping ability. The large amount of fat in cream means two things: First, when heated, cream is resistant to curdling. Second, it can be whipped into an airy cloud.

There are many types of cream. The richest contains more than 36 percent fat.

To understand why cream rarely curdles, it's first important to understand that cream is an emulsion, or a combination of two liquids that don't usually mix, like oil and water. All types of cream are oil-in-water emulsions, meaning that tiny fat droplets are suspended in water (the fat droplets are known as the dispersed phase and the water is called the continuous phase). This is why cream is a liquid, and not a solid fat like butter (page 143). Much of the protein in cream, casein, is attached to the surface of the fat droplets. More fat means more droplets, which means a greater surface area for protein to attach to. And the more surface area, the further apart the proteins. When the fat content is 30 percent or more the fat has enough surface area to prevent protein molecules from bonding together when heated. This means that when you heat most types of cream, the protein will not coagulate, and the cream will not curdle.

When cream is whipped, air bubbles are introduced. The bubbles are then surrounded by droplets of fat, which provide both rigidity and stability. Protein molecules adhere to the surface of the fat droplets, strengthening the protective coating around the air bubbles.

Here, we start with Whipped Cream (page 138), being sure not to beat the cream for too long (which can destabilize the construction and cause separation). Then we move on to Fresh Strawberry Mousse (page 139)—we use gelatin and cream cheese to achieve the perfect texture—and finish with a Triple-Chocolate Mousse Cake (page 140), which uses heavy cream to make a traditional chocolate mousse, and an easier white chocolate mousse. Heavy cream also gives a velvety texture to the sauce in our Fettuccine Alfredo (page 142).

TEST KITCHEN EXPERIMENT

Conventional wisdom says to make sure your cream is cold before whipping, but we wondered exactly how much the temperature of the cream matters, so we decided to run a few tests.

EXPERIMENT

We whipped three batches of 1 cup of pasteurized whipping cream each to stiff peaks: one that came straight from the refrigerator, 39 degrees; another that had sat out for 1 hour and reached 57 degrees; and a third that was at room temperature, 72 degrees. We recorded how long it took to whip the cream to its maximum volume without overwhipping and noted the final texture.

RESULTS

The refrigerated sample yielded 2¼ cups of smooth, stiff peaks after 1¼ minutes of whipping. The sample that sat out for an hour yielded 2 cups of slightly grainy stiff peaks after 1 minute and 50 seconds of whipping, and the room-temperature sample yielded 1¾ cups of grainy whipped cream but never reached stiff peaks, even after 2½ minutes of whipping.

TAKEAWAY

Whipping cream introduces air bubbles. When the cream is cold, these bubbles are held in place by a network of tiny globules of solid fat, which allow the cream to eventually expand into a light, airy mass. At warmer temperatures, that fat starts to soften and the globules collapse, so the cream can't whip up as fully, and it takes longer to reach its maximum (diminished) volume. This extended whipping time also gives the cream a grainy texture, as the fat forms small, irregular clumps rather than small, smooth solid globules that surround the air bubbles. So, for maximum volume and the best texture, it's crucial to use cream straight from the refrigerator. Chilling the bowl and beaters can also help ensure that your cream stays cold throughout the whipping process.

WHEN IT COMES TO WHIPPED CREAM . . . THE COLDER, THE BETTER

We whipped cream at three different temperatures (39 degrees, 57 degrees, and 72 degrees) to stiff peaks. Because the air bubbles introduced during whipping are stabilized best by solid globules of fat, the whipped cream made with the coldest cream had the greatest volume.

REFRIGERATED CREAM
This whipped cream had the greatest volume (2¼ cups), the fastest (1¼ minutes).

CREAM LEFT OUT FOR 1 HOUR
This sample yielded only 2 cups, after 1 minute and 50 seconds of whipping.

ROOM-TEMPERATURE CREAM
The warmest cream produced the least whipped cream (1¾ cups) and never reached stiff peaks.

FAMILY TREE: DAIRY

We start with milk from a cow, sheep, or goat and end up with a wide range of dairy products. (For cultured dairy products, see page 155.)

COW

SHEEP

GOAT

BUFFALO

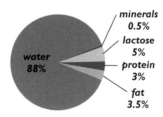

YAK

MILK

In 2015, in the U.S., 21 states banned the sale of raw milk, while 16 states limited the sale of raw milk to the farm, and 13 states allowed the sale of raw milk in retail stores. Most milks—and cheeses (page 163)—are pasteurized before sale.

water 88% · *minerals 0.5%* · *lactose 5%* · *protein 3%* · *fat 3.5%*

CREAM

When whole milk sits out—or, more often today, is centrifuged—the less-dense, fatty cream separates from the more-dense milk. The remaining liquid is used to make low-fat and skim milk. The most important flavor compounds in cream are called lactones, and include the specific compounds decalactone, dodecalactone, and octalactone. Also important are aldehydes such as hexenal, and sulfur compounds such as methional.

FAT RANGE

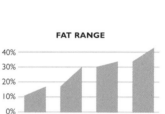

HALF & HALF · LIGHT · LIGHT | HEAVY WHIPPING

BUTTER

Butter, by law, must contain at least 80 percent fat. (It also contains 13 to 19 percent water, and 1 percent milk solids.) Butter is made by churning cream, during which globules of fat stick together to make a larger mass. (See page 143.) The leftover liquid is buttermilk.

water 13–19% · *milk solids 1%* · *80–86% fat*

SWEETENED CONDENSED MILK

Sweetened condensed milk consists of milk from which 60 percent of the water has been removed, with 40 to 45 percent added sugar (in addition to naturally occuring sugars). This makes it popular for use in sweet custards and puddings. Note: An open can of sweetened condensed milk can be left on the kitchen counter for several weeks without spoiling.

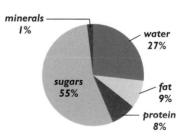

minerals 1% · *water 27%* · *sugars 55%* · *fat 9%* · *protein 8%*

Use gelatin to make whipped cream in advance.

Unlike other dessert toppings and frostings, whipped cream doesn't keep well if made in advance. After a few hours it begins to weep liquid and eventually loses the air bubbles that have been whipped into it. We often hold whipped cream in a fine-mesh strainer set over a bowl for up to 8 hours. But to see if we could stabilize the topping to avoid the strainer setup and hold it even longer, we tried a slew of additives we'd heard might help: marshmallow crème, xanthan gum, cream of tartar, confectioners' sugar, nonfat dry milk powder, instant dry vanilla pudding mix, gelatin, and buckwheat flour. Some ingredients, like cream of tartar, worked well but added unwanted flavors. Others, like xanthan gum, made the whipped topping more dense and reminiscent of sour cream. The best of the bunch proved to be gelatin, which we first heated in a bit of water to liquefy it and ensure even distribution in the cold cream. It kept liquid from weeping for a full day, contributed no additional flavors, and didn't noticeably change the texture of the whipped cream.

To make 3 cups of lightly sweetened whipped cream in advance, sprinkle ½ teaspoon of unflavored powdered gelatin over 1½ tablespoons of water in a microwave-safe bowl and let it stand for 3 minutes. Microwave the mixture in 5-second increments until the gelatin is dissolved and liquefied. Whip 1½ cups of chilled heavy cream (along with 1½ teaspoons of sugar and ½ teaspoon of vanilla extract, if desired) in a stand mixer, staying on low speed until small bubbles form and then increasing the speed to medium. When the beaters begin to leave a trail in the cream, slowly pour in the gelatin mixture and then increase the speed to high and continue to beat until soft peaks form. If well covered, the whipped cream will retain its moisture and airiness for up to 24 hours.

DEFLATED
After 2 to 3 hours, with no treatment, liquid (and air) escapes from whipped cream.

FULL OF AIR
A little gelatin whipped with the dairy keeps things stable for 24 hours.

Whipped Cream

✓ WHY THIS RECIPE WORKS

For this simple whipped cream recipe, we used cold heavy cream and a cold bowl. Heavy cream is important because it contains at least 36 percent fat—don't be tempted to use light cream or half-and-half. Cream can go from properly whipped to overwhipped in a matter of seconds. If cream becomes granular and looks curdled, you've beaten it too long and must start over with a new batch.

USE CHILLED   It's important to use cold cream when you whip cream. We tested this (see page 136) and found that the warmer the cream, the smaller the volume when whipped and the grainier the texture. This is because whipped cream is held together by tiny yet solid globules of fat. At warm temperatures, the fat softens and the globules collapse.

START LOW   We began whipping the cream on low, but then increased the speed. This accomplished two things: First, it cut down on splattering. Second, beginning slowly helped to yield a more stable final product (just like with whipped egg whites).

DON'T WHIP TOO MUCH   Whipping the cream for too long can cause the fat to clump and separate from the liquid. If you whip it way too long, you can even end up with straight butter.

WHIPPED CREAM
MAKES ABOUT 2 CUPS

For lightly sweetened whipped cream, reduce the sugar to 1½ teaspoons. For the best results, chill the mixer bowl and whisk in the freezer for 20 minutes before whipping the cream.

- 1   **cup heavy cream, chilled**
- 1   **tablespoon sugar**
- 1   **teaspoon vanilla extract**

Using stand mixer fitted with whisk, whip cream, sugar, and vanilla on medium-low speed until foamy, about 1 minute. Increase speed to high and whip until soft peaks form, 1 to 3 minutes. (Whipped cream can be transferred to fine-mesh strainer set over small bowl, covered with plastic wrap, and refrigerated for up to 8 hours.)

Fresh Strawberry Mousse

✔ WHY THIS RECIPE WORKS

When it comes to mousse desserts, recipes for the chocolate kind, or even citrus versions, abound. But it's not often that you see recipes for mousses that feature strawberries. In our opinion, this is a sad omission. The berry's bright, sweet flavor is a natural fit in other creamy desserts and should surely make a light and refreshing variation. Plus, mousse is great for warm-weather entertaining. It doesn't require turning on the oven, it looks pretty, and it's entirely make-ahead. But there's a good reason that strawberry mousse recipes aren't very prevalent: The berries contain lots of juice, which can ruin the texture of a mousse that should be creamy and rich. Plus, the fruit flavor produced by most strawberry mousse recipes is too subtle. We had our work cut out for us.

STRAWBERRY FLAVOR Even in season, the average supermarket strawberry is watery and just doesn't have a lot of flavor. Cooking the berries to drive off some of their moisture and concentrate flavor wasn't the answer. While these mousses had more discernible strawberry flavor, they also tasted cooked and jam-like, with none of the fresh taste of a berry eaten out of hand. Meanwhile, recipes that didn't cook down the berries suffered from textural problems: The large amount of juice given up by the berries made these desserts loose and runny. The solution? Macerating the finely chopped berries delivered the bright flavor and concentrated sweetness found in farmers' market specimens. By reducing the shed berry juice to just about 3 tablespoons, we were able to deepen its flavor and control the amount of liquid in the mousse.

SET IT UP We started by adding gelatin to the mousse, which acted as a stabilizer by forming a gel network that trapped liquid. Using gelatin alone made the mousse so overly set that it jiggled like Jell-O. We tried other common mousse stabilizers: pectin, whipped egg whites, and even white chocolate. Pectin was an immediate strikeout. It acts like gelatin when exposed to heat, its molecules linking up and forming a water-trapping matrix, and it made the mousse springy. Also a failure were whipped egg whites, as we disliked their foamy texture. Melted white chocolate made the mousse taste chalky. Our solution? Cream cheese. In conjunction with gelatin, the soft but dense cream cheese firmed up the mousse's texture and didn't mask the strawberry flavor.

FRESH STRAWBERRY MOUSSE
SERVES 4 TO 6

This recipe works well with supermarket strawberries and farmers' market strawberries. In step 1, be careful not to overprocess the berries. If you like, substitute 1½ pounds (5¼ cups) of thawed frozen strawberries for fresh strawberries. If using frozen strawberries skip step 1 (do not process the berries). Proceed with the recipe, adding the ½ cup of sugar and the salt to the whipped cream in step 4. For more-complex berry flavor, replace the 3 tablespoons of raw strawberry juice in step 2 with strawberry or raspberry liqueur. In addition to the diced berries, or if you're using frozen strawberries, you can serve the mousse with Lemon Whipped Cream (recipe follows).

2	pounds strawberries, hulled (6½ cups)
½	cup (3½ ounces) sugar
	Pinch salt
1¾	teaspoons unflavored gelatin
4	ounces cream cheese, cut into 8 pieces and softened
½	cup heavy cream, chilled

1. Cut enough strawberries into ¼-inch dice to measure 1 cup; refrigerate until ready to garnish. Pulse remaining strawberries in food processor in 2 batches until most pieces are ¼ to ½ inch thick (some larger pieces are fine), 6 to 10 pulses. Transfer strawberries to bowl and toss with ¼ cup sugar and salt. (Do not clean processor.) Cover bowl and let strawberries stand for 45 minutes, stirring occasionally.

2. Strain processed strawberries through fine-mesh strainer into bowl (you should have about ⅔ cup juice). Measure out 3 tablespoons juice into small bowl, sprinkle

gelatin over juice, and let sit until gelatin softens, about 5 minutes. Place remaining juice in small saucepan and cook over medium-high heat until reduced to 3 tablespoons, about 10 minutes. Remove pan from heat, add softened gelatin mixture, and stir until gelatin has dissolved. Add cream cheese and whisk until smooth. Transfer mixture to large bowl.

3. While juice is reducing, return strawberries to now-empty processor and process until smooth, 15 to 20 seconds. Strain puree through fine-mesh strainer into medium bowl, pressing on solids to remove seeds and pulp (you should have about 1⅔ cups puree). Discard any solids in strainer. Add strawberry puree to juice-gelatin mixture and whisk until incorporated.

4. Using stand mixer fitted with whisk, whip cream on medium-low speed until foamy, about 1 minute. Increase speed to high and whip until soft peaks form, 1 to 3 minutes. Gradually add remaining ¼ cup sugar and whip until stiff peaks form, 1 to 2 minutes. Whisk whipped cream into strawberry mixture until no white streaks remain. Portion into dessert dishes and chill for at least 4 hours or up to 48 hours. (If chilled longer than 6 hours, let mousse sit at room temperature for 15 minutes before serving.) Serve, garnishing with reserved diced strawberries.

PRACTICAL SCIENCE COCONUT WHIPPED CREAM

Yes, you can make dairy-free whipped "cream."

When we heard that it was possible to make dairy-free whipped "cream" using the thick layer of coconut fat from the top of a can of regular (not low-fat) coconut milk, our curiosity was piqued. Our test batches, although not as lofty as true whipped cream, had a pleasant mild coconut flavor and enough velvety billows to make us think that this unlikely ingredient could provide an acceptable dairy-free alternative. With a little more experimentation, we came up with two tips for success. First, the creamy part of coconut milk isn't always separated from the watery part; we found that refrigerating the can for a few hours helps form two distinct layers. Second, it's important to skim off only the very thick, fatty portion of the milk, or the cream won't whip properly.

To make I cup of whipped coconut cream, chill a mixing bowl and beaters in the freezer for at least 20 minutes. Using a spoon, skim the top layer of cream from a 10-ounce can of coconut milk (about ¾ cup of cream) and place it in the chilled bowl with 1½ teaspoons of sugar, ½ teaspoon of vanilla, and a pinch of salt. Beat on low speed until small bubbles form, about 30 seconds. Increase the speed to high and continue beating until the cream thickens and light peaks form, about 2 minutes. Serve immediately or cover and refrigerate for up to 4 hours.

If preferred, you can replace the lemon with lime.

½	cup heavy cream
2	tablespoons sugar
I	teaspoon finely grated lemon zest plus
	I tablespoon juice

Using stand mixer fitted with whisk, whip cream on medium-low speed until foamy, about 1 minute. Add sugar and lemon zest and juice, increase speed to high, and whip until soft peaks form, 1 to 3 minutes.

Triple-Chocolate Mousse Cake

✔ WHY THIS RECIPE WORKS

With overpoweringly rich flavor and a homogeneous texture, layered mousse cake can be more a spectacle than a tasty treat. By finessing one layer at a time, we aimed to create a tri-layered cake that was incrementally lighter in texture—and richness—with each layer.

START FLOURLESS For simplicity's sake, we decided to build the whole dessert, layer by layer, in the same springform pan. For a base layer that had the heft to support the upper two tiers, we chose flourless chocolate cake instead of the typical mousse. Our own flourless chocolate cake recipe was a bit too rich and dense to complement two layers of mousse, so we lightened it up. Folding egg whites into the batter helped lighten the cake without affecting its structural integrity. We made sure to cool the cake completely before adding the mousse layer; otherwise, the mousse would turn fluid and deflate.

TWEAK THE CHOCOLATE MOUSSE For the middle layer, we started with a traditional chocolate mousse, but the texture seemed too heavy when combined with the cake, so we removed the eggs and cut back on the chocolate a bit, resulting in a lighter, creamier layer. A combination of cocoa powder (bloomed in hot water to intensify its flavor) and bittersweet chocolate delivered a mousse with deep chocolate flavor.

TOP WITH WHITE CHOCOLATE MOUSSE And for the crowning layer, we made an easy white chocolate mousse by folding whipped cream into melted white chocolate. To prevent the soft mousse from oozing during slicing, we added a little gelatin to the mix.

TRIPLE-CHOCOLATE MOUSSE CAKE
SERVES 12 TO 16

This recipe requires a springform pan with sides that are at least 3 inches high. A cheese wire makes the neatest slices but if you don't have one, use a sharp knife and dip it in hot water before cutting each slice. It is imperative that the layers be made in sequential order. Cool the base completely before topping it with the middle layer. For best results, chill the mixer bowl before whipping the heavy cream.

BOTTOM LAYER

6	tablespoons unsalted butter, cut into 6 pieces
7	ounces bittersweet chocolate, chopped fine
¾	teaspoon instant espresso powder
4	large eggs, separated
1½	teaspoons vanilla extract
	Pinch cream of tartar
	Pinch salt
⅓	cup packed (2⅓ ounces) light brown sugar

MIDDLE LAYER

5	tablespoons hot water
2	tablespoons Dutch-processed cocoa powder
7	ounces bittersweet chocolate, chopped fine
1½	cups heavy cream, chilled
1	tablespoon granulated sugar
⅛	teaspoon salt

TOP LAYER

¾	teaspoon unflavored gelatin
1	tablespoon water
6	ounces white chocolate chips
1½	cups heavy cream, chilled
	Shaved chocolate (optional)
	Unsweetened cocoa powder (optional)

1. FOR THE BOTTOM LAYER: Adjust oven rack to middle position and heat oven to 325 degrees. Grease 9½-inch springform pan. Melt butter, chocolate, and espresso powder in large heatproof bowl set over saucepan filled with 1 inch of barely simmering water, stirring occasionally until smooth. Remove from heat and let mixture cool slightly, about 5 minutes. Whisk in egg yolks and vanilla; set aside.

2. Using stand mixer fitted with whisk, whip egg whites, cream of tartar, and salt on medium-low speed until foamy, about 1 minute. Add half of sugar and whip until combined, about 15 seconds. Add remaining sugar, increase speed to high, and whip until soft peaks form, about 1 minute longer, scraping bowl halfway through mixing. Using whisk, fold one-third of beaten egg whites into chocolate mixture by hand to lighten. Using rubber spatula, fold in remaining egg whites until no white streaks remain. Carefully transfer batter to prepared springform pan and smooth top with rubber spatula.

3. Bake cake until risen, firm around edges, and center has just set but is still soft (center of cake will spring back after pressing gently with your finger), 13 to 18 minutes, rotating pan halfway through baking. Transfer cake to wire rack and let cool completely, about 1 hour. (Cake will collapse as it cools.) Do not remove cake from pan.

4. FOR THE MIDDLE LAYER: Combine hot water and cocoa in small bowl; set aside. Melt chocolate in large heatproof bowl set over saucepan filled with 1 inch of barely simmering water, stirring occasionally until smooth. Remove from heat and let cool slightly, 2 to 5 minutes.

5. Using stand mixer fitted with whisk, whip cream, sugar, and salt on medium-low speed until foamy, about 1 minute. Increase speed to high and whip until soft peaks form, 1 to 3 minutes.

6. Whisk cocoa mixture into melted chocolate until smooth. Using whisk, fold one-third of whipped cream into chocolate mixture to lighten. Using rubber spatula, fold in remaining whipped cream until no white streaks remain. Spoon mousse into springform pan over cooled cake, smooth top with rubber spatula, and gently tap pan on counter to release air bubbles. Wipe inside edge of pan with damp cloth to remove any drips. Refrigerate cake for at least 15 minutes while preparing top layer.

7. FOR THE TOP LAYER: In small bowl, sprinkle gelatin over water and let sit for at least 5 minutes. Place white chocolate in medium heatproof bowl. Bring ½ cup cream to simmer in small saucepan over medium-high heat. Remove from heat, add gelatin mixture, and stir until fully dissolved. Pour cream mixture over white chocolate and let sit, covered, for 5 minutes. Whisk mixture gently until smooth. Let cool to room temperature, stirring occasionally (mixture will thicken slightly).

8. Using stand mixer fitted with whisk, whip remaining 1 cup cream on medium-low speed until foamy, about 1 minute. Increase speed to high and whip until soft peaks form, 1 to 3 minutes. Using whisk, fold one-third of whipped cream into white chocolate mixture to lighten. Using rubber spatula, fold remaining whipped cream into white chocolate mixture until no white streaks remain. Spoon white chocolate mousse into pan over middle layer. Smooth top with rubber spatula. Return cake to refrigerator and chill until set, at least 2½ hours. (Cake can be refrigerated for up to 1 day; leave at room temperature for up to 45 minutes before removing from pan.)

9. Garnish top of cake with shaved chocolate and/or dust with cocoa, if using. Run thin knife between cake and sides of pan; remove sides of pan. Run cleaned knife along outside of cake to smooth. Hold handles of cheese wire and pull wire taut. Using your thumbs to apply even pressure, slice down through the cake. Wipe wire clean with dry dish towel. Make second cut, perpendicular to first. Continue to make cuts around circumference. Serve.

Fettuccine Alfredo

✓ WHY THIS RECIPE WORKS

Alfredo sauce is simply cream reduced to a luxurious thick texture and then flavored with butter, the finest Parmesan cheese, salt, and pepper. We discovered that fresh pasta was essential as a base for the best fettuccine Alfredo recipe. It held onto the sauce perfectly. Turning our attention to the sauce, we found that a light hand was called for when adding two of the richer ingredients; just ¾ cup Parmigiano-Reggiano and 2 tablespoons butter were sufficient to add distinctive flavor without being overwhelming. Our real challenge was managing the heavy cream.

CREAM MANAGEMENT   Heavy cream in an Alfredo recipe is usually heated until it is reduced by half. We found that this made the sauce unpalatably thick, however. With testing, we found that if we reduced only a cup of the called-for cream, saving ½ cup and adding it, uncooked, at the end, we ended up with a supple, velvety sauce.

TIME AND TEMPERATURE MATTER   Well, a supple, velvety sauce if it was consumed within 60 seconds. The sauce soon congealed, becoming thick and gritty. Restaurants often solve this problem by adding flour to stabilize the sauce, improving its staying power. The downside is that this produces a thick, weighty sauce that is a continent removed from the delicate marriage of simple ingredients one would find in fettuccine Alfredo's native Rome. Our solution: We found that adding a little pasta water toward the end of cooking thinned the sauce just enough without compromising its body. We also heated the bowls; the warmth significantly prolonged the brief magic of this dish, delaying its transformation into bad restaurant food.

FETTUCCINE ALFREDO
SERVES 4 TO 6

Fresh pasta is the best choice for this dish. When boiling the pasta, undercook it slightly (even shy of al dente) because the pasta cooks an additional minute or two in the sauce. Note that this dish must be served immediately; it does not hold or reheat well. Heating the bowls before serving prolongues its brief life.

1½	cups heavy cream
2	tablespoons unsalted butter
	Salt
½	teaspoon pepper
1	(9-ounce) package fresh fettuccine
1½	ounces Parmesan cheese, grated (¾ cup)
⅛	teaspoon ground nutmeg

1. Bring 1 cup heavy cream and butter to simmer in large saucepan. Reduce heat to low and simmer gently until mixture measures ⅔ cup, 12 to 15 minutes. Off heat, stir in remaining ½ cup cream, ½ teaspoon salt, and pepper.

2. While cream reduces, bring 4 quarts water to boil in large pot. Add pasta and 1 tablespoon salt and cook, stirring often, until just shy of al dente. Reserve ¼ cup cooking water, then drain pasta.

3. Meanwhile, return cream mixture to simmer. Reduce heat to low and add drained pasta, Parmesan, and nutmeg to cream mixture. Cook pasta over low heat, tossing to combine, until cheese is melted, sauce coats pasta, and pasta is just al dente, 1 to 2 minutes. Add reserved cooking water as needed to adjust consistency; sauce may look thin but will gradually thicken as pasta is served. Serve immediately.

PRACTICAL SCIENCE
HOW TO MAKE CULTURED CREAMS

Crème fraîche and Mexican *crema* both start with cream.

The cultured creams crème fraîche and Mexican crema both begin with heavy cream and a natural culturing agent and end up thick, creamy, and lush. Luckily, both are easy to make at home.

For crème fraîche: Stir together 1 cup of pasteurized cream (avoid ultrapasteurized) and 2 tablespoons of buttermilk in a container. Cover and place in a warm location (75 to 80 degrees is ideal; lower temperatures will lengthen fermentation time) until the crème fraîche is thickened but still pourable, 12 to 24 hours. For crema, dissolve ⅛ teaspoon of salt in 2 teaspoons of lime juice and add to the finished crème fraîche. Refrigerate up to a month.

CHAPTER 17

Butter

This stick of (mostly) fat is the foundation for everything from flaky, layered croissants to a browned, nutty sauce for fish.

HOW THE SCIENCE WORKS

Butter is made from heavy cream by churning it into a solid and then removing the leftover buttermilk. Like cream (page 135), butter is an emulsion, a combination of two liquids that would not ordinarily mix, like oil and water. Cream is an oil-in-water emulsion, meaning tiny droplets of fat are ensconced in water, which is why it is a liquid rather than a solid. Butter, however, is the other way around. When cream is churned, the emulsion flips to become a water-in-oil emulsion, concentrating the fat and separating out the excess water. This—along with the fact that butterfat is largely saturated fat, which is more stable and given to solidify than unsaturated fat—is why butter is a solid.

There are a number of options when it comes to buying butter: regular or premium, cultured or uncultured, salted or unsalted. By law, butter manufactured in the United States contains at least 80 percent fat. The remainder is made up of water (13 to 19 percent), milk solids (namely, protein and lactose), and salt, which may be added as a preservative and flavoring. Chemically, butterfat is made of molecules called triglycerides that are composed of one molecule of glycerol attached to three molecules of fatty acids. Many of the fatty acids in butterfat are saturated, which provides the fat with a crystalline structure that melts slightly above room temperature. Butterfat also contains up to 3 percent natural emulsifiers such as lecithin, and fat-soluble vitamin A. Premium, European-style butter has a higher fat content—at least 82 percent, and up to 86 percent. Higher-fat butter has a firmer consistency and is slower to melt.

The big difference between regular butter and many European-style premium butters is culturing. Cultured butter is made from cream that has been fermented before churning. During this process, lactic acid–forming bacteria convert the lactose in cream to lactic acid, giving the cream, and then the cultured butter, a distinct sour, tangy flavor. The majority of butter manufactured in the United States, however, is regular uncultured sweet cream butter.

Finally: Butter may be manufactured with or without salt. The salt acts as a preservative and adds flavor. Salted butter contains anywhere from 1.6 to 2.5 percent added salt. The level of salt is determined by the manufacturer and can vary among brands. In addition, salted butter almost always contains more water. For these reasons, when cooking—and especially when baking—we prefer to use unsalted butter.

Butter can be difficult to work with in the kitchen because it changes so rapidly with temperature, beginning to soften between 60 and 68 degrees, beginning to melt around 84 degrees, and becoming completely melted at about 94 degrees. It grows quite firm—too firm for many applications—when refrigerated (at around 35 degrees). Getting butter's texture right can be a delicate balance. It must be chilled, but not too firm or soft to achieve the best flakiness and volume for laminated pastries—like our Croissants (page 148). The best temperature for creaming butter, which adds air pockets for optimal lift to our French Butter Cookies (page 146) and Cold-Oven Pound Cake (page 147), is between 65 and 68 degrees. Melting butter, which allows the water in the butter to interact with flour to form gluten, is key in our No-Knead Brioche (page 150). Butter that is browned develops an appealing nutty flavor and deep golden color because the protein and lactose undergo the Maillard reaction producing both color and flavor—a process we use to good effect for our Fish Meunière (page 151).

In the U.S., butter must be at least 80 percent fat.

TEST KITCHEN EXPERIMENT

For years we've advocated for using unsalted butter in recipes (especially when it comes to baking recipes, where there's no opportunity to taste and correct for seasoning) in order to retain complete control over seasoning. But many cooks report that when it comes to browning butter, salted is the better choice because it produces more total browned solids (and thus more flavor) than unsalted. We decided to put this theory to the test with an experiment.

EXPERIMENT

We browned 4 tablespoons of salted butter in one skillet and the same amount of unsalted butter in another, drained away the fat, and measured the amount of browned solids that remained. We repeated the test, adding the equivalent amount of salt found in our salted butter to the unsalted sample before browning. Again, we separated the fat and measured the amount of the nonfat solids. We also tasted both sets of samples.

RESULTS

When we compared the first set of samples, the salted butter indeed appeared to yield more than twice the volume of browned particles as the unsalted butter. It was impressive visually, but when we tasted them we found that the browned salted butter was no deeper or richer in flavor than the unsalted. (When butter is browned, the milk solids develop color during cooking and provide rich, nutty flavor.) In the second set of samples, where we added salt to unsalted butter, both yielded the same amount of browned solids. Again, tasters found no difference in flavor.

TAKEAWAY

One difference between salted and unsalted butter, besides the salt content, is the water content: Unsalted butter contains less water than salted butter. But because we evaporate the water out of butter during the browning process, this difference has no impact on the final product. Our second set of samples confirmed our suspicion that salted butter only appears to have more browned solids, when in reality the added bulk is merely salt. A look at numbers from the USDA corroborates our findings: salted and unsalted butter contain the exact same percentages of both protein (.85 percent) and sugar (.06 percent), the building

blocks of the Maillard browning process that produces the browned solids.

So while it's certainly possible to brown salted butter, there will be no browned–milk solid flavor benefit from it. In addition, we found it more difficult to avoid burning salted butter because some of the solids tended to float on the surface of the fat, obscuring the bottom of the skillet where browning was faster. The best bet? Stick with using unsalted butter.

BROWNING BUTTER: SALTED VS. UNSALTED

Salted and unsalted butter can both be browned, but there is no browned–milk solid benefit from browning salted butter—despite the fact that it may look browner.

SALTED BUTTER
Browned salted butter looks more "browned," but that is just the added bulk of the salt, not flavorful proteins and sugars.

UNSALTED BUTTER
Browned unsalted butter has the same amount of flavorful proteins and sugars, and is easier to brown.

FOCUS ON: BUTTER

As the saying goes, "Everything is better with butter." But what makes butter so great? It tastes delicious, of course. (One of the most important compounds in butter flavor is called diacetyl, which has an intense buttery aroma.) But it's also extremely versatile. Here, we break butter down into its individual elements, and take a look at five of the major, and majorly different, ways it's used in the kitchen.

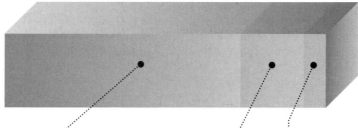

FAT

By law, butter manufactured in the U.S. must have at least 80 percent fat. (Premium European butters contain at least 82 percent and up to 86 percent fat.) This fat is made of molecules called triglycerides that are composed of one molecule of glycerol attached to three molecules of fatty acids.

WATER

Butter has between 13 and 19 percent water. Because butter is a water-in-oil emulsion, the water is suspended in the fat, creating a solid mass. A small amount of protein coats the water droplets and keeps them from coalescing until the butter is completely melted.

MILK SOLIDS

About 1 percent of butter consists of milk solids, which are everything except fat and water and include proteins, carbohydrates, vitamins, and minerals.

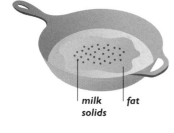

BROWNED BUTTER (245°)

Butter is browned by melting it on a stovetop until it turns, not surprisingly, brown. When this happens, the water evaporates, and the butter develops a nutty flavor and dark tan color because the protein and lactose undergo the Maillard reaction, producing both color and flavor.

CLARIFIED BUTTER (200-212°)

Butter used in restaurant kitchens is often clarified. This involves heating the butter until all the water has evaporated, and skimming off the milk solids containing protein and lactose, which cause the butter to brown when heated. Clarified butter is less likely to burn or smoke when used for searing or sautéing.

MELTED BUTTER (94°)

Butter softens between 60 and 68 degrees and melts starting at 84 degrees and liquefies at 94 degrees. The water in liquefied butter is helpful in certain applications—for example, mixing with flour to create chewy, not crunchy, cookies. Melting frees up water to hydrate wheat flour and produce stronger gluten, hence more chew in cookies or more structure in bread.

SOFTENED BUTTER (60-68°)

Creamed Butter

When you cream softened butter and sugar, the grains of sugar are forced through the fat, leaving millions of microscopic air bubbles in their wake. In the heat of the oven these bubbles expand, contributing to the lightness of the finished product. Room-temperature butter is best for aeration (about 67 degrees). If the butter is too firm and cold, air cannot be incorporated into the fat; if it's too soft and warm, the bubbles collapse.

COLD BUTTER (40°)

Laminated Dough

Croissants are made with lamination. Cold butter is sandwiched between dough, which is then folded into thirds and rolled out. This process is repeated many times, creating alternating layers of dough and fat, layers that increase exponentially with each set of folds. In the oven, the butter melts and steam fills the thin spaces left behind, creating literally hundreds of flaky layers.

French Butter Cookies

✔ WHY THIS RECIPE WORKS

The French butter cookies called sablés *offer sophistication and style from just simple pantry ingredients. That is, if you can capture their elusive sandy texture. It took some detective work to develop a French butter cookie recipe with a properly sandy texture. Cutting back on the butter helped, but the breakthrough was using a traditional French ingredient—hard-cooked egg yolk—which eliminated excess moisture and perfected the texture of the cookies.*

CUT THE BUTTER The key to sandy-textured cookies is to reduce the moisture in the dough. When cookie dough is prepared with a small amount of liquid, only a portion of the sugar will dissolve, leaving behind intact granules that deliver sandy consistency. (When the cookies are baked, some of the sugar will liquefy, but when they cool, the sugar will recrystallize, restoring sandiness.) Butter is 13 to 19 percent water, and a good candidate for reduction, because our starter recipe contained 12 tablespoons. Cookie dough needs enough butterfat to coat the flour and provide tenderness, though, so we could only cut back by 2 tablespoons.

USE A COOKED EGG YOLK We tried eliminating the egg entirely, to reduce the moisture, but that just yielded somewhat tough, pallid cookies. When we came across a sablé recipe that called for a hard-cooked egg yolk, we were tempted to ignore this unlikely ingredient. What could it possibly do, aside from fleck our cookies with unwelcome bits of yolk? But when we actually gave the cooked yolk a try, we were surprised by the results. We prepared one batch of sablé cookies with a raw yolk and compared it with another batch made with a hard-cooked yolk that had been pressed through a fine-mesh strainer. The results prepared with the hard-cooked egg yolk were markedly sandier than those prepared with the raw yolk. Even better, we could detect no bits of cooked yolk, just rich flavor. Why? An egg yolk contains about 50 percent water by weight (see page 129). When boiled, the proteins in the yolk form a solid matrix that locks in the water, making it unavailable to hydrate the flour. The sandiness in sablé cookies comes in part from undissolved sugar crystals. By reducing the amount of water available to dissolve the sugar, the cooked yolk promotes a crystalline texture in the finished cookies. By contrast, the liquid in the raw egg yolk dissolved the sugar, making the texture of the cookies smoother.

PRACTICAL SCIENCE
REHABILITATING MELTED BUTTER

Yes, you can bring back accidentally oversoftened butter.

The fat in butter is partially crystalline and highly sensitive to temperature changes. When butter is properly softened to 60 or 68 degrees, the tiny crystals can effectively surround and stabilize the air bubbles that are generated during creaming. When heated to the melting point, however, these crystals are destroyed. They can be reestablished but only if the butter is rapidly chilled. (Returning it to the refrigerator will cool it too slowly and fail to reestablish the tiny crystals.) To quickly cool down partially melted butter, we mixed in a few ice cubes. After less than a minute of stirring, the butter had cooled to a softened stage—right below 70 degrees—so we extracted the ice and prepared a couple of recipes. (The amount of icy water that leaked into the butter was negligible.)

Sugar cookies made with our rehabilitated butter were nearly identical to those made with properly softened butter, and buttercream frosting was also acceptable, if slightly softer than a control batch.

FRENCH BUTTER COOKIES (SABLÉS)
MAKES ABOUT 40 COOKIES

Turbinado sugar is commonly sold as Sugar in the Raw. Demerara sugar, sanding sugar, or another coarse sugar can be substituted. Make sure the cookie dough is well chilled and firm so that it can be uniformly sliced.

1	large egg
10	tablespoons unsalted butter, softened
1/3	cup plus 1 tablespoon (2¾ ounces) granulated sugar
1/4	teaspoon salt
1	teaspoon vanilla extract
1½	cups (7½ ounces) all-purpose flour
1	large egg white, lightly beaten with 1 teaspoon water
4	teaspoons turbinado sugar

1. Place egg in small saucepan, cover with water by 1 inch, and bring to boil over high heat. Remove pan from heat, cover, and let sit for 10 minutes. Meanwhile, fill small bowl with ice water. Using slotted spoon, transfer egg to ice water and let stand for 5 minutes. Crack egg and peel shell. Separate yolk from white; discard white. Press yolk through fine-mesh strainer into small bowl.

2. Using stand mixer fitted with paddle, beat butter, granulated sugar, salt, and cooked egg yolk on medium speed until light and fluffy, about 4 minutes, scraping down bowl as needed. Reduce speed to low, add vanilla, and mix until incorporated. Stop mixer; add flour and mix on low speed until just combined, about 30 seconds. Using rubber spatula, press dough into cohesive mass.

3. Divide dough in half. Shape each piece into log about 6 inches long and 1¾ inches in diameter. Wrap each log in parchment paper and twist ends to seal. Chill dough until firm, about 45 minutes in freezer or 2 hours in refrigerator.

4. Adjust oven racks to upper-middle and lower-middle positions and heat oven to 350 degrees. Line 2 baking sheets with parchment. Using chef's knife, slice dough into ¼-inch-thick rounds, rotating dough so that it won't become misshapen from weight of knife. Space cookies 1 inch apart on prepared baking sheets. Using pastry brush, gently brush cookies with egg white mixture and sprinkle evenly with turbinado sugar.

5. Bake until centers of cookies are pale golden brown with edges slightly darker than centers, about 15 minutes, switching and rotating sheets halfway through baking. Let cookies cool on sheets for 5 minutes; transfer cookies to wire rack and let cool to room temperature.

Cold-Oven Pound Cake

✅ WHY THIS RECIPE WORKS

This thrifty pound cake, which was designed to save on gas by not requiring a preheated oven, is an especially tall cake with a crisp crust. To create a light crumb, we used leaner whole milk instead of the heavy cream called for in most recipes. Swapping out the all-purpose flour for cake flour yielded an even finer, more delicate crumb for our pound cake. We also used baking powder, which produced carbon dioxide bubbles that gave our cake its rise. But the most important part? Putting the pound cake into a cold oven.

CREAM THE BUTTER Creaming butter, or mixing softened butter with sugar, is an incredibly important step when it comes to many cakes—and pound cakes, especially. Creaming the butter first made the butter malleable; the tiny sugar crystals then acted like extra beaters, incorporating more air into the butter. These pockets of air expanded when the cake was baked, helping to give it lift.

USE A COLD OVEN Cold-oven pound cake is a traditional recipe, and we didn't want to mess with that. But, curiosity led us to try baking our Cold-Oven Pound Cake in a preheated oven. The cake baked more quickly, but it was squat and lacked the crisp, thick crust we'd come to expect. Why? The cake was squat because putting it directly into a heated oven melted the butter so quickly that the tiny air bubbles contained within the whipped butter were destroyed before the leavener could inflate them. (Without these preformed air bubbles, leavener does little good, because its purpose is to produce gas that fills and expands the tiny air bubbles in the whipped butter.) Starting in a cool oven gave the baking powder time to begin releasing gas into the air bubbles before they collapsed. This had to start happening early in the process, before the gluten and starch began to form a strong enough structure to retain the expanded bubbles. And the crust on our Cold-Oven Pound Cake? It's in part due simply to the longer baking and therefore drying time. But it is also formed by moisture in the oven reacting with starch in the batter. A hot oven is drier than a cold oven (heat evaporates moisture), so there wasn't enough moisture in the preheated oven to form a nice, thick crust.

COLD-OVEN POUND CAKE
SERVES 12

You'll need a 16-cup tube pan for this recipe; if not using a non-stick pan, make sure to thoroughly grease a traditional pan. In step 2, don't worry if the batter looks slightly separated.

3	cups (12 ounces) cake flour
1	teaspoon salt
½	teaspoon baking powder
1	cup whole milk
2	teaspoons vanilla extract
20	tablespoons (2½ sticks) unsalted butter, softened
2½	cups (17½ ounces) sugar
6	large eggs

1. Adjust oven rack to lower-middle position. Grease and flour 16-cup tube pan. Combine flour, salt, and baking powder in bowl. Whisk milk and vanilla in measuring cup.

2. Using stand mixer fitted with paddle, beat butter and sugar on medium-high speed until light and fluffy, about 2 minutes. Beat in eggs, one at a time, until combined. Reduce speed to low and add flour mixture in 3 additions, alternating with milk mixture in 2 additions, scraping down bowl as needed. Mix on low until smooth, about 30 seconds. Give batter final stir by hand.

3. Pour batter into prepared pan and smooth top. Place cake in cold oven. Adjust oven temperature to 325 degrees and bake, without opening oven door, until cake is golden brown and skewer inserted in center comes out clean, 1 hour 5 minutes to 1 hour 20 minutes.

4. Let cake cool in pan on wire rack for 15 minutes. Remove cake from pan and let cool completely on rack about 2 hours. Serve. (Cake can be stored at room temperature for up to 2 days.)

Croissants

✔ WHY THIS RECIPE WORKS

We can think of two reasons why almost nobody makes croissants. First, most folks buy them from a bakery, or even a coffee shop or supermarket. Second, the process is long and daunting. It pairs the challenge of preparing a laminated pastry (one composed of many layers of fat) with the potential unpredictability of a yeasted item. We can also think of two reasons why making your own croissants is absolutely worth the effort. For starters, most commercial croissants are squat, dense, or just plain bland. Plus, there's nothing as satisfying as pulling off this feat yourself. We put this recipe to the test, and discovered that the type of flour and the type of butter were incredibly important for success.

TURN THRICE The layered structure that characterizes croissants is formed through a process called lamination: A relatively lean yeasted dough is wrapped around a block of butter, and then the package is rolled out and folded repeatedly to form paper-thin layers of dough separated by even thinner layers of butter. Due to increasing gluten formation, the dough becomes more difficult to roll with every turn (or each set of folds), so we were relieved to find that three turns was sufficient to yield a light pastry made up of hundreds of delicate layers.

PICK HIGH-PROTEIN FLOUR Rolling and folding the dough three times was still hard. Knowing that the protein count of the flour was directly affecting the gluten development, we made three new batches with different types of flour: one with moderate protein (10.5 percent) all-purpose flour; another with higher-protein (11.7 percent) all-purpose flour; and a final sample with high-protein (14 percent) bread flour. As expected, the higher the protein content, the more gluten development, and the more difficult to roll out. But the bread-flour croissants were great: tall, crisp, and filled with airy spirals of buttery pastry.

It turns out that gluten doesn't just make a dough more elastic; it also makes it more resistant to tearing during rolling, rising, and baking (when it expands), and

strong enough to maintain the thin sheets necessary for distinct layering. But since our hands were blistered from rolling out this extra-sturdy dough, we decided to compromise with the higher-protein all-purpose flour.

USE EUROPEAN-STYLE BUTTER Many croissant recipes call for European butter, which has a fat content starting around 82 percent, rather than sweet cream butter with 80 percent. Those that do call for sweet cream butter instruct to roll it in flour. The differences between the options were remarkable. When we tried shaping the unfloured standard butter, it broke into pieces. Flouring the standard butter helped, but it didn't compare with croissants made with European-style butter. This higher-fat dough not only proved easier to work with, but also boasted superior layering and ultrarich flavor. This is because butter with less fat contains more water. Butter with 81 percent fat, for example, contains about 18 percent water, while butter with 83 percent fat contains about 16 percent. This variance may sound small, but it was a difference significant enough that the extra water in the regular-butter dough was gluing the layers together, leading to a dense crumb. It also explained the purpose of adding flour to the standard butter: to soak up the extra moisture. Higher-fat butter remains solid over a wider temperature range, meaning that it's more pliable when cold and also holds its shape better as it warms up. This is advantageous since the butter for laminated dough must be firm to function as a barrier between distinct layers of dough and, therefore, must remain solid as the dough is handled.

FREEZE IT Finally, we froze the dough before rolling. This firmed up the dough without appreciably altering the texture of the butter (which we didn't want too cold, or too soft).

CROISSANTS
MAKES 22

These croissants take at least 10 hours to make from start to finish, but the process can be spread over two days. European-style cultured butters have a higher butterfat content, which makes it easier to fold them into the dough. Any brand of all-purpose flour will produce acceptable croissants, but we recommend using King Arthur All-Purpose Flour, which has a slightly higher protein content. Do not attempt to make these croissants in a room that is warmer than 80 degrees. If at any time during rolling the dough retracts, dust it lightly with flour, fold it loosely, cover it, and return it to the freezer to rest for 10 to 15 minutes.

3 tablespoons unsalted butter plus 24 tablespoons (3 sticks) unsalted European-style butter, very cold
1 ¾ cups whole milk
4 teaspoons instant or rapid-rise yeast
4 ¼ cups (21 ¼ ounces) all-purpose flour
¼ cup (1 ¾ ounces) sugar
Salt
1 large egg
1 teaspoon cold water

1. Melt 3 tablespoons butter in medium saucepan over low heat. Remove from heat and immediately stir in milk (temperature should be lower than 90 degrees). Whisk in yeast; transfer milk mixture to bowl of stand mixer. Add flour, sugar, and 2 teaspoons salt. Using dough hook, knead on low speed until cohesive dough forms, 2 to 3 minutes. Increase speed to medium-low and knead for 1 minute. Remove bowl from mixer, remove dough hook, and cover bowl with plastic wrap. Let dough rest at room temperature for 30 minutes.

2. Transfer dough to parchment paper–lined rimmed baking sheet and shape into 10 by 7-inch rectangle about 1 inch thick. Wrap tightly with plastic and refrigerate for 2 hours.

3. FOR THE BUTTER BLOCK: While dough chills, fold 24-inch length of parchment in half to create 12-inch rectangle. Fold over 3 open sides of rectangle to form 8-inch square with enclosed sides. Crease folds firmly. Place 24 tablespoons cold butter directly on counter and beat with rolling pin for about 60 seconds until butter is just pliable, but not warm, folding butter in on itself using bench scraper. Beat into rough 6-inch square. Unfold parchment envelope. Using bench scraper, transfer butter to center of parchment square, refolding at creases to enclose. Turn packet over so that flaps are underneath and gently roll butter packet until butter fills parchment square, taking care to achieve even thickness. Refrigerate for at least 45 minutes.

4. TO LAMINATE THE DOUGH: Transfer dough to freezer. After 30 minutes, transfer dough to lightly floured counter and roll into 17 by 8-inch rectangle with long side of rectangle parallel to edge of counter. Unwrap butter and place in center of dough so that butter and dough are flush at top and bottom. Fold 2 sides of dough over butter square so they meet in center. Press seam together with your fingertips. With rolling pin, press firmly on each open end of packet. Roll out dough, perpendicular to edge of counter, to rectangle 24 inches long and 8 inches wide.

Bring bottom third of dough up, then fold upper third over it, folding like business letter into 8-inch square. Turn dough 90 degrees counterclockwise. Roll out dough again, perpendicular to edge of counter, into 24 by 8-inch rectangle and fold into thirds. Place dough on baking sheet, wrap tightly with plastic, and return to freezer for 30 minutes.

5. Transfer dough to lightly floured counter so that top flap of dough is facing right. Roll once more, perpendicular to edge of counter, into 24 by 8-inch rectangle and fold into thirds. Place dough on baking sheet, wrap tightly with plastic, and refrigerate for 2 hours.

6. Transfer dough to freezer. After 30 minutes, transfer to lightly floured counter and roll into 18 by 16-inch rectangle with long side of rectangle parallel to edge of counter. Fold upper half of dough over lower half. Using ruler, mark dough at 3-inch intervals along bottom edge with bench scraper (you should have 5 marks). Move ruler to top of dough, measure in 1½ inches from left, then use this mark to measure out 3-inch intervals (you should have 6 marks). Starting at lower left corner, use pizza wheel or knife to cut dough into triangles from mark to mark. You will have 12 single triangles and 5 double triangles; discard scraps. Unfold double triangles and cut into 10 single triangles (making 22 equal-size triangles in total). If dough begins to soften, return to freezer for 10 minutes.

7. TO SHAPE THE CROISSANTS: Position 1 triangle on counter. (Keep remaining triangles covered with plastic while shaping.) Cut ½ inch slit in center of short end of triangle. Grasp triangle by 2 corners on either side of slit, and stretch gently, then grasp bottom point and stretch. Place triangle on counter so point is facing toward you. Fold both sides of slit down. Positioning your palms on folds, roll partway toward point. Gently grasp point again and stretch. To finish, continue to roll, tucking point underneath. Curve ends gently toward one another to create crescent shape. Repeat with remaining triangles.

8. Place 12 croissants on 2 parchment-lined baking sheets (6 croissants per sheet), leaving at least 2½ inches between croissants. Lightly wrap baking sheets with plastic, leaving room for croissants to expand. Let stand at room temperature until nearly doubled in size, 2½ to 3 hours. (Shaped croissants can be refrigerated on sheets for up to 18 hours. Remove from refrigerator to rise and add at least 30 minutes to rising time.)

9. After croissants have been rising for 2 hours, adjust oven racks to upper-middle and lower-middle positions and heat oven to 425 degrees. In small bowl, whisk together

egg, water, and pinch salt. Brush croissants with egg wash using pastry brush. Place croissants in oven and reduce temperature to 400 degrees. Bake for 12 minutes, then switch and rotate baking sheets. Continue to bake until deep golden brown, 8 to 12 minutes longer. Transfer croissants to wire rack and let cool until just warm, about 15 minutes. Serve warm or at room temperature.

TO MAKE AHEAD: After shaping, place croissants 1 inch apart on parchment-lined baking sheet. Wrap with plastic wrap and freeze until solid, about 2 hours. Transfer frozen croissants from baking sheet to zipper-lock bag and return to freezer for up to 2 months. Bake frozen croissants as directed from step 8, increasing rising time by 1 to 2 hours.

No-Knead Brioche

✓ WHY THIS RECIPE WORKS

Well-made brioche is something of a miracle: Despite being laden with butter and eggs, it manages to avoid the density of a pound cake and turn out incredibly light and airy. Yet this gossamer-wing texture still provides brioche with enough structure to serve as a base for a sandwich, a slice of toast slathered with jam, or even the foundation for bread pudding. But achieving these results is a balancing act, and a tricky one at that. Most butter-enriched doughs (like sandwich bread or dinner rolls) contain between 10 and 20 percent butter. The average brioche recipe brings the ratio up to 50 percent or more. Because fat lubricates the wheat proteins in the flour, any amount at all will inhibit their ability to form gluten, the network of cross-linked proteins that gives bread its structure. The more fat the greater interference. This can make brioche incredibly tender—or it can cause the dough to separate into a greasy mess. To make a foolproof, tender loaf, we used melted butter—and no kneading.

MELT BUTTER; DO NOT KNEAD Traditionally, making a rich dough like brioche means kneading all of the ingredients—except butter—to develop gluten. Butter (softened to 68 degrees) is added tablespoon by tablespoon only after the mixture begins to develop into dough. This is a long and painstaking process. It's an important one, too: If the butter isn't added slowly, the dough can break into a greasy mess. When we decided to ditch tradition and use a "no-knead" technique, we realized that this would also solve our tricky butter problem. In a no-knead approach, the dough (which must be very wet) sits for a long time,

stitching itself together to form gluten—all without the help of a mixer. With kneading out of the equation, we were able to melt the butter and add it all at once—a faster and far less demanding approach.

COLD REST Even with the no-knead method, at first our brioche loaves were turning out a bit too cottony and open—a sure sign that they needed more gluten. First, we decided to use the higher-protein bread flour. And then we decided to let them rest overnight in the fridge. This would not only aid in gluten development, but would add more flavor, too, since it would give the starches in the dough more time to ferment. Gluten development and fermentation are slowed but not stopped by cold temperatures, so the fridge is an excellent place for the dough's second rise.

DIVIDE AND CONQUER To build structure and ensure an even, fine crumb in the finished loaf, we divided the dough and shaped it into tight balls before placing them in the pans. Placed side by side in the pan, the two balls merged during rising and baking to form a single loaf. Even this little bit of extra manipulation made the crumb a bit finer and more uniform.

NO-KNEAD BRIOCHE
MAKES 2 LOAVES

High-protein King Arthur Bread Flour works best with this recipe, though other bread flours will suffice. If you don't have a baking stone, bake the bread on a preheated rimmed baking sheet.

3¼	cups (17¾ ounces) bread flour
2¼	teaspoons instant or rapid-rise yeast
1½	teaspoons salt
7	large eggs (1 lightly beaten with pinch salt)
½	cup water, room temperature
⅓	cup (2⅓ ounces) sugar
16	tablespoons unsalted butter, melted and cooled slightly

1. Whisk flour, yeast, and salt together in large bowl. Whisk 6 eggs, water, and sugar together in medium bowl until sugar has dissolved. Whisk in butter until smooth. Add egg mixture to flour mixture and stir with wooden spoon until uniform mass forms and no dry flour remains, about 1 minute. Cover bowl with plastic wrap and let stand for 10 minutes.

2. Holding edge of dough with your fingertips, fold dough over itself by gently lifting and folding edge of dough toward middle. Turn bowl 45 degrees; fold again. Turn bowl and fold dough 6 more times (for total of 8 folds). Cover with plastic and let rise for 30 minutes. Repeat folding and rising every 30 minutes, 3 more times. After fourth set of folds, cover bowl tightly with plastic and refrigerate for at least 16 hours or up to 48 hours.

3. Transfer dough to well-floured counter and divide into 4 pieces. Working with 1 piece of dough at a time, pat dough into 4-inch disk. Working around circumference of dough, fold edges of dough toward center until ball forms. Flip dough over and, without applying pressure, move your hand in small circular motions to form dough into smooth, taut round. (If dough sticks to your hands, lightly dust top of dough with flour.) Repeat with remaining dough pieces. Cover dough rounds loosely with plastic and let rest for 5 minutes.

4. Grease two 8½ by 4½-inch loaf pans. After 5 minutes, flip each dough ball so seam side is facing up, pat into 4-inch disk, and repeat rounding step. Place 2 rounds, seam side down, side by side in prepared pans and press gently into corners. Cover loaves loosely with plastic and let rise at room temperature until almost doubled in size (dough should rise to about ½ inch below top edge of pan), 1½ to 2 hours. Thirty minutes before baking, adjust oven rack to middle position, place baking stone on rack, and heat oven to 350 degrees.

PRACTICAL SCIENCE
REPLACING UNSALTED BUTTER WITH SALTED

Replacing unsalted butter with salted butter will require some recipe adjustment.

In the test kitchen, we always develop recipes with unsalted butter, as we like to control the amount of salt added ourselves.

If you want to use salted butter in savory recipes that call for unsalted, you will need to reduce the total amount of salt in the recipe. A stick of salted butter contains the equivalent of ⅓ to ½ teaspoon of table salt, so adjust recipes accordingly.

In baking, we strongly recommend using unsalted butter. Given its sodium content, salted butter will make many recipes inedible. For instance, our favorite butter frosting calls for just a pinch of salt, and our sugar cookies need only ¼ teaspoon salt. Each recipe calls for two sticks of butter, so if you were to use salted butter (rather than unsalted), each recipe would contain about ¾ teaspoon of salt—an amount easily detected.

---

5. Remove plastic and brush loaves gently with remaining 1 egg beaten with salt. Set loaf pans on stone and bake until golden brown and loaves register 190 degrees, 35 to 45 minutes, rotating pans halfway through baking. Let loaves cool in pans on wire rack for 5 minutes. Remove loaves from pan and let cool completely on wire rack before slicing and serving, about 2 hours.

Fish Meunière with Browned Butter and Lemon

✔ WHY THIS RECIPE WORKS

Fish meunière is a deceptively easy French restaurant dish that ought to serve as a model recipe for home cooking. Ideally, fillets are dredged lightly in flour (no need for eggs or bread crumbs) and cooked on the stovetop until a golden crust forms, leaving the inside moist and flavorful. A brown butter sauce seasoned with lemon is then poured over the fish. What could be simpler, or more delicious, or better suited to a Tuesday night dinner? That's what we thought, too, before we cooked a few test batches to get a handle on the technique. We trudged through many pale, soggy fillets in pools of greasy sauce until we figured out some answers, including dredging the fillets after seasoning and letting them sit, using a nonstick skillet with both oil and butter, and using a stainless-steel skillet for the browned butter.

CHOOSE THICK FILLETS After cooking 20 pounds of different types of white fish (see page 81), we discovered that variety, here, doesn't matter that much (tasters approved of them all). What did matter was the thickness of the fillet and its freshness. If the fillet was thinner than ⅜ inch it was nearly impossible to brown it without overcooking the inside. Fillets that were ⅜ inch thick or slightly more were perfect. They weighed 5 to 6 ounces each, and their length fit easily into a large skillet.

DREDGE IT We seasoned the fillets with salt and pepper and let them sit for a few minutes before dredging them in flour. The salt extracted water from the fish, not so much as to make it wet but just enough to give it a thin coating of moisture that helped to ensure a perfectly even coating of flour when dredged. And the flour helped the fish brown faster.

BROWN THE BUTTER Traditionally, the sauce served with meunière is *beurre noisette*, or browned butter, with the addition of lemon and parsley. Crucial to the flavor of the sauce—which adds a rich nuttiness to the fish—is proper browning of the milk solids in the butter, a task that is not easily accomplished in a nonstick skillet. The problem is that the dark surface of the pan makes it nearly impossible to judge the color of the butter. The solution was simple: We browned the butter in a medium-size stainless-steel skillet; its shiny bottom made it easy to monitor the color.

FISH MEUNIÈRE WITH BROWNED BUTTER AND LEMON
SERVES 4 TO 6

Try to purchase fillets that are of similar size, and avoid those that weigh less than 5 ounces because they will cook too quickly. A non-stick skillet ensures that the fillets will release from the pan, but for the sauce a traditional skillet is preferable because its light-colored surface will allow you to monitor the color of the butter as it browns.

FISH

½	cup all-purpose flour
4	(5- to 6-ounce) boneless, skinless sole or flounder fillets, ⅜ inch thick
	Salt and pepper
2	tablespoons vegetable oil
2	tablespoons unsalted butter, cut into 2 pieces

BROWNED BUTTER

4	tablespoons unsalted butter, cut into 4 pieces
I	tablespoon chopped fresh parsley
I½	tablespoons lemon juice, plus lemon slices for serving
	Salt

I. FOR THE FISH: Adjust oven rack to lower-middle position, set 4 heatproof plates on rack, and heat oven to 200 degrees. Place flour in shallow dish. Pat sole dry with paper towels, season both sides generously with salt and pepper, and let stand until fillets are glistening with moisture, about 5 minutes. Coat both sides of fillets with flour, shake off excess, and place in single layer on baking sheet.

2. Heat 1 tablespoon oil in 12-inch nonstick skillet over high heat until shimmering, then add 1 tablespoon butter and swirl to coat pan bottom. Carefully place 2 fillets, skinned side up, in skillet. Immediately reduce heat to medium-high and cook, without moving fish, until edges of fillets are opaque and bottom is golden brown, about 3 minutes. Using 2 spatulas, gently flip fillets and cook on second side until fish flakes apart when gently prodded with paring knife, about 2 minutes longer. Transfer each fillet to heated dinner plate, keeping skinned side down, and return plates to oven. Wipe out skillet and repeat with remaining 1 tablespoon oil, remaining 1 tablespoon butter, and remaining 2 fillets.

3. FOR THE BROWNED BUTTER: Heat butter in 10-inch skillet over medium-high heat until butter melts, 1 to 1½ minutes. Continue to cook, swirling pan constantly, until butter is golden brown and has nutty aroma, 1 to 1½ minutes. Remove skillet from heat.

4. Remove plates from oven and sprinkle fillets with parsley. Add lemon juice to browned butter and season with salt to taste. Spoon sauce over fish and serve immediately with lemon slices.

PRACTICAL SCIENCE GHEE

Ghee may be used as a slightly richer, more buttery substitute in any recipe that calls for clarified butter.

The clarified butter known as ghee is indispensable in Indian cooking, but it's also a handy ingredient to have around for other uses. Ghee is made by slowly simmering butter until all of its moisture has evaporated and its milk solids begin to brown. These solids are then strained out, and the remaining pure butter-fat has a nutty flavor and aroma and an ultrahigh smoke point (485 degrees). It can be used as a slightly richer, more buttery substitute in any recipe that calls for clarified butter (such as baklava) and can even be used for high-heat applications—such as frying and making popcorn—in which regular butter (with a smoke point of 250 to 300 degrees) would burn. Another benefit: Its pure state means that unlike regular butter or simple clarified butter (which contains water that contributes to rancidity), it doesn't have to be refrigerated, and it will keep for at least three months (or, up to a year if refrigerated). Traditionally ghee is made on the stovetop, but we like this hands-off oven method.

1. Place 1 to 2 pounds unsalted butter in Dutch oven and cook, uncovered, on lower-middle rack of 250-degree oven for 2 to 3 hours, or until all water evaporates and solids are golden brown.

2. Let cool slightly and strain ghee through fine-mesh strainer lined with cheesecloth. Pour into clean glass jar, let cool completely, and seal. Ghee can be kept, sealed, in cool, dark place for up to 3 months or refrigerated for up to 1 year.

CHAPTER 18

Yogurt

Yogurt is far more than something you eat from a plastic cup, premixed with fruit.

HOW THE SCIENCE WORKS

The dairy shelves in the supermarket can be intimidating—especially the ones that display yogurt. There are myriad varieties that include regular or Greek; cup-set or stirred yogurt (cup-set is fermented in individual containers, while stirred yogurt is fermented in a large vat); whole-milk or fat-free; plain or flavored. It's possible to make yogurt at home (page 160), but most of the yogurt consumed in the United States is bought from the store. In the test kitchen, we use yogurt for far more than eating on its own—it's a great vehicle for spices and adds both moisture and flavor in cooking and baking.

All yogurts start the same way: with milk. For manufactured yogurts sold in grocery stores, this milk is generally skim or reduced-fat cow's milk, which is then fortified with added protein, such as skim milk powder or whey protein. Many of the manufactured yogurts are also given added stabilizers—such as gelatin, starch, pectin, agar, carrageenan, or even vegetable gums—to help prevent liquid whey separation (called syneresis) in the finished yogurt. Stabilizers are not required by law, but they are required to be disclosed on the label if they are added. The final addition is often a sweetening element like sugar, high-fructose corn syrup, or an artificial sweetener.

Next up? Homogenization, which prevents fat separation, and then pasteurization of this milk mix to create "yogurt mix." The milk used to make yogurt is pasteurized at a higher temperature for a longer period of time than milk sold for drinking to ensure a greater reduction in naturally-occurring bacteria, which could affect the fermentation.

Now comes the most important step: culturing the homogenized, pasteurized yogurt mix with live bacteria.

The bacteria transform the protein in the milk to a gel with a soft, smooth texture. The fermentation temperature is critical and must be maintained at 105 to 115 degrees to promote the growth of the bacteria throughout the fermentation process, which generally lasts from 2 hours to 5 hours (until the right pH is reached).

By law, two bacteria are used in combination to make yogurt: *Streptococcus thermophilus* and *Lactobacillus bulgaricus*. At the beginning of the fermentation process, *L. bulgaricus* produces amino acids that promote the growth of *S. thermophilus*, which then continues the fermentation, rapidly producing lactic acid until the pH reaches about 5.0, when *L. bulgaricus* takes over, producing the majority of lactic acid. In addition to sour lactic acid, the major flavor compounds produced by the fermentation process are volatile acetaldehyde, and to a lesser extent the buttery-flavor compound diacetyl. At the same time, the declining pH affects texture. As the mixture turns more acidic, the casein proteins in the milk create a network of denatured proteins that traps the water, forming a soft gel.

In the test kitchen, we value plain yogurt for its tangy flavor and fat. While we rarely heat yogurt on its own (it will curdle with high heat), we use it in many ways. At its simplest, yogurt can be turned into a satisfying spread, like our Lemon-Dill Yogurt Cheese (page 156). Yogurt adds flavor and, eventually, a crust, as part of a marinade in our Tandoori Chicken (page 156). We bake with yogurt in our quick Indian Flatbread (page 158), in which it coats the flour proteins, weakening gluten formation, and helping the grilled flatbread hold on to more moisture as it cooks. And yogurt acts in interesting ways when frozen—we use that to our advantage for Frozen Yogurt (page 159).

By law, two types of bacteria are used to make yogurt.

TEST KITCHEN EXPERIMENT

Making good frozen yogurt (or ice cream or gelato, for that matter) is largely about controlling water. Generally speaking, less water in the mix translates into a smoother frozen product—one that is perceived as less icy. Since yogurt (unlike milk or cream) is a weak gel, it can be placed in a cheesecloth-lined colander and drained of excess whey, thereby reducing the amount of freezable water in the mix. We wanted to find out which low-moisture form of yogurt made for better frozen yogurt: store-bought Greek-style yogurt that has already been leached of excess whey, or plain whole-milk yogurt that we strained ourselves in the kitchen. We set up the following experiment to find out.

EXPERIMENT

We made two batches of frozen yogurt: one using full-fat Greek-style yogurt and the other using plain whole-milk yogurt (free of added thickeners), which we strained of ¾ cup of whey ourselves in a cheesecloth-lined colander. All other ingredients and procedures were identical between the two. We tasted the frozen yogurts side by side and sent samples of the unfrozen Greek-style and home-strained yogurts to an independent lab to quantify fat, protein, carbohydrate, moisture content, and pH in hopes of isolating any differences between the two. We repeated the test three times.

RESULTS

Tasters showed an overwhelming preference for the frozen yogurt made with home-strained yogurt. In terms of flavor, tasters characterized the home-strained sample as "fresher" and "brighter" than the Greek-style batch. But the largest difference was with texture: The frozen yogurt made with Greek-style yogurt was "crumbly," with a slight "dusty feel," while the home-strained frozen yogurt was "smooth" and "creamy."

The lab results lent us some insight. The Greek-style yogurt contained 5 percent fat, 82 percent moisture, 9 percent protein, and 4 percent carbohydrate. The home-strained yogurt registered 6 percent fat, 84 percent moisture, 4 percent protein, and 5 percent carbohydrate. The pH tests revealed that the two were fairly acidic, at 4.12 and 4.04, respectively. The largest difference between these analyses was protein content, with the Greek-style yogurt registering more than twice that of our home-strained yogurt. We spoke with ice cream expert John Hopkinson of DuPont, and he explained that the combination of low pH and high protein can produce the dusty, chalky quality we noticed in the frozen Greek yogurt. He added that commercially produced Greek yogurt is often strained by centrifuge, which can damage the proteins and increase the likelihood of a chalky defect.

TAKEAWAY

While it may seem like a time-saver to reach for Greek-style yogurt when making frozen yogurt, we've learned that one ultimately pays for that convenience in texture. For our Frozen Yogurt recipe (page 159), we take the time to strain our own whole-milk yogurt for the creamiest, smoothest product.

GREEK VS. STRAINED FROZEN YOGURT

We compared frozen yogurts made with Greek yogurt and strained plain yogurt and found a distinct difference in texture.

GREEK YOGURT: CRUMBLY AND DUSTY

STRAINED PLAIN YOGURT: SMOOTH AND CREAMY

FAMILY TREE: CULTURED DAIRY PRODUCTS

Cultured dairy is cream or milk with friendly live bacteria (cultures) added. The bacteria convert lactose, or milk sugar, into lactic acid, making these products thick and tangy.

MILK

CREAM

YOGURT

Add bacteria to whole, low-fat, or nonfat milk and you get yogurt. We add whole-milk yogurt to sauces, soups, and dressings, and use it to make cakes. We don't recommend cooking with nonfat yogurt. Greek yogurt (which also can be made with milks of varying fat levels) is thicker, drier, and tangier than ordinary yogurt. To bake with Greek yogurt, remember this rule: Use two-thirds of the amount of yogurt called for and make up the difference with water.

BUTTERMILK

In the old days, buttermilk was simply the liquid left behind after cream was churned into butter. As unpasteurized cream sat "ripening" for a few days before churning, naturally occurring bacteria caused it to ferment by converting milk sugars into lactic acid, which made the resulting buttermilk mildly sour and slightly thickened. But since virtually all milk and cream is now pasteurized at high temperatures, a process that kills off those bacteria, most buttermilk sold today is cultured buttermilk, made by reintroducing lactic-acid bacteria to pasteurized skim or low-fat milk. Often, it's also reinforced with salt and thickeners like carrageenan and starch.

SOUR CREAM

Sour cream is made from cultured light cream (approximately 18 to 20 percent butterfat). When we're stirring it into stews or sauces, we always do so off the heat to keep the sour cream from separating. Sour cream often makes baked goods rich and moist.

18–20% butterfat

CRÈME FRAÎCHE

Sometimes erroneously described as the French version of sour cream, crème fraîche is actually made from heavy (not light) cream, which means it contains a lot more fat (between 30 and 40 percent). This extra fat means that you can heat crème fraîche—unlike yogurt or sour cream—without the risk of it curdling.

30–40% butterfat

CULTURED BUTTER

The big difference between regular and European-style premium butters is culturing. Cultured butter is made from cream that has been fermented before churning. During this process, lactic acid–forming bacteria convert the lactose in cream to lactic acid, giving the cream, and then the cultured butter, a distinct sour, tangy flavor.

LIVE CULTURES

Yogurt is a good source of "live cultures." These beneficial bacteria (namely *Lactobacillus bulgaricus* and *Streptococcus thermophilus*) give yogurt the flavor and texture we love (tangy, thick), and, purportedly, are very good for you. But some yogurts are heated after fermentation, which can kill live bacteria. In the U.S., the National Yogurt Association has developed a program where manufacturers pay for the right to display a "Live & Active Culture" seal on containers. This requires that the yogurt contain 100 million cultures per gram at the time of manufacture.

Lemon-Dill Yogurt Cheese

☑ WHY THIS RECIPE WORKS

Strained yogurt is simply plain yogurt that has been slowly strained to remove its whey, giving it a thicker, creamier consistency and a richer flavor. Mixed with a few simple flavorings, it makes a lighter, fresher alternative to heavier dips, and it couldn't be easier to make—all it takes is a little hands-off time.

STRAIN IT To end up with about 1 cup of strained yogurt, we started with 2 cups of traditional yogurt. A strainer lined with several coffee filters or a double layer of cheesecloth was ideal for slowly draining away the whey. After about 10 hours, a full cup of whey had drained off, leaving us with thick, luscious strained yogurt with a consistency close to cream cheese.

SEASON IT For the flavorings, we chose a bright combination of lemon zest and fresh dill, plus a little salt and pepper. Both regular and low-fat yogurt worked well here. But do not use nonfat yogurt. Also avoid yogurts containing modified food starch, gelatin, or gums; they prevent the yogurt from draining. After straining, the plain yogurt also makes a good substitute for Greek yogurt or cream cheese.

LEMON-DILL YOGURT CHEESE
MAKES ABOUT 1 CUP

A colander can be used in place of the strainer.

- 2 cups plain yogurt
- 1 tablespoon minced fresh dill
- 2 teaspoons grated lemon zest
- Salt and pepper

1. Line fine-mesh strainer with 3 basket-style coffee filters or double layer of cheesecloth. Set strainer over large measuring cup or bowl (there should be enough room for about 1 cup of liquid to drain without touching strainer).

2. Spoon yogurt into strainer, cover tightly with plastic wrap (wrap should not touch yogurt), and refrigerate until yogurt has released about 1 cup whey and has creamy, cream cheese–like texture, at least 10 hours or up to 2 days.

3. Transfer drained yogurt to clean container; discard whey. Stir in dill, lemon zest, 1/8 teaspoon salt, and pinch pepper. Cover and refrigerate until flavors have blended, about 1 hour. Season with salt and pepper to taste before serving. (Yogurt can be refrigerated for up to 2 days; season with extra salt and pepper to taste before serving.)

HONEY-WALNUT YOGURT CHEESE

Omit dill, lemon zest, and pepper. Stir 3 tablespoons chopped toasted walnuts and 1 tablespoon honey into drained cheese with salt in step 3.

Tandoori Chicken

☑ WHY THIS RECIPE WORKS

When we're craving the taste of a good piece of chicken and another plain breast or thigh just won't cut it, there's no better balm than tandoori chicken. The best renditions of this famous Indian specialty feature lightly charred pieces of juicy chicken infused with smoke, garlic, ginger, and spices for a dish that manages to be exotic and homey at the same time. Authentic versions call for a 24-hour yogurt-based marinade and a tandoor, the traditional beehive-shaped clay oven that fires up to 1,000 degrees—requirements that keep the dish mainly in the realm of restaurants, even in India. We wondered: Did we really need both of those things to create a great-tasting chicken full of the same robust flavors? We decided to reinvent this dish, but instead of developing a recipe for the grill, we wanted one we could use all year round. Our tandoor-less tandoori chicken would have to work in the oven.

USE YOUR OVEN We tried cooking our working recipe in an oven cranked up to high heat, but the chicken emerged pasty and dry. We then tried cooking it using only the broiler, to mimic the incredibly high heat of the tandoor, but the placement of the broiler coils gave us some chicken pieces that were browned, some that were undercooked, and others that were dry to the bone. The solution? Start in a low oven, and then broil. We removed the chicken pieces before they were fully cooked (an internal temperature of 125 degrees for the white meat and 130 for the dark), let them rest while the broiler reached temperature, and then slid them back into the oven to finish cooking under the broiler. Success!

DUNK IN YOGURT We tried marinating the chicken for different lengths of time—from 72 hours to just a brief dip in the spiced yogurt sauce. Surprisingly, we found that we preferred the chicken that had been dipped versus soaked for any length of time—even just 30 minutes. Yogurt contains acid, which breaks down proteins to "tenderize" meat. But the longer meat is exposed to acid, the more its proteins break down, to the point where they can actually become soluble. This leads to a texture some might call tender, but we found mushy. We loved the flavor the yogurt added to the chicken and the way it clung to the chicken and created a crust of its own. This yogurt crust, in fact, functioned like chicken skin, protecting the delicate meat.

RUB IT To make up for the very short dunk in the yogurt sauce, we used a salt-spice rub on the chicken, to season the meat and help it retain moisture, and let it sit. After coating the chicken in yogurt flavored with the same spice mixture, we popped it into the oven.

TANDOORI CHICKEN
SERVES 4

We prefer this dish with whole-milk yogurt, but low-fat yogurt can be substituted. If using large chicken breasts (about 1 pound each), cut each breast into three pieces. If using smaller breasts (10 to 12 ounces each), cut each breast into two pieces. Serve with Raita (recipe follows).

2	tablespoons vegetable oil
6	garlic cloves, minced
2	tablespoons grated fresh ginger
1	tablespoon garam masala
2	teaspoons ground cumin
2	teaspoons chili powder
1	cup plain whole-milk yogurt
¼	cup lime juice (2 limes), plus lime wedges for serving
2	teaspoons salt
3	pounds bone-in chicken pieces (split breasts cut in half, drumsticks, and/or thighs), skin removed and trimmed

1. Heat oil in 10-inch skillet over medium heat until shimmering. Add garlic and ginger and cook until fragrant, about 30 seconds. Stir in garam masala, cumin, and chili powder and continue to cook until fragrant, 30 seconds longer. Transfer half of garlic mixture to medium bowl, stir in yogurt and 2 tablespoons lime juice, and set aside. In large bowl, combine remaining garlic mixture, remaining 2 tablespoons lime juice, and salt.

2. Using sharp knife, make 2 or 3 short slashes into each piece of chicken. Transfer chicken to large bowl and gently rub with salt-spice mixture until all pieces are evenly coated. Let sit at room temperature for 30 minutes.

PRACTICAL SCIENCE CUTTING OUT CURDLING IN CULTURED DAIRY PRODUCTS

Only crème fraîche won't curdle; it has enough fat.

Dishes like beef stroganoff, chicken paprikash, and many of the Moroccan stews known as tagines wouldn't be complete without a little sour cream or yogurt stirred in at the end. However, these cultured dairy products are sensitive to heat and can easily curdle if the stew is too hot or reheated. (They are also sensitive to pH, and if the pH is below 4.6, they are more likely to curdle, too.) We wondered if another dairy product would provide a more stable tang.

We stirred dollops of whole-milk yogurt, full-fat sour cream, and crème fraîche (which boasts much more fat) into water that we brought to just a simmer (185 degrees). After letting the samples sit for 10 seconds, we examined the liquid for signs of curdling. Both the yogurt and the sour cream mixtures quickly curdled, while the crème fraîche mixture remained perfectly creamy.

Curdling occurs when excessive heat causes the whey proteins in dairy to denature (unfold) and bind with casein proteins, forming clumps of larger proteins. The greater amount of butterfat in crème fraîche (30 to 40 percent, versus 18 to 20 percent and roughly 4 percent in sour cream and yogurt, respectively) protects against this process by keeping the proteins, which coat the many fat globules, further apart. Plus, with more fat, crème fraîche has far fewer proteins to bind together in the first place. It's now our go-to dairy product for hot dishes; in fact, we found that crème fraîche is so resistant to curdling that it can withstand reheating. (If you're using sour cream or yogurt, you will need to temper (or slowly warm) it before adding it to the finished dish to prevent curdling and then be ready to serve immediately—no further cooking or reheating possible.)

3. Adjust oven rack to upper-middle position and heat oven to 325 degrees. Set wire rack in aluminum foil–lined rimmed baking sheet. Pour yogurt mixture over chicken and toss until chicken is evenly coated with thick layer. Arrange chicken pieces, scored side down, on prepared wire rack. Discard excess yogurt mixture. Roast chicken until breast pieces register 125 degrees and thighs and/or drumsticks register 130 degrees, 15 to 25 minutes. (Smaller pieces may cook faster than larger pieces. Remove pieces from oven as they reach correct temperature.)

4. Adjust oven rack 6 inches from broiler element and heat broiler. Return chicken to prepared wire rack, scored side up, and broil until chicken is lightly charred in spots and breast pieces register 160 degrees and drumsticks/thighs register 175 degrees, 8 to 15 minutes. Transfer chicken to serving plate, tent loosely with foil, and let rest for 5 minutes. Serve with lime wedges.

RAITA

MAKES ABOUT 1 CUP

The raita is best made with whole-milk yogurt, although low-fat yogurt can be used. Do not use nonfat yogurt; the sauce will taste hollow and bland.

 1   cup plain whole-milk yogurt
 2   tablespoons minced fresh cilantro
 1   garlic clove, minced
     Salt
     Cayenne pepper

Mix all ingredients together and season with salt and cayenne to taste. Cover and refrigerate until needed.

Naan

✔ WHY THIS RECIPE WORKS

Naan, India's famous leavened flatbread, is considered "restaurant" bread, even in India. To create the ideal version featuring a light, airy interior and a pliant, chewy crust, the dough is baked in the traditional beehive-shaped, charcoal- or wood-fired clay oven known as a tandoor. These vessels weigh upwards of 600 pounds and often top 1,000 degrees, which explains how the crust gets so beautifully blistered—and also why few home cooks own tandoors. We wanted a light and tender naan that approached the quality of the best restaurant naan, without the need for a tandoor.

CHOOSE WHOLE-MILK YOGURT We started with a moist dough with a fair amount of fat. Whole-milk yogurt—not low-fat or nonfat—was key. The extra fat coated the flour proteins, weakening gluten formation by preventing them from binding to each other too tightly, as well as holding in more moisture for a more tender bread.

ADD MORE FAT Even using whole-milk yogurt, however, the bread turned tough as soon as it cooled off. We needed a way to keep the dough from drying out. The solution wasn't more water; that would just make the dough sticky. More fat was a better idea, since besides impeding gluten formation it limits water evaporation from the starches during baking, minimizing moisture loss. We tried adding vegetable oil, and the more we added, the more tender the dough became; we maxed out at 5 teaspoons per cup of flour. The additional fat that made it work? Egg yolk. While unusual in naan recipes, egg yolks often turn up in other types of bread just for this reason.

USE A SKILLET We initially thought that a grill or preheated pizza stone would best approximate the intense heat of a tandoor, which cooks naan mainly by heat conducted through its walls. We were wrong. A grill's searing heat came close. But it only charred the bottom of the bread, while the top was barely cooked. (Flipping only dried out the bread.) Baked on a pizza stone in the oven, the bread encountered the conductive heat of the stone, which we wanted, and the drying heat of the oven's air currents, which we didn't. But a covered skillet on the stovetop delivered heat to the bottom and top of the bread, producing naans that were nicely charred but still moist. To ensure a tender interior, we misted the dough with water.

INDIAN FLATBREAD (NAAN)

MAKES 4 PIECES

This recipe works best with a high-protein all-purpose flour such as King Arthur brand. Do not use nonfat yogurt in this recipe. A 12-inch nonstick skillet may be used in place of the cast-iron skillet. For efficiency, stretch the next ball of dough while each naan is cooking.

 ½   cup ice water
 ⅓   cup plain whole-milk yogurt
 3   tablespoons plus 1 teaspoon vegetable oil
 1   large egg yolk
 2   cups (10 ounces) all-purpose flour
 1¼ teaspoons sugar
 ½   teaspoon instant or rapid-rise yeast
 1¼ teaspoons salt
 1½ tablespoons unsalted butter, melted

 1. In measuring cup or small bowl, combine water, yogurt, 3 tablespoons oil, and egg yolk. Process flour, sugar, and yeast in food processor until combined, about 2 seconds. With processor running, slowly add water mixture; process until dough is just combined and no dry flour remains, about 10 seconds. Let dough stand for 10 minutes.

 2. Add salt to dough and process until dough forms satiny, sticky ball that clears sides of workbowl, 30 to 60 seconds. Transfer dough to lightly floured work surface and knead until smooth, about 1 minute. Shape dough into tight ball and place in large, lightly oiled bowl. Cover tightly with plastic wrap and refrigerate for 16 to 24 hours.

 3. Adjust oven rack to middle position and heat oven to 200 degrees. Place heatproof plate on rack. Transfer dough to lightly floured work surface and divide into 4 equal

pieces. Shape each piece into smooth, tight ball. Place dough balls on lightly oiled baking sheet, at least 2 inches apart; cover loosely with plastic coated with vegetable oil spray. Let stand for 15 to 20 minutes.

4. Transfer 1 ball to lightly floured work surface and sprinkle with flour. Using your hands and rolling pin, press and roll piece of dough into 9-inch round of even thickness, sprinkling dough and work surface with flour as needed to prevent sticking. Using fork, poke entire surface of round 20 to 25 times. Heat remaining 1 teaspoon oil in 12-inch cast-iron skillet over medium heat until shimmering. Wipe oil out of skillet completely with paper towels. Mist top of dough lightly with water. Place dough in pan, moistened side down; mist top surface of dough with water; and cover. Cook until bottom is browned in spots across surface, 2 to 4 minutes. Flip naan, cover, and continue to cook on second side until lightly browned, 2 to 3 minutes. (If naan puffs up, gently poke with fork to deflate.) Flip naan, brush top with about 1 teaspoon melted butter, transfer to plate in oven, and cover plate tightly with aluminum foil. Repeat rolling and cooking remaining 3 dough balls. Once last naan is baked, serve immediately.

Frozen Yogurt

✔ WHY THIS RECIPE WORKS

Twenty years ago, yogurt was swapped into ice cream recipes, in the name of calorie cutting, and then masked with strong flavors to hide its presence. The results weren't always great. Today we prize frozen yogurt for its uniquely fresh, tart flavor. We wanted a frozen yogurt that tasted like its namesake but features the rich, creamy texture we've come to expect of superpremium ice cream.

STRAIN AND DRAIN   Too much water in a frozen yogurt mix increases the formation of large ice crystals, which detract from a creamy texture (we want small crystals that our tongues cannot detect). To remove excess water from regular whole-milk yogurt, we placed it in a strainer and drained off 1¼ cups of whey. In side-by-side tests we found that draining regular yogurt produced a much creamier result than using store-bought Greek-style yogurt (see Test Kitchen Experiment, page 154).

USE SMALL SUGARS   Sugar plays an important role in controlling how much of the water in a frozen yogurt base ultimately freezes, and subsequently how icy the final product is. We found that adding "small sugars," like glucose and fructose, to the base would prevent iciness better

than a larger sugar like sucrose. We substituted Lyle's Golden Syrup (which is made up of about 50 percent glucose and fructose) for some of the granulated sugar (which is all sucrose) to get a smoother frozen yogurt.

TRAP EXCESS WATER   The final step in managing the water in our base was to trap some of it—using unflavored gelatin. By dissolving and heating just 1 teaspoon of gelatin in a portion of the strained whey, we prevented water molecules from joining together and forming large ice crystals.

FROZEN YOGURT
MAKES ABOUT 1 QUART

We prefer the flavor and texture that Lyle's Golden Syrup lends this frozen yogurt, but if you can't find it, you can substitute light corn syrup. Any brand of whole-milk yogurt will work in this recipe. You can substitute low-fat yogurt for whole-milk yogurt, but the results will be less creamy and flavorful. This recipe requires draining the yogurt for 8 to 12 hours.

- 1 quart plain whole-milk yogurt
- 1 teaspoon unflavored gelatin
- ¾ cup sugar
- 3 tablespoons Lyle's Golden Syrup
- ⅛ teaspoon salt

1. Line colander or fine-mesh strainer with triple layer of cheesecloth and place over large bowl or measuring cup. Place yogurt in colander, cover with plastic wrap (plastic should not touch yogurt), and refrigerate until 1¼ cups whey have drained from yogurt, at least 8 hours and up to 12 hours. (If more than 1¼ cups of whey drains from yogurt, simply stir extra back into yogurt.)

2. Discard ¾ cup drained whey. Sprinkle gelatin over remaining ½ cup whey in bowl and let sit until gelatin softens, about 5 minutes. Microwave until mixture is bubbling around edges and gelatin dissolves, about 30 seconds. Let cool for 5 minutes. In large bowl, whisk sugar, Lyle's Golden Syrup, salt, drained yogurt, and cooled whey-gelatin mixture until sugar is completely dissolved. Cover and refrigerate (or place bowl over ice bath) until yogurt mixture registers 40 degrees or less.

3. Churn yogurt mixture in ice cream maker until mixture resembles thick soft-serve frozen yogurt and registers about 21 degrees, 25 to 35 minutes. Transfer frozen yogurt to airtight container and freeze until firm, at least 2 hours. Serve. (Frozen yogurt can be stored for up to 5 days.)

Greek-Style Yogurt

✓ WHY THIS RECIPE WORKS

Making yogurt is a favorite ritual for many of us in the test kitchen. There are good reasons to make your own. It's easy, and quality pints don't run cheap. But perhaps most important, many brands take shortcuts, like using gelatin, pectin, or inulin (a flavorless dietary fiber) to make a thicker product, which saves money and time but degrades flavor. Instead of worrying about additives, off-textures, or sour flavors, just make your own.

HEAT IT UP We started with the best-quality milk we could find, and heated it up to 185 degrees. It is important to resist the urge to stir, we learned. Stirring will lead to small lumps in the final yogurt. At 185 degrees, the proteins in the milk reconfigure so that once cultured they will create a creamy, viscous texture, rather than separating into curds and whey. Off the heat, we gently stirred in dry milk powder, which helped thicken the yogurt.

COOL QUICKLY The milk needed to be between 110 and 112 degrees to create a friendly environment for the culture and to prevent curdling. To reach this temperature quickly, we strained the mixture into a bowl set over an ice bath.

ADD A STARTER Making yogurt from milk requires adding a starter with live cultures. Freeze-dried starters such as Yogourmet work, but the flavor was too tangy for us. Instead, we bought a small container of yogurt (with live active cultures) to use as a starter. After adding the starter, we covered the bowl with plastic wrap and pierced several holes in the top to allow the yogurt to breathe.

LET IT SIT The bacteria prosper around 100 to 110 degrees. Any lower and the culturing will take days; any higher and the milk will curdle. We kept the bowl in the oven with the light on. (If your oven goes low enough, set it to 100 degrees.) It took 5 to 7 hours for the milk to transform into yogurt; when ready, the yogurt appeared thickened, creamy, and set.

GO GREEK We like a thicker texture and richer flavor, so we strained our yogurt to mimic Greek-style. After letting it cool, we set a fine-mesh strainer over a large liquid measuring cup and lined it with a couple of coffee filters (a double layer of cheesecloth would work, too). After pouring the yogurt into the strainer, we covered it with plastic wrap and refrigerated until 2 cups of whey drained from the yogurt, which took 7 to 8 hours.

GREEK-STYLE YOGURT
MAKES 2 CUPS

This is not a quick project. It takes between 15 and 18 hours. The timing works best if you make it in the morning or afternoon and then let it drain overnight. You can use ¼ cup of the yogurt you make to help start your next batch.

- **4** cups pasteurized (not ultra pasteurized or UHT) 2 percent low-fat milk
- **¼** cup nonfat dry milk powder
- **¼** cup plain 2 percent Greek yogurt

1. Adjust oven rack to middle position. Place fine-mesh strainer over large glass bowl, then set bowl in larger bowl filled with ice water. Heat milk in large saucepan over medium-low heat (do not stir while heating), until milk registers 185 degrees. Remove pot from heat, gently stir in milk powder, and let cool to 160 degrees, 7 to 10 minutes. Strain milk through prepared strainer and let cool, gently stirring occasionally, until milk registers 110 to 112 degrees; remove from ice bath.

2. In small bowl, gently stir ½ cup warm milk into yogurt until smooth. Stir yogurt mixture back into milk. Cover tightly with plastic wrap and poke several holes in plastic. Place bowl in oven and turn on oven light, creating a warm environment of 100 to 110 degrees. Let yogurt sit undisturbed until thickened and set, 5 to 7 hours. Transfer to refrigerator until completely chilled, about 3 hours.

3. Set clean fine-mesh strainer over large measuring cup and line with double layer of coffee filters. Transfer yogurt to prepared strainer, cover with plastic, and refrigerate until about 2 cups of liquid have drained into measuring cup, 7 to 8 hours. Transfer strained yogurt to jar with tight fitting lid, discarding drained liquid. Yogurt can be refrigerated for up to 1 week.

CHAPTER 19

Goat Cheese

This tangy, bright-white cheese is soft and creamy as is—and when cooked, it works best with just a touch of heat.

HOW THE SCIENCE WORKS

In 1981, Alice Waters topped a simple green salad with a round of baked goat cheese at her Berkeley restaurant, Chez Panisse. The tangy creaminess of this supple cheese was a revelation to most Americans. For centuries, France was the primary producer of goat cheese—*chèvre* in French means goat—and at that point, it was scarcely produced domestically. But with that salad, a trend was born.

Goat's milk is similar to cow's milk, but there are important differences that impact cheese making. On average, goat's milk contains a little more fat than cow's milk (3.8 versus 3.6 percent, respectively), a little more total protein (3.4 versus 3.2 percent), and less lactose (4.1 versus 4.7 percent). But the big difference is that goat's milk contains less of a particular protein: casein. Casein, the solid component that gives cheese its structure, is, not surprisingly, essential for making cheese.

But before we unpack that, let's back up and review how cheese is made. First, the milk is filtered and then (usually) pasteurized. Next, a bacterial culture is added, which converts the milk's sugar to lactic acid and causes the milk to form a weak gel. Then enzymes, often one called rennet, which traditionally comes from the stomach of a young calf, are added. These enzymes break down only one protein in milk—casein—clipping the casein proteins so that they can bond into clumps of a stronger gel, known as curds. The curds are separated from the leftover liquid, called whey, and packed into molds to form the final cheese.

Levels of casein in goat's milk range from 2.1 to 2.4 percent by weight, compared to cow's milk, which can range from 2.6 to 2.7 percent. The difference may seem small, but it has a significant effect. Because of its lower casein content, goat's milk has a poorer coagulating ability, and therefore produces a much weaker gel, and a much softer cheese. Nearly 70 percent of all goat cheeses are considered high-moisture cheeses (containing 45 to 60 percent water), which also contributes to their soft texture. There are more than 400 varieties of goat cheese, and more than 800 kinds of cheese made with goat's milk combined with other types of milk, according to the USDA's Agricultural Handbook No. 54. Some forms of hard goat cheddar and goat blue cheeses are produced, but most varieties are soft.

Goat cheese has a distinct color and flavor. Its striking white color is due to the fact that goats convert all of the yellow-hued beta-carotene in their diet to colorless vitamin A, unlike cows, which have some free beta-carotene in their milk, producing cheese with a creamier color. The distinct "goaty" flavor of goat cheese is due to the relatively high content of short- and medium-chain fatty acids found in goat's milk (twice as many shorter-chain fatty acids as in cow's milk). In addition, goat's milk contains five different branched-chain fatty acids. Two are especially important: 4-methyloctanoic acid and 4-ethyloctanoic acid. The latter fatty acid has a threshold of only 1.8 parts per billion required for producing the goaty aroma in cheese.

While many cheeses melt freely, fresh goat cheese does not. It will soften and brown, but it crumbles rather than melts, because it is an acid-coagulated cheese (see page 169). Therefore, when heating goat cheese, we freeze it before baking it very quickly (page 164) for a salad. We also make our own fresh goat cheese (page 166), which is surprisingly easy. And, of course, we enjoy the store-bought cheese straight from the package.

There are more than 400 kinds of goat cheese.

TEST KITCHEN EXPERIMENT

Goat cheese gets its distinct flavor from the presence of short- and medium-chain fatty acids found in goat's milk. We are so sensitive to these fatty acids that we can detect many of them at concentrations around 5 parts per million, allowing us to easily distinguish between goat's milk and cow's milk. Flavor aside, we wanted to dig deeper into how the type of milk influences the texture, color, and richness of a cheese. To that end we procured raw cow's milk from Lawton's Family Farm in Foxboro, Massachusetts, and raw goat's milk from The Herb Hill Micro Dairy in Andover, Massachusetts, and made a mozzarella-style stretched cheese from each.

EXPERIMENT

We used an identical recipe for both the goat's milk and cow's milk, based on precise temperatures and pH. We added thermophilic cheese culture to 82-degree milk, which we ripened at 90 degrees until the pH dropped. We added liquid animal rennet, stirred, and let the milk coagulate. We cut the mass into curds, let them ripen in the whey, drained them, cut them, and stretched them in whey at 175 degrees.

RESULTS

For the cow's milk: We noticed that after coagulating, some fat escaped from the milk and rose to the surface of the whey. The final curds easily stretched to over a foot and resulted in a springy, off-white, mild-tasting mozzarella.

For the goat's milk: We didn't notice any fat on the surface of the whey after coagulating. The final curds stretched up to 6 inches, but broke if pulled any further. The mozzarella was soft, pure white, and tasted distinctly of goat milk.

TAKEAWAY

Goat's milk differs from cow's milk in a few important ways. Unlike cow's milk fat, the fat in goat's milk doesn't flocculate (or separate from the rest of the milk and rise to the surface). This helps explains why the fat stayed in the curd mass for the goat's milk, but separated in the cow's milk. A compound found in fat is also the culprit for the color difference. Goat's milk fat, unlike cow's milk fat, does not contain carotene (the compound that makes carrots orange) so the milk (and cheese) remains pearly white.

What about the stretching ability of the cheeses? Here things get a bit more complicated. The important milk protein when it comes to cheese making is casein. Goat's milk contains less casein (2.1 to 2.4 percent by weight) than cow's milk (2.6 to 2.7 percent by weight), and that small difference has a big impact on the milk's ability to coagulate into a firm gel. In addition, the goat's milk we used was a mixture from three different breeds: Nubian, Toggenburg, and LaMancha. Research has shown that some goats lack a functional gene for a certain form of casein, alpha-s1-casein, which can affect the curd-forming properties of their milk. Milk from Nubian goats contains higher levels of alpha-s1-casein (and is therefore thought to make better cheese) than milk from Toggenburgs. We suspect that using all Nubian goat's milk would result in a mozzarella that could stretch more similarly to the cow's milk mozzarella. The cow's milk we used came from a herd of mostly Ayrshire cattle with a few Holsteins—both breeds with a long history of milk production for quality cheese making.

IT'S A STRETCH: COW'S MILK VS. GOAT'S MILK TO MAKE CHEESE

We made mozzarella with cow's and goat's milk and, due to the unique properties of each milk, found big differences in their ability to stretch.

Our mozzarella made with cow's milk was able to stretch well over a foot and developed a springy consistency.

The mozzarella made with goat's milk was softer than the cow's milk mozzarella and was barely stretchable at all.

JOURNEY: MILK TO CHEESE

Whether made from goat's, cow's, or sheep's milk, whether made at home or in a factory, most cheeses follow the same basic general production path. Milk is made up of water and milk solids, which include proteins, fat (butterfat), and sugar (lactose). When you cause the proteins in milk to coagulate, with the help of enzymes like rennet, they produce curds. With the help of heat, time, and sometimes pressure, these curds release a protein-rich liquid called whey (which is often sprayed on fields as fertilizer as a source of nitrogen, or dried and fed to cows) and become firmer and firmer. That's cheese. Let's take a closer look.

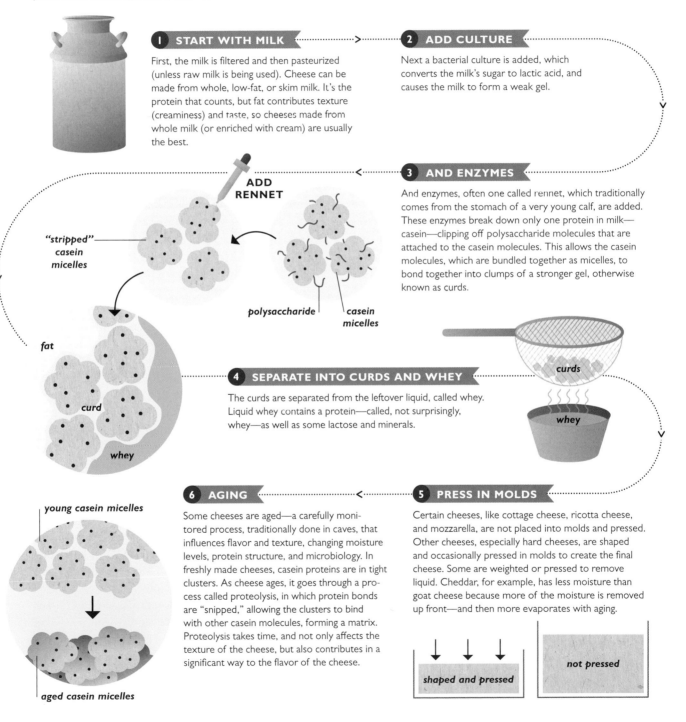

1 START WITH MILK

First, the milk is filtered and then pasteurized (unless raw milk is being used). Cheese can be made from whole, low-fat, or skim milk. It's the protein that counts, but fat contributes texture (creaminess) and taste, so cheeses made from whole milk (or enriched with cream) are usually the best.

2 ADD CULTURE

Next a bacterial culture is added, which converts the milk's sugar to lactic acid, and causes the milk to form a weak gel.

3 AND ENZYMES

And enzymes, often one called rennet, which traditionally comes from the stomach of a very young calf, are added. These enzymes break down only one protein in milk—casein—clipping off polysaccharide molecules that are attached to the casein molecules. This allows the casein molecules, which are bundled together as micelles, to bond together into clumps of a stronger gel, otherwise known as curds.

ADD RENNET

"stripped" casein micelles

polysaccharide *casein micelles*

fat

curd

whey

4 SEPARATE INTO CURDS AND WHEY

The curds are separated from the leftover liquid, called whey. Liquid whey contains a protein—called, not surprisingly, whey—as well as some lactose and minerals.

curds

whey

6 AGING

Some cheeses are aged—a carefully monitored process, traditionally done in caves, that influences flavor and texture, changing moisture levels, protein structure, and microbiology. In freshly made cheeses, casein proteins are in tight clusters. As cheese ages, it goes through a process called proteolysis, in which protein bonds are "snipped," allowing the clusters to bind with other casein molecules, forming a matrix. Proteolysis takes time, and not only affects the texture of the cheese, but also contributes in a significant way to the flavor of the cheese.

young casein micelles

aged casein micelles

5 PRESS IN MOLDS

Certain cheeses, like cottage cheese, ricotta cheese, and mozzarella, are not placed into molds and pressed. Other cheeses, especially hard cheeses, are shaped and occasionally pressed in molds to create the final cheese. Some are weighted or pressed to remove liquid. Cheddar, for example, has less moisture than goat cheese because more of the moisture is removed up front—and then more evaporates with aging.

shaped and pressed

not pressed

Herbed Baked Goat Cheese Salad

✅ WHY THIS RECIPE WORKS

Warm goat cheese salad has been a fixture on restaurant menus for years, featuring artisanal cheeses, organic baby field greens, barrel-aged vinegars, and imported oils. Marketing being what it is, the jargon is often more intriguing than the execution: tepid, crust-dusted cheese on overdressed designer greens at prices that defy reason. When we've tried to prepare this salad at home, the results have been equally disappointing, albeit less expensive. We usually ended up with flavorless warm cheese melted onto the greens. What we wanted was something different: creamy cheese rounds infused with flavor and surrounded by crisp, golden breading, all cradled in lightly dressed greens. Coating and heating the cheese was clearly our biggest challenge.

USE THE OVEN Pan-fried goat cheese develops a crisp crust, but it's very tricky to turn over rounds without crushing the melted interior and causing the cheese to ooze out. Broiling the goat cheese produced leathery skin that was dry and inedible. The answer? The oven. But goat cheese rounds coated in bread crumbs and baked in a 350-degree oven were soggy and pale. We increased the temperature of the oven. But we needed another fix.

PRACTICAL SCIENCE BLOOMED RINDS

> Eat the rinds on bloomed-rind cheeses like Brie.

Many cheeses have rinds. Some rinds are edible and some can lend flavor to other foods (like a pot of soup). There are three basic types: bloomed rinds (inoculated with mold for fuzzy white rinds and creamy cheeses, like brie), natural rinds (cheeses that are left alone to age, like cheddar), and washed rinds (rinds are washed with a brine during aging, which extracts moisture from the surface of the cheese, thus tightening up the structure of the curd as it loses moisture to the brine).

The soft, pillowy rind of Brie and other bloomed-rind cheeses, such as Camembert, is not only edible, it's the most flavorful part. The ripening process of Brie begins with the application of *Penicillium candidum*, a harmless white mold, on the surface of the immature cheese. Over the next several weeks the mold grows (or "blooms") into a tender white crust around the cheese that provides both textural contrast and concentrated flavor. The mold is also at work internally; as the cheese ages, the mold grows roots that make their way to the center of the Brie, breaking down the protein and softening the cheese as they go. You can tell that the roots have reached the middle and that the Brie is fully ripe when the center feels soft and tender to the touch. If you have an aversion to the rind, it can certainly be trimmed off, but watch where you cut. Brie ripens from the outside in, so you might be slicing off the creamiest part of the cheese with the rind.

AND USE MELBA Logic had persuaded us that higher temperatures had the potential to produce a crisp crust, but reality had shown us that we needed a more durable breading. First we tried a bound breading, with flour, egg, and then bread crumbs. That didn't work; it was gluey and heavy. We needed a sturdier crumb. In came Melba toasts, which we pulverized in a food processor. These extremely dry (and extremely hard) toasts worked well. The goat cheese coated with ground Melba crumbs, partially frozen (to minimize any oozing), and baked at 475 degrees was crisp, and maintained its shape. It had all the advantages of pan frying without any of the disadvantages.

HERBED BAKED GOAT CHEESE
MAKES 12 ROUNDS

The baked goat cheese should be served warm. Prepare the salad components (salad recipes follow) while the cheese is in the freezer and toss the greens and vinaigrette while the cheese cools a bit after baking.

3	ounces white Melba toasts (2 cups)
1	teaspoon pepper
3	large eggs
2	tablespoons Dijon mustard
1	tablespoon minced fresh thyme
1	tablespoon minced fresh chives
12	ounces firm goat cheese
	Extra-virgin olive oil

1. Process Melba toasts in a food processor to fine even crumbs, about 1½ minutes; transfer crumbs to medium bowl and stir in pepper. Whisk eggs and mustard in second medium bowl until combined. Combine thyme and chives in small bowl.

2. Using kitchen twine or dental floss, divide cheese into 12 even pieces. Roll each piece into a ball; roll each ball in herbs to coat lightly. Transfer 6 pieces to egg mixture, turn each piece to coat; transfer to Melba crumbs and turn each piece to coat, pressing crumbs into cheese. Flatten each ball into disk about 1½ inches wide and 1 inch thick and set on baking sheet. Repeat process with remaining 6 pieces cheese. Freeze cheese until firm, about 30 minutes. (Cheese may be wrapped tightly in plastic wrap and frozen for 1 week.) Adjust oven rack to top position; heat oven to 475 degrees.

3. Remove cheese from freezer and brush tops and sides evenly with oil. Bake until crumbs are golden brown and cheese is slightly soft, 7 to 9 minutes (or 9 to 12 minutes if cheese is completely frozen). Using thin metal spatula, transfer cheese to paper towel–lined plate and let cool 3 minutes before serving.

SALAD WITH HERBED BAKED GOAT CHEESE AND VINAIGRETTE
SERVES 6

Prepare the salad components while the cheese is in the freezer and toss the greens and vinaigrette while the cheese cools a bit after baking. Hearty salad greens, such as a mix of arugula and frisée, work best here.

2	tablespoons red wine vinegar
1	tablespoon Dijon mustard
1	teaspoon minced shallot
	Salt and pepper
6	tablespoons extra-virgin olive oil
14	ounces (14 cups) mixed hearty salad greens
1	recipe Herbed Baked Goat Cheese

Combine vinegar, mustard, shallot, and ¼ teaspoon salt in large bowl. Whisking constantly, drizzle in oil. Season with pepper to taste. Add greens, toss gently to coat, then divide among salad plates. Arrange warm goat cheese on greens and serve.

SALAD WITH APPLES, WALNUTS, DRIED CHERRIES, AND HERBED BAKED GOAT CHEESE
SERVES 6

Prepare the salad components while the cheese is in the freezer and toss the greens and vinaigrette while the cheese cools a bit after baking. Hearty salad greens, such as a mix of arugula and frisée, work best here.

1	cup dried cherries
2	tablespoons cider vinegar
1	tablespoon Dijon mustard
1	teaspoon minced shallot
	Salt and pepper
¼	teaspoon sugar
6	tablespoons extra-virgin olive oil
14	ounces (14 cups) mixed hearty salad greens
2	Granny Smith apples, cored, quartered, and sliced ⅛ inch thick
½	cup walnuts, toasted and chopped
1	recipe Herbed Baked Goat Cheese

1. Soak cherries in ½ cup hot water in bowl until plump, about 10 minutes; drain.

2. Combine vinegar, mustard, shallot, ¼ teaspoon salt, and sugar in large bowl. Whisking constantly, drizzle in oil. Season with pepper to taste. Add greens, toss gently to coat, then divide among salad plates. Sprinkle with cherries, apples, and walnuts. Arrange warm goat cheese on greens and serve.

SALAD WITH GRAPES, PINE NUTS, PROSCIUTTO, AND HERBED BAKED GOAT CHEESE
SERVES 6

Prepare the salad components while the cheese is in the freezer and toss the greens and vinaigrette while the cheese cools a bit after baking. Hearty salad greens, such as a mix of arugula and frisée, work best here.

2	tablespoons balsamic vinegar
1	tablespoon Dijon mustard
1	teaspoon minced shallot
	Salt and pepper
6	tablespoons extra-virgin olive oil
14	ounces (14 cups) mixed hearty salad greens
1¼	cups red seedless grapes, halved
½	cup pine nuts, toasted
6	ounces thinly sliced prosciutto
1	recipe Herbed Baked Goat Cheese

Combine vinegar, mustard, shallot, and ¼ teaspoon salt in large bowl. Whisking constantly, drizzle in oil; season with pepper to taste. Add greens, toss gently to coat, then divide among salad plates. Sprinkle with grapes and pine nuts. Arrange prosciutto and goat cheese on greens and serve.

Fresh Goat Cheese

✓ WHY THIS RECIPE WORKS

Cheese making can be an incredibly time-consuming and labor-intensive endeavor, requiring specialized equipment and a high level of expertise. But luckily, there are some cheeses that a novice can easily undertake at home. Goat cheese is one of these. Good fresh goat cheese is a beautiful thing. It should be chalky but creamy, tart and bright with an underlying richness, and above all, it should taste like what it is: little more than goat's milk and salt. (That said, you have to appreciate a "goat-y" flavor for this recipe to be worthwhile.) We tried a few different variations on the basic recipe, utilizing different coagulating agents and amounts of culture, but this one was the clear winner. For the most reliable results, use fresh homogenized and pasteurized milk here; do not use ultra-pasteurized or ultrahigh-temperature (UHT or long-life) milk in this recipe or it will not curdle properly.

HEAT IT UP Goat's milk is pricier than cow's milk, but it has its advantages. It's more acidic so it cultures faster, and, because of its structure, it produces a smoother cheese. We started by warming a half-gallon of goat's milk over low heat, stirring often to prevent scorching (which is due to the heat-sensitive whey proteins coagulating at the bottom of the pan). When the milk reached 90 degrees, we took it off the heat. Some recipes add calcium chloride to ensure good curd formation, but we found it wasn't needed and added a bitter aftertaste. (But if you're worried about the quality of your milk—if it's highly pasteurized, a process that decreases the amount of calcium, important for clotting during cheese making—you can add ⅛ teaspoon calcium chloride diluted in 2 tablespoons purified water.)

ADD CULTURE AND COAGULENT Next, we sprinkled the culture (which is just what you would guess: a bacterial culture that jump-starts the cheese-making process) over the milk and gently stirred until combined. The culture turned the lactose in the milk into lactic acid. The lactic acid is key for several reasons, including giving the cheese tangy flavor and helping the rennet, which came next, do its job. The rennet made the milk separate into curds and whey. Rennet is a collection of enzymes that, with the help of the acidic environment the starter culture creates, causes the milk to coagulate. Next up? Wait. The goat's milk mix needed to sit for 12 to 24 hours.

SEPARATE THE CURDS Now the milk mixture had separated into a raft of curds and liquid whey. We ladled the curds into a colander lined with butter muslin. The less we broke up the curds the better; whole curds drained more slowly, but they gave superior texture. The curds drained for a few hours; the goal was to thicken them but keep them moist.

SALT AND HANG We tipped the partially drained cheese from the colander into a bowl. We mixed in some coarse sea salt, and spooned half the cheese into the center of a piece of butter muslin, tied it up into a bundle, and repeated. We hung the bundles from a wooden spoon in a deep bowl for 6 to 24 hours, depending on how firm we wanted the cheese.

FRESH GOAT CHEESE
MAKES ABOUT 10 OUNCES

This recipe takes a couple days to complete. Goat's milk is sold these days in more places than you might think; just make sure you buy pasteurized milk, not ultra-pasteurized, for cheese making.

- 8   cups pasteurized (not ultrapasteurized or UHT) goat's milk
- ⅛   teaspoon direct-set mesophilic starter culture
- ⅛   teaspoon liquid animal rennet
- 1   tablespoon cold filtered water
- 1   teaspoon coarse sea salt

1. Slowly heat milk in large saucepan over low heat, stirring often, until milk registers 90 degrees, about 10 minutes. Remove from heat, sprinkle culture over surface of milk, and gently stir until combined.

2. Dilute rennet in water, then stir rennet into milk until well combined. Cover and let sit, undisturbed, at room temperature until mixture fully separates into solid curds and translucent whey, 12 to 24 hours.

3. Line colander with butter muslin or triple layer of cheesecloth and set in sink. Ladle curds into prepared colander and let drain at room temperature for 2 to 4 hours, until whey no longer runs freely from colander, and curds are thickened but still moist.

4. Transfer partially drained cheese to medium bowl, stir in salt, and divide cheese in half. Working with 1 half at a time, bundle cheese in butter muslin or triple layer of cheesecloth, then tie with kitchen twine to secure.

5. Tie cheese bundles to large spoon set over deep bowl or container, making sure bundles do not touch bottom of bowl, and refrigerate for 6 to 24 hours (depending on desired consistency). Goat cheese can be wrapped tightly in plastic wrap and refrigerated for up to 1 week.

CHAPTER 20

Parmesan

The making of traditional Parmesan is highly codified and results in an umami-rich, crystal-studded cheese. Just don't melt it too fast.

HOW THE SCIENCE WORKS

The buttery, nutty, slightly fruity taste and crystalline crunch of genuine Parmigiano-Reggiano cheese is a one-of-a-kind experience. It has been produced using traditional methods for the past 800 years in one government-designated area of northern Italy.

There, the making of Parmigiano-Reggiano is highly codified. Partly skimmed raw milk from cows that graze in a small area of Emilia-Romagna is warmed and combined with a starter culture to begin the curdling process. Rennet from calves' stomachs, which contains the coagulating enzyme rennin, is added to facilitate the formation of curds. The curds are stirred, which allows moisture and whey to escape. Eventually, the curds are formed into wheels that weigh about 80 pounds, and the words "Parmigiano-Reggiano" are stenciled onto the rind. The cheese is submerged in a saltwater brine for days. This makes the rind a bit salty, but most of the cheese is not exposed to the brine.

Finally, the cheese is aged. With aging, moisture levels decline and the cheese's characteristic crystals form. Aging also allows enzymes to break down the protein structure of the cheese, creating its crumbly, craggy texture. By law, Parmigiano-Reggiano must be aged for at least 12 months before it can be sold, and it is usually aged for 24 months.

Most of the flavor of Parmesan cheese is developed during the aging process. More aging continues to develop the complex flavors, which are formed by the natural enzymes in the cheese. The most important enzymes for both coagulating the casein proteins and forming the flavors come from mixtures of different *Lactobacillus* bacteria, combined with *Streptococcus thermophilus* bacteria. During the long aging period the enzymes do primarily two things: First, they break down the protein into flavorful fragments

When it comes to cheese:
More age means more flavor.

called peptides, and simple amino acids, a process known as proteolysis. Second, they break down the fat into shorter-chain free fatty acids, which are combined with alcohols and converted to aromatic compounds called esters. These esters give aged Parmesan cheese its fruity flavor. The free fatty acids produce its sharp, piquant flavor, while the peptides and amino acids give the cheese its delicious nutty flavors. All of these flavor components are formed as the cheese dries while it ages. The loss of moisture is important not only for forming a hard cheese texture, but also for forming the characteristic flavors of well-aged Parmesan cheese. More age means more flavor.

Hard cheeses that have been aged, like Parmesan, are difficult to melt. This is because when they age they lose a lot of water, which allows the casein clusters to come closer together and form stronger bonds. Hard cheeses like Parmesan also contain a lot of fat trapped within the protein network. This fat can melt well before the protein begins to flow, resulting in separation of the fat and protein—a problem known as "breaking." Therefore, when we cook with Parmesan, we accentuate its intense and nutty flavor, while working to not melt it too much or too fast. We take care not to brown our Parmesan-Crusted Chicken Cutlets (page 170) too deeply, to prevent the cheese from tasting sour. And we remove excess moisture from our Parmesan-Crusted Asparagus (page 171) by salting the green spears before coating them in a Parmesan-heavy crust and baking. We pair Parmesan with prosciutto to emphasize its umami-rich flavor in our tagliatelle with peas and prosciutto (page 172), and we use a food processor to pack as much Parmesan as possible in our dumplings without creating a gooey mess for our Italian Chicken Soup with Parmesan Dumplings (page 173).

TEST KITCHEN EXPERIMENT

Weighing in at 84 pounds and measuring up to 18 inches wide and 9 inches tall, a whole wheel of real Parmigiano-Reggiano is a sight to behold. In the test kitchen, we purchase quarter wheels, and each easily lasts us a couple of months. While breaking down these quarter wheels into small wedges we've often noticed that the cheese toward the rind is crumblier than that in the center. We've also noticed that the exterior cheese has better flavor and boasts more of the pleasant crunchy crystals (which are aggregates of the amino acid tyrosine) that we love—but could there really be that much variation within one cheese? There was only one way to find out.

EXPERIMENT

We first set up a blind tasting of samples of cheese taken from three locations on one wheel of 18-month-old Parmigiano-Reggiano. We excised the samples from the very center of the wheel, from a location 1 inch in from the side and bottom rind, and from a third location right between these two points. We asked tasters to describe the texture and flavor of each sample and rank them based on overall preference. Next, we took additional core samples from the center and edge locations, shaved them into thin strips, and manually counted the number of tyrosine crystals in each.

RESULTS

Tasters were clear about their preferences. The sample taken closest to the rind earned near-unanimous support for its "nutty," "complex," "sharp" flavor and "pleasantly crumbly" texture—it ranked first. The sample taken from the center of the wheel ranked third and was often described as "clean tasting" with a "smoother," "plasticky" texture. The core sample taken in between these two points scored second place and was described, fittingly, as "middle-of-the-road" in terms of both flavor and texture. The crystal count also painted a clear picture. Cheese right next to the rind averaged 20 crystals per 10 grams of cheese, while the center cheese averaged less than nine crystals per 10 grams.

TAKEAWAY

When cheese ages it undergoes a complex process called proteolysis. Proteolysis impacts the texture, melting qualities (see page 169), and flavor of a cheese. Our tests suggest that cheese changes over time in the same way that a roast heats up in the oven—from the outside in. We know that the disparity in internal temperature from the outside of a roast to the inside increases with the size of the roast; we find the same phenomenon in a wheel of Parmesan. The outer portions of cheese showed the telltale signs of advanced aging—a dry, crumbly texture, a high proportion of crunchy tyrosine crystals (as well as the larger, soft pearls of the amino acid leucine), and a complex flavor.

Going forward we'll definitely be seeking out corner pieces of Parmigiano-Reggiano at the supermarket. Not only will we get the authenticity guarantee of the stamp on the rind, we'll also be buying the best part of the wheel.

FROM RIND TO CORE: THE CHANGING TEXTURE OF PARMESAN

We tested samples from near the rind of a wheel of Parmesan to the center, and found a big difference in both texture and flavor.

quarter cheese wheel

EXTERIOR PARM
This strip of Parmesan, with visible tyrosine, was described as "nutty," "complex," and "pleasantly crumbly."

INTERIOR PARM
This strip of Parmesan, which appears plasticky in texture, was described as "clean tasting" with a "smoother" texture.

FOCUS ON: MELTING CHEESE

Different cheeses melt in different ways. Some melt smoothly. Others don't melt at all. Moisture plays a role, but the state of a cheese's proteins affects it most. There are two main stages in the cheese-making process that affect the protein structure and, eventually, the cheese's meltability: coagulation and the process of aging.

COAGULATION

All cheeses can be categorized into two groups based on how they are coagulated: with acid (such as vinegar or lemon juice) or with an enzyme known as rennet (which can be animal- or plant-derived).

RENNET-COAGULATED CHEESES

When rennet is added to a milk mixture in order to help formulate curds in the cheese-making process, enzymes present in the rennet work to strip down the bundles of protein in the milk, called casein micelles. These stripped-down proteins can then link together to form a matrix, surrounding fat and water. This matrix, though solid, is not too tightly bound. When it comes to melting, rennet-coagulated cheeses melt in two stages: First, their fat globules change from solid to liquid, which makes the cheese more supple. Then, as the temperature continues to rise, the tightly bonded casein proteins loosen their grip on one another and the cheese flows like a thick liquid. Rennet-coagulated cheeses include cheddar, Monterey Jack, and mozzarella.

ACID-SET CHEESES

Cheeses coagulated with acid resist melting because the acid dissolves the calcium ions between the casein proteins and alters their electrical charge, both of which cause the proteins to link up tightly and clump. Heat then makes the proteins bond together even more tightly, which squeezes out the water and causes the cheese to dry out and stiffen. Acid-coagulated cheeses include cottage cheese and ricotta.

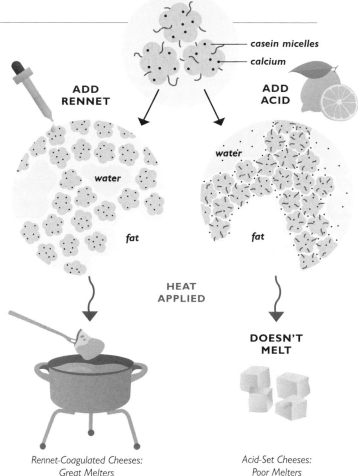

Rennet-Coagulated Cheeses: Great Melters

Acid-Set Cheeses: Poor Melters

AGING

In freshly made cheeses, casein proteins are in tightly wound clusters, allowing for little interaction with one another. As cheese ages, it goes through a process called proteolysis, in which bonds within individual casein molecules are "snipped," allowing the clusters to unwind and bind with other casein molecules, forming a matrix. Early in this process, the matrix is flexible, allowing young cheeses to melt smoothly. With time, the proteins bond together more tightly, forming a stronger network that requires more heat to melt and is less flexible when melted. This can result in more separated fat and clumps.

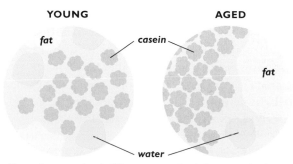

Young cheeses melt smoothly. Because their protein networks are weak, the casein flows easily, the fat dispersing evenly throughout.

Aged cheeses are harder to melt. Often, the fat melts before the protein can flow, causing it to "break."

YOUNG CHEESES

Young cheeses like mild cheddar and mozzarella melt really well. They turn from a relatively soft solid to a smooth, thin flowing mass without much heat, because their protein is held together by fairly weak forces. Young cheeses also contain high levels of water that separate the clusters of casein micelles and keep them from bonding too tightly.

AGED CHEESES

Hard cheeses that have been aged, like Parmesan, extra-sharp cheddar, and Pecorino Romano, are difficult to melt. When they age they lose a lot of water, which allows the casein clusters to come closer together and form stronger bonds. These hard cheeses also contain a lot of fat trapped within the protein network. This fat can melt well before the protein begins to flow, resulting in separation of the fat and protein—a problem known as "breaking."

Parmesan-Crusted Chicken Cutlets

✔ WHY THIS RECIPE WORKS

When it comes to Italian-style chicken cutlets, most people are familiar with two classic recipes: chicken Parmesan (breaded chicken breasts topped with melted Parmesan, mozzarella, and tomato sauce) and chicken Milanese (pan-fried chicken cutlets with a Parmesan breading). Although both offer Parmesan flavor, they're more focused on the bread crumbs. We wanted to devise an Italian-inspired cutlet recipe that put the spotlight on the cheese. To come up with a superior dish, we knew we'd have to conquer the problems of weak Parmesan flavor and mushy, patchy crusts.

PAN-FRY After some tests, we knew that the chicken would have to be pan-fried, not baked. While baking simply melted the cheese, pan frying showed potential to deliver the crisp crust we were after. Also, the chicken would need to be cooked in a nonstick skillet to keep the crust from fusing to the bottom of the pan, and it would have to be cooked quickly to prevent the cheese from burning.

MAKE A CHEESY CRUST By modifying the classic chicken Milanese breading recipes to contain a coating of flour, egg whites, and a thin layer of Parmesan, we got the cheese to adhere to the cutlet, and not act like a soufflé. But the chicken tasted only faintly of cheese. To fix this, we used a base layer of finely grated Parmesan cut on the smallest holes of a box or rasp-style grater and paired that with an exterior layer of coarsely shredded Parmesan cut on the largest holes of a box grater. This gave the chicken a substantial Parmesan-tasting crust.

NO SOUR NOTES Whenever we cooked the chicken until it was a deep brown, it tasted burnt. When we under-browned the chicken, it tasted fine. We traced the problem back to the Maillard reaction. This chemical reaction occurs when amino acids and sugars in foods are heated, causing them to combine and form new flavor compounds. Most cheeses undergo very little of this reaction when heated, because they don't contain much sugar. Parmesan cheese, however, contains fairly high levels of the sugar galactose, which undergoes the reaction quite readily. As the galactose reacts with sizable amounts of glutamic acid (an amino acid), the formation of bitter-tasting substances happens as soon as the cheese starts to brown. Turning the heat down to medium once the cutlets were in the pan—thus keeping browning at bay—allowed the chicken and cheese to cook through without tasting burnt.

PARMESAN-CRUSTED CHICKEN CUTLETS
SERVES 4

We like the flavor that authentic Parmigiano-Reggiano lends to this recipe. To make slicing the chicken easier, freeze it for 15 minutes. Although the portion size (one cutlet per person) might seem small, these cutlets are rather rich due to the cheese content. Do not be tempted to cook all four cutlets at once; this will cause excessive sticking between cutlets and make flipping them difficult. To make eight cutlets, double the ingredients and cook the chicken in four batches, transferring the cooked cutlets to the warm oven and wiping out the skillet after each batch. Serve this chicken with a simple salad.

- 2 (8-ounce) boneless, skinless chicken breasts, tenderloins removed, trimmed
- ¼ cup plus 1 tablespoon all-purpose flour
- 6½ ounces Parmesan cheese, ½ ounce grated fine (¼ cup) and 6 ounces grated coarse (2 cups)
- 3 large egg whites
- 2 tablespoons minced fresh chives (optional)
  Salt and pepper
- 4 teaspoons olive oil
  Lemon wedges

1. Adjust oven rack to middle position and heat oven to 200 degrees. Set wire rack in rimmed baking sheet. Halve chicken horizontally, then cover chicken halves with plastic wrap and pound to even ¼-inch thickness with meat pounder.

2. Combine ¼ cup flour and ¼ cup finely grated Parmesan in shallow dish. Lightly beat egg whites and chives, if using, together until slightly foamy in second shallow dish. Combine 2 cups coarsely grated Parmesan and remaining 1 tablespoon flour in third shallow dish.

3. Pat chicken dry with paper towels and season with salt and pepper. Working with 1 cutlet at a time, dredge in flour mixture, shaking off excess, then coat with egg white mixture, allowing excess to drip off. Coat all sides of cutlet with coarsely grated Parmesan mixture, pressing gently so that cheese adheres; transfer to prepared wire rack.

4. Heat 2 teaspoons oil in 12-inch nonstick skillet over medium-high heat until shimmering. Place 2 cutlets in skillet and cook until golden brown on first side, about 3 minutes. While chicken is cooking, use thin nonstick spatula to gently separate any cheesy edges that have melted together. Flip cutlets, reduce heat to medium, and continue to cook until lightly browned on second side, about 2 minutes longer. Transfer cutlets to clean wire rack set in baking sheet and keep warm in oven. Wipe out skillet with paper towels. Repeat with remaining 2 teaspoons oil and remaining 2 cutlets. Serve immediately with lemon wedges.

PRACTICAL SCIENCE STORING PARMESAN

There are many opinions, but the solution is easy: Stick it in a zipper-lock bag and squeeze out the air.

To determine the best way to store Parmesan cheese, we consulted several experts. There were several points on which everyone agreed. First, it is best to buy small pieces of cheese that will get used up in the course of a meal, thus reducing the need for storage. Assuming that there is some cheese left to store, everyone agreed that the relatively humid vegetable crisper was the best spot for it in the refrigerator.

In terms of storage, it was acknowledged that the cheese should be allowed to breathe, but just a little. Full and prolonged exposure to air oxidizes the cheese, which degrades both flavor and texture. So the cheese should be wrapped in a way that limits its breathing. The three specific wrapping recommendations were as follows: (1) wrap the cheese in a slightly moistened paper towel and then in a layer of aluminum foil; (2) wrap the cheese in parchment paper and then in either plastic wrap or foil; and (3) simply wrap the cheese in parchment, wax paper, or butcher paper alone. To these ideas we added the two methods used most often by home cooks: (1) put the cheese in a zipper-lock bag and squeeze out the air before sealing, and (2) wrap the cheese directly in plastic wrap.

To determine which method works best, we wrapped five ¾-pound pieces of Parmigiano-Reggiano, all the same size and shape and all cut fresh at the same time from a single wheel, using each of the five methods. We then stored them in the vegetable crisper of our test kitchen refrigerator for six weeks. We monitored flavor and texture by tasting each piece every other day. Differences began to show up at the one-week mark, and all the subsequent tastings remained consistent. At one week, the sample wrapped in paper towel and foil seemed slightly soft and chewy, the parchment-wrapped sample was starting to dry out a little, and some tasters felt they detected a faint "off," sour flavor in the plastic-wrapped sample (a new sheet of wrap was used every time the cheese was rewrapped after tasting). The best flavor and texture belonged to the cheese wrapped in parchment and then foil, though the cheese simply thrown in a zipper-lock bag was almost as good. And so it went. At the four-week mark, the parchment and foil–wrapped sample was still the best of show, followed closely by the zipper-lock bagged cheese. At the six-week mark, both of these samples were still fine.

Our conclusion, then, is to stick with the easiest method. If you must store a small piece of Parmesan, just toss the cheese into a small zipper-lock bag and squeeze out as much air as possible before fastening the seal.

Parmesan-Crusted Asparagus

☑ WHY THIS RECIPE WORKS

The sweet, concentrated flavor of roasted asparagus is irresistible, as is the bread-crumb-and-Parmesan crunch of asparagus gratin. We wanted to marry the two. We thought it would be a simple matter of tossing raw spears with olive oil, seasonings, and a cheese and bread-crumb mixture. But when we tried this, we found that as the asparagus roasted, it released moisture. That's no problem when the spears roast on their own—the moisture simply evaporates. But now that we'd coated them with crumbs and cheese, the moisture turned the topping soggy, and it fell off the spears in large, mucky crumbs. Clearly we had to get rid of some of the asparagus's moisture before adding the crumb topping.

SALT IT We tried roasting the spears in a 450-degree oven until the moisture evaporated, about 10 minutes, and then topping them with the cheese-crumb mixture. We gave everything a few more minutes to crisp in the oven. The finished asparagus was dehydrated and leathery, and the coating didn't adhere. We tried parcooking the asparagus in the microwave, but the spears were limp by the time the moisture was gone. What about salt? We often salt vegetables like tomatoes, eggplant, and cucumbers to draw out their moisture. We sprinkled ½ teaspoon of salt over the raw asparagus and let it sit on paper towels to drain. Thirty minutes later, the towels were sodden with exuded liquid. We tossed the asparagus with oil, sprinkled on the bread-crumb topping, and then let it roast for 20 minutes. This asparagus was markedly better. It improved further when we poked the spears with a fork before salting.

WHIP IT But the cheese-crumb mixture still refused to stick. So we decided that rather than tossing the crumbs on the spears, we'd "glue" them on. We moistened the spears in lightly beaten egg and pressed them in the cheese-crumb mixture before roasting. This "topping" was too heavy for the delicate vegetable. To lighten it, we switched to using only the egg whites. To ensure that the cheese-crumb combo would stay put, we mixed the whites with the stickiest (edible) thing we could think of: honey. Tasters liked its subtle sweetness, and we liked its adhesive properties. For the coating, we pitted ordinary bread crumbs against extra-crunchy panko crumbs. We preferred the latter. Through testing, we determined that ¾ cup of crumbs to 1½ cups of Parmesan was the best ratio. We also found that if we set aside ½ cup of the cheese to sprinkle over the coated asparagus partway through roasting, we got the crispiest coating and the best cheese flavor. With each test, the asparagus was improving, yet tasters continued to ask for more crunch. Wait a minute . . . If we whipped the egg whites before coating the asparagus, might they form peaks and valleys to grip the most possible bits of crunchy coating? Yes. Each spear was now a slim flavor-texture bomb of crunch, cheese, salt, and roasty asparagus sweetness.

PARMESAN-CRUSTED ASPARAGUS
SERVES 4 TO 6

This recipe works best with ½-inch-thick spears. Work quickly when tossing the asparagus with the egg whites, as the salt will rapidly begin to deflate the whites.

2	pounds medium-thick asparagus, trimmed
	Salt and pepper
3	ounces Parmesan cheese, grated (1½ cups)
¾	cup panko bread crumbs
1	tablespoon unsalted butter, melted and cooled
	Pinch cayenne pepper
2	large egg whites
1	teaspoon honey

1. Adjust oven rack to middle position and heat oven to 450 degrees. Line rimmed baking sheet with aluminum foil and spray with vegetable oil spray. Using fork, poke holes all over asparagus. Toss asparagus with ½ teaspoon salt and let stand for 30 minutes on paper towel–lined baking sheet.

2. Meanwhile, combine 1 cup Parmesan, panko, melted butter, ¼ teaspoon salt, ⅛ teaspoon pepper, and cayenne in bowl. Transfer half of Parmesan mixture to shallow dish and reserve remaining mixture. Using stand mixer fitted with whisk, whip egg whites with honey on medium-low speed until foamy, about 1 minute. Increase speed to medium-high and whip until soft peaks form, 2 to 3 minutes. Pour egg white mixture into 13 by 9-inch baking dish and toss asparagus with egg white mixture. Working with 1 spear at a time, dredge half of asparagus in Parmesan mixture and transfer to baking sheet. Refill shallow dish with reserved Parmesan mixture and repeat with remaining half of asparagus.

3. Bake asparagus until just beginning to brown, 6 to 8 minutes. Sprinkle with remaining ½ cup Parmesan and continue to bake until cheese is melted and panko is golden brown, 6 to 8 minutes longer. Transfer to platter. Serve.

Tagliatelle with Prosciutto, Parmesan, and Peas

✓ WHY THIS RECIPE WORKS

Good ingredients are at the heart of all Italian cooking, so we chose ours through careful testing. Opting for a dried Italian-made egg pasta over traditional dried pasta got us very close to the texture of labor-intensive fresh pasta. Frozen peas, picked at peak ripeness, offered the most consistently sweet results. To capture the full flavor of pricey prosciutto di Parma, we used it in two ways.

PEAK PROSCIUTTO To get the most from our prosciutto, we simmered a portion of it in the cream sauce and tossed the rest with the pasta as raw strips so it retained its aromatic intensity and supple texture. This way we got a background salty/umami flavor of cooked prosciutto combined with the unique fruity, nutty fragrance of raw.

USE TWO CHEESES Recent research has shown that there is much aromatic crossover between prosciutto and Parmesan cheese, which explains why the pairing is so powerful and complementary. Digging deeper, we compared the most prevalent aroma compounds in prosciutto, Parmesan, and a number of other aged cheeses. It turned out that aged Gruyère—a cheese that is especially meaty and fruity tasting—contains two important compounds present in prosciutto but not in Parmesan: methanethiol, which aroma experts describe as meaty, fishy, and cheesy, and ethyl-2-methylbutyrate, which provides fruity apple and strawberry scents. Subbing in unconventional aged Gruyère for a portion of the Parmesan cheese made the prosciutto taste, well, more prosciutto-y. Sold!

TAGLIATELLE WITH PROSCIUTTO, PARMESAN, AND PEAS
SERVES 4 TO 6

We prefer imported prosciutto di Parma or domestically made prepackaged Volpi Traditional Prosciutto. If using sliced-to-order prosciutto, ask for it to be sliced ¹⁄₁₆ inch thick. Look for a hard Gruyère that is aged for at least 10 months and use a rasp-style grater or the small holes of box grater to grate it. Tagliatelle is a long, flat, dry egg pasta that is about ¼ inch wide. If you cannot find tagliatelle, substitute pappardelle.

6	ounces thinly sliced prosciutto
1	tablespoon unsalted butter
1	shallot, minced

Salt and pepper
1 cup heavy cream
1 pound tagliatelle
1½ cups frozen petite peas, thawed
1 ounce Parmesan cheese, grated (½ cup)
1 ounce Gruyère cheese, grated (½ cup)

1. Slice 5 ounces prosciutto crosswise into ¼-inch-wide strips; set aside. Mince remaining 1 ounce prosciutto. Melt butter in 10-inch skillet over medium-low heat. Add shallot and ¼ teaspoon salt and cook until softened, about 2 minutes. Stir in cream and minced prosciutto and bring to simmer. Cook, stirring occasionally, until cream mixture measures 1 cup, 5 to 7 minutes. Remove pan from heat and cover to keep warm.

2. Meanwhile, bring 4 quarts water to boil in large pot. Add pasta and 1 tablespoon salt and cook, stirring often, until al dente. Reserve 2 cups cooking water, then drain pasta and return it to pot.

3. Add 1 cup reserved cooking water, cream mixture, prosciutto strips, peas, Parmesan, Gruyère, and 1 teaspoon pepper to pasta. Gently toss until pasta is well coated. Transfer pasta to serving bowl and serve immediately, adjusting consistency with remaining reserved cooking water as needed.

Italian Chicken Soup with Parmesan Dumplings

✓ WHY THIS RECIPE WORKS

Passatelli are tender dumplings formed by pressing dough made from bread crumbs, eggs, and Parmesan cheese—and in the best versions, beef marrow—through the holes of a specialized tool. The resulting skinny, noodle-shaped dumplings are so deeply flavorful that as a first course they need nothing more than to be poached in a light chicken broth. But, we quickly found, making this dish in our own kitchen would require some significant adjustments. For one thing, if we were going to make dumplings from scratch, we didn't want them to be an appetizer, we wanted them to be the main course. This meant that the broth would need some bulking up. Then there was the matter of the dumpling-making tool. Surely there was a way to shape dough that would cook up light and chewy without having to buy a whole new gadget.

PROCESS THE PARM We began by rolling a batch of round dumplings made from coarse, crisp Japanese-style

bread crumbs, whole eggs, and finely grated Parmesan, and simmered them in broth. Unfortunately these dumplings were rather dull. We switched to homemade crumbs, but we wanted more Parmesan flavor. Increasing it to 3 ounces gave our dumplings a jump, but when cooked, all that melting cheese turned the dough into gluey balls: The finely grated wisps created by our rasp style grater were gluing too tightly to one another upon heating. Would the food processor change that? Yes. Making the cheese roughly the same size and shape as the bread crumbs prevented the cheese crumbs from clinging to each other and melting together. The use of egg whites also lightened up the dumplings.

AMP UP THE BROTH Instead of using a light and delicate broth, we wanted to create a richer, more satisfying broth, but without spending all day on it. We turned to our trick of enriching store-bought broth with chicken thighs and aromatic vegetables, including onions, carrots, and celery. Browning only the skin side of the thighs produced flavorful fond on the bottom of the pot, and to avoid any need for skimming fat off the finished broth, we poured off the rendered fat and removed the skin before simmering the thighs with the vegetables and broth.

ITALIAN CHICKEN SOUP WITH PARMESAN DUMPLINGS

SERVES 4 TO 6

Use the large holes of a box grater to shred the Parmesan. To ensure that the dumplings remain intact during cooking, roll them until the surfaces are smooth and no cracks remain.

4	(5- to 7-ounce) bone-in chicken thighs, trimmed
	Salt and pepper
1	teaspoon vegetable oil
1	fennel bulb, 1 tablespoon fronds minced, stalks discarded, bulb halved, cored, and cut into ½-inch pieces
1	onion, chopped fine
2	carrots, peeled and cut into ¾-inch pieces
½	cup dry white wine
8	cups chicken broth
1	Parmesan cheese rind, plus 3 ounces Parmesan, shredded (1 cup)
2	slices hearty white sandwich bread, torn into 1-inch pieces
2	large egg whites
¼	teaspoon grated lemon zest
	Pinch ground nutmeg
½	small head escarole (6 ounces), trimmed and cut into ½-inch pieces

1. Pat chicken dry with paper towels and season with salt and pepper. Heat oil in Dutch oven over medium-high heat until just smoking. Add chicken, skin side down, and cook until well browned, 6 to 8 minutes. Transfer chicken to plate. Discard skin.

2. Pour off all but 1 teaspoon fat from pot and reserve 1 tablespoon fat for dumplings. Return pot to medium heat. Add fennel bulb, onion, carrots, and ½ teaspoon salt and cook, stirring occasionally, until vegetables soften and begin to brown, about 5 minutes. Add wine and cook, scraping up any browned bits, until almost dry, about 2 minutes. Return chicken to pot; add broth and Parmesan rind and bring to boil. Reduce heat to low, cover, and simmer until chicken is tender and registers 175 degrees, about 30 minutes. Transfer chicken to plate. Discard Parmesan rind. Cover broth and remove from heat. When cool enough to handle, use 2 forks to shred chicken into bite-size pieces. Discard bones.

3. While broth is simmering, adjust oven rack to middle position and heat oven to 350 degrees. Pulse bread in food processor until finely ground, 10 to 15 pulses. Measure out 1 cup bread crumbs and transfer to parchment paper–lined rimmed baking sheet (set aside remainder for another use). Toast until light brown, about 5 minutes. Transfer to medium bowl, reserving sheet and parchment, and let bread crumbs cool completely.

4. Pulse shredded Parmesan in now-empty food processor until finely ground, 10 to 15 pulses. Transfer Parmesan to bowl with cooled bread crumbs and add egg whites, lemon zest, nutmeg, ⅛ teaspoon pepper, and reserved 1 tablespoon fat. Mix until thoroughly combined. Refrigerate dough for 15 minutes.

5. Working with 1 teaspoon dough at a time, roll into smooth balls and place on parchment-lined sheet (you should have about 28 dumplings).

6. Return broth to simmer over medium-high heat. Add escarole and chicken and return to simmer. Add dumplings and cook, adjusting heat to maintain gentle simmer, until dumplings float to surface and are cooked through, 3 to 5 minutes. Stir in fennel fronds. Season with salt and pepper to taste, and serve.

TO MAKE AHEAD: Prepare recipe through step 5. Refrigerate broth, shredded chicken, and dumplings separately for up to 24 hours. To serve, proceed with step 6 as directed.

PRACTICAL SCIENCE
THE CRYSTALS OF PARMESAN

The mystery of Parmesan's crystal structure has been solved.

Well-aged Parmigiano-Reggiano cheese is characterized by the visible presence of very small white crystals, and larger round "pearls." These are not defects, but contribute to the satisfying crunch of really good cheese that has been aged for about two years. Similar crystals and pearls are seen in cheddar and gouda cheeses aged for two years. For a long time cheese experts have wondered about the composition of these crunchy artifacts. Early studies suggested they might be crystals of amino acids formed by the proteolysis of proteins. Other studies suggested they could be crystals of salts such as calcium lactate or calcium phosphate, or even mixtures of these compounds. Thanks to research conducted at the University of Vermont using a sophisticated method called powder x-ray diffractometry we now know the answer, which was published in *Dairy Science and Technology* in 2015. The tiny white crystals in Parmigiano-Reggiano are composed of the amino acid called tyrosine, while the small pearls turn out to be a crystalline form of the amino acid called leucine. Mystery solved! (See experiment, page 168.)

CHAPTER 21

Green Beans

These legumes are one the few green vegetables that stay together during long cooking.

HOW THE SCIENCE WORKS

Green beans are legumes, members of a family of plants that contain seeds within a pod. There are more than 130 different varieties with the Latin name *Phaseolus vulgaris*, the most common including snap beans, string beans, and the long, thin haricots verts. While string beans once had a "string" attached, keeping the pod closed, the beans were bred to grow without the string in the late 1800s, making true "string" beans uncommon today. What we do find in the supermarket: green beans with round pods and immature seeds inside.

One of the key differences between the cells in plants and animals is that plant cells are surrounded by thick, strong cell walls in addition to the thin cell membranes that surround animal cells. The strong cell walls in plants provide extra protection for the contents inside, but also contribute most of the texture we associate with eating vegetables. Because the seeds inside green beans are immature and small, most of the texture of green beans is provided by the pods.

Green beans contain about 90 percent water. The remaining 10 percent is made up of protein (about 2 percent) and equal amounts of cell wall polysaccharides and free sugars (about 7 percent). And the polysaccharides (composed of cellulose, hemicellulose, and pectin) are important, as they make up the majority of green beans' nondigestible dietary fiber. The hemicellulose and pectin are embedded within the cellulose and also form a tightly bound coating around it, providing a rigid cell wall structure that makes fresh green beans firm enough to snap when broken in half.

The pectin acts like glue that holds the cell walls together. During cooking, however, it breaks down, weakening the structure of the cell walls, which then collapse.

Beans were bred to grow without the string in the late 1800s, making true "string" beans uncommon today.

This is what makes the beans tender. Notably, pectin is sensitive not only to heat, but also to the pH of the cooking liquid. It is very stable in acidic liquids, but becomes progressively less stable as the pH increases (becoming more alkaline). This is why beans take longer to cook in acidic tomato sauce than water, and why adding baking soda can shorten cooking times.

We cook green beans in two ways: fast and slow. Fresh green beans are great after a quick roast in the oven (page 178), maintaining their bright color and crunchy texture. We steam them for just a few minutes before adding them to our Pasta with Pesto, Potatoes, and Green Beans (page 181). If the beans are cooked quickly, much of the volatile compounds, the pectin, and chlorophyll will remain intact, keeping the beans a bright green with a firm texture. Want access to crunchy-tender green beans all year round? Can them yourself with our Dilly Beans recipe (page 182).

But beans are rugged. The strong and abundant cellulose molecules in the cell walls, as well as a small amount of a substance called lignin, are very resistant to heat. So even though the beans become tender and dull in color, they can be braised for a long time without falling apart. Unlike other green vegetables, green beans will not turn into mush after 20 minutes. The long cooking time, instead, gives the beans a silky yet stable texture. While they lose volatile flavor compounds, they do gain the rich flavor of the braising liquid. Our braised green beans (page 178) are cooked for over an hour, partly with acidic tomatoes, to give them a rich texture. Our Sesame-Ginger Braised Green Beans (page 179) are in the slow cooker for up to a full 8 hours.

TEST KITCHEN EXPERIMENT

There are many green vegetables that don't fare too well when cooked past crisp-tender (mushy snap peas or broccoli, anyone?), but green beans are not among them. In fact, green beans are a surprisingly versatile veggie, performing equally well in a quick stir-fry as they do in a long, slow braise. We used the classic Mediterranean recipe of green beans braised with tomatoes to examine how changes in pH impact green bean cookery.

EXPERIMENT

We cooked 1½ pounds of green beans in three different cooking liquids and tracked how long it took for each batch to reach the same final tenderness, which we measured using a CT3 Texture Analyzer (see page 3). We also tasted each sample and noted differences in texture beyond tenderness (creamy, silky, chalky, etc.). The first cooking liquid contained water, tomato paste, canned diced tomatoes, and salt and registered a relatively acidic pH of 4. In the second batch we ditched the tomato products and cooked the beans in water with baking soda and salt—a mixture that registered an alkaline pH of 8. The final batch was cooked in water and salt and registered a neutral pH of 7.

RESULTS

The beans cooked with tomatoes took 70 minutes to turn tender, but even at that point the interiors never reached the same silky quality as the other samples. The exteriors of these beans remained intact. The beans cooked in the water spiked with baking soda softened rapidly. At the 20-minute mark their exteriors were extremely soft and some beans had blown out. The sample cooked in neutral water reached comparable tenderness in 35 minutes, and featured relatively creamy interiors and intact exteriors.

TAKEAWAY

Traditional recipes for braised green beans with tomatoes feature long cooking times (often on the order of a couple of hours), as the acidity introduced by the tomatoes reinforces the pectin holding the beans together. As we saw in this experiment, turning the cooking liquid alkaline with a small amount of baking soda can speed the breakdown of the pectin significantly. In our recipe for Mediterranean Braised Green Beans (see page 178) we use our knowledge of this relationship to achieve the best of both worlds. We start cooking the beans in baking soda–spiked water to speed cooking and turn their interiors silky and creamy. Then we add the tomato product, which neutralizes the cooking liquid and helps prevent the exteriors of the beans from turning mushy.

GREEN BEANS AND PH: A DELICATE BALANCE

COOKED WITH ACIDIC TOMATOES
It took 70 minutes for these beans to cook, remaining relatively tender and intact.

COOKED WITH BASIC BAKING SODA
These beans cooked in 20 minutes, becoming incredibly soft and blown out.

COOKED IN NEUTRAL WATER
After 35 minutes, these beans were tender and intact.

FOCUS ON: GREEN BEANS

There are many types of green beans, but we most often see string beans or haricots verts in the market. At their most basic, green beans are immature, unripe seeds surrounded by a pod. Let's take a closer look.

POD

Most of the texture of cooked green beans is provided by the protective pod. Like many other vegetables, green beans contain about 90 percent water. The remaining 10 percent is made up of protein (about 2 percent), and equal amounts of cell wall polysaccharides and free sugars (about 7 percent total). The majority of the texture of green beans comes from the pod.

STEM

Green beans grow either as bush beans or pole beans. Both are attached to the plant via their stem, which is often removed before cooking.

SEEDS

The seeds inside green beans are immature at harvest.

CLOSE UP: GREEN BEAN CELLS

Plant cells are surrounded by a thick, strong cell wall in addition to the thin cell membranes that typically surround animal cells. The strong cell walls in plants provide extra protection for the contents inside, and contribute most of the texture we associate with plant foods.

And in green beans? The firm texture of fresh green beans comes from their especially rigid cell wall structure. This is largely due to the relatively substantial amount of polysaccharides found in the cell walls. These polysaccharides are composed of three components: cellulose, hemicellulose, and pectin. The hemicellulose and pectin are embedded within the tough strands of cellulose and they also form a tightly bound coating around the cellulose. This gives green beans enough firmness that they snap when bent in half.

cell nucleus

vacuole

cell wall

cell membrane

chloroplast

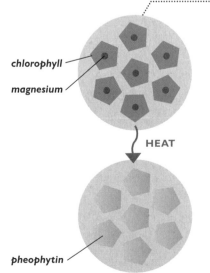

chlorophyll

magnesium

HEAT

pheophytin

COLOR

Fresh green beans are a vibrant green, a color caused by the molecule chlorophyll, which occurs in two closely related chemical forms—chlorophyll a and chlorophyll b—and is responsible for photosynthesis in the plant. Chlorophyll contains an atom of magnesium in the middle of its chemical structure. If the magnesium atom is removed, a new molecule called pheophytin is formed, which is responsible for the dull olive-green color of long-cooked green beans. In acidic conditions, the magnesium atom is lost more rapidly, so cooking green beans in tomato sauce, or vinegar, or soaking them in lemon juice (such as salad dressing) turns them dull green very quickly.

POLYSACCHARIDE

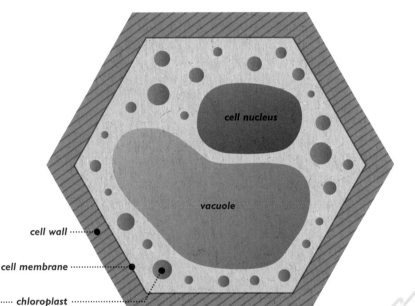

pectin

hemicellulose

cellulose fiber

Roasted Green Beans

✓ WHY THIS RECIPE WORKS

Delicate and slender, garden-fresh haricots verts need only a few minutes of steaming, a pat of butter, and a sprinkle of salt and pepper to be ready for the table. In fact, they are so sweet, crisp, and tender that it's not uncommon to eat them raw. Take the same route with mature supermarket green beans, however, and you'll regret it. Unlike their lithe cousins, overgrown store-bought beans are often tough and dull, demanding special treatment. Roasting is commonplace for root vegetables like potatoes and carrots, and the technique is becoming popular for other vegetables, too. Would a stint in the oven have a positive effect on out-of-season green beans?

ROAST 'EM We had our answer when an embarrassingly simple test produced outstanding results. Roasted in a hot oven with only oil, salt, and pepper, an entire baking sheet of beans disappeared faster than French fries. Repeated tests confirmed that roasting consistently transforms geriatric specimens into deeply caramelized, full-flavored beauties. Here's why: As green beans mature, their fibers toughen and their sugars are converted to starch. The hot, dry heat of the oven helps to reverse the aging process. Fibers break down and an enzymatic reaction causes the starch to turn back into sugar, restoring sweetness. Roasting encourages the Maillard reaction—a chemical response that creates flavor through browning, a benefit lost in moist cooking techniques.

ROASTED GREEN BEANS
SERVES 4

An aluminum foil liner prevents burning on dark nonstick baking sheets. When using baking sheets with a light finish, foil is not required, but we recommend it for easy cleanup.

- l pound green beans, trimmed
- l tablespoon olive oil
  Salt and pepper

1. Adjust oven rack to middle position and heat oven to 450 degrees. Line rimmed baking sheet with aluminum foil and spread beans on baking sheet. Drizzle with oil and, using your hands, toss to coat. Sprinkle with ½ teaspoon salt, toss to coat, and distribute in even layer. Transfer to oven and roast for 10 minutes.

2. Remove baking sheet from oven. Using tongs, redistribute beans. Continue roasting until beans are dark golden brown in spots and have started to shrivel, 10 to 12 minutes. Season with salt and pepper to taste, and serve.

Mediterranean Braised Green Beans

✓ WHY THIS RECIPE WORKS

Quickly steamed or sautéed, lightly crisp green beans are commonplace. But there's a lesser-known approach—a slow braise—that turns beans into something altogether different. The time-honored Mediterranean take on the method calls for sautéing garlic and onions in olive oil, adding tomatoes and green beans along with water, and then simmering until the sauce is thickened and the beans are infused with tomato and garlic. The best part is the texture of the beans: The slow cooking renders them so meltingly tender that they're almost creamy. There are just two problems: First, it takes at least 2 hours of cooking to turn the beans ultra-tender. (Some recipes call for shorter cooking times, but they don't produce the truly silky texture that makes this dish so special.) Second, we often find that by the time the skins have fully softened, the interiors have practically disintegrated. We wanted the beans to turn velvety-soft but remain intact. We also wanted a reasonable cooking time—no more than an hour.

ADD BAKING SODA Before we started cooking, we brushed up on the makeup of green beans. Their pods are composed primarily of cellulose and pectin, polysaccharides that are the main building blocks of most plant cell walls. The tough fibers of cellulose are impossible to dissolve, but when pectin breaks down during cooking, water is able to enter the fibers, over time swelling and softening them. The key to speedier cooking, then, would be to focus on the pectin. Pectin is affected by pH and will break down more slowly in an acidic environment. It was therefore likely that one of the key components of this dish—tomatoes—was lengthening the cooking time. To confirm our hunch, we made one batch of beans with tomatoes and another without. Sure enough, the tomato-free beans needed far less time to soften. Tomatoes are integral to the dish, and ditching them wasn't an option. But fortunately, it's just as easy to speed up the breakdown of pectin as it is to slow it down: All you need is an alkaline environment, which is as simple as adding baking soda to the pot.

USE A LOW OVEN One minor outstanding issue: The beans were a bit ragged around the edges. So for the next test, after incorporating the tomatoes, we moved the pot to a low oven where the beans could finish cooking in the more gentle heat. These beans were perfect, with tender skins, intact interiors, and rich flavor. To brighten things, we stirred in a little red wine vinegar, along with chopped parsley for freshness. We also threw together an equally good variation with mint and feta.

MEDITERRANEAN BRAISED GREEN BEANS
SERVES 4 TO 6 AS A SIDE DISH

A dollop of yogurt spooned over the beans adds a nice tang. To make a light entrée, serve the beans with rice or crusty bread.

5	tablespoons extra-virgin olive oil
1	onion, chopped fine
4	garlic cloves, minced
	Pinch cayenne pepper
1½	cups water
½	teaspoon baking soda
1½	pounds green beans, trimmed and cut into 2- to 3-inch lengths
1	(14.5-ounce) can diced tomatoes, drained with juice reserved, chopped coarse
1	tablespoon tomato paste
1	teaspoon salt
¼	teaspoon pepper
¼	cup chopped fresh parsley
	Red wine vinegar

1. Adjust oven rack to lower-middle position and heat oven to 275 degrees. Heat 3 tablespoons oil in Dutch oven over medium heat until shimmering. Add onion and cook, stirring occasionally, until softened, 3 to 5 minutes. Add garlic and cayenne and cook until fragrant, about 30 seconds. Add water, baking soda, and green beans and bring to simmer. Reduce heat to medium-low and cook, stirring occasionally, for 10 minutes. Stir in tomatoes and their juice, tomato paste, salt, and pepper.

2. Cover pot, transfer to oven, and cook until sauce is slightly thickened and green beans can be easily cut with side of fork, 40 to 50 minutes. Stir in parsley and season with vinegar to taste. Drizzle with remaining 2 tablespoons oil and serve warm or at room temperature.

MEDITERRANEAN BRAISED GREEN BEANS WITH MINT AND FETA

Add ¾ teaspoon ground allspice with garlic and cayenne. Substitute 2 tablespoons chopped fresh mint for parsley. Omit 2 tablespoons oil in step 2. Sprinkle green beans with ½ cup crumbled feta cheese before serving.

Sesame-Ginger Braised Green Beans

✔ WHY THIS RECIPE WORKS

Braised green beans are a classic and healthy vegetable side. But braising can be time-consuming, and we wanted an easy, hands-off approach. The solution? A slow cooker. We found that cooking just half of the ginger and sesame oil with the green beans infused the beans with flavor, and stirring in a fresh portion of each once the beans were tender preserved their vibrant taste. A mixture of aromatics, hoisin sauce, and a tablespoon of water created a sauce with the perfect consistency for coating the green beans as they gently simmered and soaked up flavor. Finally, sprinkling the beans with toasted sesame seeds and thinly sliced scallions provided the finishing touch for this easy vegetable side.

USE SESAME OIL Raw sesame oil, which is very mild and light in color, is used mostly for cooking, while toasted sesame oil, which has a deep amber color, is primarily used for seasoning because of its intense flavor. For the biggest hit of flavor, we chose toasted sesame oil. Just a couple teaspoons of this oil gave the dish a deep, nutty flavor without being overpowering.

BLOOM AROMATICS IN THE MICROWAVE It seems silly to pull out a skillet to sauté the aromatics (onion, garlic, ginger) when making a slow-cooker recipe. But if you just toss these ingredients into the slow cooker with the liquid ingredients, you don't necessarily develop their potential flavors. As we do for many slow-cooker recipes, we mixed the aromatics with a little oil and then microwaved the mixture to create a greater variety of complex flavors. We scraped the contents of the bowl into the slow cooker, added the beans, water, and hoisin sauce, and then cooked it all for hours and hours.

SESAME-GINGER BRAISED GREEN BEANS
SERVES 6

This recipe cooks for 7 to 8 hours on low or 4 to 5 hours on high in a 5½- to 7-quart slow cooker.

1	onion, chopped fine
2	teaspoons toasted sesame oil
2	teaspoons grated fresh ginger
2	garlic cloves, minced
⅓	cup hoisin sauce
1	tablespoon water
2	pounds green beans, trimmed
	Salt and pepper
2	scallions, sliced thin
1	teaspoon sesame seeds, toasted

1. Microwave onion, 1 teaspoon oil, 1 teaspoon ginger, and garlic in bowl, stirring occasionally, until onion is softened, about 5 minutes; transfer to slow cooker. Stir in hoisin and water, then stir in beans. Cover and cook until beans are tender, 7 to 8 hours on low or 4 to 5 hours on high.

2. Stir in remaining 1 teaspoon oil and remaining 1 teaspoon ginger. Season with salt and pepper to taste. (Green beans can be held on warm or low setting for up to 2 hours.) Sprinkle with scallions and sesame seeds before serving.

Southern-Style Green Beans

✔ WHY THIS RECIPE WORKS

Some cooks we know preach the gospel of crisp-tender vegetables and will ardently caution against the sin of overcooking them. But we think that vegetables are just as often undercooked and can sometimes benefit from more thorough cooking. One dish that illustrates this point well is Southern-style green beans, in which the beans are boiled with potatoes and pork for upwards of an hour until they are silky-soft and infused with deliciously salty, meaty, full flavor. As a bonus, you get to drink the rich cooking liquid known as pot liquor (or pot likker). We gathered a bunch of recipes for this dish and found that many of them suffered from the same problem: a lack of specifics. In particular, several simply called for water without giving an amount; others listed "potatoes" without saying what kind or how they should be prepped. As for the pork, recipes called for bacon, ham hock, salt pork, or country-ham trimmings. Some recipes included sugar or lemon, while others went virtually unseasoned. We selected a sample of recipes that represented these variables and got busy cooking.

ADD EXTRAS Starting with 1½ pounds of beans, we ran a few tests and determined that 4 cups of water was the right amount. We tested different types of potatoes and landed on a pound of red potatoes cut into 1-inch pieces, which we added after the beans had simmered for about 20 minutes and then let cook for another half-hour, until everything was perfectly tender. As for the pork products, we tried them all (save for the country-ham trimmings, which are hard to find in much of the country) and settled on meaty-tasting ham hocks, which we started with the beans and then removed at the end so we could pick the meat and return it to the pot.

SOUTHERN-STYLE GREEN BEANS AND POTATOES
SERVES 6 TO 8

Do not drain off the cooking liquid before serving: This flavorful, savory pot liquor should be sipped with the meal. Leftover pot liquor can be used as a soup base.

1	tablespoon vegetable oil
1	onion, halved and sliced thin
4	cups water
1½	pounds green beans, trimmed and cut into 1½-inch lengths
2	(12-ounce) smoked ham hocks
3	garlic cloves, crushed and peeled
	Salt and pepper
1	pound red potatoes, unpeeled, cut into 1-inch pieces
1	teaspoon cider vinegar (optional)

1. Heat oil in Dutch oven over medium-high heat until shimmering. Add onion and cook until translucent, about 4 minutes.

2. Add water, green beans, ham hocks, garlic, and 2¼ teaspoons salt and bring to boil. Reduce heat to low, cover, and simmer for 20 minutes. Stir in potatoes, cover, and continue to simmer until potatoes are tender, about 30 minutes longer, stirring halfway through cooking.

3. Off heat, remove ham hocks and let cool for 5 minutes. Chop meat and return to pot; discard skin and bones. Gently stir in vinegar, if using, to avoid breaking up potatoes. Season with salt and pepper to taste. Serve.

Pasta with Pesto, Potatoes, and Green Beans

✓ WHY THIS RECIPE WORKS

We're relatively oblivious when it comes to trends, but even we know that carbohydrates are out of fashion. That's why the notion of putting pasta and potatoes in the same dish initially struck us as just plain wrong. But we were intrigued to learn that the preferred way to serve pesto in Liguria, Italy—the birthplace of the basil sauce—involved just that combination. Wondering what the Italians knew that we didn't, we found a handful of recipes and gave them a whirl. Some variations were dull and heavy, but we were surprised that many boasted a creamy lightness. Why? It all came down to how the potatoes were treated. The most successful versions called for cutting the potatoes into chunks and then, once cooked, vigorously mixing them with the pesto, pasta, and green beans. The agitation sloughed off their corners, which dissolved into the dish, pulling the pesto and cooking water together to form a simple sauce. But the recipe still needed work. The sauce was slightly grainy and the sharp, raw garlic dominated. Timing was another issue: The green beans could be jarringly firm and the pasta way too soft—or vice versa. And the traditional mortar and pestle? No thanks. We'd opt for the convenience of the food processor.

PICK WAXY We knew that the potatoes were the key to the sauce, and we wondered if our choice of russets was the reason for the grainy texture. Sure enough, when we subbed waxy red potatoes for russets, the graininess disappeared. Why? Waxy red potatoes contain about 25 percent less starch than russet potatoes do. When waxy potatoes are boiled, they absorb less water and their cells swell less and do not separate and burst as those in russet potatoes do. As a result, waxy potatoes produce a smooth, creamy texture, while russets can be mealy and grainy.

TIME WELL The traditional method of staggering the addition of the ingredients to the pot doesn't allow for much variation in the size or quality of each, making it difficult to cook each element perfectly—especially the green beans. But cooking each ingredient sequentially took too long, and boiling them simultaneously in separate pots dirtied too many dishes. By recycling our pine nut–toasting skillet to steam the beans, and by fully cooking the potatoes in the water before the pasta went in, we were able to cook everything separately using only two pots. Cooking the beans only briefly kept them tender and crunchy.

PASTA WITH PESTO, POTATOES, AND GREEN BEANS
SERVES 6

If gemelli is unavailable, penne or rigatoni make good substitutes. Use large red potatoes measuring 3 inches or more in diameter.

¼	cup pine nuts
3	garlic cloves, unpeeled
1	pound large red potatoes, peeled and cut into ½-inch pieces
	Salt and pepper
12	ounces green beans, trimmed and cut into 1½-inch lengths
2	cups fresh basil leaves
1	ounce Parmesan cheese, grated (½ cup)
7	tablespoons extra-virgin olive oil
1	pound gemelli
2	tablespoons unsalted butter, cut into ½-inch pieces and chilled
1	tablespoon lemon juice

1. Toast pine nuts and garlic in 10-inch skillet over medium heat, stirring frequently, until pine nuts are golden and fragrant and garlic darkens slightly, 3 to 5 minutes. Transfer to bowl and let cool. Peel garlic and chop coarse.

2. Bring 3 quarts water to boil in large pot. Add potatoes and 1 tablespoon salt and cook until potatoes are tender but still hold their shape, 9 to 12 minutes. Using slotted spoon, transfer potatoes to rimmed baking sheet. (Do not discard water.)

3. Meanwhile, bring ½ cup water and ¼ teaspoon salt to boil in now-empty skillet over medium heat. Add green beans, cover, and cook until tender, 5 to 8 minutes. Drain green beans and transfer to sheet with potatoes.

4. Process basil, Parmesan, oil, pine nuts, garlic, and ½ teaspoon salt in food processor until smooth, about 1 minute.

5. Add pasta to water in large pot and cook, stirring often, until al dente. Set colander in large bowl. Drain pasta in colander, reserving cooking water in bowl. Return pasta to pot. Add butter, lemon juice, potatoes and green beans, pesto, 1¼ cups reserved cooking water, and ½ teaspoon pepper and stir vigorously with rubber spatula until sauce takes on creamy appearance. Add additional cooking water as needed to adjust consistency and season with salt and pepper to taste. Serve immediately.

Dilly Beans

✔ WHY THIS RECIPE WORKS

Dilly beans are crunchy, sweet-sour pickled green beans flavored—as the name implies—with dill, plus the classic pickling spices of garlic, mustard seeds, and peppercorns. The biggest hurdles? Keeping the green beans both tender and crisp, and incorporating the flavor of dill without it becoming medicinal.

PRESERVE THE CRUNCH We tried various techniques for preparing our beans before packing them into jars, and we found that raw packing gave us leathery beans. Instead, to tenderize our beans and preserve their crunch, we found that a quick blanch in boiling water (followed by an ice bath) did the trick. Just 1 minute of boiling gave us the texture we were looking for in our pickles.

ADD DILL We experimented with different ways of infusing our beans with dill and found that a large bunch of chopped fresh dill steeped in the brine for 15 minutes produced the most well-rounded flavor. To infuse the brine with potent dill flavor without adding small pieces of dill that look like grass clippings to the jars, we made a sachet using cheesecloth and kitchen twine.

DILLY BEANS
FOUR 1-PINT JARS

¼ cup canning and pickling salt

2 pounds green beans, trimmed and cut into 4-inch lengths

2 cups chopped fresh dill

3 cups distilled white vinegar

3 cups water

6 tablespoons sugar

1 tablespoon black peppercorns

6 garlic cloves, peeled and quartered

1. Fill large bowl with ice water. Bring 6 quarts water and 1 tablespoon salt to boil in Dutch oven over high heat. Add beans and cook until crisp-tender but still crunchy at core, about 1 minute. Transfer beans to ice water and let cool for 2 minutes; drain well, discard ice, and pat dry with paper towels.

2. Bundle dill in cheesecloth and secure with kitchen twine. Bring dill sachet, vinegar, water, sugar, peppercorns, and remaining 3 tablespoons salt to boil in large saucepan over medium-high heat. Cover, remove from heat, and let steep for 15 minutes; discard sachet.

3. Meanwhile, set canning rack in large pot, place four 1-pint jars in rack, and add water to cover by 1 inch. Bring to simmer over medium-high heat, then turn heat off and cover to keep hot.

4. Place dish towel flat on counter. Using jar lifter, remove jars from pot, draining water back into pot. Place jars upside down on towel and let dry for 1 minute. Distribute garlic evenly among jars, then pack tightly with beans.

5. Return brine to brief boil. Using funnel and ladle, pour hot brine over beans to cover, distributing peppercorns evenly and leaving ½ inch headspace. Slide wooden skewer along inside of jar, pressing slightly on beans to remove air bubbles, and add extra brine as needed.

6A. FOR SHORT-TERM STORAGE: Let jars cool to room temperature, cover with lids, and refrigerate for at least 1 week before serving. (Beans can be refrigerated for up to 3 months; flavor will continue to mature over time.)

6B. FOR LONG-TERM STORAGE: While jars are warm, wipe rims clean, add lids, and screw on rings until fingertip-tight; do not overtighten. Return pot of water with canning rack to boil. Lower jars into water, cover, bring water back to boil, then start timer. Cooking time will depend on your altitude: Boil 10 minutes for up to 1,000 feet, 15 minutes for 1,001 to 3,000 feet, 20 minutes for 3,001 to 6,000 feet, or 25 minutes for above 6,000 feet. Turn heat off and let jars sit in pot for 5 minutes. Remove jars from pot and let cool for 24 hours. Remove rings, check seal, and clean rims. (Sealed jars can be stored for up to 1 year.)

PRACTICAL SCIENCE GREEN VS. WAX BEANS

There is no flavor difference.

Green beans get their color from chlorophyll, and yellow wax beans are simply green beans that have been bred to have none of this pigment. So the questions are, does chlorophyll contribute to the flavor of green beans and will you miss it if it's not there?

We tasted green and wax beans steamed until crisp-tender and braised in our Mediterranean Braised Green Beans recipe. In both applications, tasters found very little difference in the flavors of the two beans, calling both sweet and "grassy." But wax beans did have one advantage over green: Because they have little color to lose during prolonged braising, their appearance changes less than that of green beans, which tend to turn a drab olive. So if you're making a long-cooked bean dish and are picky about aesthetics, go for the gold.

CHAPTER 22

Sweet Potatoes

There are many differences between white and sweet potatoes. The biggest? A tiny enzyme.

HOW THE SCIENCE WORKS

All potatoes are not created equal. The deep orange, earthy sweet potatoes, which we focus on here, are only distantly related to the starchy white russets perched nearby in the market. The sweet potato, *Ipomoea batatas*, is a member of the *Convolvulaceae* family, which contains fleshy storage roots and also garden flowers called morning glories.

Sweet potatoes are one of the most important food crops in the world, yet in the United States they are mostly used as an occasional vegetable, covered in marshmallows and served for Thanksgiving. But the world of sweet potatoes extends far beyond these marshmallow-crusted confines. Ninety percent of the world's sweet potatoes are grown in Asia, where they are mostly white-fleshed and neither as sweet nor as soft as the traditional orange-fleshed varieties. (Sweet potatoes are not related to true yams, which have thick, fibrous skin and are starchy and fairly bland tasting.)

Sweet potatoes come in different forms, but the most common in the United States are the deep-orange Beauregard and Jewel. These varieties have a moist, soft texture and are very sweet when cooked. Interestingly, the moist orange varieties are not favored in the rest of the world.

All sweet potatoes are "cured" for four to seven days immediately after harvest, stored at 84 degrees and around 95 percent relative humidity. (All potatoes are cured, though the conditions are different depending on the variety.) Curing heals wounds from harvesting and handling, and decreases the potential for microbial decay during storage. Perhaps most important, the curing phase facilitates the synthesis of amylase enzymes, which are important for flavor development during cooking (more on this later).

> **Sweet potatoes are only distantly related to starchy white russets.**

Following curing, sweet potatoes are stored. They can last for up to a year without sprouting, at the right temperature. Sweet potatoes must be kept in a cool, dark pantry.

Most of the sweet flavor of sweet potatoes is developed during storage and cooking. Freshly harvested raw sweet potatoes are high in tasteless starch. Like the average white potato, they contain a combination of amylose and amylopectin starches. But in sweet potatoes, these starches are converted to sugars by a family of enzymes known as amylases. This happens first during storage, when up to 27 percent of the starch can be converted over a period of 10 weeks. The amylase enzymes become more active with heat, especially between 140 and 170 degrees, and so during cooking the amylases can convert as much as 75 percent of the total starch to sugars.

Though sweet potatoes have a very similar moisture content to most white potatoes, more starch is broken down in sweet potatoes during the cooking process, meaning more moisture is released from the starch granules. This is why many sweet potatoes are soft and moist rather than mealy. (For example: our Baked Sweet Potatoes, page 186.) Because of the differences in starch breakdown and moisture release, we treat sweet potatoes differently than we do white potatoes. For our Thick-Cut Sweet Potato Fries (page 188), we first blanch them in water and then add a cornstarch slurry before giving them their final fry. We use the moisture-release levels of sweet potatoes to our advantage, braising them in mostly their own liquid for our Mashed Sweet Potatoes (page 186); or we work to get rid of the extra moisture, as by using an elevated rack for our Roasted Sweet Potato Wedges (page 187) so they don't become mushy.

TEST KITCHEN EXPERIMENT

Common sweet potato varieties contain an enzyme called amylase that has the ability to break down starch and convert it to the sugar maltose. The conversion is most active in the range of 140 to 170 degrees. We were inspired by J. Kenji Lopez-Alt's 2014 experiment on seriouseats.com, where he used sous vide to hold sweet potatoes in this enzymatic sweet spot. We decided to gather our own data to find out if a longer time resulted in a sweeter spud.

EXPERIMENT

To control for the fact that the starch and sugar composition can vary among individual sweet potatoes, we worked with one large sweet potato, and repeated the test two more times with different sweet potatoes. We peeled the sweet potato, cut it into thin slices, and sealed each piece in a separate vacuum bag. For a control, we boiled three samples for 1 minute to ensure the enzyme was completely denatured (and therefore no longer able to convert starch to maltose). We placed all of the samples (including the controls) in a 150-degree temperature-controlled water bath. At 1, 2, and 3 hours we removed three of the test samples plus one of the controls. We boiled the test samples for 1 minute to denature the enzyme. Finally, we cooked all samples in a water bath at 190 degrees until tender (150 degrees is too low for sweet potatoes to actually soften). Tasters tried the warm samples for each time period next to the control for that time period. The results are an average of our three tests.

RESULTS

The controls were identical to one another in sweetness, flavor, and texture, confirming that the enzyme had indeed been denatured by boiling. After 1 hour of cooking, tasters noted a subtle difference in the sweetness and flavor of the test samples compared to the control, often describing it as "molasses-y." The difference became more noticeable at the 2-hour mark, and registered the strongest at 3 hours. Beyond flavor differences, we were surprised to see a marked difference in texture. All of the test samples cooked up with a "firm," "cooked carrot-like" texture, while the controls were consistently "creamy" and "smooth."

TAKEAWAY

Maltose is not a very sweet sugar. It's roughly one-third as sweet as sucrose (granulated sugar). So while amylase had clearly converted starch to maltose, it's not surprising that tasters didn't find the potatoes to be a lot sweeter. More intriguing was the change in flavor, from simply sweet to molasses-like. A few tasters preferred the flavor of the samples cooked at 150 degrees for 3 hours, but no one preferred their texture. And the firmness, it turns out, is caused by a completely separate enzymatic reaction: Sweet potatoes contain another enzyme, pectin methylesterase, which, at temperatures between 120 and 160 degrees, allows pectin in the potato's cell walls to readily link with calcium ions and become reinforced. The result is sweet potatoes that stay firmer, even when later cooked at a higher temperature.

This experiment demonstrates the effect that amylase has on sweet potato starch. There are times when it's worth it to cook low and slow to maximize starch conversion but in most cases we found that adding even a small amount of molasses or brown sugar masked any differences in flavor.

NOT-SO-SWEET SWEET POTATOES

While sweet potatoes are pretty sweet no matter what, we wondered if cooking them especially low and slow would make for sweeter spuds. After all, the enzyme amylase present in sweet potatoes converts starch to the sugar maltose most actively between 140 and 170 degrees. But after cooking many samples in a temperature-controlled water bath (shown here at 149.7 degrees), we found that, while a tiny bit sweeter, maltose just isn't sweet enough to make a huge difference.

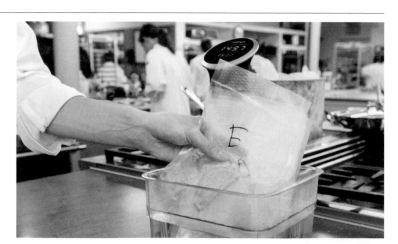

FAMILY TREE: POTATOES

Although all vegetables vary by size and freshness, most markets carry only a single variety. Broccoli is broccoli, carrots are carrots. Even when there are several varieties (as with heirloom tomatoes), most can be used interchangeably in recipes. Yes, one tomato might look a bit different or be a bit sweeter than another, but they all will taste fine in salads. With potatoes, this is not the case.

SWEET POTATOES

Like white potatoes, sweet potatoes contain a mix of starches and moisture. There are many differences—white potato starch granules are larger than in sweet potatoes, and white potato granules swell and gelatinize at a lower temperature. But the biggest is the presence of enzymes, specifically amylase enzymes, which are found in all sweet potatoes and not found at all in white potatoes. They are important because amylase enzymes convert starches to sugars during the cooking process.

SOFT, MOIST FLESHED

Moist, soft sweet potatoes contain more amylase enzymes, meaning more of the starch in these sweet potatoes is broken down. With less starch these potatoes release more moisture and have a moist, soft texture.

Beauregard, Jewel, Red Garnet, Hernandez, Centennial

FIRM, MEALY FLESHED

These firm potatoes have fewer amylase enzymes, meaning that less starch is turned into sugar, and they cook up less moist and more mealy. Many are white-fleshed and popular outside the U.S.

O'Henry, Jersey, White Triumph, Southern Queen, Kotobuki, Okinawan

WHITE POTATOES

White potatoes are categorized into two major eating types: High-starch, low-moisture (which can be dry and mealy); and low-starch, high-moisture (also classified as smooth and waxy). These two types of potatoes differ in total starch content and the composition of the starch. Waxy potatoes have less starch. But most importantly, the composition of the starch is quite different. Most starch in plants is made of two molecules: amylose and amylopectin. High-starch mealy potatoes contain about 25 percent amylose with the rest being amylopectin. But low-starch waxy potatoes contain almost no amylose.

HIGH STARCH

These potatoes generally lose their shape when simmered. Because they have so little moisture, they soak up liquid as they cook and explode.

MEDIUM STARCH

Medium-starch potatoes do a better job of holding their shape but share many traits in common with high-starch potatoes.

LOW STARCH

Low-starch/high-moisture potatoes hold their shape better than other potatoes when simmered. They contain little amylose.

YAMS

Yams are not potatoes. On a dry basis they contain about 90 percent starch, of which around 20 percent is amylose. So they do contain more starch than potatoes, and a little bit less moisture. The small number of varieties of edible yams are not toxic. But wild yams contain a toxic alkaloid called dioscorine.

SWEET POTATOES: HOW STARCH TURNS TO SUGAR

When sweet potatoes cook, a family of enzymes call amylases work to convert the starch present into a sugar called maltose. The amylase enzymes break down the starch, which is made up of chains of glucose molecules. The resulting maltose consists of two glucose molecules linked together, and is less sweet than glucose alone.

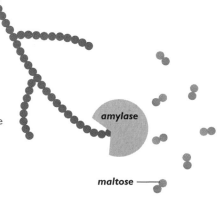

starch ⎯

amylase

maltose ⎯

Baked Sweet Potatoes

✔ **WHY THIS RECIPE WORKS**

We wanted to find the perfect baked sweet potato recipe, moist inside with a soft, caramelized skin. We pierced the potatoes' skins with a fork, rubbed the potatoes with oil, and then baked them on a foil-lined baking sheet set on the middle rack of a 400-degree oven. We learned not to turn the potatoes during baking; turning will keep the perfectly browned bottom skin from caramelizing.

PICK MOIST POTATOES Sweet potatoes (occasionally labeled "yams" in the grocery store, though they are not actually yams), come in two distinct types: dry and moist. The endless varieties, sizes, and shapes can be confusing, but the basic rule is that dry sweet potatoes have white to yellow flesh while moist ones are varying deep shades of orange. This recipe is for the moist, orange-fleshed varieties of sweet potatoes.

PIERCE AND OIL We did a number of tests to find the best way to deal with the skin, which is thin and very delicious when cooked properly. Uncoated skin stayed tough and unappealing, but coating it with butter tended to cause burning. Lightly rubbing with fresh vegetable or olive oil, though, softened the skin just the right amount. Piercing the skin, we found, was essential to prevent the infamous exploding potato.

BAKED SWEET POTATOES
SERVES 4

You can cook up to six potatoes at one time without altering the cooking time. Buying potatoes of the same size is a good idea because it standardizes cooking time.

- 4 medium sweet potatoes (about 2 pounds), washed, dried, and lightly pricked with a fork in 3 places
- 2 tablespoons olive oil or vegetable oil
  Salt and pepper
  Unsalted butter

1. Adjust oven rack to middle position and heat oven to 400 degrees. Rub potatoes with oil, then arrange on aluminum foil–lined baking sheet as far apart as possible.

2. Bake until knife tip slips easily into potato center, 40 to 50 minutes. Slit each potato lengthwise; using dish towel, hold ends and squeeze together slightly until soft flesh mounds up. Season with salt and plenty of pepper to taste. Dot with butter to taste, and serve.

Mashed Sweet Potatoes

✔ **WHY THIS RECIPE WORKS**

For the holidays, mashed sweet potatoes are often overdressed in a Willie Wonka–style casserole topped with marshmallows and whipped cream. But this candied concoction doesn't hold a candle to an honest sweet potato mash in terms of flavor. With a deep, natural sweetness that doesn't require much assistance, the humble sweet potato, we thought, would taste far better if prepared using a modicum of ingredients. Yet even with a simple recipe, mashed sweet potatoes would pose some problems. Nailing a fork-friendly puree every time is a form of cooking roulette. Mashed sweet potatoes often turn out overly thick and gluey or, at the other extreme, sloppy and loose. We also found that most recipes overload the dish with pumpkin pie seasonings that obscure the potatoes' natural flavor. We wanted a recipe that would push their deep, earthy flavor to the fore and that would produce a silky puree with enough body to hold its shape while sitting on a fork.

BRAISE 'EM To determine the best cooking method, we tested a variety of techniques: baking unpeeled potatoes; boiling whole, unpeeled potatoes; boiling peeled and diced potatoes; and microwaving whole unpeeled potatoes. Adding a little butter and salt to the potatoes after they were mashed, we found huge differences in texture, flavor, and ease of preparation. The baked potatoes made a mash with deep flavor and bright color, but took a long time to bake (over an hour) and handling them hot was tricky. Boiling created a watery, flavorless mash. It was easy to overmicrowave the potatoes, which created a pasty mouthfeel and odd plastic flavor. But then we tried braising. Cut into uniform pieces and cooked over low heat in a covered pan, the sweet potatoes released their own moisture slowly, basically braising themselves and remaining flavorful.

ADD CREAM Rather than adding water to the pot to help jump-start the braising, we figured we might as well add the butter and dairy (why water down the flavor?). When comparing batches with added cream, milk, or half-and-half, tasters unanimously preferred cream. Two pounds of potatoes tasted best when blended with 4 tablespoons of butter and 2 tablespoons of heavy cream. This may seem like a minuscule amount of cream, but more simply ran over the sweet potatoes' delicate flavor. Adding salt brought out even more of that flavor, and just a teaspoon of sugar bolstered their sweetness.

MASHED SWEET POTATOES
SERVES 4

Cutting the sweet potatoes into slices of even thickness is important in getting them to cook at the same rate. A potato masher will yield slightly lumpy sweet potatoes; a food mill will make a perfectly smooth puree.

- 2 pounds sweet potatoes, peeled, quartered lengthwise, and cut crosswise into ¼-inch-thick slices
- 4 tablespoons unsalted butter, cut into 4 pieces
- 2 tablespoons heavy cream
- 1 teaspoon sugar
  Salt and pepper

1. Combine potatoes, butter, cream, sugar, and ½ teaspoon salt in large saucepan and cook, covered, over low heat, stirring occasionally, until potatoes fall apart when poked with fork, 35 to 45 minutes.

2. Off heat, mash potatoes in saucepan with potato masher until smooth. Season with salt and pepper to taste, and serve.

MAPLE-ORANGE MASHED SWEET POTATOES

Stir in 2 tablespoons maple syrup and ½ teaspoon grated orange zest along with pepper just before serving.

INDIAN-SPICED MASHED SWEET POTATOES WITH RAISINS AND CASHEWS

Substitute dark brown sugar for granulated sugar and add ¾ teaspoon garam masala to saucepan along with sweet potatoes in step 1. Stir ¼ cup golden raisins and ¼ cup roasted unsalted cashews, chopped coarse, into mashed sweet potatoes along with pepper just before serving.

GARLIC MASHED SWEET POTATOES WITH COCONUT AND CILANTRO

Substitute ½ cup coconut milk for butter and cream, and add 1 small minced garlic clove and ¼ teaspoon red pepper flakes to pot with potatoes. Stir in 1 tablespoon minced fresh cilantro just before serving.

Roasted Sweet Potato Wedges

✓ WHY THIS RECIPE WORKS

Roasting vegetables is one of the most flavorful ways to cook them. The recipe, if it can be called one, is basic: Toss vegetables in oil, season, throw onto baking sheet, roast at 450 degrees. The method concentrates the flavor of vegetables, coaxing out and intensifying their natural sugars. But if you roast wedges of sweet potatoes, they can cook unevenly and become soggy inside and leathery outside. They never develop the caramelized exterior, creamy interior, and intense flavor of other roasted vegetables. We wanted to solve these problems. The solution? We ended up cooking them in two steps.

RAISE THEM   As sweet potatoes cook, moisture leaks out, so the potatoes stew in their own liquid instead of roasting. Which means they never brown. To raise the potatoes out of that liquid, we began by roasting them at a low temperature on a wire rack set in a baking sheet to dry them out—and allow the enzymes present to turn starch to sugar.

BROWN THEM   We finished them on a preheated rimmed baking sheet in a hot oven so the natural sugars in the potatoes caramelized on the exterior.

ROASTED SWEET POTATO WEDGES
SERVES 4 TO 6

Let the potatoes cool for 10 minutes after the first bake before tossing with the oil (hot potatoes will stick to the pan).

- 2 pounds sweet potatoes, peeled
- 1 tablespoon vegetable oil
- 2 teaspoons sugar
- ½ teaspoon salt
- ¼ teaspoon pepper

1. Adjust oven rack to middle position and heat oven to 325 degrees. Cut each potato in half crosswise, then cut each half into 6 to 8 wedges. Arrange wedges on wire rack set in rimmed baking sheet and bake until just tender, about 30 minutes. Remove potatoes from oven and increase heat to 475 degrees. Wipe off baking sheet and return to oven. Let potatoes cool on wire rack for 10 minutes.

2. Gently toss potatoes with oil, sugar, salt, and pepper in large bowl. Remove baking sheet from oven. Arrange potatoes in single layer on hot sheet and roast, flipping once, until deep golden brown, 15 to 20 minutes. Serve.

Thick-Cut Sweet Potato Fries

✔ WHY THIS RECIPE WORKS

Though white potatoes and sweet potatoes contain roughly the same amount of starch and water, they cook very differently—a fact that is nowhere more apparent than when making fries. It's very hard to make sweet potato fries that rival classic French fries made from russets. Sweet potato fries are typically soggy or burnt—and often they hit both marks at once. Occasionally a restaurant manages to deliver crispy sweet potato fries, but they never taste much like the tuber. These fries are usually not even house-made: They're frozen fries purchased from a food processing plant. Furthermore, they're frequently cut too thin for our liking, offering little in the way of a supercreamy, sweet-tasting interior—in our opinion, the biggest selling point of this vegetable. Fueled by a serious hunger for good thick-cut sweet potato fries, we ordered 50 pounds of the orange spuds and got to work.

BLANCH Our first thought was to go the classic French fry route and treat the uncoated wedges to a quick blanch in lower-temperature (around 250-degree) oil before frying them again at the proper higher temperature to crisp the coating. We gave it a try, and while the interior texture turned soft and sweet, the exterior never crisped up like white potatoes. So we switched to blanching in water rather than in oil, simmering the wedges in a couple of quarts of salted water until their exteriors were tender but their very centers remained slightly firm. Adding baking soda to the water made them tacky on the outside.

COAT While commercial frozen sweet potato fries lack flavor, we have to respect their ability to turn (and stay) supercrispy. How do they do it? When we compared the ingredient lists of a few products, we found a common theme: starch. A starchy coating on these frozen fries makes all the difference. This discovery didn't come entirely by surprise. After all, it's the high-starch composition of russet potatoes that makes them so suited to frying, and we use starchy coatings to give all kinds of low-starch foods (like chicken) a crispy fried exterior. Although, while raw sweet potatoes contain about the same amount of starch and moisture as white potatoes, sweet potatoes contain an enzyme that, when heated, converts much of the starch in the sweet potatoes into sugars. All this translates into a serious handicap in the world of deep frying. We created a cornstarch slurry that stayed put, thanks in part to the parcooked wedges' tacky exteriors, and it crisped up beautifully in the hot oil.

FRY Our last move was to try to simplify and fool-proof the frying process. Up to this point we'd been using our standard setup: frying in batches in 2 quarts of oil in a large Dutch oven and keeping the fries warm in a low oven. But the supersticky coating mixture meant that now our fries were pretty likely to stick to one another, as well as to the bottom of the pot. To eliminate the bottom-sticking issue, we opted for nonstick cookware. At first a skillet seemed like an odd choice, but we found that we could drop the oil from 2 quarts to just 3 cups and still keep the wedges fully submerged. To limit how much the fries stuck to one another, we added them to the pan individually with tongs to ensure that there was good spacing around them—a simple step, considering we were

---

PRACTICAL SCIENCE WHY STARCH GETS CRISPY WHEN FRIED

It all comes down to starch molecules forming a rigid network.

While you can certainly fry food in hot oil as is (think skin-on chicken pieces), we often dip food in a coating first. Such coatings provide a few benefits: They help protect the food from moisture loss, and they shield the food from direct contact with the hot frying oil for more-gentle cooking. And perhaps most important, we know that these coatings—starchy coatings, specifically—become incredibly crispy when fried. But until now we've never really asked ourselves the deeper question: What exactly is happening that makes starch the key?

Here's what we've learned. First, the starch granules in the coating absorb water, whether from the wet surface of the food itself or because we combine them with a liquid to make a slurry before coating the food (as we do for our Thick-Cut Sweet Potato Fries). The hydrated granules swell when they are initially heated in the oil, allowing the starch molecules to move about and separate from one another. As water is driven away during the frying process, these starch molecules lock into place, forming a rigid, brittle network with a porous, open structure.

Furthermore, the two types of starch molecules (amylose and amylopectin)—which are present in varying amounts in all forms of starch, including sweet potatoes—form some cross-links with one another at high frying temperatures, further reinforcing the coating's structure. Thus, the molecules in this porous network have room to compress and fracture, providing the sensation of crispiness. Interestingly, cornstarch contains 25 to 28 percent amylose, which is higher than the amount in wheat or potato starch (which are 20 to 22 percent amylose), and this is why cornstarch works the best for making crispy coatings on fried foods.

---

using thick-cut wedges rather than shoestring fries. Any fries that did manage to stick together were easily pried apart with tongs or two forks either during or after frying. Finally (and optionally), we ditched commonplace super-sweet ketchup in favor of an easy spicy, creamy fry sauce for serving.

THICK-CUT SWEET POTATO FRIES
SERVES 4 TO 6

If your sweet potatoes are shorter than 4 inches in length, do not cut the wedges crosswise. We prefer peanut oil for frying, but vegetable oil may be used instead. Leftover frying oil may be saved for further use; strain the cooled oil into an airtight container and store it in a cool, dark place for up to one month or in the freezer for up to two months. We like these fries with our Spicy Fry Sauce (recipe follows), but they are also good served plain.

½   cup cornstarch
    Kosher salt
1   teaspoon baking soda
3   pounds sweet potatoes, peeled and cut into ¾-inch-thick wedges, wedges cut in half crosswise
3   cups peanut oil

1. Adjust oven rack to middle position and heat oven to 200 degrees. Set wire rack in rimmed baking sheet. Whisk cornstarch and ½ cup cold water together in large bowl.

2. Bring 2 quarts water, ¼ cup salt, and baking soda to boil in Dutch oven. Add potatoes and return to boil. Reduce heat to simmer and cook until exteriors turn slightly mushy (centers will remain firm), 3 to 5 minutes. Whisk cornstarch slurry to recombine. Using wire skimmer or slotted spoon, transfer potatoes to bowl with slurry.

3. Using rubber spatula, fold potatoes with slurry until slurry turns light orange, thickens to paste, and clings to potatoes.

4. Heat oil in 12-inch nonstick skillet over high heat to 325 degrees. Using tongs, carefully add one-third of potatoes to oil, making sure that potatoes aren't touching one another. Fry until crispy and lightly browned, 7 to 10 minutes, using tongs to flip potatoes halfway through

frying (adjust heat as necessary to maintain oil temperature between 280 and 300 degrees). Using wire skimmer or slotted spoon, transfer fries to prepared wire rack (fries that stick together can be separated with tongs or forks). Season with salt to taste, and transfer to oven to keep warm. Return oil to 325 degrees and repeat in 2 more batches with remaining potatoes. Serve immediately.

SPICY FRY SAUCE
MAKES ABOUT ½ CUP

For a less spicy version, use only 2 teaspoons of Asian chili-garlic sauce. The sauce can be made up to four days in advance and stored, covered, in the refrigerator.

6   tablespoons mayonnaise
1   tablespoon Asian chili-garlic sauce
2   teaspoons white vinegar

Whisk all ingredients together in small bowl.

Sweet Potato Salad

✓ WHY THIS RECIPE WORKS

For a picnic-worthy sweet potato salad, we had to rethink our typical potato salad protocol. Unlike their starchy white counterparts, sweet potatoes quickly become waterlogged and mushy when they are boiled. Steaming, however, is a relatively gentle process, which avoids any waterlogging, giving the potatoes the moist, tender texture we love.

STEAM THEM We steamed the sweet potatoes to get a perfect tender texture without turning them soggy. Adding crisp bell pepper to the steaming basket during the final minutes of cooking helped to temper its raw crunch. Then we tossed the vegetables with a seasoned vinegar mixture to ensure that they were well flavored throughout.

AND CHILL THEM Chilling the sweet potatoes in the refrigerator before finishing the salad with vinaigrette, some scallions, and a sprinkling of parsley also prevented them from having a mushy texture. Cilantro can be substituted for the parsley.

SWEET POTATO SALAD

SERVES 4 TO 6

2	pounds sweet potatoes, peeled and cut into ¾-inch pieces
1	red bell pepper, stemmed, seeded, and chopped fine
2½	tablespoons cider vinegar
1½	tablespoons Dijon mustard
	Salt and pepper
	Pinch cayenne pepper
¼	cup extra-virgin olive oil
2	scallions, sliced thin
2	tablespoons minced fresh parsley

1. Fill Dutch oven with 1 inch water and bring to boil over high heat. Reduce heat to medium-low and carefully lower steamer basket into pot. Add sweet potatoes to basket, cover, and cook until potatoes are nearly tender, about 15 minutes.

2. Add bell pepper to basket, cover, and cook until sweet potatoes and pepper are tender, 2 to 4 minutes. Transfer vegetables to large bowl.

3. Whisk vinegar, mustard, ½ teaspoon salt, ¼ teaspoon pepper, and cayenne together in small bowl. Drizzle half of vinegar mixture over vegetables, toss gently to combine, and refrigerate until vegetables are cool, about 45 minutes.

4. Whisking constantly, drizzle oil into remaining vinegar mixture, then gently stir into vegetables. Stir in scallions and parsley, season with salt and pepper to taste, and serve.

ASIAN-STYLE SWEET POTATO SALAD

Replace bell pepper with 4 ounces snow peas, strings removed and sliced ½ inch thick on bias. In step 3, replace cider vinegar with 1 tablespoon lime juice and 1 tablespoon rice vinegar, mustard with 1 tablespoon grated fresh ginger, and salt with 1 tablespoon soy sauce. Replace 1 tablespoon olive oil with 1 tablespoon toasted sesame oil. In step 4, add ⅓ cup salted, dry-roasted peanuts, chopped along with scallions and parsley.

PRACTICAL SCIENCE
CHILLING INJURIES FOR SWEET POTATOES

One potential chilling injury is hard-core formation.

What does that mean? It means that the sweet potato forms a core of hard tissue in its center, which remains even after cooking. It can occur to varying degrees in all varieties of sweet potatoes that have been subjected to improper storage below 55 degrees followed by storing at room temperatures. Why? Normally, when vegetables are cooked they become soft due to the breakdown of pectin, which holds the cell walls together (see page 177). However, when sweet potatoes are stored below 55 degrees, an enzyme called pectin methylesterase (PME) is activated. PME actually changes the pectin so that it combines with calcium ions in the cells, strengthening the pectin and keeping the cell walls, particularly in the center of the sweet potato, from softening, even during prolonged cooking. The solution? Keep your sweet potatoes in a cool (but not too cool), dry spot.

CHAPTER 23

Cauliflower

We can manipulate the flavor of this cruciferous vegetable by cooking it … longer.

HOW THE SCIENCE WORKS

Cauliflower is a cruciferous vegetable, part of the *Brassicaceae* family, related to broccoli, Brussels sprouts, cabbage, collard greens, and kale. We eat the flowering head of the cauliflower plant, called the curd, which is made up of individual florets. The oldest references to cauliflower date back to about 2,600 years ago. It originated in the Mediterranean and Asia Minor regions. Today it's popular as a substitute for carbs (see Cauliflower Rice, page 196), and it can also be treated like meat (seared in slabs, to make cauliflower "steaks").

Hundreds of varieties of cauliflower are consumed around the world, with about 80 varieties grown in North America alone. Most of the cauliflower sold in North America is white, but it also comes in green, orange, and purple. White cauliflower is produced by allowing the leaves surrounding the flowering head to cover it completely and protect it from light. If the leaves are removed from the cauliflower head, it turns green from the development of chlorophyll. Orange varieties obtain their color from carotenoids, while the purple varieties contain purple-colored pigments called anthocyanins.

There are hundreds of varieties of cauliflower—not only white, but green, orange, and purple, too.

All cauliflower grown in the United States is hand-harvested because the heads bruise very easily, leading to diseases such as the dark patches of a mold called downy mildew. Cauliflower is very sensitive to external sources of the ripening hormone ethylene gas, and therefore should not be stored near apples, melons, or tomatoes.

Cauliflower, like all cruciferous vegetables, has a characteristic pungent, nutty flavor and aroma—but they don't exist in the intact vegetable. However, when the vegetable's cells are damaged by cutting, chopping, or chewing, an enzyme called myrosinase is released. The myrosinase comes in contact with sulfur-containing compounds, called glucosinolates, that are contained within the cells. (One glucosinolate, called sinigrin, is responsible for the bitter taste of cauliflower.) The myrosinase enzyme rapidly converts the glucosinolates to volatile pungent compounds called isothiocyanates. Interestingly, cauliflower's flavor not only changes with the act of cooking, but also changes drastically depending on how long it's cooked (see Test Kitchen Experiment, page 192).

When cooking, we use the changing nature of cauliflower's flavor to our advantage, most strikingly in our Creamy Cauliflower Soup (page 194), in which we cook some of the cauliflower for only 15 minutes, and the rest for a full 30 minutes. The soup also takes advantage of the unique composition of cauliflower's fiber. All vegetables have both soluble and insoluble fiber, but only the soluble kind fully breaks down during cooking, which contributes viscosity to, say, a soup. Insoluble fiber remains intact. Cauliflower has a leg up on other vegetables: It has very little fiber overall, and only half of it is insoluble. This means that cauliflower is easily pureed into a silky-smooth soup with no cream at all.

Cauliflower is also delicious cooked for an even longer amount of time, treated more like a piece of meat than a vegetable. We discovered that steaming (in a covered pan in the oven) followed by roasting produces nicely caramelized cauliflower with a creamy texture (page 195). Finally, we use cauliflower to make—yes!—rice (page 196).

TEST KITCHEN EXPERIMENT

One of the most interesting dynamic processes in the kitchen is flavor change as a result of cooking. Everyone knows that a seared steak tastes very different from beef tartare, but it's not always as simple as the difference between raw and cooked. Vegetables belonging to the cruciferous family often go through particularly complex flavor changes throughout the cooking process. Here, we analyze how the flavor of cauliflower changes over the course of an hour.

EXPERIMENT

We cooked six batches of 8 ounces of cauliflower florets in 1 cup of simmering water for 10, 20, 30, 40, 50, and 60 minutes, respectively. We asked tasters to sample both the cauliflower and the cooking liquid at each interval and describe the flavor and aroma.

RESULTS

Tasters' comments showed a great deal of agreement across the board. The 10- and 20-minute samples were characterized at "sulfurous" while the 30- and 40-minute batches were described at "nutty" and "sweet." Tasters found very few descriptors for the longer-cooked 50- and 60-minute batches; a number of tasters deemed these samples "bland."

TAKEAWAY

In the beginning of cooking, cauliflower's glucosinolates are converted to new volatile sulfur compounds called isothiocyanates, which give it the characteristic sulfurous aroma that tasters noted in the 10- and 20-minute samples. These compounds dissipate with further cooking, and, at the same time, other compounds form from the slower oxidation of the essential fatty acids linoleic acid and linolenic acid. As the sulfurous aroma is driven off, these new compounds make a more significant contribution to flavor: a "grassy" odor from an aldehyde called hexanal and a buttery, caramel aroma from a compound called 2, 3-butanedione. The characteristic nuttiness of cooked cauliflower, which tasters noted as particularly strong in the 30- and 40-minute samples, is caused by the formation of nonvolatile and more-stable compounds called thioureas. After a full hour of cooking, enough of the important volatile compounds boil off that the cauliflower tastes bland. We take full advantage of this transformation to create complex flavor in our Creamy Cauliflower Soup (page 194).

WHEN CAULIFLOWER TASTES BEST

The flavor of cauliflower changes with cooking. Volatile sulfur compounds are present in the first 20 minutes of cooking. Around 30 to 40 minutes, stable compounds called thioureas are formed, giving cauliflower its characteristic nutty flavor we love. Later, the flavor grows bland.

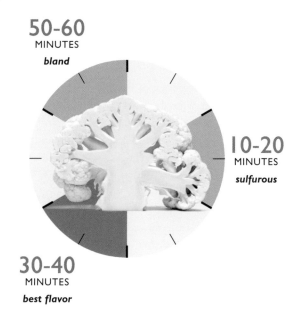

50-60
MINUTES
bland

10-20
MINUTES
sulfurous

30-40
MINUTES
best flavor

FAMILY TREE: BRASSICA VEGETABLES

Often called cruciferous vegetables, or the "cabbage family," the Brassica family of vegetables includes cauliflower, as well as broccoli, kale (page 205), Brussels sprouts, kohlrabi, cabbage (page 213), and more. They are all known for having strong flavors, brought out only when the cells are damaged by chopping, chewing, or massaging.

TURNIP

Turnips are recognizable by their off-white skin capped with a purple halo. When young, turnips are tender and sweet, but as they age they become increasingly "sulfurous" and "tough."

RUTABAGA

A close relative of the turnip, this large root has thin skin and sweet, golden flesh. Its flavor is reminiscent of "broccoli and mustard," with a "horseradish aftertaste" and "dense, crunchy" texture.

KOHLRABI

Kohlrabi is sometimes referred to as a cabbage turnip. The greens have an "earthy, mineral quality" when sautéed; the bulbs are "slightly bitter" with a "garlicky kick."

BROCCOLI

However you choose to cook broccoli, give the heartier peeled stems a minute or two head start before adding the tender florets. Look for broccoli with dark green, tightly packed florets and stems that are firm and not shriveled or dried-out.

BROCCOLINI

Broccolini is a hybrid of Chinese kale and broccoli. It is typically sold in bunches like asparagus, and it can be prepared similarly. Its flavor is "slightly mineral," "sweet, like a cross between spinach and asparagus."

BROCCOFLOWER

Broccoflower is a trademarked hybrid of broccoli and cauliflower, developed in Holland. While the tightly packed curd is similar in texture to cauliflower, the flavor skews more toward broccoli, with a "mild wheatiness" and subtle sweetness.

COLORED CAULIFLOWER

There is more to these vegetables than just aesthetics: The orange variety has roughly 25 times more vitamin A than traditional cauliflower and tastes a bit "like winter squash." Purple cauliflower is high in antioxidants and has a "slightly bitter" flavor.

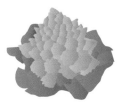

ROMANESCO

The delicate, intricately spiraled florets of this vegetable make it instantly recognizable. Its flavor combines "green beans and cauliflower," with an "aftertaste of fresh corn." Sprinkle steamed florets with lemon juice or sauté them in olive oil and finish with minced garlic.

CAULIFLOWER

Although the dense, pebbled curd of this vegetable is often served raw, the "chalky" texture and "bland" flavor of cauliflower are improved with cooking. Steam, boil, or roast florets to bring out their "subtle, earthy sweetness" and "firm, crunchy texture."

BOK CHOY

Also called Chinese white cabbage, bok choy looks like a wide-stalked version of Swiss chard. Its "tender, spinachy" leaves and "crisp" stalks are common ingredients in stir-fries; for the best texture, add the crisp white stalks first and the tender leaves toward the end of cooking.

BRUSSELS SPROUTS

Brussels sprouts, which grow in clusters on long stalks, are so named because they originated in Belgium. Smaller sprouts are "tender and sweet," but those larger than an inch across can be "bitter." Trim the stem ends and remove any discolored leaves.

Creamy Cauliflower Soup

✓ WHY THIS RECIPE WORKS

If you judged cauliflower by typical cauliflower soups, you might think of it as a characterless white vegetable with no flavor of its own. This is because most classic cauliflower soups go overboard on the heavy cream; thicken with flour; or incorporate ingredients like bacon, tomatoes, or curry powder, whose potent flavors smother this vegetable's more delicate ones. But if you've ever experienced the full spectrum of cauliflower's flavors, which can range from bright and cabbage-like to nutty and even sweet, you know that cauliflower is eminently worthy of being the real focal point of the recipe. We set out to create a soup that was creamy without being stodgy and that highlighted, rather than covered up, the flavors of this often mistreated vegetable. We did this by using the amount and type of cauliflower's fiber (not that much insoluble), and the ability of its flavor to change over time (great), to our benefit.

USE NO CREAM We started by stripping down the soup to just cauliflower and water, and were immediately struck by its texture: supremely silky and smooth. This is because how much a vegetable breaks down when it is cooked and pureed depends largely on one thing: fiber. Vegetables have two kinds: soluble and insoluble. When subjected to heat and liquid, soluble fiber readily breaks down and dissolves, providing viscosity, while insoluble fiber remains stable even when pureed. Cauliflower is remarkably low in overall fiber, and especially in insoluble fiber (just ½ gram per ½-cup serving, or about one-third as much insoluble fiber as found in green peas). No wonder cauliflower can be blended to an ultrasmooth creamy consistency—no cream needed.

COOK DIFFERENT TIMES We stumbled upon a cauliflower soup recipe from chef and restaurateur Thomas Keller that calls for cooking cauliflower for almost an hour. Our interest was piqued, so we tried simmering the cauliflower in our working recipe for 30 minutes (twice as long as we had been up to this point). Even when we added back a little water to the pot to make up for the liquid that had evaporated over the longer cooking time, we were surprised by how much sweeter and nuttier tasting this vegetable had become. We ran some experiments, and discovered that shorter cooking times bring out cauliflower's cabbage-like flavors, while longer cooking times turn it nuttier and sweet. Too much cooking drives off all its flavor. To bring the full spectrum of possible flavors into

our soup, we cooked some of the cauliflower for 15 minutes and the remainder for 30 minutes.

FINISH WITH BUTTER We wanted to bring some of the nuttiness of roasted cauliflower to the soup. To bring that intensity, we cut a cup of ½-inch florets from the cauliflower before slicing up the rest for the soup. We melted a few more tablespoons of butter in a small skillet and fried the florets to a golden-brown color. Tossed with a little sherry vinegar and sprinkled over the soup, they served as the ideal complement to our clean-tasting puree. But during frying, the cauliflower wasn't the only thing cooking—the butter turned a nice golden brown. That gave us an idea: Cook the cauliflower in extra butter, and use that browned butter as a second garnish. Just a teaspoon or two of browned butter brought richness to each bowl of soup.

CREAMY CAULIFLOWER SOUP
SERVES 4 TO 6

White wine vinegar may be substituted for the sherry vinegar. Be sure to thoroughly trim the cauliflower's core of green leaves and leaf stems, which can be fibrous and contribute to a grainy texture in the soup.

1	head cauliflower (2 pounds)
8	tablespoons unsalted butter, cut into 8 pieces
1	leek, white and light green parts only, halved lengthwise, sliced thin, and washed thoroughly
1	small onion, halved and sliced thin
	Salt and pepper
4½–5	cups water
½	teaspoon sherry vinegar
3	tablespoons minced fresh chives

1. Pull off outer leaves of cauliflower and trim stem. Using paring knife, cut around core to remove; slice core thin and reserve. Cut heaping 1 cup of ½-inch florets from head of cauliflower; set aside. Cut remaining cauliflower crosswise into ½-inch-thick slices.

2. Melt 3 tablespoons butter in large saucepan over medium-low heat. Add leek, onion, and 1½ teaspoons salt; cook, stirring frequently, until leek and onion are softened but not browned, about 7 minutes.

3. Increase heat to medium-high; add 4½ cups water, sliced core, and half of sliced cauliflower; and bring to

simmer. Reduce heat to medium-low and simmer gently for 15 minutes. Add remaining sliced cauliflower, return to simmer, and continue to cook until cauliflower is tender and crumbles easily, 15 to 20 minutes longer.

4. While soup simmers, melt remaining 5 tablespoons butter in 8-inch skillet over medium heat. Add reserved florets and cook, stirring frequently, until florets are golden brown and butter is browned and imparts nutty aroma, 6 to 8 minutes. Remove skillet from heat and use slotted spoon to transfer florets to small bowl. Toss florets with vinegar and season with salt to taste. Pour browned butter in skillet into small bowl and reserve for garnishing.

5. Process soup in blender until smooth, about 45 seconds. Rinse out pan. Return pureed soup to pan and return to simmer over medium heat, adjusting consistency with remaining water as needed (soup should have thick, velvety texture but should be thin enough to settle with flat surface after being stirred) and seasoning with salt to taste. Serve, garnishing individual bowls with browned florets, drizzle of browned butter, and chives and seasoning with pepper to taste.

Roasted Cauliflower

✔ WHY THIS RECIPE WORKS

Roasting vegetables is all about caramelizing sugars to produce big flavor. And we wanted to add flavor to cauliflower without drowning it in cheese sauce, so we developed a recipe that gave us cauliflower with a golden, nutty exterior and sweet interior. Cutting it into wedges, using a good amount of oil, and oven steaming and then roasting gave us flavorful, caramelized cauliflower with a still-creamy interior.

CUT INTO WEDGES If the cauliflower is cut too small, the florets disintegrate into small pieces and burn when roasting. Instead, we cut the cauliflower through the core to keep the florets from separating. And since browning takes place only where the vegetables are in contact with the hot pan, we sliced a head of cauliflower into eight wedges, creating more flat surface area than we'd get with florets.

STEAM, THEN ROAST To keep the cauliflower from drying out, we started it covered in a hot oven, letting it steam for 10 minutes until barely soft and then removed the aluminum foil so it could brown. Flipping each slice halfway through roasting ensured even cooking and color.

ROASTED CAULIFLOWER
SERVES 4 TO 6

Wedges are easy to flip and have a lot of surface area in contact with the pan, which leads to great browning.

1	head cauliflower (2 pounds)
¼	cup extra-virgin olive oil
	Kosher salt and pepper

1. Adjust oven rack to lowest position and heat oven to 475 degrees. Trim outer leaves of cauliflower and cut stem flush with bottom of head. Cut head into 8 equal wedges, keeping core and florets intact. Place wedges cut side down on parchment paper–lined rimmed baking sheet. Drizzle with 2 tablespoons oil and season with salt and pepper to taste; rub gently to distribute oil and seasonings.

2. Cover sheet tightly with aluminum foil and cook for 10 minutes. Remove foil and continue to roast until bottoms of cauliflower wedges are golden, about 15 minutes. Remove sheet from oven and, using spatula, carefully flip wedges. Return sheet to oven and continue to roast until cauliflower is golden all over, about 15 minutes longer. Season with salt and pepper to taste, transfer to platter, drizzle with remaining 2 tablespoons oil, and serve.

ROASTED CAULIFLOWER WITH BACON AND SCALLIONS

In step 1, combine 2 tablespoons oil and 4 minced garlic cloves in small bowl before drizzling over cauliflower. Distribute 6 slices bacon, cut into ½-inch pieces, and ½ onion, cut into ½-inch-thick slices, on baking sheet around cauliflower before roasting. In step 2, whisk remaining 2 tablespoons oil with 2 teaspoons cider vinegar in large bowl. Toss roasted cauliflower mixture with oil-vinegar mixture. Season with salt and pepper to taste, transfer to platter, and sprinkle with 2 thinly sliced scallions.

ROASTED CAULIFLOWER WITH CURRY AND LIME

In step 1, combine 2 tablespoons oil and 1½ teaspoons curry powder in small bowl before drizzling over cauliflower. Distribute ½ onion, cut into ½-inch-thick slices, on baking sheet around cauliflower before roasting. In step 2, whisk remaining 2 tablespoons oil with 2 teaspoons lime juice in large bowl. Toss roasted cauliflower with oil–lime juice mixture. Season with salt and pepper to taste; transfer to platter; and sprinkle with ¼ cup cashews, toasted and chopped, and 2 tablespoons chopped fresh cilantro.

ROASTED CAULIFLOWER WITH PAPRIKA AND CHORIZO

In step 1, combine 2 tablespoons oil and 1½ teaspoons smoked paprika in small bowl before drizzling over cauliflower. Distribute ½ red onion, cut into ½-inch-thick slices, on baking sheet around cauliflower before roasting. In step 2, when removing aluminum foil, distribute 6 ounces chorizo sausage, halved lengthwise and sliced ½ inch thick, on sheet. In step 2, whisk remaining 2 tablespoons oil with 2 teaspoons sherry vinegar in large bowl. Toss roasted cauliflower mixture with oil-vinegar mixture. Season with salt and pepper to taste, transfer to platter, and sprinkle with 2 tablespoons chopped fresh parsley.

Cauliflower Rice

✓ WHY THIS RECIPE WORKS

In some diets, cauliflower is used in place of rice, since it's easy to process the florets into rice-size granules and it cooks up pleasantly fluffy. This is in part due to its low levels of overall fiber, half of which is soluble fiber, which easily breaks down to help give the fluffy, creamy texture of cooked rice. We decided to take on the challenge of creating a foolproof cauliflower "rice" of our own.

CHOP IT RIGHT To make our cauliflower rice foolproof, we first needed to figure out the best way to chop the florets to the right size. We found that using the food processor made quick work of breaking down the florets and created a fairly consistent texture. Working in batches helped to ensure that all of the florets broke down evenly.

START COVERED Next, we needed to give our neutral-tasting cauliflower a boost in flavor; a shallot and a small amount of chicken broth did the trick. To ensure that the cauliflower was tender but still maintained a pleasant, rice-like chew, we first steamed the "rice" in a covered pot and then finished cooking it uncovered to evaporate any remaining moisture.

CAULIFLOWER RICE
SERVES 4

This recipe can be doubled; use a Dutch oven and increase the cooking time to about 25 minutes in step 2.

- 1 head cauliflower (2 pounds), cored and cut into 1-inch florets (7 cups)
- 1 tablespoon extra-virgin olive oil
- 1 shallot, minced
- ½ cup chicken broth
  Kosher salt and pepper
- 2 tablespoons minced fresh parsley (optional)

1. Working in 2 batches, pulse cauliflower in food processor until finely ground into ¼- to ⅛-inch pieces, 6 to 8 pulses, scraping down sides of bowl as needed; transfer to bowl.

2. Heat oil in large saucepan over medium-low heat until shimmering. Add shallot and cook until softened, about 3 minutes. Stir in processed cauliflower, broth, and 1½ teaspoons salt. Cover and cook, stirring occasionally, until cauliflower is tender, 12 to 15 minutes.

3. Uncover and continue to cook until cauliflower rice is almost completely dry, about 3 minutes. Off heat, stir in parsley, if using, season with salt and pepper to taste, and serve.

CURRIED CAULIFLOWER RICE

Add ¼ teaspoon ground cardamom, ¼ teaspoon ground cinnamon, and ¼ teaspoon ground turmeric to saucepan with shallot. Substitute 1 tablespoon minced fresh mint for parsley and stir ¼ cup toasted sliced almonds into cauliflower rice with mint.

TEX-MEX CAULIFLOWER RICE

Add 2 minced jalapeños, 1 minced garlic clove, 1 teaspoon ground cumin, and 1 teaspoon ground coriander to saucepan with shallot. Substitute 2 tablespoons minced fresh cilantro for parsley and stir 1 teaspoon lime juice into cauliflower rice with cilantro.

CHAPTER 24

Mushrooms

To get the best flavor from these waterlogged fungi, you must deal with the moisture.

HOW THE SCIENCE WORKS

Mushrooms are neither plant nor animal but belong to a kingdom of organisms called fungi, which also contains yeasts and molds. Unlike plants, mushrooms do not produce chlorophyll for the conversion of sunlight into energy. They rely on decomposed organic matter as a source of nutrients, so wild mushrooms are found growing on the forest floor. The common name mushroom is adapted from the French word *mousseron*. But long before mushrooms became popular in France, they were eaten by the ancient Greeks and Romans, who employed food tasters to determine if gathered mushrooms were safe.

There are around 1,000 edible varieties of mushrooms; only about 20 are commercially cultivated. The mushrooms we buy in the supermarket are grown under highly controlled conditions in mushroom farms. Today, approximately 50 percent of all edible mushrooms are produced in China.

Edible mushrooms belong to many different families, the most common being *Agaricaceae*, which includes white (or button), cremini, and portobello mushrooms. Cremini are a darker variety of white mushrooms, while portobellos are mature cremini on (figurative) steroids. Other species include shiitake, maitake, hen-of-the-woods, oyster, and enoki. All of these species grow above ground, though there are some that grow below ground, like truffles.

Mushrooms are often referred to as the "meat" of the vegetable world, and for good reason. Cell walls in plants are made primarily of cellulose (a polymer made from simple glucose), while the membranes of animal cells contain proteins (made from nitrogen-containing amino acids). The cell wall material in mushrooms is made of a substance called chitin, a polymer composed of a nitrogen-containing sugar called N-acetylglucosamine.

Mushrooms are neither plant nor animal.

What does that mean? Chitin is chemically related to both cellulose and proteins and in this sense bridges the gap between plants and animals. In addition, chitin is very heat stable. This is why mushrooms do not get soft and mushy when cooked, instead retaining their firm, chewy texture. But like plants, mushrooms contain a lot of water, much of which is expelled on cooking. This allows them to become porous sponges that soak up flavors and cooking oils.

Mushrooms are noted for their characteristic flavor when cooked, providing a savory, meaty umami taste to dishes. That's because they are an excellent source of both glutamic acid and the nucleotides IMP and GMP that combine to produce a strong umami taste. Since both glutamic acid and the nucleotides are nonvolatile and heat-stable, cooking does not destroy the mushroom's ability to enhance the taste of food.

It's important to think about moisture when cooking with mushrooms, as most contain up to 90 percent water. To get the most of their earthy, deep flavor, often the first step is to rid the mushrooms of that excess liquid. To do this, we often precook mushrooms, either in the oven, as in our Stuffed Portobello Mushrooms recipe (page 201), or in the microwave as in our silky (and not too cream-heavy) Mushroom Bisque (page 202). Crosshatching and a flip help save the mushrooms for our Grilled Portobello Burgers (page 203) from being water-logged. (We also use this technique when roasting portobellos that will be stuffed.) On the other hand, some mushroom recipes benefit from water, in the form of a brine. In our Roasted Mushrooms (page 200), we quickly brine our mushrooms in salted water to help season them evenly before their stint in the oven.

TEST KITCHEN EXPERIMENT

Cooks often lump mushrooms into the category of vegetables, which, aside from being a taxonomy faux pas, can be problematic in the kitchen. While these fungi display characteristics of both meat (their savory flavor, for instance) and vegetables (their high water content), they are unique in important ways. Chief among these differences is their ability to maintain a pleasant texture over a wide range of cooking times. We set up the following experiment to illustrate how mushroom texture changes with cooking in relationship to a green vegetable and a cut of beef.

EXPERIMENT

We cut ½-inch-thick planks of portobello mushroom, zucchini, and beef tenderloin and spaced them out evenly in a steamer basket. We set the basket over boiling water in a large Dutch oven, covered it with a lid, and steamed the samples for 40 minutes. At 5-minute intervals we used a CT3 Texture Analyzer (see page 3) to test the tenderness of each sample and then graphed the data as a function of tenderness over cook time.

RESULTS

After 5 minutes of steaming, the tenderloin, portobello, and zucchini required 186, 199, and 239 grams of force, respectively, to be compressed 3 millimeters. Tasters noted that all of these samples were tender. This picture changed

rapidly with 5 more minutes of steaming: at the 10-minute mark, the tenderloin, portobello, and zucchini samples required 524, 195, and 109 grams of force, respectively. Tasters found the tenderloin to be tough and leathery, and the zucchini overly soft. The portobello, on the other hand, remained largely unchanged. As the graph below shows, over the course of the next 30 minutes, the tenderloin continued to toughen, eventually turning a whopping 293 percent tougher, while the zucchini decreased in firmness 83 percent and turned mushy and structure-less. The portobello, meanwhile, increased in firmness just 57 percent over the same period of time; after a full 40 minutes of cooking, tasters found the mushroom to be properly tender.

TAKEAWAY

While many foods we cook require precise attention to internal temperature and cook time, mushrooms are remarkably forgiving. The key to their resiliency lies in their cell walls, which are made of a polymer called chitin. Unlike the proteins in meat, or pectin in vegetables, chitin is very heat stable. This unique structure allows us to quickly sauté mushrooms for a few minutes or roast them for the better part of an hour, all the while achieving well-browned, perfectly tender specimens.

TENDERNESS AND COOK TIME: TENDERLOIN, PORTOBELLO, AND ZUCCHINI

Not many ingredients are as forgiving as mushrooms when it comes to internal temperature and cook time. We steamed portobellos, tenderloin, and zucchini and compared their textures over the course of 40 minutes. The only ingredient that stayed texturally steady? Mushrooms.

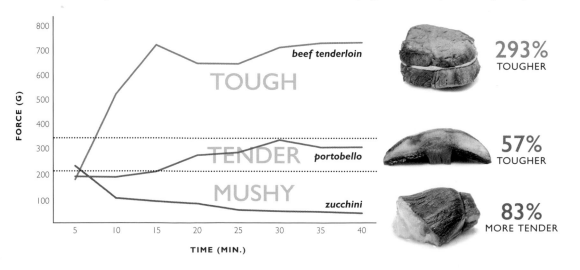

FOCUS ON: MUSHROOMS

Mushrooms are neither plant nor animal but fungi, made up of gills, spores, chitin, and more.

GILLS

Mushrooms reproduce by releasing spores from the gills located under the cap. When a mushroom is immature the gills are closed, but they open to release spores as the mushroom matures. The presence of gills under the cap can be a sign of age, so careful attention should be given to the gills when purchasing mushrooms. On good-quality mushrooms the gills should be clean, not too dark, uniform, and unbroken.

SPORES

Spores, from which the mushrooms grow, are produced in the gills of the mushroom. Often, they are used to help identify different species—placing a mushroom gill-side down overnight will leave a powdery impression, called a spore print.

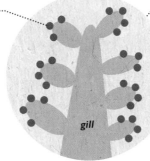

gill

VITAMINS

Mushrooms are excellent sources of vitamin B12 as well as vitamin D2. Mushrooms use the ultraviolet rays in sunlight to convert a compound called ergosterol to vitamin D2. In fact, in mushrooms just a few minutes of exposure to ultraviolet light following harvest can form up to four times the FDA recommended daily requirement of vitamin D2.

CLEANING

Contrary to popular belief, the caps of mushrooms can be washed under gently running tap water to remove debris. Because the caps of mushrooms are covered with water-repelling proteins called hydrophobins, they can grow without becoming overly soggy when it rains. However, exposed gills should not be wetted as they will absorb water and make the mushroom soggy.

CAP

The caps of mushrooms contain water-repelling proteins called hydrophobins. That's why mushrooms can grow in the forest without becoming soggy when it rains.

CHITIN

The cell wall material in mushrooms is made of a substance called chitin, a polymer composed of a nitrogen-containing sugar called N-acetylglucosamine. Chitin gives the mushroom structure and keeps it firm during cooking. (Strikingly, it is also the substance found in the exoskeleton of crustaceans like lobsters, though the chitin in the tough exoskeleton of crabs, lobsters, and shrimp is combined with protein and high levels of calcium carbonate that help make the exoskeleton rigid and tough. See page 99.)

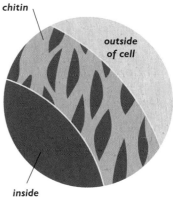

cell wall chitin

outside of cell

inside of cell

WATER CONTENT IN MUSHROOMS

While different varieties of mushrooms may look very different, they are all high in water content.

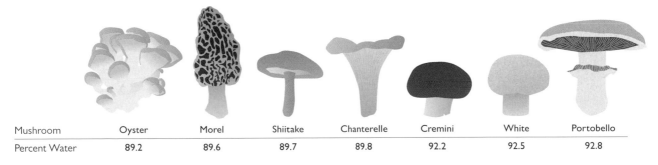

Mushroom	Oyster	Morel	Shiitake	Chanterelle	Cremini	White	Portobello
Percent Water	89.2	89.6	89.7	89.8	92.2	92.5	92.8

*Data are all from the USDA Nutrient Database.

Roasted Mushrooms

✔ WHY THIS RECIPE WORKS

We love the side dishes at a steakhouse: wedge salad, potatoes au gratin, and creamed spinach. But there's an exception: the mushroom sides, which are often uninspired. Awful? No. Dull? You bet. Still, rich, meaty-tasting mushrooms are an ideal side dish since they partner well with almost any protein. Outdoing the restaurants ought to be a cinch. But when we began testing, right away we knew that sautéing was out since we didn't want to labor with multiple batches (crowding the pan would cause them to steam, not brown). That left roasting—the best way to develop flavorful browning without requiring constant attention. We jumped right in.

CHOOSE MULTIPLE MUSHROOMS We wanted to avoid relatively bland white mushrooms, so we decided to go for a handful of other, more full-flavored varieties. This meant four types: cremini, portobellos, oysters, and shiitakes to start. In the end, a duo of cremini and shiitakes took top honors, the former providing pronounced earthiness and the latter a meaty taste.

BRINE 'EM But while we were testing oven temperatures—we settled on 450 degrees—a problem popped up. No matter how carefully we sprinkled on the salt, the mushrooms emerged unevenly seasoned. Then we thought of brining. We knew that the cap of any fungi is covered with a layer of hydrophobic (water-repellent) proteins that prevent water from seeping in. But could salt water soak through the gills? We dissolved 3 tablespoons

of salt in 2 quarts of water, dumped in the mushrooms, and left them to soak for 10 minutes. After blotting the mushrooms dry, we proceeded with oiling and roasting. Now they were too salty, but, encouragingly, they were all too salty. A tweak of the brine, and we were heading in the right direction.

Why did brining work? Because the mushrooms already contain a good deal of water (about 90 percent), they didn't absorb enough water to noticeably alter their texture, yet they held on to enough salt from the brine to be well seasoned.

ROASTED MUSHROOMS WITH PARMESAN AND PINE NUTS
SERVES 4

Quarter large (more than 2-inch) mushrooms, halve medium (1- to 2-inch) ones, and leave small (under 1-inch) ones whole.

	Salt and pepper
1½	pounds cremini mushrooms, trimmed and left whole if small, halved if medium, or quartered if large
1	pound shiitake mushrooms, stemmed, caps larger than 3 inches halved
2	tablespoons extra-virgin olive oil
2	tablespoons unsalted butter, melted
1	teaspoon lemon juice
1	ounce Parmesan cheese, grated (½ cup)
2	tablespoons pine nuts, toasted
2	tablespoons chopped fresh parsley

1. Adjust oven rack to lowest position and heat oven to 450 degrees. Dissolve 5 teaspoons salt in 2 quarts room-temperature water in large container. Add cremini mushrooms and shiitake mushrooms to brine, cover with plate or bowl to submerge, and let stand for 10 minutes.

2. Drain mushrooms in colander and pat dry with paper towels. Spread mushrooms evenly on rimmed baking sheet, drizzle with oil, and toss to coat. Roast until liquid from mushrooms has completely evaporated, 35 to 45 minutes.

3. Remove sheet from oven (be careful of escaping steam when opening oven) and, using thin metal spatula, carefully stir mushrooms. Return to oven and continue to roast until mushrooms are deeply browned, 5 to 10 minutes longer.

PRACTICAL SCIENCE
EFFECTS OF AGE ON WHITE MUSHROOM FLAVOR

Older mushrooms have more flavor.

Freshly harvested white mushrooms have firm caps, stems, and gills that are free of dark spots. That said, some chefs advocate the use of slightly older, blemished mushrooms, claiming that they are more flavorful than pristine, ultrafresh specimens. To test this claim for ourselves, we sautéed two batches of mushrooms, one fresh from the supermarket and one showing signs of age after a week in the refrigerator. In a side-by-side comparison, the results surprised us. Tasters found that the older mushrooms actually had a deeper, earthier flavor and were substantially more "mushroomy" than the unblemished samples. This is likely because some moisture had evaporated and flavors were concentrated. In addition, during aging (as with aged cheese), some of the proteins are broken down to peptides and amino acids such as glutamic acid that add to the umami taste. The takeaway: There's no need to discard old mushrooms. In fact, their imperfections may actually improve the flavor of your dish. Do not, however, use mushrooms that smell fermented or look slimy.

4. Combine melted butter and lemon juice in large bowl. Add mushrooms and toss to coat. Add Parmesan, pine nuts, and parsley and toss. Season with salt and pepper to taste; serve immediately.

Stuffed Portobello Mushrooms

✔ WHY THIS RECIPE WORKS

Stuffed mushrooms aren't bad—but we've never eaten any worth raving about. For one thing, they're often marred by a soggy, gluey, or just plain messy filling. Furthermore, although white mushrooms have an ideal shape for finger food, they're no prize in terms of flavor and are easily overshadowed. We wanted the ultimate stuffed mushrooms: meaty, earthy, and intense, with a filling that contributed complementary flavors and textures.

PICK PORTOBELLOS First, we needed more mushroom flavor. Many exotic mushrooms fit that requirement, but they're the wrong shape for stuffing. Two cultivated kinds stood out for consideration: cremini (also called "baby bellas") and portobellos. Both boast rich flavor and are widely available. We went with portobellos for two reasons. As mushrooms mature, their flavor intensifies, giving portobellos (which are mature creminis) the edge on that front. And while small mushrooms are great for passing on trays to grazing guests, a sit-down meal with knife and fork calls for one large mushroom per portion.

GET RID OF MOISTURE To extract moisture from the whole mushroom caps, we tried salting and draining them before cooking—a trick we often use with watery veggies such as eggplant and zucchini. But the method succeeded only in making the caps slimy. It turns out that the exterior of any mushroom is covered with a layer of hydrophobic (water-repellent) proteins that prevents water from going in—and keeps moisture from going out. Instead, we removed liquid by cutting slits in the caps, which allowed water to drip out and evaporate as we precooked the mushrooms in a 400-degree oven.

FILL THEM When it comes right down to it, you can stuff a mushroom with anything so long as it fits in the cap. But after testing dozens of combinations, we developed some basic rules. First, chopped stems make a good stuffing base. Portobello caps hold plenty of filling, so it made sense to use the parts already on hand rather than rely solely on new ingredients. Next, some sort of binder is essential. The most common are bread crumbs and béchamel, but we found that each had its share of problems. The

bread crumb fillings were typically soggy and did nothing for flavor, while the béchamel versions turned out gluey and were a pain to make. Could we simply use cheese as a binder? After sautéing the chopped stems, we added ½ cup of cheddar with a splash of cream. Success: The cheese kept the stuffing intact, and the cream added welcome lushness. Tasters then sampled a few different kinds, preferring goat cheese for its tangy flavor, with blue cheese coming in a close second.

STUFFED PORTOBELLO MUSHROOMS WITH SPINACH AND GOAT CHEESE
SERVES 8 AS A SIDE DISH OR 4 AS A MAIN DISH

The filling can be made up to two days ahead and refrigerated. Rewarm the filling before stuffing the mushrooms. We do not recommend roasting the mushrooms in advance, as they become leathery once rewarmed. When shopping, choose dense mushrooms with a cupped shape. Blue cheese can be substituted for the goat cheese. This recipe can be easily halved.

10	portobello mushrooms (4 to 5 inches in diameter), stems removed and reserved
¼	cup olive oil
	Salt and pepper
12	ounces (12 cups) baby spinach
2	tablespoons water
2	slices hearty white sandwich bread, torn into quarters
2	tablespoons unsalted butter
2	onions, chopped fine
4	garlic cloves, minced
½	cup dry sherry
2	tablespoons chopped fresh thyme
4	ounces goat cheese, crumbled (1 cup)
¼	cup heavy cream
1	cup walnuts, toasted and chopped coarse
2	teaspoons lemon juice

1. Adjust oven rack to upper-middle position, place rimmed baking sheet on rack, and heat oven to 400 degrees. Using tip of sharp knife, lightly score top of 8 mushroom caps in crosshatch pattern. Dice remaining 2 mushroom caps and reserved stems into ½-inch pieces; set aside (you should have about 3 cups).

2. Brush both sides of caps with 2 tablespoons oil and sprinkle evenly with 1 teaspoon salt. Carefully place caps, gill side up, on preheated baking sheet. Roast until mushrooms have released some of their juices and begin to brown around edges, 8 to 12 minutes. Flip caps over and continue to roast until liquid has completely evaporated and caps are golden brown, 8 to 12 minutes longer. Remove mushrooms from oven and heat broiler.

3. Meanwhile, place spinach and water in large bowl. Cover bowl with large dinner plate (plate should completely cover bowl and not rest on spinach). Microwave until spinach is wilted and decreased in volume by half, 3 to 4 minutes. Using potholders, remove bowl from microwave and keep covered for 1 minute. Carefully remove plate and transfer spinach to colander set in sink. Using back of rubber spatula, gently press spinach against colander to release excess liquid. Transfer spinach to cutting board and chop coarse. Return spinach to colander and press again. Set aside.

4. Pulse bread in food processor to coarse crumbs, about 10 pulses (you should have about 1½ cups). Heat 1 tablespoon oil and 1 tablespoon butter in 12-inch skillet over medium heat until butter is melted. Add bread crumbs and ¼ teaspoon salt; cook, stirring frequently, until light golden brown, 5 to 8 minutes. Transfer crumbs to small bowl and wipe out skillet with paper towels.

5. Return now-empty skillet to medium-high heat, add remaining 1 tablespoon oil, and heat until smoking. Add chopped mushrooms and cook without stirring for 2 minutes. Continue cooking, stirring occasionally, until lightly browned, 4 to 6 minutes longer. Transfer to medium bowl.

6. Add remaining 1 tablespoon butter and onions to skillet; cook, stirring occasionally, until onions are light brown, 5 to 6 minutes. Add garlic and cook until fragrant, about 30 seconds. Stir in sherry and cook until almost no liquid remains, 1 to 2 minutes. Reduce heat to low and stir in reserved cooked mushrooms, spinach, thyme, goat cheese, cream, and walnuts. Continue cooking until cheese is melted and vegetables are well coated, 1 to 2 minutes. Remove pan from heat, stir in lemon juice, and season with salt and pepper to taste.

7. Flip caps gill side up and distribute filling evenly among mushroom caps; top each with 2 tablespoons breadcrumb mixture. Broil mushrooms until crumbs are golden brown, 1 to 3 minutes. Serve immediately.

Mushroom Bisque

✔ WHY THIS RECIPE WORKS

Mushroom bisque should be a far more sophisticated version of cream of mushroom soup: smoother, more luxurious, and with greater savory depth. And yet the abundance of dairy that gives a bisque its signature velvety texture can also mute its flavor. Decreasing the cream makes the soup more flavorful, but then it's too austere to merit the name "bisque." Our goal was to reconcile an indulgent texture with robust mushroom flavor.

BRING TO MICROWAVE Mushrooms are 90 percent water, and we wanted to get rid of as much as we could for two reasons: First, the more moisture we removed, the more mushrooms (and therefore mushroom flavor) we could add to our bisque. Second, browning is an avenue to flavor, but mushrooms won't brown if they're wet. Most of the recipes we'd tried started with cooking the sliced mushrooms in the pot to dehydrate them, but it took as long as 25 minutes for them to dry out enough to begin browning. We knew it would be quicker to move this part of the operation to the microwave.

KEEP WHOLE We fit a full 2 pounds of mushrooms into our bisque but didn't need to slice or chop them. Because mushrooms lack a thick outer layer, they give up moisture readily even when left whole. We simply tossed them with salt and microwaved them until most of their liquid was released. Then we browned the shriveled mushrooms to deepen their flavor and used the reserved mushroom liquid to help form the base of the soup.

USE YOLKS For a bisque with both pleasing body and a more pronounced mushroom flavor, we turned to an old-school French thickener—a so-called liaison, which replaces a large portion of the cream with egg yolks. As the bisque heats, proteins in the yolks cross-link into coagulated spheres that, like the fat in cream, interfere with the movement of water molecules. Egg yolks also contain the powerful emulsifier lecithin, which has a twofold effect: It breaks up the fat droplets into smaller particles that disperse more completely throughout the liquid for an even thicker consistency. It also keeps the bisque smooth by holding the fat droplets suspended in the liquid so they don't separate out. If yolks can do all this, why did we use cream? Because the fat it contains provides an appealing mouthfeel that yolks alone can't match.

MUSHROOM BISQUE

SERVES 6 TO 10

Tying the thyme sprig with twine makes it easier to remove from the pot. For the smoothest result, use a conventional blender rather than an immersion blender.

1	pound white mushrooms, trimmed
8	ounces cremini mushrooms, trimmed
8	ounces shiitake mushrooms, stemmed
	Kosher salt and pepper
2	tablespoons vegetable oil
1	small onion, chopped fine
1	sprig fresh thyme, tied with kitchen twine
2	tablespoons dry sherry
4	cups water
3½	cups chicken broth
⅔	cup heavy cream, plus extra for serving
2	large egg yolks
1	teaspoon lemon juice
	Chopped fresh chives

1. Toss white mushrooms, cremini mushrooms, shiitake mushrooms, and 1 tablespoon salt together in large bowl. Cover with large plate and microwave, stirring every 4 minutes, until mushrooms have released their liquid and reduced to about one-third their original volume, about 12 minutes. Transfer mushrooms to colander set in second large bowl and drain well. Reserve liquid.

2. Heat oil in Dutch oven over medium heat until shimmering. Add mushrooms and cook, stirring occasionally, until mushrooms are browned and fond has formed on bottom of pot, about 8 minutes. Add onion, thyme sprig, and ¼ teaspoon pepper and cook, stirring occasionally, until onion is just softened, about 2 minutes. Add sherry and cook until evaporated. Stir in reserved mushroom liquid and cook, scraping up any browned bits. Stir in water and broth and bring to simmer. Reduce heat to low and simmer for 20 minutes.

3. Discard thyme sprig. Working in batches, process soup in blender until very smooth, 1½ to 2 minutes per batch. Return soup to now-empty pot. (Soup can be refrigerated for up to 2 days. Warm to 150 degrees before proceeding with recipe.)

4. Whisk cream and egg yolks together in medium bowl. Stirring slowly and constantly, add 2 cups soup to cream mixture. Stirring constantly, slowly pour cream mixture into simmering soup. Heat gently, stirring constantly, until soup registers 165 degrees (do not overheat). Stir in lemon juice and season with salt and pepper to taste. Serve immediately, garnishing each serving with 1 teaspoon extra cream and sprinkle of chives.

PRACTICAL SCIENCE SHIITAKE SUBSTITUTE

You can substitute cremini for shiitakes; just cook them longer.

The goal of cooking mushrooms is to evaporate their liquid so they can brown and their flavor can intensify. To identify any difference in water weight between cremini and shiitake mushrooms that would affect cooking times, we chopped 8 ounces of each and placed them in separate pots with no liquid or oil. We covered the pots and cooked each batch for 10 minutes over medium-low heat. We then removed the mushrooms from the pans and weighed them again. The shiitakes lost 1.1 ounces of water, or about 14 percent of their weight, while the cremini mushrooms lost 4.8 ounces, or about 60 percent of their weight. The higher water content of the cremini was confirmed when we sautéed a batch of each mushroom. The cremini took nearly 5 minutes longer than the shiitakes to release their liquid and begin to brown. In the end, we decided that it's fine to make a substitution, keeping in mind that the cremini will have a slightly softer texture and a bit less-intense flavor. Just remember to sauté or stir-fry cremini for a few extra minutes until their excess liquid completely evaporates.

Grilled Portobello Burgers

✓ WHY THIS RECIPE WORKS

For a grilled mushroom burger that would please even the staunchest beef lover, we started with meaty portobello caps. We love portobellos, but most "burgers" made from them simply are not very good. Seeing no reason why that should be so, we set ourselves the goal of making portobello mushroom burgers that were worthy of the name.

SCRAPE AND MARINATE We began with an established test kitchen technique for portobellos: scraping out the dark brown gills on the underside of the mushrooms in order to help them fit on a burger bun and hold whatever fixings may come. Then we put the caps into a zipper-lock bag with a simple mixture of olive oil, vinegar, garlic, salt, and pepper and let them soak for 30 minutes before heading to the grill.

HATCH AND GRILL A few trial runs led us to the best cooking method: We grilled the caps gill side up over a medium-hot fire until the tops were nicely charred and they had released their liquid. Then we flipped them over to let the liquid drain and sear the other side. These mushrooms were seasoned throughout and had great grill flavor. Unfortunately, the tops were still slightly tough. To fix this, we turned to a technique we use for meat, crosshatching. Cutting a shallow crosshatch pattern into the tops of the mushrooms created a textured surface and thus eliminated the chewy "skin" on the exterior. As an added bonus, the crosshatched caps soaked up even more marinade.

FILL 'ER UP As for the filling, we chose Mediterranean flavors to complement the simple marinade. We experimented with fillings featuring Parmesan, olives, capers, anchovies, and every other Mediterranean ingredient we could think of. After several rounds of testing, we landed on a combination of chopped roasted red peppers and sun-dried tomatoes, plus feta cheese for a powerful, briny kick. After mixing the filling together, we went back out to the grill and quickly learned that stuffing the raw mushrooms was a nonstarter: The filling tumbled out as the mushrooms softened, and there was no way to flip them. We found it best to grill them as before, then transfer the cooked caps to a plate, add the filling, and place them back on the grill to quickly warm through.

GRILLED PORTOBELLO BURGERS
SERVES 4

Our favorite feta cheese is Mt. Vikos Traditional Feta from Greece. If the mushrooms absorb all the marinade, simply brush the onions with olive oil before grilling them in step 4.

4	portobello mushrooms (4 to 5 inches in diameter), stems and gills removed
½	cup extra-virgin olive oil
3	tablespoons red wine vinegar
1	garlic clove, minced
	Salt and pepper
4	ounces feta cheese, crumbled (1 cup)
½	cup jarred roasted red peppers, patted dry and chopped
½	cup oil-packed sun-dried tomatoes, patted dry and chopped
½	cup mayonnaise
½	cup chopped fresh basil
4	(½-inch-thick) slices red onion
4	kaiser rolls, split
1	ounce (1 cup) baby arugula

1. Using tip of paring knife, cut ½-inch crosshatch pattern on tops of mushroom caps, 1/16 inch deep. Combine oil, vinegar, garlic, 1 teaspoon salt, and ½ teaspoon pepper in 1-gallon zipper-lock bag. Add mushrooms, seal bag, turn to coat, and let sit for at least 30 minutes or up to 1 hour.

2. Combine feta, red peppers, and sun-dried tomatoes in bowl. Whisk mayonnaise and basil together in separate bowl. Push 1 toothpick horizontally through each onion slice to keep rings intact while grilling.

3A. FOR A CHARCOAL GRILL: Open bottom vent completely. Light large chimney starter filled with charcoal briquettes (6 quarts). When top coals are partially covered with ash, pour evenly over grill. Set cooking grate in place, cover, and open lid vent completely. Heat grill until hot, about 5 minutes.

3B. FOR A GAS GRILL: Turn all burners to high, cover, and heat grill until hot, about 15 minutes. Turn all burners to medium-high.

4. Clean and oil cooking grate. Remove mushrooms from marinade, reserving excess. Brush onions all over with reserved mushroom marinade. Place onions and mushrooms, gill side up, on grill. Cook (covered if using gas) until mushrooms have released their liquid and are charred on first side, 4 to 6 minutes. Flip mushrooms and onions and continue to cook (covered if using gas) until mushrooms are charred on second side, 3 to 5 minutes.

5. Transfer onions to platter; remove toothpicks. Transfer mushrooms to platter, gill side up, and divide feta mixture evenly among caps, packing down with your hand. Return mushrooms to grill, feta side up, and cook, covered, until heated through, about 3 minutes.

6. Return mushrooms to platter and tent with aluminum foil. Grill rolls cut sides down until lightly charred, about 1 minute. Spread basil-mayonnaise on roll bottoms and top each with 1 mushroom and 1 onion slice. Divide arugula evenly among burgers, then cap with roll tops. Serve.

CHAPTER 25

Kale

The key to kale, a nutritional powerhouse, is to minimize the bitterness and accentuate its sweet, underlying flavor.

HOW THE SCIENCE WORKS

Kale, the bitter, leafy cousin of cabbage, has come into its own. Heralded as one of the "trendiest vegetables in the last 50 years" by *Bon Appetit*, it has inspired countless dishes, not to mention whole diets, a veggie for the stars. But strip away its media attention and what you're left with is a seriously flavor-packed green with possibilities.

Kale is one of approximately 36 cruciferous vegetables consumed around the world, related to cauliflower (page 191), broccoli, and bok choy. Its name comes from the latin *caulis*, which means "stem" or "stalk." There are many varieties of kale, from curly to colorful, all with the characteristic bittersweet pungent flavor. Similar to alliums like onions and garlic, which are odorless until sliced, the particular flavor of cruciferous vegetables like kale comes into existence only after the vegetable is chopped or massaged or chewed.

What's going on? Vegetables are made up of countless numbers of cells, each including proteins, enzymes, sugars, color pigments, and lots of water, all surrounded by a membrane. Cells in kale contains two key things: the enzyme myrosinase and sulfur-containing organic compounds called glucosinolates. When left alone, each element remains distinct and separate. But when the structure of a leaf of kale is disturbed, whether by chopping or massaging or chewing, the cell barriers are broken, and the myrosinase and glucosinolates begin to interact. Together, they create isothiocyanates, or new sulfur-containing compounds that provide kale's familiar bitter pungency.

Perhaps the reason kale has gotten so much press is its highly heralded health properties. Kale is high in vitamins A and C. The presence of some specific isothiocyanates has been shown to reduce the risk of certain cancers. Kale also contains high levels of the carotenoids lutein and ß-carotene, both strong antioxidants. Kale has 45 flavonoids, chemical compounds found in plants (they do everything from provide color pigments to act as chemical messengers) that purportedly have antioxidant and anti-inflammatory activity.

The flavor of kale can vary depending on growing conditions, such as the sulfur level in the soil, as well as whether or not the plant has survived a frost (see page 207). Another way to vary the flavor is through cooking: Blanching cruciferous vegetables like kale inactivates the myrosinase enzyme, resulting in a milder, less bitter flavor. Soaking kale in a hot water bath, like we do for our Kale Caesar Salad (page 212), works in the same way, albeit more mildly. Massaging raw kale, on the other hand, breaks down the cell structure to bring out the pungent bitter taste.

When it comes to cooking, kale is versatile. Sometimes we want to highlight kale's deep flavor, complementing its sweetness and the bitterness with additional ingredients: In our Braised Kale (page 208), we cook it for about 40 minutes with garlic and red pepper flakes and chicken broth so that it is creamy and sweet. Lightly braised kale adds texture and flavor to our Gemelli with Caramelized Onions, Kale, and Bacon (page 209) and Caldo Verde (page 210). We use a slow cooker to bring out the best flavor and texture in our Hearty Braised Kale with Garlic and Chorizo (page 211). We massage raw kale to make it tender in our Overnight Kale Salad (page 208). To round out our collection? Microwave Kale Chips (page 211).

> **The unique flavor of kale exists only after it is chopped, massaged, or chewed.**

TEST KITCHEN EXPERIMENT

Raw kale salads have grown enormously in popularity as Americans realize the health benefits of eating this leafy brassica. We love kale leaves as a refreshingly substantial alternative to more delicate, traditional salad greens, but we've noticed that most recipes and restaurant versions tend to overdress them in the name of masking their pungency. This bitter pungency is created when the cell walls are damaged during cutting, massaging, or chewing (see page 207). We wondered if we could dress kale with a lighter hand by creating and then mitigating some of its intensity during preparation.

EXPERIMENT

We sliced stemmed kale leaves into ¼-inch strips and then massaged them by placing them in an open zipper-lock bag and running a rolling pin firmly back and forth over them for 15 seconds. Both steps heavily damaged cell walls, thereby releasing the enzyme myrosinase and creating pungent isothiocyanates.

Having read that changes in pH can affect myrosinase activity in regular cabbage, we tried mitigating the kale's pungency by rinsing batches of the massaged leaves in water at different pH levels. We acidified one batch of water with lemon juice to pH 3 and alkalized another to pH 8 using baking soda. We also left one batch of water untreated—it registered a pH of 6.7. After agitating the leaves in the water for 1 minute, we drained each, spun them dry, and tasted them plain for pungency next to kale leaves that were cut and massaged but not rinsed, as well as raw untouched leaves.

RESULTS

Tasters found the kale leaves from both the acidified and alkalized rinses to be just as mild and sweet as those rinsed in plain water. All rinsed samples were milder than both the cut and massaged and the untouched leaves.

TAKEAWAY

While we found no strong correlation between pH and pungency in cut and massaged kale leaves, this experiment does show that order of operations is important when prepping kale salad. Isothiocyanates will form in kale once cell walls are broken, whether during cutting, massaging, or chewing. By forming some of these pungent compounds before chewing we can rinse some of them away, leading to milder kale that needs less dressing to taste balanced. Since we already recommend washing kale leaves thoroughly to remove dirt and sand, this process doesn't add much to the prep time, but it makes a big difference in terms of flavor.

PUNGENCY AND KALE: IT'S THE ORDER OF OPERATIONS THAT COUNTS

We had a hunch that altering the pH of massaged kale would mitigate its pungency. Turns out what matters most is when you rinse it in water.

CHOPPED, RAW, UNTOUCHED KALE
Kale that underwent zero treatment (no massage, no rinse) tasted pungent and bitter.

CHOPPED, MASSAGED, RINSED KALE
Rinsing the kale after massaging caused it to taste much more mild and sweet.

FOCUS ON: KALE

Kale comes in many forms, curly and smooth, green and purple and red, and one variety that grows so tall its stem can be turned into a walking stick. But all types have the same basic structure.

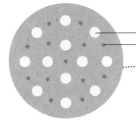

— **myrosinase**
— **glucosinolates**

BEFORE CHOPPING

Before chopping, the cells in kale leaves contain two important elements—the enzyme myrosinase and sulfur-containing organic compounds called glucosinolates. In undisturbed leaves, they remain separate.

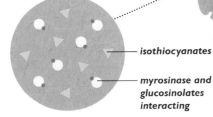

isothiocyanates

myrosinase and glucosinolates interacting

AFTER CHOPPING

When you start chopping up that kale leaf, the structure of the cells is disturbed. This means that the myrosinase and glucosinolates begin to interact. And when they interact the two come together to create isothiocyanates, or new sulfur-containing compounds that taste like the bitter, pungent kale you know.

STEM

Kale's thick stalk is tough, especially the bottom portion below the leafy green. In the test kitchen, we trim it before cooking, holding each leaf at the base of the stem and using a knife to slash the leafy portion from either side of the tough stem.

LEAF

After discarding the stem, we are left with the leaf, which is what we mainly cook with. Known for their health benefits, kale leaves are also packed with flavor—a flavor that doesn't come out until the leaf has been chopped, chewed, or massaged.

STORING

Store kale and other hearty greens in an open plastic produce bag or an open zipper-lock bag. In tests, we've found that trapped gases and too much constriction encourage rotting. This is because in plastic bags the moisture and heat are retained, which encourages the growth of spoilage-promoting fungi and molds. Ripening enzymes in the vegetable do become more active, which leads to softening, but the fungi and molds are responsible for most of the damage.

GROWING

Many cruciferous vegetables, including kale, grow well in colder temperatures, and can even taste better as a result. Kale, in fact, is frost-resistant. Not only that, but when subjected to a frost, a kale plant will convert stored starches into soluble sugars. This helps prevent the water in the kale's leaves from freezing, expanding, and rupturing cell walls. It also makes kale that has survived a frost taste demonstrably sweeter.

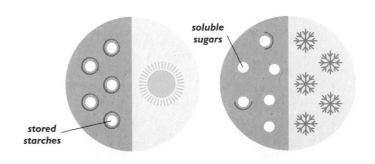

soluble sugars

stored starches

Braised Kale

✔ WHY THIS RECIPE WORKS

In the South, meaty greens like kale are traditionally thrown into a pot of water with a ham hock and boiled to death. Other recipes first blanch and then sauté in order to retain the still-al-dente greens' deep color and earthy flavor. We wanted a flavorful one-pot kale recipe—with no parcooking. To achieve this, we first sautéed, and then added liquid.

SKIP THE BLANCHING Rather than blanching the greens in a big pot of water, we first sautéed half of them before adding the rest with a little bit of liquid and covering the pot. When the greens almost had the tender-firm texture we wanted, we removed the lid to allow the liquid to cook off. The result? A kale recipe that highlighted the greens' cabbage-like flavor and firm texture.

ADD FLAVOR The characteristic bittersweet flavor of kale could only gain more depth with some additions. We added a dash of red pepper flakes with the garlic and onions, and substituted a bit of chicken broth for water. This moved the flavor from one-dimensional to full-bodied.

BRAISED KALE
SERVES 4

For the best results, be sure the greens are fully cooked and tender in step 1 before moving on to step 2. Collard greens can be substituted for kale; after covering the pot in step 1, increase the cooking time to 35 to 45 minutes.

3	tablespoons olive oil
1	onion, chopped fine
5	garlic cloves, minced
1/8	teaspoon red pepper flakes
2	pounds kale, stemmed and chopped into 3-inch pieces
1	cup chicken broth
1	cup water
	Salt and pepper
2–3	teaspoons lemon juice

1. Heat 2 tablespoons oil in Dutch oven over medium heat until shimmering. Add onion and cook, stirring frequently, until softened and beginning to brown, 4 to 5 minutes. Add garlic and pepper flakes and cook until garlic is fragrant, about 1 minute. Add half of kale and stir until beginning to wilt, about 1 minute. Add remaining kale, broth, water, and 1/4 teaspoon salt. Quickly cover pot and reduce heat to medium-low. Cook, stirring occasionally, until kale is tender, 25 to 35 minutes.

2. Remove lid and increase heat to medium-high. Cook, stirring occasionally, until most of liquid has evaporated (bottom of pot will be almost dry and greens will begin to sizzle), 8 to 12 minutes. Off heat, stir in 2 teaspoons lemon juice and remaining 1 tablespoon oil. Season with salt, pepper, and lemon juice to taste, and serve.

Overnight Kale Salad

✔ WHY THIS RECIPE WORKS

We love the earthy, nutty flavor of uncooked kale. But unless we're using hard-to-find baby kale, its texture can be tough. We wanted to find a way to tenderize standard supermarket kale without subjecting it to heat. Many recipes call for tossing kale with oil or salad dressing and letting it sit to tenderize in the refrigerator overnight. We found an improvement in the texture of the kale with this method, but it didn't quite deliver the tender leaves we were after. In addition to storing the dressed kale overnight, we found another technique that got great results: a quick massage.

TENDERIZE THE KALE For a raw kale salad with greens that were fresh and crisp—but not tough—we needed to find a way to tenderize the kale. The trick turned out to be a quick massage; we kneaded the kale vigorously for 5 minutes until the leaves were darkened and slightly wilted. This broke down the cell walls of the kale in a manner similar to the effects of heat. Then we tossed the salad with a vinaigrette and refrigerated it overnight to tenderize the greens further. The kale leaves have a protective waxy cuticle layer that prevents water-based liquids from having much effect on them, but oil easily penetrates the film and helps to wilt and tenderize the kale.

ADD FLAVOR To complement the earthy kale, we made a tangy dressing with pomegranate molasses and cider vinegar balanced by a touch of honey. Caramelized roasted sweet potatoes, shredded radicchio, and crunchy pecans plus a sprinkling of Parmesan cheese and pomegranate seeds turned our salad into a hearty meal.

OVERNIGHT KALE SALAD WITH SWEET POTATOES AND POMEGRANATE VINAIGRETTE
SERVES 4

Pomegranate molasses can be found in the international aisle of supermarkets; if you can't find it, substitute 2 tablespoons of lemon juice, 2 teaspoons of mild molasses, and 1 teaspoon of honey. Green curly kale, Tuscan kale (also known as dinosaur or Lacinato kale), or red kale can be used in this recipe; do not use baby kale. If you prefer your kale to be less bitter, give it a quick rinse after the massage (see Test Kitchen Experiment, page 206).

1½	pounds sweet potatoes, peeled, quartered lengthwise, and cut crosswise into ½-inch pieces
⅓	cup plus 1 tablespoon extra-virgin olive oil
	Salt and pepper
2	tablespoons water
1½	tablespoons pomegranate molasses
1	shallot, minced
1	tablespoon honey
1	tablespoon cider vinegar
12	ounces kale, stemmed and sliced into 1-inch strips
½	head radicchio (5 ounces), cored and sliced thin
½	cup pecans, toasted and chopped
⅓	cup pomegranate seeds (optional)
1	ounce Parmesan cheese, shaved

1. Adjust oven rack to middle position and heat oven to 400 degrees. Toss sweet potatoes with 1 tablespoon oil, ½ teaspoon salt, and ½ teaspoon pepper until evenly coated. Arrange in single layer in rimmed baking sheet and roast until bottom edges of potatoes are browned, about 15 minutes. Flip potatoes and continue to roast until second side is spotty brown, 10 to 15 minutes. Transfer potatoes to large plate and let cool to room temperature, about 20 minutes.

2. Meanwhile, whisk water, pomegranate molasses, shallot, honey, vinegar, ¼ teaspoon salt, and ¼ teaspoon pepper together in medium bowl. Whisking constantly, drizzle in remaining ⅓ cup oil.

3. Vigorously knead and squeeze kale with your hands until leaves are uniformly darkened and slightly wilted, about 5 minutes. Toss kale, roasted potatoes, and radicchio with ⅓ cup vinaigrette in large bowl; cover. Cover remaining vinaigrette.

4. Refrigerate kale mixture and vinaigrette separately for up to 24 hours.

5. Remove kale mixture and vinaigrette from refrigerator and let sit at room temperature for 15 minutes. Whisk vinaigrette to recombine, then drizzle over kale mixture. Add pecans and pomegranate seeds, if using, and toss to combine. Season with salt and pepper to taste, and top with Parmesan. Serve.

Gemelli with Caramelized Onions, Kale, and Bacon

✔ WHY THIS RECIPE WORKS
Glossy caramelized onions, braised kale, and crisped bacon give this pasta dish a sweet, savory, and highly addictive flavor profile. We gave the onions a jump start and braised the kale with water we would later use for cooking the pasta. Grated Parmesan cheese brought the sauce together and reinforced the meaty, salty notes of the bacon.

JUMP-START THE ALLIUMS We jump-started the caramelization of our onions by cooking them covered so they'd release their moisture. Then we removed the lid and sautéed them to let the liquid evaporate and give the onions a chance to become deeply browned and tender.

BRAISE THE KALE For the kale, we simply added it to the pan with the onions. The pasta cooking water did double duty—before adding the pasta, we added a scoop of the boiling water to the pan to braise the kale.

GEMELLI WITH CARAMELIZED ONIONS, KALE, AND BACON
SERVES 4 TO 6

Do not dry the kale completely after washing; a little extra water clinging to the leaves will help them wilt when cooking in step 2.

8	slices bacon, cut into ½-inch pieces
3	onions, halved and sliced thin
	Salt and pepper
4	garlic cloves, minced
1	pound kale, stemmed and chopped into 1-inch pieces
1	pound gemelli
2	ounces Parmesan cheese, grated (1 cup), plus extra for serving

1. Bring 4 quarts water to boil in large pot for pasta. Cook bacon in 12-inch nonstick skillet over medium-high heat until crisp, about 5 minutes; using slotted spoon, transfer to paper towel–lined plate. Add onions and ½ teaspoon salt to fat left in pan, cover, and cook over medium-high heat until soft, about 5 minutes. Remove lid and continue to cook onions, stirring often, until lightly browned, about 10 minutes.

2. Stir in garlic and cook until fragrant, about 30 seconds. Stir in half of kale and cook until it begins to wilt, about 2 minutes. Add remaining kale and 1½ cups of boiling water for pasta (skillet will be very full). Cover and simmer, tossing occasionally, until kale is tender, about 15 minutes.

3. Meanwhile, add pasta and 1 tablespoon salt to boiling water and cook, stirring often, until al dente. Reserve ½ cup cooking water, then drain pasta and return it to pot. Add kale mixture, bacon, and Parmesan and toss to combine. Add reserved cooking water as needed to adjust consistency and season with salt and pepper to taste. Serve with extra Parmesan.

Caldo Verde

✔ WHY THIS RECIPE WORKS

Caldo verde, a traditional Portuguese soup of shredded greens, potatoes, and sausage, is traditionally slightly thickened by partially mashing some of the potatoes. Our soup, thickened with pureed potatoes and olive oil, is silky-smooth, and by increasing the amount of potato and sausage, we turned this simple first course into a hearty and filling meal.

CHOP IT UP The problem with using shredded kale, we discovered, is that the wilted strips dangled from the spoon, making this soup messy to eat. Chopping into bite-size pieces made them more spoon-friendly.

PUREE THOSE TATERS The traditional method for creating a smooth soup is vigorously stirring the broth once the potatoes have softened so that they break down and produce body. It was clear that this method would not produce the smoothness we desired. Instead, we pureed some of the softened potatoes with the liquid. This way, the broth thickened up and became uniformly silky. As for the potatoes left intact in the soup, lower-starch Yukon Gold potatoes held their shape even during the long cooking.

Collard greens can be substituted for kale. Serve this soup with hearty bread and, for added richness, a final drizzle of extra-virgin olive oil.

¼	cup extra-virgin olive oil
12	ounces Spanish-style chorizo sausage, cut into ½-inch pieces
1	onion, chopped fine
4	garlic cloves, minced
	Salt and pepper
¼	teaspoon red pepper flakes
2	pounds Yukon Gold potatoes, peeled and cut into ¾-inch pieces
4	cups chicken broth
4	cups water
1	pound kale, stemmed and cut into 1-inch pieces
2	teaspoons white wine vinegar

1. Heat 1 tablespoon oil in Dutch oven over medium-high heat until shimmering. Add chorizo and cook, stirring occasionally, until lightly browned, 4 to 5 minutes. Transfer chorizo to bowl and set aside. Reduce heat to medium and add onion, garlic, 1¼ teaspoons salt, and pepper flakes and season with pepper to taste. Cook, stirring frequently, until onion is translucent, 2 to 3 minutes. Add potatoes, broth, and water; increase heat to high and bring to boil. Reduce heat to medium-low and simmer, uncovered, until potatoes are just tender, 8 to 10 minutes.

2. Transfer ¾ cup solids and ¾ cup broth to blender jar. Add kale to pot and simmer for 10 minutes. Stir in chorizo and continue to simmer until greens are tender, 8 to 10 minutes longer.

PRACTICAL SCIENCE WILTING

Kale and other greens will shrink during cooking due to the loss of something called turgor pressure.

Why will a huge pile of kale shrink to almost nothing when left out too long on the counter, or cooked? It has to do with something called "turgor pressure," or the pressure that builds up in each plant cell when filled with water. In crisp, healthy greens, the turgor pressure is high, the cell walls of each leaf bulging and taut. But with time—or cooking—the water from inside the cells passes through the cell membranes and evaporates, reducing turgor pressure within the cells, and causing the leaves to wilt.

---

3. Add remaining 3 tablespoons oil to soup in blender and process until very smooth and homogeneous, about 1 minute. Remove pot from heat and stir pureed soup mixture and vinegar into soup. Season with salt and pepper to taste, and serve. (Soup can be refrigerated for up to 2 days.)

Hearty Braised Kale with Garlic and Chorizo in a Slow Cooker

✓ WHY THIS RECIPE WORKS

Using the slow cooker to prepare our hearty kale was a no-brainer— after all, a long cooking time helps to turn kale meltingly tender and tempers its assertive flavor. Braising the kale with chorizo and garlic gave these simple greens a meaty, spicy kick.

SLOW COOKING NEEDS LITTLE LIQUID   A slow cooker works best in most recipes with a modest amount of liquid. There's very little evaporation. Plus, little liquid means more concentration of flavor over the longer cooking time period. Also, less liquid means less time for the slow cooker to do its work, and the final result isn't a soupy mess. We found it was important that the kale still had a little liquid clinging to the leaves. We relied on a lot of garlic, because slow cookers dull other flavors.

HEARTY BRAISED KALE WITH GARLIC AND CHORIZO IN A SLOW COOKER
SERVES 4 TO 6

You will need a 5½- to 7-quart slow cooker for this recipe. Collard greens can be substituted for kale. Chicken broth can be a substitute for the water.

- 2   pounds kale, stemmed and sliced into 1-inch-wide strips
- 8   ounces chorizo sausage, halved and sliced ½ inch thick
- ½   cup water
- 2   tablespoons minced garlic
     Salt and pepper

1. Combine kale, chorizo, water, and garlic in slow cooker. Cover and cook until kale is tender, 5 to 6 hours on low or 3 to 4 hours on high.

2. Season with salt and pepper to taste. Serve. (Braised greens can be held on warm or low setting for up to 2 hours.)

Microwave Kale Chips

✓ WHY THIS RECIPE WORKS

If you've somehow missed that kale chips are a "thing," trust us: Tossing torn leaves of kale with oil and salt and baking them until crispy is a worthwhile endeavor. The slightly browned leaves take on a nutty, sweet taste and a pleasing, brittle texture. But the standard oven approach isn't perfect: It's hard to get the leaves evenly browned; plus, it's difficult to drive off enough moisture so that the chips stay crispy when stored for more than a few hours. An easy fix? The microwave. We found that the microwave dehydrates the leaves evenly and thoroughly, so they stay crispy longer—and the chips cook a whole lot faster than they do in the oven.

WATCH THE SPARK   Sometimes, when making kale chips in the microwave, the kale can spark. The phenomenon even has a name: arcing. There are a few theories about what causes it. It could be that the mineral or moisture content of certain vegetables makes them more prone to spark. Others say it's more likely to happen when pieces of food with sharp (rather than rounded) edges are arranged too closely together in the microwave. While we could not make it happen in the test kitchen, we did some research on how to make it stop. Using a reduced power level won't solve the issue. Waves can be emitted by a microwave at only one energy level, so the appliance just cycles on and off when set on a lower power setting—one burst of waves can still cause arcing. We suggest making sure that the kale is dried thoroughly and that the pieces are spread out on the plate. If this doesn't help, best to stop using the microwave to make kale chips (according to the USDA, prolonged arcing can damage your microwave).

MICROWAVE KALE CHIPS
SERVES 2

For the best texture, we prefer to use flatter Lacinato kale. We found that collard greens also work well, but we don't recommend curly-leaf kale, Swiss chard, or curly-leaf spinach, all of which turn dusty and crumbly when crisped.

- 5   ounces kale (about ½ bunch), stemmed and torn into 2-inch pieces
- 4   teaspoons oil
     Kosher salt

1. Wash and thoroughly dry kale, then toss well with oil in large bowl.

2. Spread roughly one-third of leaves in single layer on large plate and season lightly with kosher salt.

3. Microwave for 3 minutes. If leaves are crispy, transfer to serving bowl; if not, continue to microwave leaves in 30-second increments until crispy. Repeat with remaining leaves in 2 batches. Serve. (Chips can be stored in airtight container for up to 1 week.)

Kale Caesar Salad

✔ WHY THIS RECIPES WORKS

Kale is notorious for being fibrous and tough. In order to break down the leaves and make them more palatable, we soaked them in a hot-water bath. The hot-water soak eliminated the need for cooking or massaging the sturdy kale, making the leaves tender enough— yet still crunchy—for this unique take on a classic salad. To balance the strong flavor of kale, we made an extra-potent dressing, with a stronger dose of lemon juice and anchovies than is typical. Marinating the kale in the Caesar dressing in the refrigerator gave the salad time to cool back down and the flavors time to meld. Even better? We could make this salad ahead of time—dressing it up to 6 hours in advance.

GIVE THE LEAVES A BATH Letting the leaves soak in a bath of hot tap water (about 112 degrees Fahrenheit) helped wilt them slightly, creating a tender yet still crunchy texture. The hot water is like a very mild form of blanching, which damages the cells in the kale leaf and releases enzymes that begin the process of breaking down cell walls. Once released, these enzymes—primarily polygalacturonase, or the same enzyme that starts to break down cell walls as fruits like tomatoes ripen—become more active as they warm up.

MARINATE WARM Marinating the warm kale leaves in the dressing for 20 minutes likewise helps to tenderize the salad. This is mainly due to the oil in the dressing. It turns out that salad leaves like kale have a protective waxy cuticle layer that prevents water-based liquids (vinegar) from having much effect on them, but oil easily penetrates this film.

KALE CAESAR SALAD
SERVES 4

The kale can be dressed up to 6 hours in advance. We prefer curly-leaf kale for this recipe.

SALAD

- 12 ounces kale, stemmed and cut into 1-inch pieces (16 cups)
- 1 ounce Parmesan cheese, grated (½ cup)

CROUTONS

- 3 ounces baguette, cut into ¾-inch cubes (3 cups)
- 2 tablespoons extra-virgin olive oil
- ¼ teaspoon pepper
- ⅛ teaspoon salt

DRESSING

- ½ cup mayonnaise
- ¼ cup grated Parmesan cheese
- 2 tablespoons lemon juice
- 1 tablespoon white wine vinegar
- 1 tablespoon Worcestershire sauce
- 1 tablespoon Dijon mustard
- 3 anchovy fillets, rinsed
- 1 garlic clove, minced
- ½ teaspoon salt
- ½ teaspoon pepper
- ¼ cup extra-virgin olive oil

1. FOR THE SALAD: Place kale in large bowl and cover with hot tap water. Swish kale around with your hand to remove grit. Let kale sit in hot-water bath for 10 minutes. Remove kale from water and spin dry in salad spinner in multiple batches. Pat leaves dry with paper towels if still wet.

2. FOR THE CROUTONS: Adjust oven rack to middle position and heat oven to 350 degrees. Toss all ingredients together in bowl. Bake on rimmed baking sheet until golden and crisp, about 15 minutes. Let croutons cool completely on sheet. (Cooled croutons can be stored in airtight container at room temperature for up to 24 hours.)

3. FOR THE DRESSING: Process mayonnaise, Parmesan, lemon juice, vinegar, Worcestershire, mustard, anchovies, garlic, salt, and pepper in blender until pureed, about 30 seconds. With blender running, slowly add oil until emulsified. Set aside ¼ cup dressing for serving.

4. Toss kale with remaining ¾ cup dressing in large bowl. Refrigerate dressed kale and reserved dressing for at least 20 minutes or up to 6 hours. Toss Parmesan and croutons with dressed kale. Serve, passing reserved dressing at table.

CHAPTER 26

Cabbage

Cabbage may not seem wildly exciting, but it can be a flavor powerhouse.

HOW THE SCIENCE WORKS

Cabbage is a cruciferous vegetable, a member of the same family as cauliflower (page 191), kale (page 205), broccoli, and Brussels sprouts. The cabbage we know today evolved from wild field cabbage, also known as colewort, and has been domesticated as a food for more than 2,500 years.

As with all cruciferous vegetables, the pungent taste and aroma of cabbage does not exist in intact leaves. The compounds responsible for eliciting the taste and smell are formed only when the cells are damaged. Damaging the cells releases an enzyme called myrosinase, which acts on glucosinolates, compounds that exist in all cruciferous vegetables (see page 193), to create compounds called isothiocyanates. These compounds give cruciferous vegetables their pungent, bitter flavor.

> *To this day, previously unknown bacteria are being discovered in kimchi.*

When it comes to cooking? Poor cabbage. Alternately viewed as a pauper's vegetable or a dieter's frenemy, cabbage can become overbearing, limp, and smelly when cooked. To manage the potentially pungent sulfur-tasting compounds—including hydrogen sulfide (typical of rotten eggs) and ammonia, which are produced with longer cooking—we soak it in water to wash away the precursors of these compounds (the glucosinolates) for our Sautéed Cabbage (page 218). We balance all the flavors present in our longer-cooked Braised Red Cabbage (page 219) by including red wine and orange juice concentrate to give it a sweet-and-sour depth.

Here we also want to concentrate on one of the most common ways of preparing cabbage: fermentation. Fermentation has been used to preserve food ever since the earliest agricultural settlements in China, the Middle East, and South America. But it was only 150 years ago that Louis Pasteur discovered that microorganisms were essential for fermenting food. These microorganisms, such as bacteria, yeast, and mold, exist everywhere in the air, soil, water, and even in the gastrointestinal tracts of animals and humans. Fermentation refers to the process by which these microorganisms convert natural sugars to metabolites such as lactic acid, alcohol, and carbon dioxide.

The fermentation of cabbage provides a great example of how it works—especially Sauerkraut (page 216). The process is simple: Chop cabbage, add salt, weigh it down in a container protected from air, and wait. The salt pulls liquid from the cabbage via osmosis. The juices dissolve the salt to form a brine. The brine encourages the growth of some coliform bacteria (found in the air, water, and soil) while discouraging the growth of harmful microorganisms. The bacteria also convert a small amount of the sugars present in the cabbage into lactic acid, lowering the pH of the brine and encouraging the growth of *Leuconostoc* bacteria, and then *Lactobacillus* bacteria. Several different species of *Lactobacillus* bacteria grow, each better at a different pH, together creating enough lactic acid to produce the tangy taste of sauerkraut. (Refrigeration slows the process.) The low pH of the finished product prevents the growth of harmful microorganisms, preserving the food.

Kimchi (page 217) takes this fermentation process one step further. Traditional kimchi is made from cabbage (plus other ingredients, often including radish, red pepper, green onion, ginger, garlic, salt, and a fermented fish product). Fermentation is carried out in tightly sealed containers, which favor the growth of anaerobic bacteria. Because of the variety of ingredients, kimchi contains hundreds of different varieties of bacteria. In fact, previously unknown bacteria are being discovered in kimchi to this day.

Traditional forms of vegetable preservation, like naturally pickled cucumbers, sauerkraut, and kimchi, rely on an important balance of salt and bacteria for preservation. Salt prohibits the growth of unwanted bacteria, giving beneficial, largely salt-resistant species enough time to dominate and lower the pH to safe levels (under pH 4.6). Beyond preservation, these bacteria also produce the desirable characteristic flavors. Temperature impacts both the speed at which fermentation progresses and the resulting flavors. To explore the relationship between temperature and fermentation in kimchi, and to aid in development of our Kimchi recipe (page 217), we set up the following experiment.

EXPERIMENT

We mixed up four identical batches of our Kimchi recipe, packed them into ½-gallon glass jars, and stored them at four different temperatures—39 degrees, 50 degrees, 65 degrees, and 70 degrees—for nine days. We then tasted each batch and sent samples to the Tufts University Biology Department, where Assistant Professor Benjamin Wolfe and graduate student Esther Miller ran analysis of their respective bacterial compositions.

RESULTS

We were surprised to find remarkable differences among the four batches of kimchi. The sample stored at 39 degrees featured crisp cabbage, a thin brine, and one-dimensional, mildly fishy flavor, while the sample at the other extreme of 70 degrees was effervescent, on the verge of mushy, and tasted sharp and overly cheesy. The batch at 50 degrees was nearly as crisp as the 39-degree sample, with slightly more complex, funky flavor, and a slightly thickened brine. The 65-degree sample, while slightly softer than the 50-degree sample, featured the most complex mix of bright acidity, pleasant fermented flavor, and a thickened brine.

While the types of bacteria in a given batch of kimchi can vary considerably based on the specific vegetables used, research has shown that often a type of bacteria called *Leuconostoc* dominates in the early stages of fermentation. *Leuconostoc* lower the pH of the kimchi and decrease oxygen, creating an environment that favors the growth of *Lactobacillus* bacteria. The results from Tufts University suggest that this progression took place in our samples. The 39-degree sample contained almost entirely *Leuconostoc* species, while the 50-degree sample was a mixture of both *Leuconostoc* species and *Lactobacillus* species. The 65-degree and 70-degree batches were composed almost entirely of *Lactobacillus* species.

TAKEAWAY

The temperature of kimchi fermentation has an impact on not only the assortment of bacteria present but also the speed at which the bacteria do their work. Our results suggest that at refrigerator temperature, *Leuconostoc* stay active for much longer than at higher temperatures, leading to milder flavor. As the temperature increases, so too does the presence of *Lactobacillus* species that provide greater acidity and more complex flavor. In this test we found that 65 degrees for nine days provided the optimal environment for kimchi with a thickened, tangy brine, crunchy cabbage, and well-rounded flavor.

KIMCHI: FERMENTATION TEMPERATURE MATTERS

We stored kimchi at four different temperatures for nine days each, and found remarkable differences in the ratio and amount of the two types of bacteria produced. Our preference? The sample stored at 65 degrees, which had a thick, tangy brine and crunchy cabbage.

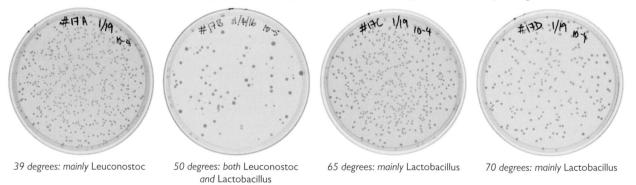

39 degrees: mainly Leuconostoc   *50 degrees: both* Leuconostoc *and* Lactobacillus   *65 degrees: mainly* Lactobacillus   *70 degrees: mainly* Lactobacillus

FAMILY TREE: PRESERVED FOODS

You might be surprised to learn that familiar items like bread, coffee, beer, and chocolate wouldn't exist without fermentation. This ancient, natural process—which relies on the transformative powers of friendly bacteria—not only helps preserve food but also alters its textures, flavors, and aromas. Here, we take a look at a wide assortment of foods whose production involves fermentation.

PLANTS

KIMCHI

While this spicy, crunchy Korean pickle is most commonly made with napa cabbage, it can be made with radish, cucumber—even watermelon rind.

SAUERKRAUT

True sauerkraut is the result of wild fermentation (meaning that it uses lactic acid bacteria already present in and on the vegetable). It's bacteria that lend sauerkraut its trademark flavor.

PRESERVED LEMONS

This savory take on citrus has North African origins. Lemons are scored, packed with salt and lemon juice, and fermented for six to eight weeks. The rinds soften and mellow in flavor.

SOUR PICKLES

Unlike sweet pickles, true sour pickles are the product of fermentation. After as little as a week in solution, the lactic acid bacteria have done their work and the pickles are salty, sour, and crisp.

VINEGAR

Grape juice's initial fermentation turns it into wine, but if left exposed to air and room temperature, over time bacteria and yeasts in the wine convert the alcohol into acid.

ANIMALS

FISH SAUCE

This highly concentrated liquid, made from salted, fermented fish; water; salt; and sometimes sugar, adds complexity to foods—and when used carefully, no trace of fishiness.

SALAMI

Salting and drying is essential for cured meat. Salami recipes also include a starter culture of lactic acid–producing bacteria that act as a preservative and lend a signature, faintly sour flavor.

YOGURT

Milk is heated and then cooled to just over 100 degrees before a bacterial culture is added. After 4 to 8 hours, the mixture thickens into yogurt. (For more on yogurt, see page 153.)

KEFIR

Kefir cultures are added to milk and left to ferment at room temperature for as little as 24 hours and then refrigerated. As it ferments, it becomes thicker and takes on a tart, bubbly quality.

BEANS

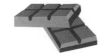

CHOCOLATE

Cacao beans and pulp are left outdoors for up to seven days. Naturally occurring yeasts and bacteria grow, decreasing pH. (See page 399 for more.)

MISO

Miso is made by mashing cooked soybeans with salt; grains; flavorings; and *koji*, or rice that has grown a healthy mold that produces a sweet fragrance.

SOY SAUCE

Made from soybeans and wheat, salty soy sauce is left to ferment for up to four years, which can explain the widely divergent flavors and quality.

Sauerkraut

✓ WHY THIS RECIPE WORKS

A classic pairing with brats and Reubens, sauerkraut packs a big punch and yet it's nothing more than shredded cabbage and salt that have been left to ferment. Naturally occurring bacteria do all the work: They devour sugars in the cabbage, producing lactic acid. This acidity and the complex flavor compounds these bacteria produce lend that trademark sour flavor. We set to work finding out the best method.

CHOP IT Cutting the cabbage into similar-size shreds, we found, ensured that the jar would ferment at the same rate. To do this easily, we first quartered and cored the cabbage. Then, working with smaller stacks of cabbage leaves, we pressed the leaves flat to the counter and carefully sliced them into thin, uniform strips.

TOSS AND MASSAGE We then tossed the cabbage with 4 teaspoons salt in a large bowl, kneading it with our hands until it had softened and began to release some liquid. (This liquid is necessary to help start the fermentation process and keep the cabbage submerged in the jar.)

SALT IT WELL Salt keeps bad bacteria that break down the cabbage at bay, so the salinity here is crucial. Too little salt, and our kraut wilted and spoiled too quickly. Too much salt and the fermentation slowed to a halt; this meant that our sauerkraut didn't become acidic enough, and bad bacteria were free to take over. We found that 2.8 percent salinity was the "sweet spot" for a crunchy, pleasantly sour-tasting kraut. (Canning salt is specifically designed for pickle making and contains no iodine or anti-caking agents.)

SUBMERGE IT As we filled the jar with the salted cabbage, we used our fists to pack it as tightly as possible and remove any air pockets. This ensured that the cabbage would stay submerged during fermentation. When done, we pressed a parchment round flush against the cabbage. To help the cabbage stay fully submerged, we placed a bag of brine on top to weigh it down. We decided to use the brine (rather than water) because if the bag broke it wouldn't ruin the careful balance of salinity we'd created inside the jar (we learned that the hard way. . .).

KEEP THE RIGHT TEMP Placing a triple layer of cheesecloth over the mouth of the jar helped the fermentation gases escape while keeping out debris and bugs. The ideal environment for fermenting is between 50 and 70 degrees (do not ferment above 70 degrees). The fermentation temperature will affect the timing and flavor of the sauerkraut; warmer temperatures will ferment more quickly and produce sharper, more pungent flavors. For a balanced flavor, we preferred a fermentation temperature of 65 degrees. (For more on this, see Test Kitchen Experiment, page 214.)

SAUERKRAUT
MAKES ABOUT 6 CUPS

This sauerkraut cannot be processed for long-term storage. Kosher salt can be substituted for canning salt.

- 1   head green cabbage (2½ pounds), quartered, cored, and sliced into ⅛-inch-thick shreds (7 cups)
- 2   tablespoons pickling and canning salt
- 1½ teaspoons juniper berries
- 2   cups water

1. Cut out parchment paper round to match diameter of ½-gallon wide-mouth glass jar. Toss cabbage with 4 teaspoons salt in large bowl. Using your hands, forcefully knead salt into cabbage until it has softened and begins to release moisture, about 3 minutes. Stir in juniper berries.

2. Tightly pack cabbage mixture and any accumulated liquid into jar, pressing down firmly with your fist to eliminate air pockets as you pack. Press parchment round flush against surface of cabbage.

3. Dissolve remaining 2 teaspoons salt in water and transfer to 1-quart zipper-lock plastic bag; squeeze out air and seal bag well. Place bag of brine on top of parchment and gently press down. Cover jar with triple layer of cheesecloth and secure with rubber band.

4. Place jar in 50- to 70-degree location away from direct sunlight and let ferment for 6 days; check jar daily, skimming residue and mold from surface and pressing to keep cabbage submerged. After 6 days, taste sauerkraut daily until it has reached desired flavor (this may take up to 7 days longer; sauerkraut should be pale and translucent with a tart and floral flavor).

5. When sauerkraut has reached desired flavor, remove cheesecloth, bag of brine, and parchment, and skim off any residue or mold. Serve. (Sauerkraut and accumulated juices can be transferred to clean jar, covered, and refrigerated for up to 6 weeks; once refrigerated, flavor of sauerkraut will continue to mature.)

Sauerkraut is made by salting shredded cabbage, packing it in containers, and leaving it to ferment at room temperature for one to six weeks. During this time, natural bacteria and yeasts eat away at sugars in the cabbage, leaving behind tart lactic acid. To find out which kraut is king, we tried six nationally available sauerkrauts plain, with hot dogs, and in pierogi.

Our tasters detected off-flavors in three lower-ranked brands. The ingredient labels revealed that these products all added preservatives. With so few other ingredients to mask off-flavors, sauerkrauts with chemical preservatives had a prominent "sulfuric," almost "ammonia-like" quality. Tasters preferred "brighter" products that contained just cabbage, salt, and water. We also liked the "punchy," "zippy" flavor of sauerkrauts with 200 milligrams of sodium or more per 2-tablespoon serving; those with any less just tasted like wet cabbage.

These brighter-tasting krauts were packaged in shelf-stable jars or cans, while lower-ranked products were packed in refrigerated plastic bags. Though we often assume that the products we buy in the refrigerated section are fresher than their shelf-stable counterparts, our science editor explained that unlike jars and cans, plastic bags let in small amounts of air over time, which degrades some of the sauerkraut's pungent flavor. This is also why bagged products are the only ones to add preservatives to prevent the growth of microorganisms.

Canned and jarred sauerkrauts also had a softer, more tender texture. Bagged sauerkrauts were tough and crunchy, which tasters found distracting on hot dogs and in pierogi; we preferred softer krauts with only a hint of crunch to complement a dish. Lower-ranked products also had strands that were large and uneven, while our favorite krauts had small and uniform shreds.

Our favorite was Eden Organic Sauerkraut, a jarred kraut with punchy, tangy flavor and even, delicate shreds.

Kimchi

✓ WHY THIS RECIPE WORKS

Kimchi is a Korean pickle of fermented vegetables, typically napa cabbage and scallions, and sometimes leeks, radishes, and carrots. The fermentation process gives kimchi its signature flavor. We wanted to figure out exactly what flavors to add, how to long to ferment it, and at what temperature.

SALT IT AND ADD FLAVOR We first salted the cabbage to remove excess water. For flavor, we made a paste of garlic, ginger, Korean chili powder, sugar, fish sauce, and soy sauce—this brought complexity and heat. We limited our vegetable selection to napa cabbage, scallions, and carrots.

SUBMERGE IT To eliminate air pockets and keep the cabbage submerged in its juices, we placed a plastic bag of water on top; we used two bags to help prevent it from leaking.

FERMENT IT The ideal environment for fermenting is between 50 and 70 degrees (do not ferment above 70 degrees). The fermentation temperature will affect the timing and flavor of the kimchi; warmer temperatures will ferment more quickly and produce sharper flavors. For a balanced flavor, we prefer fermenting at 65 degrees. (For more on this, see Test Kitchen Experiment, page 214.)

KIMCHI
MAKES ABOUT 6 CUPS

You can find Korean chili powder (which has a mild, fruity flavor) at Asian markets and online. If Korean chili powder is unavailable, you can substitute 1/3 cup red pepper flakes. This kimchi cannot be processed for long-term storage. Kosher salt can be substituted for canning salt.

1	head napa cabbage (2½ pounds), cored and cut into 2-inch pieces
2½	teaspoons canning and pickling salt
20	garlic cloves, peeled
½	cup Korean chili powder
⅓	cup sugar
¼	cup low-sodium soy sauce
3	tablespoons fish sauce
1	(2-inch) piece fresh ginger, peeled and chopped coarse
16	scallions, cut into 2-inch pieces
1	carrot, peeled and cut into 2-inch matchsticks

1. Toss cabbage with salt in bowl, cover, and let sit at room temperature for 1 hour. Transfer cabbage to colander, squeeze to drain excess liquid, and return to now-empty bowl. Cut out parchment paper round to match diameter of ½-gallon wide-mouth glass jar.

2. Process garlic, chili powder, sugar, soy sauce, fish sauce, and ginger in food processor until no large pieces of garlic or ginger remain, about 20 seconds. Add chili mixture, scallions, and carrot to cabbage and toss to combine. Tightly pack vegetable mixture into jar, pressing down

firmly with your fist to eliminate air pockets as you pack. Press parchment round flush against surface of vegetables.

3. Fill 1-quart zipper-lock bag with 1 cup water, squeeze out air, and seal well. Place inside second zipper-lock bag, press out air, and seal well. Place bag of water on top of parchment and gently press down. Cover jar with triple layer of cheesecloth and secure with rubber band.

4. Place jar in 50- to 70-degree location away from direct sunlight and let ferment for 9 days; check jar daily, skimming residue and mold from surface and pressing to keep mixture submerged. After 9 days, taste kimchi daily until it has reached desired flavor (this may take up to 11 days longer; cabbage should be soft and translucent with a pleasant cheesy, fishy flavor.)

5. When kimchi has reached desired flavor, remove cheesecloth, bag of water, and parchment and skim off any residue or mold. Serve. (Kimchi and accumulated juice can be transferred to clean jar, covered, and refrigerated for up to 3 months; once refrigerated, kimchi will continue to soften and develop flavor.

PRACTICAL SCIENCE
SUBSTITUTING RED AND GREEN CABBAGE

It is possible.

Although both are part of the *Brassicaceae* family, red and green cabbage are two different varieties. However, it's not uncommon for us to use them interchangeably in recipes.

To compare their flavors, we made batches of buttermilk coleslaw and Braised Red Cabbage (page 219) with green cabbage and red cabbage and tasted the batches side by side. Tasters didn't notice textural differences. But the green cabbage tasted notably milder in both applications, with tasters commenting on its vegetal flavor while raw. The red cabbage was sweeter and "fruitier" in both recipes, though this was more pronounced in the braised sample.

In conclusion? While they behave similarly and can be used interchangeably in recipes, red and green cabbage have slightly different flavor profiles: Green cabbage is mellower and more vegetal, while red is sweeter and more floral.

Sautéed Cabbage

✓ WHY THIS RECIPE WORKS

Unlike kale and Brussels sprouts, which have undergone a recent resurgence, cabbage is still considered boring and bland at best and mushy and smelly at worst. We wanted to restore cabbage's reputation by highlighting its mild sweetness and maintaining a crisp-tender texture, all the while avoiding objectionable flavors and odors.

SOAK IT   The trouble begins with cabbage's pungent-tasting sulfur compounds called isothiocyanates. Cooking can temper their taste, but it's possible to go overboard: The longer cabbage is cooked, the more odoriferous compounds—including hydrogen sulfide (typical of rotten eggs) and ammonia—are produced. To avoid such aromas and flavors, then, it would be necessary to cook the vegetable as rapidly as possible. We also knew another tip: Immerse the cut cabbage in water to draw out the precursors of the pungent isothiocyanates—the odorless glucosinolates, which are water-soluble and bitter. Putting both tricks to work, we soaked sliced cabbage for various amounts of time, drained it, and then quickly sautéed it and compared it with unsoaked samples. Great news: A mere 3-minute soak, along with swift cooking, produced a noticeable reduction in unwanted flavors.

COVER UP, AND OFF   But all was not perfect: Cooked uncovered over medium-high heat, the cabbage lightly caramelized in some areas, adding nuttiness, but only some slices emerged tender while others were downright crunchy. Conversely, when we cooked the cabbage covered over lower heat, it emerged uniformly tender and sweet, yet slightly soggy and missing the depth provided by browning. What if we used a hybrid method—starting with the lid on to create steam (generated by the moisture clinging to the cabbage after soaking) and then uncovering the pan to evaporate liquid and encourage browning? Sure enough, this cabbage was crisp-tender, with plenty of sweetness and nuttiness.

SAUTÉED CABBAGE WITH PARSLEY AND LEMON
SERVES 4 TO 6

1	small head green cabbage (1¼ pounds), cored and sliced thin
2	tablespoons vegetable oil
1	onion, halved and sliced thin
	Salt and pepper
¼	cup chopped fresh parsley
1½	teaspoons lemon juice

1. Place cabbage in large bowl and cover with cold water; let stand for 3 minutes. Drain well and set aside. Meanwhile, heat 1 tablespoon oil in 12-inch nonstick skillet over medium-high heat until shimmering. Add onion and ¼ teaspoon salt and cook, stirring occasionally, until softened and lightly browned, 6 to 7 minutes. Transfer onion to bowl.

2. Return now-empty skillet to medium-high heat, add remaining 1 tablespoon oil and heat until shimmering. Add cabbage and sprinkle with ½ teaspoon salt and ¼ teaspoon pepper. Cover and cook, without stirring, until cabbage is wilted and lightly browned on bottom, about 3 minutes.

3. Stir and continue to cook, uncovered, until cabbage is crisp-tender and lightly browned in places, about 4 minutes longer, stirring once halfway through cooking. Remove skillet from heat. Stir in onion, parsley, and lemon juice. Season with salt and pepper to taste, transfer to serving bowl, and serve.

SAUTÉED CABBAGE WITH BACON AND CARAWAY SEEDS

Substitute red cabbage for green. Whisk 1 tablespoon cider vinegar and 2 teaspoons packed brown sugar together in medium bowl. Omit oil. Cook 4 slices chopped bacon in skillet over medium-high heat until crisp, 5 to 7 minutes. Transfer bacon to paper towel–lined plate and pour off all but 1 tablespoon fat into bowl (reserve fat). Substitute red onion for onion and cook in fat in skillet until almost tender, 5 to 6 minutes. Add 1 teaspoon caraway seeds and cook for 1 minute. Transfer to bowl with vinegar mixture. Cook cabbage in 1 tablespoon reserved fat. Stir bacon into cabbage with onion mixture before serving.

SAUTÉED CABBAGE WITH CHILE AND PEANUTS

Substitute red onion for onion. Cook 1 thinly sliced jalapeño, seeds reserved (optional), with onion in step 1. Once onion is crisp-tender, about 4 minutes, add 2 garlic cloves, minced to paste, and continue to cook until fragrant, about 30 seconds. Substitute 4 teaspoons fish sauce and 2 teaspoons packed brown sugar for salt and pepper in step 2. Substitute ½ cup chopped fresh cilantro for parsley and 1 tablespoon lime juice for lemon juice. Add reserved jalapeño seeds, if desired. Sprinkle cabbage with 2 tablespoons chopped dry-roasted peanuts before serving.

SAUTÉED CABBAGE WITH FENNEL AND GARLIC

Substitute savoy cabbage for green. Substitute extra-virgin olive oil for vegetable oil and 1 cored and thinly sliced fennel bulb for onion. Cook fennel bulb until softened, 8 to 10 minutes, then add 2 garlic cloves, minced to paste, and ¼ teaspoon red pepper flakes and continue to cook until fragrant, about 30 seconds. Omit pepper. Substitute fennel fronds for parsley and increase lemon juice to 2 teaspoons. Drizzle cabbage with 1 tablespoon extra-virgin olive oil and sprinkle with 2 tablespoons grated Parmesan before serving.

Braised Red Cabbage

✔ WHY THIS RECIPE WORKS

Sweet-and-sour braised red cabbage is a classic German side that has a bright flavor ideal for pairing with rich, meaty entrées. Braising humble cabbage with brown sugar and orange juice transforms it by bringing out its sweet flavor and giving it a silky texture. The key is to not make it too sweet, or too sour, or too mushy—a surprisingly tall order.

USE CONCENTRATE To add a gentle sweetness, we started with a braising liquid of equal parts orange juice and red wine. But, while the version with orange juice was good, we found that using orange juice concentrate boosted the dish's flavor and helped it cook faster (since we didn't have to wait for the concentrate to, well, concentrate).

LIFT THE LID Leaving the lid of the Dutch oven on the entire time resulted in too much liquid in the pot when the cabbage was done. A better method was to braise the cabbage for 45 minutes, covered, and then remove the cover and simmer the cabbage for another 25 to 30 minutes. This gave us perfectly tender cabbage that was nicely coated in the sweet, sour, and syrupy glaze. Finishing the dish with a tart Granny Smith apple, butter, and minced parsley brought everything together.

BRAISED RED CABBAGE
SERVES 4

We developed this recipe with inexpensive Cabernet Sauvignon, but any dry red wine will work. Our favorite frozen orange juice concentrate is Minute Maid Original Frozen Concentrated Orange Juice.

3	tablespoons unsalted butter
1	onion, halved and sliced thin
1	head red cabbage (2 pounds), cored and sliced ½ inch thick
1	cup red wine
½	cup frozen orange juice concentrate
1½	tablespoons packed brown sugar
	Salt and pepper
1	Granny Smith apple, peeled, cored, and cut into ¼-inch pieces
3	tablespoons minced fresh parsley

1. Melt 2 tablespoons butter in Dutch oven over medium heat. Add onion and cook until golden, 7 to 9 minutes. Stir in cabbage, wine, orange juice concentrate, sugar, 1¼ teaspoons salt, and ½ teaspoon pepper and bring to boil. Cover, reduce heat to low, and simmer for 45 minutes.

2. Stir in apple. Increase heat to medium-low and continue to simmer, uncovered, until cabbage is tender and liquid is syrupy, 25 to 30 minutes longer.

3. Off heat, stir in parsley and remaining 1 tablespoon butter. Season with salt and pepper to taste. Serve.

PRACTICAL SCIENCE
TURNING RED CABBAGE BLUE

Cooking with an alkaline component can turn cabbage blue.

Red onions—as well as other red produce, including cabbage and cherries—are rich in pigments called anthocyanins. When they're cooked with acid, their color intensifies, but when combined with an alkaline component, they can turn a startling bluish-green color.

Just for fun, we decided to see if we could reverse the color change once a fruit or vegetable with anthocyanin turns blue. We sautéed red cabbage and then added a pinch of baking soda to turn it blue. We found that a splash of vinegar brought its red color right back. This trick may not have a practical application, but it might impress your friends.

CHAPTER 27

Tomatoes

Garden-fresh tomatoes taste amazing. But when they're store-bought you need to maximize their flavor . . . in the kitchen.

HOW THE SCIENCE WORKS

Tomatoes are a member of the nightshade family, or *Solanaceae*, which includes eggplant, potatoes, peppers, and *Atropa belladonna*, also known as deadly nightshade. (This poisonous cousin is what once gave tomatoes a bad reputation, preventing their consumption in Europe for many years.) The tomato originated in Central America, was domesticated around 2,500 years ago in southern Mexico, and spread through the Americas with the Spanish colonists in the 1400s. (The word "tomato" comes from the Spanish word *tomate,* and the Nahuatl word *tomatl.*) Today over 7,500 varieties are grown for consumption worldwide.

Botanically, tomatoes are classified as a fruit, not a vegetable. This is because they grow from the ovary of the parent plant and contain the seeds for the next generation. All fruits are classified as either climacteric (they continue to ripen after harvest) or nonclimacteric (they do not). Tomatoes are climacteric. After harvest, they turn from green to red or yellow or orange, and continue to change over time, producing less acid, more sugar, and more flavor compounds.

When it comes to tomatoes, one thing is clear: Fresh, ripe tomatoes from the garden are far more flavorful than tomatoes purchased at the supermarket. Why? Being a climacteric fruit, many commercial tomatoes are harvested when they are still unripe and green. At this stage they are very firm and have relatively little flavor—and therefore are much less susceptible to damage during harvest and shipping. Once at the local distributor, green tomatoes are turned into red tomatoes by treatment with a little ethylene gas (the same chemical produced by fruits as they ripen). The color change occurs rapidly, allowing the tomatoes to be shipped to market soon after treatment. Unfortunately, the flavor development is a slower process. So even though supermarket tomatoes may be bright red, they lack the flavor of garden-ripened tomatoes.

Most of the true flavor of ripe tomatoes comes from the formation of about 400 aroma compounds. These compounds are produced either during ripening in the intact fruit or by tissue damage caused by slicing, chopping, or chewing—similar to cruciferous vegetables (page 193). Cell disruption releases enzymes that rapidly catalyze the formation of volatile aroma compounds. A ripe tomato may have plenty of aroma, but chopping tomatoes increases it. Other sources of volatile flavor compounds formed during ripening are the amino acids, including glutamic acid, known for its savory umami taste. The highest levels of glutamic acid are found in the jelly located in the middle of the tomato.

Cooking undeniably changes the flavor of fresh tomatoes. With heat, many of the volatile aroma compounds in tomatoes are lost, while less-volatile compounds become more concentrated, building flavor. Also, potent volatile sulfur compounds are formed during cooking—including one called dimethyl sulfide, which is one of the characteristic flavor compounds in tomato paste. We work hard to improve the less-flavorful supermarket tomatoes with heat. Roasting slices of tomatoes (Roasted Tomatoes, page 224) concentrates their flavor. And roasting vine-ripened tomatoes from the supermarket—with tomato paste, for a deeper tomato flavor—creates a rich, hearty Roasted Tomato Sauce (page 224). Our Greek Cherry Tomato Salad (page 225) is amplified by first salting and draining the tomatoes and then reducing the glutamate-rich jelly to add back to the salad. We likewise salt and drain tomatoes for our Pasta with Raw Tomato Sauce (page 226) and then cook the pasta in the tomato juice for additional flavor.

A tomato is not a vegetable, but a fruit.

TEST KITCHEN EXPERIMENT

In 2003, Chef Paul Bertolli popularized the technique of adding fresh tomato leaves to cooked tomato sauce to supposedly boost its fresh, tomato-y flavor. Years later, Harold McGee hopped on the bandwagon, both to dispel any lingering beliefs that tomato leaves are poisonous and to provide his own spin on the recipe. With our curiosity piqued, we decided to run some taste tests of own.

EXPERIMENT

We cooked up one large batch of a basic tomato sauce, split it in half, and steeped ¼ cup of chopped fresh tomato leaves from one test cook's garden in one portion for 10 minutes. We placed the leaves in a cheesecloth bag so that they could be easily removed before serving. We also repeated the test with the leaves and vines taken from store-bought vine-ripe tomatoes.

RESULTS

Tasters found the batch doctored with garden-fresh tomato leaves less sweet and more complex than the untreated batch. Some tasters noted that it featured more fresh tomato flavor, while others found it smelled earthy and leafy. The test with store-bought vine-ripe tomato leaves was less conclusive. A few tasters picked up, and appreciated, a "greener" flavor, but most had a difficult time telling the two batches apart.

TAKEAWAY

The primary compounds responsible for the aroma of fresh tomato leaves are Z-3-hexenal and 2-isobutylthiazole. Interestingly, both of these highly volatile flavor compounds are also found in raw tomatoes. The compound 2-isobutylthiazole is actually isolated and added to a wide range of commercial products, including condiments like ketchup. We found that both canning and freezing the treated tomato sauce greatly decreased the fresh, leafy aroma and flavor. But if you grow tomatoes or buy garden-fresh vine-ripe tomatoes at the farmers' market, we think it's worth trying. Use ¼ cup chopped leaves per 8 cups tomato sauce and steep for the final 10 minutes of cooking (remove and discard leaves before serving).

THE FLAVOR OF TOMATO LEAVES

Adding chopped-up tomato leaves to tomato sauce can add a "greener" flavor, which many tasters enjoyed.

Fresh leaves from the garden, or even the stems and tops from vine-ripened tomatoes from the grocery store, will add fresh flavor to sauces.

FOCUS ON: TOMATOES

Tomatoes come in many forms and sizes—cherry, plum, beefsteak, vine-ripened, heirloom, and more—but every tomato shares the same basic structure. Here, we take a closer look.

STEM

There are two basic types of tomato plants: determinate and indeterminate. Determinate tomatoes, or bush tomatoes, have vines that grow only 1 to 3 feet and then stop. Vines of indeterminate tomatoes can grow up to 20 feet long, and need to be pruned and supported by a trellis or tomato cage.

SEEDS

Old wives' tales have long implied that the seeds of tomatoes are bitter and should be removed before cooking a sauce or a stew. But this isn't true. They are in fact quite benign in flavor. The only reason to remove seeds is to avoid a lumpy texture.

JELLY

The jelly surrounding the seeds in the middle of a raw tomato is incredibly flavorful, containing high levels of glutamates—even more than the flesh itself.

FLESH

Most of the aroma of fresh tomatoes is formed in the flesh. The aroma compounds develop during ripening—or by tissue damage (cutting, slicing, chewing). This "disruption" causes the release of an enzyme that forms volatile aroma compounds.

LEAVES

Some chefs add tomato leaves to enhance the flavor of a sauce. Why? A variety of aroma compounds are formed in tomato leaves when they are torn or damaged. These volatile compounds are formed by the rapid oxidation of the two essential fatty acids linoleic acid and linolenic acid when they come in contact with the enzyme known as lipoxygenase. Many of these compounds are the same that are formed in ripe tomatoes, which is why tomato leaves smell like ripe tomatoes. Thus, torn tomato leaves added at the end of cooking a tomato sauce deliver back the volatile fresh aroma compounds that may have evaporated during the slow cooking of the sauce. To be most effective the leaves must be torn into small pieces rather than simply added as whole leaves. So when you harvest your tomatoes save some of the leaves.

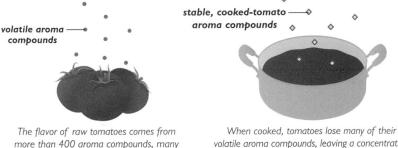

volatile aroma compounds

stable, cooked-tomato aroma compounds

The flavor of raw tomatoes comes from more than 400 aroma compounds, many volatile, formed by ripening or chopping.

When cooked, tomatoes lose many of their volatile aroma compounds, leaving a concentration of more-stable aroma compounds.

Adding fresh tomato leaves to a cooked tomato sauce delivers back some of the volatile aroma compounds from raw tomatoes.

Roasted Tomatoes

✓ WHY THIS RECIPE WORKS

If you've never roasted tomatoes, you should. It's a largely hands-off technique that yields the ultimate condiment: bright, concentrated tomatoes that are soft but retain their shape. They can be used right away or frozen. That said, many people shy away from roasting because most recipes take hours. Faster recipes yield bland results—an unappealing phase between raw and roasted. We wanted bright-tasting, soft-but-intact tomatoes in less time.

USE LARGE TOMATOES We started with larger round tomatoes, which boast a higher ratio of the flavorful "jelly" to skin than do the denser plum variety, and a lower ratio of chewy skin to flesh than smaller cherry or grape tomatoes. And since the main goal of roasting tomatoes is to evaporate much of their moisture, we sliced them into ¾-inch-thick rounds—a shape that maximized their surface area for efficient evaporation and allowed us to fit 3 pounds in a single layer on a foil-lined rimmed baking sheet.

COAT IN OIL With just a drizzle of oil, it took up to 5 hours for the tomatoes to collapse and shrivel sufficiently. Starting with a blast of heat and then lowering the temperature only helped a bit. Then we thought about how oil is more efficient than air at transferring heat. Sure enough, when we roasted a batch in ¾ cup of oil, they cooked up nicely concentrated and caramelized in half the time.

ROASTED TOMATOES
MAKES 1½ CUPS

Avoid using tomatoes smaller than 3 inches in diameter, which have a smaller ratio of flavorful jelly to skin than larger tomatoes. To double the recipe, use two baking sheets, increase the baking time in step 2 to 40 minutes, and rotate and switch the sheets halfway through baking. In step 3, increase the roasting time to 1½ to 2½ hours.

- 3 pounds large tomatoes, cored, bottom ⅛ inch trimmed, and sliced ¾ inch thick
- 2 garlic cloves, peeled and smashed
- ¼ teaspoon dried oregano
  Kosher salt and pepper
- ¾ cup extra-virgin olive oil

1. Adjust oven rack to middle position and heat oven to 425 degrees. Line rimmed baking sheet with aluminum foil. Arrange tomatoes in even layer on prepared sheet, with larger slices around edge and smaller slices in center. Place garlic cloves on tomatoes. Sprinkle with oregano and ¼ teaspoon salt and season with pepper to taste. Drizzle oil evenly over tomatoes.

2. Bake for 30 minutes, rotating sheet halfway through baking. Remove sheet from oven. Reduce oven temperature to 300 degrees and prop open door with wooden spoon to cool oven. Using thin spatula, flip tomatoes.

3. Return tomatoes to oven and continue to cook until spotty brown, skins are blistered, and tomatoes have collapsed to ¼ to ½ inch thick, 1 to 2 hours. Remove from oven and let cool completely, about 30 minutes. Discard garlic and transfer tomatoes and oil to airtight container. (Tomatoes can be refrigerated for up to 5 days or frozen for up to 2 months.)

Roasted Tomato Sauce

✓ WHY THIS RECIPE WORKS

A sauce made with supermarket tomatoes lacks the meaty intensity of a sauce made with garden tomatoes. Is there a way to make a great fresh tomato sauce when the garden is covered with snow? We wondered if roasting could transform those characterless tomatoes in the supermarket produce section in the dead of winter. Roasting caramelizes natural sugars, intensifies flavors, and adds a light touch of smokiness. Could roasting work its magic with crummy tomatoes?

PICK THE RIGHT TOMATO Most supermarkets offer three tomato choices—vine-ripened, plum, and beefsteak. We roasted each variety and were surprised by the winner. The large, out-of-season beefsteaks produced a watery, bland sauce after roasting. Most plum tomatoes worked fine in our tests, but a few mealy samples created a sauce that was too dry. But vine-ripened tomatoes had the brightest flavor and best texture. These juicy tomatoes were absolutely consistent in our testing.

USE A RACK Elevating the vegetables on a rack set in a foil-lined rimmed baking sheet maximized charring and flavor development; it also prevented the vegetables from stewing in their own juices. We tried seeding the tomatoes before roasting, to eliminate extra moisture. But we found that keeping the seeds kept more of that fresh flavor, combined with a roasted flavor.

ADD TOMATO PASTE We discovered that a couple tablespoons of tomato paste deepened the tomato flavor in our sauce and improved its color. We simply coated the fresh tomatoes, onion slices, and garlic cloves with tomato paste before they went into the oven. The paste darkened as it roasted, and its flavor became more intense. We've found that tomato paste performs a similar function in other recipes, adding depth to countless stews and sauces. We usually add the tomato paste once the aromatic vegetables have been cooked and before the liquid goes into the pan—exposing the tomato paste directly to dry heat intensifies its flavor and color.

ROASTED TOMATO SAUCE
MAKES ENOUGH FOR 1 POUND OF PASTA

This sauce is best served with short pasta shapes, such as ziti, penne, or fusilli. It can also be served over chicken Parmesan or grilled fish.

- 2 tablespoons tomato paste
- 2 tablespoons extra-virgin olive oil
- 2 teaspoons minced fresh thyme
- Salt and pepper
- ⅛ teaspoon red pepper flakes
- 3 pounds tomatoes, cored and halved
- 1 small onion, sliced into ½-inch-thick rounds
- 6 garlic cloves, peeled
- 1 teaspoon red wine vinegar
- Sugar
- 2 tablespoons chopped fresh basil

1. Adjust oven rack to middle position and heat oven to 475 degrees. Combine tomato paste, 1 tablespoon oil, thyme, ¾ teaspoon salt, ¼ teaspoon pepper, and pepper flakes in large bowl. Add tomatoes, onion, and garlic and toss until evenly coated. Set wire rack in aluminum foil–lined rimmed baking sheet and place 4-inch square of foil in center of rack. Place garlic cloves and onion rounds on foil and arrange tomatoes, cut side down, around garlic and onion. Roast until vegetables are soft and tomato skins are well charred, 45 to 55 minutes.

2. Remove baking sheet from oven and let cool for 5 minutes. Transfer garlic and onion to food processor and pulse until finely chopped, about 5 pulses. Add tomatoes, vinegar, and remaining 1 tablespoon oil to food processor and pulse until tomatoes are broken down but still chunky, about 5 pulses, scraping down bowl as needed. Season mixture with salt, pepper, and sugar to taste, and pulse until sauce is slightly chunky, about 5 pulses. Transfer mixture to bowl and stir in basil.

Greek Cherry Tomato Salad

✔ WHY THIS RECIPE WORKS

Cherry tomatoes are often considered a support player in salad. But when summertime cherry tomatoes are especially sweet and juicy, they are more than worthy of taking center stage. We knew from experience, however, that we couldn't merely slice them in half, toss them with vinaigrette, and call it a salad. Like bigger, meatier beefsteak and plum varieties, cherry tomatoes exude lots of liquid when cut, quickly turning a salad into a soup.

SALT AND SPIN To get rid of some of the tomato juice without throwing away flavor, we quartered and salted the tomatoes before whirling them in a salad spinner to separate the seeds and jelly from the flesh.

REDUCE After we strained the juice and discarded the seeds, we reduced the tomato jelly to a flavorful concentrate (adding garlic, oregano, shallot, olive oil, and vinegar) and reunited it with the tomatoes.

GREEK CHERRY TOMATO SALAD
SERVES 4 TO 6

If cherry tomatoes are unavailable, substitute grape tomatoes cut in half along the equator. If you don't have a salad spinner, wrap the bowl tightly with plastic wrap after the salted tomatoes have sat for 30 minutes and gently shake to remove seeds and excess liquid. Strain the liquid and proceed with the recipe as directed. If you have less than ½ cup of juice after spinning, proceed with the recipe using the entire amount of juice and reduce it to 3 tablespoons as directed (the cooking time will be shorter).

- 1½ pounds cherry tomatoes, quartered
- ½ teaspoon sugar
- Salt and pepper
- 1 shallot, minced
- 1 tablespoon red wine vinegar
- 2 garlic cloves, minced
- ½ teaspoon dried oregano
- 2 tablespoons extra-virgin olive oil
- 4 ounces feta cheese, crumbled (1 cup)
- 1 small cucumber, peeled, halved lengthwise, seeded, and cut into ½-inch dice
- ½ cup pitted kalamata olives, chopped
- 3 tablespoons chopped fresh parsley

1. Toss tomatoes, sugar, and ¼ teaspoon salt together in bowl and let sit for 30 minutes. Transfer tomatoes to

salad spinner and spin until seeds and excess liquid have been removed, 45 to 60 seconds, stopping to redistribute tomatoes several times during spinning. Return tomatoes to bowl. Strain ½ cup tomato liquid through fine-mesh strainer into liquid measuring cup; discard any extra liquid.

2. Bring tomato liquid, shallot, vinegar, garlic, and oregano to simmer in small saucepan over medium heat and cook until reduced to 3 tablespoons, 6 to 8 minutes. Transfer to small bowl and let cool to room temperature, about 5 minutes. Whisking constantly, drizzle in oil. Season with salt and pepper to taste.

3. Add feta, cucumber, olives, and parsley to bowl with tomatoes. Drizzle with dressing and toss gently to coat. Serve.

Pasta with Raw Tomato Sauce

✔ WHY THIS RECIPE WORKS

Summer's tomatoes are most flavorful when eaten raw. But to make a pasta sauce without cooking the tomatoes presented challenges. Many recipes had trouble getting the texture right. We wanted a mixture thick enough to cling nicely to the pasta, but not so thick that it would seem like a salsa.

SALT 'EM We first concentrated on figuring out how to avoid a thin, watery sauce. For this, we turned to a trick that the test kitchen often uses when faced with this challenge: salting the tomatoes. This technique extracts liquid from the tomatoes and softens their flesh. After many tests, we figured out that an hour was the optimal amount of time to let seasoned tomatoes sit. Two pounds of tomatoes released a full cup of liquid! To get the ideal texture, we mashed half of the tomatoes for the sauce.

USE THE LIQUID We found ourselves wondering what to do with the drained tomato liquid; we were not about to toss it out, because we knew it had a ton of flavor. What if we used this liquid to cook the pasta? Diluted by the amount of water used to cook pasta in the traditional method, it wouldn't have much of an effect. But we have a skillet method of cooking pasta that requires much less liquid: The pasta absorbs the water as it cooks and is never drained. Using this as our guide, we combined the tomato liquid with enough water to bring the total amount to 4 cups (enough for 1 pound of pasta with our skillet method) in a Dutch oven. We stirred in 1 pound of

pasta and cooked it until the pasta was al dente and most of the liquid was gone. After stirring the mashed and reserved tomatoes into the now-cooked pasta, we were relieved to see a sauce. Stirring the pasta as it cooked released starch and helped it to thicken. When the liquid was all gone, the pasta was cooked well, infused with tomato flavor, and coated with a light rose–colored tomato sheen.

PASTA WITH RAW TOMATO SAUCE
SERVES 4

Use the ripest tomatoes you can find.

- 2 pounds very ripe tomatoes, cored and cut into ½-inch pieces
- 1½ tablespoons chopped fresh oregano
- 2 teaspoons plus 2 tablespoons extra-virgin olive oil, plus extra for serving
- 2 garlic cloves, minced
  Salt and pepper
- ¼ teaspoon sugar
- 3 cups water
- 1 pound short pasta, such as campanelle, penne, or fusilli
- ½ cup fresh basil leaves, torn
- 1 ounce Parmesan cheese, grated (½ cup), plus extra for serving

1. Combine tomatoes, oregano, 2 teaspoons oil, garlic, 1½ teaspoons salt, and sugar in large bowl. Let sit until tomatoes soften and release their juice, at least 1 hour or up to 3 hours.

2. Drain tomato mixture in fine-mesh strainer set over bowl and reserve juice. (You should have 1 cup tomato juice; if not, add water as needed to equal 1 cup.) Divide drained tomato mixture evenly between 2 bowls. Using potato masher, mash 1 bowl of tomato mixture to pulp.

3. Combine water, pasta, and reserved tomato juice in Dutch oven. Cover, set over medium-high heat, and cook at vigorous simmer, stirring often, until pasta is al dente and liquid has nearly evaporated, 12 to 15 minutes. Off heat, stir in basil, Parmesan, mashed and unmashed tomato mixtures, and remaining 2 tablespoons oil. Season with salt and pepper to taste. Serve with extra oil and extra Parmesan.

CHAPTER 28

Garlic

The flavor of this tiny yet powerful allium must be managed carefully.

HOW THE SCIENCE WORKS

Garlic is an allium, part of the large genus of (750 different) plants that includes onions (page 233), chives, leeks, scallions, ramps, and shallots. The word "allium" derives from the Greek "to avoid"—and for a long time, that's what humans did with potent, aromatic, spicy garlic. But ever since the ancient Greeks embraced garlic as a food, it's been lodged firmly in our culinary oeuvre.

Garlic falls into two categories: hard-neck and soft-neck, depending on how the stalk, or the scape, grows. The stalk of hard-neck garlic coils like a pig's tail while the soft-neck stalk grows relatively straight. Soft-neck garlic contains a circle of plump cloves shrouding a second circle of smaller cloves, all enveloped by many papery layers. Because soft-neck garlic is heat tolerant and produces and stores well, it has become the favored commercial garlic. Hard-neck garlic has a relatively sparse parchment wrapper that makes it easier to peel, and damage. Its thinly wrapped cloves lose moisture quickly, however, and do not winter over. In the test kitchen, we tasted eight varieties, soft-neck and hard-neck, raw and cooked, and found a wide range of flavors. We enjoyed several soft-neck and hard-neck varieties, but our favorites were Porcelain Zemo and Rocambole Carpathian, both hard-necks.

The potent aroma of raw garlic is due to the formation of volatile sulfur-containing compounds, which are created when the cells are crushed, chopped, or chewed. When garlic cells are damaged, an enzyme called alliinase is released. Alliinase reacts with a sulfur-containing amino acid called alliin, converting it to a totally new compound. This new compound, called allicin, is chemically classified as a thiosulfinate, a chemical relative of the isothiocyanates formed in cruciferous vegetables (page 193). And it's allicin that produces the characteristic pungent aroma of raw crushed garlic. Smell an intact clove and you will not smell any classic garlic odor unless the tissue is beginning to break down. Allicin is not the only thiosulfinate created when raw garlic is crushed, but it does make up about 70 percent of all the thiosulfinates formed. It is somewhat water-soluble, but very oil-soluble, which means that in a vinaigrette most of the garlic flavor will be located in the oil.

And so the key to cooking with garlic is knowing how to manage its flavor—whether that means aiding and abetting its pungency or mellowing it out. Because chopping or crushing damages cells, mincing garlic ahead of time increases its flavor. To maximize the formation of allicin, let minced garlic stand for a few minutes before cooking (the formation of allicin slows down after 10 minutes). To mellow the harsh bite of garlic, deactivate the alliinase enzyme. How? Heat. To deactivate alliinase, you must raise the clove's temperature to 140 degrees or above. Heat also quickly converts the harsh aroma of raw garlic to milder-flavored compounds called polysulfides. Cooking garlic eliminates its harsh, raw flavor, but overcooking to the point that it browns produces bitter-tasting compounds.

Our favorite way to mellow the flavor of garlic is by toasting unpeeled garlic cloves until they are slightly browned, a technique we use in our Classic American Garlic Bread (page 231) and Toasted Nut and Parsley Pesto (page 231). We use garlic in three different ways to obtain the most nuanced, full flavor in our Garlic-Parmesan Mashed Potatoes (page 230), including a novel use of garlic powder (for more, see Test Kitchen Experiment, page 228).

In a vinaigrette, most of the garlic flavor will be located in the oil.

TEST KITCHEN EXPERIMENT

Garlic powder, which is simply dehydrated garlic that's ground to a powder, has never jumped out at us as a particularly potent form of garlic flavor, but when we were developing our Garlic-Parmesan Mashed Potatoes (page 230), we decided to explore all our options, including this ingredient. Knowing that the primary flavor in garlic is not only water-soluble but fat-soluble, we devised a quick test to find out if we could coax more flavor from garlic powder by treating it as we would a spice: blooming it in fat before adding it to the recipe.

EXPERIMENT

For one batch of mashed potatoes, we added ½ teaspoon of garlic powder straight from the jar. For the second batch, we sautéed an equal amount of garlic powder in butter and then stirred it into the potatoes. We asked tasters to compare the garlic in each sample.

RESULTS

The potatoes with untreated garlic powder tasted harsh and garlicky but not particularly complex, similar to what you'd find with raw minced garlic, while the batch with garlic powder that had been sautéed in butter had almost no garlic flavor at all. How could it be that sautéing the powder in butter not only didn't lead to more-complex flavor but seemed to lessen its flavor?

TAKEAWAY

A little research informed us that there was more going on here than the garlic flavor's solubility in water and fat. Garlic develops flavor when its cells are ruptured, releasing an odorless sulfur-containing amino acid called alliin and the enzyme alliinase. Alliinase converts alliin to the primary flavor component in garlic: allicin. Garlic powder producers are careful to dry garlic at temperatures low enough to remove water without destroying alliinase, which will happen at temperatures higher than 140 degrees. Once the water has been removed, the enzyme exists in an inactive state. Only with the reintroduction of water does alliinase "wake up" and begin producing allicin. Adding garlic powder as-is to the mashed potatoes allowed the powder to hydrate in the potatoes' natural moisture, so allicin was able to form. The sample with garlic powder sautéed in butter tasted dull because the alliinase had been exposed to high heat and thus any chance of allicin forming was eliminated.

The bottom line? It's important to first "wake up" the dormant flavor-producing enzyme in garlic powder by hydrating it—and to avoid heating the powder before doing so since that will destroy the enzyme. The best method? When using garlic powder, for the fullest flavor hydrate it in an equal amount of water and then sauté it in fat (as with fresh garlic) before adding it to your dish.

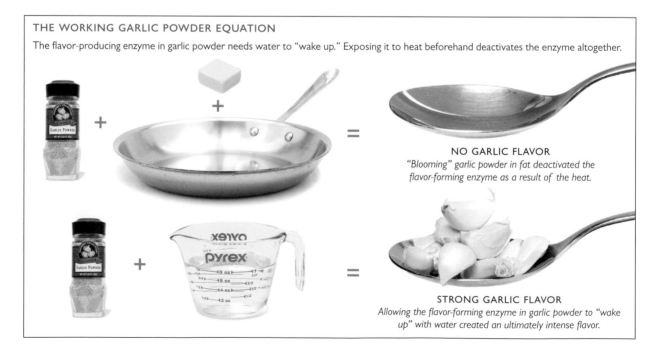

THE WORKING GARLIC POWDER EQUATION

The flavor-producing enzyme in garlic powder needs water to "wake up." Exposing it to heat beforehand deactivates the enzyme altogether.

NO GARLIC FLAVOR
"Blooming" garlic powder in fat deactivated the flavor-forming enzyme as a result of the heat.

STRONG GARLIC FLAVOR
Allowing the flavor-forming enzyme in garlic powder to "wake up" with water created an ultimately intense flavor.

FOCUS ON: GARLIC

Garlic is a staple in many kitchens. The sharp, pungent flavor of that familiar cloved bulb is released with chopping or crushing or chewing. Let's take a closer look.

HARD-NECK GARLIC

Hard-neck garlic, which is the original cultivated garlic variety, is distinguished by its stiff center staff, around which large uniform cloves hang. Hard-neck garlic has a relatively sparse parchment wrapper that makes it easier to peel (and damage) than soft-neck. It is considered superior in flavor—more complex and intense than soft-neck. Its thinly wrapped cloves lose moisture quickly, however, and do not winter over, as do the cloves of the robust soft-neck.

GARLIC SCAPES

Slim stems growing from the top of hard-neck garlic, garlic scapes can be found in farmers' markets and some grocery stores. They have a mild garlic flavor, and are great grilled.

SOFT-NECK GARLIC

The garlic that most of us cook with is soft-neck garlic, so called because its neck is soft and braidable. Soft-neck garlic contains a circle of plump cloves shrouding a second circle of smaller cloves, all enveloped by many papery layers. It is the favored commercial version because not only is it heat tolerant, but it also stores well. You will see soft-neck garlic in the supermarket almost exclusively.

STORAGE

Garlic is highly sensitive to the length of sunlight and temperature it is exposed to. Following harvest, garlic should be stored away from direct sunlight in low humidity to prevent drying out. For long-term commercial storage garlic is normally refrigerated in a nitrogen atmosphere to prevent sprouting. Garlic should not be stored in the refrigerator, as the combination of low temperature, oxygen, and moisture will initiate spoilage.

clove

bulb

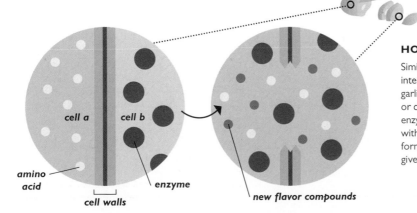

cell a *cell b*

amino acid

cell walls

enzyme

new flavor compounds

HOW FLAVOR IS MADE

Similar to that of cruciferous vegetables, the intense flavor of garlic is only formed after the garlic cells are damaged by chopping, crushing, or chewing. When the cells are damaged, an enzyme, called alliinase, is released, and interacts with a sulfur-containing amino acid, alliin, to form a compound called allicin. Allicin is what gives garlic its spicy, pungent flavor.

Garlic-Parmesan Mashed Potatoes

✔ WHY THIS RECIPE WORKS

Whenever we want something more inspired than plain old mashed potatoes, we turn to potent additions like garlic and Parmesan. Achieving good cheese flavor is as simple as mixing in a handful of the freshly grated stuff, but the garlic is a different story. If it isn't too subtle, it's often overpowering—whether too sharp, too sweet, or even unpleasantly bitter. We envisioned moderately rich potatoes with complex, balanced garlic flavor accentuated by nutty Parmesan.

PICK YOUR POTATO We've developed a lot of mashed potato recipes over the years. Dipping into our expansive archive, it didn't take us long to settle on a potato plan. We started with one of our favorite varieties for mashing: buttery-tasting, moderately starchy Yukon Golds, simmered for about 20 minutes until tender. We drained the slices and then riced the potatoes back into the pot set over low heat. This move helped evaporate excess water, avoiding a soggy mash. Next we stirred in a modest amount of melted butter and warm whole milk.

GARLIC THREE WAYS To get truly complex garlic flavor, we added it in three ways. We incorporated garlic paste sautéed in butter for clean, mellow flavor; a very small amount of raw garlic paste for assertiveness; and a small amount of rehydrated garlic powder, also sautéed in butter, for complex, lightly roasted flavor. In order to maximize the garlic powder's flavor, we first bloomed it in water to reactivate the enzyme that produces the compound allicin, which is responsible for garlic's characteristic flavor (see Test Kitchen Experiment, page 228).

GARLIC-PARMESAN MASHED POTATOES
SERVES 4 TO 6

Our favorite brand of garlic powder is Spice Islands.

- 2 pounds Yukon Gold potatoes, peeled and sliced ½-inch-thick
- ½ teaspoon garlic powder
- 4 tablespoons unsalted butter, cut into 4 pieces
- 1¼ teaspoons garlic, minced to paste
- 1½ ounces Parmesan cheese, grated (¾ cup)
  Salt and pepper
- ⅔ cup warm whole milk

1. Place potatoes in large saucepan and add cold water to cover by 1 inch. Bring water to simmer over medium-high heat. Adjust heat to maintain gentle simmer until paring knife can be slipped into and out of center of potatoes with no resistance, 18 to 22 minutes. Drain potatoes.

2. While potatoes cook, combine garlic powder and ½ teaspoon water in small bowl. Melt butter in 8-inch skillet over medium-low heat. Stir in 1 teaspoon garlic paste and garlic powder mixture; cook, stirring constantly, until fragrant and golden, about 1 minute. Transfer butter mixture to medium bowl and thoroughly stir in Parmesan, 1¼ teaspoons salt, ½ teaspoon pepper, and remaining ¼ teaspoon garlic paste.

3. Place now-empty saucepan over low heat; set ricer or food mill over saucepan. Working in batches, transfer potatoes to hopper and process. Using rubber spatula, stir in butter-Parmesan mixture until incorporated. Stir in warm milk until incorporated. Season with salt and pepper to taste; serve immediately.

PRACTICAL SCIENCE GARLIC SCAPES

The long stems that grow from garlic are good to eat, too.

Garlic scapes—slim, serpentine flower stems—grow from the tops of hard-neck garlic. Farmers have long known that removing them encourages the plant to direct its energy toward growing a plump underground bulb, but only recently has this agricultural byproduct begun to find its way to farmers' markets and community-supported agriculture boxes, usually in late spring.

Our tasters found that raw garlic scapes have an assertive garlic flavor that's less fiery and more grassy than that of raw cloves. Because garlic scapes have a tough and fibrous texture, we found that they worked best minced or pureed for raw applications. Pureed with olive oil, Parmesan cheese, and pine nuts, they produced a simple yet potent pesto.

When the scapes were cooked, tasters noted that the garlic flavor became more muted and sweet—more like roasted garlic than raw—and the texture was impressively dense and meaty. For the simplest preparation, we tossed the scapes with oil, salt, and pepper and cooked them on the grill over medium-high heat until they were softened and lightly charred. We also found that they worked very well when substituted for the green beans in a spicy stir-fry, as their mellow garlic flavor complemented the heat.

Garlic scapes are very hardy; we found that they can be refrigerated in a zipper-lock bag, left slightly open, for up to three weeks. The stem ends and the flower pods can be quite fibrous even when cooked, so we recommend trimming them before use.

Classic American Garlic Bread

✓ WHY THIS RECIPE WORKS

For our best garlic bread recipe, we wanted a lightly toasted surface with a crisp crust that shattered when bitten. The bread within should be warm and chewy, light yet substantial. The garlic flavor should be full and prominent without being harsh. Would it be possible? We set to work.

COOK THE GARLIC The cry for a full, resonant garlic flavor necessitated the use of many more cloves than the usual two or three. But upping the ante created another problem: near overpowering harshness. Since the flavor of garlic mellows with heat, we decided to precook the cloves. We tried sautéing them in butter, but the results were too mild, lacking character and depth. Instead, we toasted unpeeled cloves until just fragrant. After toasting, we minced the cloves and added them to the butter.

PICK BUTTER AND CHEESE We wanted to go with butter, rather than olive oil, for this American-style bread. The right amount would make the garlic bread moist, not soggy or saturated. Six tablespoons did the trick, giving the bread ample richness without marring its texture. A bit of grated Parmesan cheese added depth and complexity without interfering with the garlic flavor.

BAKE IT Wrapping the garlic bread in foil to bake it turned it soggy. We settled on baking an unwrapped loaf at 500 degrees, which produced a beautifully crunchy crust and a nicely browned surface in just 9 minutes or so, with no broiling necessary.

CLASSIC AMERICAN GARLIC BREAD
SERVES 6 TO 8

Plan to pull the garlic bread from the oven when you are ready to serve the other dishes—it is best served piping hot.

- 10 garlic cloves, unpeeled
- 6 tablespoons unsalted butter, softened
- 2 tablespoons grated Parmesan cheese
  Salt and pepper
- 1 (1-pound) loaf Italian bread (preferably football-shaped), halved horizontally

1. Adjust oven rack to middle position and heat oven to 500 degrees. Meanwhile, toast garlic cloves in 8-inch skillet over medium heat, shaking pan occasionally, until

fragrant and color of cloves deepens slightly, about 8 minutes. When cool enough to handle, peel and mince cloves (you should have about 3 tablespoons). Using dinner fork, mash garlic, butter, Parmesan, and ½ teaspoon salt in bowl until thoroughly combined.

2. Spread cut sides of loaf evenly with garlic and butter mixture; season with pepper. Transfer loaf halves, buttered side up, to rimmed baking sheet and bake until surface of bread is golden brown and toasted, 5 to 10 minutes, rotating baking sheet halfway through baking. Cut each half into 2-inch slices; serve immediately.

Toasted Nut and Parsley Pesto

✓ WHY THIS RECIPE WORKS

There are good reasons why pesto has gone from obscure Italian sauce to American favorite. It's incredibly delicious and incredibly easy. But what happens in the winter months, when basil isn't fresh and readily available? We turned to parsley. Whether basil or parsley, however, this bright sauce is too often overloaded with cheese and oil and bludgeoned by harsh garlic. Our goal: Tame that garlic.

TOAST IT We started by putting together a recipe of standard ratios to dress a pound of pasta, and pureed everything in the food processor. We stirred Parmesan in at the end. Just as we feared, the garlic overpowered the parsley and the nuts. The solution? Heat. Toasting the garlic cloves halts the activity of the alliinase enzyme, which creates the pungent flavor of garlic. Here, the technique adequately mellowed the intensely flavored paste.

TOASTED NUT AND PARSLEY PESTO
MAKES 1½ CUPS, ENOUGH FOR 1 POUND OF PASTA

Note that when adding any pesto to cooked pasta it is important to include 3 or 4 tablespoons of the cooked pasta water for proper consistency and even distribution. This pesto can be kept in the refrigerator for up to three days if covered with a sheet of plastic wrap or a thin film of oil.

3	garlic cloves, unpeeled
1	cup pecans, walnuts, whole blanched almonds, skinned hazlenuts, unsalted pistachios, or pine nuts, or any combination thereof
¼	cup fresh parsley leaves
7	tablespoons extra-virgin olive oil
¼	cup grated Parmesan cheese
	Salt and pepper

1. Toast garlic in 10-inch skillet over medium heat, shaking pan occasionally, until softened and spotty brown, about 8 minutes; when cool, remove and discard skins.

2. Toast nuts in now-empty skillet over medium heat, stirring frequently, until golden and fragrant, 4 to 5 minutes.

3. Process garlic, nuts, parsley, and oil in food processor until smooth, about 1 minute, scraping down bowl as necessary. Transfer mixture to small bowl and stir in Parmesan; season with salt and pepper to taste.

PRACTICAL SCIENCE ELEPHANT GARLIC

Elephant garlic is not a substitute for real garlic.

Despite the name, elephant garlic is not actually garlic. Though both aromatics are part of the allium genus, they belong to different species. Elephant garlic belongs to *ampeloprasum*, the same species as leeks; garlic is from the species *sativum*. And while at first glance elephant garlic might look like garlic on steroids (it's two to three times larger), closer examination reveals some differences. Conventional garlic heads can boast as many as 20 cloves, but elephant garlic never has more than about six, and its cloves have a yellowish cast.

To see how their tastes compared, we made aïoli and garlic-potato soup, using regular garlic in one batch and the same amount of elephant garlic in another. Raw in aïoli, the elephant garlic had a mild, garlicky onion flavor. This weak flavor virtually disappeared when it was simmered in soup. Tasters much preferred the sharper, more pungent taste of regular garlic in both recipes. It turns out that elephant garlic produces the same flavor compounds as regular garlic when it's crushed, as well as those produced by onions and leeks—just less of each type. The upshot is that elephant garlic doesn't taste as potent as its allium cousins.

In short: Elephant garlic is not a substitute for true garlic. If you want milder garlic flavor, use less of the real stuff.

ELEPHANT GARLIC

CONVENTIONAL GARLIC

CHAPTER 29

Onions

The common everyday onion can add surprisingly meaty flavors to dishes.

HOW THE SCIENCE WORKS

"It is hard to imagine a civilization without onions; in one form or another their flavor blends into almost everything in the meal except the dessert," wrote Julia Child in *Mastering the Art of French Cooking*. We agree. And we're not alone. Today, onions are the most widely consumed allium in the world, ranked third among all produce, following tomatoes and cabbage. Botanically named *Allium cepa*, onions are in the same genus as garlic, chives, leeks, scallions, ramps, and shallots.

Onions are divided into two categories, sweet onions and storage onions. Sweet onions are generally available in the spring and early summer, while storage onions are available year-round. Sweet onions are milder, sweeter, and contain more water, while storage onions are more pungent and more suitable for long-term storage.

When it comes to creating their characteristic flavor, garlic (page 227) and onions share very similar chemistry—up to a point. As with garlic, the pungent flavor of onions is created only when the cells are damaged and an enzyme is released. (The enzyme in onions, like that in garlic, is called alliinase, and it reacts with a compound called isoalliin.) But onions contain another very important enzyme, one that is absent in garlic, that is responsible for creating the compound—called propanethial-S-oxide, or PSO—that gives onions their particular flavor and makes our eyes tear.

Like in garlic, the pungent flavor compounds in onions contain a sulfur atom. Therefore, it's no surprise that the sulfur content of the soil in which onions are grown plays a significant role in the intensity of their flavor. Soils with higher sulfur content produce more intensely flavored onions. Conversely, sweet onions are grown in regions with sulfur-poor soils.

Don't be fooled by the term "caramelized."

That raw bite to onions changes drastically when cooked. Often in recipes onions are "caramelized." But don't be fooled by the term, as it doesn't refer to caramelization alone. It's true that when subjected to temperatures of 300 degrees and above the simple sugars present (about 4 percent) do undergo a reaction: Molecules of water are eliminated from the sugar molecules, resulting in the formation of sweet-smelling compounds such as hydroxymethylfurfural (HMF). But other elements are at play: Onions contain about 1 percent protein. Above 300 degrees, broken down into amino acids, the protein interacts with some of the sugar molecules in what is known as the Maillard reaction. The Maillard reaction produces a deep brown color and intensely aromatic compounds that contribute a roasted, meaty, nutty flavor to onions.

But sautéing isn't the only way to build flavor in onions, although that is how they are most popularly used. In this chapter, we highlight other ways—no browning needed—to get onions to lend their flavor to dishes. In our Rigatoni with Beef and Onion Ragu (page 236), we cook onions (a lot of them) with water to help release the volatile sulfur-containing compound called 3-mercapto-2-methylpentan-1-ol, or MMP, which has an intensely meaty flavor (see Test Kitchen Experiment, page 234). Our Simple Pot-au-Feu (page 237) uses quartered onions—not browned, not sautéed—to add deep flavor to a clear, complex broth. Of the many different types of onions, each with slightly different flavors, we chose mildly sweet yellow onions to complement the crunchy crust for our Shoestring Onions (page 239). And in our Rice and Lentils with Crispy Onions (page 240), we use the microwave to remove excess water and help the onions obtain the right texture.

TEST KITCHEN EXPERIMENT

When developing our recipe for Rigatoni with Beef and Onion Ragu (see page 236), we noticed that recipes that included pounds of onions, but relatively little beef, turned out especially meaty. And unlike French onion soup, which calls for caramelizing the onions, recipes for this rustic ragu opt instead to cook the onions in plain water. Intrigued by what we tasted, we set up an experiment to figure out what was going on.

EXPERIMENT

We cooked multiple batches of a stripped-down version of our beef and onion ragu (using beef, water, onions, and salt), changing only the way we treated the 2½ pounds of onions. In one batch we sliced the onions and started them in 2 cups of water. For the second batch we finely chopped the onions in the food processor before starting them in 2 cups of water. We also made two more batches identical to the first, except that we let the cut onions sit for 10 minutes before adding them to the water. We cooked all four batches of ragu for 2 hours. Finally, we had tasters sample the ragus and comment on how meaty they tasted.

RESULTS

The batches where the onions sat for 10 minutes before being cooked tasted meatier than those that were cooked immediately. And how the onions were cut made a difference as well: the food-processed onions that sat for 10 minutes were deemed the meatiest of the bunch.

TAKEAWAY

When an onion is cut, some of its sulfur compounds combine to form a new compound: propanethial-S-oxide—the stuff that makes your eyes tear. The more an onion is cut, and the longer it sits before being cooked (as when it is chopped in a food processor and rested for 10 minutes), the more propanethial-S-oxide is formed. This compound turns into another compound, a water-soluble one called 3-mercapto-2-methypentan-1-ol (MMP), a conversion that speeds up when the onions are heated. Though derived from a vegetable, MMP tastes remarkably meaty. And because MMP is water-soluble, there's no need to sauté the onions to develop their meaty flavor.

ONIONS: NICE TO MEAT YOU

When an onion is chopped or sliced, one of the compounds released is called propanethial-S-oxide, which is responsible for making your eyes tear up. Interestingly, it is also responsible for a meaty, savory taste, which can be extracted into water.

FAMILY TREE: ALLIUMS

These bulbous, pungent vegetables in the allium family are most frequently used to build flavor in a range of recipes.

ONIONS

YELLOW ONION

Yellow onions are the most common onions in the U.S. Tasters found this onion to strike a "good balance between savory and sweet."

WHITE ONION

These onions are slightly mellower than yellow onions. Some tasters liked this onion's simple, "sugary," "mellow" flavor, while others found it "too sweet."

SPANISH ONION

These onions are larger and sweeter than yellow onions. Most tasters liked this onion for its "deep and complex" flavor and "meaty" texture.

RED ONION

Red onions are pungent and spicy, often pickled or even eaten raw. They are available year round.

VIDALIA ONION

Vidalia onions are grown near the Vidalia region of Georgia. They are one of the mildest onion options—mild enough to eat raw.

GARLIC

Garlic (see page 227) comes in hard-neck and soft-neck varieties. Like onions, garlic gets its flavor from an enzymatic reaction after it is chopped or crushed.

CHIVE

Chives are a perennial plant that grow with a bulb, though we often eat only the scapes, which are generally treated as an herb. They have a mild flavor.

LEEK

Leeks, unlike onions, garlic, and shallots, do not grow a bulb. Instead, the edible portions of this vegetable are in its long and leafy stalk. Its flavor is mild, and leeks are often used in stocks and soups.

RAMP

The ramp sprouts up in early spring in woodlands as far-flung as Canada, North Carolina, Missouri, and Minnesota. Both bulb and leaves can be used raw or cooked in applications that call for onions, leeks, or scallions.

SCALLION

These long, thin, mild onion relatives can be cooked or eaten raw.

SHALLOT

Shallots are a type of onion, which, like garlic, contain a head with multiple cloves.

PUNGENCY: TWO VARIABLES

The pungent taste of alliums varies for two reasons. One is variety. The second is soil chemistry. The pungent flavor in onions contains a sulfur atom. Therefore, the more sulfur in the soil, the more intense the onion flavor.

VS

VARIETY

Different alliums have different inherent levels of pungency (see: yellow onions vs. chives).

SOIL CHEMISTRY

The pungency of onions has much to do with the presense of sulfur: the more sulfur in the soil, the stronger the flavor.

Rigatoni with Beef and Onion Ragu

✓ WHY THIS RECIPE WORKS

There are those who have the best of everything, and there are those who make the best of everything. The residents of 16th-century Naples fell into the latter category. Faced with a population explosion that caused severe food shortages, they created a thrifty yet supremely satisfying gravy of beef and aromatic vegetables known, ironically, as la Genovese. *Later in the 19th century, onions took center stage, and the dish became one of the region's most beloved. The classic preparation is straightforward: A piece of beef, usually from the round, is placed in a pot and covered with approximately twice its weight in sliced onions, along with chopped aromatic vegetables, salt, and perhaps some herbs. Then several cups of water and a bit of wine go into the pot, and the mixture is simmered for anywhere from 3 to 6 hours, until the liquid has evaporated, the beef is tender, and the onions have cooked down into a soft, pulpy mass. Traditionally, frugal cooks served the beef-flavored onion gravy as a sauce for sturdy tubular pasta like rigatoni. The meat itself was typically reserved for a second meal, or at least a second course, with a vegetable. But in these comparatively prosperous times, the beef is more likely to be shredded and incorporated into the sauce for a substantial single dish—exactly the kind of pasta sauce we love to make in cold weather months.*

CHOOSE CHUCK EYE Beef round's tight grain makes this cut a good candidate for slicing, but since we were in pursuit of more tender meat that we could shred and return to the sauce, we moved to our favorite braising cuts: short ribs, blade steaks, and chuck-eye roast. The latter won for its beefy flavor, tenderness, and relatively low price tag. The only glitch? Cooked whole, it took upwards of 3½ hours to turn tender. Cutting it into four chunks reduced the cooking time to 2½ hours and allowed us to trim away intramuscular fat pockets. We also seasoned the roast with salt and pepper before cooking and moved the braising to a low (300-degree) oven, where the meat would cook more evenly. And we cut way back on the water—down to 3 cups—hoping to drastically shorten the reduction time. But even with that little amount, it still took about a half-hour of stovetop reduction to turn the onions and cooking liquid saucy. We wondered: Did we have to add water at all? In the next batch we omitted the water and simply nestled the beef in the onion mixture and sealed the pot tightly with foil (to lock in steam) and then the lid. This worked well; the meat braised to

perfect tenderness in the released juices, and the sauce required less stovetop reduction time—just 10 minutes. But strangely, this version tasted less savory.

MEATY CONUNDRUM To ramp up meatiness, we turned to innovations that started to show up in later Genovese recipes: pancetta and salami and tomato paste. They all made the ragu more savory, particularly the umami-rich tomato paste when we browned it in the pot before adding the onions. The tomato paste also warmed up the color of the formerly drab-looking sauce. But while this batch tasted meatier than our previous attempts, it still was not as savory as the first versions without them. We were baffled. We had not only added meaty ingredients but also taken away the world's most neutral ingredient: water.

USE THE ONIONS Believe it or not, much of the meaty flavor in our Genovese ragu actually comes from the 2½ pounds of onions. Specifically, the flavor stems from a compound formed in onions called 3-mercapto-2-methylpentan-1-ol, or MMP for short. When an onion is cut, some of its sulfur compounds combine to form a new compound: propanethial-S-oxide—the stuff that makes your eyes tear. When heated, this compound turns into MMP. And what does MMP taste like? Meat broth. To harness MMP 's full savory power, we switched from slicing to finely chopping the onions in a food processor to create even more opportunities for sulfur compounds to be released and transformed into MMP. And here's the secret: MMP's meat flavor can be extracted into water, but there's a limit on how much the water can hold. By using 2 cups of water (versus allowing the onions to simmer in their own juices) we extract more of the flavor into the liquid, creating an especially meaty broth.

RIGATONI WITH BEEF AND ONION RAGU
SERVES 6 TO 8

If marjoram is unavailable, substitute an equal amount of oregano. Pair this dish with a lightly dressed salad of assertively flavored greens.

1	(1- to 1¼-pound) boneless beef chuck-eye roast, cut into 4 pieces and trimmed of large pieces of fat Kosher salt and pepper
2	ounces pancetta, cut into ½-inch pieces
2	ounces salami, cut into ½-inch pieces
1	small carrot, peeled and cut into ½-inch pieces
1	small celery rib, cut into ½-inch pieces
2½	pounds onions, halved and cut into 1-inch pieces
2	tablespoons tomato paste
1	cup dry white wine
2	tablespoons minced fresh marjoram
1	pound rigatoni
1	ounce Pecorino Romano cheese, grated (½ cup), plus extra for serving

1. Sprinkle beef with 1 teaspoon salt and ½ teaspoon pepper and set aside. Adjust oven rack to lower-middle position and heat oven to 300 degrees.

2. Process pancetta and salami in food processor until ground to paste, about 30 seconds, scraping down sides of bowl as needed. Add carrot and celery and process 30 seconds longer, scraping down sides of bowl as needed. Transfer paste to Dutch oven and set aside; do not clean out processor bowl. Pulse onions in processor in 2 batches, until ⅛- to ¼-inch pieces form, 8 to 10 pulses per batch.

3. Cook pancetta mixture over medium heat, stirring frequently, until fat is rendered and fond begins to form on bottom of pot, about 5 minutes. Add tomato paste and cook, stirring constantly, until browned, about 90 seconds. Stir in 2 cups water, scraping up any browned bits. Stir in

onions and bring to boil. Stir in ½ cup wine and 1 tablespoon marjoram. Add beef and push into onions to ensure that it is submerged. Transfer to oven and cook, uncovered, until beef is fully tender, 2 to 2½ hours.

4. Transfer beef to carving board. Place pot over medium heat and cook, stirring frequently, until mixture is almost completely dry. Stir in remaining ½ cup wine and cook for 2 minutes, stirring occasionally. Using 2 forks, shred beef into bite-size pieces. Stir beef and remaining 1 tablespoon marjoram into sauce and season with salt and pepper to taste. Remove from heat, cover, and keep warm.

5. Bring 4 quarts water to boil in large pot. Add rigatoni and 2 tablespoons salt and cook, stirring often, until just al dente. Drain rigatoni and add to warm sauce. Add Pecorino and stir vigorously over low heat until sauce is slightly thickened and rigatoni is fully tender, 1 to 2 minutes. Serve, passing extra Pecorino separately.

Simple Pot-au-Feu

✓ WHY THIS RECIPE WORKS

By many accounts, pot-au-feu—which translates literally to "pot on the fire"—has been France's most celebrated dish since the French Revolution, extolled for providing sustenance to rich, poor, and everyone in between. Typically, several cuts of meat are simmered in a pot of water with potatoes and other root vegetables until tender, at which point the meat is carved and portioned into bowls with the vegetables and the clear, complex-tasting broth is ladled over the top. To give the dish kick, pungent condiments like mustard and the tiny French pickles known as cornichons are served alongside. Most recipes are complex, time-sucking affairs. We wanted to simplify—yet still keep the complex flavors, as tailor-made for a special occasion as for a family dinner.

PICK ONE CUT Most recipes call for a slew of different meats. To streamline, we settled on just one cut: chuck-eye roast, which delivers tender, beefy-tasting meat with a fraction of the effort or expense required by many classic renditions. This roast also needs very little prep.

ADD BONES One thing our chuck-eye roast didn't deliver was the silky body and almost buttery flavor of a broth made from bone-in cuts. The solution was simple: Add marrow bones. The soft tissue found inside the bones is packed with the amino acids responsible for meaty, umami flavors. It also contains the volatile compound diacetyl, a component of natural butter flavor, and it brought a subtle buttery taste to the broth. As an added bonus, at the end of cooking, we scraped the marrow from the bones and stirred it into our sauce to give it a beefy, rich boost.

MAKE FLAVORFUL STOCK Onions are an important part of the traditional, flavorful broth. They are not browned, but instead braised along with the meat in the pot and then removed, adding their meaty, delicate flavor. Cut in quarters, they are easily retrieved. For a clear broth without the fuss, we skipped the skimming step most recipes require and simply kept the pot at a gentle simmer, which we guaranteed by transferring the pot to a low oven.

SIMPLE POT-AU-FEU
SERVES 6 TO 8

Marrow bones (also called soup bones) can be found in the freezer section or the meat counter at most supermarkets. Use small red potatoes measuring 1 to 2 inches in diameter.

MEAT

1	(3½- to 4-pound) boneless beef chuck-eye roast, pulled into 2 pieces at natural seam and trimmed Kosher salt
1½	pounds marrow bones
1	onion, quartered
1	celery rib, sliced thin
3	bay leaves
1	teaspoon black peppercorns

PARSLEY SAUCE

⅔	cup minced fresh parsley
¼	cup Dijon mustard
¼	cup minced fresh chives
3	tablespoons white wine vinegar
10	cornichons, minced
1½	teaspoons pepper

VEGETABLES

1	pound small red potatoes, halved
6	carrots, halved crosswise, thick halves quartered lengthwise, thin halves halved lengthwise
1	pound asparagus, trimmed Kosher salt and pepper
	Flake sea salt

1. FOR THE MEAT: Adjust oven rack to lower-middle position and heat oven to 300 degrees. Season beef with 1 tablespoon salt. Using 3 pieces of kitchen twine per piece, tie each into loaf shape for even cooking. Place beef, bones, onion, celery, bay leaves, and peppercorns in Dutch oven. Add 4 cups cold water (water should come halfway up roasts). Bring to simmer over high heat. Partially cover pot and transfer to oven. Cook until beef is fully tender and sharp knife easily slips in and out of meat (meat will not be shreddable), 3¼ to 3¾ hours, flipping beef over halfway through cooking.

2. FOR THE PARSLEY SAUCE: While beef cooks, combine all ingredients in bowl. Cover and set aside.

3. Remove pot from oven and turn off oven. Transfer beef to large platter, cover tightly with aluminum foil, and return to oven to keep warm. Transfer bones to cutting board and use end of spoon to extract marrow. Mince marrow into paste and add 2 tablespoons to parsley sauce (reserve any remaining marrow for other applications). Using ladle or large spoon, skim fat from surface of broth and discard fat. Strain broth through fine-mesh strainer into large liquid measuring cup; add water to make 6 cups. Return broth to pot. (Meat can be returned to broth, cooled, and refrigerated for up to 2 days. Skim fat from cold broth, then gently reheat and proceed with recipe.)

4. FOR THE VEGETABLES: Add potatoes to broth and bring to simmer over high heat. Reduce heat to medium and simmer for 6 minutes. Add carrots and cook 10 minutes longer. Add asparagus and continue to cook until all vegetables are tender, 3 to 5 minutes longer.

5. Using slotted spoon, transfer vegetables to large bowl. Toss with 3 tablespoons parsley sauce and season with salt and pepper to taste. Season broth with salt to taste.

6. Transfer beef to cutting board, remove twine, and slice ½ inch thick against grain. Arrange servings of beef and vegetables in large, shallow bowls. Dollop beef with parsley sauce, drizzle with ⅓ cup broth, and sprinkle with flake sea salt. Serve, passing remaining parsley sauce and flake sea salt separately.

Shoestring Onions

✓ WHY THIS RECIPE WORKS

Let's be honest: Thick beer-battered rings are more about the puffy, crunchy coating than about the onions themselves. Shoestring onions, on the other hand, have a thinner, crisp coating that highlights the onions. At their best, shoestrings arrive at the table a salty, crunchy tangle of feathery fried onions that are hard to stop eating. At their worst, they're a greasy, soggy pile of breading.

PICK YELLOW   Our initial task was to determine what variety of onion had the sweet-yet-robust flavor that would work best here. We started with a simple recipe that called for tossing thinly sliced onions in flour seasoned with salt and pepper. We sliced red, white, yellow, and sweet onions, tossed each in the flour, and fried them separately in peanut oil. Red onions browned faster than the flour coating did, while sweet onions were (duh) too sweet and didn't have much oniony oomph. White onions were a little flat and lacked sweet-savory balance, but yellow onions were identifiably "onion" without being offensively pungent. Now we had the correct onions, but the seasoned flour coating was limp and greasy.

ADD ACID FOR CRUNCH   In search of something that would give these onions more crunch, we dug through dozens of recipes for fried foods. Some recipes call for soaking the sliced onions in milk or buttermilk for about 30 minutes before dredging in flour. We soaked one batch in milk and another in buttermilk and then dredged and fried them alongside a batch that hadn't been soaked. Only the buttermilk-soaked onions were really crisp, but they held on to so much flour that the onion flavor was diminished. Why the crunch? Buttermilk is made by adding live cultures to milk; the cultures produce lactic acid, which gives buttermilk its signature tang. The acid in the buttermilk was helping the coating fry up crisper by speeding up the gelatinization of the starch and drawing more amylose out of the starch granules in the flour. We wondered if another acidic liquid would yield the same crunch yet release more of the flour. White vinegar worked, but made the onions way too sour. Cider vinegar, while also too tart, improved matters, so we tried diluting it with an equal amount of water. That worked pretty well, but what worked even better was trading the water for apple juice.

The juice contributed more acid (hence more crunch) than water did; plus, it added sweetness to balance the vinegar. As a bonus, we discovered that the onions didn't need to soak for 30 minutes—a quick dip did the trick.

USE CREAM OF TARTAR   Having unlocked the secret to maximum crunch (acid), we wondered if we could take it one step further. The wet ingredients were working hard to create crunch, but what about the flour? Was there a dry acidic ingredient that we could add to the flour to promote even more crispness? Searching the test kitchen pantry, we came across cream of tartar, which is often used as an acidic activator in baked goods leavened with baking soda (the soda requires an acid to release its lift-giving bubbles). A few tests of cream of tartar in varying amounts determined that ¾ teaspoon added a crunchy boost without leaving a flavor trail.

PRACTICAL SCIENCE
PREPPING AND CUTTING ONIONS

Here are some tips to control flavor.

- Avoid using an onion's core in raw applications. We've found that the outer layers of an onion taste noticeably milder than the inner layers. The inner layers contain a higher concentration of flavor precursors than the outer layers do, and therefore have stronger flavor.

- For fuller, more complex flavor in cooked applications, cut onions fine. The more you process an onion, the more flavor-producing enzymes are released, and the more potential there will be for the development of complex flavor during cooking.

- For milder flavor in raw applications, slice onions with the grain. We sniffed and tasted eight onions sliced pole to pole (with the grain) and parallel to the equator (against the grain). Because slicing pole to pole ruptures fewer cell walls, thus leading to the creation of fewer sulfur molecules, we weren't surprised that these onions were clearly less pungent in taste and odor than those cut along the equator.

- For even milder flavor, give them a soak. Many sources recommend soaking chopped raw onions in milk or vinegar to remove sulfur compounds from their surface; we found that a 15-minute soak in plain water was just as effective. That said, if you like the flavor of lightly pickled onions, go ahead and soak them in vinegar instead.

- Beware of cutting onions in advance. Whether you're cutting pungent or mild onions, their flavor will degrade as they sit. We found that pungent onions can turn "sour," while mild onions can taste harsh. If you must cut onions in advance, store them in a zipper-lock bag, give them a quick rinse before using, and use them only in cooked applications.

SHOESTRING ONIONS
SERVES 4

You will need at least a 6-quart Dutch oven for this recipe. We prefer yellow onions here, but white onions will also work.

2	quarts peanut or vegetable oil
1½	cups all-purpose flour
	Salt and pepper
¾	teaspoon cream of tartar
1	pound onions, sliced into ¼-inch-thick rings
½	cup apple juice
¼	cup cider vinegar

1. Adjust oven rack to middle position and heat oven to 200 degrees. Heat oil in large Dutch oven over medium-high heat to 350 degrees. Set wire rack in rimmed baking sheet.

2. While the oil heats, combine flour, 1 teaspoon salt, cream of tartar, and ½ teaspoon pepper in large bowl. Toss onions with apple juice and vinegar to coat in second large bowl. Drain onions and transfer to flour mixture, tossing to coat.

3. Fry half of onion rings, stirring occasionally and adjusting burner as necessary to maintain oil temperature between 325 and 350 degrees, until golden brown and crisp, 3 to 4 minutes. Drain onions on prepared wire rack and place in oven. Bring oil back to 350 degrees and repeat with remaining onions. Season with salt and pepper to taste, and serve.

PRACTICAL SCIENCE
COOKING WITH MILD ONIONS?

Stick with the pungent ones.

Thanks to their higher ratio of flavor-packed tissue to water and the potential to deliver more-complex taste, pungent onions are referred to as cooking onions. But since mild onions have even more sugars that, when caramelized, can contribute new flavors, is it really so bad to cook with them? To find out, we made rice pilaf and French onion soup with both pungent and mild onions. In pilaf, where onions were sautéed until softened, tasters preferred the batch made with pungent onions, which tasted noticeably more complex, though the pilaf with mild onions was acceptable. When we caramelized the onions for the soup, the mild onions brought a one-dimensional sweetness to the soup, while the pungent onions contributed a deeper sweetness. Plus, the mild onions cooked down about 15 percent more—which makes sense, since water takes up far more of their mass. With mainly sugars contributing to their flavor during cooking, mild onions can't help but taste less complex. Stick with pungent ones.

Rice and Lentils with Crispy Onions

✓ WHY THIS RECIPE WORKS

Essentially the "rice and beans" of the Middle East, this might be the most spectacular example of how a few humble ingredients can add up to a dish that's satisfying, complex, and deeply savory. Though every household and restaurant differs in its approach to this dish, it's simple to throw together. Basically: Boil basmati rice and lentils together until each component is tender but intact, then work in warm spices such as coriander, cumin, cinnamon, allspice, and pepper, as well as a good measure of minced garlic. But the real showpiece of the dish is the onions—either fried or caramelized—which get stirred into and sprinkled over the pilaf just before serving. Their flavor is as deep as their mahogany color suggests, and they break up the starchy components. Finished with a bracing garlicky yogurt sauce, this pilaf is comfort food at its best.

USE GREEN LENTILS Many lentil dishes benefit from the firm, distinct texture of the French variety known as *lentilles du Puy*. But in this dish, the softer (but still intact) texture of green or brown lentils is best because it pairs well with the tender grains of rice. A bonus: Green and brown lentils are also easier to find and cheaper than the French kind.

BALANCE LENTILS AND RICE Cooking lentils with rice is a different ball game than cooking them alone, since we needed both components, which cook at different rates, to emerge evenly tender and also form a cohesive pilaf. We decided to try a variation on the absorption approach, in which the rice and parcooked lentils are cooked pilaf-style—that is, toasted in fat before liquid is added. Giving the lentils a 15-minute head start ensured that they finished cooking on pace with the rice. This step also allowed us to drain away their muddy cooking liquid before combining them with the rice, which made for a cleaner-looking dish. Toasting the rice in oil brought out the grain's nutty flavor and let us deepen the flavor of the spices and garlic by cooking them in the fat, too. The one snag: Even after we parcooked the lentils, they still absorbed quite a bit of water, robbing the rice of the liquid it needed to cook through. Adding more water didn't help; the lentils simply soaked it up faster than the rice and turned mushy. Fortunately, we had a quick fix in mind: We soaked the raw rice in hot water for 15 minutes, which softened the grains' exteriors so that they could absorb water more easily. Plus, this step loosened and washed away some of the excess starches, helping the rice cook up fluffy, not sticky.

MICROWAVE THE ONIONS We pared down the typically fussy process of batch-frying onions in several cups of oil to a single batch of onions fried in just 1½ cups of oil. The trick: removing a good bit of the onions' water before frying by tossing them with salt, microwaving them for 5 minutes, and drying them thoroughly.

RICE AND LENTILS WITH CRISPY ONIONS (MUJADDARA)
SERVES 4 TO 6

Do not substitute smaller French lentils for the green or brown lentils. When preparing the Crispy Onions, be sure to reserve 3 table-spoons of the onion cooking oil for cooking the rice and lentils.

YOGURT SAUCE

1	cup plain whole-milk yogurt
2	tablespoons lemon juice
½	teaspoon minced garlic
½	teaspoon salt

RICE AND LENTILS

8½	ounces (1¼ cups) green or brown lentils, picked over and rinsed
	Salt and pepper
1¼	cups basmati rice
1	recipe Crispy Onions, plus 3 tablespoons reserved oil (recipe follows)
3	garlic cloves, minced
1	teaspoon ground coriander
1	teaspoon ground cumin
½	teaspoon ground cinnamon
½	teaspoon ground allspice
⅛	teaspoon cayenne pepper
1	teaspoon sugar
3	tablespoons minced fresh cilantro

1. FOR THE YOGURT SAUCE: Whisk all ingredients together in bowl. Refrigerate while preparing rice and lentils.

2. FOR THE RICE AND LENTILS: Bring lentils, 4 cups water, and 1 teaspoon salt to boil in medium saucepan over high heat. Reduce heat to low and cook until lentils are tender, 15 to 17 minutes. Drain and set aside. While lentils cook, place rice in medium bowl and cover by 2 inches with hot tap water; let stand for 15 minutes.

3. Using your hands, gently swish rice grains to release excess starch. Carefully pour off water, leaving rice in bowl. Add cold tap water to rice and pour off water. Repeat adding and pouring off cold tap water 4 to 5 times, until water runs almost clear. Drain rice in fine-mesh strainer.

4. Heat reserved onion oil, garlic, coriander, cumin, cinnamon, allspice, ¼ teaspoon pepper, and cayenne in Dutch oven over medium heat until fragrant, about 2 minutes. Add rice and cook, stirring occasionally, until edges of rice begin to turn translucent, about 3 minutes. Add 2¼ cups water, sugar, and 1 teaspoon salt and bring to boil. Stir in lentils, reduce heat to low, cover, and cook until all liquid is absorbed, about 12 minutes.

5. Off heat, remove lid, fold dish towel in half, and place over pot; replace lid. Let stand for 10 minutes. Fluff rice and lentils with fork and stir in cilantro and half of crispy onions. Transfer to serving platter, top with remaining crispy onions, and serve, passing yogurt sauce separately.

PRACTICAL SCIENCE FREEZING ONIONS

Frozen onions simply aren't as good as fresh in raw dishes like salsas and salads.

Frozen diced onions are available in the freezer section of many grocery stores, so it stands to reason that you should be able to preserve your extra onions in the freezer. To find out how the texture and flavor of frozen onions stack up against fresh, we froze both whole peeled onions and diced onions in zipper-lock bags. But then we took it a step further. Commercial frozen goods are often individually quick frozen ("individually" to prevent the product from freezing into a solid mass, and "quick" to prevent textural damage by the formation of large ice crystals). For our third batch of onions, we set out to simulate individual quick freezing by spreading diced onions in one layer on a rimmed baking sheet, freezing them, and only then loading them into zipper-lock bags for storage. We tested all three batches of onions against fresh in recipes that used them raw and cooked.

Whole onions came out of the freezer mushy and flavorless: They were unacceptable used either raw or cooked. Tasters found both sets of frozen diced onions acceptable in our cooked preparation of baked rice. (You don't need to thaw them.) The simply diced and bagged batch finished slightly ahead, so there's no need to freeze the diced onions before bagging. The frozen diced onions didn't fare well, however, when we made salsa with them. Tasters panned all three salsas made with frozen onions for being "dull," "sulfuric," and "squishy."

CRISPY ONIONS
MAKES 1 ½ CUPS

It is crucial to thoroughly dry the microwaved onions after rinsing. The best way to accomplish this is to use a salad spinner. Reserve 3 tablespoons of oil when draining the onions to use in Rice and Lentils with Crispy Onions. Remaining oil may be stored in an airtight container and refrigerated for up to four weeks.

2   pounds onions, halved and sliced crosswise
    into ¼-inch-thick pieces
2   teaspoons salt
1 ½ cups vegetable oil

1. Toss onions and salt together in large bowl. Microwave for 5 minutes. Rinse thoroughly, transfer to paper towel–lined baking sheet, and dry well.

2. Heat onions and oil in Dutch oven over high heat, stirring frequently, until onions are golden brown, 25 to 30 minutes. Drain onions in colander set in large bowl. Transfer onions to paper towel–lined baking sheet to drain.

PRACTICAL SCIENCE
CARAMELIZING ONIONS CHOPPED IN ADVANCE

You can caramelize onions that have been chopped up to two days in advance.

We caramelized four batches of onions that had been stored from one to four days after chopping. We found very little difference in the onions stored for up to two days. However, beyond that we noticed a marked difference in both the flavor and texture of the onions. Onions that had been stored for at least three days began to brown sooner than the fresher onions and tended to take at least 5 fewer minutes to caramelize. But instead of the moist, jammy texture of caramelized onions made with recently chopped onions, these older onions cooked into distinct pieces that had an unpleasant, dry, leathery texture and lacked sweetness.

Why? Chopping the onions damages their cells and allows water to leak out during storage. This surface water quickly evaporates during cooking, causing the onions to dry out faster than onions that are cooked immediately after chopping. As for the flavor difference, chopping also causes the enzymes that create the pungent taste in onions to be released and become active. These reactions occur immediately but continue over time, so the chopped onions will develop more pungency the longer they are stored. It's not that the older onions are less sweet, but rather that other flavor compounds are more prominent.

CHAPTER 30

Ginger

This spicy rhizome has a pungent flavor that changes with cooking.

HOW THE SCIENCE WORKS

Ginger is a rhizome—a swollen, root-like mass that grows, often horizontally, underground—of a flowering plant belonging to the family *Zingiberaceae*, which includes galangal, turmeric, and cardamom. Ginger originated in southern China and is now grown in India, the Caribbean, Jamaica, West Africa, the Spice Islands, and Hawaii.

To produce the ginger we buy in the market, the rhizomes are harvested after the stalk withers. They are then either scalded in hot water or washed and scraped in order to inactivate the rhizome, preventing it from sprouting.

The flavor of ginger is due to both volatile aroma compounds and more-stable, more-pungent compounds. Ginger is characterized as having a citrus-like odor, due to the presence of two volatile compounds called geranial and neral. The strong taste of ginger actually comes from compounds that are chemically related to those that give hot peppers their heat, known as capsaicins (see page 251).

Dried ginger is more pungent than fresh ginger.

Unlike the pungent compounds in cruciferous vegetables, which are formed only when the cells are damaged, the pungent compounds in ginger are formed as the plant develops and are present in the fresh tissue. The dominant pungent compound in ginger is called gingerol.

We eat ginger in a number of different forms, the two most common being fresh, and dried and powdered. Interestingly, as the form changes, so does the flavor. When ginger is heated, dried, and ground to a powder, many of the gingerol molecules lose a molecule of water (a process called dehydration) to form a new compound called shogaol, which has about twice the pungency of gingerol. Thus, powdered ginger is more pungent than fresh ginger, which is one of the reasons why recipes calling for fresh ginger use up to six times as much fresh ginger as powder.

Cooking also changes the flavor of ginger. When fresh ginger is cooked, gingerol is converted to another compound, called zingerone, which is far less pungent. Because of the chemical reactivity of gingerol, the pungency of the ginger can vary widely depending on how the ginger was stored, its age, and where it was grown.

Ginger does more than impart flavor—it contains an enzyme that breaks down proteins. These types of enzymes are called protease enzymes, and the one in ginger is named zingibain. (Other natural protease enzymes include papain from papaya and bromelain from pineapple, which are often used as meat tenderizers.) Zingibain is especially active against collagen, the primary protein in tough connective tissue, though it is not very stable, so it cannot be isolated as a powder and sold as a commercial meat tenderizer. However, fresh ginger is capable of tenderizing meat, with optimum activity at 140 degrees and a pH between 6 and 8 (which is more alkaline than most meat). "Tenderizing" is not always a good thing, however—instead it can make meat quite mushy (see page 244).

Because the flavor and pungency of ginger changes with drying or cooking, we often use more than one form in our recipes. Using a mixture of ginger products (crystallized and grated fresh), we were able to get bright, refreshing ginger flavor with a moderate kick of heat for our Carrot-Ginger Soup (page 246). We use a healthy amount of dried ground ginger, plus some fresh, to add depth to our Gingersnaps (page 247) and our Classic Gingerbread Cake (page 249). For a more straight-up taste of ginger, we pickle it, a process that turns young ginger a vibrant pink, though it keeps the more-mature supermarket ginger an understated, yet still delicious, warm brown (page 250).

TEST KITCHEN EXPERIMENT

There are a handful of fruits, like papaya and pineapple, that contain enzymes able to break down meat proteins. Isolated forms of these enzymes are readily available at the supermarket in the form of meat tenderizers. They may sound like an easy path to tenderness, but we've found that in reality they deliver mushy meat. In the test kitchen, we noticed when raw meat comes in contact with ginger (as in a marinade) it often suffers the same fate. With some research we learned that ginger contains its own protein-destroying enzyme called zingibain. We also discovered that the enzyme's impact on protein could potentially be decreased with both acidity and cooking, allowing us to incorporate ginger in meat marinades without the risk of mushiness. We designed the following experiment to test that theory out.

EXPERIMENT

We procured pork loin, four kinds of steak (flank steak, sirloin steak tips, tenderloin, and blade steaks), and chicken breast and split each into five portions. For one portion of each we applied grated fresh ginger directly to the meat. For the second we mixed grated fresh ginger into a simple marinade of soy sauce, garlic, and brown sugar and applied that to the meat. For the third we microwaved the grated fresh ginger for 30 seconds before mixing it into an identical marinade. For the fourth we added lime juice to an identical marinade to acidify it before adding the grated fresh ginger. We allowed all of the treatments to sit on the meats for 30 minutes before wiping off the excess and cooking them. We compare the texture of each to a control that was marinated with no added ginger or lime.

RESULTS

The results were largely consistent across all meat, so our conclusions apply equally to pork, beef, and chicken. The samples where grated fresh ginger was applied directly featured a thick layer of pasty meat on the surface and a broken down structure. The simple marinade with grated fresh ginger (and no lime juice) caused slightly less damage, but still featured an unappealing pasty surface. The addition of lime juice to the marinade resulted in even less damage to the meat, but tasters still noticed a slight pastiness on the surface. (Though acidic ingredients can create mushiness, it takes more than 30 minutes.) Neither the sample where the grated fresh ginger was first microwaved, nor the no-ginger control, showed any signs of mushiness.

TAKEAWAY

Completely omitting ginger from a marinade is obviously one way to prevent the meat from turning mushy, but the loss of ginger flavor is less than ideal. Scientific literature suggests that zingibain activity decreases rapidly below pH 5, and that it must be heated well beyond 158 degrees to be completely denatured. Our tests show that using an acidic marinade does limit zingibain's effect on meat, but that heating ginger to the boiling point in the microwave is an even more effective measure. (Don't worry, microwaved ginger still contributed plenty of ginger flavor.) In the future we won't hesitate to use ginger in marinades, but we will be sure to treat it properly.

HOW TO USE GINGER IN MARINADES

If grated raw ginger is left in contact with meat, it will give it a mushy texture. Adding acid to the marinade helps. Heat helps even more.

MUSHY MEAT
Raw ginger on meat allowed the zingibain enzyme to wreak havoc.

SLIGHTLY MUSHY MEAT
Adding ginger to an acidic marinade lessened the effect of zingibain.

NOT MUSHY MEAT
Microwaving ginger beforehand deactivated the enzyme completely.

FOCUS ON: GINGER

The familiar fresh ginger root that we find in the supermarket is a rhizome, meaning it grows in large, root-like masses horizontally underground. It is spicy when used fresh—a flavor that grows even more pungent when dried.

THE SPICINESS OF GINGER . . . AND PEPPER

Our ability to detect taste, smell, and oral pain (chemesthesis) is due to the interaction of chemical compounds with receptors in our mouth, nose, and throat. Receptors bind with chemical compounds in very specific ways, like keys into a lock. When a key fits, the lock is activated, sending electrical signals to the brain. Certain chemical compounds, such as capsaicin in hot chile peppers (page 251), produce a sense of pain in the mouth and throat. Molecules with a similar size and shape can activate the capsaicin receptor and produce a sense of pain. This is true for the pungent compound in ginger called gingerol, and even more for the similar compound formed when ginger is dried, called shogaol. And both fit better than the breakdown product of gingerol called zingerone.

COMPOUND	RELATIVE PUNGENCY
Capsaicin	250
Shogaol	1.5
Gingerol	0.8
Zingerone	0.5

ginger rhyzome

capsaicin ····> hot peppers

shogaol ······> dried ginger

gingerol ······> fresh ginger

zingerone ···> cooked ginger

Look at the chemical structures of compounds from hot peppers and dried, fresh, and cooked ginger. Shogaol is most similar to capsaicin and, therefore, the spiciest.

ON THE TONGUE: GINGER

The TRPV1 receptors in our mouth detect capsaicin, the pain-inducing chemical in hot peppers. They are also activated by molecules with a similar shape. This is true for the pungent compound in ginger, gingerol, and the compound formed when ginger is dried, called shogaol. Shogaol actually fits into the receptor better than gingerol, producing a more pungent, spicy taste.

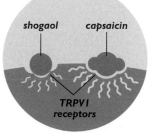

shogaol   capsaicin

TRPV1 receptors

DRYING GINGER

When dried, gingerol loses a molecule of water to form a compound called shogaol—a similar compound with a very different level of pungency. This is why dried ginger is so much more potent than fresh.

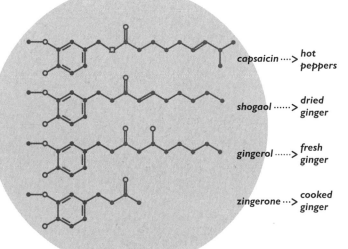

H_2O

Carrot-Ginger Soup

✓ WHY THIS RECIPE WORKS

The coupling of sweet carrots and pungent ginger has the potential to produce an elegant, flavorful soup. It's troubling, then, that we've been unable to truly taste either ingredient in most of the versions we've tried. That's due primarily to the hapless addition of other vegetables, fruits, or dairy—all of which mask the starring flavors. Another irritating problem is a grainy consistency; we like our pureed soups to be perfectly smooth and creamy. Could we bring this soup to its full potential?

GET CARROT FLAVOR   We started by making a barebones soup, but the carrot flavor was muddled. And while the soup had a fiery kick, it had not even a hint of the fresh, bright flavor associated with ginger. For unadulterated carrot flavor, it made sense to ditch the broth in favor of plain water. But what was really missing was ultrafresh carrot flavor. Maybe if we just used raw carrots—in the form of carrot juice? After a few tries, we settled on swapping some carrot juice for some of the water and stirring in more right before serving. Between the sweet cooked carrots and the bright, raw carrot juice, this was a well-balanced soup.

PUMP UP THE GINGER   On to the ginger. Our soup had the peppery heat associated with the root but almost none of its vibrant fruitiness. We rounded up the different forms of ginger—fresh juice, fresh grated, ground, and crystallized—and started sampling. Ginger juice offered plenty of heat but little flavor. Ground ginger simply tasted bitter. A combo of fresh and crystallized ginger was the best of the bunch, with the former supplying spiciness and the latter delivering the almost citrusy freshness that ginger is prized for. We sautéed some grated fresh ginger and some minced crystallized ginger (plus 1 teaspoon of sugar to counter their spiciness) with the other aromatics and then continued with the recipe. In the finished soup, the duo struck an ideal balance of flavor and heat.

ADD BAKING SODA   For the silkiest possible consistency in the soup, we tried cooking the carrots until they were mushy and breaking apart. After we pureed it, the soup was still not smooth enough. We wanted to avoid straining, so it made sense to turn to one of the test kitchen's secret weapons: baking soda. We have used it on numerous occasions to break down the cell walls of a vegetable as it cooks in water. Sure enough, with a bit of baking soda and 20 minutes of simmering, the soup was smoother than any we'd ever had. In fact, it was downright velvety—all without the need for lengthy cooking or fussy straining.

CARROT-GINGER SOUP
SERVES 6

In addition to the sour cream and chives, you can serve this soup with Buttery Croutons (recipe follows).

2	tablespoons unsalted butter
2	onions, chopped fine
¼	cup minced crystallized ginger
1	tablespoon grated fresh ginger
2	garlic cloves, peeled and smashed
	Salt and pepper
1	teaspoon sugar
2	pounds carrots, peeled and sliced ¼ inch thick
4	cups water
1½	cups carrot juice
2	sprigs fresh thyme
½	teaspoon baking soda
1	tablespoon cider vinegar
	Chopped chives
	Sour cream

1. Melt butter in large saucepan over medium heat. Add onions, crystallized ginger, fresh ginger, garlic, 2 teaspoons salt, and sugar; cook, stirring frequently, until onions are softened but not browned, 5 to 7 minutes.

2. Increase heat to high; add carrots, water, ¾ cup carrot juice, thyme sprigs, and baking soda and bring to

---

PRACTICAL SCIENCE
DOES SHRIVELED GINGER HAVE LESS FLAVOR?

Old, shriveled ginger does lose some of its potency.

We rarely use up an entire knob of fresh ginger in one go, and we routinely store the remainder in the fridge. But after a few weeks, the root tends to shrivel and dry out. Is this an indication that it's no longer suitable for cooking?

After preparing two batches of stir-fried broccoli, we had our answer. Though tasters found both dishes acceptable, the sample made with fresh, plump ginger packed spicy heat and "zing," while the broccoli made with a more wizened specimen turned out "mild" and "flat." Why? As ginger ages, it loses its signature pungency from the compound gingerol. During storage—and even as it's heated—gingerol converts into a more mild-flavored compound called zingerone, which, despite its sharp-sounding name, is far less assertive than its precursor. Lesson learned: If possible, buy small pieces of ginger and use it while it's fresh. And if you're polishing off an older piece, be prepared to use more than the recipe calls for and add it as close as possible to the end of cooking.

simmer. Reduce heat to medium-low and simmer, covered, until carrots are very tender, 20 to 25 minutes.

3. Discard thyme sprigs. Working in batches, process soup in blender until smooth, 1 to 2 minutes. Return soup to clean pot and stir in vinegar and remaining ¾ cup carrot juice. (Soup can be refrigerated for up to 4 days.) Return to simmer over medium heat and season with salt and pepper to taste. Serve with sprinkle of chives and dollop of sour cream.

BUTTERY CROUTONS
MAKES ABOUT 2 CUPS

- 3 tablespoons unsalted butter
- 1 tablespoon olive oil
- 3 slices hearty sandwich bread,
  cut into ½-inch cubes
  Salt

Melt butter and oil in 12-inch skillet over medium heat. Add bread cubes and cook, stirring frequently, until golden brown, about 10 minutes. Transfer croutons to paper towel–lined plate and season with salt to taste.

Gingersnaps

✔ WHY THIS RECIPE WORKS

Sweetened dough spiced with ginger has been around since medieval times, but the term "gingersnap" wasn't coined until the 19th century. To our minds, this nomenclature should have settled once and for all the question of whether a ginger cookie should be crisp or chewy. We've never doubted that "snap" speaks to a cookie that breaks cleanly in half and crunches with every bite. "Snap" also sums up assertive ginger flavor and heat. But most gingersnap recipes that we've tried don't live up to the name. We wanted freshly baked gingersnaps with a crackly top and a texture to rival the store-bought kind, but with all-natural ginger flavor and lingering heat.

SLASH THE SUGAR We turned to the sugar first. We knew that brown sugar was a double-edged sword. It contributes rich molasses flavor but also creates chewiness in cookies. This is because brown sugar is even more hygroscopic than granulated sugar, attracting moisture during baking. Switching to granulated sugar did produce a crispier, less chewy cookie, but the loss of flavor wasn't worth it. Our only choice was to cut back on the sweetener. We found that slashing the brown sugar almost in half—from 2 cups to 1¼ cups—resulted in cookies noticeably drier and crunchier (albeit not yet worthy of their eponymous "snap"). Reducing the sugar also allowed the ginger flavor to move to the fore.

BROWN THE BUTTER On to the butter, which is about 16 percent water. Using less butter dehydrated the cookies a bit, but new problems emerged. Without ample fat, the leaner, stiffer dough refused to spread as it baked. More important, these cookies didn't taste as good. It occurred to us that if we browned the butter, we'd eliminate some of its water while keeping its fat (and creating richer, nutty flavor). Of course, this meant that we could no longer cream the butter with the sugar, so we tried simply whisking the browned butter with the sugar. We were pleased to find that this lower-moisture dough yielded considerably firmer cookies, and the subtle nutty taste of the browned butter turned out to be an ideal backdrop for the ginger. But all was not perfect. The center of the cookie was still a little too moist and didn't have the crackly top we wanted.

LOAD UP ON LEAVENING Previous experiments in the test kitchen gave us an idea for creating crackles: increase the leavening. Using a full 2 teaspoons of baking soda in our cookie dough instead of the more typical ½ to 1 teaspoon not only helped create desirable fissures in the final cookie but also helped it dry out. Baking soda is an alkaline substance that weakens the gluten (the network of proteins that gives most baked goods their structure) in a dough or batter. Weaker gluten means a more porous structure from which air bubbles and moisture can escape. It also means that the dough will collapse after its initial rise in the oven, leading to cracks that also allow more moisture to escape.

UP THE GINGER All that remained was to punch up their rather mild flavor. Doubling the amount of dried ginger was an obvious starting point, as was incorporating freshly grated ginger. Warm spices seemed appropriate here, and we followed the lead of many other recipes by incorporating cinnamon and cloves. But we wanted yet another layer of heat. We perused the spice cabinet once more, landing on cayenne and black pepper. The combination lent the cookies a judicious but lingering heat. Finally, to make the spices really sing, we bloomed them in the browned butter, the hot fat helping to fully release the spices' pungent aromatic compounds.

GINGERSNAPS

MAKES 80 1½-INCH COOKIES

For the best results, use fresh spices. For efficiency, form the second batch of cookies while the first batch bakes. The 2 teaspoons of baking soda are essential to getting the right texture.

2½	cups (12½ ounces) all-purpose flour
2	teaspoons baking soda
½	teaspoon salt
12	tablespoons unsalted butter
2	tablespoons ground ginger
1	teaspoon ground cinnamon
¼	teaspoon ground cloves
¼	teaspoon pepper
	Pinch cayenne pepper
1¼	cups packed (8¾ ounces) dark brown sugar
¼	cup molasses
2	tablespoons finely grated fresh ginger
1	large egg plus 1 large yolk
½	cup granulated sugar

1. Whisk flour, baking soda, and salt together in bowl. Heat butter in 10-inch skillet over medium heat until melted. Lower heat to medium-low and continue to cook, swirling pan frequently, until foaming subsides and butter is just beginning to brown, 2 to 4 minutes. Transfer butter to large bowl and whisk in ground ginger, cinnamon, cloves, pepper, and cayenne. Let cool slightly, about 2 minutes. Add brown sugar, molasses, and fresh ginger to butter mixture and whisk to combine. Add egg and yolk and whisk to combine. Add flour mixture and stir until just combined. Cover dough tightly with plastic wrap and refrigerate until firm, about 1 hour.

2. Adjust oven racks to upper-middle and lower-middle positions and heat oven to 300 degrees. Line 2 baking sheets with parchment paper. Place granulated sugar in shallow dish. Divide dough into heaping teaspoon portions; roll dough into 1-inch balls. Working in batches of 10, roll balls in sugar to coat. Evenly space dough balls on prepared baking sheets, 20 dough balls per sheet.

3. Place 1 baking sheet on upper rack and bake for 15 minutes. Transfer partially baked top sheet to lower rack, rotating 180 degrees, and place second sheet of dough balls on upper rack. Continue to bake until cookies on lower sheet just begin to darken around edges, 10 to 12 minutes longer. Remove lower sheet of cookies and transfer upper sheet to lower rack, rotating 180 degrees, and continue to bake until cookies begin to darken around edges, 15 to 17 minutes longer. Slide baked cookies, still on parchment, to wire rack and let cool completely before serving. Let sheets cool slightly and line with parchment again. Repeat step 3 with remaining dough balls. (Cooled cookies can be stored at room temperature for up to 2 weeks.)

TO MAKE AHEAD: Dough can be refrigerated for up to 2 days or frozen for up to 1 month. Let frozen dough thaw overnight before proceeding with recipe. Let dough stand at room temperature for 30 minutes before shaping.

PRACTICAL SCIENCE FREEZE TO GRATE

Freezing ginger does make it easier to grate. It also makes it easier to clean the grater.

We froze several pieces of ginger and then we had a group of testers each grate one frozen and one fresh piece of ginger on the same rasp-style grater. All the testers found the frozen ginger easier to grate—it didn't shred or break down like fresh ginger sometimes does with vigorous grating. We also found that the grater was much easier to clean after grating frozen ginger because the fibers neatly sheared crosswise and didn't leave frayed bits stuck in the grater. After precisely 30 seconds of grating, the piles of frozen ginger measured, on average, almost twice as much by volume as the fresh.

But when we weighed each sample, we found that the frozen ginger actually weighed much less (about 9 grams compared with about 14 grams for the fresh ginger), essentially because the frozen ginger made a fluffier pile. To get accurate volume measurements, we had to either let the grated ginger thaw or pack it gently into the measuring spoon.

GRATED FROZEN GINGER
Frozen ginger grates up taller and airier.

GRATED GINGER
Room-temperature ginger grates up dense and wet.

Classic Gingerbread Cake

✓ WHY THIS RECIPE WORKS

Gingerbread cakes date back to the Colonial era. Our ideal version would be moist through and through and utterly simple—a snack cake that we could bake in a square pan. But almost without exception, all the modern recipes we tried suffered from a dense, sunken center. Equally disappointing, flavors ran the gamut from barely gingery to so addled with spice to make a curry fan cry for mercy. We started with a basic recipe, and began experimenting.

MAXIMIZE THE SPICE Bumping the ground ginger up to 2 tablespoons yielded an assertive bite, though it lacked complexity. We tried folding in grated fresh ginger with the dried. Sure enough, the pungent notes of the fresh root made the flavor sing. What about other spices? Options like cardamom, nutmeg, and cloves weren't terrible but shifted the gingerbread too far into spice-cake territory. In the end, only two "guest" spices made the cut: cinnamon and, in an unexpected twist, fresh-ground black pepper, which worked in tandem with all that potent ginger to produce a warm, complex, lingering heat.

ADD STOUT Eyeing the liquid components, we suspected that using water was a missed opportunity. Buttermilk added tanginess but dulled the ginger. Ginger ale, ginger beer, and hard apple cider all seemed likely contenders, but baking rendered them undetectable. Dark stout, on the other hand, had a bittersweet flavor that brought out the caramel undertones of the molasses. To minimize its booziness, we tried gently heating the stout to cook off some of the alcohol—a somewhat fussy step that side-by-side tests nonetheless proved worthwhile.

STOP SINKING To keep our gingerbread recipe from sinking in the middle, we incorporated the baking soda with the wet ingredients and roughed up some of the batter to strengthen the flour, giving our gingerbread a more sturdy texture while maintaining its moistness.

CLASSIC GINGERBREAD CAKE
SERVES 16

This cake packs potent yet well-balanced heat. If you're particularly sensitive to spice, decrease the amount of ground ginger to 1 tablespoon. Guinness Draught is the test kitchen's favorite stout. If your pan has thin walls, consider wrapping it with cake strips. Serve the gingerbread plain or with lightly sweetened whipped cream.

¾ cup stout
½ teaspoon baking soda
¾ cup packed (5¼ ounces) light brown sugar
⅔ cup molasses
¼ cup (1¾ ounces) granulated sugar
1½ cups (7½ ounces) all-purpose flour
2 tablespoons ground ginger
½ teaspoon baking powder
½ teaspoon salt
¼ teaspoon ground cinnamon
¼ teaspoon pepper
2 large eggs
⅓ cup vegetable oil
1 tablespoon finely grated fresh ginger

1. Adjust oven rack to middle position and heat oven to 350 degrees. Grease and flour 8-inch square baking pan.

2. Bring stout to boil in medium saucepan over medium heat, stirring occasionally. Off heat, stir in baking soda (mixture will foam vigorously). When foaming subsides, stir in brown sugar, molasses, and granulated sugar until dissolved; set aside. Whisk flour, ground ginger, baking powder, salt, cinnamon, and pepper together in large bowl; set aside.

3. Transfer stout mixture to second large bowl. Whisk in eggs, oil, and fresh ginger until combined. Whisk stout-egg mixture into flour mixture in 3 additions, stirring vigorously until completely smooth after each addition.

4. Transfer batter to prepared pan and gently tap on counter to release air bubbles. Bake until top of cake is just

---

PRACTICAL SCIENCE BLUE GINGER

Fresh ginger sometimes has a blue-gray color because it loses acidity.

When ginger is stored for a long period of time in a cold environment, it becomes less acidic, and this causes some of its anthocyanin pigments to change to a blue-gray color. It is still safe to eat, but we wondered if there was a difference in the flavor.

We started by finely grating some ginger that had changed color and some that had not and then squeezing out the juice from each and adding it to water (to make it palatable). The majority of our tasters found the flavor of the water with the blue ginger to be less potent and spicy than that containing the regular ginger. However, when we compared the two gingers in a soy dipping sauce and a gingerbread cake, no one could detect a difference, due to all the competing flavors.

The takeaway? Ginger that has turned blue is perfectly safe to eat, and while its flavor is slightly milder, it's unlikely you'll notice when using it in a recipe.

firm to touch and toothpick inserted in center comes out clean, 35 to 45 minutes, rotating pan halfway through baking. Let cake cool in pan on wire rack, about 1½ hours. Cut into 2-inch squares and serve warm or at room temperature. (Leftover cake can be wrapped in plastic wrap and stored at room temperature for up to 2 days.)

Pickled Ginger

✔ WHY THIS RECIPE WORKS

Unlike wasabi, pickled ginger isn't just a condiment. Traditionally, the pickled root is eaten between bites of sushi, since ginger is a natural palate cleanser. We are accustomed to seeing piles of neon-pink ribbons on our sushi boats, but we wanted to find a way to make a recipe for pickled ginger ourselves.

PINK GINGER? The blushing of pickled ginger does occur naturally, but with a bit more subtlety than the commercial stuff. Spring ginger, or young ginger root, is what is traditionally used; it contains pigments called anthocyanins that turn pink when in contact with acid. Because young ginger isn't commonly found in grocery stores year round, we wanted to develop this recipe using the readily available mature ginger root. While it may not always turn pink when pickled (though some of our batches still did), we found our pickled ginger to be equally delicious.

PRACTICAL SCIENCE THE COLOR OF GINGER

The color of ginger is determined by pigments called anthocyanins—and its environment.

The flesh of fresh ginger rhizomes is characterized by a light yellow color due to the presence of pigments called anthocyanins. Recently (in 2003), the two anthocyanins responsible for the color of fresh ginger were identified as cyanidin 3-glucoside, and peonidin-3-rutinoside, with the latter being present at significantly higher levels. Like other anthocyanins, the color of these two pigments is dependent on the pH of the environment. At neutral pH the pigments are light yellow, but at acid pH they change to a pink color. This is why pickling in vinegar gives ginger a pink hue, which is why ginger served with sushi is pink instead of the normal light yellow of fresh ginger. But most interestingly, the discovery of these two pigments in ginger showed that their formation and abundance varies with the variety, and place of cultivation. That's why ginger from Japan turns pink when pickled, but Chinese ginger does not!

MAKE IT TENDER Unfortunately, our thin strips of pickled mature ginger were tough and fibrous. We sliced the root thin against the grain into small coins to eliminate the tougher texture and added sugar to our recipe to balance the pungency of the mature ginger and tang of the vinegar. We found that a brief 40-second boil helped to soften our ginger and mellow its flavor. The ginger should be refrigerated in its brine for four days to allow the vegetable to be fully pickled.

PICKLED GINGER
MAKES 2 1-CUP JARS

For best flavor and texture, we recommend using fresh, young ginger. This pickled ginger cannot be processed for long-term storage. Kosher salt can be substituted for canning salt.

14	ounces ginger, peeled
1	cup rice vinegar
1	tablespoon canning and pickling salt
6	tablespoons sugar

1. Using mandoline, cut ginger against grain into paper-thin slices. Line rimmed baking sheet with several layers paper towels. Bring 2 quarts water to boil over high heat in medium saucepan. Add ginger and boil until slightly darker and softened, about 40 seconds. Drain ginger through colander, then spread out over paper towels.

2. Bring vinegar, salt, and sugar to boil in now-empty saucepan over medium-high heat, stirring occasionally to dissolve sugar; cover and remove from heat.

3. Meanwhile, place two 1-cup jars in bowl and place under hot running water until heated through, 1 to 2 minutes; dry thoroughly. Pack ginger tightly into hot jars, pressing down as needed, leaving ½-inch space at the top.

4. Return brine to brief boil. Using funnel and ladle, pour hot brine over ginger to cover. Slide wooden skewer along inside of jar, pressing slightly on ginger to remove air bubbles, and add extra brine as needed.

5. Let jars cool to room temperature, cover with lids, and refrigerate for at least 4 days before serving. (Pickled ginger can be refrigerated for up to 6 months; ginger flavor will mellow over time.)

CHAPTER 31

Dried Chiles

We use these desiccated specimens to add deep, earthy flavor.

HOW THE SCIENCE WORKS

Peppers are the fruit of plants belonging to the genus *Capsicum*, which includes mild sweet peppers like bell peppers, and hot, spicy peppers commonly called chiles or chili peppers. Like tomatoes, peppers are a member of the nightshade family, botanically named *Solanaceae*.

Peppers originated in the Americas and were first domesticated as a food more than 6,000 years ago in Mexico; though evidence shows they have been part of the human diet for almost 9,500 years. Christopher Columbus is given credit for first calling them "peppers," when he realized they could serve as a substitute for the much more costly, rare black peppercorns. Today, India is the world's largest producer of peppers.

The characteristic flavor and aroma of all peppers is largely due to a group of compounds called pyrazines—namely, one called 2-isobutyl-3-methoxypyrazine. Pyrazines are naturally formed in the tissue of the fruit as it ripens, so chopping and chewing are not necessary for the formation of pepper flavor. Pyrazines are among the most potent aroma compounds, with extremely low odor thresholds; humans can detect some of these compounds dissolved in water at concentrations as low as a part per trillion. In fact, bell and jalapeño peppers have been found to contain levels of only a few nanograms (or billionths of a gram) of 2-isobutyl-3-methoxypyrazine per gram of dried pepper.

Chile peppers owe their heat to a family of compounds called capsaicinoids. At least 12 different capsaicinoids have been identified in hot peppers, but two compounds, capsaicin and dihydrocapsaicin, account for about 90 percent of the heat, both having similar potency. (The capsaicinoids are produced in the cells of the white pith, and migrate to the nearby seeds.) Capsaicin and dihydrocapsaicin have been shown to bind to a specific receptor in the mouth—called the TRPV1 receptor, which is the capsaicin receptor—responsible for detecting pain in mammals. This pain is called a "chemesthetic sensation," a description that also applies to touch and heat and is different than taste or smell. Not all animals possess the same taste and smell receptors as humans, but chemesthetic receptors are widely distributed throughout the animal world.

Drying a chile pepper reduces the weight of the pepper and therefore increases the relative hotness of the dried pepper by as much as 10 times. In addition, slowly drying peppers with heat, such as in the oven or a food dehydrator, increases the rich, sweet, raisin-like flavor characteristics of peppers, due primarily to the formation of 2-methylpropanal, 2-methylbutanal, and 3-methylbutanal. Smoking is another drying method, which adds the complexity of smoky flavor, like that in chipotle peppers. Generally, whole dried pods retain more flavor than crushed pods. Drying chiles results in a decrease in green, floral notes due to the loss of volatile compounds such as (Z)-3-hexenal and hexanal.

> **You can detect the aroma of a chile at concentrations as low as one part per trillion.**

We make good use of dried chiles in the test kitchen, often toasting them and grinding them ourselves to create flavorful, fresh rubs or marinades. We use guajillo chiles to create the base of a marinade for pork in our spicy Tacos al Pastor (page 254), and New Mexican chiles to create a rub for our Grilled Steak (page 255). We toast (to bring out the best flavor), seed (to remove some heat), and puree a mixture of dried chiles for two very different types of chilis: our Ultimate Beef Chili (page 259) and our Ultimate Vegetarian Chili (page 257).

TEST KITCHEN EXPERIMENT

Chiles get their heat from a class of chemical compounds called capsaicinoids, the most important of which is capsaicin. Capsaicin binds to receptors on our skin and tongue and causes a temporary burning sensation in even minute quantities. This pain response adds complexity to untold dishes and cuisines, but it's not always welcome. Anyone who's seeded chiles without gloves or gotten a bigger hit of spicy food than expected knows that sometimes all you want is relief. There are plenty of purported home remedies for cooling the burn, but do any of them actually work? To find out, we ran an unusual experiment.

EXPERIMENT

We rounded up some brave testers to seed chiles without gloves, smear chile paste onto patches of their skin, and eat scrambled eggs doused in hot sauce. On these affected areas we tested a number of home remedies. For the skin, we washed with soap and water, and rubbed with oil, vinegar, tomato juice, a baking soda slurry, and a 3 percent hydrogen peroxide solution. For the mouth, we asked tasters to swish with (but not swallow) water, whole milk, 5 percent alcohol-by-volume beer, and a 1.5 percent hydrogen peroxide solution.

RESULTS

All testers noted that soap and water helped lessen the burn on their skin slightly, while rubbing oil, vinegar, tomato juice, or baking soda on their skin didn't help at all. As for their mouths, water and beer failed to lessen the burn, too. Milk, on the other hand, had a slight impact. Interestingly, the hydrogen peroxide treatment was deemed effective by a majority of testers at reducing the burning sensation both on the skin and in the mouth.

TAKEAWAY

Why does hydrogen peroxide work? It turns out that it has the ability to oxidize capsaicin to a compound that does not readily bind with pain receptors. Hydrogen peroxide's oxidizing activity has been shown to increase in the presence of a weak alkali, such as sodium bicarbonate (baking soda). With some further testing we found that a solution of 1 tablespoon of 3 percent hydrogen peroxide, 1 tablespoon of water, and ⅛ teaspoon of baking soda worked best as a wash for the affected area or as a mouthwash (swish vigorously for 30 seconds). Toothpaste containing hydrogen peroxide and baking soda proved a somewhat less effective remedy. It's important to note that while the burn of capsaicin in your eyes can be very painful, you should not use hydrogen peroxide or baking soda (or toothpaste!) on your eyes—use warm water instead.

FEELING THE BURN

We had brave tasters seed chiles without gloves, smear chile paste onto their skin, and eat scrambled eggs doused in hot sauce, and then try a handful of home remedies to help ease the pain. The best solution? Hydrogen peroxide, which, it turns out, has the ability to oxidize capsaicin (the spicy chemical compound in chiles) into a compound that does not readily bind with our pain receptors.

FAMILY TREE: CHILE PEPPERS

DRIED CHILES

Just as dried fruit has a more concentrated taste than its fresh counterpart, chiles gain a more intense character when dried. Because they're allowed to ripen on the plant, chiles often taste sweeter dried.

ANCHO (DRIED POBLANO)
Appearance: Wrinkly; dark red
Flavor: Rich, with raisiny sweetness
Substitutions: Pasilla, mulato
Heat: ●○○○○

MULATO (DRIED SMOKED POBLANO)
Appearance: Wrinkly; deep brown
Flavor: Very smoky, with hints of licorice and dried cherry
Substitutions: Ancho
Heat: ●○○○○

CHIPOTLE (DRIED SMOKED JALAPEÑO)
Appearance: Wrinkly; brownish red
Flavor: Smoky, chocolaty, with tobacco-like sweetness
Substitutions: None
Heat: ●●○○○

CASCABEL
Appearance: Small, round; reddish brown
Flavor: Nutty, woodsy
Substitutions: New Mexican
Heat: ●●○○○

NEW MEXICAN
Appearance: Smooth; brick red
Flavor: Slightly acidic, earthy
Substitutions: Cascabel, guajillo
Heat: ●●○○○

ARBOL
Appearance: Smooth; bright red
Flavor: Bright, with smoky undertones
Substitutions: Pequin
Heat: ●●●○○

PEQUIN
Appearance: Small, round; deep red
Flavor: Brighty, citrusy
Substitutions: Arbol
Heat: ●●●○○

FRESH CHILES

The same chile can go by different names in different parts of the country and can range from green to red, depending on when it was harvested.

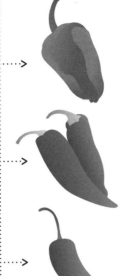

POBLANO
Appearance: Large, triangular; dark green to red-brown
Flavor: Crisp, vegetal
Substitutions: Anaheim, bell pepper
Heat: ●○○○○

ANAHEIM
Appearance: Large, long, skinny; yellow-green to red
Flavor: Mildly tangy, vegetal
Substitutions: Poblano, bell pepper
Heat: ●●○○○

JALAPEÑO
Appearance: Small, smooth, shiny; green or red
Flavor: Bright, grassy
Substitutions: Serrano
Heat: ●●○○○

SERRANO
Appearance: Small; dark green
Flavor: Bright, citrusy
Substitutions: Jalapeño
Heat: ●●●○○

THAI
Appearance: Narrow and petite; bright red
Flavor: Rich, fruity
Substitutions: Serrano
Heat: ●●●◑○

HABANERO
Appearance: Bulbous; bright orange to red
Flavor: Deeply floral, fruity
Substitutions: Double dose Thai
Heat: ●●●●○

WHERE IS THE HEAT IN HOT PEPPERS?

The heat is not in the flesh but in the pith and the seeds. We separated the flesh, pith, and seeds of 40 jalapeños and sent them to our lab. There were 5 milligrams of capsaicin per kilogram of flesh, 73 mg in the seeds, and 512 mg in the pith. Seeds are hotter than the flesh because they are embedded in the pith. They are hot by association.

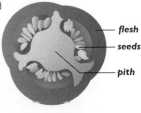

flesh
seeds
pith

Spicy Pork Tacos

✓ WHY THIS RECIPE WORKS

Tacos al pastor, or "shepherd-style" tacos, are a Mexican taqueria classic made from thin slices of chile-marinated pork that's been tightly packed onto a vertical spit with layers of pork fat and then broiled. The cone-shaped stack is often topped with a whole pineapple whose tangy, sweet juices trickle down, encouraging the meat to brown as it turns. When the exterior is browned and crisp, thin shavings of the roasted pork and pineapple are carved off directly onto a warm tortilla and then topped with garnishes that contrast with the rich meat: minced raw onion, cilantro, and a squeeze of fresh lime. It's an adaptation of the lamb shawarmas (themselves inspired by Turkish doner kebabs) introduced to Mexico by Arab immigrants in the late 19th century, and it's one of our favorite kinds of taco filling. We've often given thought to a homemade version but have always been deterred by the fact that home kitchens lack what you'd think would be an essential piece of equipment: a vertical spit. We decided to see what it would take to make this superflavorful meat at home.

BRAISE IN SPICES We started with the braising liquid. Most recipes include some assortment of whole dried guajillo, pasilla, and/or chipotle chiles (all readily available at most supermarkets), toasted in a skillet and then combined with tomatoes or tomatillos, cumin, garlic, citrus juices, herbs and spices, and water. We followed suit, picking guajillo chiles, which are a mild, fruity dried chile, and the toasting them brought out their deep flavor. We simmered the mixture until the chiles were soft and then pureed and strained them to create a complexly flavored marinade in which to braise the meat. We tried a number of different cooking methods to mimic the rotisserie, until we stumbled upon the technique used by chef Jorge Calderon, who runs the kitchen of Taqueria el Amigo, in Waltham, Massachusetts. He makes tacos al pastor the way his grandmother did at her roadside stand in Mexico: First he braises the pork in the tomato-based chile sauce, and then he griddles it. We took note, starting by gently simmering the pork roast (cut into ½-inch slabs) in the chile sauce, which tenderized the meat and infused it with rich flavor.

GRILL AND BASTE Searing the braised pork on the grill crisped up the edges. But we still wished it were as succulent as the spit-roasted versions we'd had. That's when it dawned on us that a crucial part of the classic setup was missing: the melted fat that drips down, basting the meat as it cooks. We weren't about to start grilling pieces of pork fat, but we did have a potful of braising liquid that was loaded up with rendered drippings. We brushed the unctuous liquid over both sides of each pork slab before grilling and then, just before serving, tossed a little more of it, spiked with a bit of lime juice for brightness, with the grilled slices.

SPICY PORK TACOS (AL PASTOR)
SERVES 6 TO 8

Boneless pork butt is often labeled Boston butt. If you can't find guajillo chiles, New Mexican chiles may be substituted, although the dish may be spicier. To warm the tortillas, place them on a plate, cover with a damp dish towel, and microwave for 60 to 90 seconds. Keep the tortillas covered and serve immediately.

- 10 large dried guajillo chiles, wiped clean
- 1¼ pounds plum tomatoes, cored and quartered
- 1½ cups water
- 8 garlic cloves, peeled
- 4 bay leaves
- Salt and pepper
- ¾ teaspoon sugar
- ½ teaspoon ground cumin
- ⅛ teaspoon ground cloves
- 3 pounds boneless pork butt roast
- 1 lime, cut into 8 wedges
- ½ pineapple, peeled, cored, and cut into ½-inch-thick rings
- Vegetable oil
- 18 (6-inch) corn tortillas, warmed
- 1 small onion, chopped fine
- ½ cup coarsely chopped fresh cilantro leaves

1. Toast guajillos in large Dutch oven over medium-high heat until softened and fragrant, 2 to 4 minutes. Transfer to large plate and, when cool enough to handle, remove stems.

2. Bring toasted guajillos, tomatoes, water, garlic, bay leaves, 2 teaspoons salt, ½ teaspoon pepper, sugar, cumin, and cloves to simmer in now-empty Dutch oven over medium-high heat. Cover, reduce heat, and simmer, stirring occasionally, until guajillos are softened and tomatoes mash easily, about 20 minutes.

3. While sauce simmers, trim excess fat from exterior of pork, leaving ¼-inch-thick fat cap. Slice pork against grain into ½-inch-thick slabs.

4. Transfer guajillo-tomato mixture to blender and process until smooth, about 1 minute. Strain puree through fine-mesh strainer, pressing on solids to extract as much liquid as possible. Return puree to pot, submerge pork slices in liquid, and bring to simmer over medium heat. Partially cover, reduce heat, and gently simmer until pork is tender but still holds together, 1½ to 1¾ hours, flipping and rearranging pork halfway through cooking. (Pork can be left in sauce, cooled to room temperature, and refrigerated, covered, for up to 2 days.)

5. Transfer pork to large plate, season both sides with salt, and cover tightly with aluminum foil. Whisk sauce to combine. Transfer ½ cup to bowl for grilling; pour off all but ½ cup remaining sauce from pot and reserve for another use. Squeeze 2 lime wedges into sauce in pot and add spent wedges; season with salt to taste.

6A. FOR A CHARCOAL GRILL: Open bottom vent halfway. Light large chimney starter filled with charcoal briquettes (6 quarts). When top coals are partially covered with ash, pour evenly over grill. Set cooking grate in place, cover, and open lid vent halfway. Heat grill until hot, about 5 minutes.

6B. FOR A GAS GRILL: Turn all burners to high, cover, and heat grill until hot, about 15 minutes. Turn all burners to medium.

7. Clean and oil cooking grate. Brush 1 side of pork with ¼ cup reserved sauce. Place pork on 1 side of grill, sauce side down, and cook until well browned and crisp, 5 to 7 minutes. Brush pork with remaining ¼ cup reserved sauce, flip, and continue to cook until second side is well browned and crisp, 5 to 7 minutes longer. Transfer to cutting board. Meanwhile, brush both sides of pineapple rings with vegetable oil and season with salt to taste. Place on other half of grill and cook until pineapple is softened and caramelized, 5 to 7 minutes per side; transfer pineapple to cutting board.

8. Coarsely chop grilled pineapple and transfer to serving bowl. Using tongs or carving fork to steady hot pork, slice each piece crosswise into ⅛-inch pieces. Bring remaining ½ cup sauce in pot to simmer, add sliced pork, remove pot from heat, and toss to coat pork well. Season with salt to taste.

9. Spoon small amount of pork into each warm tortilla and serve, passing chopped pineapple, remaining 6 lime wedges, onion, and cilantro separately.

Grilled Steak with New Mexican Chile Rub

✔ WHY THIS RECIPE WORKS

As dedicated practitioners of the silk-purse-out-of-a-sow's-ear approach to cooking, we enjoy the challenge of transforming inexpensive ingredients into a memorable meal. But we've always conceded that when it comes to grilled steaks, there's no way around it: You get what you pay for. With their tender texture and big-time beef flavor, pricey cuts from the middle of the steer (like rib eyes and T-bones) need little more than salt, pepper, and a few minutes over a hot fire to render them impressive. Try that minimalist technique on cheaper steaks from farther down the animal (the sirloin and the round) and you get meat that's chewy and dry, with flavors that veer toward liver-y and gamy. It's probably these flavor and texture challenges that inspire cooks to take a page from the barbecue manual and apply spice rubs to less-expensive steaks. Unfortunately, in our experience that approach doesn't really work. Because cheap steaks exude little fat to bond with the spices, the rub tends to fall off in chunks. Surely there was a way to create a recipe for inexpensive grilled steak that was also tender and juicy, with a flavorful, crunchy crust that stayed in place.

USE GLUTAMATES We knew from past test kitchen experience that certain ingredients high in glutamates can amp up savory, meaty flavors without imparting their own distinguishing flavors. Tomato paste and fish sauce are two of the most potent carriers of glutamates, and they did their job well here as a wet rub for the steak: The flavor of the meat was noticeably deeper, without tasting like fish or tomatoes. We then built on that base by adding basic spices. Since the flavor compounds in garlic powder and onion powder are water-soluble, we were able to infuse the steak with flavor even before we added the rub.

CHOOSE THE RIGHT SPICES Dried herbs and other delicate spices can lose their flavor in the intense heat of the grill, but spices containing capsaicin, such as paprika, chiles (like dried New Mexican chiles), and peppers, fare well. We preferred the taste and texture of whole spices that we toasted and ground ourselves, and we eliminated the raw spice flavors by spritzing the steaks with vegetable oil, allowing the spices to bloom right on the steaks.

MAKE SLITS Making a series of very small slits on both sides of the steaks proved to be doubly advantageous: It increased the flavor-grabbing surface area for our initial rub, and it helped the second spice rub to stick to the meat (instead of the grill grate).

GRILLED STEAK WITH NEW MEXICAN CHILE RUB

SERVES 6 TO 8

Shell sirloin steak is also known as top butt, butt steak, top sirloin butt, top sirloin steak, and center-cut roast. Spraying the rubbed steaks with oil helps the spices bloom, preventing a raw flavor.

STEAK

2	teaspoons tomato paste
2	teaspoons fish sauce
1½	teaspoons kosher salt
½	teaspoon onion powder
½	teaspoon garlic powder
2	(1½- to 1¾-pound) boneless shell sirloin steaks, 1 to 1¼ inches thick, trimmed

SPICE RUB

2	dried New Mexican chiles, stemmed, seeded, and torn into ½-inch pieces (½ cup)
4	teaspoons cumin seeds
4	teaspoons coriander seeds
½	teaspoon red pepper flakes
½	teaspoon black peppercorns
1	tablespoon sugar
1	tablespoon paprika
¼	teaspoon ground cloves
	Vegetable oil spray

1. FOR THE STEAK: Combine tomato paste, fish sauce, salt, onion powder, and garlic powder in bowl. Pat steaks dry with paper towels. With sharp knife, cut 1/16-inch-deep slits on both sides of steaks, spaced ½ inch apart, in crosshatch pattern. Rub salt mixture evenly on both sides of steaks. Place steaks on wire rack set in rimmed baking sheet; let stand at room temperature for at least 1 hour. After 30 minutes, prepare grill.

2. FOR THE SPICE RUB: Toast chiles, cumin, coriander, pepper flakes, and peppercorns in 10-inch skillet over medium-low heat, stirring frequently, until just beginning to smoke, 3 to 4 minutes. Transfer to plate to cool, about 5 minutes. Grind spices in spice grinder or in mortar with pestle until coarsely ground. Transfer spices to bowl and stir in sugar, paprika, and cloves.

3A. FOR A CHARCOAL GRILL: Open bottom vent completely. Light large chimney starter mounded with charcoal briquettes (7 quarts). When top coals are partially covered with ash, pour two-thirds evenly over grill, then pour remaining coals over half of grill. Set cooking grate in place, cover, and open lid vent completely. Heat grill until hot, about 5 minutes.

3B. FOR A GAS GRILL: Turn all burners to high, cover, and heat grill until hot, about 15 minutes. Leave primary burner on high and turn other burner(s) to medium.

4. Clean and oil cooking grate. Sprinkle half of spice rub evenly over 1 side of steaks and press to adhere until spice rub is fully moistened. Lightly spray rubbed side of steak with oil spray, about 3 seconds. Flip steaks and repeat process of sprinkling with spice rub and coating with vegetable oil spray on second side.

5. Place steaks over hotter part of grill and cook until browned and charred on both sides and center registers 125 degrees (for medium-rare) or 130 degrees (for medium), 3 to 4 minutes per side. If steaks have not reached desired temperature, move to cooler side of grill and continue to cook. Transfer steaks to clean wire rack set in rimmed baking sheet, tent loosely with aluminum foil, and let rest for 10 minutes. Slice meat thin against grain and serve.

PRACTICAL SCIENCE BLOOMING SPICES

Blooming spices in fat can extract far more flavor than simply simmering these ingredients in water.

We've long advocated "blooming" spices and certain herbs in oil or fat before adding liquid to the pot, which our tastebuds tell us extracts more of their flavors. But we wondered if we could get at a more objective assessment of blooming's impact.

We steeped 50 grams of crushed red pepper flakes in 100 grams of canola oil and another batch in 100 grams of water, holding both liquids at a constant 200 degrees and steeping for 20 minutes. We then strained out the pepper flakes and sent the oil and water to a lab to test for capsaicin (the compound responsible for a chile pepper's heat). We repeated the experiment with thyme and sent the oil and water samples to the lab to test for its main flavor compound, thymol.

The pepper-infused oil had a stronger flavor, with more than double the amount of heat-producing capsaicin than the pepper-infused water. The results for thyme were even more dramatic: The herb-infused oil contained 10 times as much thymol as the herb-infused water.

The main flavor compounds in many spices and some herbs (including thyme, rosemary, lavender, sage, savory, and bay leaves) are largely fat-soluble. So by briefly heating spices (or herbs) in fat before the liquid goes into the pot, you can extract far more flavor than you could by simply simmering these ingredients in water.

Ultimate Vegetarian Chili

✓ WHY THIS RECIPE WORKS

We love chili, but we admit that vegetarian versions are usually the last kind we'd think to make. Most lack depth and complexity, so while they may taste lively and bright initially, their flavor fades. They rely on beans and chunky veggies for heartiness—but in truth that heartiness is just an illusion. Neither ingredient offers any real replacement for the flavor, texture, and unctuous richness that meat provides. It doesn't help matters that such chilis are typically made with canned beans and lackluster commercial chili powder. But do vegetarian chilis really have to be this way? We set out to build a version as rich, savory, and deeply satisfying as any meat chili out there—one that even meat lovers would make on its own merits, not just to serve to vegetarian friends.

USE CHILES The first ingredient to tackle was the seasoning that gives the dish its name. Though we've found premade chili powders to recommend, even the best can't compete with a powder that you grind yourself from dried chiles. Plus, the commercial products tend to have a gritty, dusty texture that comes from grinding whole chiles, including the stems and seeds, which never fully break down. For our homemade blend, we opted for two widely available dried chiles: mild, sweet ancho and earthy New Mexican. We toasted them to bring out their flavor and then, after removing the stems and seeds, pulverized the peppers to a fine powder in a spice grinder with some dried oregano.

BRINE YOUR BEANS For greater complexity, we wanted to use a mix of beans with different characteristics, singling out sweet, nutty cannellinis and meaty, earthy pintos. Canned beans are certainly convenient, but they also tend to be bland and mushy, so we opted for dried, calling on our quick-brining method. This entails bringing the beans to a boil in a pot of salted water and then letting them sit, covered, for an hour. The brine ensures soft, creamy beans (sodium ions from salt weaken the pectin in the bean skins, for a softer texture) that are well seasoned and evenly cooked.

USE BULGUR Besides the beans, most vegetarian chilis replace the bulk that meat contributes with some combination of diced vegetables. But these recipes miss a major point: In addition to adding volume and flavor, meat gives chili its distinctive texture. Properly made meat chili is a homogeneous mixture of ground or diced meat napped with a thick, spicy sauce. No matter how you slice or dice them, cut vegetables can't deliver that same sturdy texture.

They also tend to water down the dish. We'd come across vegetarian chilis that called for nuts, seeds, or grains. We tried a few of these more unusual add-ins and hit the jackpot: bulgur. Even after the long simmer, these precooked wheat kernels (which are normally plumped up by a quick soak in water) retained their shape, giving the chili the textural dimension that it had been missing.

AND GLUTAMATES We still didn't have the rich depth of flavor that could help turn what was a good chili into something great. Canned tomatoes were introducing some savory flavor, but we needed a more potent source, so we added a few dollops of umami-packed tomato paste as well as a few tablespoons of soy sauce. But the flavor was still too one-dimensional. Umami boosters fall into two categories, glutamates and nucleotides, which have a synergistic effect when used together. Dried mushrooms are rich in nucleotides and could amplify the effect of the glutamate-rich soy sauce and tomatoes. Since we were already grinding our chile peppers, we simply tossed in some chopped, dried shiitake mushrooms at the same time, in order to take advantage of their flavor-boosting qualities without adding distinct chunks of mushroom. Sure enough, this batch was the meatiest yet. But could we take things even further? Yes. Walnuts contain more than twice the amount of glutamates as tomatoes. In they went.

GIVE IT A REST To capitalize on the ability of the fat in the chili to create body in the sauce, we gave the chili a vigorous stir and a 20-minute rest after we took it out of the oven. Stirring helped to release starch from the beans and the bulgur. The starch then clustered around the fat droplets in the chili, preventing them from coalescing and helping to create a thick, velvety emulsion that never left a slick of oil on top of the chili, no matter how many times we reheated it.

ULTIMATE VEGETARIAN CHILI
SERVES 6 TO 8

We prefer to make our own chili powder from whole dried chiles, but jarred chili powder can be substituted. If using jarred chili powder, grind the shiitakes and oregano and add them to the pot with ¼ cup of chili powder in step 4. We also recommend a mix of at least two types of beans, one creamy (such as cannellini or navy) and one earthy (such as pinto, black, or red kidney). For a spicier chili, use both jalapeños. Serve the chili with lime wedges, sour cream, diced avocado, chopped red onion, and shredded Monterey Jack or cheddar cheese, if desired.

Jarred chili powder can contain many different ingredients, depending on brand. We chose two winners.

Chili powder is a seasoning blend made from ground dried chiles and an assortment of other ingredients. Much like curry powder, there is no single recipe, but cumin, garlic, and oregano are traditional additions. Chili powder is not to be confused with the lesser-known chile powder (also often spelled chili powder), made solely from chiles without additional seasonings. We use the blend to season batches of chili and in spice rubs and marinades.

But which brand is best? Wanting a bold, complex powder with a warming but not scorching heat, we chose seven widely available chili powders (including two from industry giant McCormick) and tasted them sprinkled over potatoes—to assess each uncooked on a neutral base—and cooked in beef-and-bean chili. What did we learn?

Top picks won praise for bold heat; those we liked less we faulted as "meek." Capsaicin is the chemical that gives chile peppers their heat; its strength is measured on the Scoville scale in Scoville heat units (SHU). We contacted each manufacturer to ask which peppers they use in their powders; three manufacturers deemed that information proprietary, but four were willing to share. Our top two products, which tasters liked for their "bold" heat, both use cayenne (30,000 to 50,000 SHU) in combination with milder peppers. The third- and fourth-place products use a single pepper named "6–4," developed at New Mexico State University (300 to 500 SHU). The 6–4 wasn't hot enough for our tasters. Manufacturers of the lowest-ranked products declined to reveal which peppers they use, but tasters found their heat levels lacking.

Yet a great chili powder is more than just heat. As we noted, our top two products—Morton & Bassett Chili Powder, and Penzeys Spices Medium Hot Chili Powder—used a combination of peppers to achieve complexity; both add paprika, which is made from dried sweet red peppers (0 SHU), and one added ancho peppers (1,000 to 2,000 SHU). This layering of multiple peppers created depth that tasters preferred to the "flat" single-pepper powders.

Supporting spices also played a role. Manufacturers of two of the bottom three products also refused to share information about their "spices"; tasters found them sweet and not much else. Two less-preferred products branched off into Indian-influenced spice blends with coriander, cloves, and allspice. Tasters found these products "muddled" and their flavor odd in a bowl of chili. Our top picks stuck with the classics: cumin, oregano, and garlic, with minor deviations, such as black pepper and parsley. The supporting spices rounded out flavor, complementing the peppers without dominating or distracting from them. Our two recommended products had something else in common: no added salt.

1 pound (2½ cups) dried beans, picked over and rinsed
    Salt
2 dried ancho chiles
2 dried New Mexican chiles
½ ounce dried shiitake mushrooms, chopped coarse
4 teaspoons dried oregano
½ cup walnuts, toasted
1 (28-ounce) can diced tomatoes, drained, with juice reserved
3 tablespoons tomato paste
1–2 jalapeño chiles, stemmed and chopped coarse
3 tablespoons soy sauce
6 garlic cloves, minced
¼ cup vegetable oil
2 pounds onions, chopped fine
1 tablespoon ground cumin
⅔ cup medium-grind bulgur
¼ cup chopped fresh cilantro

1. Bring 4 quarts water, beans, and 3 tablespoons salt to boil in large Dutch oven over high heat. Remove pot from heat, cover, and let stand for 1 hour. Drain beans and rinse well. Wipe out pot.

2. Adjust oven rack to middle position and heat oven to 300 degrees. Arrange anchos and New Mexican chiles on rimmed baking sheet and toast until fragrant and puffed, about 8 minutes. Transfer to plate and let cool, about 5 minutes. Do not turn off oven. Stem and seed anchos and New Mexican chiles. Working in batches, grind mushrooms, oregano, and toasted chiles in spice grinder or with mortar and pestle until finely ground.

3. Process walnuts in food processor until finely ground, about 30 seconds. Transfer to bowl. Process drained tomatoes, tomato paste, jalapeño(s), soy sauce, and garlic in food processor until tomatoes are finely chopped, about 45 seconds, scraping down sides of bowl as needed.

4. Heat oil in now-empty Dutch oven over medium-high heat until shimmering. Add onions and 1¼ teaspoons salt; cook, stirring occasionally, until onions begin to brown, 8 to 10 minutes. Lower heat to medium and add cumin and ground chile mixture; cook, stirring constantly, until fragrant, about 1 minute. Add rinsed beans and 7 cups water and bring to boil. Cover pot, transfer to oven, and cook for 45 minutes.

5. Remove pot from oven. Stir in bulgur, ground walnuts, tomato mixture, and reserved tomato juice. Cover pot and return to oven. Cook until beans are fully tender, about 2 hours.

6. Remove pot from oven, stir chili well, and let stand, uncovered, for 20 minutes. Stir in cilantro and serve. (Chili can be made up to 3 days in advance.)

Ultimate Beef Chili

✔ WHY THIS RECIPE WORKS

Our goal in creating an "ultimate" beef chili was to determine which of the "secret ingredients" recommended by chili experts around the world were spot-on—and which were expendable.

CHOOSE YOUR MEAT   After deciding to use diced—not ground—beef, we began by testing six different cuts: flap meat, brisket, chuck-eye roast, skirt steak, blade steak, and short ribs. Though the short ribs were extremely tender, some tasters felt that they tasted too much like pot roast. The brisket was beefy but lean and a bit tough. The clear winner was blade steak, favored for its tenderness and rich flavor. Chuck-eye roast is a good second option.

BRINE THE BEANS   It's important to brine your beans (see page 351) in order to get them to cook quickly, with a lasting tender and creamy texture. We used a quick brine because beans were not the central focus and, after all, the rest of the recipe took a fair amount of work. The timing worked out perfectly: By the time the beans were done brining (1 hour), the rest of the work was done.

SEED, TOAST, PUREE   For complex chile flavor, we traded in commercial chili powder in favor of ground dried ancho and arbol chiles; for a grassy heat, we added fresh jalapeños. We toasted the anchos to develop their flavor and seeded all our chiles to control the heat. We also included oregano, cumin, cocoa, and salt. Adding broth to this chile paste as we pureed it allowed us to cook the ground chiles longer, without danger of scorching them.

ADD FLAVOR   A combination of beer and chicken broth outperformed red wine, coffee, and beef broth as the liquid component. To balance the sweetness, mild molasses beat out other offbeat ingredients (including prunes and Coca-Cola). For the right level of thickness, flour and

peanut butter didn't perform as promised; instead, a small amount of ordinary cornmeal (which we processed with the chiles and spices) sealed the deal, providing just the right consistency in our ultimate beef chili.

ULTIMATE BEEF CHILI
SERVES 6 TO 8

Because much of the chile flavor is held in the fat of this dish, refrain from skimming fat from the surface. Dried New Mexican or guajillo chiles make a good substitute for the anchos; each dried arbol may be replaced with ⅛ teaspoon cayenne pepper. If you prefer not to work with any whole dried chiles, the anchos and arbols can be replaced with ½ cup commercial chili powder and ¼ to ½ teaspoon cayenne pepper, though the texture of the chili will be slightly compromised. Good choices for condiments include diced avocado, finely chopped red onion, chopped cilantro, lime wedges, sour cream, and shredded Monterey Jack or cheddar cheese.

8	ounces (1¼ cups) dried pinto beans, picked over and rinsed
	Salt
6	dried ancho chiles, stemmed, seeded, and torn into 1-inch pieces
2–4	dried arbol chiles, stemmed, seeded, and split into 2 pieces
3	tablespoons cornmeal
2	teaspoons dried oregano
2	teaspoons ground cumin
2	teaspoons unsweetened cocoa powder
2½	cups chicken broth
2	onions, cut into ¾-inch pieces
3	small jalapeño chiles, stemmed, seeded, and cut into ½-inch pieces
3	tablespoons vegetable oil
4	garlic cloves, minced
1	(14.5-ounce) can diced tomatoes
2	teaspoons molasses
3½	pounds beef blade steak, ¾ inch thick, trimmed and cut into ¾-inch pieces
1½	cups mild lager, such as Budweiser

1. Combine 4 quarts water, beans, and 3 tablespoons salt in Dutch oven and bring to boil over high heat. Remove pot from heat, cover, and let stand for 1 hour. Drain and rinse well.

2. Adjust oven rack to lower-middle position and heat oven to 300 degrees. Toast ancho chiles in 12-inch skillet over medium-high heat, stirring frequently, until fragrant, 2 to 6 minutes. Transfer to food processor and let cool. Do not wash out skillet.

3. Add arbol chiles, cornmeal, oregano, cumin, cocoa, and ½ teaspoon salt to food processor with toasted ancho chiles; process until finely ground, about 2 minutes. With processor running, slowly add ½ cup broth until smooth paste forms, about 45 seconds, scraping down sides of bowl as necessary. Transfer paste to small bowl. Place onions in now-empty processor and pulse until roughly chopped, about 4 pulses. Add jalapeños and pulse until consistency of chunky salsa, about 4 pulses, scraping down bowl as necessary.

4. Heat 1 tablespoon oil in Dutch oven over medium-high heat. Add onion mixture and cook, stirring occasionally, until moisture has evaporated and vegetables are softened, 7 to 9 minutes. Add garlic and cook until fragrant, about 1 minute. Add chile paste, tomatoes and their juice, and molasses; stir until chile paste is thoroughly combined. Add drained beans and remaining 2 cups broth; bring to boil, then reduce heat to simmer.

5. Meanwhile, heat 1 tablespoon oil in now-empty 12-inch skillet over medium-high heat until shimmering. Pat beef dry with paper towels and sprinkle with 1 teaspoon salt. Add half of beef and cook until browned on all sides, about 10 minutes. Transfer meat to Dutch oven. Add ¾ cup beer to skillet, scraping up browned bits from bottom of pan, and bring to simmer. Transfer beer to Dutch oven. Repeat with remaining 1 tablespoon oil, remaining beef, and remaining ¾ cup beer. Stir to combine and return mixture to simmer.

6. Cover pot and transfer to oven. Cook until meat and beans are fully tender, 1½ to 2 hours. Let chili stand, uncovered, for 10 minutes. Stir well, season with salt to taste, and serve. (Chili can be refrigerated for up to 3 days.)

PRACTICAL SCIENCE TOASTING DRIED CHILES

You can use the oven!

Just as roasting fresh chiles deepens their flavor, toasting dried ones improves their taste. While many recipes recommend pan toasting, it's not the only way. (It's easier to scorch the chiles, which can impart bitterness, when pan-toasting.) You can toast yours in the oven, too. To do so: Clean chiles with damp paper towel. Arrange on baking sheet and toast in 350-degree oven just until fragrant and puffed, about 6 minutes.

CHAPTER 32

Apples

When there are more than 6,000 types of apples, the key to cooking with them is to pick the right one.

HOW THE SCIENCE WORKS

Apples, which belong to the genus *Malus*, a member of the rose family botanically named *Rosaceae*, have been grown for thousands of years. DNA mapping has shown them to originate from the wild apple, *Malus sieversii*, in a region of Central Asia that includes southern Kazakhstan and Kyrgyzstan. And they are more complicated than you'd think: Apples have the largest genome of any known plant, containing 57,000 genes. (Even the human genome contains only about 30,000 genes.) Today there are around 6,000 cultivars of apples (though only a dozen or so in the average supermarket). China is the world's largest producer, with the United States ranking number two.

Over the years, apples have been bred for one of three purposes: eating, cooking, or juice production. This means that varieties that are best for eating are not the best for cooking, and vice versa. It all comes down to the texture, which depends on a few things: the structure and composition of the cell walls, the amount of air between the apple cells, and the amount of acid in the apple. Storage conditions are also important (see Practical Science, page 265).

First, the cell walls of apples are made of cellulose and hemicellulose, held together with pectin. Pectin is a complex polysaccharide that holds the cells of many fruits and vegetables together, as well as forms part of the cell wall structure, providing strength. Pectin is strengthened by calcium ions that link its molecules together. Apples that are best for cooking tend to have pectin reinforced with more calcium than apples that are best for eating. In addition, about 25 percent of the volume of an apple is composed of air held in open spaces between the cells. These air pockets expand with steam during cooking and can result in rupture, collapse, and release of juice, especially in eating apples. And, finally, acid strengthens pectin and keeps it from dissolving so readily when heated. Naturally acidic apples, such as Granny Smiths, are more likely to hold their shape than other varieties. This is why we like to use Granny Smiths for baking.

Apples are a climacteric fruit, meaning they continue to ripen following harvest. Like most climacteric fruit (see Tomatoes, page 221), they are harvested before becoming fully ripe. At this stage apples still contain a lot of tart, sour-tasting malic acid and starch, which means they tend to be more sour than sweet. A few important things take place during ripening: First, apples use some of the acid for energy and metabolism; second, they convert much of their starch to sugars; finally, an enzyme known as polygalacturonase gradually breaks down some of the pectin.

When it comes to cooking, we stick to only a few types of apples—apples that are readily available in the supermarket, all year round, and apples that are better equipped to deal with heat. This means apples with more calcium-reinforced pectin, more acid, and less space between their cells. First place? Granny Smith. Here, we use them to make a double-layered French Apple Cake, in which the Granny Smiths remain intact with the help of a little precooking (page 264). We lightly caramelize whole, hollowed-out Granny Smiths, which stand up to the oven in our Best Baked Apples (page 267). Finally, for our French Apple Tart (page 265), we use Golden Delicious apples, which break down more readily, in two ways—reduced into a puree as the base of the tart, and in slightly precooked, still-intact slices arranged in a rosette—for a dessert that's simple and fancy at the same time.

> *Apples have the largest genome of any known plant, with 57,000 genes.*

TEST KITCHEN EXPERIMENT

In the test kitchen we turn to Granny Smith apples again and again for baking applications. Their high acidity provides great balance in sweet applications, but often it's their firm texture (and ability to retain that firmness during cooking) that makes them our top pick. We were curious how some of the lesser-known, less-available, or newer apples measured up. We set up the following experiment.

EXPERIMENT

We gathered 10 apple varieties and measured their initial firmness using a CT3 Texture Analyzer (see page 3). We then cooked slices of each apple at 185 degrees (a temperature at which pectin quickly breaks down) until they registered the same soft texture. We tracked how long each variety took to reach the same endpoint and compared that to the initial firmness to look for a potential correlation. For a more visual (and real-world) representation, we also baked each type of apple whole, on a baking sheet in a 350-degree oven until they softened. We used the data for Granny Smith apples as a benchmark for comparison.

RESULTS

We found a clear correlation between the initial firmness of a particular apple and how long that sample took to soften. Specifically, the firmer the raw apple, the longer it took to soften. When we organized the results by apple variety, we noticed clear trends that can help dictate best uses for a given variety.

TAKEAWAY

Based on our tests we were able to group the apple varieties into a few categories. McIntosh, Red Delicious, and Golden Delicious soften rapidly and are better suited to applesauce or apple butter where the end goal is a completely soft texture. At the other end of the spectrum we found that Pink Lady, Braeburn, and Honeycrisp perform similarly to our perennial pie favorite, Granny Smith. These apples start out firm and retain their texture well during extended cooking. In the middle of the pack we grouped Gala, Jonagold, and Empire apples together. Many factors contribute to apple texture when both raw and cooked. Chief among them is the strength of the pectin, which provides structure in the cell walls of the apple. Apples that are higher in calcium and acidity, which both reinforce pectin, generally hold up better to cooking. (Tart apples also tend to be firmer than sweet apples.)

Beyond texture, each type of apple varies in sweetness and acidity so that should be a consideration when choosing an apple for a particular application. While apple varieties performed relatively consistently from test to test, there were exceptions among individual apples within a variety. The bottom line? If you start with a mealy, soft apple it will turn to mush quickly, no matter the variety.

FROM APPLE TO SAUCE: HOW QUICKLY WILL YOUR APPLE BREAK DOWN?

We tested apples of 10 varieties, measuring their firmness and timing how long it took them break down during cooking. We found a correlation between initial firmness and tendency to break down. The takeaway? Soft apples are better for sauce. Hard apples will better retain their texture.

MCINTOSH
This apple started soft and quickly turned to mush. Best used for applesauce.

GALA
This apple landed firmly in the middle of initial firmness and breakdown during cooking.

GRANNY SMITH
This apple started out crisp and retained much of its texture over the cooking time.

APPLES BY THE NUMBERS

TYPE OF APPLE	AVERAGE INITIAL HARDNESS (GRAMS FORCE)	TIME TO TURN TO MUSH AT 185° (MINUTES)
McIntosh	188.2	2.3
Red Delicious	195.6	2.0
Golden Delicious	232.8	2.3
Gala	246.8	4.7
Jonagold	251.7	3.7
Empire	270.0	4.7
Honeycrisp	352.2	24.4
Granny Smith	475.3	14.7
Braeburn	601.9	24.7
Pink Lady	607.1	34.0

FOCUS ON: APPLES

There are around 6,000 varieties of apples grown in North America today. (There used to be more. See Practical Science, page 266.) When it comes to choosing which particular apple to eat or bake with, it's between more than simply red and green.

RED-FLESHED APPLES

A group of apples are known as "red-fleshed" apples due to (you guessed it!) their red-colored flesh. These apples get their color from the presence of anthocyanin pigments in the flesh. Red-fleshed apples are descendents of a European apple called "Surprise" and were cultivated and developed by California-based apple growers in the early 1920s. Among Surprise's descendents is the Pink Pearl apple.

SEEDS

Apple seeds contain amygdalin, which releases hydrogen cyanide when digested. But the human body can detoxify small amounts of cyanide, and apple seeds have a tough outer coating that is largely impervious to digestive juices. So don't worry.

SKIN

Much of the aroma of apples is formed in the skin.

STEM

FLESH

The structure of apple cells comes from cellulose and hemicellulose. There is also pectin, which is a complex polysaccharide found in apples (and other vegetables and fruits), and acts as the glue that holds cells together. Pectin is strengthened by calcium, meaning apples with pectin more reinforced with calcium are better for baking. Acid likewise strengthens the pectin found in apples. In addition, it keeps pectin from readily dissolving when heated. Acidic apples, like Granny Smiths, hold their shape better when baked.

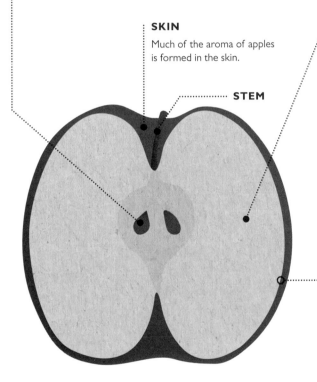

air pockets
Twenty-five percent of an apple consists of air pockets, which expand with steam, rupture, and collapse often during cooking.

skin

cells

Baldwin Apple   **1930s**   **McIntosh Apple**

THE DISAPPEARANCE OF THE BALDWIN

Baking apples used to be more prevalent in the American kitchen, partially due to the fact that a lack of refrigeration meant that apples were stored in cellars, and the hardy skins of baking apples lent them very good storage attributes under these conditions. In fact, a baking apple called "Baldwin" used to be America's #1 apple. But then, according to University of Massachusetts professor of pomology Wesley Autio, a succession of exceptionally cold temperatures in New England in the 1930s killed off many of the trees. The survivor? The less than universally loved McIntosh.

French Apple Cake

✓ WHY THIS RECIPE WORKS

We wanted to create an apple cake with a custardy base—rich and creamy and dense, but not the least bit heavy. We wanted butter-soft apple slices, simultaneously tart and sweet, perfectly intact despite their tender texture. And above the rich custard, we wanted a double layer of real cake—light and airy on the inside, with a beautifully golden-brown, crisp top. It was a tall order. We set to work.

PICK GRANNIES We started with the apples. We didn't want soft and mushy apples, but we did want a variety of apple flavors. In order to avoid creating sodden patches in the cake here and there because of different varieties releasing different levels of moisture, we stuck with one kind. Since we wanted the apples to hold their shape entirely, we opted for Granny Smiths; among the firmer apples, their tartness stood out most clearly against the sweet, dense background of a cake. A splash of Calvados added the depth we wanted.

ENSURE TENDERNESS To get our apples to the right texture, however, we had to precook them just a bit in the microwave. Why do apples that go straight into the cake batter bake up too firm, while those same raw apples come out soft and tender if microwaved a bit before heading into the oven? Common sense might suggest that precooking simply hastens the fruit's breakdown. But there's more to the answer than that. As so often happens in cooking, an enzyme is involved, in this case a temperature-sensitive enzyme called pectin methylesterase (PME). As the batter's temperature climbs and lingers between 120 and 160 degrees, the PME sets the pectin in the fruit, so the slices will remain relatively firm no matter how long they are cooked. The catch, though, is that PME is deactivated at temperatures above 160 degrees. Enter the microwave. A 3-minute zap quickly brought the apples to

180 degrees—high enough to permanently kill any activity of the PME—so the precooked fruit emerged fully soft in the finished cake. We even double-checked the science with a side test: heating vacuum-sealed batches of both raw and microwaved apples in a sous vide machine to the final temperature of the cake (208 degrees) for the same amount of time it bakes, giving the apples plenty of time to linger between 120 and 160 degrees. The microwaved apples were predictably tender, while the slices that we didn't microwave remained firm. Furthermore, these slices never fully softened, even after we continued to cook them for another 40 minutes.

MAKE TWO BATTERS (KIND OF) To produce the cake's distinct layers, we started with a simple base batter, and discovered that key additions could make it work in two ways. First, we added extra flour to 1 cup of the base batter to create a tender, airy top. Adding two extra yolks to the remaining base batter created a creamy, dense bottom.

FRENCH APPLE CAKE
SERVES 8 TO 10

The microwaved apples should be pliable but not completely soft when cooked. To test for doneness, take one apple slice and try to bend it. If it snaps in half, it's too firm; microwave it for an additional 30 seconds and test again. If Calvados is unavailable, 1 tablespoon of apple brandy or white rum can be substituted.

1½	pounds Granny Smith apples, peeled, cored, cut into 8 wedges, and sliced ⅛ inch thick crosswise
1	tablespoon Calvados
1	teaspoon lemon juice
1	cup (5 ounces) plus 2 tablespoons all-purpose flour
1	cup (7 ounces) plus 1 tablespoon granulated sugar
2	teaspoons baking powder
½	teaspoon salt
1	cup vegetable oil
1	cup whole milk
1	large egg plus 2 large yolks
1	teaspoon vanilla extract
	Confectioners' sugar

1. Adjust oven rack to lower-middle position and heat oven to 325 degrees. Spray 9-inch springform pan with vegetable oil spray. Place prepared pan on rimmed baking sheet lined with aluminum foil. Place apple slices in glass

---

> **PRACTICAL SCIENCE**
> **ARE APPLE SEEDS POISONOUS?**
>
> Yes, and no.
>
> Apple seeds contain amygdalin, which releases hydrogen cyanide when digested. But there are two reasons why you shouldn't be concerned: First, the human body can detoxify small amounts of cyanide; second, apple seeds have a tough outer coating that is largely impervious to digestive juices. In other words, you would have to chew and swallow the seeds from several pounds of apples to be in any real danger.

pie plate, cover, and microwave until apples are pliable and slightly translucent, about 3 minutes. Toss apple slices with Calvados and lemon juice and let cool for 15 minutes.

2. Whisk 1 cup flour, 1 cup granulated sugar, baking powder, and salt together in bowl. Whisk oil, milk, egg, and vanilla together in second bowl until smooth. Add dry ingredients to wet ingredients and whisk until just combined. Transfer 1 cup batter to separate bowl and set aside.

3. Add egg yolks to remaining batter and whisk to combine. Using rubber spatula, gently fold in cooled apples. Transfer batter to prepared pan; using offset spatula, spread batter evenly to pan edges, gently pressing on apples to create even, compact layer, and smooth surface.

4. Whisk remaining 2 tablespoons flour into reserved batter. Pour over batter in pan and spread batter evenly to pan edges and smooth surface. Sprinkle remaining 1 tablespoon granulated sugar evenly over cake.

5. Bake until center of cake is set, toothpick inserted in center comes out clean, and top is golden brown, about 1¼ hours, rotating pan halfway through baking. Transfer pan to wire rack; let cool for 5 minutes. Run thin knife around sides of pan and let cool completely, 2 to 3 hours. Dust lightly with confectioners' sugar, cut into wedges, and serve.

French Apple Tart

✓ WHY THIS RECIPE WORKS

A classic French apple tart is little more than apples and pastry, but such simplicity means that imperfections like tough or mushy apples, unbalanced flavor, and a sodden crust are hard to hide. In its simplest form, the tart has a crisp pastry shell that's filled with a concentrated apple puree and then topped with a spiraling fan of paper-thin apple slices. It's usually finished with a delicate glaze, which caramelizes during baking, providing an extra layer of flavor and a distinctly European flair. We were drawn to the idea of a showstopper dessert that could be made with a short list of pantry staples. Our challenge would be perfecting each component to produce a tart with a lively, intense apple flavor and a crust that stayed crisp. And we were unwilling to sacrifice integrity for beauty; we wanted both.

MAKE A STURDY BASE For a dough that would hold its shape and maintain a crisp texture even after being filled with the puree, we tried out puff pastry, pâte brisée, and pâte sucrée—the triumvirate of classic French pastry options. None were perfect, but a modified pâte sucrée

did the trick. Why? Traditional French pastry crusts that call for cold butter require a series of chilling, resting, and rolling steps to ensure that the dough doesn't shrink or slump during baking. For our modified dough, we used melted butter, which allowed us to skip the fussy prebaking steps—and offered a couple other benefits, too. First, melted butter thoroughly coats the flour proteins, preventing them from linking up and forming the elastic network known as gluten that causes pie dough to retract during baking. The fat also "waterproofs" the dough by coating the flour's starch granules, preventing them from absorbing the moisture from the tart filling. Finally, melted butter makes this dough not only easy to throw together (just pour the butter over the dry ingredients and stir) but also so malleable when raw that it can simply be pressed into the pan rather than rolled out.

PACK WITH APPLES For intense fruit flavor, we packed the tart with a whopping 5 pounds of Golden Delicious apples, which broke down easily to make a puree. We got a concentrated fruit flavor by cooking the puree down until it measured about 2 cups. But we wanted the flavor to be more distinctive. We found what we were looking for in Julia Child's recipe for *tarte aux pommes*, in which she adds butter and apricot preserves to her puree. We did the same for a richer, brighter-tasting filling.

PARCOOK, TOO A problem we ran into was that the apple slices on top of the tart never became tender enough for us to cut the tart without their resisting and becoming dislodged. We swapped the traditional wafer-thin slices of apples for more generous slices and then sautéed them for 10 minutes to jump-start the softening before placing them on the tart. (Because sautéing brings the temperature of the apples quickly above 160 degrees—the temperature at which the enzyme pectin methylesterase, which can cause the fruit to remain firm, is deactivated—this step ensures a soft, sliceable fruit.) Formed into a rosette pattern, the apple topping was elegant and easy, especially with a simple apricot glaze.

PRACTICAL SCIENCE HEIRLOOM APPLES

> There have been more than 16,000 different types of apples grown in North America.

Walking into the typical grocery store today and glancing at the produce section, it's easy to think that there are only a handful of different apples to choose from. Not so, says Dan Bussey, orchard manager and apple historian at Seed Savers Exchange, a nonprofit organization that works to collect and save heirloom plants and seeds. ("Heirloom" means any species that's more than 50 years old, Bussey explains.) Bussey, who began researching heirloom apples while homesteading in the 1970s, recently finished the seven-volume *Illustrated History of Apples in North America*, which covers the 16,468 apple varietals on record as having grown here. Today there are only around 6,000 varieties of apples growing in North America, the remainder lost to time or commercial demands. The flavors and textures of many heirloom apples are "exquisite," says Bussey. "But humans eat with their eyes, and if an apple doesn't look good, they think it won't taste good. That's not the case." Some apple varietals date way beyond the last 50 years—try the 1200s. Or even earlier. The Decio, says Bussey, is the oldest apple, from Italy, and legend has it dating back to 450 AD. A Roman general named Ezio supposedly took this apple with him as he chased Attila the Hun. "Probably because it traveled well," Bussey explains. "It's hard and gnarly, but a tasty treat."

FRENCH APPLE TART
SERVES 8

You may have extra apple slices after arranging the apples in step 6. If you don't have a potato masher, you can puree the apples in a food processor. For the best flavor and texture, be sure to bake the crust thoroughly until it is deep golden brown. To ensure that the outer ring of the pan releases easily from the tart, avoid getting apple puree and apricot glaze on the crust. The tart is best served the day it is assembled.

CRUST

1⅓	cups (6⅔ ounces) all-purpose flour
5	tablespoons (2¼ ounces) sugar
½	teaspoon salt
10	tablespoons unsalted butter, melted

FILLING

10	Golden Delicious apples (8 ounces each), peeled and cored
3	tablespoons unsalted butter
1	tablespoon water
½	cup apricot preserves
¼	teaspoon salt

1. FOR THE CRUST: Adjust 1 oven rack to lowest position and second rack 5 to 6 inches from broiler element. Heat oven to 350 degrees. Whisk flour, sugar, and salt together in bowl. Add melted butter and stir with wooden spoon until dough forms. Using your hands, press two-thirds of dough into bottom of 9-inch tart pan with removable bottom. Press remaining dough into fluted sides of pan. Press and smooth dough with your hands to even thickness. Place pan on wire rack set in rimmed baking sheet and bake on lower rack until crust is deep golden brown and firm to touch, 30 to 35 minutes, rotating pan halfway through baking. Set aside until ready to fill. Do not turn off oven.

2. FOR THE FILLING: Meanwhile, cut 5 apples lengthwise into quarters and cut each quarter lengthwise into 4 slices. Melt 1 tablespoon butter in 12-inch skillet over medium heat. Add apple slices and water and toss to combine. Cover and cook, stirring occasionally, until apples begin to turn translucent and are slightly pliable, 3 to 5 minutes. Transfer apples to large plate, spread into single layer, and set aside to cool. Do not clean skillet.

3. While apples cook, microwave apricot preserves until fluid, about 30 seconds. Strain preserves through fine-mesh strainer into small bowl, reserving solids. Set aside 3 table-spoons strained preserves for brushing tart.

4. Cut remaining 5 apples into ½-inch-thick wedges. Melt remaining 2 tablespoons butter in now-empty skillet over medium heat. Add remaining apricot preserves, reserved apricot solids, apple wedges, and salt. Cover and cook, stirring occasionally, until apples are very soft, about 10 minutes.

5. Mash apples to puree with potato masher. Continue to cook, stirring occasionally, until puree is reduced to 2 cups, about 5 minutes.

6. Transfer apple puree to baked tart shell and smooth surface. Select 5 thinnest slices of sautéed apple and set aside. Starting at outer edge of tart, arrange remaining slices, tightly overlapping, in concentric circles. Bend reserved slices to fit in center. Bake tart, still on wire rack in sheet, on lowest rack, for 30 minutes. Remove tart from oven and heat broiler.

7. While broiler heats, warm reserved preserves in microwave until fluid, about 20 seconds. Brush evenly over surface of apples, avoiding tart crust. Broil tart, checking every 30 seconds and turning as necessary, until apples are attractively caramelized, 1 to 3 minutes. Let tart cool for at least 1½ hours. Remove outer metal ring of tart pan, slide thin metal spatula between tart and pan bottom, and carefully slide tart onto serving platter. Cut into wedges and serve.

PRACTICAL SCIENCE BROWNING APPLES

Browned apples may not look good, but they still taste fine.

As anyone who has brought sliced apples to school for lunch knows: Cut apples will turn brown, and quickly. This browning reaction is quite different than the browning we know as the Maillard reaction. Here, it is due to an enzyme called polyphenol oxidase, or PPO. And PPO reacts with compounds called polyphenols—including tannins, which are responsible for the astringent taste of apples, as well as tea and red wine—that are quite abundant in apples. The brown compounds produced are called melanins, and are perfectly safe to eat, although not very appealing. Polyphenol oxidase is most active at a neutral pH of 7.0, and much less active at acidic pH. This is why soaking sliced apples in water with a bit of lemon juice (which is about 10 times more acidic than apples), or brushing the slices with lemon juice alone, greatly slows down the browning reaction. Scientists have been working on curing this problem for the schoolchildren of the world: In 2015 the USDA approved the genetically modified "Arctic Apple," which has been bred not to turn brown after slicing, for sale in the United States.

TO MAKE AHEAD: Baked crust, apple slices, and apple puree can be made up to 24 hours in advance. Apple slices and apple puree should be refrigerated separately in airtight containers. Assemble tart with refrigerated apple slices and puree and bake as directed, adding 5 minutes to baking time.

Best Baked Apples

✔ WHY THIS RECIPE WORKS

The charms of a fresh apple aren't difficult to grasp. Sweet with a touch of ripe tartness, the flesh bursts with all the crisp, juicy complexity of a young white wine. But slide that same fruit into the oven, and the dry heat makes quick work of killing off every ounce of apple appeal. The crunchy texture turns to mush. The skin becomes chewy. The interior cells rupture, releasing a rush of moisture that dilutes the once-flavorful sugars and acids. The end result: a bland, squishy "dessert" that makes you wish you'd gone with the chocolate soufflé. We had some work to do.

GO WITH GRANNY SMITH Previous pie testing has taught us that good apple cookery is as much about picking the right variety of fruit as it is about how you bake with it. We tried several of the most widely available apples—both sweet and tart—in a basic working recipe. We removed the cores with a paring knife, leaving 1-inch-diameter cavities, then placed the apples in a baking dish, stuffed them with a simple filling, and wet the dishes with apple cider, which we hoped would cook down into a sauce. We baked them at 375 degrees until they were easily pierced with a paring knife, which took between 30 and 45 minutes, depending on the apple type. To our surprise, the winner wasn't any of our favorites for eating out of hand, like the Jonagold or the Fuji. Even the flesh of a McIntosh, a variety prized for both snacking and baking, broke down under the oven's heat and turned to mush. The very qualities that made for a great snacking apple proved too delicate to survive a stint in the oven. Best in show was the Granny Smith—firm and nicely tart, yes, but only mildly fruity and sweet. They held up fairly well in the heat, and their acerbic bite balanced nicely with the sweetness of the filling and sauce.

PEEL THEM But we couldn't ignore a persistent problem: apples that "blew out" and collapsed in the oven. Could removing the skin solve the issue? To find out, we prepared two batches of six baked Granny Smith apples each, one skin-on, the other skin-off, using our place-holder filling and sauce. Then we baked each batch in a 13 by 9-inch baking dish in a 375-degree oven until the apples could be pierced easily with a knife. To our surprise, all the skin-off apples held their shape, without a single blowout. Within the skin-on batch, half of the apples collapsed. Why? In nature, the peel protects an apple; in the oven, it traps moisture that's been transformed into steam. As the steam attempts to escape, its outward pressure ruptures cells and eventually bursts through the apple's skin, causing blowouts. Removing all the skin allows the steam to escape without damaging the fruit's structure.

CARAMELIZE THEM After enlarging the cavity to hold a filling, we still wanted more flavor. The apple vessels themselves still lacked the concentrated, rich flavor of other cooked fruit desserts, but we thought of the French classic tarte Tatin, and had an idea. For this popular Parisian bistro tart, peeled, sliced apples are sautéed in butter and sugar to coax an intense, candy-like caramelized flavor from the fruit. Of course, we couldn't slice the apples—but maybe we could create a flat surface that would caramelize on the stovetop. Setting aside the baking dish we'd been using, we melted a tablespoon of butter in a large nonstick skillet, sliced ½ inch off the top of the apples, and added them upside down. It took about 3 minutes for them to turn golden brown over medium heat. We then flipped them and added the filling. Instead of transferring the stuffed fruit back to the baking dish, we simply added the sauce and transferred the entire skillet to the oven. To our delight, the skillet turned out to be an ideal container, giving us ample room to baste the apples during cooking.

PRACTICAL SCIENCE
APPLE CIDER VS. APPLE JUICE

When it comes to cooking, don't swap apple juice for cider.

To make cider, apples are simply cored, chopped, mashed, and then pressed to extract their liquid. Most cider is pasteurized before sale, though unpasteurized cider is also available. To make apple juice, manufacturers follow the same steps used to make cider, but they also filter the extracted liquid to remove pulp and sediment. Apple juice is then pasteurized, and potassium sorbate (a preservative) is often mixed in to prevent fermentation. Finally, apple juice is sometimes sweetened with sugar or corn syrup.

We tried using unsweetened apple juice in recipes for pork chops and glazed ham that call for cider. Tasters were turned off by excessive sweetness in the dishes made with apple juice, unanimously preferring those made with cider. This made sense: The filtration process used in making juice removes some of the complex, tart, and bitter flavors that are still present in cider. (When we tested the pH level of both liquids, the cider had a lower pH than the apple juice, confirming its higher level of acidity.)

BEST BAKED APPLES
SERVES 6

If you don't have an ovensafe skillet, transfer the browned apples to a 13 by 9-inch baking dish and bake as directed. The recipe calls for seven apples; six are left whole and one is diced and added to the filling. Serve with vanilla ice cream, if desired.

7	large Granny Smith apples (8 ounces each)
6	tablespoons unsalted butter, softened
⅓	cup dried cranberries, chopped coarse
⅓	cup pecans, toasted and chopped coarse
¼	cup packed (1¾ ounces) brown sugar
3	tablespoons old-fashioned rolled oats
1	teaspoon finely grated orange zest
½	teaspoon ground cinnamon
	Pinch salt
⅓	cup maple syrup
⅓	cup plus 2 tablespoons apple cider

1. Adjust oven rack to middle position and heat oven to 375 degrees. Peel, core, and cut 1 apple into ¼-inch dice. Combine diced apple, 5 tablespoons butter, cranberries, pecans, sugar, oats, orange zest, cinnamon, and salt in bowl; set aside.

2. Shave thin slice off bottom (blossom end) of remaining 6 apples to allow them to sit flat. Cut top ½ inch off stem end of apples and reserve. Peel apples and use melon baller or small measuring spoon to remove 1½-inch-diameter core, being careful not to cut through bottom of apples.

3. Melt remaining 1 tablespoon butter in 12-inch ovensafe nonstick skillet over medium heat. Add apples, stem side down, and cook until cut surface is golden brown, about 3 minutes. Flip apples, reduce heat to low, and spoon filling inside, mounding excess filling over cavities; top with reserved apple caps. Add maple syrup and ⅓ cup cider to skillet. Transfer skillet to oven and bake until skewer inserted into apples meets little resistance, 35 to 40 minutes, basting every 10 minutes with maple syrup mixture in pan.

4. Transfer apples to serving platter. Stir up to 2 tablespoons of remaining cider into sauce in skillet to adjust consistency. Pour sauce over apples and serve.

CHAPTER 33

Strawberries

To make the most of this "false fruit" when cooking: macerate, concentrate, puree.

HOW THE SCIENCE WORKS

Strawberries have been prized since ancient Roman times, when they were a small, wild fruit. The French are given credit for developing the first culinary applications for strawberries in the 1300s. The dessert of strawberries and cream was created in the 1500s by Thomas Wolsey, a cardinal of the Roman Catholic Church in England.

But the large, bright-red, flavorful fruit we eat today has its roots in North America. It's actually a hybrid—a cross between two species, *Fragaria virginiana* from North America and *Fragaria chiloensis* from Chile. The two were crossbred in Brittany in the 1750s, producing the standard variety now consumed all over the world. Today, the United States is by far the leading producer.

Most fruit grows from the ovary, or the flowering part of the plant. But strawberries are different—a difference you can see, especially in the seeds, which are enclosed in seed-like structures, called *achenes*, on the outside of the strawberry flesh rather than within. This is because strawberries are an "aggregate" fruit, or a "false" fruit, meaning the strawberry flesh is derived from the swollen base of the flower, or the receptacle that holds the ovary, and not the ovary itself.

Strawberries are a nonclimacteric fruit, meaning they do not ripen after harvesting. This is why strawberries are picked when they are dark red, at the peak of ripeness. Strawberries contain pockets of air, which weaken the structure of the fruit, causing it to become soft and mushy very easily. Their relatively weak cell structure is an indication that they contain fairly low levels of pectin (the polysaccharide that holds cells together and reinforces the structure and strength of the cell walls) compared with other fruits.

> *"Strawberries and cream" was invented by a cardinal of the Roman Catholic Church in the 1500s.*

This is why strawberries need help in the form of added pectin and sugar when made into a jam (page 276).

Strawberries are known for their sweet taste and their unique fruity, floral aroma. The sweet taste is due to a combination of three sugars: fructose, glucose, and sucrose. The formation of all three sugars occurs during ripening, which is also when the two dominant tart-tasting acids, malic and citric, decrease in concentration.

The strong aroma of strawberries is due to a combination of volatile esters, aldehydes, and ketones. Eleven of these compounds create the characteristic aroma, but two are especially significant. First is a compound called furaneol, or HD3F. It has a strong, sweet, caramel-like aroma, and is also an important contributor to the aroma of pineapple. The second compound is an aldehyde called (Z)-3-hexenal, which contributes a green, fruity scent.

Because it's not always strawberry season, and even when it is we're not always in spots with seasonal strawberries available, we turn to the larger, blander supermarket varieties in our cooking. Because these strawberries are less flavorful, we often macerate them with sugar to release some of their liquid, and concentrate the remaining flavors by cooking the juice down, or mashing or pureeing the remaining flesh. We do both in our Strawberry-Rhubarb Pie (page 273). In our Fresh Strawberry Pie (page 272) we tackle the amount of liquid in the whole, uncooked strawberries by using a combination of thickeners (low-sugar pectin and cornstarch). For our (slightly unconventional) Strawberry Pretzel Salad (page 275), we use strained frozen strawberries to make an intensely strawberry-flavored Jell-O layer. Don't forget our Fresh Strawberry Mousse (page 139).

TEST KITCHEN EXPERIMENT

Pectin can be confusing. Some fruits have lots of it while others are deficient. You can also add it in powdered form from the supermarket, but dumping lots of pectin into a recipe is no guarantee your jelly will set up properly. Even buying it at the store can be fraught. The two most common forms of pectin at the supermarket are high methoxyl (HM) and low methoxyl (LM) pectin, but you won't likely see those terms on the labels. High methoxyl pectin relies on a combination of low pH and high sugar concentration to gel, while low methoxyl pectin gels with low pH and the assistance of added calcium. We wanted to better understand how the two most commonly available forms of commercial pectin—Sure-Jell Pectin (HM) and Sure-Jell for Less or No Sugar Needed Recipes Pectin (LM)—work so that we could make smarter recipe decisions and ultimately better jams and jellies. Specifically, we wanted to find out how sensitive they are to the quantity of sugar in our jam.

EXPERIMENT

For both types of pectin (Sure-Jell Pectin and Sure-Jell For Less or No Sugar Needed Recipes Pectin) we made five batches of a barebones jam recipe with just water, red food coloring, sugar, and pectin (both pectin products contain enough added acidity to drop the pH into the ideal range of 2.8 to 3.5 without added lemon juice). We added varying amounts of sugar to achieve five sugar concentrations: 34, 42, 52, 65, and 79 percent. After allowing all of the jams to cool completely in the refrigerator overnight, we unmolded them and examined their texture.

RESULTS

There were drastic textural differences among the various sugar concentrations for a particular type of pectin as well as between the two types of pectin at the same sugar concentration. The low methoxyl pectin formed varying degrees of gels over the full range of sugar concentrations—34 to 79 percent—while the regular, high methoxyl pectin formed gels only at 52, 65, and 79 percent. At the low end of the spectrum, the high methoxyl pectin failed to thicken at all.

TAKEAWAY

According to Harold McGee in *On Food and Cooking*, pectin gels best when the sugar concentration falls between 60 and 65 percent. In that concentration range, there is sufficient sugar to draw enough water away from the pectin molecules that they are forced to link up with one another into a web-like structure. Our tests support this statement.

Low methoxyl pectins don't require as much sugar because their gelling power is assisted by the presence of calcium (found either in the pectin mix itself, or from another source such as tap water). This makes low methoxyl pectins less dependent on exact sugar quantities. In the test kitchen we often prefer the flavor of jams and jellies with less sugar, so if you only want to keep one type of pectin on hand, we'd recommend choosing a low methoxyl type, as it will yield successful jams and jellies over a much wider range of sugar. That said, it's worth noting tasters did prefer the texture of the 65 percent sugar jelly made with high methoxyl pectin to the one made with low methoxyl pectin. If you often make classic, full-sugar jam recipes (which are around 65 percent sugar), go for a high methoxyl pectin. But there are other options: In our recipe for Classic Strawberry Jam (page 276) we add grated high-pectin Granny Smith apple to naturally augment low-pectin strawberries.

THE RELATIONSHIP BETWEEN PECTINS AND SUGAR

We tested two forms of commercial pectin with varying sugar concentrations. Low-sugar (LM) pectin had a wider margin in which it set. Regular (HM) pectin did not set at 34 and 42 percent sugar.

REGULAR (HM) PECTIN		LOW-SUGAR (LM) PECTIN
	34% SUGAR	
	42% SUGAR	
	52% SUGAR	
	65% SUGAR	
	79% SUGAR	

Technique 101: Water-Bath Canning

Canning is a fantastic way to preserve foods you love, from jams and jellies to all manner of pickles, so that you can enjoy them throughout the year. It may seem intimidating processing sterilized jars of food in hot water, but water-bath canning is in fact quite simple. A boiling-water canner is basically a big pot with a lid and a rack in the bottom. It can usually process up to nine 1-cup jars or 7 quarts. Filled jars are submerged in a pot of boiling water and simmered for a prescribed amount of time. Boiling the filled jars ensures that any contaminants in the jars are killed. During cooking, gases inside the jar expand and escape through the lid. When the jars are removed from the canner and start to cool, the pressure inside the jar is lower than the pressure outside, so the lid is pushed in and sealed. This is what keeps the food fresh and shelf-stable.

LARGE CANNING POT

An 18- to 21-quart canning pot is key for processing the jars. It should be large and deep enough to accomodate a range of jar sizes.

MASON JARS

Glass canning jars are sold with flat metal lids and threaded metal screw bands that hold the lids in place during processing.

JAR LIFTER

This works better than tongs when pulling filled jars out of a water bath because it allows you to grasp the jars firmly.

CANNING INSERT

This insert will fit in the pot to make pulling the jars out of boiling water easy. Often canning pots are sold with a rack, but we prefer the insert, since it makes the canning process simple.

STEEL FUNNEL

A wide-mouth stainless-steel funnel makes pouring liquids, like jams, into jars tidy and easy.

CAN YOU CAN IT?

For preserving purposes, all foods are categorized as either high-acid or low-acid, and their relative acidity determines which heat-processing method to use. High-acid foods with a pH of 4.6 or lower (most fruits, jams, jellies, and pickles) as well as fermented foods (such as sauerkraut and fermented pickles) can be safely heat-processed in boiling water. A boiling-water canner heats food to the boiling point (212 degrees F), a temperature sufficient to kill molds, yeasts, and some bacteria. Bacteria are not easily destroyed. Certain bacteria, especially those found in low-acid foods (with a high pH), actually thrive without air in a moist environment at temperatures that destroy molds and yeasts. Foods that have very little natural acid include vegetables, meats, poultry, seafood, and dairy. All low-acid foods must be processed in a pressure canner, which heats food to 240 degrees F, the temperature required to destroy toxin-producing bacterial spores including *Clostridium botulinum*, which causes botulism, a potentially fatal food-borne illness. Tomatoes (along with figs and mangos) are a special case because they are on the borderline between low-acid and high-acid foods. They need to be acidified for safe canning and require the addition of bottled lemon juice or citric acid to ensure safe water-bath canning. (Because the pH level of fresh lemons can vary, bottled lemon juice is recommended for canning.)

CAN IT?	FRUITS/VEGETABLES
These fruits have pH values (from 2.0 to 4.6) suitable to be safely processed in a water-bath canner.	Apples, Apricots, Blackberries, Blueberries, Cherries, Gooseberries, Grapefruit, Grapes, Lemons, Nectarines, Oranges, Yellow Peaches, Pears, Plums, Raspberries, Rhubarb, Strawberries
These fruits and vegetables have pH values (near or above 4.6) that require added acid (bottled lemon juice or citric acid) to bring their pH to 4.6 or below for safe water-bath processing.	Figs, Mangos, Tomatoes
These low-acid fruits and vegetables must be pickled to lower their pH for safe processing.	Asparagus, Green Beans, Beets, Cabbage, Carrots, Cauliflower, Corn, Cucumbers, Dates, Eggplant, Garlic, Ginger, Okra, Yellow Onions, White Peaches, Bell Peppers, Cherry Peppers, Chile Peppers, Turnips, Watermelon

Fresh Strawberry Pie

✔ WHY THIS RECIPE WORKS

Fresh strawberry pie can be a revelation: This sweet, juicy dessert trades on nothing more than fresh berries, a sheer glaze that just barely holds the fruit together while making it sparkle, and a flaky, buttery crust. Because uncooked berries shed so much liquid (even when left whole), the filling needs to be firmed up with some sort of thickener.

USE TWO THICKENERS We knew that the success of our pie hinged on the thickener. We tried cornstarch, gelatin, and pectin, but none worked on its own, producing a pie that was either way too runny or stiff. To create a filling with just enough sticking power to hold the berries together gently, we turned to a thickener more common in jam than pie—low-sugar (or low methoxyl) pectin—and used it in combination with cornstarch. Both products work similarly: When combined with liquid, then heated and cooled, some of their molecules bond together, trapping water and creating a solid, jelly-like structure. But the strength and properties of the two structures differ. Amylose, one of two types of starch molecules in cornstarch, forms a weak structure that easily comes apart under the weight of heavy, juice-filled strawberries. Low-sugar pectin (which, unlike regular pectin, gels without added sugar and acid) contains bigger molecules that form a firmer structure held together more forcefully by calcium ions. Once created, this matrix resists coming apart. When used independently, neither product resulted in a suitable pie filling, but together they yielded a glaze with just the right texture.

FOOLPROOF DOUGH Most pie crusts are stingy with water. Although scant water makes the dough hard to roll, it prevents too much gluten from forming, which would make the crust tough. We replaced some of the water with vodka. Because vodka is 40 percent ethanol, a liquid in which gluten does not form, the dough stays supple, tender, and easy to roll. Don't worry; your pie will not taste boozy. The alcohol evaporates in the oven.

FRESH STRAWBERRY PIE
SERVES 8

Use Foolproof Single-Crust Pie Shell (recipe follows) for this pie; you will need to bake it ahead of time. To account for any imperfect strawberries, the ingredient list calls for several more ounces of berries than will be used in the pie. If possible, use ripe, farmers' market–quality berries. Make sure to thoroughly dry the berries. Make certain that you use Sure-Jell engineered for low- or no-sugar recipes (packaged in a pink box) and not regular Sure-Jell (in a yellow box); otherwise, the glaze will not set properly. The pie is at its best after 2 or 3 hours of chilling; as it continues to chill, the glaze becomes softer and wetter, though the pie will taste just as good.

3	pounds strawberries, hulled (9 cups)
¾	cup (5¼ ounces) sugar
2	tablespoons cornstarch
1½	teaspoons Sure-Jell for Less or No Sugar Needed Recipes
	Pinch salt
1	tablespoon lemon juice
1	recipe Foolproof Single-Crust Pie Shell (recipe follows), fully baked and cooled

1. Select 6 ounces misshapen, underripe, or otherwise unattractive berries, halving those that are large; you should have about 1½ cups. Process berries in food processor to smooth puree, 20 to 30 seconds, scraping down bowl as needed (you should have about ¾ cup puree).

2. Whisk sugar, cornstarch, Sure-Jell, and salt together in medium saucepan. Stir in berry puree, making sure to scrape corners of pan. Cook over medium-high heat, stirring constantly, and bring to boil. Boil, scraping bottom and sides of pan to prevent scorching, for 2 minutes to ensure that cornstarch is fully cooked (mixture will appear frothy when it first reaches boil, then will darken and thicken with further cooking). Transfer glaze to large bowl and stir in lemon juice; let cool to room temperature.

3. Meanwhile, pick over remaining berries and measure out 2 pounds of most attractive ones; halve only extra-large berries. Add berries to bowl with glaze and fold gently with rubber spatula until berries are evenly coated. Scoop berries into cooled prebaked pie crust, piling into mound. If any cut sides face up on top, turn them face down. If necessary, rearrange berries so that holes are filled and mound looks attractive. Refrigerate pie until filling is chilled and has set, about 2 hours. Serve within 5 hours of chilling.

FOOLPROOF SINGLE-CRUST PIE SHELL
MAKES ENOUGH FOR ONE 9-INCH PIE

Vodka is essential to the tender texture of this crust and imparts no flavor—do not substitute water. This dough is unusually moist and requires a full ¼ cup of flour when rolling it out to prevent it from sticking. A food processor is essential to making this dough—it cannot be made by hand.

- 1¼   cups (6¼ ounces) all-purpose flour
- 1   tablespoon sugar
- ½   teaspoon salt
- 6   tablespoons unsalted butter, cut into ¼-inch pieces and chilled
- 4   tablespoons vegetable shortening, cut into 2 pieces and chilled
- 2   tablespoons vodka, chilled
- 2   tablespoons ice water

1. Process ¾ cup flour, sugar, and salt together in food processor until combined, about 5 seconds. Scatter butter and shortening over top and continue to process until incorporated and mixture begins to form uneven clumps with no remaining floury bits, about 10 seconds.

2. Scrape down bowl and redistribute dough evenly around processor blade. Sprinkle remaining ½ cup flour over dough and pulse until mixture has broken up into pieces and is evenly distributed around bowl, 4 to 6 pulses.

3. Transfer mixture to medium bowl. Sprinkle vodka and ice water over mixture. Stir and press dough together, using stiff rubber spatula, until dough sticks together.

4. Turn dough onto sheet of plastic wrap and flatten into 4-inch disk. Wrap tightly in plastic and refrigerate for 1 hour. Before rolling dough out, let it sit on counter to soften slightly, about 10 minutes. (Dough can be wrapped tightly in plastic and refrigerated for up to 2 days or frozen for up to 1 month. If frozen, let dough thaw completely on counter before rolling it out.)

5. Adjust oven rack to middle position and heat oven to 425 degrees. Roll dough into 12-inch circle on floured counter. Loosely roll dough around rolling pin and gently unroll it onto 9-inch pie plate, letting excess dough hang over edge. Ease dough into plate by gently lifting edge of dough with your hand while pressing into plate bottom with your other hand. Leave any dough that overhangs plate in place. Wrap dough-lined pie plate loosely in plastic and refrigerate until dough is firm, about 30 minutes.

6. Trim overhang to ½ inch beyond lip of pie plate. Tuck overhang under itself; folded edge should be flush with edge of pie plate. Crimp dough evenly around edge of pie using your fingers. Wrap dough-lined pie plate loosely in plastic and refrigerate until dough is fully chilled and firm, about 15 minutes, before using.

7. Line chilled pie shell with parchment paper or double layer of aluminum foil, covering edges to prevent burning, and fill with pie weights.

8. Bake until pie dough looks dry and is pale in color, about 15 minutes. Remove weights and foil and continue to bake crust until deep golden brown, 8 to 12 minutes longer. Transfer pie plate to wire rack and let crust cool completely, about 1 hour.

Strawberry-Rhubarb Pie

✔ WHY THIS RECIPE WORKS
American cooks have been pairing strawberries and rhubarb for a very long time, which might make you think they're a good match, but they're not. The trouble lies not in their differences—fruit and vegetable, sweet and sour—but in a similarity: Both are loaded with water (92 and 95 percent water by weight, respectively). When the two are enclosed in pastry and baked, that water heats up and causes both to soften dramatically, albeit differently: Rhubarb often blows out, releasing all that moisture into the filling and collapsing into mush, while strawberries remain intact but become bloated. We wanted to bring together delicately sweet strawberries and bracingly tart rhubarb in a bright-tasting filling that gelled softly and contained plenty of intact fruit and vegetable pieces.

MACERATE AND DRAIN To rid the rhubarb of some water, we tossed the cut-up pieces with sugar (which helped draw out moisture) and briefly microwaved them. Resting the sugared rhubarb for 30 minutes drew out even more moisture that we then drained off. We further minimized the juices by reducing the shed liquid with the rest of the berries until the mixture turned jammy. This solved the problem of bloated strawberries, as, cooked down, they gave the syrup more body and an extra boost of fruity flavor, while also giving up some of their own moisture. We gave strawberries their own presence in the pie by macerating some cut-up berries along with the rhubarb.

FINISH STRONG The filling tasted bright and pleasantly tart, so we thought that an extra burst of sugar on the top crust would be a subtle way to add contrasting sweetness, not to mention a hint of crystalline crunch against the soft filling. But when we sprinkled any more than a couple of teaspoons of sugar onto the pastry before baking, most of the granules didn't stick. The solution? Water. Lots of it. We topped our double-crust pie with a generous amount of water and sugar, which baked to a crackly finish. That heavy coat of sugar worked its hygroscopic magic once again: The ample amount of water allowed the sugar granules to dissolve and then dry into a glassy candy-like shell.

STRAWBERRY-RHUBARB PIE
SERVES 8

This dough is unusually moist and requires a full ¼ cup of flour when rolling it out to prevent it from sticking. Rhubarb varies in the amount of trimming required. Buy 2 pounds to ensure that you end up with 7 cups of rhubarb pieces. If desired, serve the pie with whipped cream or ice cream.

CRUST
- 2½ cups (12½ ounces) all-purpose flour
- 2 tablespoons sugar, plus 3 tablespoons for sprinkling
- 1 teaspoon salt
- 12 tablespoons unsalted butter, cut into ¼-inch slices and chilled
- ½ cup vegetable shortening, cut into 4 pieces and chilled
- ¼ cup vodka, chilled
- ¼ cup cold water, plus extra for brushing

FILLING
- 2 pounds rhubarb, trimmed and cut into ½-inch pieces (7 cups)
- 1¼ cups (8¾ ounces) sugar
- 1 pound strawberries, hulled, halved if less than 1 inch, quartered if more than 1 inch (3 to 4 cups)
- 3 tablespoons instant tapioca

1. FOR THE CRUST: Process 1½ cups flour, 2 tablespoons sugar, and salt in food processor until combined, about 5 seconds. Scatter butter and shortening over top and process until incorporated and mixture begins to form uneven clumps with no remaining floury bits, about 15 seconds.

2. Scrape down sides of bowl and redistribute dough evenly around processor blade. Sprinkle remaining 1 cup flour over dough and pulse until mixture has broken up into pieces and is evenly distributed around bowl, 4 to 6 pulses.

3. Transfer mixture to large bowl. Sprinkle vodka and cold water over mixture. Using rubber spatula, stir and press dough until it sticks together.

4. Divide dough in half. Turn each half onto sheet of plastic wrap and form into 4-inch disk. Wrap disks tightly in plastic and refrigerate for 1 hour. Let chilled dough sit on counter to soften slightly, about 10 minutes, before rolling. (Wrapped dough can be refrigerated for up to 2 days or frozen for up to 1 month. If frozen, let dough thaw completely on counter before rolling.)

5. FOR THE FILLING: While dough chills, combine rhubarb and sugar in bowl and microwave for 1½ minutes. Stir and continue to microwave until sugar is mostly dissolved, about 1 minute longer. Stir in 1 cup strawberries and set aside for 30 minutes, stirring once halfway through.

6. Drain rhubarb mixture in fine-mesh strainer set over large saucepan. Return drained rhubarb mixture to bowl and set aside. Add remaining strawberries to rhubarb liquid and cook over medium-high heat until strawberries are very soft and mixture is reduced to 1½ cups, about 10 to 15 minutes. Mash berries with fork (mixture does not have to be smooth). Add strawberry mixture and tapioca to drained rhubarb mixture and stir to combine. Set aside.

7. Roll 1 disk of dough into 12-inch circle on well-floured counter. Loosely roll dough around rolling pin and gently unroll onto 9-inch pie plate, letting excess dough hang over edge. Ease dough into plate by gently lifting edge of dough with your hand while pressing into plate bottom with your other hand. Wrap dough-lined plate loosely in plastic and refrigerate until dough is firm, about 30 minutes.

8. Roll other disk of dough into 12-inch circle on well-floured counter, then transfer to parchment paper–lined baking sheet; cover with plastic and refrigerate for 30 minutes. Adjust rack to middle position and heat oven to 425 degrees.

9. Transfer filling to chilled dough-lined plate and spread into even layer. Loosely roll remaining dough round around rolling pin and gently unroll it onto filling. Trim overhang to ½ inch beyond lip of plate. Pinch edges of top and bottom crusts firmly together. Tuck overhang under itself; folded edge should be flush with edge of plate. Crimp dough evenly around edge of plate using your fingers or butter knife. Brush surface thoroughly with extra water and sprinkle with 3 tablespoons sugar. Cut eight 2-inch slits in top crust.

10. Place pie on parchment-lined rimmed baking sheet and bake until crust is set and begins to brown, about 25 minutes. Rotate pie and reduce oven temperature to 375 degrees; continue to bake until crust is deep golden brown and filling is bubbling, 30 to 40 minutes longer. If edges of pie begin to get too brown before pie is done, cover loosely with aluminum foil. Let cool on wire rack for 2½ hours before serving.

Strawberry Pretzel Salad

✔ WHY THIS RECIPE WORKS

In the Midwest, an unlikely yet beloved dish holds a place of honor at backyard barbecues, potlucks, and holiday dinners: the pretzel salad. A baking pan is filled with a mix of crushed pretzels, sugar, and melted butter and baked into a crust; then it is spread with a combination of sweetened cream cheese and whipped topping; and then it is covered with a layer of strawberry Jell-O mixed with syrupy berries. You might think this is for dessert, but it's actually eaten for dinner. Confused? So were many of us in the test kitchen. Until we tasted it.

START WITH THE CRUST Many crusts were way too crumbly when we began testing this recipe. But that was an easy fix. It was simply a matter of using pretzel sticks instead of classically shaped pretzels. The sticks crushed evenly, making for a sturdier crust.

USE CREAM Next up, we replaced the traditional Cool Whip with homemade whipped cream. We folded it into cream cheese that we'd beaten with sugar in a stand mixer. While this worked, it was too fussy. We tried slowly pouring the cream into the mixer with the cream cheese and sugar instead of whipping it separately. To our surprise, the mixture whipped up fine.

USE FROZEN STRAWBERRIES For the gelatin layer, we hoped to ditch the artificially flavored boxed Jell-O and overly sweet frozen berries in syrup and pack in as much real strawberry flavor as we could. To do so, we'd make homemade Jell-O. After some experimentation, we had our game plan: Puree berries, strain to extract strawberry juice, heat liquid with sugar, and thicken with gelatin. By the time we were done, we were whizzing 2 entire pounds of frozen (for year-round consistency), thawed berries in the food processor and setting things to a relaxed wiggle with just 4½ teaspoons of gelatin. Instead of the strawberries in syrup, we folded in another full pound of sliced berries. The result? An intense strawberry flavor.

STRAWBERRY PRETZEL SALAD

SERVES 10 TO 12

For a sturdier crust, use (thinner) pretzel sticks not (fatter) rods. Thaw the strawberries in the refrigerator the night before you begin the recipe. You'll puree 2 pounds of the strawberries and slice the remaining 1 pound.

6½	ounces pretzel sticks
2¼	cups (15¾ ounces) sugar
12	tablespoons unsalted butter, melted and cooled
8	ounces cream cheese
1	cup heavy cream
3	pounds (10½ cups) frozen strawberries, thawed
¼	teaspoon salt
4½	teaspoons unflavored gelatin
½	cup cold water

1. Adjust oven rack to middle position and heat oven to 400 degrees. Spray 13 by 9-inch baking pan with vegetable oil spray. Pulse pretzels and ¼ cup sugar in food processor until coarsely ground, about 15 pulses. Add melted butter and pulse until combined, about 10 pulses. Transfer pretzel mixture to prepared pan. Using bottom of measuring cup, press crumbs into bottom of pan. Bake until crust is fragrant and beginning to brown, about 10 minutes, rotating pan halfway through baking. Set aside crust, letting it cool slightly, about 20 minutes.

2. Using stand mixer fitted with whisk, whip cream cheese and ½ cup sugar on medium speed until light and fluffy, about 2 minutes. Increase speed to medium-high and, with mixer still running, slowly add cream in steady stream. Continue to whip until soft peaks form, scraping down bowl as needed, about 1 minute longer. Spread whipped cream cheese mixture evenly over cooled crust. Refrigerate until set, about 30 minutes.

3. Meanwhile, process 2 pounds strawberries in now-empty food processor until pureed, about 30 seconds. Strain mixture through fine-mesh strainer set over medium saucepan, using underside of small ladle to push puree through strainer. Add remaining 1½ cups sugar and salt to strawberry puree in saucepan and cook over medium-high heat, whisking occasionally, until bubbles begin to appear around sides of pan and sugar is dissolved, about 5 minutes; remove from heat.

4. Sprinkle gelatin over water in large bowl and let sit until gelatin softens, about 5 minutes. Whisk strawberry puree into gelatin. Slice remaining strawberries and stir into strawberry-gelatin mixture. Refrigerate until gelatin thickens slightly and starts to cling to sides of bowl, about 30 minutes. Carefully pour gelatin mixture evenly over whipped cream cheese layer. Refrigerate salad until gelatin is fully set, at least 4 hours or up to 24 hours. Serve.

Classic Strawberry Jam

✔ WHY THIS RECIPE WORKS

Strawberry jam is a universal favorite. But because strawberries are naturally low in pectin, a carbohydrate found in some fruits (and extracted into a powder you can buy) that helps jam keep its structure, we needed to find the right mix of acidity, sugar, and other means of procuring pectin to end up with the jam we wanted.

ADD NATURAL PECTIN Naturally low in pectin, strawberries are often cooked too long in order to concentrate the pectin, causing the fruit to lose its bright flavor. We shortened the cooking time by cutting the strawberries into pieces and mashing them to release their juices and jump-start the cooking process. Apples are naturally higher in pectin. We found that adding shredded apple gave our jam enough natural pectin plus some good fresh flavor.

USE LEMON Lemon juice added acidity to balance the sugar's sweetness. Acidity also plays a key role in the gelling abilities of pectin; without a consistent pH it can be difficult to predict how a jam or jelly will set. Fresh lemon juice has too much variation from lemon to lemon to consistently predict how much it will increase the acidity of a given preserve; bottled lemon juice, however, has a tightly controlled pH that is always consistent no matter the time of year or variety used. Citric acid can also be used to ensure acidity, but we found bottled lemon juice easier to find and more likely to be already on hand.

CLASSIC STRAWBERRY JAM
MAKES FOUR 1-CUP JARS

Small, fragrant berries produce the best jam. Do not try to make a double batch of this jam in a large pot; it will not work. Rather, make two single batches in separate pots.

3 pounds strawberries, hulled and cut into ½-inch pieces (10 cups)
3 cups sugar
1¼ cups peeled and shredded Granny Smith apple (1 large apple)
2 tablespoons bottled lemon juice

1. Place 2 small plates in freezer to chill. Set canning rack in large pot, place four 1-cup jars in rack, and add water to cover by 1 inch. Bring to simmer over medium heat, then turn off heat and cover to keep hot.

2. In Dutch oven, crush strawberries with potato masher until fruit is mostly broken down. Stir in sugar, apple, and lemon juice and bring to boil, stirring often, over medium-high heat. Once sugar is completely dissolved, boil mixture, stirring and adjusting heat as needed, until thickened and registers 217 to 220 degrees, 20 to 25 minutes. (Temperature will be lower at higher elevations; see Practical Science, page 283.) Remove pot from heat.

3. To test consistency, place 1 teaspoon jam on chilled plate and freeze for 2 minutes. Drag your finger through jam on plate; jam has correct consistency when your finger leaves distinct trail. If runny, return pot to heat and simmer for 1 to 3 minutes longer before retesting. Skim any foam from surface of jam using spoon.

4. Place dish towel flat on counter. Using jar lifter, remove jars from pot, draining water back into pot. Place jars upside down on towel and let dry for 1 minute. Using funnel and ladle, portion hot jam into hot jars, leaving ¼ inch headspace. Slide wooden skewer along inside edge of jar and drag upward to remove air bubbles.

5A. FOR SHORT-TERM STORAGE: Let jam cool to room temperature, cover, and refrigerate until jam is set, 12 to 24 hours. (Jam can be refrigerated for up to 2 months.)

5B. FOR LONG-TERM STORAGE: While jars are hot, wipe rims clean, add lids, and screw on rings until fingertip-tight; do not overtighten. Return pot of water with canning rack to boil. Lower jars into water, cover, bring water back to boil, then start timer. Cooking time will depend on your altitude: Boil 10 minutes for up to 1,000 feet, 15 minutes for 1,001 to 3,000 feet, 20 minutes for 3,001 to 6,000 feet, or 25 minutes for 6,001 to 8,000 feet. Turn off heat and let jars sit in pot for 5 minutes. Remove jars from pot and let cool for 24 hours. Remove rings, check seal, and clean rims. (Sealed jars can be stored for up to 1 year.)

CHAPTER 34

Oranges

The secret to cooking with oranges? Use the peel.

HOW THE SCIENCE WORKS

Oranges. We drink their juice. We candy their peels. We eat them sliced into wedges. We cook with oranges, too, adding them to everything from Chinese-style beef to pound cake. But when it comes to cooking, the flavor of orange juice can be fleeting. This is why we use the whole fruit.

The name of this fruit does not refer to its color—the word "orange" comes from the ancient Tamil word *naru*, which means "fragrant." Oranges belong to a large family of flowering plants botanically named *Rutaceae*, within the genus *Citrus*, which also includes grapefruits, lemons, limes, citron, and pomelos. Oranges are divided into two kinds: sweet (*Citrus sinensis*) and sour (*Citrus aurantium*). Seventy percent of the varieties grown today are sweet.

Like all citrus fruits, oranges are nonclimacteric, meaning they will not continue to ripen following harvest. Nearly all commercial oranges are harvested at the mature stage, when they are pale orange in color, still containing patches of green. (Most are treated with a small amount of ethylene gas in order for them to develop their bright orange color. Some are even dyed orange.)

The most popular varieties of sweet oranges include the seedless thick-skinned navel orange, thin-skinned juice oranges such as Valencia, and blood oranges. Blood oranges owe their distinctive purple-red color to anthocyanin pigments, while the orange color of all varieties is created by the presence of many different carotenoid pigments, such as beta-carotene and lycopene, as well as some very unusual ones named cryptoxanthin, cryptoflavin, and violaxanthin. Sour oranges contain higher levels of sour-tasting citric acid and bitter flavonoids, such as neohesperidin. In contrast to sweet oranges, sour oranges also contain higher levels of

Oranges contain a good deal of the amino acid glutamate, a key source of umami.

pectin, which is why they are often used to make a marmalade that includes their pectin-rich peel (page 283).

The flavor of oranges comes, in part, from the volatile aroma compounds found in both the juice and the oils of the skin, including a complex mixture of aldehydes, esters, ketones, alcohols, and hydrocarbons called terpenes. The majority of these volatile aroma compounds are easily lost with the heat of cooking, which is why orange or lemon zest are usually added toward the end of the cooking process.

It may come as a surprise: Oranges contain a relatively high amount of the amino acid glutamate (between 60 and 90 milligrams per 100 grams of edible portion), which is the key ingredient in the savory taste called umami. When glutamates are combined with sources of nucleotides, such as meat, poultry, shrimp, anchovies, and shiitake mushrooms, they enhance umami by as much as 20 times that of glutamate alone. (Grapefruits contain even more: around 246 milligrams of glutamate per 100 grams, which is similar to the amount of glutamate in tomatoes.) We maximize the flavor of glutamates by pairing oranges with beef in our Crispy Orange Beef (page 280).

We love to eat oranges—and all citrus, really, straight up (like we do in our Citrus Salads, page 282), but when it comes to cooking, we tend to focus on maximizing the flavor of the peel, which contains flavors that are not as volatile as those in the juice. We use pith and zest in our Crispy Orange Beef to add some more-complex bitter notes to the dish. In our Orange Bundt Cake (page 281), we use zest, fresh juice, and orange juice concentrate to get the most possible orange flavor into each bite. But, of course, you can always just squeeze them and drink the juice alone.

TEST KITCHEN EXPERIMENT

We love eating and cooking with fresh oranges, but the fact of the matter is that most of the orange juice we consume comes out of a bottle from the supermarket. We designed the following experiment to find out which brands taste best, and why.

EXPERIMENT

We blind-tasted seven brands of store-bought orange juice, including two frozen brands. We rated them on freshness, sweetness, acidity, and overall appeal. We sent samples of each to an independent lab to assess levels of ethyl butyrate, a compound that occurs naturally in oranges and that is added back to most commercial orange juice to make its flavor seem fresher, as well as Brix (sugar content) and acidity percentages.

RESULTS

Interestingly, all brands featured similar levels of both sugar and acidity: Sugar ranged from 11.6 percent to 12.7 percent and acidity (from citric acid) from 0.64 percent to 0.71 percent. Flavor, however, varied greatly. Three of the juices that were ranked highest for fresh flavor by our tasters—Minute Maid Pure Squeeze Never from Concentrate Pasteurized 100% Orange Juice, Simply Orange Not from Concentrate Pasteurized 100% Orange Juice, and Florida's Natural 100% Pure Florida Orange Juice—contained relatively high levels of ethyl butyrate (as high as 4.92 mg per liter). The top-ranked juice, Natalie's 100% Florida Orange Juice, Gourmet Pasteurized, contained only 1.01 mg per liter of ethyl butyrate but nonetheless tasted "superfresh."

TAKEAWAY

Because different varieties of oranges are in season at different times, most manufacturers squeeze the juice immediately and store it for months to maintain a year-round supply of particular varieties. To keep the juice from turning rancid, most companies strip away the juice's oxygen and store it in million-gallon tanks topped with a layer of nitrogen. But stripping the oxygen out of juice also strips out the juice's flavor-providing compounds. That's where blend technicians come in: Their jobs involve restoring flavor to the juice through the addition of "flavor packs." These highly engineered additives are made from essential orange flavor volatiles that have been harvested from the fruit and its skin and then chemically reassembled by scientists at leading fragrance companies. Fresh orange juice flavor is one of the toughest to imitate because none of the compounds that contribute to the orange's aroma individually smell of orange. To recoup fresh flavor, juice makers include ethyl butyrate in the flavor packs. This compound isn't an artificial flavor: It occurs naturally in fresh-squeezed orange juice as an aroma, but because it's volatile, much of it is driven off during processing. Adding more ethyl butyrate to the juice actually restores the impression of freshness. So why did our top choice, Natalie's 100% Florida Orange Juice, not have a high level of ethyl butyrate? Because it's never doctored: Natalie's squeezes its juice within 24 hours of shipping and doesn't manipulate its flavor. Natalie's exhibited a level of ethyl butyrate consistent with fresh fruit, and a complex flavor to boot.

WHICH ORANGE JUICE IS BEST?

Our favorite juice, Natalie's 100% Florida Orange Juice, tasted the freshest without any added "fresh" flavor in the form of ethyl butyrate.

VS.

TRULY FRESH
Just juice.

NOT SO FRESH
Many had high levels of ethyl butyrate, a natural compound often added to mimic a fresher flavor.

FOCUS ON: ORANGES

Sweet, tart, and high in vitamin C, citrus fruits are a favorite across the globe. Oranges are some of the most common citrus, especially in the U.S. Here, we take a closer look at their anatomy.

ALBEDO (OR PITH)

The edible portion is protected by a spongy white layer called the albedo, where most of the pectin and bitter flavonoids are found.

SEEDS

Common navel oranges are seedless (and therefore a favorite for eating), but other varieties do contain small white seeds throughout the fruit.

JUICE

The edible portion of oranges is composed of numerous individual segments, each containing hundreds of elongated vesicles filled with juice cells full of liquid.

ZEST

Oranges are covered by a skin containing numerous tiny glands that secrete and store the fragrant orange oils. Unlike the water-soluble acids and sugars in the juice, these oils are water-insoluble but are capable of adding significant orange flavor to an emulsified sauce.

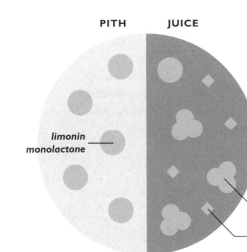

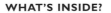

PITH   JUICE

limonin monolactone

limonin

acid molecule

WHY ORANGE JUICE CAN TURN BITTER

A complex non-bitter compound called limonin monolactone is present in the albedo. When liquid is extracted from the orange, however, some of this compound may be transferred to the juice. There, it is hydrolyzed by the acid present to become a very bitter compound called limonin. This is why fresh sweet orange juice can quickly become bitter.

JUICE IT

A good juicer should extract maximum juice with minimum mess. We compared several styles of juicing tools. Styles include simple stick-like reamers, squeeze-style juice presses, and reamers with built-in strainers and collecting cups. We preferred the latter style, especially when paired with an electric motor. Our favorite is the Dash Go Dual Citrus Juicer. It's cheap, light, and easy to clean, with a screen for adjusting pulp levels and a quiet motor that won't wake late sleepers.

WHAT'S INSIDE?

The edible portion of oranges contains about 89 percent by weight water and from 8.0 to 9.5 percent sugars made up of about 3.4 percent sucrose, 2.4 percent glucose, and 2.4 percent fructose. In addition to sweet sugars and sour citric and malic acids, the juice contains many different volatile aroma compounds that contribute to flavor. (The same variety of oranges grown in California and Florida differ in their juiciness, color, and texture because of differences in soil and climate—another example of *terroir*.)

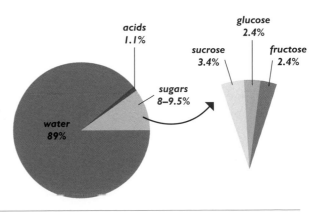

acids
1.1%

glucose
2.4%

sucrose
3.4%

fructose
2.4%

sugars
8–9.5%

water
89%

Crispy Orange Beef

✓ WHY THIS RECIPE WORKS

Most versions of this Chinese restaurant standard are better dubbed "Soggy Orange Beef." We wanted truly crispy strips of beef doused in a sweet, savory, tangy citrus sauce.

DRY YOUR MEAT In order to achieve a perfectly crisp coating, we needed to dry the surface of the meat as much as possible. To start, we simplified the coating, replacing the traditional multi-ingredient batter with only a dredge in cornstarch. Cornstarch absorbed the excess surface moisture. To supplement the drying effect of the cornstarch, we put the coated pieces of meat in the freezer for 45 minutes to remove even more surface moisture, guaranteeing that the crisp coating wouldn't have any competition.

CUT BACK THE OIL While frying beef in vats of oil may work for restaurants, it's not practical for the home cook. We made our recipe work with only 3 cups of oil by cooking the beef in three batches. To prevent the pieces of meat from folding over and sticking together in the oil, we cut them into matchsticks.

BROWN THE ORANGE Traditionally, this dish gets its pungent depth from dried tangerine peels, a difficult ingredient to find in most grocery stores. To imitate the flavor profile, we used pieces of more readily available orange peels. Keeping some of the pith on the peels added a subtle bitterness, and browning them in oil introduced deeper, caramelized notes to the sauce. We further enhanced the orange flavor with freshly squeezed orange juice.

PRACTICAL SCIENCE STORING ORANGES

Keep them in the refrigerator.

Unlike bananas or peaches, which ripen at room temperature, citrus fruits stop ripening the moment they are picked, thus beginning a slow and steady decline in texture and flavor. To improve their shelf life, commercially grown citrus are buffed with a thin layer of food-safe wax that prevents moisture from escaping through the fruits' porous rind. To test how well the wax coating works, we bought lemons, limes, and oranges and stored half in the refrigerator and half at room temperature. The fruit that was refrigerated remained firm and juicy for about three weeks, while citrus that was left at room temperature began to discolor and dehydrate in as little as five days. Ultimately, the only downside to storing citrus in the fridge is that it's more difficult to squeeze juice from a cold citrus fruit. To make life easier, let your citrus sit at room temperature for about 15 minutes before juicing.

CRISPY ORANGE BEEF
SERVES 4

Use a vegetable peeler on the oranges and make sure that your strips contain some pith. Do not use low-sodium soy sauce. Serve this dish with steamed rice.

1½ pounds beef flap meat, trimmed
3 tablespoons soy sauce
6 tablespoons cornstarch
10 (3-inch) strips orange peel, sliced thin lengthwise (¼ cup), plus ¼ cup juice (2 oranges)
3 tablespoons molasses
2 tablespoons dry sherry
1 tablespoon rice vinegar
1½ teaspoons toasted sesame oil
3 cups vegetable oil
1 jalapeño chile, stemmed, seeded, and sliced thin lengthwise
2 tablespoons grated fresh ginger
3 garlic cloves, minced
½ teaspoon red pepper flakes
2 scallions, sliced thin on bias

1. Cut beef along grain into 2½- to 3-inch-wide lengths. Slice each piece against grain into ½-inch-wide slices. Cut each slice lengthwise into ½-inch-thick strips. Toss beef with 1 tablespoon soy sauce in bowl. Add cornstarch and toss until evenly coated. Spread beef in single layer on wire rack set in rimmed baking sheet. Transfer sheet to freezer until meat is very firm but not completely frozen, about 45 minutes.

2. Whisk orange juice, molasses, sherry, vinegar, sesame oil, and remaining 2 tablespoons soy sauce together in bowl.

3. Line second rimmed baking sheet with triple layer of paper towels. Heat vegetable oil in large Dutch oven over medium heat until oil registers 375 degrees. Carefully add one-third of beef and fry, stirring occasionally to keep beef from sticking together, until golden brown, about 1½ minutes. Using spider, transfer meat to paper towel–lined sheet. Return oil to 375 degrees and repeat twice more with remaining beef. After frying, reserve 2 tablespoons frying oil.

4. Heat reserved oil in 12-inch skillet over medium-high heat until shimmering. Add orange peel and jalapeño and

cook, stirring occasionally, until about half of orange peel is golden brown, 1½ to 2 minutes. Add ginger, garlic, and pepper flakes; cook, stirring frequently, until garlic is beginning to brown, about 45 seconds. Add soy sauce mixture and cook, scraping up any browned bits, until slightly thickened, about 45 seconds. Add beef and scallions and toss. Transfer to platter and serve immediately.

Orange Bundt Cake

✓ WHY THIS RECIPE WORKS

An orange Bundt cake should be moist, rich, and tender. While the correct texture is relatively easy to achieve, developing assertive orange flavor is more of a challenge. All citrus dulls when baked, but while a lemon is tart and bright—thanks to its high acidity— the mild flavor of an orange is especially fleeting. We armed ourselves with a crate of Florida's finest and headed to the test kitchen to create an orange Bundt cake that tasted like it was straight from the grove.

USE ZEST AND JUICE We started with a basic recipe that used added fresh orange zest for the orange flavor. And the zest did produce a fair amount of orange flavor, but it was one-dimensional and flat. We wondered if any other orange ingredients might help. We baked cakes with powdered Tang, orange juice concentrate, orange extract, and orange oil. The cakes made with Tang and juice concentrate were sickeningly sweet, with weak orange flavor, while the cakes made with extract and oil tasted like furniture polish. We returned our attention to fresh oranges— but this time, to their juice. Bundt cake recipes typically call for about a cup of dairy, usually milk or buttermilk. We wondered if we could replace the dairy with fresh orange juice. We made a cake with each of the three liquids. It was clear that the juice lent a mellow orange background flavor to the more astringent and perfumed zest, whereas the cakes made with milk and buttermilk seemed bland.

ORANGE GLAZE For more orange flavor, we made a thin confectioners' sugar glaze that easily absorbed into the hot cake, then added more confectioners' sugar to the mixture to thicken it for an eye-catching glaze. We had been using a mixture of orange juice, lemon juice (for brightness), and confectioners' sugar in the glaze, but replacing the orange juice with undiluted orange juice concentrate provided an extra punch of flavor. A dusting of granulated sugar flavored with orange zest lent a final burst of flavor and delicate crunch to our cake.

ORANGE BUNDT CAKE
SERVES 12

When grating orange zest, remove just the outer orange part of the peel, as the inner white part is very bitter. You should be able to get enough zest for both the cake and the orange sugar topping from the two oranges.

CAKE
4	large eggs, room temperature
2	tablespoons finely grated orange zest plus ¾ cup juice (2 oranges)
1	teaspoon vanilla extract
2½	cups (12½ ounces) all-purpose flour
2	cups (14 ounces) granulated sugar
1	teaspoon salt
1	teaspoon baking powder
½	teaspoon baking soda
18	tablespoons (2¼ sticks) unsalted butter, cut into 18 pieces and softened

GLAZE AND ORANGE SUGAR
2	cups (8 ounces) confectioners' sugar
½	cup frozen orange juice concentrate, thawed
4	teaspoons lemon juice
	Pinch salt
3	tablespoons granulated sugar
1½	teaspoons grated orange zest

1. FOR THE CAKE: Adjust oven rack to middle position and heat oven to 350 degrees. Grease and flour 12-cup nonstick Bundt pan. Whisk eggs, orange zest and juice, and vanilla together in medium bowl.

2. Using stand mixer fitted with paddle, mix flour, sugar, salt, baking powder, and baking soda on low speed until combined. Add butter, 1 piece at a time, and mix until only pea-size pieces remain, about 1 minute. Add egg mixture in steady stream. Scrape down bowl, increase speed to medium-high, and beat until light and fluffy, about 2 minutes (batter may look slightly curdled). Give batter final stir by hand.

3. Pour batter into prepared pan and smooth top with rubber spatula. Bake until skewer inserted in center comes out clean, 45 to 55 minutes.

4. FOR THE GLAZE AND ORANGE SUGAR: While cake bakes, whisk 1½ cups confectioners' sugar, orange juice concentrate, lemon juice, and salt together in bowl until smooth. Let cake cool in pan on wire rack for 20 minutes, remove cake from pan, and transfer to wire rack set in rimmed baking sheet. Brush cake with ¼ cup glaze and let stand until just warm, about 1 hour. Whisk remaining ½ cup confectioners' sugar into remaining glaze and pour evenly over top of cake. Using fork, mix granulated sugar and orange zest together in small bowl and sprinkle over glaze. Let cake cool completely, about 2 hours. (Cooled cake can be wrapped tightly in plastic wrap and kept at room temperature for up to 3 days.)

Citrus Salads

✔ WHY THIS RECIPE WORKS

Call it fate: Smack in the middle of the coldest part of the year, just as the hefty braises of winter begin to pall on us, citrus season begins, swooping in with brilliant hues and bracing flavors. But we rarely take full advantage, usually limiting ourselves to eating oranges out of hand and grapefruits only at breakfast. A more impressive setting for these seasonal fruits is a salad, and savory versions—augmented with crisp greens, crunchy nuts, and dried fruit—provide a particularly nice context. We set to work.

SLICE 'EM For maximum color, we decided to use both red grapefruits and navel oranges, the latter of which could easily be switched out for other varieties like blood oranges or tangelos. Painstakingly trimming the citrus into slim, membrane-free segments (or supremes) was too time-consuming, and simply dicing the flesh into chunks left diners contending with large, chewy pieces of membrane. We compromised and sliced the halved, peeled fruit into delicate half-moons that were easy on the eye—and on the teeth.

TONE IT DOWN But when we dressed the citrus with a simple vinaigrette and tossed it with the other components, the results were disheartening. The assertive grapefruits overpowered even these hearty flavors, and the heavier ingredients sank to the bottom of the bowl while the dressed greens sat irrelevantly on top. To temper the grapefruits' sourness, we seasoned them with a bit of sugar and also salt, a trick we use to tone down bitterness in foods like eggplant and coffee. Rather than attempt to defy gravity's influence on the weighty fruit and nuts, we embraced it by composing the salad instead of tossing it: We arranged the citrus slices on a platter and layered the remaining salad ingredients on top.

DRAIN AND SERVE To remove excess liquid, we treated both the sliced grapefruits and oranges with salt, let their tangy juices drain off, and reserved them before plating the citrus. Since the olive oil had caused the watercress to droop, we drizzled it over the citrus instead, tossing the greens only with mustard, shallot, and some reserved juice instead of the vinegar. We mixed half of the nuts and cranberries into the greens and sprinkled the remainder on top.

CITRUS SALAD WITH WATERCRESS, DRIED CRANBERRIES, AND PECANS
SERVES 4 TO 6

You may substitute tangelos or Cara Caras for the navel oranges. Valencia and blood oranges can also be used, but since they are smaller, increase the number of fruit to four.

- 2 red grapefruits
- 3 navel oranges
- 1 teaspoon sugar
- Salt and pepper
- 1 teaspoon unsalted butter
- ½ cup pecans, chopped coarse
- 3 tablespoons extra-virgin olive oil
- 1 small shallot, minced
- 1 teaspoon Dijon mustard
- 4 ounces (4 cups) watercress, torn into bite-size pieces
- ⅔ cup dried cranberries

1. Cut away peel and pith from grapefruits and oranges. Cut each fruit in half from pole to pole, then slice crosswise into ¼-inch-thick pieces. Transfer fruit to bowl and toss with sugar and ½ teaspoon salt. Set aside for 15 minutes.

2. Melt butter in 8-inch skillet over medium heat. Add pecans and ½ teaspoon salt and cook, stirring often, until lightly browned and fragrant, 2 to 4 minutes. Transfer pecans to paper towel–lined plate and set aside.

3. Drain fruit in colander, reserving 2 tablespoons juice. Transfer fruit to platter, arrange in even layer, and drizzle with oil. Whisk reserved juice, shallot, and mustard in medium bowl. Add watercress, ⅓ cup cranberries, and ¼ cup pecans and toss to coat. Arrange watercress mixture over fruit, leaving 1-inch border around edges. Sprinkle with remaining ⅓ cup cranberries and remaining ¼ cup pecans. Season with salt and pepper to taste. Serve immediately.

CITRUS SALAD WITH ARUGULA, GOLDEN RAISINS, AND WALNUTS

Substitute coarsely chopped walnuts for pecans, arugula for watercress, and ½ cup golden raisins for cranberries.

CITRUS SALAD WITH RADICCHIO, DATES, AND SMOKED ALMONDS

Substitute coarsely chopped smoked almonds for pecans, omitting butter and step 2. Substitute 1 small head radicchio, halved, cored, and sliced ¼ inch thick, for watercress, and chopped pitted dates for cranberries.

Seville Orange Marmalade

✓ WHY THIS RECIPE WORKS

Marmalade is commonly defined as a fruit preserve that includes pieces of rind in the jelly base. Although historically made from quinces ("marmalade" comes from the Portuguese word marmalada, meaning "quince jam"), most marmalade today is made from citrus fruits, especially oranges. Because of the sour tang derived from both the rind and the flesh of the Seville oranges customarily used as the base fruit, good orange marmalade should have a complexity and depth not associated with sweeter jams and jellies. With its thick, difficult-to-peel skin and its bitter, seed-ridden interior, the highly aromatic Seville orange, also known as bitter orange or sour orange, is unattractive as a table fruit but perfect for making intensely flavored, pleasantly tart marmalade. We tested several methods of preparing the fruit, and we found that the simplest method—simmering the fruit whole in a tightly covered pot before chopping the peels and mashing the pulp—yielded the best results.

USE SEVILLES Seville oranges are a rugged, persnickety lot. They're available only for about three weeks in January but can be frozen whole for several months before using.

SIMMER WHOLE We started by weighing out 1 pound of Seville oranges, making sure that none had soft spots (green skin or blemishes were OK). We added a whole lemon for its bright flavor and natural pectin, plus just the right amount of sugar to balance the fruits' tartness. We tightly sealed our covered pot with aluminum foil to prevent any of the liquid from evaporating as it simmered.

COOK HIGH To achieve the proper consistency, we found that our marmalade—made without commercial pectin—needed to cook to a slightly higher temperature (220 to 222 degrees) than our jams made without commercial pectin (which achieve a jam-like texture at 217 to 220 degrees). It was only within this higher temperature range that our marmalade passed the "wrinkle test," indicating that the liquid in which our candied fruit rind was suspended had gelled into marmalade.

SEVILLE ORANGE MARMALADE

MAKES FOUR (1-CUP) JARS

Seville oranges are available for about three weeks in January and can be frozen whole for several months before using. In their absence, Jamaican Ugli fruit—a hybrid of Seville orange, grapefruit, and tangerine—can be used as a substitute.

4	cups water
1	pound Seville oranges, scrubbed
1	lemon, scrubbed
3½	cups sugar

1. Bring water, oranges, and lemon to brief boil in large saucepan over high heat, then reduce heat to low. Cover pot with heavy-duty aluminum foil, crimp edges to seal, and cover with lid. Gently simmer until fruit is easily pierced with skewer, about 1½ hours. Remove pot from heat and let cool to room temperature, covered, about 5 hours or overnight.

2. Set canning rack in large pot, place four 1-cup jars in rack, and add water to cover by 1 inch. Bring to simmer over medium heat, then turn heat off and cover to keep hot.

3. Place 2 small plates in freezer to chill. Transfer oranges and lemon to cutting board; cut fruits into quarters. Using paring knife, scrape pulp with most of pith from peels; reserve pulp and peels separately. Return pulp to pot with liquid, mash lightly with potato masher, bring to simmer over medium heat, and cook for 10 minutes. Meanwhile, slice peels into thin strips, then cut crosswise into ¼-inch pieces.

4. Strain liquid through fine-mesh strainer into large bowl, pressing firmly on solids to extract as much liquid as possible; discard solids. Combine strained juice, chopped peels, and sugar in Dutch oven. Bring to vigorous boil over medium-high heat, stirring and adjusting heat as needed, until thickened and registers 220 to 222 degrees, 15 to 25 minutes. (This temperature depends on altitude; see Practical Science page 283.) Remove pot from heat.

5. To test consistency, place 1 teaspoon marmalade on chilled plate and freeze for 2 minutes. Gently push cooled marmalade with your finger; marmalade should wrinkle around edges when set. If runny, return pot to heat and simmer for 1 to 3 minutes longer before retesting. Skim any foam from surface of marmalade using large spoon.

6. Place dish towel flat on counter. Using jar lifter, remove jars from pot, draining water back into pot. Place jars upside down on towel and let dry for 1 minute. Using funnel and ladle, portion hot marmalade into hot jars, leaving ¼ inch headspace. Slide wooden skewer along inside edge of jar and drag upward to remove air bubbles.

7A. FOR SHORT-TERM STORAGE: Let marmalade cool to room temperature, cover, and refrigerate until marmalade is set, 12 to 24 hours. (Marmalade can be refrigerated for up to 2 months).

7B. FOR LONG-TERM STORAGE: While jars are hot, wipe rims clean, add lids, and screw on rings until fingertip-tight; do not overtighten. Return pot of water with canning rack to boil. Lower jars into water, cover, bring water back to boil, then start timer. Cooking time will depend on your altitude: Boil 10 minutes for up to 1,000 feet, 15 minutes for 1,001 to 3,000 feet, 20 minutes for 3,001 to 6,000 feet, or 25 minutes for above 6,000 feet. Turn off heat and let jars sit in pot for 5 minutes. Remove jars from pot and let cool for 24 hours. Remove rings, check seals, and clean rims. (Sealed jars can be stored for up to 1 year.)

PRACTICAL SCIENCE ORANGE JUICE COLOR

Any variance in a natural, minimally processed product like freshly squeezed orange juice is, well, natural.

The color of orange juice depends on the variety of orange used and when in the season it was harvested. The earliest juice is virtually clear, while late-harvest juice has that familiar deep-orange color of carton juice. Though color doesn't necessarily have anything to do with flavor, manufacturers of carton juice try to ensure their juice always looks the same. They squeeze and store juice from the early-, mid-, and late-season harvests in super-chilled vats that preserve flavor, then mix the juices together to make them consistent from carton to carton. To further enhance color, manufacturers add up to 10 percent vividly colored mandarin orange juice as well as pigment from orange peels. When you buy freshly squeezed orange juice, you're getting the juice direct from harvesting, with no mixing and matching, so the color may change as the season goes on. Also, it tends to separate, while carton juice doesn't. Carton juice is pasteurized at a high temperature (over 190 degrees) to extend shelf life and to deactivate an enzyme called pectin methylesterase that causes the juice to separate upon standing. Freshly squeezed juice is "flash pasteurized" at a lower temperature that doesn't impact this enzyme.

CHAPTER 35

Coconut

This stone fruit (yes!) contains many elements, from husk to seed. We use variations of its edible parts in our recipes.

HOW THE SCIENCE WORKS

Despite their name, coconuts are not nuts. They are botanically classified as drupes, or stone fruits, like peaches. They come from the coconut tree, and are members of the *Arecaceae* family, which contains all palm plants. All drupes have a seed, surrounded by a shell, surrounded again by a fleshy or protective layer. In the case of coconuts, the outer protective layer is a fibrous husk, which is removed, leaving the hard brown shell that we recognize as a fresh coconut. Inside the hard shell is the edible fleshy portion of coconut meat, coconut water, and the coconut seed. The meat is known as the endosperm, which is deposited in layers as the maturing coconut develops.

It takes about one year for the coconut to reach maturity and be ready for harvest. At maturity, the meat makes up about 15 percent of the weight of the coconut, and contains about 45 percent by weight water, 35 percent fat, 10 percent carbohydrate, and 5 percent protein. (The rest is seed and hard shell.)

Coconuts aren't nuts. They're drupes, or stone fruits, like peaches.

The earliest written record of the coconut palm tree dates to about 545 AD, yet fossils of coconut have been found in Australia and India that date as far back as 37 to 55 million years. The coconut palm tree originated in the tropics, where it flourishes in the high humidity and heat. Frost is fatal to the tree, yet it's able to withstand significant salinity in the soil.

In addition to being eaten fresh, coconuts can be made into a number of cooking products. The meat can be dried, sweetened, or toasted, cut to sizes that range from large shreds to fine flakes. There is also coconut water (the clear liquid from the center of the coconut), coconut milk (made by combining grated coconut meat with hot water and filtering the liquid), and coconut cream (the fat that separates from coconut milk). And, finally, there is coconut oil.

Coconut oil has enjoyed widespread use in cooking, as well as interest in its influence on health. Coconut oil is unique in that it has a high percentage of saturated fat (about 90 percent by weight) and about 8 percent monounsaturated. This high level of saturation means that coconut oil is a solid, which melts a little above room temperature, and which has a long shelf life (two years). It also has a very high smoke point (up to 450 degrees). But what makes it even more unique is its molecular makeup: Most of coconut oil's fatty acids are shorter carbon chains than the fatty acids in other plants and animal fats. (The majority in coconut oil contain 8 to 12 carbon atoms, while animal and plant fats and oils mostly contain fatty acids with 18 carbon atoms.) These shorter chains of fatty acids are metabolized by humans differently than the longer-chained fatty acids, and while the effects of this are still unknown, some studies have shown that coconut oil helps to reduce levels of unhealthy cholesterol.

Because the flavor of each coconut product can be delicate, we often pair multiple products together to get deep coconut flavor. For our Coconut Layer Cake (page 288) we use three different coconut products in the batter and frosting: coconut extract, shredded coconut, and cream of coconut. In our Coconut Cream Pie (page 289) we use shredded coconut in both the crust and filling; the filling also contains coconut milk. Coconut milk likewise adds depth to the spice-heavy sauce of our streamlined Thai Chicken Curry (page 291). Finally, you can make your own Homemade Coconut Milk (page 292), with little more than shredded coconut, water, and baking soda.

TEST KITCHEN EXPERIMENT

Choosing the right milk for a recipe used to be as simple as picking a desired fat content. Nowadays, the world of alternative milks makes matters much more complicated. We were curious about which milk alternatives could be swapped directly into recipes calling for cow's milk (with no other ingredient adjustments needed), and which could not. We rounded up unsweetened soy milk, unsweetened almond milk, canned coconut milk, and a relatively new product called coconut beverage (a milk alternative that's a combination of coconut milk, water, and thickeners) and ran the following experiment.

EXPERIMENT

We chose three recipes that called for a relatively high amount of milk—white cake, simple baked custard, and scones—and prepared each using unsweetened soy milk, unsweetened almond milk, canned coconut milk, and coconut beverage. We examined the results of each compared to a control we made with whole cow's milk.

RESULTS

For the white cake, we found almond milk and coconut beverage to be fully successful swaps—both turned out a fine, moderately tender crumb with no off-flavors. Soy milk was deemed unacceptable as it produced a coarse crumb and left a bean-like aftertaste. Canned coconut milk was also ruled out because it created a fine pound cake–like crumb that tasted strongly of coconut.

The tests with custards were far less successful. Only the original recipe with cow's milk resulted in a smooth, creamy, perfectly set custard. Interestingly, the soy milk, almond milk, and coconut beverage custards all turned an unappetizing brown color, despite the fact that the milks themselves were white to begin with. While the majority of the alternative-milk custards appeared thin and broken, the one made with coconut milk was too thick and grainy.

For the scones, almond milk and soy milk performed as well as cow's milk, delivering a fluffy interior and well-browned exterior. Canned coconut milk produced scones with a slightly gummy interior and a strong coconut flavor. The interior of the scones made with coconut beverage was fine, but the scones lacked exterior browning.

TAKEAWAY

Overall, our tests showed that while alternative milks may work just fine poured over a bowl of cereal, they have unique limitations when it comes to baking. Almond milk was successful in two of the applications, whereas canned coconut milk failed to deliver acceptable results across the board. Why? Fat is a big reason. Coconut milk is much more fatty than all the other milks; it significantly boosted the overall fat content and therefore resulted in drastically denser, less airy textures. (It's important to keep in mind that for this test we did straight one-to-one substitutions, without any further adjustments to the recipes.) Moving forward, if we want to use an alternative milk in a baked good, we'll plan on rebuilding a recipe from the ground up.

CAN YOU SUBSTITUTE ALTERNATIVE MILKS IN BAKED GOODS?

Here's how alternative milks stack up in baked goods in a 1:1 substitution.

	COW	ALMOND	SOY	COCONUT MILK	COCONUT BEVERAGE
White Cake	Good	Good	Bad	Bad	Good
Custard	Good	Bad	Bad	Bad	Bad
Scones	Good	Good	Good	Bad	Bad
Verdict		Good alternative	Fine for scones	Save for curries	Can work for cake

FOCUS ON: COCONUT

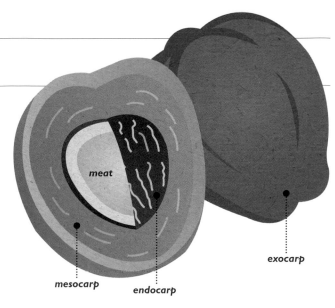

Botanically, the coconut fruit is a drupe, or stone fruit, and not a nut at all. Either way, we use coconut in myriad ways, from drinking its water to baking with its meaty flakes.

meat

exocarp

mesocarp   endocarp

COCONUT

While we see processed coconut in all its different forms in the market, we rarely find whole coconuts. And whole coconuts may surprise you. They consist of many layers—the exocarp (the outer husk often removed before sale), mesocarp (the fleshy middle layer), and endocarp (the harder woody layer that encases the seed). The seed itself contains both solid and liquid, and is what we eat.

COCONUT FLAKES

Desiccated coconut is made by reducing the water content of the fresh meat from about 45 percent to less than 5 percent, leaving the dried coconut containing a significant amount of coconut oil (about 64 percent fat by weight). Simple sugars make up 7 percent of the total weight.

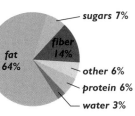

sugars 7%
fiber 14%
fat 64%
other 6%
protein 6%
water 3%

SWEETENED COCONUT FLAKES

Sweetened desiccated coconut is made by cooking coconut meat with sugar before drying. This dried form of coconut contains about 28 percent fat and 15 percent water. Simple sugars make up about 37 percent of the total weight of the dried, sweetened coconut. The water content is higher than in unsweetened desiccated coconut because sugar is hygroscopic and makes it more difficult to remove as much water. Because of the higher water content, sweetened coconut often contains glycerine to keep the flakes soft, and sulfites to keep the product white.

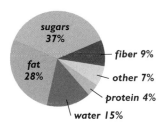

sugars 37%
fat 28%
fiber 9%
other 7%
protein 4%
water 15%

COCONUT WATER

Coconut water is the clear liquid in the center of the coconut.

COCONUT MILK

Coconut milk is made by combining grated coconut meat with hot water and filtering the liquid. Coconut milk is unsweetened and available in cans. Its composition is 73 percent water, 21 percent fat, 3 percent carbohydrate, and 2 percent protein. The protein in coconut milk can be coagulated like cow's milk when acidified.

COCONUT CREAM

The rich fat in coconut milk often floats to the top where it is separated and sold as coconut cream. Unsweetened coconut cream contains about 54 percent water, 35 percent fat, and 7 percent carbohydrate.

CREAM OF COCONUT

Not to be confused with coconut cream, cream of coconut is a sweetened product based on coconut cream that also contains thickeners and emulsifiers.

Coconut Layer Cake

✔ WHY THIS RECIPE WORKS

To us, coconut cake should be perfumed inside and out with the cool, subtle, mysterious essence of coconut. Its layers of snowy white cake should be moist and tender, with a delicate, yielding crumb, and the icing a silky, gently sweetened coat covered with a deep drift of downy coconut. So it's irksome and disappointing that coconut cakes are often frauds, no more than plain white cakes with plain white icing slapped with shredded coconut. We decided to find a coconut cake that fulfilled our dreams.

PICK CREAM OF COCONUT We started with a base recipe that included both coconut milk and coconut extract. But we found that, from batch to batch, the coconut milk could produce mystifyingly different results: sometimes a flat cake, sometimes a mounded cake, sometimes a heavy, greasy cake. This is because the fat content of coconut milk can vary as much as 33 percent from brand to brand. Cream of coconut, a sweetened coconut product that contains a few emulsifiers, seemed to be a more consistent product, perhaps because there are fewer brands, Coco López being the best known. We cut back on some of the sugar that went into the batter, and used cream of coconut instead of coconut milk. These cakes baked up beautifully, their exteriors an appealing burnished brown color that the coconut milk versions lacked, and they tasted more strongly of coconut as well.

LEVEL IT OUT The downside to our cream of coconut cakes was that they baked up with a big mound in the center. To even the layers out, we lowered the oven temperature to 325 degrees for a more even rise while baking.

START WITH MERINGUE We tested out many different types of frostings, starting with cream cheese frosting, which was not a hit. We settled on a buttercream, specifically an egg white buttercream, which was incredibly lithe, significantly silky and smooth, and not too sweet. This type of buttercream begins life as a meringue, with softened butter eventually beaten in.

TOAST THE COCONUT The crowning glory of a coconut cake is its woolly coconut coat. Pure white shredded coconut straight from the bag made for a maidenly cake. But we were after a more intense coconut flavor, as well as textural contrast. We toasted the coconut, not to the point of even brownness, but just until it resembled a toss of white and bronze confetti. Sprinkled on top and pressed onto the sides, the toasted coconut gave this cake a celebratory air.

COCONUT LAYER CAKE

SERVES 10 TO 12

Be sure to use cream of coconut (such as Coco López) and not coconut milk here. One 15-ounce can is enough for both the cake and the icing; make sure to stir it well before using because it separates upon standing.

CAKE

1	large egg plus 5 large whites
¾	cup cream of coconut
¼	cup water
1	teaspoon vanilla extract
1	teaspoon coconut extract
2¼	cups (9 ounces) cake flour
1	cup (7 ounces) sugar
1	tablespoon baking powder
¾	teaspoon salt
12	tablespoons unsalted butter, cut into 12 pieces and softened
2	cups (6 ounces) sweetened shredded coconut

ICING

4	large egg whites
1	cup (7 ounces) sugar
	Pinch salt
1	pound unsalted butter (4 sticks), each stick cut into 6 pieces and softened
¼	cup cream of coconut
1	teaspoon coconut extract
1	teaspoon vanilla extract

1. FOR THE CAKE: Adjust oven rack to lower-middle position and heat oven to 325 degrees. Grease two 9-inch round cake pans, line with parchment paper, grease parchment, and flour pans.

2. Whisk egg and whites together in 2-cup liquid measuring cup. Add cream of coconut, water, vanilla, and coconut extract and whisk until thoroughly combined.

3. Using stand mixer fitted with paddle, mix flour, sugar, baking powder, and salt on low speed until combined. Add butter, 1 piece at a time, and mix until only pea-size pieces remain, about 1 minute. Add half of egg mixture, increase speed to medium-high, and beat until light and fluffy, about 1 minute. Reduce speed to medium-low, add remaining egg mixture, and beat until incorporated, about 30 seconds. Give batter final stir by hand.

4. Divide batter evenly between prepared pans and smooth tops with rubber spatula. Bake cake until toothpick inserted in centers comes out clean, about 30 minutes. Do not turn off oven. Let cakes cool in pans on wire rack for 10 minutes. Remove cakes from pans, discard parchment, and let cool completely, about 2 hours, before frosting. (Cooled cakes can be wrapped tightly in plastic wrap and kept at room temperature for up to 1 day. Wrapped tightly in plastic, then aluminum foil, cakes can be frozen for up to 1 month. Defrost cakes at room temperature before unwrapping and frosting.)

5. While cakes are cooling, spread shredded coconut on rimmed baking sheet; toast in oven until shreds are a mix of golden brown and white, about 15 to 20 minutes, stirring 2 or 3 times. Let cool to room temperature.

6. FOR THE ICING: Combine egg whites, sugar, and salt in bowl of stand mixer and set over medium saucepan filled with 1 inch of barely simmering water (do not let bottom of bowl touch water). Whisk constantly until mixture is opaque and warm to the touch and registers about 120 degrees, about 2 minutes.

7. Remove bowl from heat. Fit stand mixer with whisk and whip egg white mixture on high speed until barely warm (about 80 degrees), glossy, and sticky, about 7 minutes. Reduce speed to medium-high and whip in butter, 1 piece at a time, followed by cream of coconut, coconut extract, and vanilla, scraping down bowl as needed. Continue to whip at medium-high speed until combined, about 1 minute.

8. TO ASSEMBLE THE CAKE: Using long serrated knife, cut 1 horizontal line around sides of each layer; then, following scored lines, cut each layer into 2 even layers.

9. Line edges of cake platter with 4 strips of parchment paper to keep platter clean. Place 1 cake layer on prepared platter. Place about ¾ cup icing in center of bottom cake layer and, using large spatula, spread in even layer right to edge of cake. Carefully place second cake layer on top of icing and press lightly to adhere. Repeat, using remaining cake layers and more icing, spreading icing until slightly over edge of top layer. Gather more frosting on tip of spatula and gently spread icing onto side of cake. Smooth icing by gently running edge of spatula around cake and leveling ridge that forms around top edge. Sprinkle top of cake evenly with toasted coconut, then press remaining toasted coconut into sides of cake. Carefully pull out pieces of parchment from beneath cake before serving. (Assembled cake can be refrigerated for up to 1 day. Bring to room temperature before serving.)

Coconut Cream Pie

✔ WHY THIS RECIPE WORKS

The first bite of a coconut cream pie almost always disappoints, generally tasting like a redecorated vanilla cream pie and nothing more. A handful of coconut shreds stirred into the filling or sprinkled on the whipped cream might be enough to give it a new name, but certainly not to give it flavor. Then there's the crust: soft and soggy—and the miserable texture of the filling: rubbery, resilient, and starchy. The essence of a great coconut cream pie ought to be the exotic and elusive flavor of tropical coconut rather than a thinly disguised vanilla custard. We set to work.

PICK ANIMAL CRACKERS—AND COCONUT After testing a handful of recipes, it became clear that when it came to the crust, a toasty, sweet, sandy, and crisp crumb crust was a better match for the filling than the common and more labor-intensive pastry crust, whose plain-Jane personality tended to disappear into the filling and turn sodden, to boot. In the end, we used not-too-sweet animal crackers to create a delicate crust that wouldn't overshadow the coconut filling. For added coconut flavor, we ground a couple of tablespoons of shredded coconut in the food processor along with the crackers.

USE A COCONUT COMBO For the filling itself, we used a combination of coconut products to get the best texture and vibrant coconut flavor. We preferred unsweetened shredded coconut over sweetened because it gave the pie more coconut flavor and better texture, and didn't add too much sweetness. Cream of coconut, we found, gave our pie a slimy texture. Coconut milk had a solid coconut flavor and didn't harm the texture of the pie, as long as it was cut with some whole milk so that it contained a bit less fat.

FILL 'ER UP The common thickeners for cream pie fillings are flour and cornstarch. We tested both of them, as well as arrowroot. Flour was a loser. It made a filling with a heavy, starchy feel and a flavor to match. The arrowroot and cornstarch fillings were better. Both were clean-tasting and nicely set, but whereas the cornstarch filling was lilting and creamy, the honorable-mention arrowroot filling was slightly bouncy and gelatin-like. We went with cornstarch.

COCONUT CREAM PIE
SERVES 8

Do not use light coconut milk here because it does not have enough flavor. Also, don't confuse coconut milk with cream of coconut. The filling should be warm when poured into the cooled pie crust. To toast the coconut, place it in a small skillet over medium heat and cook, stirring often, for 3 to 5 minutes. It burns quite easily, so keep a close eye on it.

CRUST

6	ounces animal crackers
2	tablespoons unsweetened shredded coconut
I	tablespoon granulated sugar
4	tablespoons unsalted butter, melted and cooled

FILLING

I	(13.5-ounce) can coconut milk
I	cup whole milk
½	cup unsweetened shredded coconut
½	cup plus I tablespoon (4 ounces) granulated sugar
⅜	teaspoon salt
5	large egg yolks
¼	cup cornstarch (I ounce)
2	tablespoons unsalted butter, cut into 2 pieces
I	teaspoon vanilla extract

WHIPPED CREAM AND GARNISH

I ½	cups heavy cream, chilled
2	tablespoons granulated sugar
½	teaspoon vanilla extract
I	tablespoon unsweetened shredded coconut, toasted

I. FOR THE CRUST: Adjust oven rack to lower-middle position and heat oven to 325 degrees. Pulse animal crackers, coconut, and sugar in food processor to fine crumbs, 18 to 20 pulses, then process until powdery, about 5 seconds. Transfer crumbs to medium bowl and add butter; stir to combine until crumbs are evenly moistened. Empty crumbs into 9-inch glass pie plate; using bottom of ½-cup dry measuring cup, press crumbs evenly into bottom and up sides of pie plate. Bake until fragrant and medium brown, about 15 minutes, rotating pie shell halfway through baking. Set on wire rack and let cool to room temperature, about 30 minutes.

2. FOR THE FILLING: Bring coconut milk, whole milk, shredded coconut, ½ cup sugar, and salt to simmer over medium-high heat, stirring occasionally to ensure that sugar dissolves. Whisk yolks, cornstarch, and remaining 1 tablespoon sugar in medium bowl until thoroughly combined. Whisking constantly, gradually ladle about 1 cup hot milk mixture over yolk mixture; whisk well to combine. Whisking constantly, gradually add remaining milk mixture to yolk mixture in 3 or 4 additions; whisk well to combine. Return mixture to saucepan and cook until thickened and mixture reaches boil, whisking constantly, about 1 minute; filling must boil in order to fully thicken. (To determine whether filling has reached boil, stop whisking; large bubbles should quickly burst on surface.) Off heat, whisk in butter and vanilla until butter is fully incorporated. Pour hot filling into cooled pie shell and smooth surface with rubber spatula; press plastic wrap directly against surface of filling and refrigerate until firm, at least 3 hours or up to 12 hours.

3. FOR THE WHIPPED CREAM: Just before serving, using stand mixer fitted with whisk, whip cream, sugar, and vanilla on medium-low speed until frothy, about 1 minute. Increase speed to high and continue to whip until soft peaks form, 1 to 3 minutes. Top pie with whipped cream and then sprinkle with coconut. Cut pie into wedges and serve.

PRACTICAL SCIENCE
HOW TO CRACK COCONUT CREAM

You can "crack" coconut milk for traditional curries at home.

Traditional Thai curry recipes call for frying the spice paste in coconut cream that's been "cracked"—that is, simmered until its oil separates out. Besides drawing out the oil, simmering the coconut cream also forces water to evaporate, making for a slightly more concentrated curry. We skip this step in our Thai Chicken Curry with Potatoes and Peanuts and fry the paste in vegetable oil to keep things simple, but if you want to achieve a slightly richer-tasting curry, follow the steps below and then proceed with step 4 of the recipe, adding the curry paste to the saucepan and omitting the oil. (Add the remaining coconut milk with the broth.) In step 5, add up to ¾ cup of water to ensure that the chicken pieces are just submerged in the liquid. Note that some products contain emulsifiers and stabilizers that discourage the formation of the cream layer. We have found that Thai Kitchen Coconut Milk works best for this process.

1. Skim solid layer of cream from can of coconut milk to yield roughly ¾ cup.

2. Simmer cream in large saucepan over medium heat, stirring constantly, until cream is texture of yogurt and sizzles at edges, 7 to 12 minutes.

Thai Chicken Curry with Potatoes and Peanuts

✔ WHY THIS RECIPE WORKS

Unlike many Thai dishes that feature hot, sour, salty, and sweet elements, massaman curry trades on a warm, faintly sweet, and not overly spicy profile, thanks to the mix of warm spices like cinnamon, cloves, cardamom, and cumin, as well as roasted dried chiles and aromatics like shallots, garlic, and fresh galangal (a sweet-spicy cousin of ginger) that make up its paste. A last-minute addition of either shrimp paste or fish sauce and a few teaspoons of tangy tamarind balance the rich sauce, which is typically paired with chicken (or beef), potato chunks, and roasted peanuts. Massaman is a dish that presents challenges in an American kitchen. Ingredients like galangal and tamarind are hard to track down. Plus, precooking dried chiles and aromatic vegetables and toasting and grinding whole spices (another traditional step) make for one heck of a prep job—and that's just for the paste. We were determined to produce a massaman curry as fragrant and rich-tasting as any Thai restaurant would make, but with less work.

MAKE A PASTE To see what would happen if we cut the precooking step for both the dried chiles and aromatics, we compared the dish made with two different batches of paste: One used oven-toasted chiles and broiled skin-on garlic and shallots; the other used the same ingredients without precooking. The flavor differential was extreme. Precooking was essential. But we could make a streamlining decision: Since the spices would bloom in oil, they didn't absolutely need to be toasted ahead of time.

CRACKED CREAM IS OPTIONAL Traditional Thai curry recipes call for frying the paste in coconut cream (either skimmed from the top of a can of coconut milk or bought separately) that's first heated until its oil separates out, or "cracks." We pitted a batch of curry in which we had fried the paste in the skimmed, cracked cream against our working recipe, which called for simply frying the paste in vegetable oil. Admittedly, a few tasters picked up on the more concentrated flavor of the cracked cream curry, but most agreed that vegetable oil worked fine. (If you want to try cracking coconut cream yourself, see Practical Science, page 290.)

ADD LIME Our tasters were also clamoring for a bit of brightness, so we tried finishing the curry with a few teaspoons of lime juice—our best guess for a tamarind substitute. Alas, its effect was too sharp for massaman, and scaling back on the juice flattened its effect altogether. What did work: changing when we added the lime juice rather than how much we added. When we replaced some of the water in the paste with a few teaspoons of juice, the lime's acid mellowed as it cooked in the curry but didn't disappear. Finishing the curry with lime zest and cilantro freshened it even more.

THAI CHICKEN CURRY WITH POTATOES AND PEANUTS
SERVES 4 TO 6

Serve the curry with jasmine rice. The ingredients for the curry paste can be doubled to make extra for future use. Refrigerate the paste for up to one week or freeze it for up to two months. Be sure to zest the lime before juicing it.

CURRY PASTE

6	dried New Mexican chiles
4	shallots, unpeeled
7	garlic cloves, unpeeled
½	cup chopped fresh ginger
¼	cup water
1½	tablespoons lime juice
1½	tablespoons vegetable oil
1	tablespoon fish sauce
1	teaspoon five-spice powder
½	teaspoon ground cumin
½	teaspoon pepper

CURRY

1	teaspoon vegetable oil
1	(13.5-ounce) can coconut milk
1¼	cups chicken broth
1	pound Yukon Gold potatoes, unpeeled, cut into ¾-inch pieces
1	onion, cut into ¾-inch pieces
⅓	cup dry-roasted peanuts
¾	teaspoon salt
1	pound boneless, skinless chicken thighs, trimmed and cut into 1-inch pieces
2	teaspoons grated lime zest
¼	cup chopped fresh cilantro

1. FOR THE CURRY PASTE: Adjust oven rack to middle position and heat oven to 350 degrees. Line rimmed baking sheet with aluminum foil. Arrange chiles on prepared sheet and toast until puffed and fragrant, 4 to 6 minutes. Transfer chiles to large plate. Heat broiler.

2. Place shallots and garlic on foil-lined sheet and broil until softened and skin is charred, 6 to 9 minutes.

3. When cool enough to handle, stem and seed chiles and tear into 1½-inch pieces. Process chiles in blender until finely ground, about 1 minute. Peel shallots and garlic. Add shallots, garlic, ginger, water, lime juice, oil, fish sauce, five-spice powder, cumin, and pepper to blender. Process to smooth paste, scraping down sides of blender jar as needed, 2 to 3 minutes. You should have 1 cup paste.

4. FOR THE CURRY: Heat oil in large saucepan over medium heat until shimmering. Add curry paste and cook, stirring constantly, until paste begins to brown, 2½ to 3 minutes. Stir in coconut milk, broth, potatoes, onion, peanuts, and salt, scraping up any browned bits. Bring to simmer and cook until potatoes are just tender, 12 to 14 minutes.

5. Stir in chicken and continue to simmer until chicken is cooked through, 10 to 12 minutes. Remove pan from heat and stir in lime zest. Serve, passing cilantro separately.

PRACTICAL SCIENCE COCONUT OIL

> Refined coconut oil makes a perfectly good substitute for butter (or oil, for that matter) in baking and sautéing.

Once demonized, coconut oil is experiencing a comeback. As long as the oil isn't hydrogenated (which creates the dreaded trans fats that clog arteries), some scientists say that it isn't as bad as once thought. The jury is still out, but coconut oil may even have health benefits. It's also gaining popularity with vegans as a nondairy butter substitute. Coconut oil is sold in two forms, both solid at room temperature: refined, which has virtually no taste or aroma, and virgin, which retains a strong coconut flavor. Since we have limited use for an oil that makes food smell and taste like a piña colada, we tested only the refined product.

We tried the melted oil in chocolate chip cookies and found that it performed just as well as melted butter, though we missed butter's sweet dairy flavor. Ditto when we creamed the oil for cake and used it to sauté carrots. (Because of its steep price—about $8 for 16 ounces—coconut oil is impractical for deep frying.) In an all-butter pie crust, subbing coconut oil for butter required an adjustment. Most pie dough needs to be chilled before rolling, but coconut oil becomes hard and brittle when refrigerated, leading to dough that is too firm to roll out without cracking. The simple fix: Rest the dough on the counter instead of in the fridge.

Homemade Coconut Milk

✔ WHY THIS RECIPE WORKS

Much of the coconut milk found in stores contains a great number of additives, preservatives, and stabilizers, and the one or two brands that don't are difficult to find. Homemade coconut milk is easy to make and can be stored for up to two weeks.

USE BOILING WATER We tested blending shredded coconut with water of varying temperatures and determined that near-boiling water worked best; the heat softened the coconut and extracted the most flavor. We wanted our recipe to make the equivalent of one can of coconut milk; after some testing, we landed on using 1¾ cups each of water and unsweetened shredded coconut meat. We strained the processed coconut mixture through a fine-mesh strainer lined with cheesecloth so that our milk would turn out perfectly smooth.

AND BAKING SODA Since the milk tended to curdle when heated to a simmer, we added a touch of baking soda if we planned on cooking with it. This made the milk more alkaline and discouraged the milk proteins from clumping.

HOMEMADE COCONUT MILK

MAKES 1¾ CUPS (THE EQUIVALENT OF ONE
13.5-OUNCE CAN COCONUT MILK)

For an accurate measurement of water, bring a full pot of water to a near-boil and then measure out the desired amount. We do not recommend using coconut flakes here. This recipe can be doubled.

- 1¾ cups water, 200 to 205 degrees
- 1¾ cups unsweetened shredded coconut
- ¼ teaspoon baking soda

Combine water and coconut in blender and process for 2 minutes. Transfer to fine-mesh strainer set over large measuring cup and press to extract as much liquid as possible; let cool for 15 minutes. Transfer shredded coconut to clean dish towel in large bowl. Gather sides of dish towel around coconut and squeeze remaining milk into measuring cup. Whisk baking soda into milk. Discard shredded coconut and use milk as desired or refrigerate for up to 2 weeks.

CHAPTER 36

Pasta

You think you know how to cook it. But there's more than one way to produce perfect pasta.

HOW THE SCIENCE WORKS

Pasta is a versatile food, used in cuisines all over the world. In the test kitchen, we have developed hundreds of pasta recipes over the years—baked or boiled, fresh or dried. But at its core, pasta is a simple product made from flour and water and, sometimes, eggs. While different cultures use different types of flour, with different levels of protein, and different techniques to produce and cook it, here we'll concentrate (mainly) on the classic dried Italian-style noodles.

Noodle-shaped foods were first made in China, as far back as 200 BCE. Although a food similar to lasagna was known to ancient Romans, it was not until later that references were made to anything resembling pasta: In the early 12th century, the Arab geographer Al-Idris reported the first production of dried pasta in Sicily.

While simple, dried pastas (which account for 90 percent of all pastas sold today) are anything but haphazard. In fact, there are standards of identity in place for pasta products in Italy and the United States. Italian standards require the use of durum semolina flour, made from durum wheat, for all forms of dried pasta. The U.S. standards don't specify the type of flour, but do require that only certain names be used for defined products. For instance, spaghetti must be cord-shaped (not tubular) with a diameter between 0.06 inches and 0.11 inches, while vermicelli must be less than 0.06 inches in diameter.

Dried pasta made from durum semolina flour is the most common—a pasta with a nice yellow color, resistance to overcooking, firm bite, and nutty flavor. These traits are in part because durum semolina flour contains a high level of protein (about 13 percent protein, with 13 percent water, 73 percent starch, and around 1 percent fat).

By law, U.S.-made spaghetti must be cord-shaped with a diameter between 0.06 inches and 0.11 inches.

And why is protein so important? The two main components of pasta are starch and protein. In dried pasta, the starch remains in whole, intact granules, just as it occurs in the raw flour (see illustration, page 295). The proteins exist in the form of gluten, arranged between and around the starch granules. During cooking, the starch granules absorb water and swell. The proteins, however, coagulate and form a net-like structure surrounding the swollen granules, effectively trapping the granules inside the protein network, and ensuring a firm consistency and lack of stickiness. If the protein network is weak and inelastic, or insufficient to surround all the granules, then the granules will not be confined. Instead they will continue to swell and release starch molecules that make the pasta sticky and soft. Escaping starch molecules can be observed as a milky appearance in the cooking water. Therefore, good pasta quality is dependent on a high protein content that is capable of forming gluten during the preparation and manipulation of the dough. (For more, see Practical Science, page 298.)

We use a number of different methods to cook pasta, in order to produce the flavors and textures we desire. To create a starch-heavy cooking liquid, we cook dried pasta in a relatively small amount of water: For our Cacio e Pepe (page 296), we use that semolina-infused water as the base of a smooth sauce. For our Spanish-Style Toasted Pasta with Shrimp (page 297) we toast the dried, raw pasta before cooking it in a flavorful broth. We use a risotto method on our Spring Vegetable Pasta (page 299), optimizing the combo of broth, wine, and starch to make a bright, creamy vegetarian dish. And for a different take? Try our Fresh Pasta without a Machine (page 301).

TEST KITCHEN EXPERIMENT

Adding salt to pasta's cooking water ensures that the pasta (and not just the sauce) is flavorful. Throughout the years we've zeroed in on a preferred ratio of 1 tablespoon of table salt to 4 quarts of cooking water per pound of pasta for the most well-seasoned pasta. We were curious to find out exactly how much sodium actually makes it into the pasta, so we ran the following experiment.

EXPERIMENT

We cooked 1 pound each of six different pasta shapes—spaghetti, linguini, penne, rigatoni, campanelle, and orzo—in 4 quarts of boiling water with 1 tablespoon of table salt until al dente. After draining and cooling the pastas, we sent samples of each to an independent lab to test for sodium content.

RESULTS

Penne, rigatoni, and campanelle contained the least sodium, all averaging 135 mg for 4 ounces of cooked pasta. Linguine and spaghetti were higher with 147 and 158 mg, respectively, and orzo topped the group with 170 mg. To put these numbers in perspective, $\frac{1}{16}$ teaspoon of table salt contains 150 mg of sodium. Tasters had trouble tasting the difference in salt level between each type of pasta. They all tasted seasoned.

TAKEAWAY

It may seem odd that even though we used the identical amount of salt for each type of pasta, the sodium content varied among shapes. But, in fact, these differences correlate quite closely with surface area. For a given weight, the smaller and/or thinner the pasta shape, the more relative surface area it has to absorb sodium from the cooking water. The Dietary Guidelines for Americans recommend less than 2,300 milligrams daily for people under 51 and less than 1,500 milligrams for those 51 and older, so even if you are watching your sodium intake, the amount pasta actually absorbs is so small that it's probably not an issue.

HOW MUCH SALT DOES YOUR PASTA ABSORB?

When we cook pasta, we add 1 tablespoon of table salt to 4 quarts of cooking water per pound of pasta. But how much salt does that pasta actually absorb? It all comes down to surface area. The smaller and thinner the pasta, the more surface area it has to absorb salt from the cooking water. Though, in reality, no pasta shape absorbs so much salt that you should worry about it.

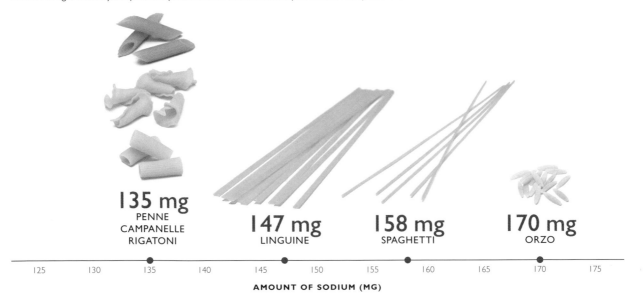

135 mg
PENNE
CAMPANELLE
RIGATONI

147 mg
LINGUINE

158 mg
SPAGHETTI

170 mg
ORZO

| 125 | 130 | 135 | 140 | 145 | 150 | 155 | 160 | 165 | 170 | 175 |

AMOUNT OF SODIUM (MG)

JOURNEY: COMMERCIAL DRIED PASTA

Today the process for making dry pasta is completely automated. It involves durum semolina flour, known for its high protein content, water, and not a whole lot else.

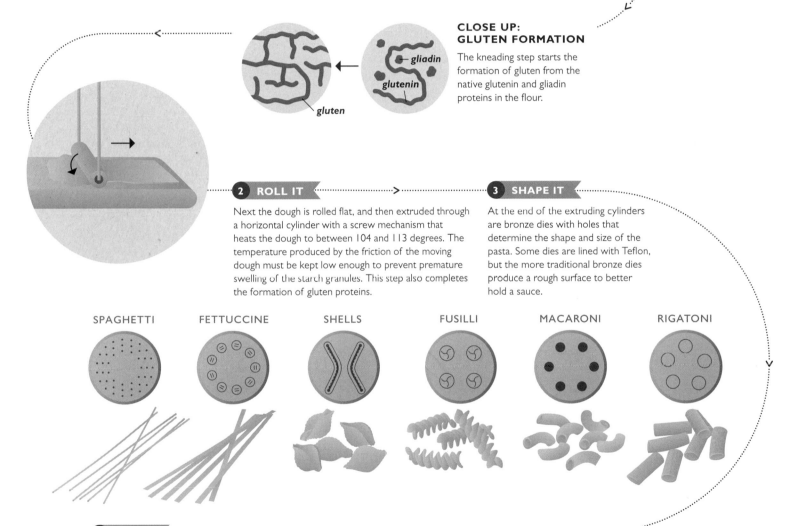

1 MIX AND KNEAD

To begin, the semolina flour is mixed with water and kneaded into a lumpy dough that contains about 30 percent moisture (typical sandwich bread dough, by comparison, contains about 50 to 60 percent moisture). During the mechanical kneading process that lasts for about 15 to 20 minutes, it is important to ensure that all of the water becomes evenly dispersed to avoid white spots in the finished product.

water

semolia flour

CLOSE UP: GLUTEN FORMATION

The kneading step starts the formation of gluten from the native glutenin and gliadin proteins in the flour.

gliadin

glutenin

gluten

2 ROLL IT

Next the dough is rolled flat, and then extruded through a horizontal cylinder with a screw mechanism that heats the dough to between 104 and 113 degrees. The temperature produced by the friction of the moving dough must be kept low enough to prevent premature swelling of the starch granules. This step also completes the formation of gluten proteins.

3 SHAPE IT

At the end of the extruding cylinders are bronze dies with holes that determine the shape and size of the pasta. Some dies are lined with Teflon, but the more traditional bronze dies produce a rough surface to better hold a sauce.

SPAGHETTI   FETTUCCINE   SHELLS   FUSILLI   MACARONI   RIGATONI

4 DRY IT

The final step in the process involves drying the extruded pasta. This is the most important step for ensuring good quality because it creates the characteristic flavor, aroma, and texture of the cooked pasta. The drying time and temperature must be very carefully controlled. The drying process must also lower the water content to no more than 13 percent, dictated by the standards of identity. This ensures that the moisture level will be low enough to prevent the growth of harmful microorganisms and provide a shelf life of at least three years (see Practical Science, page 300).

Cacio e Pepe

✓ WHY THIS RECIPE WORKS

There are dozens of approaches to this simple dish that combines long, thin pasta with Pecorino Romano and fresh-cracked black pepper, but it's hard to find any that produce a creamy sauce without lumps of cheese. To solve the inherent problems, we played with the amount of pasta water and the addition of an emulsifier.

USE STARCHY WATER Cheese consists mainly of three basic substances: fat, protein, and water. In a hard lump of Pecorino, the three are locked into position by the solid structure of the cheese. But when the cheese is heated, its fat begins to melt and its proteins soften. Cornstarch is useful for coating the cheese and preventing the proteins from sticking together, so we added some as we tossed the pasta. It worked, but by the time we used enough cornstarch to prevent clumping, it dulled the flavor of the cheese. Was there another way to get starch into the mix? Pasta releases starch into the cooking water as it boils, so maybe we could use this to our advantage. We reduced our cooking water from 4 quarts all the way down to 2 quarts per pound of pasta. After cooking the spaghetti, we whisked some grated cheese into a cup of the semolina-infused water that remained. Our results were the best yet, but some of the cheese was still clumping.

PRACTICAL SCIENCE LOW TEMPERATURE PASTA

You don't have to boil your pasta.

We already broke with this conventional wisdom by showing that you can cook pasta in a lot less water than is typically called for, as long as you don't mind stirring it frequently. Now we've learned that you don't need to hold your pasta water at a rolling boil either. In fact, you don't even need to keep the pot on the heat. The pasta will cook just fine if you take the pot off the burner as soon as you add the pasta, cover it immediately, stir once or twice during the first minute, cover again, and leave it to sit for the recommended cooking time. We tested this method with spaghetti, shells, farfalle, and ziti, using the full 4 quarts of water recommended per pound, and we found that the texture was identical to that of pasta we boiled the conventional way. Here's why the approach works: Starches absorb water at approximately 180 degrees. As long as the water is at a rolling boil (212 degrees) when you add the pasta and your kitchen is at normal room temperature, the water will remain well above 180 degrees off the heat for longer than the typical 8 to 10 minutes it takes for the pasta to cook through. In our tests, the water temperature had cooled to only about 195 degrees by the time the pasta was al dente. (In a cooler-than-normal kitchen, the pasta might take a minute or two longer to reach the proper texture.)

ADD CREAM Another factor that affects how proteins and fat interact: emulsifiers. Milk, cream, and fresh cheeses have special molecules called lipoproteins that can associate with both fat and protein, acting as a sort of liaison between the two and keeping them from separating. But as cheese ages, the lipoproteins break down, losing their emulsifying power. No wonder our Pecorino Romano, which is aged for at least eight months, was clumping. How could we get an infusion of totally intact lipoproteins? The answer was simple: add milk or cream. Since we were already using butter, why not replace it with the same amount of cream? This time, the cheese easily formed a light, perfectly smooth sauce when we tossed it with the spaghetti. Now for the real test: We placed a serving of pasta on the table and let it cool for a full 5 minutes. Even as it cooled, there wasn't a clump in sight.

SPAGHETTI WITH PECORINO ROMANO AND BLACK PEPPER (CACIO E PEPE)
SERVES 4 TO 6

High-quality ingredients are essential in this dish, most importantly imported Pecorino Romano. For a slightly less rich dish, substitute half-and-half for the heavy cream. Do not adjust the amount of water for cooking the pasta; the amount used is critical to the success of the recipe. Make sure to stir the pasta frequently while cooking so that it doesn't stick to the pot. Draining the pasta water into the serving bowl warms the bowl and helps keep the dish hot until it is served. Letting the dish rest briefly before serving allows the sauce to thicken.

6	ounces Pecorino Romano cheese, 4 ounces grated fine (2 cups) and 2 ounces grated coarse (1 cup)
1	pound spaghetti
1½	teaspoons salt
2	tablespoons heavy cream
2	teaspoons extra-virgin olive oil
1½	teaspoons pepper

1. Place finely grated Pecorino in medium bowl. Set colander in large bowl.

2. Bring 2 quarts water to boil in large pot. Add pasta and salt and cook, stirring often, until al dente. Drain pasta into prepared colander, reserving cooking water. Pour 1½ cups cooking water into liquid measuring cup and discard remainder. Return drained pasta to now-empty bowl.

3. Slowly whisk 1 cup reserved cooking water into finely grated Pecorino until smooth, then whisk in heavy cream, oil, and pepper. Gradually pour cheese mixture over pasta and toss to combine. Let pasta rest for 1 to 2 minutes, tossing frequently and adding remaining cooking water as needed to adjust consistency. Serve, passing coarsely grated Pecorino separately.

Spanish-Style Toasted Pasta with Shrimp

✔ WHY THIS RECIPE WORKS

The biggest star of traditional Spanish cooking is arguably paella, but there's another closely related dish equally deserving of raves: fideuà. This richly flavored dish swaps the rice for thin noodles that are typically toasted until nut-brown before being cooked in a garlicky, tomatoey stock loaded with seafood and sometimes chorizo sausage. As with the rice in paella, the noodles (called fideos) should be tender but not mushy. But whereas paella tends to be moist but not soupy, fideuà is often a little brothy. One thing that paella and fideuà have in common: a lengthy and involved cooking process. Almost all of the recipes we tried called for the same series of steps: Simmer fish and shellfish scraps to create stock. Toast the fideos and put together a flavorful base (the sofrito) by slowly reducing fresh tomatoes with aromatics and seasonings. Combine the sofrito with the stock and then simmer the toasted noodles and seafood in this rich-tasting liquid until cooked. Finally, put the whole thing in the oven to create a crunchy layer of pasta on top. Our crash course in the genre taught us that the results were often well worth the effort. But just as with paella, tinkering with fideuà is part of the art. We decided that our tweaks would be aimed at streamlining a recipe but leaving it every bit as deeply flavorful as the more time-consuming versions.

SHRIMP AND EASY STOCK Our first decision was to keep things simple in the seafood department and go with shrimp alone. Our next step was to make a stock without even dirtying a pot. We knew that shrimp shells can build a surprisingly flavorful broth without much help (see page 98), so we combined the shells from 1½ pounds of shrimp in a bowl with some water and a bay leaf and microwaved until the shells turned pink and the water was hot. The resulting broth wasn't bad for something that took such little effort, but its taste improved when we replaced a portion of the water with chicken broth and added a small measure of white wine for brightness.

APPROXIMATE FIDEOS Fideos come in varying thicknesses and shapes, including short, straight strands and coiled nests of thin, vermicelli-like noodles. We found that snapping spaghettini (more widely available than fideos) into pieces gave us a fine approximation of the first type of fideos. Not all fideuà recipes call for toasting the pasta, but skipping that step led to a dish that tasted weak and washed-out. So what was the best way to toast? The oven provided controlled heat but required repeatedly moving a baking sheet in and out in order to stir the noodles, which added another item to the dirty-dish pile. Toasting on the stovetop in a skillet—the same skillet in which the dish would be cooked and served—also required stirring, but this was much easier to monitor.

MAKE AN EFFICIENT SOFRITO Next we examined the sofrito. This flavor base shows up in a variety of forms in Spanish dishes but always features some combination of aromatics (onion, garlic, celery, and bell pepper are common) slow-cooked in oil to soften and concentrate their flavors. In fideuà, onion and garlic are typical, along with tomato. In the interest of efficiency, we ruled out preparing the sofrito separately, in another skillet. We also finely chopped our onion so that it would cook quickly and added ¼ teaspoon of salt to help draw out moisture so that the onion softened and browned even faster in the oil. Fresh tomatoes would take time to cook down, so we opted for canned diced tomatoes that we drained well and chopped fine. Added to the skillet with the softened onion, they reduced to a thick paste in a matter of minutes. Then we introduced minced garlic and cooked the mixture for a minute to bloom the flavors. When we pitted fideuà made with our abbreviated sofrito against a traditional slow-cooked version, tasters were hard pressed to taste any difference.

SPANISH-STYLE TOASTED PASTA WITH SHRIMP
SERVES 4

In step 5, if your skillet is not broiler-safe, once the pasta is tender transfer the mixture to a broiler-safe 13 by 9-inch baking dish lightly coated with olive oil; scatter the shrimp over the pasta and stir them in to partially submerge. Broil and serve as directed. Serve this dish with lemon wedges and Garlic Aïoli (recipe follows), stirring it into individual portions at the table.

3   tablespoons plus 2 teaspoons extra-virgin olive oil

3   garlic cloves, minced

     Salt and pepper

1½   pounds extra-large shrimp (21 to 25 per pound), peeled and deveined, shells reserved

2¾   cups water

1   cup chicken broth

1   bay leaf

8   ounces spaghettini or thin spaghetti, broken into 1- to 2-inch lengths

1   onion, chopped fine

1   (14.5-ounce) can diced tomatoes, drained and chopped fine

1   teaspoon paprika

1   teaspoon smoked paprika

½   teaspoon anchovy paste

¼   cup dry white wine

1   tablespoon chopped fresh parsley

     Lemon wedges

1. Combine 1 tablespoon oil, 1 teaspoon garlic, ¼ teaspoon salt, and ⅛ teaspoon pepper in medium bowl. Add shrimp, toss to coat, and refrigerate until ready to use.

2. Place water, broth, bay leaf, and reserved shrimp shells in medium bowl. Cover and microwave until liquid is hot and shells have turned pink, about 6 minutes. Set aside until ready to use.

3. Toss pasta and 2 teaspoons oil in broiler-safe 12-inch skillet until pasta is evenly coated. Toast pasta over medium-high heat, stirring frequently, until browned and nutty in aroma (pasta should be color of peanut butter), 6 to 10 minutes. Transfer pasta to bowl. Wipe out skillet with paper towel.

4. Heat remaining 2 tablespoons oil in now-empty skillet over medium-high heat until shimmering. Add onion and ¼ teaspoon salt; cook, stirring frequently, until onion is softened and beginning to brown around edges, 4 to 6 minutes. Add tomatoes and cook, stirring occasionally, until mixture is thick, dry, and slightly darkened in color, 4 to 6 minutes. Reduce heat to medium and add paprika, smoked paprika, anchovy paste, and remaining garlic. Cook until fragrant, about 1½ minutes. Add pasta and stir to combine.

5. Adjust oven rack 5 to 6 inches from broiler element and heat broiler. Pour shrimp broth through fine-mesh strainer into skillet. Add wine, ½ teaspoon pepper, and ¼ teaspoon salt and stir well. Increase heat to medium-high and bring to simmer. Cook, uncovered, stirring occasionally, until liquid is slightly thickened and pasta is just tender, 8 to 10 minutes. Scatter shrimp over pasta and stir into pasta to partially submerge. Transfer skillet to oven and broil until shrimp are opaque and surface of pasta is dry with crisped, browned spots, 5 to 7 minutes. Remove from oven and let stand, uncovered, for 5 minutes. Sprinkle with parsley and serve immediately, passing lemon wedges separately.

PRACTICAL SCIENCE HOW WHEAT FLOUR WORKS

The network of gluten proteins is key.

Flour can be produced from almost any hard, dry food source such as cereal grains, nuts, or legumes by grinding them to very fine particles. But one among them stands out: Wheat. All flours contain two principle components, starch and protein. But the proteins in wheat provide just the right properties for making baked goods and pasta. When water is added to wheat flour the two major proteins in wheat, called glutenin and gliadin, chemically bond together to form a new protein called gluten. Unlike either glutenin or gliadin, gluten is a very elastic protein, meaning it can stretch and form airtight films much like the latex in balloons. This unique property of gluten enables the preparation of leavened bread by trapping the gases produced by yeast, and the creation of firm chewy pasta.

The most abundant component of flour by far is starch, which is composed of two molecules called amylopectin and amylose in a ratio of roughly 4 to 1. Amylose is a small linear polymer while amylopectin is a giant complex polymer with many branches that make it resemble a tree. The starch molecules are tightly organized into microscopic particles called granules. When starch is heated in water, the granules absorb the water as it heats, causing the granules to swell many times their normal size. This process is called gelatinization. Near the boiling point starch granules can absorb so much water that they literally burst and release their cache of molecules. The primary role of gluten is to surround and control the granules and prevent them from bursting. Constraining the starch granules gives baked goods and pasta their structure and texture. If the granules escape and release the amylose and amylopectin molecules, the food will become sticky.

Although starch granules from different plants vary in size, they all behave very similarly when heated in water. But the proteins in wheat flour are unique in that they combine in the presence of water to form gluten, which is essential for harnessing the more abundant starch granules, creating the desired texture and structure of soft bread, and nonsticky al dente pasta. Semolina flour from durum wheat is high in protein (about 13 percent) forming lots of gluten that provides the needed control of the unruly starch granules. Semolina flour is also more coarsely ground than other flours such as bread and all-purpose flour.

GARLIC AÏOLI
MAKES 1¼ CUPS

Using a combination of vegetable oil and extra-virgin olive oil is crucial to the flavor of the aïoli.

2	large egg yolks
2	teaspoons Dijon mustard
2	teaspoons lemon juice
1	garlic clove, minced
¾	cup vegetable oil
1	tablespoon water
½	teaspoon salt
¼	teaspoon pepper
¼	cup extra-virgin olive oil

Process yolks, mustard, lemon juice, and garlic in food processor until combined, about 10 seconds. With processor running, slowly drizzle in vegetable oil, about 1 minute. Transfer mixture to medium bowl and whisk in water, salt, and pepper. Whisking constantly, slowly drizzle in olive oil. (Aïoli can be refrigerated for up to 4 days.)

Spring Vegetable Pasta

✔ WHY THIS RECIPE WORKS

You'd never know that pasta primavera, a pseudo-Italian dish that appears on virtually every chain restaurant menu, actually has roots in French haute cuisine. The usual reproduction—a random jumble of produce tossed with noodles in a heavy, flavor-deadening cream sauce—tastes nothing like spring. Surprisingly, when we dug up the original recipe from New York's famed Le Cirque restaurant, we found it wasn't all that inspiring either, despite taking about 2 hours to prepare and dirtying five pans. First, the vegetables (which had been painstakingly blanched one by one) were bland. Second, the cream-, butter-, and cheese-enriched sauce dulled flavor and didn't really unify the dish. If we wanted a true spring-vegetable pasta—with a few thoughtfully chosen vegetables and a light but full-bodied sauce that clung well to the noodles and brought the dish together—we'd have to start from the beginning.

CHOOSE YOUR VEGETABLES WISELY Freely testing our way through various spring staples, we landed on a pair of classics—asparagus and green peas—plus garlic

and leeks for their aromatic depth and sweetness, chives for their fresh bite and oniony overtones, and mint, a natural match for peas. We also decided at the outset to do away with the tedious blanching step. We found that by sautéing the vegetables in stages in a large Dutch oven, we were able to ensure that each one maintained its crisp-tender texture while taking on a touch of flavorful browning. First went the leeks, followed by the chopped asparagus, the minced garlic, and finally the frozen baby peas, which needed only a minute over the heat to lend sweetness to the mix. But the vegetables alone weren't enough to give the dish flavor.

USE THE RISOTTO METHOD Italian cookery has a tradition of parboiling pasta in water and then letting it finish cooking for a minute or two in whatever sauce is being served. The technique has a twofold benefit: As the pasta cooks, it absorbs some of the sauce and takes on its flavors. In exchange, the noodles release some of their starches into the sauce, which helps build body. If we were going to add the pasta to the broth eventually, why not get the full benefit of the broth's flavor and use it to cook the pasta from the start? The concept was nothing new, of course: It's a classic risotto technique, in which the rice and broth work together to produce a glossy, full-bodied "sauce" that thoroughly flavors and coats each grain. When we tried the approach with pasta, the results weren't quite perfect, but they were promising: The noodles, which we had boiled in a modest 5 cups of liquid (4 cups of broth, 1 cup of water) until they were al dente and the Dutch oven was almost dry, emerged more flavorful and lightly coated with the silky, starchy pot liquor. In fact, the sauce was thick enough that we didn't even need to add any cream or butter to give it body.

PICK CAMPANELLE Traditionally, the raw rice grains "toast" for a few minutes in some hot fat before the liquid is added, taking on a nutty richness. Adapting this technique for our pasta recipe seemed like a natural move, except for the problem of the long spaghetti strands, which we'd need to break up first. It seemed easier to just change the shape of the noodle. After testing half a dozen shorter shapes, we opted for bell-shaped campanelle: They held on to the sauce nicely, without clinging to one another or compressing into a mass. (Bow tie–shaped farfalle and penne quills made fine substitutes.)

SPRING VEGETABLE PASTA

SERVES 4 TO 6

Campanelle is our pasta of choice in this dish, but farfalle and penne are acceptable substitutes.

1½	pounds leeks, white and light green parts halved lengthwise, sliced ½-inch-thick, and washed thoroughly; 3 cups coarsely chopped dark green parts, washed thoroughly
1	pound asparagus, tough ends trimmed, chopped coarse, and reserved; spears cut on bias into ½-inch lengths
2	cups frozen peas, thawed
4	garlic cloves, minced
4	cups vegetable broth
1	cup water
2	tablespoons minced fresh mint
2	tablespoons minced fresh chives
½	teaspoon grated lemon zest plus 2 tablespoons juice
6	tablespoons extra-virgin olive oil
	Salt and pepper
¼	teaspoon red pepper flakes
1	pound campanelle
1	cup dry white wine
1	ounce Parmesan cheese, grated (½ cup), plus extra for serving

1. Bring leek greens, asparagus trimmings, 1 cup peas, half of garlic, broth, and water to simmer in large saucepan. Reduce heat to medium-low and simmer gently for 10 minutes. While broth simmers, combine mint, chives, and lemon zest in bowl; set aside.

2. Strain broth through fine-mesh strainer into large liquid measuring cup, pressing on solids to extract as much liquid as possible (you should have 5 cups broth; add water as needed to measure 5 cups). Discard solids and return broth to saucepan. Cover and keep warm.

3. Heat 2 tablespoons oil in Dutch oven over medium heat until shimmering. Add leeks and pinch salt and cook, covered, stirring occasionally, until leeks begin to brown, about 5 minutes. Add asparagus and cook until asparagus is crisp-tender, 4 to 6 minutes. Add remaining garlic and pepper flakes and cook until fragrant, about 30 seconds.

Add remaining 1 cup peas and continue to cook 1 minute longer. Transfer vegetables to plate and set aside. Wipe out pot.

4. Heat remaining ¼ cup oil in now-empty pot over medium heat until shimmering. Add pasta and cook, stirring often, until just beginning to brown, about 5 minutes. Add wine and cook, stirring constantly, until absorbed, about 2 minutes.

5. When wine is fully absorbed, add warm broth and bring to boil. Cook, stirring frequently, until most of liquid is absorbed and pasta is al dente, 8 to 10 minutes. Off heat, stir in half of herb mixture, vegetables, lemon juice, and Parmesan. Season with salt and pepper to taste, and serve immediately, passing additional Parmesan and remaining herb mixture separately.

PRACTICAL SCIENCE
WATER ACTIVITY AND DRIED PASTA

Measuring water activity ensures safety.

High-moisture foods are very susceptible to the growth of harmful microorganisms such as bacteria, yeast, and mold. To prevent contamination, foods containing a significant amount of water, such as fresh pasta, milk, meat, poultry, cheese, and bread, must be preserved by refrigeration, pasteurization, sterilization, drying, or the addition of antibacterial agents.

Water exists in food in three forms: free, adsorbed, and bound. Free water is water than can be squeezed from a food such as an orange. Adsorbed water is water that is bonded to the surface of proteins and polysaccharides in food. Bound water is trapped within crystals such as the crystalline regions of starch granules. The first two forms of water are available for the growth of microorganisms, while bound water is not.

The water activity of a food, designated Aw, is a measure of the amount of free and adsorbed water in a food and is therefore a measure of how susceptible a food is to the growth of microorganisms. It is equal to the vapor pressure of the food divided by the vapor pressure of pure water, and can be measured by a simple instrument in 5 minutes. Water activity is a dimensionless scale that runs from 0 to 1, with 1 being the water activity of pure water, while a food with a water activity of 0 would contain no water.

Most bacteria will not grow in foods with a water activity of less than 0.85. But yeasts and molds can grow in foods with water activities as low as around 0.6. When pasta is dried it must be dried to a water activity of 0.6, which is about 12.5 percent water by weight. At this low water activity no microorganisms will grow in dry pasta. What does this all mean? Rather than measure the percent of water in dried pasta, the quality control laboratory measures the water activity of the dried product to ensure it will be safe and shelf-stable.

Fresh Pasta without a Machine

✔ WHY THIS RECIPE WORKS

One challenge we've always wanted to set for ourselves is figuring out how to make pasta with nothing more than the dough, a rolling pin, and some elbow grease. While mechanical pasta rollers aren't all that expensive, many home cooks don't own them. But as anyone who has ever attempted to roll out a block of hard pasta dough by hand knows, it's no easy task. The dough has a tendency to spring back—and if it isn't rolled out gossamer-thin, the pasta will never achieve the right al dente texture when cooked. So how do Italian cooks manage to pull off this feat? One answer: years of perseverance. While we're typically game for a hard-won lesson in authenticity, even we have limits. We wanted a dough that any cook could roll out with ease on the first try and that would cook up to that incomparably tender, silky yet slightly springy texture that makes fresh pasta so worth making.

USE OLIVE OIL   Traditional pasta dough is about 30 percent water (compared with around 50 to 60 percent hydration for a basic sandwich bread dough), all of which comes from the eggs. We figured that simply upping the hydration level would create a softer dough that would be easier to roll out, so we experimented with adding plain water to a batch of dough and an extra egg white (the white accounts for 80 percent of an egg's moisture) to another. Just as we'd hoped, these more hydrated doughs were more extensible—at least initially. But they had their downsides: First, the wetter surface of the dough caused considerable sticking, which required the heavy use of bench flour during rolling and led to cooked pasta with a starchy, gummy surface. Second, by adding more water, we'd allowed for too much gluten development, creating dough that, although easier to roll out at first, developed a greater tendency to snap back to its original shape once stretched out; this also meant pasta that cooked up tough and chewy. Still, we felt we were on to something by increasing the liquid in the recipe. Olive oil is a common addition to many fresh pasta recipes. What if we introduced it instead of water? We mixed up a few more batches of dough, adding increasing amounts of olive oil. As the oil amount increased, the dough became more supple and easier to roll out. But because fat coats the proteins, inhibiting gluten formation, too much oil weakened the dough's structure, leading to excess starch loss in the water and a compromised texture.

AND YOLKS   Up to this point we had tried adding water, protein (from egg whites), and fat to our dough, but we hadn't experimented with the one ingredient that contains all three: yolks. Many pasta doughs substitute yolks for some of the whole eggs, and for good reason. While yolks still contain about 50 percent water, they are also loaded with fat and emulsifiers, both of which limit gluten development. However, unlike doughs made with cake flour or excessive amounts of oil, dough made with extra yolks still has plenty of structure thanks to the coagulation of the egg proteins. To 2 cups of flour, two whole eggs, and 2 tablespoons of olive oil, we kept adding yolks until we had a truly soft, easy-to-work dough that also boiled up nice and tender. The magic number proved to be six extra yolks. This dough took on a beautiful yellow hue, yielded to gentle pressure with a rolling pin, and cooked into delicate ribbons with a springy bite. While tasters had been concerned that the pasta would taste too eggy, they needn't have feared. The sulfurous compounds responsible for the flavor we associate with eggs reside primarily in the whites, not the yolks.

LONG REST   After being mixed, pasta dough is often rested for 20 to 30 minutes to allow the flour to fully hydrate and the newly formed gluten to cross-link into a network and then relax. Given that 30 minutes makes for a friendlier dough, would longer be even better? To find out, we made a batch and let the dough sit at room temperature for an extended period of time, cutting and rolling out pieces every 30 minutes. As we suspected, after an hour, our dough was significantly more malleable—and it continued to soften over the next 3 hours (we found 4 hours of resting time to be ideal, though not critical for success).

ROLL IT OUT   This dough was worlds away from the dense blocks we'd struggled with in the past, but it still required a bit of technique. We knew we needed to avoid using too much bench flour: A little cling is a good thing, as it prevents the dough from springing back too easily. Plus, as we'd already learned, excess flour doesn't get incorporated into the dough and turns the surface of the pasta coarse and gummy. With that in mind, we first cut the dough into six manageable pieces. Working with one at a time, we dusted each piece lightly with flour and used our fingers to flatten it into a 3-inch square. From there we switched to a rolling pin and doubled it to a 6-inch square. After another light dusting of flour, we began working the dough. We started with the pin in the middle of the dough and first rolled away, returned to the middle, and then rolled toward us. When the dough reached 6 by

12 inches, we gave it another dusting of flour and then repeated the rolling process until the dough measured roughly 6 by 20 inches. From here, the possibilities were limitless. Lasagna was a given. For ribbon-style pasta, we allowed the sheets to dry on dish towels until firm around the edges (a step that enabled us to avoid dusting with more flour) before folding them up in 2-inch intervals and slicing crosswise to the desired thickness.

FRESH PASTA WITHOUT A MACHINE
MAKES 1 POUND; SERVES 4 TO 6

If using a high-protein all-purpose flour like King Arthur brand, increase the amount of egg yolks to seven. The longer the dough rests in step 2 the easier it will be to roll out. When rolling out the dough, avoid adding too much flour, which may result in excessive snapback. Serve with a sauce of your choosing.

- 2 cups (10 ounces) all-purpose flour
- 2 large eggs plus 6 large yolks
- 2 tablespoons olive oil
- 1 tablespoon salt

1. Process flour, eggs and yolks, and oil in food processor until mixture forms cohesive dough that feels soft and is barely tacky to touch, about 45 seconds. (If dough sticks to your fingers, add up to ¼ cup flour, 1 tablespoon at a time, until barely tacky. If dough doesn't become cohesive, add up to 1 tablespoon water, 1 teaspoon at a time, until it just comes together; process 30 seconds longer.)

2. Turn dough ball onto dry surface and knead until smooth, 1 to 2 minutes. Shape dough into 6-inch-long cylinder. Wrap with plastic wrap and set aside at room temperature to rest for at least 1 hour or up to 4 hours.

3. Cut cylinder crosswise into 6 equal pieces. Working with 1 piece of dough (rewrap remaining dough), dust both sides with flour, place cut side down on clean work surface, and press into 3-inch square. Using heavy rolling pin, roll into 6-inch square. Dust both sides of dough lightly with flour. Starting at center of square, roll dough away from you in 1 motion. Return rolling pin to center of dough and roll toward you in 1 motion. Repeat steps of rolling until dough sticks to counter and measures roughly 12 inches long. Lightly dust both sides of dough with flour and continue rolling dough until it measures roughly 20 inches long and 6 inches wide, frequently lifting dough to release it from counter. (You should be able to easily see outline of your fingers through dough.) If dough firmly sticks to counter and wrinkles when rolled out, dust dough lightly with flour.

4. Transfer pasta sheet to clean dish towel and let stand, uncovered, until firm around edges, about 15 minutes; meanwhile, roll out remaining dough. Starting with 1 short end, gently fold pasta sheet at 2-inch intervals until sheet has been folded into flat, rectangular roll. With sharp chef's knife, slice crosswise into ³⁄₁₆-inch-wide noodles. Use your fingers to unfurl pasta and transfer to baking sheet. Repeat folding and cutting remaining sheets of dough. Cook noodles within 1 hour.

5. Bring 4 quarts water to boil in large Dutch oven. Add salt and pasta and cook until tender but still al dente, about 3 minutes. Reserve 1 cup cooking water. Drain pasta and toss with sauce of your choosing; serve immediately.

TO MAKE AHEAD: Follow recipe through step 4, transfer baking sheet of pasta to freezer, and freeze until pasta is firm. Transfer to zipper-lock bag and store for up to 2 weeks. Cook frozen pasta straight from freezer as directed in step 5.

PRACTICAL SCIENCE
COOKING PASTA IN ALKALINE TAP WATER

Alkaline water can make for sticky pasta.

While pure water has a pH of 7 (neither acidic nor basic), tap water is often alkaline. Water may be naturally alkaline if it contains lots of calcium or magnesium, or your local water authority may be adding alkali to reduce pipe corrosion.

When pasta is immersed in boiling water, its starches begin to absorb water and swell at the same time that the protein network surrounding them grows more elastic. Here's where pH comes into play: Alkaline water will weaken the protein network, which acts as a sort of protective mesh to contain the starches. This allows starches at the surface of the pasta to absorb water and burst, leaving a sticky residue that causes strands to stick together. Water that's even slightly acidic, however, can strengthen the protein mesh and prevent starch granules from swelling to the point that they burst.

If you think you have alkaline water, here's a quick fix: Add 2 teaspoons of lemon juice or white vinegar to 4 quarts of pasta water. This will help prevent your pasta from sticking without affecting its flavor.

CHAPTER 37

Whole-Wheat Flour

This nutty, earthy flour adds intense flavor to baked goods. And it doesn't have to ruin their texture. It just needs a soak.

HOW THE SCIENCE WORKS

Unlike refined white flour, which is derived from just the grain's stripped-down inner core, or endosperm, whole-wheat flour is made from the entire wheat berry: endosperm, germ, and bran. Because of this, it boasts a light brown color and a more pronounced wheat flavor.

Within a kernel of wheat, the endosperm comprises about 83 percent of the weight. The endosperm also contains nearly all of the starch and the proteins gliadin and glutenin, which combine when moisture is introduced to produce gluten, the protein that is essential for making leavened bread, among other things. The germ, which makes up about 2.5 percent of the wheat kernel, is high in fat for fuel (about 10 percent of its weight), numerous active enzymes, and other proteins (though none that form gluten), as well as nutrients needed for the growth of the seed. The fat in the germ is the reason that whole-wheat flour has a shorter shelf life; the unsaturated molecules of fat are easily oxidized and become rancid within a few months. The bran, which makes up about 4.5 percent of the kernel, is the protective covering. It contains many layers of tough fibrous material. The remaining 10 percent of the weight of a wheat kernel? Water.

Whole-wheat flour is more nutritious than refined white flour, providing a good supply of B vitamins, essential minerals, trace minerals, and dietary fiber. But whole-wheat flour is less functional than refined white flour for making bread and other leavened baked goods. And that's not because it has less protein—in fact it has more, around 15 percent, compared to white flour, which contains 7 to 13 percent, give or take. But not all of the proteins in whole-wheat flour are capable of forming gluten. And there are other components of whole wheat that limit its functionality. First, ground particles of bran are sharp and easily pierce the gluten protein network when it forms. Second, the germ contains a small peptide called glutathione, which chemically combines with the gliadin and glutenin proteins, reducing their ability to cross-link and form a strong gluten network. Gluten formed in the presence of glutathione is weaker and less capable of holding the expanding gases during bread baking.

Manufacturers that produce whole-wheat bread help to minimize these limitations by grinding the bran to very fine particle sizes or adding emulsifying agents. But even with these changes, whole-wheat flour is not ideal for bread making, and this is why federal regulations allow loaves labeled "whole-wheat bread" to contain up to 49 percent white flour.

We use various techniques to bypass the limitations of whole-wheat flour in order to create baked goods with intensely nutty flavor, and yet still an enjoyable texture. For our Thin-Crust Whole-Wheat Pizza (page 306), we cut the whole-wheat flour with bread flour and let the dough sit, in order to both strengthen and then loosen the gluten network. For our Whole-Wheat Sandwich Bread (page 307), we soak the wheat flour to soften the sharp bran. Similarly, for our Honey-Wheat Dinner Rolls (page 309), we use a superhydrated dough in order to soften the bran, and we use ingredients that are especially high in moisture for our Whole-Wheat Blueberry Muffins (page 310). The only recipe we don't have to worry about? 100 Percent Whole-Wheat Pancakes (page 311). Here, a lack of gluten is a good thing—making for tender, nutty-flavored pancakes.

Federal regulations allow loaves labeled "whole-wheat bread" to contain up to 49 percent white flour.

There's no denying it. Whole-wheat flour still gets a bad rap for making baked goods taste bitter and unpleasant. But is that a fair judgment? Is whole wheat really to blame, or is it perhaps our fault for how we store it? We set up the following experiment to find out.

EXPERIMENT

We made three batches of our 100 Percent Whole-Wheat Pancakes (page 311). For one batch we used flour from a bag that had been opened and stored at room temperature for a few months. For the second we used flour from a fresh bag straight from the supermarket. For the final batch we made our own flour by grinding fresh wheat berries in a blender. We had tasters sample pancakes from each batch and comment on texture and flavor.

RESULTS

Our tasters couldn't have been clearer in their preferences. While there was no discernable difference in texture among the three batches, there were drastic differences in flavor. The pancakes made with bagged flour fresh from the supermarket and those made with our homemade flour were touted as "sweet" and "nutty" with "no trace of bitterness." The batch made with the flour left at room temperature for a few months, however, was unanimously panned as "bitter."

TAKEAWAY

It turns out that what we consider "whole-wheat flavor" is really a combination of two distinct flavors. The toasty, slightly tannic flavor we often describe as "nutty" primarily comes from phenolic acids found in the bran. This flavor is inherent to whole wheat and is relatively stable over time. The bitter flavor, on the other hand, develops as a result of oxidation of the fat found mostly in the germ. It is the flavor of rancidity.

So does this mean that whole-wheat flour stored for any appreciable amount of time will necessarily taste bitter? Luckily, no. While we've found that whole-wheat flour left in its original bag can go rancid in as little as three months at room temperature, that process slows down considerably when the temperature drops. In previous tests we've stored whole-wheat flour in a sealed container in the freezer for up to 12 months without it developing the unpleasant flavors of oxidation. In the future we'll always use fresh flour, frozen flour, or flour we grind ourselves right in the kitchen.

THE BITTER EDGE TO WHOLE WHEAT

Sometimes baked goods (or pancakes) made with whole-wheat flour can taste a bit bitter. What's going on? It turns out the bitterness has everything to do with how you store your flour. A bitter flavor can develop when whole-wheat flour is stored at room temperature, allowing the fat found in the germ to more easily oxidize. Our preference? Use fresh flour from the market, frozen flour, or even grind your own flour yourself, like we are doing here (for more, see page 312).

Technique 101: Yeasted Bread

Yeasted breads can be intimidating. Making them involves multiple steps—and a lot of time. But once you understand the science underlying the recipes, it becomes much more manageable. Here, we take a closer look at choosing yeast, developing gluten, and giving your loaf of bread all the time it needs to ferment.

LET IT RISE

Fermentation is a key step that occurs after the dough has been mixed and kneaded. In this stage, the yeast consumes sugars and starches in the dough, producing not only carbon dioxide, which is critical to give the dough the proper rise, but also numerous flavor and aroma molecules.

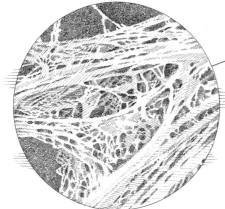

CLOSE UP: GLUTEN

The two proteins in flour important for gluten development are glutenin and gliadin. Glutenin is large and coiled, providing strength and elasticity in dough. Gliadin is smaller and more tightly coiled, providing stretch. When water and flour mix, glutenin and gliadin form a loose, disorganized matrix. With kneading (or resting), these proteins are aligned, better linking up, and creating a stronger network.

START WITH FLOUR AND WATER

The ratio of water to flour can drastically change bread's texture. When flour hits water, the individual wheat proteins begin to change shape, connecting to form strands of gluten. Too much water can dilute and weaken the gluten. Too little water, and the gluten network cannot form. Without a strong gluten network, the gas bubbles created in the dough cannot hold and rise, creating either loaves with a small and dense crumb or ones that are unable to rise. We vary the hydration of our loaves depending on our desired texture. But it's important to measure your ingredients well.

MAXIMIZE GLUTEN DEVELOPMENT

In bread baking, kneading is an incredibly important step. Proper kneading incorporates air, distributes ingredients, and, most importantly, develops gluten, which gives yeasted bread chew. Mixing starts the process by creating a weak, disorganized matrix of gluten proteins. Then, kneading is required to do the bulk of the work, the mechanical action straightening out these proteins and aligning them so they can cross-link into a strong gluten network that gives bread the structure it needs to expand without bursting.

TAKE YOUR TIME

After kneading comes fermentation. If fermentation happens too quickly, the yeast can produce an excess of sour-smelling volatile acids. We use two techniques to combat this: pre-ferments and cool fermentation. Pre-ferments (also known as sponges or starters) are made before the bread dough is even mixed together. Cool fermentation is all about temperature, or allowing bread doughs to rise overnight in the fridge. At lower temperatures, yeast will produce less carbon dioxide and more alcohols and desirable acids, making more flavorful bread.

YEAST PRIMER

There are three main types of yeast: fresh, active dry, and instant (or rapid-rise). All are derived from the powerful brewer's yeast known as *Saccharomyces cerevisiae*, but each is processed in a slightly different way. Instant and active dry yeast may be substituted for each other if you follow this formula: 1 teaspoon active dry yeast equals ¾ teaspoon instant yeast.

ACTIVE DRY Active dry yeasts arrive at their granular state by undergoing processes that reduce them to 95 percent dry matter. Because a layer of dead cells encapsulates living cells, active dry yeast must first be dispersed in a relatively hot liquid to slough off dead cells from the living cells.

INSTANT Instant yeasts are also processed to 95 percent dry matter, but are subjected to a gentler drying process than active dry. As a result, most of the dried particles are living, or active. This means the yeast can be mixed directly with recipe ingredients without first being dispersed in water.

FRESH The original commercial yeast, known as fresh, compressed, or cake yeast is about 70 percent water by weight and is composed of 100 percent living cells. It is soft and requires no proofing—fresh yeast will disperse if it is simply rubbed into sugar or dropped into warm liquid.

Thin-Crust Whole-Wheat Pizza

✔ WHY THIS RECIPE WORKS

A quick survey of pizza parlor menus suggests that pies are going the way of rustic bread: They're no longer a white flour–only affair. Even most supermarkets offer a partial whole wheat–flour dough alongside their standard white. In theory, this is good news, since whole wheat can lend rich, nutty flavor and satisfying depth to almost any kind of baked good. But in practice, we often find the marriage of whole wheat and pizza crust to be strained at best. Most recipes seem to fear commitment to the style, casually throwing a scant amount of whole-wheat flour into a white flour formula. The resulting pies may have decent texture, but if they have zilch when it comes to nuttiness or flavor complexity, what's the point? At the other end of the spectrum, we've tried following pizza dough recipes with a high ratio of whole-wheat flour (some with as much as 100 percent), and we've found that for the most part they produce dense pies devoid of satisfying chew or crisp crust. Not to mention that these crusts have an overly wheaty flavor that competes for attention with even the most potent toppings. We decided to rethink whole-wheat pizza, examining it through the lens of a bread baker in order to formulate a dough (and a baking technique) that would give us a crust with it all: good—but not overwhelming—wheat flavor; a crisp bottom; and a moist, chewy interior.

ADD BREAD FLOUR We started by using both whole-wheat flour and white bread flour. Bread flour contains more of the proteins (glutenin and gliadin) that form gluten than all-purpose flour. And because whole-wheat flour has less gluten potential (due to the types of proteins in the mix and to the presence of both the germ and the bran, which inhibit gluten development), we would need to punch up the gluten potential in other ways to increase chewiness.

USE ICE WATER We highly hydrated the dough to help strengthen the gluten network. (More water allows for a stronger, more stretchable gluten network.) Ice water kept it from overheating while kneaded in the food processor.

REST A LONG TIME A long rest (read: overnight rise) gave enzymes in the dough time to slightly weaken the gluten strands, increasing extensibility. It also allowed for more flavor-boosting fermentation.

USE THE BROILER We know that a wet steak takes much longer to sear than a dry one and that by the time you achieve a good crust on the former, much of the interior is overcooked. This holds true for pizza as well: A wetter dough will take longer to brown and crisp because more of the oven's energy is going into driving off the extra moisture, leaving less available for crisping. This is why we decided to preheat the pizza stone under the broiler's high heat. It was essential for a nicely browned crust.

DITCH THE TOMATOES The sweet-tart flavors of tomato sauce clashed with earthy whole wheat. Instead, we topped our pizza with three cheeses, garlicky oil, and basil.

THIN-CRUST WHOLE-WHEAT PIZZA WITH GARLIC OIL, THREE CHEESES, AND BASIL
MAKES TWO 13-INCH PIZZAS

We recommend King Arthur brand bread flour for this recipe. Some baking stones, especially thinner ones, can crack under the intense heat of the broiler. Our recommended stone, by Old Stone Oven, is fine if you're using this technique. If you use another stone, you might want to check the manufacturer's website.

DOUGH

- 1½ cups (8¼ ounces) whole-wheat flour
- 1 cup (5½ ounces) bread flour
- 2 teaspoons honey
- ¾ teaspoon instant or rapid-rise yeast
- 1¼ cups ice water
- 2 tablespoons extra-virgin olive oil
- 1¾ teaspoons salt

GARLIC OIL

- ¼ cup extra-virgin olive oil
- 2 garlic cloves, minced
- 2 anchovy fillets, rinsed, patted dry, and minced (optional)
- ½ teaspoon pepper
- ½ teaspoon dried oregano
- ⅛ teaspoon red pepper flakes
- ⅛ teaspoon salt

- 1 cup fresh basil leaves
- 1 ounce Pecorino Romano cheese, grated (½ cup)
- 8 ounces whole-milk mozzarella cheese, shredded (2 cups)
- 6 ounces (¾ cup) whole-milk ricotta cheese

1. FOR THE DOUGH: Process whole-wheat flour, bread flour, honey, and yeast in food processor until combined, about 2 seconds. With processor running, add ice water and process until dough is just combined and no dry flour remains, about 10 seconds. Let dough stand for 10 minutes.

2. Add oil and salt to dough and process until it forms satiny, sticky ball that clears sides of workbowl, 45 to 60 seconds. Remove from bowl and knead on oiled countertop until smooth, about 1 minute. Shape dough into tight ball and place in large, lightly oiled bowl. Cover tightly with plastic wrap and refrigerate for at least 18 hours or up to 2 days.

3. FOR THE GARLIC OIL: Heat oil in 8-inch skillet over medium-low heat until shimmering. Add garlic; anchovies, if using; pepper; oregano; pepper flakes; and salt. Cook, stirring constantly, until fragrant, about 30 seconds. Transfer to bowl and let cool completely before using.

4. One hour before baking pizza, adjust oven rack 4½ inches from broiler element, set pizza stone on rack, and heat oven to 500 degrees. Remove dough from refrigerator and divide in half. Shape each half into smooth, tight ball. Place balls on lightly oiled baking sheet, spacing them at least 3 inches apart. Cover loosely with plastic coated with vegetable oil spray; let stand for 1 hour.

5. Heat broiler for 10 minutes. Meanwhile, coat 1 ball of dough generously with flour and place on well-floured countertop. Using your fingertips, gently flatten into 8-inch disk, leaving 1 inch of outer edge slightly thicker than center. Lift edge of dough and, using back of your hands and knuckles, gently stretch disk into 12-inch round, working along edges and giving disk quarter turns as you stretch. Transfer dough to well-floured peel and stretch into 13-inch round. Using back of spoon, spread half of garlic oil over surface of dough, leaving ¼-inch border. Layer ½ cup basil leaves over pizza. Sprinkle with ¼ cup Pecorino, followed by 1 cup mozzarella. Slide pizza carefully onto stone and return oven to 500 degrees. Bake until crust is well browned and cheese is bubbly and partially browned, 8 to 10 minutes, rotating pizza halfway through baking. Remove pizza and place on wire rack. Dollop half of ricotta over surface of pizza. Let pizza rest for 5 minutes, slice, and serve.

6. Heat broiler for 10 minutes. Repeat process of stretching, topping, and baking with remaining dough and toppings, returning oven to 500 degrees when pizza is placed on stone.

THIN-CRUST WHOLE-WHEAT PIZZA WITH PESTO AND GOAT CHEESE

Process 2 cups basil leaves, 7 tablespoons extra-virgin olive oil, ¼ cup pine nuts, 3 minced garlic cloves, and ½ teaspoon salt in food processor until smooth, scraping down sides of bowl as needed, about 1 minute. Stir in ¼ cup finely grated Parmesan or Pecorino Romano and season with salt and pepper to taste. Substitute pesto for garlic oil. In step 5, omit basil leaves, Pecorino Romano, mozzarella, and ricotta. Top each pizza with ½ cup crumbled goat cheese before baking.

Whole-Wheat Sandwich Bread

✓ WHY THIS RECIPE WORKS

Most recipes for whole-wheat sandwich bread lead to one of two pitfalls. They either pay lip service to being "whole wheat," yielding loaves containing so little of the whole-grain stuff that they resemble the fluffy, squishy bread you find at the supermarket, or they call for so much whole wheat that the loaves bake up coarse and dense, crumbling as soon as you slice into them. (The challenge when making whole-wheat bread is that the very thing that gives it character and distinguishes it from white bread—the presence of bran—is also an impediment to gluten development.) We wanted a sandwich bread with a full-blown nutty (but not bitter) taste and a hearty yet soft crumb that sliced neatly.

INCREASE THE WHOLE WHEAT AND SOAK Using bread flour, with its extra gluten-forming ability, in place of all-purpose flour allowed us to increase the amount of whole-wheat flour from 40 to 50 percent. But to up the percentage even more, we gave the whole-wheat flour a prolonged soaking, which accomplished three things: First and foremost, it softened the grain's bran, thereby preventing the sharp edges from puncturing and deflating the dough. Second, the hydrating effect also prevented the grains from robbing moisture from the dough, which would toughen the crumb. Third, steeping the grains activated the wheat's enzymes, converting some starches into sugars and, in turn, reducing bitterness and coaxing out a sweet flavor. Using a soaker, we increased the whole-wheat content to 60 percent, producing a considerably wheatier final product.

ADD WHEAT GERM   To bring our already wheaty wheat bread up to the next level, we added extra wheat germ, which is removed along with the bran during the milling process for refined flour and is a significant source of not only the whole grain's nutrition but also its sweet flavor. To add even more flavor to our bread, we added some honey for a complex sweetness and cut back on the fat, swapping some of the butter for oil, for a hearty yet soft-textured loaf.

USE A SPONGE   The difference between a good-tasting loaf and one that offers the most robust, well-developed flavor can boil down to the use of a sponge. When left to sit overnight, this mixture of flour, water, and yeast develops a full range of unique flavors that give bread even more character. Because we were already soaking the whole-wheat flour overnight, we made our sponge at the same time and let it ferment overnight.

TURN, SLASH, AND STEAM   We turned the dough midway through the first rise in order to remove large gas bubbles and promote even fermentation. We slashed the top of the dough before baking to make it easier for the dough to rise suddenly in the oven. And before putting the bread in the oven, we poured boiling water into an empty loaf pan that we positioned on the bottom rack. This supplied steam—a common bread baker's technique that prevented the crust from drying out before the loaves had fully expanded.

PRACTICAL SCIENCE
WHITE WHOLE-WHEAT FLOUR

White whole-wheat flour may be substituted for traditional whole-wheat flour, though it has a milder flavor.

White whole-wheat flour is milled from hard white wheat, whereas traditional whole-wheat flour is milled from hard red wheat. Both types of flour include the whole grain (the bran, germ, and endosperm) and are nutritionally similar, though traditional whole wheat has slightly more calories, fiber, and sugar. We compared the King Arthur brand of each in the test kitchen's recipe for whole-wheat bread and unanimously preferred the traditional whole wheat for its heartier texture and nuttier flavor. It tasted "more like whole wheat is supposed to," one taster said. Even so, we wouldn't go so far as to rule out white whole-wheat flour; it worked just as well as regular whole wheat in the recipe, and some folks may prefer a milder taste.

WHOLE-WHEAT SANDWICH BREAD
MAKES 2 LOAVES

If you don't have a stand mixer, you can mix the dough by hand. To do this, stir the wet and dry ingredients together along with the soaker and sponge with a stiff rubber spatula until the dough comes together and looks shaggy. Transfer the dough to a clean counter and knead by hand to form a smooth, round ball, 15 to 25 minutes, adding additional flour, if necessary, to prevent the dough from sticking to the counter. Proceed with the recipe as directed. The test kitchen's preferred loaf pan measures 8½ by 4½ inches; if you use 9 by 5-inch loaf pans, start checking for doneness 5 minutes earlier than advised in the recipe. If you don't have a baking stone, bake the bread on an overturned and pre-heated rimmed baking sheet set on the middle oven rack.

SPONGE

2	cups (11 ounces) bread flour
1	cup warm water (110 degrees)
½	teaspoon instant or rapid-rise yeast

SOAKER

3	cups (16½ ounces) whole-wheat flour
½	cup wheat germ
2	cups whole milk

DOUGH

6	tablespoons unsalted butter, softened
¼	cup honey
2	tablespoons instant or rapid-rise yeast
2	tablespoons vegetable oil
4	teaspoons salt

1. FOR THE SPONGE: Combine flour, water, and yeast in large bowl and stir with wooden spoon until uniform mass forms and no dry flour remains, about 1 minute. Cover bowl tightly with plastic wrap and let sit at room temperature for at least 8 hours or up to 24 hours.

2. FOR THE SOAKER: Combine flour, wheat germ, and milk in second large bowl and stir with wooden spoon until shaggy mass forms, about 1 minute. Transfer dough to lightly floured counter and knead by hand until smooth, 2 to 3 minutes. Return soaker to bowl, cover tightly with plastic, and refrigerate for at least 8 hours or up to 24 hours.

3. FOR THE DOUGH: Tear soaker apart into 1-inch pieces and place in bowl of stand mixer fitted with dough hook. Add sponge, butter, honey, yeast, oil, and salt and mix on low speed until cohesive mass starts to form, about 2 minutes. Increase speed to medium and knead until dough is smooth and elastic, 8 to 10 minutes. Transfer dough to lightly floured counter and knead by hand to form smooth, round ball, about 1 minute. Place dough in lightly greased large bowl. Cover tightly with plastic and let rise at room temperature for 45 minutes.

4. Gently press down on center of dough to deflate. Spray rubber spatula or bowl scraper with vegetable oil spray; fold partially risen dough over itself by gently lifting and folding edge of dough toward middle. Turn bowl 90 degrees; fold again. Turn bowl and fold dough 6 more times (total of 8 folds). Cover tightly with plastic and allow to rise at room temperature until doubled in size, about 45 minutes.

5. Grease two 8½ by 4½-inch loaf pans. Transfer dough to well-floured counter and divide in half. Press 1 piece of dough into 17 by 8-inch rectangle, with short side facing you. Roll dough toward you into firm cylinder, keeping roll taut by tucking it under itself as you go. Turn loaf seam side up and pinch it closed. Place loaf seam side down in prepared pan, pressing gently into corners. Repeat with second piece of dough. Cover loaves loosely with greased plastic and let rise at room temperature until nearly doubled in size, 1 to 1½ hours (top of loaves should rise about 1 inch over lip of pan).

6. One hour before baking, adjust oven racks to middle and lowest positions, place baking stone on upper rack, place empty loaf pan or other heatproof pan on lower rack, and heat oven to 400 degrees. Bring 2 cups water to boil on stovetop. Using sharp serrated knife or single-edge razor blade, make one ¼-inch-deep slash lengthwise down center of each loaf. Working quickly, pour boiling water into empty loaf pan in oven and set loaves in pans on baking stone. Reduce oven temperature to 350 degrees. Bake until crust is dark brown and loaves register 200 degrees, 40 to 50 minutes, rotating loaves front to back and side to side halfway through baking. Transfer pans to wire rack and let cool for 5 minutes. Remove loaves from pans, return to rack, and let cool to room temperature, about 2 hours, before slicing and serving. (Bread can be wrapped in double layer of plastic wrap and stored at room temperature for up to 3 days. Wrapped with additional layer of aluminum foil, bread can be frozen for up to 1 month.)

Honey-Wheat Dinner Rolls

✔ WHY THIS RECIPE WORKS

In our experience, there are two types of honey–whole wheat dinner rolls, and neither hits the mark: Commercially produced versions are light and fluffy, but they're usually too sweet and taste only faintly of wheat. Commercial bakeries rely on chemical dough softeners to lighten their rolls and use more artificial sweeteners than honey. Homemade honey-wheat rolls present a different set of problems. The ones we tried tasted wheaty and nutty all right, but they were as dense as wet sand. In both cases, these rolls are often honey in name only. We wanted tender, fluffy honey-wheat rolls that actually tasted like their namesake ingredients.

MIX WHOLE-WHEAT AND WHITE FLOUR Since we love the texture of the test kitchen's favorite white dinner roll, we decided to start with that recipe and reverse-engineer it into a whole-wheat roll. Our recipe calls for all-purpose flour, yeast, milk, butter, honey, and salt. As a starting point, we exchanged all the white flour for an equal amount of whole-wheat flour. We knew we'd need more liquid than usual, so we dutifully added an extra ¼ cup of milk. Then we kneaded the dough, let it rise, shaped it into rolls, let it rise again, and baked. A few hours later, we stared unhappily at the tray of tough, dense honey-wheat rolls we'd produced. Also, using all whole-wheat flour had made the rolls almost bitter. We tried adding more butter, and more eggs. But nothing worked. No matter what we added, the rolls were heavy, coarse, and bitter. We finally admitted that a 100 percent–wheat dinner roll wasn't going to work. That's because wheat flour and white flour function differently. The bran in whole-wheat flour inhibits gluten development, which is why whole-wheat rolls don't rise as well as white flour rolls. To get a light, fluffy roll we'd have to put some all-purpose white flour back into the dough, letting more gluten develop. After a few tests, we figured out that a volume ratio of about 3 parts wheat to 2 parts white flour was where we had to stop.

INCREASE LIQUID Whole-wheat flour has a lot more bran than white flour. And bran is sharp, so sharp that it can slice right through the gluten strands that give height and structure to bread (and cakes, for that matter). To stop the bran from doing so, we realized, we needed to soften it. How? By letting it absorb a lot of water. (Alternatively, we could let the bran soak for a long time, but we were unwilling to wait around any longer than necessary for these rolls.) And with that, we'd found the key to fluffy wheat rolls—a superwet (or "superhydrated") dough. With this in mind, we once again increased the amount of liquid called for in our recipe to make an especially sticky dough. To force the loose dough to rise up, not spread out, we snuggled the shaped rolls against one another in a baking dish. Placing them close together also translated into less crust and a more fluffy interior. Indeed, these rolls were the best yet: tall and soft yet still unequivocally wheaty.

HONEY-WHEAT DINNER ROLLS
MAKES 16 ROLLS

Expect this dough to be sticky; resist the urge to add more flour, which will turn the rolls dense.

1¾ cups warm whole milk (110 degrees), plus 1 tablespoon
6 tablespoons plus 1 teaspoon honey
5 tablespoons unsalted butter, melted and cooled
1 large egg
2½ cups (13¾ ounces) whole-wheat flour
1¾ cups (8¾ ounces) all-purpose flour
1 tablespoon instant or rapid-rise yeast
2¼ teaspoons salt

1. Adjust oven rack to lower-middle position and heat oven to 200 degrees. When oven temperature reaches 200 degrees, turn off oven. Grease large bowl and 13 by 9-inch baking dish. Combine 1¾ cups warm milk, 6 tablespoons honey, 4 tablespoons melted butter, and egg in 4-cup liquid measuring cup.

2. Using stand mixer fitted with dough hook, mix whole-wheat flour, all-purpose flour, yeast, and salt on low speed until combined. Slowly add milk mixture and mix until dough comes together, about 1 minute. Increase speed to medium and knead until dough is smooth and almost clears sides of bowl yet still sticks to bottom, 6 to 8 minutes.

3. Scrape down bowl and transfer dough to greased bowl. Cover with plastic wrap and transfer to turned-off oven. Keep dough in oven until dough has doubled in size, about 45 minutes.

4. Punch down dough on lightly floured counter. Cut dough into quarters and cut each quarter into 4 equal pieces. Form each piece into rough ball by pinching and pulling dough edges under so that top is smooth. On clean counter, cup each ball with your palm and roll into smooth,

tight ball. Arrange in prepared dish, 6 balls down center and five on either side. Cover with plastic and refrigerate for at least 8 hours or up to 24 hours.

5. When ready to serve rolls, adjust oven rack to lower-middle position and heat oven to 400 degrees. Remove rolls from refrigerator and let sit at room temperature for 30 minutes. Combine remaining 1 tablespoon melted butter and remaining 1 teaspoon honey in bowl. Brush rolls with remaining 1 tablespoon milk. Bake rolls until golden brown and rolls register 200 degrees, about 20 minutes, rotating dish halfway through baking. Brush with honey butter and let cool in dish on wire rack for 10 minutes before serving.

Whole-Wheat Blueberry Muffins

✓ WHY THIS RECIPE WORKS
One hundred percent whole-wheat muffins can often be dense, squat sinkers that nobody wants to eat. Our goal was to fix that problem. We played with leavener choice, and tried ingredients with differing amounts of moisture to find the solution.

HIGH MOISTURE After trying out a bunch of recipes, we settled on a base recipe that had an unusually high amount of liquid—not just a cup of buttermilk, but also 1½ cups of blueberries, two eggs, and 4 tablespoons each of melted butter and vegetable oil. This high water content produced more steam during baking, which served as another kind of leavening. The liquid also softened the bran in the whole wheat, which helped create lighter, more tender, less dense muffins. The combination of melted butter and oil also reduced gluten development and helped tenderize the muffins. Likewise, the acid from the buttermilk lowered the pH, again inhibiting gluten development and therefore producing a more tender crumb.

TWO LEAVENERS We did a side-by-side test of our working recipe using just baking powder versus powder plus soda, and there was a clear difference. The muffins that used both leaveners were lighter in texture, the tops were domed, and they were more golden brown in color. This is because the baking soda was helping neutralize the acid in the buttermilk, which in turn allowed the baking powder to function more effectively. Without the added baking soda, much of the baking soda already in the baking powder was being neutralized and losing its leavening power.

WHOLE-WHEAT BLUEBERRY MUFFINS
MAKES 12 MUFFINS

Do not overmix the batter. You can substitute unthawed frozen blueberries for fresh in this recipe.

STREUSEL

3	tablespoons granulated sugar
3	tablespoons packed brown sugar
3	tablespoons whole-wheat flour
	Pinch salt
2	tablespoons unsalted butter, melted

MUFFINS

3	cups (16½ ounces) whole-wheat flour
2½	teaspoons baking powder
½	teaspoon baking soda
1	teaspoon salt
1	cup (7 ounces) granulated sugar
2	large eggs
4	tablespoons unsalted butter, melted
¼	cup vegetable oil
1¼	cups buttermilk
1½	teaspoons vanilla extract
7½	ounces (1½ cups) blueberries

1. FOR THE STREUSEL: Combine granulated sugar, brown sugar, flour, and salt in bowl. Add melted butter and toss with fork until evenly moistened and mixture forms large chunks with some pea-size pieces throughout; set aside.

2. FOR THE MUFFINS: Adjust oven rack to middle position and heat oven to 400 degrees. Spray 12-cup muffin tin, including top, generously with vegetable oil spray. Whisk flour, baking powder, baking soda, and salt together in large bowl. Whisk sugar, eggs, melted butter, and oil together in separate bowl until combined, about 30 seconds. Whisk buttermilk and vanilla into sugar mixture until combined.

3. Stir sugar mixture into flour mixture until just combined. Gently stir in blueberries until incorporated. Using heaping ¼-cup dry measuring cup, divide batter evenly among prepared muffin cups (cups will be filled to rim); sprinkle muffin tops evenly with streusel.

4. Bake until golden brown and toothpick inserted in center comes out with few crumbs attached, 18 to 20 minutes, rotating muffin tin halfway through baking. Let muffins cool in muffin tin on wire rack for 5 minutes. Remove muffins from muffin tin and let cool 5 minutes longer. Serve.

100 Percent Whole-Wheat Pancakes

✔ WHY THIS RECIPE WORKS

We've always liked the nutty flavor and slightly rustic texture of whole-wheat flour, so we're glad to see it being added to everything from muffins to pizza crusts. But where, we wondered, were all the pancake recipes? A pancake would be a perfect place to swap whole-wheat flour for white flour because its robust flavor would be an ideal foil for the caramel-y sweetness of maple syrup—and the health benefits of eating whole grains don't hurt either. Pancake recipes that feature a portion of whole-wheat flour do exist, of course, but those that call for 100 percent whole-wheat flour are surprisingly rare. Most cut the whole-wheat flour with an equal amount of white flour, while others call for grains like oats or buckwheat. We wanted something different: a no-frills, all whole-wheat pancake that was simple to prepare and as light, tender, and fluffy as a pancake made with white flour.

BITTER BE GONE We tried just swapping in whole-wheat flour in our regular pancake recipe. The texture was fine, but the flavor was not. Even when we used only 50 percent whole-wheat flour, the pancakes had a bitter flavor that overpowered the nuttiness. We did some testing, and found out why: We had used an open bag of flour we'd been keeping in our cupboard. (See Test Kitchen Experiment, page 304, for more on why.) For our next batch of pancakes, we made sure to use a fresh bag of flour (just opened and well within its expiration date). The results tasted much better. These pancakes were nutty and sweet.

DON'T WORRY Recipes for white-flour pancakes always warn against overmixing. That's because it will create a strong, restrictive gluten network, and that makes for tough, dense cakes. But we discovered that the same rule doesn't apply to pancakes made with whole-wheat flour for two reasons. The first is that cup for cup, whole-wheat flour has fewer gluten-forming proteins than white flour. Second, whole-wheat flour contains bran, which is sharp and will cut through gluten strands that do form. When the gluten strands are shorter, the gluten network is weakened and the pancakes become even more tender. So even using 100 percent whole-wheat flour meant that we ended up with tender, flavorful pancakes.

GRIND YOUR OWN The little bits of bran and germ in whole-wheat flour are a nutritional boon, but they're also a storage liability because they contain fats that are vulnerable to oxidation. If unchecked, this oxidation can give the flour a bitter taste. For the best flavor, we recommend starting with a freshly opened bag or one that you've stored in the freezer. Or you can take it to the next level and grind your own grain. Sound hard-core? We thought so, too, until we tried it. The method is simple: Pulverize wheat berries (which are simply dried wheat kernels and widely available in the bulk section of supermarkets), sugar, and salt in a blender and then add liquid (we use buttermilk); keep blending and then add the rest of the pancake ingredients to create a batter that you can pour directly from the blender jar into the skillet. The whole process barely takes 5 minutes, and the result is the sweetest, nuttiest-tasting whole-wheat pancake you've ever experienced.

100 PERCENT WHOLE-WHEAT PANCAKES
MAKES 15 PANCAKES

An electric griddle set at 350 degrees can be used in place of a skillet. If substituting buttermilk powder and water for fresh buttermilk, use only 2 cups of water to prevent the pancakes from being too wet. To ensure the best flavor, use either recently purchased whole-wheat flour or flour that has been stored in the freezer for less than 12 months. Serve with maple syrup and butter.

2	cups (11 ounces) whole-wheat flour
2	tablespoons sugar
1½	teaspoons baking powder
½	teaspoon baking soda
¾	teaspoon salt
2¼	cups buttermilk
5	tablespoons plus 2 teaspoons vegetable oil
2	large eggs

1. Adjust oven rack to middle position and heat oven to 200 degrees. Spray wire rack set in rimmed baking sheet with vegetable oil spray; place in oven.

2. Whisk flour, sugar, baking powder, baking soda, and salt together in medium bowl. Whisk buttermilk, 5 tablespoons oil, and eggs together in second medium bowl. Make well in center of flour mixture and pour in buttermilk mixture; whisk until smooth. (Mixture will be thick; do not add more buttermilk.)

3. Heat 1 teaspoon oil in 12-inch nonstick skillet over medium heat until shimmering. Using paper towels, carefully wipe out oil, leaving thin film on bottom and sides of pan. Using ¼-cup dry measuring cup or 2-ounce ladle,

portion batter into pan in 3 places. Gently spread each portion into 4½-inch round. Cook until edges are set, first side is golden brown, and bubbles on surface are just beginning to break, 2 to 3 minutes. Using thin, wide spatula, flip pancakes and continue to cook until second side is golden brown, 1 to 2 minutes longer. Serve pancakes immediately or transfer to wire rack in oven. Repeat with remaining batter, using remaining 1 teaspoon oil as necessary.

WHEAT BERRY PANCAKES
MAKES 12 PANCAKES

The recipe directions below are for mixing only. For cooking directions refer to steps 1 and 3 of 100 Percent Whole-Wheat Pancakes and be sure to have extra vegetable oil on hand for the skillet. For efficient blending of the buttermilk and wheat berry mixture, it's important for the blender to create and maintain a vortex, which looks like a whirlpool. Watch the batter as it is mixing; if the vortex closes (or does not form), changing the blender speed or adding more buttermilk will bring it back. Because pulverizing the wheat berries creates some stress on a blender's motor, we recommend using a machine with at least a 450-watt motor and ice-crushing capability. If you are using a high-end blender like a Vitamix or Blendtec, the blending times will be shorter.

1½	cups wheat berries
2	tablespoons sugar
¾	teaspoon salt
1½	cups buttermilk
5	tablespoons vegetable oil
2	large eggs
1½	teaspoons baking powder
½	teaspoon baking soda

Process wheat berries, sugar, and salt in blender on high speed until as fine as possible, about 3 minutes. Transfer mixture to bowl. Add 1 cup buttermilk to blender and pour wheat berry mixture on top. Blend on high speed, adding additional buttermilk and changing speed as necessary to maintain vortex, until mixture is thick and has only small lumps, about 3 minutes. Add oil, eggs, and any remaining buttermilk and continue to blend until fully incorporated, about 30 seconds longer. With blender running, add baking powder and baking soda, and blend until incorporated, about 15 seconds.

CHAPTER 38

Brown Rice

Unlike white rice, brown rice isn't a bland, blank canvas. It's sweet, earthy, and even nutty. You just need to cook it right.

HOW THE SCIENCE WORKS

Rice, a seed from the plant *Oryza sativa,* originally produced in China thousands of years ago, is today routinely found on dinner plates around the world. The varieties of rice, and ways to cook it, can seem endless.

When rice is harvested, every grain of every cultivar and variation is covered with a protective husk. Once the husk is mechanically removed, you are left with brown rice, which includes the fiber-rich bran, oil- and enzyme-heavy aleurone layers, and fatty germ, as well as the starchy endosperm (see page 315). White rice is milled to remove the bran and germ, and polished to remove the aleurone layer, leaving only the endosperm. Keeping all of these elements intact means that, sure, brown rice can be harder to cook, but brown rice also contains more nutrition—and more flavor.

Brown rice is often a starchy, unseasoned mess. It doesn't have to be that way.

While we think of brown rice as a single ingredient, the reality is more complex. There are thousands of different cultivars grown around the world, though the majority of the rice that we buy at the store falls into two: the longer, firmer *indica* rice and the shorter, stickier *japonica*. Within the cultivars, there are even more categories: long-, medium-, and short-grain rice, labels that, not surprisingly, describe the ratio of length to width of each grain. Each type varies significantly in texture when cooked, differences that depend primarily on the amount and composition of starch present.

Starch in rice is composed of two molecules, the smaller amylose and much larger amylopectin. Many studies have shown that amylose is the most important factor in determining the texture of cooked rice. Long-grain rice has the highest level of amylose (22 to 28 percent of the total starch), while medium-grain rice contains less (15 to 18 percent) and most short-grain varieties contain little

to none. Starch granules in long-grain rice cook into firm, dry, fluffy grains of rice. Short-grain rice, also known as waxy or glutinous rice, forms soft, sticky rice and is prized for making sushi. It is sticky in part because the starch granules of short-grain rice begin to absorb water, swell, and gelatinize at a lower temperature than the two other types of rice. Medium-grain rice falls in the middle.

The particular cultivar and the ratio of starches determines whether rice cooks up fluffy and separate or sticky and soft. Yes, the cooking method can affect the texture of the cooked rice, but a lot of the variation is baked into the recipe once you make your selection at the market.

The health food movement of the 1960s and '70s wasn't kind to brown rice. Back then, brown rice, frequently found in macrobiotic restaurants, was often served as a starchy, unseasoned mess. But it doesn't have to be that way. Because brown rice still contains the nutritious (and flavorful) bran, it absorbs water much more slowly than white rice does. Many older recipes cook brown rice the same way as white rice—and either just add more time or more water. The problem with the "more time" method is pretty obvious—if you keep simmering a pot of rice for 45 minutes you will end up with seriously burned rice on the bottom while the grains at the top of the pot are still crunchy. And it turns out brown rice doesn't need to absorb more water than white rice to cook up fluffy and separate. Our favorite way to cook brown rice? In your oven. We bake brown rice in the oven with varying amounts of water, depending on the vessel, for a range of dishes: simple Baked Brown Rice (page 316), Hearty Baked Brown Rice (page 316), Mexican Brown Rice (page 318), and Brown Rice Paella (page 319).

TEST KITCHEN EXPERIMENT

Even well-seasoned home cooks, diligently following back-of-the-bag ratios, often struggle when it comes to cooking a good pot of rice. What if the problem had little to do with a cook's competence and everything to do with the rice-to-water ratios themselves? A survey of common rice-to-water ratios suggests that long-grain rice absorbs more water than short-grain rice and that brown rice absorbs more than white rice. And yet when we researched how rice is cooked commercially, we found that 1 cup of water should be sufficient to hydrate 1 cup of rice, regardless of type. The water in excess of this 1:1 ratio is included to account for evaporation during cooking, according to commercial producers. To find out if this theory holds water, we ran the following experiment.

EXPERIMENT

We gathered 17 different varieties of rice, including white and brown short-grain, medium-grain, long-grain, basmati, and jasmine rice plus two varieties of red and black rice. After rinsing the rice to remove excess surface starch, we placed 1 cup of each type with 1 cup of water in a vacuum bag and sealed them to ensure that no water could evaporate during cooking. We then submerged the bags in a 200-degree water bath until the grains turned tender—25 minutes for white rice types and 65 minutes for brown, red, and black rice types. After letting the cooked rice sit in the bags for 10 minutes, we emptied each into a separate bowl, fluffed the grains with a fork, and tasted for doneness. We repeated this test three times.

RESULTS

To the surprise of our tasting panel, every variety of rice was properly cooked using the 1:1 ratio of rice to water. All of the rice types were tender throughout with no chalky or mushy grains. In addition, the water had been completely absorbed in each sample.

TAKEAWAY

Our findings support the claim that all rice cooks to the proper doneness with a 1:1 ratio of rice to water in the absence of evaporation. How does this translate to traditional rice cookery, where evaporation is always a factor? We have a better understanding of the purpose of published rice-cooking ratios. A cup of long-grain brown rice doesn't require more water than a cup of long-grain white rice, but it does need to cook for a significantly longer period of time in order for the water to work its way through the tough bran layer. That extended cooking time results in a greater amount of water lost to evaporation. But there are other factors that influence evaporation, including the size and shape of the cooking vessel, how tightly the pot is covered, and the source and intensity of the heat. In addition, scaling ratios can be problematic because the amount of evaporation doesn't necessarily double when we double the quantity of rice. All of these variables demonstrate why set-in-stone ratios fail the home cook. The solution? Knowing your equipment and using a trusted recipe. We test our brown rice recipes extensively to determine the ideal amount of water for a given cooking setup. It is important to follow our instructions on pan size and oven or stove temperature, and to choose a properly fitting pan lid.

RICE: 1:1 RATIOS WORK

We cooked 17 different types of rice, in vacuum-sealed bags to prevent evaporation, with a 1:1 ratio of rice to water. We were shocked to find that it worked for every type, including white, brown, red, and black rice. The problem for home cooks? You have to account for evaporation, pan size, and how tightly the lid fits on the pan.

FOCUS ON: BROWN RICE

Brown rice got a bad rap during the health movement of the 1960s and '70s. It doesn't have to be a bland, chewy grain; it's highly flavorful and nutritious.

ALEURONE LAYER

This layer of cells is protected by the bran. It covers the endosperm and is rich in oils and enzymes.

ENDOSPERM

The center portion of the rice grain is high in starch, and is all that's left when white rice is milled.

GERM

The oil-rich germ is responsible for reproduction in a grain of rice—though, along with the bran, it is removed through milling to make the more shelf-stable white rice.

BRAN

The outer, protective bran layer is fiber-rich, contains proteins and minerals, and can be light brown, black, or red in color.

BROWN RICE TYPE	TEXTURE	FLAVOR
Aromatic Rice: Basmati	Distinctly separate grains with an elastic, almost spongy texture	Mildly sweet with clean nut and barley flavors
Aromatic Rice: Jasmine	Moderately firm, separate grains	Nutty, buttery, and rich-tasting
Short-Grain	Soft and creamy	Very sweet and malty-tasting
Long-Grain	Very firm, separate grains with almost no elasticity	Earthy-tasting with a slightly chalky finish

GROWING

Rice can grow in many conditions, from wetlands to desert. In the U.S., rice is most commonly grown in Arkansas, California, Louisiana, Mississippi, Missouri, and Texas. The combination of heavy clay soil, which holds water, and hot, dry weather, which does not encourage disease and insects, is what makes California a good place to grow rice, says Bryce Lundberg of Lundberg Family Farms, where they produce 18 types of rice, both brown and white.

Any variety of rice can be left in its brown form or milled to produce a white variety. From a grower's perspective, the difference between brown and white rice "has to do with how we're harvesting it," says Lundberg. "For brown rice, we want it to be harvested at a lower moisture, which helps the bran layer turn a golden brown. We wait until it dries out. We harvest white rice at a higher moisture, in part because this builds more elasticity into the grain."

Baked Brown Rice

✓ WHY THIS RECIPE WORKS

For our brown rice recipe, we cooked the rice in the oven to approximate the controlled heat of a rice cooker, eliminating the risk of scorching. Experimenting with proportions, we discovered why so much brown rice is sodden and overcooked: Most brown rice recipes call for a 2:1 water-to-rice ratio. For our brown rice recipe, we found that 2⅓ cups water to 1½ cups rice gave us just what we wanted—rice that was tender yet chewy, and not sodden at all.

USE LESS WATER   While many brown rice recipes suggest a conventional ratio of 2 parts water to 1 part rice, we found this caused our brown rice to turn out sodden and overcooked. Brown rice doesn't need more water than white rice, but it does need more time. Instead, the ratio of 3 parts water to 2 parts rice—plus trapping the moisture in a covered baking dish—produced a much better final texture.

START BY BOILING   To reduce what was a long baking time of 90 minutes at 350 degrees, we decided to start with boiling water instead of cold tap water—and to raise the oven to 375 degrees. These steps reduced the brown rice baking time to a reasonable 1 hour. (An even hotter oven would cause some of the fragile grains to explode.)

ADD FAT   While toasting the rice dry in the oven imparted a little flavor, it was a slightly off-flavor. Sautéing the rice in fat before baking, however, caused the grains to fray slightly. The solution? Adding fat to the cooking water. A small amount of butter added mild flavor while keeping the rice fluffy.

PRACTICAL SCIENCE SOAKING BROWN RICE

Soak brown rice for a speedier cook time.

Since brown rice can take 45 minutes to an hour to cook, we wondered if soaking it ahead of time could speed up the cooking (just as it does with dried beans). We're pleased to report success: After soaking in water for at least 6 hours in the refrigerator, brown rice cooked in only 30 minutes. The simplest approach is to place the rice and premeasured cooking water (use 1½ cups of water per cup of rice) directly into a pot (before leaving for work, for example) and let it soak in the refrigerator. Then it's merely a question of adding salt and turning on the heat when you're ready to cook. Besides the abbreviated cooking time, there's an added benefit: The long soak softens the hard outer bran layer much better than simmering alone does, resulting in rice that's far more tender and fluffy. (Just don't soak rice for longer than 24 hours: It can start to sprout or ferment.)

BAKED BROWN RICE
SERVES 4 TO 6

To minimize any loss of water through evaporation, cover the saucepan and use the water as soon as it reaches a boil. An 8-inch ceramic baking dish with a lid may be used instead of the baking dish and aluminum foil. To double the recipe, use a 13 by 9-inch baking dish; the baking time does not need to be increased.

1½	cups long-grain, medium-grain, or short-grain brown rice
2⅓	cups water
2	teaspoons unsalted butter or vegetable oil
½	teaspoon salt

1. Adjust oven rack to middle position and heat oven to 375 degrees. Spread rice in 8-inch square baking dish.

2. Bring water and butter to boil, covered, in medium saucepan. Once boiling, immediately stir in salt and pour water over rice in baking dish. Cover baking dish tightly with 2 layers of aluminum foil. Transfer baking dish to oven and bake rice until tender, about 1 hour.

3. Remove baking dish from oven and uncover. Fluff rice with fork, then cover dish with dish towel and let rice stand for 5 minutes. Uncover and let rice stand 5 minutes longer. Serve immediately.

Hearty Baked Brown Rice with Onions and Roasted Red Peppers

✓ WHY THIS RECIPE WORKS

To bump up the flavor of our basic brown rice recipe, we turned to a Dutch oven and made a few easy additions. Caramelizing onions in the Dutch oven before stirring in the rice, and incorporating chicken broth into the cooking liquid, had a positive impact. In variations we used peas, black beans, or andouille sausage as rich additions. Fresh herbs and a squeeze of citrus just before serving, or the addition of strong cheeses like Parmesan or feta, also brightened this brown rice recipe.

GO DUTCH   While in our simple baked brown rice recipe we cooked the rice in a baking dish covered in foil, in this recipe, we decided to go with a lidded Dutch oven. Why? Because we were adding ingredients like garlic and onions, which needed to be sautéed, using a Dutch oven meant we could eliminate the use of an extra sauté pan.

USE MORE WATER Because we were using a Dutch oven, which has a greater surface area than an 8-inch baking dish, more water evaporated during the cook time. Therefore, we increased the liquid to 3¼ cups to achieve perfectly chewy rice.

HEARTY BAKED BROWN RICE WITH ONIONS AND ROASTED RED PEPPERS
SERVES 4 TO 6

Short-grain brown rice can also be used.

4	teaspoons olive oil
2	onions, chopped fine
2¼	cups water
I	cup chicken broth
I½	cups long-grain brown rice
I	teaspoon salt
¾	cup chopped jarred roasted red peppers
½	cup minced fresh parsley
¼	teaspoon pepper
I	ounce Parmesan cheese, grated (½ cup)
	Lemon wedges

1. Adjust oven rack to middle position and heat oven to 375 degrees. Heat oil in Dutch oven over medium heat until shimmering. Add onions and cook, stirring occasionally, until well browned, 12 to 14 minutes.

2. Add water and broth, cover, and bring to boil. Off heat, stir in rice and salt. Cover, transfer pot to oven, and bake rice until tender, 1 hour 5 minutes to 1 hour 10 minutes.

3. Remove pot from oven and uncover. Fluff rice with fork, stir in roasted red peppers, and replace lid; let sit for 5 minutes. Stir in parsley and pepper. Serve, passing Parmesan and lemon wedges separately.

HEARTY BAKED BROWN RICE WITH PEAS, FETA, AND MINT

Reduce amount of olive oil to 1 tablespoon and omit 1 onion. Substitute 1 cup thawed frozen peas for roasted red peppers, ¼ cup minced fresh mint for parsley, ½ teaspoon grated lemon zest for pepper, and ½ cup crumbled feta for Parmesan.

HEARTY BAKED BROWN RICE WITH BLACK BEANS AND CILANTRO

Substitute 1 finely chopped green bell pepper for 1 onion. Once vegetables are well browned in step 1, stir in 3 minced garlic cloves and cook until fragrant, about 30 seconds. Substitute one 15-ounce can black beans for roasted red peppers and ¼ cup minced fresh cilantro for parsley. Omit Parmesan and substitute lime wedges for lemon wedges.

HEARTY BAKED BROWN RICE WITH ANDOUILLE, CORN, AND RED PEPPERS

If you cannot find andouille sausage, substitute chorizo, linguiça, or kielbasa.

Omit 1 onion. Reduce amount of olive oil to 1 tablespoon. Heat olive oil in Dutch oven over medium heat until shimmering. Add 6 ounces andouille sausage, cut into ½-inch pieces, to pot and cook until lightly browned, 4 to 6 minutes. Using slotted spoon, transfer sausage to paper towel–lined plate; set aside. Add onion and 1 finely chopped red bell pepper to fat left in pot and cook, stirring occasionally, until well browned, 12 to 14 minutes; add 3 minced garlic cloves and cook until fragrant, about 30 seconds, before adding water and broth. Substitute ½ cup thawed frozen corn for roasted red peppers; add reserved sausage with corn. Substitute ¼ cup chopped fresh basil for parsley and omit Parmesan.

PRACTICAL SCIENCE HOW SAFE IS LEFTOVER RICE?

Be careful with your leftover rice.

While it's one of the most common foods (in some countries providing up to three-quarters of daily energy intake), rice may not be the best choice to eat as leftovers. Why? Rice of all types can be contaminated with the spore-forming bacteria called *Bacillus cereus*. Present but dormant in all raw brown and white rice varieties, the spores are not killed by the boiling cooking water—instead, they are actually revived and converted into potentially harmful live bacteria as the rice cools. If the rice is consumed shortly after cooking there is no problem, as very few bacteria have had the time to multiply. But if the rice is saved, and even stored in the refrigerator for a significant period of time, the amount of bacteria will grow. With enough time, the bacteria, which is responsible for 2 to 5 percent of all reported food-borne illnesses, can form enough heat-stable toxin to make a consumer sick within a few hours. The risk is not high, but has most commonly been observed in cooked rice that has been left out for several hours, then refrigerated, and then fried.

Mexican Brown Rice

✔ WHY THIS RECIPE WORKS

Mexican-style rice is a pilaf-style rice dish—with a hearty bunch of additions. We wanted our Mexican rice recipe to be rich but not oily, and moist but not watery. Furthermore, it had to boast clean, balanced flavors and tender, perfectly cooked rice. We produced superior grains by sautéing long-grain brown rice in canola oil until it toasted before adding the cooking liquid. Baking the rice in the oven (rather than keeping it on the stovetop) ensured even cooking.

RIB THOSE CHILES The fleshy white pith of the chile—not the seeds, as is commonly assumed—contains the majority of the spicy heat. The seeds contain heat simply because they are embedded in the pith, making them guilty by association (see page 253). Because the spiciness of jalapeños varies from chile to chile, we controlled the heat by removing the ribs and seeds from the two chiles that we cooked in the rice.

TIME FOR TOMATOES Cooking cereal grains, vegetables, and even legumes with tomatoes can do more than add flavor. Tomatoes are acidic, and acid stabilizes the pectin in the cell walls of these ingredients, preventing them from breaking down quickly. For our recipe development, this meant that the presence of tomatoes slowed down the softening of the cell walls in the bran layer and endosperm of our brown rice, prolonging cooking time. In the end, our Mexican rice needed to cook for 1¼ to 1½ hours in the oven.

PRACTICAL SCIENCE BROWN RICE SYRUP

Yes, you can substitute brown rice syrup for corn syrup.

Like corn syrup, brown rice syrup is made by treating the cooked grain with enzymes that convert starches into glucose and oligomers of glucose called maltodextrins; the resulting sweet liquid is reduced until thick. To see if it makes a suitable substitute, we tasted Lundberg Organic Sweet Dreams Brown Rice Syrup plain and used it in two recipes in which we normally use corn syrup: chocolate frosting and glazed chicken.

Corn syrup is approximately 45 percent as sweet as table sugar, or sucrose. Lundberg claims that its rice syrup is about 50 percent as sweet as sugar, and we found the sweetness levels comparable when we sampled the products plain. But the rice syrup did have a prominent viscosity and pronounced cereal aroma.

To our surprise, tasters found the frosting and chicken samples very similar in taste, texture, and appearance—the complex flavors of the other ingredients masked the brown rice syrup's toasty notes. Rice syrup tends to be more expensive than corn syrup, but is otherwise a suitable alternative.

MEXICAN BROWN RICE
SERVES 6 TO 8

Use an ovensafe pot about 12 inches in diameter so that the rice cooks evenly and in the time indicated. The pot's depth is less important than its diameter; we've successfully used both a straight-sided sauté pan and a Dutch oven. Whichever type of pot you use, it should have a tight-fitting, ovensafe lid. Vegetable broth can be substituted for chicken broth.

2	tomatoes, cored and quartered
1	onion, preferably white, peeled, trimmed of root end, and quartered
3	jalapeño chiles
⅓	cup canola oil
2	cups long-grain brown rice
4	garlic cloves, minced
2½	cups chicken broth
1	tablespoon tomato paste
1½	teaspoons salt
½	cup minced fresh cilantro
	Lime wedges

1. Adjust oven rack to middle position and heat oven to 350 degrees. Process tomatoes and onion in food processor until smooth and thoroughly pureed, about 15 seconds, scraping down bowl if necessary. Transfer mixture to liquid measuring cup; you should have 2 cups (if necessary, spoon off excess so that volume equals 2 cups). Remove ribs and seeds from 2 jalapeños and discard; mince flesh and set aside. Mince remaining jalapeño, including ribs and seeds; set aside.

2. Heat oil in 12-inch ovensafe straight-sided sauté pan or Dutch oven over medium-high heat, 1 to 2 minutes. Drop 3 or 4 grains rice in oil; if grains sizzle, oil is ready. Add rice and fry, stirring frequently, until rice is light golden and translucent, 3 to 3½ minutes. Reduce heat to medium, add garlic and seeded minced jalapeños, and cook, stirring constantly, until fragrant, about 1½ minutes. Stir in pureed tomatoes and onion, broth, tomato paste, and salt; increase heat to medium-high and bring to boil. Cover pan and transfer to oven; bake until liquid is absorbed and rice is tender, 1¼ to 1½ hours, stirring well every 30 minutes.

3. Stir in cilantro and reserved minced jalapeño with seeds to taste. Serve immediately, passing lime wedges separately.

Brown Rice Paella

✓ WHY THIS RECIPE WORKS

The key to our paella recipe was finding equipment and ingredients that stayed true to the dish's heritage, while also finding ways to create a simpler, less daunting recipe that could be made in a reasonable amount of time. First, we substituted a Dutch oven for a single-purpose paella pan. Then we pared down our ingredients, dismissing lobster (too much work), diced pork (sausage would be enough), fish (flakes too easily), and rabbit and snails (too unconventional). For our streamlined paella recipe, we were left with chorizo, chicken (boneless, skinless thighs), shrimp, and mussels (favored over scallops, clams, and calamari). When we focused on the rice, we liked long-grain brown rice.

GO DUTCH To find a substitute for a traditional paella pan, we looked to other recipes. While none were perfect, some offered good clues. One was that if the rice and proteins were to cook uniformly, they had to be arranged in a not-too-thick, relatively even layer. Crowding or mounding the ingredients in a pile was a surefire route to disaster, as a recipe for eight in a 12-inch skillet quickly proved. A Dutch oven held the same amount of ingredients as a 13- to 15-inch paella pan, fit perfectly on the stovetop, and offered the best distribution and retention of heat.

PICKING BROWN RICE Traditionally, paella is made with Valencia white rice. To replace white with brown, we used an equal amount of long-grain brown rice. Because brown rice has the bran and germ still intact, as we know, it usually takes longer to cook. We found it necessary to bake the rice in the oven for 30 minutes before adding the browned chicken and chorizo. However, the amount of liquid in the recipe (from the chicken broth, tomatoes, and wine) was just the same as it was when using white rice. Because our paella is baked in a Dutch oven, very little liquid can escape from the pot. (For more on evaporation and rice-to-water ratio, see Test Kitchen Experiment, page 314.)

BUILD A BASE Whereas French cooking depends on a sautéed aromatic base of carrots, onions, and celery and Cajun cuisine relies on a trinity of bell peppers, onions, and celery, Spanish cuisine uses a trio of onions, garlic, and tomatoes—called *sofrito*—as the building block for its rice dishes. We began by sautéing one finely diced onion until soft and adding a hearty dose of garlic. Traditionally, the final ingredient, tomato, is added in seeded, grated form.

To avoid the mess (as well as skinned fingers), we used a can of drained diced tomatoes instead, mincing the pieces for a similarly fine consistency and cooking the resulting pulp until thick and slightly darkened.

BROWN RICE PAELLA
SERVES 6

This recipe is for making paella in a Dutch oven (the Dutch oven should be 11 to 12 inches in diameter with at least a 6-quart capacity). Dry cured Spanish chorizo is the sausage of choice for paella, but fresh chorizo or linguiça are acceptable substitutes.

- 1 pound extra-large shrimp (21 to 25 per pound), peeled and deveined
  Salt and pepper
- 2 tablespoons olive oil, plus extra as needed
- 8 garlic cloves, minced
- 1 pound boneless, skinless chicken thighs, trimmed and halved crosswise
- 1 red bell pepper, stemmed, seeded, and cut lengthwise into ½-inch-wide strips
- 8 ounces Spanish chorizo, sliced ½-inch-thick on bias
- 1 onion, chopped fine
- 1 (14.5-ounce) can diced tomatoes, drained, minced, and drained again
- 2 cups long-grain brown rice
- 3 cups chicken broth
- ⅓ cup dry white wine
- ½ teaspoon saffron threads, crumbled
- 1 bay leaf
- 1 dozen mussels, scrubbed and debearded
- ½ cup frozen green peas, thawed
- 2 teaspoons chopped fresh parsley
  Lemon wedges

1. Adjust oven rack to lower-middle position and heat oven to 350 degrees. Toss shrimp, ¼ teaspoon salt, ¼ teaspoon pepper, 1 tablespoon oil, and 1 teaspoon garlic in medium bowl; cover with plastic wrap and refrigerate until needed. Season chicken thighs with salt and pepper; set aside.

2. Heat 2 teaspoons oil in Dutch oven over medium-high heat until shimmering. Add bell pepper and cook, stirring occasionally, until skin begins to blister and turn

spotty black, 3 to 4 minutes. Transfer bell pepper to small plate and set aside.

3. Heat 1 teaspoon oil in now-empty pot until shimmering. Add chicken pieces in single layer; cook, without moving, until browned, about 3 minutes. Turn pieces and brown on second side, about 3 minutes longer; transfer chicken to medium bowl. Reduce heat to medium and add chorizo to pot. Cook, stirring frequently, until deeply browned and fat begins to render, 4 to 5 minutes. Transfer chorizo to bowl with chicken and set aside.

4. Add enough oil to fat in pot to equal 2 tablespoons; heat over medium heat until shimmering. Add onion and cook, stirring frequently, until softened, about 3 minutes; stir in remaining garlic and cook until fragrant, about 1 minute. Stir in tomatoes; cook until mixture begins to darken and thicken slightly, about 3 minutes. Stir in rice and cook until grains are well coated with tomato mixture, 1 to 2 minutes. Stir in chicken broth, wine, saffron, bay leaf, and ½ teaspoon salt; increase heat to medium-high and bring to boil, uncovered, stirring occasionally.

5. Cover pot and transfer to oven; cook until rice absorbs most of liquid, about 30 minutes. Remove pot from oven, add chicken and chorizo, cover pot, and return to oven; cook for 15 minutes. Remove pot from oven; scatter shrimp over meat and rice, insert mussels hinged side down into rice (so they stand upright), arrange bell pepper strips in pinwheel pattern, and scatter peas over top. Cover and return to oven; cook until shrimp are opaque and mussels have opened, about 12 minutes.

6. Let paella stand, covered, about 5 minutes. Discard any mussels that have not opened and bay leaf, if it can be easily removed. Sprinkle with parsley and serve, passing lemon wedges separately.

PRACTICAL SCIENCE WHY BROWN RICE FLOUR MAKES THE BEST GLUTEN-FREE PASTA

It is high in protein and fiber and makes a stronger pasta.

Most gluten-free pastas are starchy and gummy. In traditional Italian-style dried pasta, gluten is critically important. This protein matrix provides the structure that keeps noodles intact and pleasantly springy. For people who are avoiding gluten in their diets, finding good wheat-free pasta with the right texture and flavor is a challenge, one which has been met in a variety of ways by pasta manufacturers. We sampled eight brands of gluten-free spaghetti made from substitute grains—mainly rice, quinoa, and corn—that lack the specific proteins necessary to form gluten. Each pasta was boiled and tasted with olive oil, and then with tomato sauce in a second round.

The results were unambiguous: Most brands absolutely failed to meet our standards. Tomato sauce provided some distraction that improved scores, but not by much. Most of these pastas disappointed with textures that managed, despite careful cooking, to be both "mushy" and "gritty." And many tasters complained about flavors that ranged from "bland" to "fishy." But there was a lone standout that tasters described as "clean" and "springy."

We examined the labels, looking for clues to our preferences. Our first discovery was that two brands that billed themselves as "quinoa" pasta were frankly misleading: One contained more rice flour than quinoa and the other was principally made of corn. We definitely didn't enjoy any of the pastas containing corn; all three fell in the bottom half of our rankings.

Our favorite pasta is made with brown rice, and it contains a relatively high combined total of fiber and protein (the combined total matters more than the amount of either fiber or protein alone). It turns out that protein and fiber keep the noodles intact during cooking, forming a barrier around the starch granules, which prevents the amylose molecules from escaping and leaving the cooked pasta sticky and soft. If the protein network fails, the amylose leaches into the cooking water, turning it cloudy—something we observed when cooking the lower-rated brands. Corn and quinoa pastas have less protein and fiber and cooked up mushy and starchy.

High-protein, high-fiber brown rice makes a stronger pasta, and the flavor is surprisingly close to that of whole-wheat pasta. If you're looking for decent pasta without gluten, our advice is to stick with our taste-test winner, Jovial Gluten Free Brown Rice Spaghetti.

CHAPTER 39

Cornmeal

The most important thing about cornmeal is the size to which you grind it.

HOW THE SCIENCE WORKS

Like wheat, corn is a cereal grain. It therefore contains the same three parts as wheat: endosperm, germ, and bran. The endosperm makes up the largest portion of the kernel (82 percent) and contains all of the starch. The germ contains all of the oil (25 percent of the weight of the germ), while the tough bran is rich in dietary fiber.

Corn was first domesticated in Mexico, from a wild grass called *teosinte*, as long as 8,000 years ago. (Corn of that era was small and multicolored.) Corn, also known as maize, is one of the most widely cultivated crops in the world, and more than 40 percent of it is produced by the United States. In 2014, the total acreage of corn planted in this country was almost as large as the state of California. Yet despite this incredible abundance of corn, only about 15 percent in the United States is actually used for human food. The rest is used for animal feed, fuel alcohol, or export. And the vast majority of corn used for human consumption is not the sweet, high-sugar variety we like to eat off the cob. Instead it is yellow dent corn, which contains yellow-colored carotenoids and is high in starch and low in sugars.

Like wheat, corn kernels are dry milled to various sizes depending on the intended application. Unlike wheat, dry corn kernels are also processed by a method known as wet milling, in which the kernels are first steeped in a dilute solution of sulfur dioxide gas dissolved in water. This mildly acidic solution softens the hulls, making it easier to separate the individual components of the kernels into starch, oil, germ, protein (called corn gluten meal), and fiber.

Cornstarch and cornmeal are the two most important corn-based ingredients for the home cook. While cornstarch is produced by wet milling, cornmeal is made by dry milling corn, and it's produced in three particle sizes: coarse, medium, and fine. Most of the cornmeal produced in the United States is ground with steel rollers that physically remove most of the bran and germ. In the absence of the germ, steel-ground cornmeal has a low fat content and is stable for about one year. A small proportion of corn is ground with stone mills, which crushes the corn in a way that retains some of the bran and germ, producing a cornmeal that has more flavor and nutrients but must be refrigerated to prevent oxidation of the fat.

Cornmeal contains a moderate amount of protein (about 7 to 8 percent). The proteins in corn, called prolamins, do not form gluten, so when cornmeal is cooked in water there is no gluten to constrain the abundant starch granules, which swell and gelatinize. With stirring, the granules release starch molecules to form a viscous and pasty network, which solidifies on cooling (think polenta).

One of the most important decisions when it comes to cooking with cornmeal is which grind to use. We use steel-ground cornmeal—the most common kind of cornmeal, which no longer contains the bran or germ—pre-cooking it a bit, to help with moisture retention during baking in our Savory Corn Muffins (page 324). We use a more flavorful (and slightly more perishable) stone-ground cornmeal, which does retain some of the bran and germ, in our heartier Fresh Corn Cornbread (page 325). Grits are coarser-ground cornmeal, and the star of our Creamy Cheese Grits (page 326)—a Southern staple. Finally, we use masa harina, which is cornmeal heated in an alkaline solution before grinding, to help with the malleability in doughs, to make our Corn Tortillas (page 327).

> *In 2014, the total acreage of corn in the United States was as large as California.*

TEST KITCHEN EXPERIMENT

When we explore individual ingredients in the test kitchen, we often find that it's most valuable to break them down even further into their constituent parts in order to understand exactly how they impact a recipe. An obvious example of how this thinking can be useful is the chicken egg. Instead of viewing it as a single ingredient, we separate it into the white and the yolk, each of which provides starkly different uses. A less obvious example is cornmeal. Cornmeal is rich in both protein and starch, two building blocks that perform unique functions in a baked good. We designed the following experiment to explore how the starch component of cornmeal can be put to use in the pursuit of a better corn muffin.

EXPERIMENT

We made three batches of cornmeal muffins with a ratio of 2 parts cornmeal to 1 part all-purpose flour. We kept the recipes identical with the exception of how much milk we added and how the milk was incorporated. For the first batch we used ⅔ cup of milk, stirred into the cornmeal with the rest of the wet ingredients. For the second batch we doubled the amount of milk to 1⅓ cups and again stirred it into the cornmeal with the wet ingredients. For the final batch, we used 1⅓ cups of milk but mixed it with ½ cup of the total amount of cornmeal and cooked it in the microwave to a porridge-like consistency before mixing it into the rest of the batter. We baked the muffins and examined each for appearance and texture.

RESULTS

There was an immediate visual difference between the first and second batch of muffins. While the muffins in the first batch, with ⅔ cup of milk, formed attractive domes, the muffins in the batch where we doubled the milk to 1⅓ cups were flat and spilled out of the muffin cups. Interestingly, the muffins in the third batch, where we cooked the 1⅓ cups of milk with ½ cup of cornmeal, were domed and attractive just like the first batch.

Tasters found the muffins made with ⅔ cup milk to be dry and crumbly, while both muffins made with 1⅓ cups of milk were moist and tender. The only batch that delivered both ideal appearance and texture was the third.

TAKEAWAY

So why the big difference? The starch granules in cornmeal absorb only a limited amount of moisture (less than 30 percent of their own weight) when mixed into a cold liquid. You can see this phenomenon when mixing up a cornstarch slurry with cold water—left to sit for a few minutes, the cornstarch simply settles back to the bottom of the bowl. But when the liquid is heated, it weakens the starch granules so that they are able to soak up much more fluid (up to 40 times their own weight). Consider that same cornstarch slurry mixed into a hot pot of soup—the granules absorb massive amounts of water and effectively thicken it.

So, in the two batches of muffins where we didn't heat up the milk, the raw cornmeal absorbed and trapped less liquid. For the muffins with less milk, this meant that while they baked into a nice shape, they tasted dry. For the muffins with more milk, this meant that the batter contained so much unabsorbed liquid that it spilled out of the muffin cups, despite the fact that the muffins were moist and tender. Only the cornmeal that was cooked, and therefore capable of absorbing a large amount of liquid, baked into a moist, tender muffin with a proper shape. We used this knowledge for our Savory Corn Muffins recipe (page 324).

CORNMEAL CONUNDRUM: HOW MUCH MILK?

MOIST AND TENDER
Cooking some cornmeal with a lot of milk made for moist muffins.

DRY AND CRUMBLY
The cornmeal absorbs only a limited amount of liquid when cold. Less liquid led the muffins to bake up dry.

FAMILY TREE: CORN PRODUCTS

The United States produces 42 percent of the world's corn—three times as much as any other nation. With all that corn, it's little wonder that we use it in so many ways.

DENT CORN

The vast majority of corn grown in the U.S. is dent corn, which has more starch and less sugar than sweet corn.

SWEET CORN

Sweet corn is harvested in its immature "milk stage" while the kernels are smooth and filled with a milk-like juice; it's cooked and eaten as a vegetable.

POPCORN

Kernels of popping corn consist of a moist, starchy center sealed inside a tough, dried hull. Heating the kernels softens the starch and turns the moisture into steam, which increases pressure inside until the hull pops into a "flake."

CORNSTARCH

This thickener is made from the dried ground corn endosperm (which contains starch and protein). It's often used to thicken sauces.

CORNMEAL

Cornmeal is ground processed corn kernels. Stone-ground cornmeal has a coarse texture due to the rough grinding surface of stone; a fine, uniform grind comes from steel rollers.

GRITS

Another form of ground cornmeal, grits usually have a coarser grain than most packaged cornmeal. They are often cooked up into a porridge-like dish.

MASA HARINA

This flour is made by heating corn in an alkaline solution and rinsing, drying, and grinding it. It's dried again and ground to a fine powder, which is used to form a malleable dough.

POLENTA

Italian polenta is a porridge made with water or stock and coarsely ground cornmeal, which is often labeled "polenta" by Italian manufacturers.

HOMINY

Hominy, an essential ingredient in posole, is dried corn that has been soaked or cooked in an alkaline solution of water and calcium hydroxide to remove the germ and hull.

CORN SYRUP

Corn syrup is made from cornstarch, a complicated process that results in a sweet food syrup. It is about 45 percent as sweet as sugar, is very thick, and doesn't crystallize.

BOURBON

In order for whiskey to be called bourbon, its fermented grain mash (also including wheat, rye, and malted barley) must be U.S.-made and contain at least 51 percent corn.

CORN OIL

A relatively modern invention, corn oil was refined for cooking in 1910. The oil is bleached and deodorized; only some trace amounts of flavor compounds remain.

Savory Corn Muffins

✓ WHY THIS RECIPE WORKS

A great sweet cornmeal muffin might be easy to come by, but a passable version of the savory type is the Bigfoot of the muffin world: We've all heard of its existence, but good luck finding physical evidence to support the claim. Most often, these muffins are unappealing, with insufficient cornmeal flavor and/or a dense, heavy crumb. Could we tip the scales in favor of the cornmeal? We knew the reason for the flavor deficit: Recipes generally call for only 1 part cornmeal to 1 part wheat flour. Using more cornmeal would surely produce the distinctive flavor we wanted. But it would also affect texture: Wheat flour helps form an elastic network of gluten that provides structure and traps gas during baking. Cornmeal, on the other hand, can't form gluten. For an attractive rise, some wheat flour would be essential, but we wanted to use as little as possible to keep the cornmeal flavor at the fore.

USE A LITTLE SUGAR We tested several proportions before settling on 2 cups cornmeal to 1 cup flour, along with milk, melted butter, baking powder and soda, salt, and eggs. These muffins boasted excellent flavor with enough gluten to push the batter above the rim of the muffin tin, but they were way too dry. Muffins stay moist with the help of a few key ingredients, namely, water, fat, and sugar. Because a batter that's too runny won't form the proper shape during baking, we wanted to avoid, at least for the moment, increasing the milk we were already using or even adding water. Instead we tried sour cream, which has some water and a lot of fat. But the thick dairy wasn't enough to turn the tide: These muffins were still on the dry side. Next on the docket? Sugar. Yes, sugar makes things sweet, but it also has a huge impact on the moisture level of baked goods. That's because sugar is hygroscopic, meaning that it attracts and traps moisture. It's not uncommon for a sweet muffin to call for more than 1 cup of sugar, an absolute nonstarter for savory muffins. But a little sugar could provide some moisture retention without making the muffins sweet. We started small, maxing out at 3 tablespoons of sugar before the muffins began to taste too sweet.

PRECOOK THE CORNMEAL But frustratingly, even with the help of sour cream and sugar, the crumb was still dry. In the past, we've improved moistness by adding a surplus of liquid to other types of batter and then letting it rest to thicken up prior to baking. The upshot is extra liquid in the mix without having to sacrifice the attractive dome achieved by a drier, stiffer batter. We tried it,

increasing the milk and letting the batter rest for 20 minutes. No dice: The cornmeal-rich batter never fully absorbed the extra liquid and the muffins baked up flat. But could we add more moisture without thinning the batter by precooking the cornmeal with extra milk? We'd give it a try. We microwaved some of the cornmeal with a bit of milk until a thick, polenta-like porridge formed. We then whisked in the rest of the ingredients, divided the batter among the muffin tin cups, and placed the tin in the oven. Fifteen minutes later, we pulled out 12 idyllic muffins: golden brown, rich with buttery cornmeal flavor, and, most important, perfectly moist. Why did this work? The starch granules in cornmeal absorb only a limited amount of moisture (less than 30 percent of their own weight) when mixed into a cold liquid. But when the liquid is heated, it weakens the starch granules so that they are able to soak up more fluid. Using this technique, we could add nearly twice the amount of liquid to our batter without turning it too thin to form a dome.

SAVORY CORN MUFFINS
MAKES 12 MUFFINS

Don't use coarse-ground or white cornmeal.

2	cups (10 ounces) cornmeal
1	cup (5 ounces) all-purpose flour
1½	teaspoons baking powder
1	teaspoon baking soda
1¼	teaspoons salt
1¼	cups whole milk
1	cup sour cream
8	tablespoons unsalted butter, melted and cooled slightly
3	tablespoons sugar
2	large eggs, beaten

1. Adjust oven rack to upper-middle position and heat oven to 425 degrees. Grease 12-cup muffin tin. Whisk 1½ cups cornmeal, flour, baking powder, baking soda, and salt together in medium bowl.

2. Combine milk and remaining ½ cup cornmeal in large bowl. Microwave milk-cornmeal mixture for 1½ minutes. Whisk thoroughly and continue to microwave, whisking every 30 seconds, until thickened to batter-like consistency (whisk will leave channel in bottom of bowl that slowly fills in), 1 to 3 minutes longer. Whisk in sour

cream, melted butter, and sugar until combined. Whisk in eggs until combined. Fold in flour mixture until thoroughly combined. Using portion scoop or large spoon, divide batter evenly among prepared muffin cups (about ½ cup batter per cup; batter will mound slightly above rim).

3. Bake until tops are golden brown and toothpick inserted in center comes out clean, 13 to 17 minutes, rotating muffin tin halfway through baking. Let muffins cool in muffin tin on wire rack for 5 minutes. Remove muffins from muffin tin and let cool 5 minutes longer. Serve warm.

Fresh Corn Cornbread

✔ WHY THIS RECIPE WORKS

Cornbread falls into two main styles: the sweet, cakey Northern type and the crusty, savory kind often found in Southern kitchens. Each has its diehard fans, but let's face the facts—neither tastes much like sweet corn. This is because most cornbreads are made with cornmeal, and no fresh corn at all. Furthermore, the dent or "field" corn used to make cornmeal is far starchier (read: less flavorful) than the sweet corn grown to eat off the cob. So what would it take to get real corn flavor in cornbread? It wouldn't be as simple as just tossing some fresh-cut kernels into the batter. When we tried, we found that we needed to add at least 2 whole cups of kernels for the corn flavor to really shine, and that created a slew of problems. Since fresh kernels are full of moisture, the crumb of the cornbread was now riddled with unpleasant gummy pockets. What's more, the kernels turned chewy and tough as the bread baked. But there had to be a way to get true sweet corn flavor in cornbread, and we were determined to figure it out.

BATTER UP We decided to work on the cornbread base first. In our earlier tests, tasters found that the little bit of sweetener added to the Northern-style versions helped fresh corn flavor break through, so we settled on that cornbread archetype. For our working recipe, we used slightly more cornmeal than flour and decided to abandon fine-ground cornmeal in favor of the stone-ground type, which contains both the hull and the oil-rich germ of the corn kernel. The upshot: a more rustic texture and fuller flavor. For sweetness, honey, maple syrup, and brown sugar all masked the fresh corn taste, but 2 tablespoons of regular granulated sugar fell neatly in line. For the liquid component, we would stick with traditional tangy buttermilk. Three tablespoons of melted butter and two eggs provided richness, and baking the cornbread in a cast-iron skillet allowed it to develop a crisp brown crust.

PRACTICAL SCIENCE
ARE WHITE AND YELLOW CORNMEAL THE SAME?

You can interchange them. Just pay attention to the grind.

The color of cornmeal comes from the variety of corn from which it is milled. To see if there is a noticeable flavor difference, we made our Savory Corn Muffins, Hushpuppies, and Easy Baked Polenta with yellow cornmeal and then with white cornmeal.

With the corn muffins, a few tasters did detect sweeter notes, stronger corn flavor, and a slightly more delicate crumb in the batch made with yellow cornmeal. However, in the tastings of the hushpuppies and polenta, we did not find strong flavor or textural differences (though many tasters preferred the look of the yellow cornmeal).

While most of our recipes work with yellow or white cornmeal, our testing here did confirm a more important distinction: Coarseness is key. When a recipe calls for a specific grind of cornmeal, be sure to use what's called for, as it can greatly affect the texture of the final product. If the recipe does not specify, use finely ground. The test kitchen's favorite finely ground cornmeal is Arrowhead Mills Organic Yellow Cornmeal.

MAKE CORN BUTTER We wondered if we could get rid of the unpleasantly steamed, chewy texture of the kernels by soaking them in a solution of water and baking soda before adding them to the batter—a technique we recently used to tenderize kernels for a fresh corn salsa. The alkaline environment provided by the baking soda helps soften the hulls of the kernels. Sure enough, the kernels were tender . . . that is, until they were baked in the bread and the heat of the oven toughened them right back up. And we still had the issue of all those wet, gummy pockets. With no new ideas to try, we were idly flipping through cookbooks when we came across a recipe for "corn butter" made by pureeing fresh kernels and then reducing the mixture on the stove until thick. We tried it using three large ears of corn and found that the puree thickened and turned deep yellow in minutes, transforming into a "butter" packed with concentrated corn flavor. While the recipes we found used the corn butter as a spread, we had another idea: We added the reduced puree to a batch of batter, baked it—and rejoiced. For the first time, our cornbread tasted like real corn—and without any distracting chewiness. This method offered another benefit: Since cooking the corn puree drove off moisture, our bread no longer had gummy pockets surrounding the kernels. In fact, the bread was almost too dry and even a little crumbly—a result of the large amount of natural cornstarch (released by pureeing the kernels) that was now absorbing surrounding moisture in the batter. Happily, this problem was easy to solve by simply increasing the amount of fat in the batter: an extra egg yolk and 2 more tablespoons of butter did the trick.

FRESH CORN CORNBREAD
SERVES 6 TO 8

We prefer to use a well-seasoned cast-iron skillet in this recipe, but an ovensafe 10-inch skillet can be used in its place. Alternatively, in step 4 you can add 1 tablespoon of butter to a 9-inch cake pan and place it in the oven until the butter melts, about 3 minutes.

1⅓	cups (6⅔ ounces) stone-ground cornmeal
1	cup (5 ounces) all-purpose flour
2	tablespoons sugar
1½	teaspoons baking powder
¼	teaspoon baking soda
1¼	teaspoons salt
3	ears corn, kernels cut from cobs (2¼ cups)
6	tablespoons unsalted butter, cut into 6 pieces
1	cup buttermilk
2	large eggs plus 1 large yolk

1. Adjust oven rack to middle position and heat oven to 400 degrees. Whisk cornmeal, flour, sugar, baking powder, baking soda, and salt together in large bowl.

2. Process corn kernels in blender until very smooth, about 2 minutes. Transfer puree to medium saucepan (you should have about 1½ cups). Cook puree over medium heat, stirring constantly, until very thick and deep yellow and it measures ¾ cup, 5 to 8 minutes.

3. Remove pan from heat. Add 5 tablespoons butter and whisk until melted and incorporated. Add buttermilk and whisk until incorporated. Add eggs and yolk and whisk until incorporated. Transfer corn mixture to bowl with cornmeal mixture and, using rubber spatula, fold together until just combined.

4. Melt remaining 1 tablespoon butter in 10-inch cast-iron skillet over medium heat. Scrape batter into skillet and spread into even layer. Bake until top is golden brown and toothpick inserted in center comes out clean, 23 to 28 minutes. Let cool on wire rack for 5 minutes. Remove cornbread from skillet and let cool for 20 minutes before cutting into wedges and serving.

Creamy Cheese Grits

✓ WHY THIS RECIPE WORKS

Grits should be creamy, rich, full of real corn flavor, and have an amazingly buttery, cheesy finish. Like polenta, grits are cornmeal. The primary difference between grits and polenta is how they're prepared. Unlike polenta, which can require 20 minutes of intermittent stirring, grits are simplicity itself: You whisk a cup into 4 or 5 cups of boiling water; stir occasionally over low heat for about 15 minutes, until the mixture is thick, pudding-like, and soft, with a hint of gritty texture; and stir in a few pats of butter at the end. Recipes for cheese grits usually just swap milk or cream for a bit of the water and whisk in a few handfuls of shredded cheese before serving. Easy? Not so fast. It's tricky to get great corn flavor out of corn grits.

PICK MILK We started by focusing on the cooking liquid. Initially, we thought a combination of heavy cream and water would be ideal, but cream, even in scant amounts, made the grits dense. Eventually we found that a combination of 1 cup of milk and 3½ cups of water was much better. The grits were creamy, with a nice milky sweetness.

AND MONTEREY JACK Next we turned to the cheese. Most recipes call for sharp cheddar (a few recipes suggest Brie or goat cheese, but grits are from the South, not the south of France). But the cheddar made the grits chalky. Even mild, thus moister, cheddar didn't solve the problem. We tried Monterey Jack and mozzarella instead. Though mild, these two are supercreamy and boast a full, milky taste. Mozzarella was too stringy here, but Monterey Jack fit the bill. Ultimately, our tasters decided on a combination of 1 cup of sharp cheddar and 1 cup of Monterey Jack for grits that were creamy and cheesy, with a hint of sharpness.

ADD CORN It took us a while to figure out just what was missing, but eventually we realized it was the corn flavor. In the South, many restaurants (and home cooks, too) use locally milled, stone-ground grits, which have more flavor than the grits available in most grocery stores. Could we coax more flavor out of the regular grits? To amplify the corn flavor, we tried toasting the grits in a dry pan, hoping to bring out the corn taste. This technique did change the flavor, but not in the way we intended—it gave the grits an off-putting, slightly bitter taste. We tried frying the grits in oil and butter at the outset, as though they were rice and we were making risotto, but the result was the same. We were back to square one. We were getting ready to throw in the towel when someone suggested a fix of forehead-slapping ease: "If you want corn flavor, why don't you add corn?" That was it. By pureeing ½ cup of sweet corn kernels along with ¼ cup of water and stirring the mixture into the grits just before serving, we were able to mimic the deep corn flavor of fancy stone-ground grits.

CREAMY CHEESE GRITS
SERVES 4 TO 6

The grits are ready when they are mostly creamy but still retain a little bite. If the grits get too thick, whisk in a little water.

3½	cups water
½	cup fresh or thawed frozen corn
4	tablespoons unsalted butter
4	scallions, white parts minced, green parts sliced thin
I	cup milk
½	teaspoon hot sauce
	Salt and pepper
I	cup old-fashioned grits
4	ounces Monterey Jack cheese, shredded (I cup)
4	ounces sharp cheddar cheese, shredded (I cup)

I. Process ¼ cup water with corn in blender until smooth, about 1 minute; set aside. Melt 2 tablespoons butter in medium saucepan over medium heat. Add scallion whites and cook until softened, about 2 minutes. Stir in milk, hot sauce, ½ teaspoon salt, ½ teaspoon pepper, and remaining 3¼ cups water and bring to boil.

2. Slowly whisk grits into pan until no lumps remain. Reduce heat to low and cook, stirring frequently, until grits are thick and creamy, about 15 minutes.

3. Off heat, stir in Monterey Jack, cheddar, reserved corn mixture, and remaining 2 tablespoons butter until combined. Season with salt and pepper to taste. Sprinkle with scallion greens and serve.

Corn Tortillas

✔ WHY THIS RECIPE WORKS

Fresh corn tortillas have a lightly sweet flavor and a soft, springy texture unmatched by store-bought kinds. We rested the dough for 5 minutes before pressing the tortillas to ensure that the masa was fully hydrated. Vegetable oil, although nontraditional, made the dough soft, pliable, and easy to work with. Be sure to use masa harina or Maseca brand Instant Masa Corn Flour.

ROLL 'EM We like to use a tortilla press for perfectly even tortillas (but you can also press the dough with a pie plate). To use the press, knead the dough until it is soft and tacky. Cover and set aside for 5 minutes. Then, divide the dough into 12 equal pieces, rolling each into a ball. Finally, place the ball in the center of the tortilla press in a split-open zipper-lock bag. Press gently and evenly into a 6½-inch tortilla.

COOK 'EM Tortillas are, of course, used as a serving vessel for tacos and tostadas, and served on the side of countless other Mexican dishes. But when they are incorporated into a dish, such as enchiladas, they are often softened by briefly frying them, one at a time, in hot oil. This helps to make the tortillas pliable and decreases the risk that they'll crack or fall apart in the sauce. Since frying tortillas one at a time is time-consuming and messy, we often warm the tortillas all at once in the microwave instead. In some recipes, we opt to toast the tortillas to both deepen their flavor and help them hold together when covered in sauce.

CORN TORTILLAS
MAKES TWELVE 6-INCH TORTILLAS

The dough should be very wet; if it is too dry, the tortillas will be crisp and brittle. If the dough becomes too dry to work with, knead in additional water. Using two skillets to toast the tortillas in step 4 saves time. Don't skip the final step of laying the toasted tortillas between damp dish towels; it's crucial for attaining a soft texture. To reheat tortillas quickly, stack them on a plate, sprinkle them with a little water, cover them with microwave-safe plastic wrap, and microwave them on high until warm and soft, I to 2 minutes. This method can also be used to heat store-bought tortillas.

2   cups (5 ounces) masa harina
I   teaspoon vegetable oil
¼   teaspoon salt
2   cups warm water

1. Cut twenty-four 8-inch squares of parchment paper; set aside.

2. Mix masa harina, oil, and salt together in medium bowl. Stir in 1¼ cups water with rubber spatula to form soft dough. Using hands, knead dough in bowl, adding additional water as needed, until dough is very soft and has texture of very wet cookie dough (nearly too wet to handle). Cover and set dough aside for 5 minutes.

3. Pinch off 3-tablespoon-size piece of dough and roll into ball. Lay 1 square of parchment on bottom of tortilla press, place ball of dough in middle, and lay second piece of parchment over top. Press ball gently into ⅛-inch-thick tortilla (about 6 inches in diameter). Remove parchment-encased tortilla from press and set aside; repeat with remaining dough and parchment.

4. Line baking sheet with 2 clean damp dish towels; set aside. Heat 8- or 10-inch nonstick skillet (or griddle) over medium-high heat until hot, about 2 minutes. Working with 1 tortilla at a time, gently peel off parchment, 1 side at a time, and lay tortilla in dry skillet. Cook, without moving, until tortilla moves freely when skillet is shaken, about 30 seconds. Flip tortilla over and cook until edges curl and bottom is spotty brown, 30 to 60 seconds. Flip tortilla back over and continue to cook until first side is spotty brown,

30 to 60 seconds. Lay toasted tortilla between damp dish towels; repeat with remaining tortillas.

TO MAKE AHEAD: Uncooked tortillas can be held, covered, at room temperature for up to 4 hours before cooking. Cooked tortillas can be transferred to zipper-lock bag and refrigerated for up to 5 days.

PRACTICAL SCIENCE DIFFERENT TYPES OF MAIZE

Nixtamalization differentiates masa-based products.

Masa and masa harina are both made from hominy, which is dried corn that has been soaked or cooked in an alkaline solution of water and calcium hydroxide to remove the germ and hull. This process, called nixtamalization, imparts a distinctive flavor that differentiates masa-based products from other forms of dried corn like polenta and cornmeal.

Masa is a moist dough made from finely ground hominy. It can be flattened into thin rounds to make corn tortillas or enriched with other ingredients to make tamales (small, moist corn cakes wrapped in corn husks) and *pupusas* (thick tortillas filled with cheese or meat and beans). Highly perishable fresh masa is difficult to find outside Mexico and the Southwest.

More commonly available masa harina is made by drying fresh masa and processing it into a flour. It can be cooked with water and used in place of fresh masa to make tortillas, tamales, or pupusas, but it has a less intense corn flavor.

Unlike masa and masa harina, *masarepa*, a form of instant precooked corn flour, has not been treated with calcium hydroxide. In the test kitchen, we found that it had the weakest flavor of the three products. Masarepa is typically mixed with cold water to make arepas, corn cakes that are split and filled like a sandwich, and then grilled, fried, or baked.

CHAPTER 40

Oats

How to cook the perfect bowl of oatmeal: Pick the right oats.

HOW THE SCIENCE WORKS

Oats are another cereal grain comprised of three parts: outer husk (or hull), endosperm, and germ. The hull is tough and must be removed before processing. Beneath the hull you'll find layers of bran, which contain nearly all of the fiber. The whole grain minus the hull is called a groat; all the familiar oat products we see in the store are made from oat groats.

In general, oat groats require extensive cooking in water to make them soft enough to eat. In the late 19th century, however, quick-cooking rolled oats were developed, changing the face of American breakfast. Today a number of whole-grain oat products are available: regular rolled oats, quick-cooking rolled oats, instant oatmeal, steel-cut oats, and oat bran. Rolled oats are produced from groats that are steamed, squeezed between drum rollers, and dried. Pregelatinization of the starch enables the oats to cook more rapidly, while the thin, flat surface rapidly absorbs cooking water. Quick-cooking oats are squeezed even thinner, while the oats in instant oatmeal are cut in pieces and then rolled thinner still. Steel-cut oats are whole oat groats that have been cut into two to four pieces, producing a chewier texture when cooked.

In the late 19th century, quick-cooking rolled oats were invented, changing the face of American breakfast.

Oats contain the highest level of fat of all the cereal grains (6 to 7 percent of total weight, compared with 2 to 4 percent in wheat and corn). The fat is distributed in the bran, germ, and endosperm, while in other grains it is located almost exclusively in the germ. The fat in oats is easily oxidized due to the presence of several enzymes called lipoxygenases that catalyze the oxidation and therefore lead to the early onset of rancidity. Fortunately, steam treatment and drying early in the processing of oats deactivates the enzymes. As in corn, the proteins in oats, called avenins, present at 13 to 16 percent by weight, do not form gluten, so oat flour is not suitable for making bread.

Oats are especially healthy because oat bran is rich in dietary fiber, especially a soluble fiber called beta-glucan. Studies show that beta-glucan lowers harmful LDL cholesterol in the blood, thus reducing the risk of coronary heart disease. Clinical studies conducted between 1980 and 1995 by the Quaker Oats Company showed that consuming 3 grams of beta-glucan (contained in 60 grams of oatmeal or 40 grams of oat bran) reduced serum cholesterol by 5 percent. On the basis of these studies, the U.S. Food and Drug Administration awarded the first food-specific health claim to oats in January 1997. In order to qualify for a health claim on the label an oat product must contain 13 grams of oat bran or 20 grams of oatmeal (about ¼ cup) providing at least 1 gram of beta-glucan per serving without fortification.

When it comes to cooking oats, it matters what type you choose—the "grind" will determine the texture, and some of the flavor, of your finished dish. We rarely use quick or instant oats, as they contain little of the sweet oat flavor we love. We chose traditional rolled oats for our Oatmeal Muffins (page 332) for their flavor, but turned them into a homemade flour of sorts in order to prevent gummy, starchy patches. We likewise use traditional oats for our Almond Granola with Dried Fruit (page 333), taking care to bake the granola mix without stirring, so that we end up with large and crunchy chunks. Interested in straight-up oatmeal? Try our Ten-Minute Steel-Cut Oatmeal (page 334), made possible by an overnight soak before cooking.

TEST KITCHEN EXPERIMENT

When it comes to flavor and texture, few oatmeal fans swear allegiance to rolled or instant oats. Sure, they're quick cooking, but these processed forms of the oat groat trade the nutty, satisfying bite of minimally processed steel-cut oats for convenience. We were curious if we could find a way to cut the lengthy (up to 40 minutes) cooking time down and make steel-cut oats a weekday breakfast option. We set up the following experiment to find out.

EXPERIMENT

To try to cut down on cooking time, we tested three pre-soaking methods using a ratio of 4 cups water to 1 cup of oats. For the first batch we combined the oats with room-temperature water; for the second we combined the oats and water and brought them to a boil before turning off the heat; and for the third we brought the water to a boil, removed it from the heat, and then stirred in the oats. Each batch sat overnight for 12 hours. The next day we brought each batch to a simmer and cooked until just tender. We also prepared a control batch of oatmeal where we cooked the oats straight through without soaking.

RESULTS

The control batch of oatmeal required 37 minutes of simmering for the oats to turn creamy and just tender. While each of the soaked batches cooked faster, the oats soaked in room-temperature water still took 25 minutes to reach the same consistency. The batches where we used boiling water both turned tender in a mere 10 minutes. In the end, the batch in which the water was brought to a boil separately and then the oats were added produced the finest texture— tender but intact. For the oats that were combined with the water and then brought to a boil, the final simmer turned them mushy and pasty.

TAKEAWAY

We often think of heat as having the greatest influence on speed of cooking. And when it comes to grilling a steak or poaching an egg, that's accurate. But when dealing with dried grains, such as oats, this experiment illustrates that hydration is the real gatekeeper, with heat playing the role of accelerant. By starting the process of hydration well in advance, we can cut our active oatmeal-cooking time from a whopping 37 minutes to just 10. We use the results of the experiment in our Ten-Minute Steel-Cut Oatmeal (see page 334).

CUTTING DOWN ON COOKING TIME

We tested three presoaking techniques for steel-cut oats: soaking them in room-temperature water overnight; bringing water and oats to a boil and then letting them sit overnight; and bringing water to a boil, adding the oats, and letting the mixture sit overnight. We compared each of these to the control: cooking steel-cuts traditionally. The result? Bringing the water to a boil drastically reduced the time it took the oats to finish cooking the following day. Our preference is to bring the water to a boil and then add the oats.

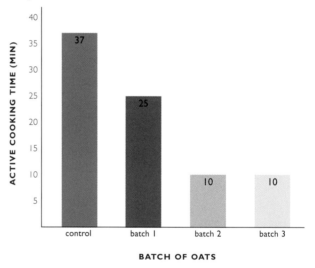

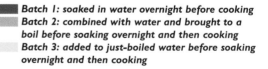

Batch 1: soaked in water overnight before cooking
Batch 2: combined with water and brought to a boil before soaking overnight and then cooking
Batch 3: added to just-boiled water before soaking overnight and then cooking

FOCUS ON: OATS

In the 19th century, quick-cooking oats were invented, a revolution that changed the face of American breakfast. Today, you can buy a whole slew of oat varieties, from steel-cut to instant, which vary in flavor and cooking time.

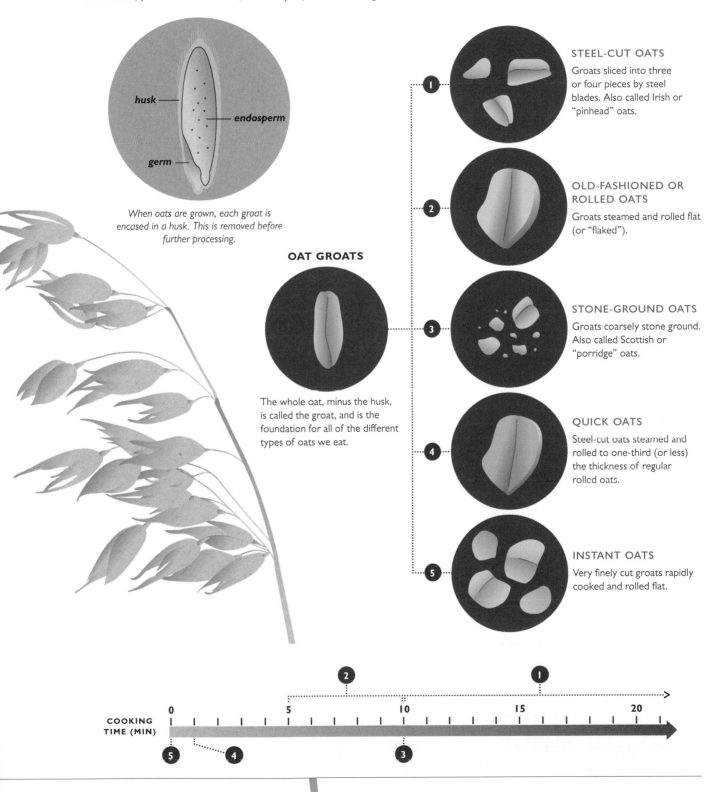

husk — endosperm — germ

When oats are grown, each groat is encased in a husk. This is removed before further processing.

OAT GROATS

The whole oat, minus the husk, is called the groat, and is the foundation for all of the different types of oats we eat.

1 STEEL-CUT OATS
Groats sliced into three or four pieces by steel blades. Also called Irish or "pinhead" oats.

2 OLD-FASHIONED OR ROLLED OATS
Groats steamed and rolled flat (or "flaked").

3 STONE-GROUND OATS
Groats coarsely stone ground. Also called Scottish or "porridge" oats.

4 QUICK OATS
Steel-cut oats steamed and rolled to one-third (or less) the thickness of regular rolled oats.

5 INSTANT OATS
Very finely cut groats rapidly cooked and rolled flat.

COOKING TIME (MIN)

0   5   10   15   20

Oatmeal Muffins

✔ WHY THIS RECIPE WORKS

We've always been interested in the idea of a breakfast that boasts the best qualities of a great bowl of oatmeal—lightly sweet, oaty flavor and satisfying heartiness—in the convenient, portable form of a muffin. But we've yet to find a decent example of the confection. We suppose it isn't all that surprising: Oats are dry and tough, making them difficult to incorporate into a tender crumb. And what chance does their mild, nutty flavor have of shining through when it is clouded by loads of spices and sugar? Determined to bake our way to a richly flavored, moist, and tender oatmeal muffin, we headed into the kitchen and got to work.

BLITZ THE OATS It was clear that simply stirring raw whole oats into the batter wasn't enough to sufficiently hydrate and cook them. Sticking with old-fashioned rolled oats, we set about trying to find the best way to ensure that they would cook through. Soaking and precooking didn't work. It turns out that when oats are hydrated and heated, they release gobs of starch. The oat starch ends up trapping some of the moisture in the batter, thus preventing the flour from evenly hydrating. The result: ruinous thick gummy patches. What if we processed our rolled oats? We broke out the food processor and whizzed 2 cups of chunky rolled oats into a pile of fine oat flour. The finely ground meal readily absorbed milk and fully softened once incorporated into the batter and baked.

LET IT REST But our home-ground oat flour absorbed liquid much more slowly than wheat flour did. We found that if we mixed up the batter and immediately portioned it into a muffin tin, its consistency was too thin and the muffins spread and ran into one another during baking. So after mixing the batter, we gave it a 20-minute rest to fully hydrate.

TOAST IN BUTTER To add flavor, we turned to toasting. We evaluated two options: tossing the whole oats in a dry skillet over medium heat until they turned golden and sautéing them in a couple tablespoons of butter. No contest: The muffins made with butter-toasted oats won for their richer, more complex taste and aroma.

WHISK-FOLD When mixed with the wet ingredients, the oat flour occasionally developed a few large clumps that stubbornly refused to hydrate and dissolve into the batter during baking, leaving dry, floury pockets in the finished muffins. We tried vigorously folding with a spatula, whisking energetically, and even processing the mixture in a blender. But manhandling the batter to smooth it out only resulted in a crumb with a tough texture—a repercussion of overworking the oat starch and wheat gluten. Then we tried a lesser-known technique called whisk folding. In this method, a whisk is gently drawn down and then up through the batter before being tapped lightly against the side of the bowl to knock any clumps back into the mixture. Sure enough, whisk folding made all the difference.

OATMEAL MUFFINS
MAKES 12 MUFFINS

Do not use quick or instant oats in this recipe. Walnuts may be substituted for the pecans. The easiest way to grease and flour the muffin tin is with a baking spray with flour.

TOPPING

½	cup (1½ ounces) old-fashioned rolled oats
⅓	cup (1⅔ ounces) all-purpose flour
⅓	cup pecans, chopped fine
⅓	cup packed (2⅓ ounces) light brown sugar
1¼	teaspoons ground cinnamon
⅛	teaspoon salt
4	tablespoons unsalted butter, melted

MUFFINS

2	tablespoons unsalted butter, plus 6 tablespoons melted
2	cups (6 ounces) old-fashioned rolled oats
1¾	cups (8¾ ounces) all-purpose flour
1½	teaspoons salt
¾	teaspoon baking powder
¼	teaspoon baking soda
1⅓	cups packed (9⅓ ounces) light brown sugar
1¾	cups milk
2	large eggs, beaten

1. FOR THE TOPPING: Combine oats, flour, pecans, sugar, cinnamon, and salt in medium bowl. Drizzle melted butter over mixture and stir to thoroughly combine; set aside.

2. FOR THE MUFFINS: Grease and flour 12-cup muffin tin. Melt 2 tablespoons butter in 10-inch skillet over medium heat. Add oats and cook, stirring frequently, until oats turn golden brown and smell of cooking popcorn, 6 to 8 minutes. Transfer oats to food processor and process into fine meal, about 30 seconds. Add flour, salt, baking powder, and baking soda to oats and pulse until combined, about 3 pulses.

3. Stir 6 tablespoons melted butter and sugar together in large bowl until smooth. Add milk and eggs and whisk until smooth. Using whisk, gently fold half of oat mixture into wet ingredients, tapping whisk against side of bowl to release clumps. Add remaining oat mixture and continue to fold with whisk until no streaks of flour remain. Set aside batter for 20 minutes to thicken. Meanwhile, adjust oven rack to middle position and heat oven to 375 degrees.

4. Using ice cream scoop or large spoon, divide batter equally among prepared muffin cups (about ½ cup batter per cup; cups will be filled to rim). Evenly sprinkle topping over muffins (about 2 tablespoons per muffin). Bake until toothpick inserted in center comes out clean, 18 to 25 minutes, rotating muffin tin halfway through baking.

5. Let muffins cool in muffin tin on wire rack for 10 minutes. Remove muffins from muffin tin and serve warm or let cool completely on wire rack before serving.

Almond Granola With Dried Fruit

✔ WHY THIS RECIPE WORKS

Sure, do-it-yourself granola affords you the opportunity to choose exactly which nuts and dried fruit you want to include, as well as how much. But there is a downside: The slow baking and frequent stirring that most recipes recommend results in a loose, granular texture. We wanted something altogether different: substantial clumps of toasty oats and nuts. Our ideal clusters would be markedly crisp yet tender enough to shatter easily when bitten; we definitely didn't want the density or tooth-chipping crunch of a hard granola bar. We set to work.

CHOOSE THE RIGHT OATS We baked test batches using instant, quick, steel-cut, and old-fashioned whole rolled oat varieties. It was no surprise that instant and quick oats baked up unsubstantial and powdery. Steel-cut oats suffered the opposite problem: Chewing them was like munching gravel. Whole rolled oats were essential for a hearty, crisp texture.

ADD FAT When we mixed up a batch of granola in which we left out the oil, the resulting cereal was a real flop, the oats having taken on a crisp but overly dry consistency. It turns out that fat is essential for creating a likable crispness. Here's why: When the water in a viscous liquid sweetener (like the maple syrup in our recipe) evaporates in the heat of the oven, the sugars left behind develop into a thin coating on the oats and nuts. But without any fat, the sugar coating will become brittle and dry. Only oil can provide a pleasantly crisp coating with a sense of moistness.

BAKE IN A LAYER Next up: Getting substantial chunks. We'd been reaching into the oven to repeatedly stir the granola as it baked, so we decided to try skipping this step. Sure enough, some olive-size pieces did form in a no-stir sample—but we wanted more (and larger) chunks. Since the raw granola mixture was so sticky with syrup and oil, we wondered if muscling it into a tight, compact layer in the pan before baking would yield larger nuggets. We gave it a try, happily finding that when we pulled the cereal from the oven, it remained in a single sheet as it cooled. Now the end product was more of a granola "bark," which was ideal, since we could break it into clumps of any size.

ALMOND GRANOLA WITH DRIED FRUIT
MAKES ABOUT 9 CUPS

Chopping the almonds by hand is best for superior crunch. Use a single type of your favorite dried fruit or a combination. Do not substitute quick or instant oats.

- ⅓ cup maple syrup
- ⅓ cup packed (2⅓ ounces) light brown sugar
- 4 teaspoons vanilla extract
- ½ teaspoon salt
- ½ cup vegetable oil
- 5 cups (15 ounces) old-fashioned rolled oats
- 2 cups (10 ounces) whole almonds, chopped coarse
- 2 cups (10 ounces) raisins or other dried fruit, chopped

1. Adjust oven rack to upper-middle position and heat oven to 325 degrees. Line rimmed baking sheet with parchment paper.

2. Whisk maple syrup, sugar, vanilla, and salt together in large bowl. Whisk in oil, then fold in oats and almonds until thoroughly coated.

3. Transfer oat mixture to prepared sheet and spread into thin, even layer (about ⅜ inch thick). Using stiff metal spatula, compress oat mixture until very compact. Bake until lightly browned, 40 to 45 minutes, rotating sheet halfway through baking. Transfer sheet to wire rack and let cool completely, about 1 hour. Break cooled granola into pieces of desired size. Stir in raisins. (Granola can be stored at room temperature for up to 2 weeks.)

Ten-Minute Steel-Cut Oatmeal

✔ WHY THIS RECIPE WORKS

Steel-cut oats, which are dried oat groats cut crosswise into coarse bits, are gently simmered in lightly salted water until the hard oats swell and soften and release some of their starch molecules into the surrounding liquid. Those freed starches bond with the liquid, thickening it until the oatmeal forms a substantial yet fluid mass of plump, tender grains. So what's the problem? That transformation from gravelly oats to creamy, thick porridge takes 30 minutes minimum; closer to 40 minutes is preferable. To reduce the prebreakfast rush, some cooks allow steel-cut oats to just barely bubble in a slow cooker overnight, but we've never had luck with that approach. After 8 hours the oats are mushy and blown out and lack the subtle chew of traditionally prepared oatmeal. Our goal: perfect porridge that required fewer than 10 minutes of active engagement.

PREHYDRATE THE OATS Surely boiling water would hasten the softening of the oats faster than room-temperature water, right? To find out, we brought the oats and the water to a boil together, cut the heat, covered the pot, and left it to sit overnight. When we uncovered the pot the next morning, we knew we were getting somewhere. Thanks to this head start, the coarse, gravelly oats we'd started with had swelled and fully softened. We were encouraged and flipped on the burner to medium to see how long it would take before the cereal turned creamy and thickened. About 10 minutes of simmering later, the porridge was heated through and viscous—but was also mushy and pasty like the slow-cooker oats. Simmering the oats for less time wasn't the answer: It left the liquid in the pot thin and watery. As surprising as it seemed, we could only conclude that parcooking by bringing the oats up to a boil with the water was too aggressive, causing too many starch molecules to burst, which turned the oats to mush and caused the surrounding liquid to become pasty. Instead of bringing the oats to a boil with the water, we boiled the water by itself, poured in the oats, covered the pot, and then left them to hydrate overnight. The next morning we got the pot going again. With this slightly more gentle method, 10 minutes later the oatmeal was perfectly creamy and not at all blown out or sticky. (See Test Kitchen Experiment, page 330.)

CUT THE HEAT EARLY Though the finished oatmeal looked appropriately creamy in the pot, the mixture continued to thicken after we poured it into the bowl as the starches continued to absorb the water. By the time we dug in, the result was so thick and pasty that we could stand our spoons in it. That's when we seized on our last adjustment: We would cut the heat before the oatmeal had achieved its ideal thickness and then let it sit for a few minutes, until it thickened up just enough. We gave it a whirl, simmering the oatmeal for a mere 5 minutes and then moving the pot off the heat to rest. Five minutes later we dug into a bowl of perfect porridge: creamy and viscous and not the least bit pasty. Goal achieved.

TEN-MINUTE STEEL-CUT OATMEAL
SERVES 4

The oatmeal will continue to thicken as it cools. If you prefer a looser consistency, thin the oatmeal with boiling water. Customize your oatmeal with toppings such as brown sugar, toasted nuts, maple syrup, or dried fruit.

4	cups water
1	cup steel-cut oats
¼	teaspoon salt

1. Bring 3 cups water to boil in large saucepan over high heat. Remove pan from heat; stir in oats and salt. Cover pan and let stand overnight.

2. Stir remaining 1 cup water into oats and bring to boil over medium-high heat. Reduce heat to medium and cook, stirring occasionally, until oats are softened but still retain some chew and mixture thickens and resembles warm pudding, 4 to 6 minutes. Remove pan from heat and let stand for 5 minutes. Stir and serve, passing desired toppings separately.

> **PRACTICAL SCIENCE**
> **ANOTHER WAY TO THICKEN SOUPS**
>
> Whole oats can be used instead of bread to thicken soup.
>
> Many pureed-soup recipes call for sliced white sandwich bread as a thickener. Since we don't always have sandwich bread on hand, we wondered if oats might work just as well. We made three of our soups that we thicken with bread—potato-leek, creamy tomato, and Italian garlic soup—subbing in ½ cup of oats for each slice of bread called for in the recipe. The oats worked well in the potato and garlic soups, but tasters found that they dulled the bright flavor of the tomato soup and created a slightly gelatinous consistency. We fixed both issues simply by reducing the amount of oats by half. In sum: Use ½ cup oats per slice of bread for most pureed soups. For tomato-based soups, only use ¼ cup oats per slice.

CHAPTER 41

Quinoa

To serve this incredibly healthy seed (yes, seed), we start by rinsing and toasting.

HOW THE SCIENCE WORKS

For many years, quinoa sat in obscurity. Americans didn't eat it. Barely anyone knew about it. But in the last decade it has been discovered, suddenly popping up everywhere, and not just in the health food industry. In January 2005 the term "quinoa" appeared in headlines nine times, according to Google Trends. In January 2015? Ninety-six times. The United Nations even named 2013 "The Year of Quinoa."

Why? To start, quinoa is a seed, not a grain. Like its relatives buckwheat and amaranth, it is officially classified as a "pseudocereal." Its botanical name is *Chenopodium quinoa*; it belongs to the same family as beets, spinach, and chard. Quinoa has been cultivated for thousands of years, first domesticated in the south-central Andes of southern Peru and Bolivia, where seeds have been dated to between 5,000 and 7,000 years old.

More than 2,000 different varieties of quinoa have grown throughout the Andes, says Stephen Gorad, one of the first importers of quinoa outside of the Andes. "Quinoa was always grown by a family for themselves on a farm. A family on a certain side of the mountain was growing one version, and someone on the other side of the mountain was growing it with a slightly different seed. So many different types of quinoa grow with just slight variations." Today in the United States there are three colors available—white, red, and black. They are essentially the same, though black and red quinoas have an extra shell, which makes them slightly crunchier when cooked.

What attracts many to quinoa today is the fact that it's highly nutritious. It contains high levels of protein (about 14 to 15 percent by weight of the dry seed), which is composed of all of the essential amino acids. The protein content of quinoa is higher than most cereal crops, but even more important is that quinoa contains the essential amino acid lysine, while cereals such as wheat and rice are lysine-deficient. The proteins in quinoa do not form gluten.

The cooked quinoa seed contains about 72 percent water, 4.5 percent protein, 2 percent fat, and 21 percent carbohydrate, of which 3 percent by weight functions as dietary fiber. The relatively low amount of fat is composed of almost 90 percent healthy mono- and polyunsaturated fatty acids. Almost 50 percent is the essential omega-6 fatty acid linoleic acid, while 7 percent is the essential omega-3 fatty acid linolenic acid. Quinoa is also a good source of iron and the B-vitamin riboflavin. In conclusion? It's not just hype: Quinoa truly is a superfood.

When it comes to cooking, the first thing to think about is the seed coating on quinoa, which contains bitter-tasting complex compounds called saponins. These saponins have the positive impact of repelling birds before harvest, and can be removed by brief washing before cooking. Most commercial quinoa seeds have been processed by brief polishing and washing to remove the saponins. But we've found it helpful to rinse quinoa, whether prewashed or not (see page 336).

After rinsing, we toast quinoa in a dry pan. Toasting it in fat, we've found, accentuates the bitter nature of the seed. A ratio of 1 part water to 1 part quinoa works far better than the soggy ratio of 2 to 1 that many recipes employ. We add herbs and lemon to our quinoa pilaf (page 338), and jalapeño and red bell pepper to our quinoa salad (page 338). We bind quinoa together with egg and Monterey Jack cheese to make flavorful and moist quinoa patties (page 339)—a hearty, protein-packed vegetarian entrée.

The United Nations named 2013 "The Year of Quinoa."

TEST KITCHEN EXPERIMENT

With a high protein content, 10 essential amino acids, a firm, satisfying texture, and a nutty flavor, there's a lot to recommend quick-cooking quinoa. The only real downside? It can be unpleasantly bitter, thanks to a concentration of bitter-tasting compounds called saponins on the surface of the seeds. In addition to being unpalatable, saponins are mildly toxic, causing low-level gastrointestinal distress in some people. Some brands of quinoa come prewashed, while others don't. To find out if prewashing guarantees less bitter quinoa, and if you should still rinse the prewashed stuff, we set up the following experiment.

EXPERIMENT

We purchased all available brands of both prewashed and unwashed white quinoa and rinsed half of each under cool water in a strainer for 1 minute while leaving the other half unrinsed. We cooked each sample using 1¾ cups water to 1½ cups quinoa (following our recipe for quinoa pilaf, page 338) and tasted them blind, side by side. Tasters were asked to rank the samples according to bitterness.

RESULTS

We found no consensus on comparative bitterness between prewashed quinoa that we did not rinse and unwashed quinoa that we rinsed, suggesting that it doesn't matter who does the rinsing, as long it gets done. Both of these samples fell in the middle of the pack for bitterness. However, we did have strong agreement on the other samples. The prewashed quinoa that we rinsed was deemed the least bitter while the unwashed quinoa that we did not rinse was by far the most bitter.

TAKEAWAY

Our results show that making the best-tasting quinoa begins at the supermarket, where you want to buy brands that are labeled as prewashed (in previous tests we found no texture or flavor disadvantage to prewashed quinoa—only the bitterness had been removed). But your work isn't done yet—even prewashed quinoa benefits from a quick rinse with cold tap water in a fine-mesh strainer to produce the least bitter pilaf.

TO PREWASH OR NOT TO PREWASH?

It's important to rinse your quinoa, in order to remove the bitter-tasting compounds called saponins on the surface of the seed. We tested prewashed and unwashed brands and found that both benefit from rinsing at home.

FOCUS ON: QUINOA

Quinoa is truly a superfood, a seed with high protein levels and all of the essential amino acids.

RAW

Raw quinoa seeds contain about 14 percent protein, 13 percent water, 6 percent fat, and 64 percent carbohydrate, of which 7 percent by weight functions as dietary fiber.

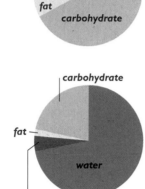

protein

water

fat

carbohydrate

COOKED

Boiling quinoa seeds breaks down some of the proteins, and changes the composition to about 72 percent water, 4.5 percent protein, 2 percent fat, and 21 percent carbohydrate, with almost 3 percent functioning as dietary fiber.

carbohydrate

fat

water

protein

SEED

Quinoa seeds are covered in a coating that can be white, red, or black. Each seed coating contains bitter-tasting saponins.

LEAF

Leaves of the quinoa plant are edible but high in oxalic acid, so the leaves should not be eaten in excess. The leaves often change color as the plant matures—from green to red, yellow, or purple.

STEM

Quinoa stems are thick and hardy.

GLOBAL PRODUCTION OF QUINOA

The main quinoa-producing countries in the Andean region and the world are Peru and Bolivia. In 2008, these two countries accounted for 92 percent of quinoa produced in the world. They are followed by the United States, Ecuador, Argentina, and Canada.

Peru

Bolivia

ROOT

The roots of quinoa plants are branched and fibrous, making them highly resistant to drought.

Quinoa Pilaf

✔ WHY THIS RECIPE WORKS

While in theory cooked quinoa seeds have an appealingly nutty flavor and crunchy texture, in practice they more often turn into a mushy mess, with washed-out flavor and an underlying bitterness. Pilaf recipes that call for cooking the seed with onion and other flavorings don't help matters. If it's blown-out and mushy, quinoa pilaf is no better than the plain boiled seed on its own. We were determined to develop a foolproof approach to quinoa pilaf that we'd want to make not because it was healthy but because it tasted great.

USE A 1:1 RATIO We put together a basic working recipe: Soften finely chopped onion in butter in a saucepan, stir in quinoa and water, cover, and cook until tender. We then tested a range of water-to-quinoa ratios and found that while 2 to 1 might be the common rule, 1 to 1 was nearly perfect. To allow for evaporation, we tweaked this ratio just slightly, using a bit more water than quinoa (1¾ cups water to 1½ cups quinoa).

STIR AND REST After about 20 minutes of covered simmering, most of the quinoa was tender, with a satisfying bite. But there was a ½-inch ring of overcooked seeds around the pot's circumference. The heat of the pot was cooking the outer seeds faster than the interior ones. To even things out, our first thought was to stir the quinoa halfway through cooking. We feared that we would turn our pilaf into a starchy mess, as so easily happens with rice, but we needn't have worried. A few gentle stirs at the midway point gave us perfectly cooked quinoa, with no ill effects. Why? While quinoa is quite starchy—more so than long-grain white rice—it also contains twice the protein of white rice. That protein is key, as it essentially traps the starch in place so you can stir it without creating a gummy mess. The texture of the quinoa improved further when we let it rest, covered, for 10 minutes before fluffing. This allowed the seeds to finish cooking gently and firm up, making them less prone to clump.

TOAST DRY It was time to think about the toasting step. While the majority of quinoa on the market has been debittered, some bitter-tasting compounds (called saponins) remain on the exterior. We have found that toasting quinoa in fat can exacerbate this bitterness, so we opted to dry-toast the seeds in the pan before sautéing the onion. After about 5 minutes in the pan, the quinoa smelled like popcorn. This batch was nutty and rich-tasting, without any bitterness.

QUINOA PILAF WITH HERBS AND LEMON
SERVES 4 TO 6

Rinse the quinoa in a fine-mesh strainer, drain it, and then spread it on a rimmed baking sheet lined with a dish towel and let dry for 15 minutes before proceeding with the recipe. Any soft herbs, such as cilantro, parsley, chives, mint, and tarragon, can be used.

1½	cups prewashed quinoa, rinsed and dried
2	tablespoons unsalted butter, cut into 2 pieces
1	small onion, chopped fine
¾	teaspoon salt
1¾	cups water
3	tablespoons chopped fresh herbs
1	tablespoon lemon juice

1. Toast quinoa in medium saucepan over medium-high heat, stirring frequently, until quinoa is very fragrant and makes continuous popping sound, 5 to 7 minutes. Transfer quinoa to bowl and set aside.

2. Melt butter in now-empty pan over medium-low heat. Add onion and salt; cook, stirring frequently, until onion is softened and light golden, 5 to 7 minutes.

3. Increase heat to medium-high, stir in water and quinoa, and bring to simmer. Cover, reduce heat to low, and simmer until grains are just tender and liquid is absorbed, 18 to 20 minutes, stirring once halfway through cooking. Remove pan from heat and let sit, covered, for 10 minutes. Fluff quinoa with fork, stir in herbs and lemon juice, and serve.

Quinoa Salad

✔ WHY THIS RECIPE WORKS

To take advantage of the versatility of quinoa, we wanted to make a protein-packed quinoa salad. Crisp, sweet bell pepper, jalapeño, red onion, and fresh cilantro provided a sweet and spicy contrast to the hearty, chewy quinoa. We tossed the vegetables and seeds with a bright dressing flavored with lime juice, mustard, garlic, and cumin.

USE THE PILAF METHOD We started by rinsing our quinoa to remove the majority of the bitter-tasting saponins. And then? We toasted the quinoa, dry, in a pan. (We found that toasting it in fat could accentuate the underlying bitter taste of quinoa.) We then added water and cooked the seeds until just tender.

COOL ON A BAKING SHEET After 12 minutes of cooking, there was still a little bit of water in the pan. This water evaporated, though, when we spread the cooked quinoa over a baking sheet to cool it to room temperature quickly. Last, we tossed the quinoa with the additional ingredients and a dressing.

QUINOA SALAD WITH RED BELL PEPPER AND CILANTRO
SERVES 4

Rinse the quinoa in a fine-mesh strainer, drain it, and then spread it on a rimmed baking sheet lined with a dish towel and let dry for 15 minutes before proceeding with the recipe. To make this dish spicier, add the chile seeds. The quinoa salad can be refrigerated in an airtight container for up to two days; season with additional salt, pepper, and lime juice to taste before serving.

I	cup prewashed quinoa, rinsed and dried
I½	cups water
	Salt and pepper
½	red bell pepper, chopped fine
½	jalapeño chile, minced
2	tablespoons minced red onion
I	tablespoon minced fresh cilantro
2	tablespoons fresh lime juice
I	tablespoon extra-virgin olive oil
2	teaspoons Dijon mustard
I	small garlic clove, minced
½	teaspoon ground cumin

I. Toast quinoa in large saucepan over medium heat, stirring frequently, until quinoa is lightly toasted and aromatic, about 5 minutes. Stir in water and ¼ teaspoon salt and bring to simmer. Reduce heat to low, cover, and continue to simmer until water is mostly absorbed and quinoa is nearly tender, about 12 minutes. Spread quinoa out over rimmed baking sheet and set aside until tender and cool, about 20 minutes.

2. Transfer cooled quinoa to large bowl. Stir in bell pepper, jalapeño, onion, and cilantro. In separate bowl, whisk lime juice, oil, mustard, garlic, and cumin together, then pour over quinoa mixture and toss to coat. Season with salt and pepper to taste, and serve.

Quinoa Patties with Spinach and Sun-Dried Tomatoes

✔ WHY THIS RECIPE WORKS

We set out to develop a recipe for quinoa patties—a protein-packed vegetarian entrée—with bright, fresh flavors and enough add-ins to make them hearty and satisfying. To make these patties weeknight accessible, we wanted to distribute the work so we could come home and have a filling dinner in just 30 minutes.

PICK WHITE QUINOA While we liked the earthy flavor of red quinoa, it did not soften enough to form cohesive patties. Classic white (or golden) quinoa performed much better, and upping the amount of cooking liquid delivered even more cohesive patties, since the quinoa was extra-moist from absorbing the extra liquid overnight. We skipped the usual toasting step because it encourages the individual seeds to separate rather than stick together.

BIND IT As for the binder, we tried mashed beans and potatoes, a variety of cheeses, bread, and processing some of the quinoa itself, but only one whole egg plus one yolk and melty Monterey Jack cheese bound the seeds together perfectly.

COOK ON THE STOVETOP Chilling the patties ensured that they stayed together during cooking. Baking was an appealing hands-off cooking method, but the heat of the oven dried the patties out. It was much easier on the stovetop to get a crisp crust and moist interior. Because the patties needed at least 5 minutes on each side to set up and cook through, cooking them over medium-low heat prevented burning but still resulted in a nice crust.

ADD FLAVOR To give the patties interesting flavor, we mixed in chopped sun-dried tomatoes, scallions, delicate baby spinach, and a little lemon zest and juice. Sautéing the aromatics in some of the tomatoes' packing oil infused them with even more flavor.

QUINOA PATTIES WITH SPINACH
AND SUN-DRIED TOMATOES
SERVES 4

Rinse the quinoa in a fine-mesh strainer, drain it, and then spread it on a rimmed baking sheet lined with a dish towel and let dry for 15 minutes before proceeding with the recipe.

½   cup oil-packed sun-dried tomatoes,
      chopped coarse, plus 1 tablespoon oil
4   scallions, chopped fine
4   garlic cloves, minced
2   cups water
1   cup prewashed white quinoa, rinsed and dried
1   teaspoon salt
1   large egg plus 1 large yolk, lightly beaten
2   ounces (2 cups) baby spinach, chopped
2   ounces Monterey Jack cheese, shredded (½ cup)
½   teaspoon grated lemon zest plus
      2 teaspoons juice
2   tablespoons vegetable oil

1. Heat tomato oil in large saucepan over medium heat until shimmering. Add scallions and cook until softened, 3 to 5 minutes. Stir in garlic and cook until fragrant, about 30 seconds. Stir in water, quinoa, and salt and bring to simmer. Reduce heat to medium-low, cover, and continue to simmer until quinoa is tender, 16 to 18 minutes.

2. Remove pot from heat and let sit, covered, until liquid is fully absorbed, about 10 minutes. Transfer quinoa to large bowl and let cool for 15 minutes. Stir in sun-dried tomatoes, egg and yolk, spinach, Monterey Jack, and lemon zest and juice.

3. Line rimmed baking sheet with parchment paper. Divide quinoa mixture into 8 equal portions and pack firmly into 3½-inch-wide patties; place on prepared sheet. Refrigerate, uncovered, until patties are chilled and firm, about 30 minutes.

4. Heat 1 tablespoon vegetable oil in 12-inch non-stick skillet over medium heat until shimmering. Gently lay 4 patties in skillet and cook until set and well browned on both sides, 16 to 20 minutes, turning gently halfway through cooking; transfer to plate and cover to keep warm. Repeat with remaining 1 tablespoon vegetable oil and patties. Serve.

PRACTICAL SCIENCE MANY COLORS OF QUINOA

You can use white and red interchangeably.

White quinoa is the most commonly found variety of these tiny seeds native to South America, but red and black varieties are increasingly available. To see if color made a difference, we put together batches of our quinoa pilaf recipe (page 338) using all three types.

White quinoa, the largest seeds of the three, had a slightly nutty, vegetal flavor with a hint of bitterness; it also had the softest texture of the three quinoas. The medium-size red seeds offered a heartier crunch, thanks to their additional seed coat, and a predominant nuttiness. Black quinoa seeds, the smallest of the three, have the thickest seed coat. They were notably crunchy in our recipe and retained their shape the most during cooking, but many tasters disliked their slightly sandy texture. These seeds had the mildest flavor, with a hint of molasses-like sweetness.

We'll definitely use white and red quinoa interchangeably in our quinoa pilaf recipe and most other recipes, but black quinoa is better off in recipes specifically tailored to its distinctive texture and flavor.

WHITE

RED

BLACK

CHAPTER 42

Cannellini Beans

Don't be afraid of cooking with canned beans. Just don't throw out their liquid.

HOW THE SCIENCE WORKS

We go through a lot of cannellini beans in the test kitchen. Their creamy texture and mildly nutty flavor round out soups, casseroles, pasta dishes, and dips. Our readers love them, too. Seventy-one percent say that they regularly buy cannellini beans, outstripping the next two most popular white beans: great northern and navy.

Cannellini beans bear the botanical name *Phaseolus vulgaris* and were first domesticated in the Andes mountains of Peru sometime between 4,300 and 5,000 years ago. They were first cultivated in Italy in the early 1800s, and they soon became quite popular, especially in Tuscany. Cooked, they are characterized by a thin skin and creamy flesh.

And the texture of this flesh? It actually has a lot to do with calcium. This is because within beans, insoluble calcium pectate provides strength to the cell walls, holding the cells together. Therefore, sufficient calcium pectate must be present to prevent the beans from blowing out and becoming mushy when cooked. Much of this calcium, interestingly, comes from the soil in which they're grown. (See Test Kitchen Experiment, page 342.)

Seventy-one percent of our readers say that they regularly buy cannellini beans over others.

When it comes to producing beans today, about 1.35 million acres of beans intended for drying are planted in the United States annually. Bean plants signal when they are ready to harvest by turning from green to gold as they dry. Plants are cut down to finish drying and then threshed to separate the now-dried beans from pods. Beans to be sold dried are passed over screens to remove stunted beans, stones, and dirt; color-sorted; and then stored in giant totes until they're ready to be packaged.

The exact canning procedure varies from brand to brand, but generally starts with a thorough cleaning and then automatic size sorting and computerized optical inspection. Then the beans are blanched in hot water and sealed in cans with water and often salt. The salt works like a brine, not only improving flavor but also helping tenderize the skins. Most brands add calcium chloride, which maintains firmness and prevents splitting, and calcium disodium EDTA, a preservative that binds iron in the water and prevents white beans from turning brown. The final step is pressure-cooking the beans right in their cans.

We tasted both canned and dried cannellini beans in the test kitchen, and found that the canned beans were largely better. Top scores for canned beans actually edged out top scores for dried beans. Sure, we disliked a few brands of canned, whose mushy textures and tinny flavors lived up to our preconceptions, but the best canned beans were excellent: firm and intact, with meltingly tender skins, creamy texture, and clean bean flavor. And, above all, they were perfectly uniform.

And when we cook with canned cannellini beans? We use the whole can, with at least some if not all of the liquid included. Why? That starchy liquid is the key to great consistency in many a sauce or soup. We use the bean liquid (from cannellini beans, as well as pinto beans) in our Pasta with Beans, Chard, and Rosemary (page 344) to create a deeply flavorful sauce. The bean liquid in our modern take on succotash (page 345) likewise brings it all together, delicately binding the ingredients while not overpowering the flavors. And using a similar technique, with a different type of bean, look to our Best Ground-Beef Chili (page 346), where pinto beans, and their starchy liquid, take center stage alongside ground beef, which we cook for a surprisingly long time.

TEST KITCHEN EXPERIMENT

Canned beans are a remarkably consistent product. That might not sound surprising, but compare that to most cooks' experiences with cooking dried beans at home: tough beans that never soften, ruptured skins, and interiors that are either chalky or mushy. What's different about canned beans and those you cook at home? Besides the cooking process itself (canned beans are cooked under pressure), canned beans usually contain added calcium chloride, which, according to manufacturers, maintains firmness and prevents splitting. We had to wonder if some dried beans naturally contained more calcium than others, and if that would translate to better home-cooked beans. To find out, we ran the following experiment.

EXPERIMENT

We tasted five brands of dried white beans—plain, in dip, and in soup—rating their flavor, texture, and overall appeal. We also sent samples of each to an independent laboratory to determine the dried beans' calcium contents.

RESULTS

While many of the beans had good flavor, most lost points for textural issues: blown-out skins and mushy or chalky interiors. Our top-ranked bean, from Rancho Gordo, had great flavor, but it was its creamy, intact texture that won rave reviews. When we compared the beans' rank to their calcium content we were shocked to find a perfect correlation: The beans containing the most calcium ranked the highest, and the beans with the least ranked the lowest. In addition, there were even two brands of beans that contained essentially the same amount of calcium and that tied in the taste ranking.

TAKEAWAY

Calcium in beans is mostly associated with the pectin that holds the cells together as well as strengthens the cell walls. It was anticipated that more calcium would result in less "blow out" (bursting of the outer shell) of the beans and a better interior texture, and our results support that hypothesis. So why does one bean have more calcium than another? Research studies have shown that the level of calcium in beans is related to both the genotype and the calcium content of the soil in which they are grown. The bottom line? Mail-order bean purveyors like Rancho Gordo that pick heirloom varieties and grow them in the right soil might just be worth the extra expense.

HOW MUCH CALCIUM IN YOUR BEANS? IT MATTERS.

We tested five brands of dried white beans, cooking them in a range of dishes, and sending samples to the lab to determine the beans' calcium content. Without fail, the more calcium, the better the bean ranked in taste tests.

LESS CALCIUM
Beans with less calcium meant beans that blew out during cooking. The calcium provides strength to the cell walls.

MORE CALCIUM
Beans with more calcium held together while cooking. The calcium content has a lot to do with the soil in which the beans were grown.

COOKED DRIED CANNELLINI BEANS

RANK	BRAND	CALCIUM (MG/100G)
1	Rancho Gordo (Dried Cassoulet Beans)	362
2	Zursun Idaho Dried Cannellini Beans	204
Tie	Bob's Red Mill Dried Cannellini Beans	176
Tie	Jansal Valley Dried Cannellini Beans	175
5	Goya Dried Cannellini Beans	168

JOURNEY: CANNED BEANS

Seventy-one percent of our readers say that they regularly buy cannellini beans. We tested dried vs. canned cannellini beans, and found that the canned were largely better. How do these creamy, uniform beans get from farm to can? Let's take a closer look.

1 GROW BEANS

1.35 million acres of beans intended for drying are planted in the U.S. every year. Beans are ready to harvest after the leaves and pods turn from green to gold on the stalk as they dry.

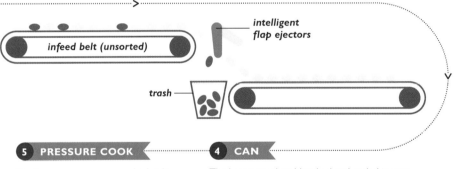

2 DRY THEM

The plants finish drying after they are cut. The now-dried beans are then separated from their pods. (Historically, this was done by hand; today, machines collect the beans and chop the rest into compost.)

3 SORT

Because dried beans are never washed (which would introduce moisture and the possibility of rot), they are sorted by being passed over screens to remove flawed beans and dirt. They are also sorted by color and size, and go through a computerized optical inspection.

intelligent flap ejectors

infeed belt (unsorted)

trash

5 PRESSURE COOK

The beans are pressure-cooked right in their can. This preserves them and keeps them shelf-stable for sale.

4 CAN

The beans are then blanched and sealed in cans with water and salt. (The salt works as a brine.) Calcium chloride is often added, to maintain firmness, as well as calcium disodium EDTA, which prevents beans from turning brown.

GOYA CANNELLINI

Tasters' favorite canned beans were "well seasoned" (they had the highest sodium level of the five products we tested), "big and meaty," and "very satisfying," with both "earthy sweetness" and "savory flavor." Their texture was consistently "ultracreamy and smooth," with a "nice, firm bite"—all evidence of carefully calibrated processing.

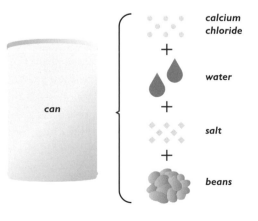

calcium chloride

+

water

+

can

salt

+

beans

Pasta with Beans, Chard, and Rosemary

✔ WHY THIS RECIPE WORKS

Recipes for pasta with beans and greens abound, but are generally unremarkable. Most feature cannellini beans, plus sausage for heft, while everything from kale to spinach is fair game for the greens. And the sauce? There really aren't guidelines, but it's typically bare-bones. Yet even with numerous variations on the theme, the results are the same: a bland mix of thrown-together ingredients. We thought we could do better.

CHOOSE CANNELLINI In Italy, this dish often features borlotti, staple beans in Italian cooking, which are creamy but also wonderfully meaty. Red-speckled borlotti beans (part of the cranberry bean family) aren't readily available at the average American supermarket, so we needed a substitute. Cannellini would be fine for simulating borlotti creaminess, and to provide the right meaty flavor we'd also use an equal amount of pintos.

USE CANNED—AND LIQUID As for canned versus dried beans, we know that canned cannellini are often a good alternative, and not just because they are convenient. The best have a uniform tenderness that dried beans can lack. And because canned beans are simply dried beans sealed in cans with salted water (along with a few benign additives) and cooked under pressure, the canning liquid is pretty much the same mixture of bean starch and water that you get when you cook dried beans. While nearly every recipe using canned beans calls for draining and rinsing said beans, we would do no such thing. That starchy canning liquid would lend richness and body to our sauce.

PICK SWISS CHARD For the greens, we settled on Swiss chard: We finely chopped its hearty stems to cook at the outset, and we chopped the tender leaves and set them aside to add toward the end. We sautéed an onion and the chard stems with garlic, red pepper flakes, and rosemary, and then we added 1½ cups of water and one can each of cannellini and pinto beans, scraping all their liquid and starch into the pot. Knowing that the Swiss chard leaves would turn mushy if overcooked, we took a more gentle approach. After simmering the mixture for 10 minutes to let the flavors meld, we spread the chard leaves over the surface, covered the pot, and allowed them to steam off the heat for about 5 minutes. We then stirred in some penne, which we'd cooked separately, and sprinkled Parmesan on top.

DEVELOP FLAVOR We still wanted more flavor. We decided to start by sautéing 3 ounces of pancetta, not enough to become a primary ingredient but, we hoped, sufficient to provide a meaty backbone. We also tossed in the rind from the Parmesan when we added the beans. For the pasta, we switched to fusilli since the deep grooves of its spiral shape would better capture what we hoped would be a delicious broth. We also decided to cook the pasta less, to just shy of al dente, so that we could finish cooking it through in the broth, allowing it to soak up flavor. When the short simmer was done, we stirred in the pasta, sprinkled the chard on top, and left it to finish, covered and off the heat.

PASTA WITH BEANS, CHARD, AND ROSEMARY
SERVES 6

The sauce will thicken as it cools.

- 2 tablespoons vegetable oil
- 3 ounces pancetta, diced
- 1 onion, chopped fine
- 10 ounces Swiss chard, stems chopped fine, leaves chopped coarse
- 2 teaspoons minced fresh rosemary
- 1 garlic clove, minced to paste
- ¼ teaspoon red pepper flakes
- 1 (15-ounce) can cannellini beans (do not drain)
- 1 (15-ounce) can pinto beans (do not drain)
- 1 Parmesan cheese rind (optional), plus 1 ounce Parmesan, grated (½ cup), plus extra for serving
- 8 ounces (2½ cups) fusilli
  Salt
- 1 tablespoon red wine vinegar

1. Heat oil in Dutch oven over medium-high heat until smoking. Add pancetta and cook, stirring occasionally, until pancetta begins to brown, 2 to 3 minutes. Stir in onion and chard stems and cook, stirring occasionally, until slightly softened, about 3 minutes. Add 1 teaspoon rosemary, garlic, and pepper flakes and cook until fragrant, about 1 minute. Stir in beans and their liquid, 1½ cups water, and Parmesan rind, if using, and bring to boil. Reduce heat to medium-low and simmer for 10 minutes.

2. Meanwhile, bring 2 quarts water to boil in large saucepan. Add pasta and 1½ teaspoons salt and cook until pasta is just shy of al dente. Drain. Stir pasta into beans and spread chard leaves on top. Cover, remove from heat, and let sit until pasta is fully cooked and chard leaves are wilted, 5 to 7 minutes. Discard Parmesan rind, if using. Stir in remaining 1 teaspoon rosemary, ½ cup Parmesan, and vinegar. Season with salt to taste, and serve, passing extra Parmesan separately.

Modern Succotash

✓ WHY THIS RECIPE WORKS

In 17th-century Plymouth, Massachusetts, Pilgrims and Native Americans frequently cooked up what was later referred to as "Plymouth succotash"—a stew of corn or hominy, dried beans, and bits of dried or fresh meat or fish. By the 19th century, succotash had evolved into the meatless side dish that we know today. But just because a dish boasts longevity doesn't mean that it's well liked. In fact, many folks crinkle their noses at the mention of succotash, since they have always known it as a dish of canned or frozen corn and lima beans swamped in a thick, dull cream sauce. This is a shame, since a quick, easy mix of crisp, sweet corn and creamy beans should be a summertime staple. We set out to modernize succotash by nixing the dull dairy and freshening up the lackluster vegetables.

CHOOSE CANNED CANNELLINIS The quality of the corn and beans would be crucial to success, so using fresh corn was a must. But fresh limas are hard to come by, so we tried alternatives—with no luck. Dried limas took hours to cook; frozen were inconsistent, as some cooked up creamy while others were grainy; and canned were unattractively washed out in flavor and color. But canned limas did boast a pleasant creamy texture that made us wonder if other canned beans might fare better. After surveying the possibilities, we decided to try cannellini beans. Sure enough, the cannellini offered mild flavor, decent looks, and the same appealing texture. After stripping the kernels from four ears of corn, we sautéed them in butter with the rinsed and drained beans. This warmed the beans through while retaining the crispness of the corn.

ADD BEAN LIQUID We were happy with the way the dish was shaping up but had one lingering concern: Without the traditional cream sauce to bind the ingredients, the

dish resembled salsa instead of succotash. We tried "milking" the corn after removing the kernels by scraping the cob with the back of a knife, but there wasn't enough liquid to create a light coating for the vegetables. Mixing chicken broth with a little cornstarch did a better job of giving the dish some cohesion, but the chicken flavor was distracting. The cornstarch gave us an idea, though: We could add a splash of the starchy bean "broth" in the can—a sleeper ingredient we sometimes call on to lend body to bean soups and pasta dishes. Just 2 tablespoons delicately bound the ingredients and accentuated the bean taste without overpowering the other flavors.

MODERN SUCCOTASH WITH FENNEL AND SCALLIONS
SERVES 4

Do not use frozen or canned corn in this dish.

- 1 (15-ounce) can cannellini beans, 2 tablespoons liquid reserved, beans rinsed
- 2 teaspoons lemon juice
- 3 tablespoons unsalted butter
- 4 scallions, white and green parts separated and sliced thin on bias
- 1 fennel bulb, stalks discarded, bulb halved, cored, and cut into ¼-inch pieces
  Salt and pepper
- 2 garlic cloves, minced
- ¼ teaspoon ground fennel
- 4 ears corn, kernels cut from cobs (3 cups)

1. Stir reserved bean liquid and lemon juice together in small bowl; set aside. Melt butter in 12-inch nonstick skillet over medium-high heat. Add scallion whites, fennel, and ½ teaspoon salt and cook, stirring frequently, until softened and beginning to brown, 4 to 5 minutes. Add garlic and ground fennel and cook until fragrant, about 30 seconds.

2. Reduce heat to medium and add corn and beans. Cook, stirring occasionally, until corn and beans have cooked through, about 4 minutes. Add bean liquid mixture and cook, stirring constantly, for 1 minute. Remove skillet from heat, stir in scallion greens, and season with salt and pepper to taste. Serve.

Best Ground-Beef Chili

✓ WHY THIS RECIPE WORKS

We've rarely encountered a ground beef chili that can hold its own against the chunky kind. It often suffers from dry, grainy, somewhat tough meat. We set ourselves the challenge of changing that. We wanted a big batch of thick, spicy, ultrabeefy chili—the kind we'd pile into a bowl with tortilla chips or rice and enjoy with a beer. In order to create that, we would first have to sort out how to give the ground meat the same juicy, tender texture found in chili made with chunks of beef.

COOK THE BEEF A LONG TIME   Our ground beef chili uses 85 percent lean ground beef for richness and flavor. You might think that just because ground beef is made up of tiny pieces of meat, it doesn't need much time to cook. But ground chuck is exactly that—cut-up pieces of chuck roast—and as such contains the same proteins and collagen that require adequate exposure to moist heat to properly break down. Many chili recipes cook the ground meat for 45 minutes or even less. For optimally tender results, we simmered ours for 1½ to 2 hours—almost as long as we do stew meat.

USE TOMATOES AND BEANS   We used only small amounts of pureed whole canned tomatoes and pinto beans to create a thick, rich dish. The starchy liquid from the can of beans helped to keep the saucy chili together.

USE BAKING SODA   Browning ground beef is a challenge since it expels juices more rapidly than chunks of meat do, and most of that moisture needs to evaporate before browning can occur. To limit the amount of liquid, the usual solution is to brown in batches. We stuck with one batch but tossed the meat with baking soda before cooking, which helped lock in moisture. To quantify baking soda's impact, we ran a simple experiment: We cooked three batches of ground beef treated with baking soda and compared them with three otherwise identical untreated batches. We calculated the pre- and postcooking moisture level of each batch and compared degrees of browning. The results? On average, the untreated meat lost about 10 percent more moisture during cooking than the treated meat. That may not sound like much, but it makes a significant difference in how well ground meat browns: The treated batches were deeply browned, whereas the untreated batches didn't brown at all. (If we kept cooking the untreated meat, it would have eventually browned but would have been overdone.) Raising the pH of meat increases its water-holding capacity, meaning that the proteins attract more water and are better able to hold on to it—not just during browning but throughout cooking. Besides keeping the meat from losing water that would make it steam versus brown, a higher pH also speeds up the Maillard reaction, making the treated meat brown even better and more quickly.

AND LOTS OF SPICES   Finally, we made our own chili powder using a combination of toasted dried ancho chiles, chipotle chiles in adobo, and paprika, along with a blend of herbs and spices to round it out. We made sure to stir in any fat that collected on the top of the chili before serving since it contains much of the flavor from the fat-soluble spices in the chile powder.

BEST GROUND-BEEF CHILI
SERVES 8 TO 10

Diced avocado, sour cream, and shredded Monterey Jack or cheddar cheese are also good options for garnishing. This chili is intensely flavored and should be served with tortilla chips and/or plenty of steamed white rice.

2	pounds 85 percent lean ground beef
2	tablespoons plus 2 cups water
	Salt and pepper
¾	teaspoon baking soda
6	dried ancho chiles, stemmed, seeded, and torn into 1-inch pieces
1	ounce tortilla chips, crushed (¼ cup)
2	tablespoons ground cumin
1	tablespoon paprika
1	tablespoon garlic powder
1	tablespoon ground coriander
2	teaspoons dried oregano
½	teaspoon dried thyme
1	(14.5-ounce) can whole peeled tomatoes
1	tablespoon vegetable oil
1	onion, chopped fine
3	garlic cloves, minced
1–2	teaspoons minced canned chipotle chile in adobo sauce
1	(15-ounce) can pinto beans (do not drain)

2   teaspoons sugar
2   tablespoons cider vinegar
     Lime wedges
     Coarsely chopped cilantro
     Chopped red onion

1. Adjust oven rack to lower-middle position and heat oven to 275 degrees. Toss beef with 2 tablespoons water, 1½ teaspoons salt, and baking soda in bowl until thoroughly combined. Set aside for 20 minutes.

2. Meanwhile, place anchos in Dutch oven set over medium-high heat; toast, stirring frequently, until fragrant, 4 to 6 minutes, reducing heat if anchos begin to smoke. Transfer to food processor and let cool.

3. Add tortilla chips, cumin, paprika, garlic powder, coriander, oregano, thyme, and 2 teaspoons pepper to food processor with anchos and process until finely ground, about 2 minutes. Transfer mixture to bowl. Process tomatoes and their juice in now-empty processor until smooth, about 30 seconds.

4. Heat oil in now-empty pot over medium-high heat until shimmering. Add onion and cook, stirring occasionally, until softened, 4 to 6 minutes. Add garlic and cook until fragrant, about 1 minute. Add beef and cook, stirring with wooden spoon to break meat up into ¼-inch pieces, until beef is browned and fond begins to form on pot bottom, 12 to 14 minutes. Add ancho mixture and chipotle; cook, stirring frequently, until fragrant, 1 to 2 minutes.

5. Add remaining 2 cups water, beans and their liquid, sugar, and tomato puree. Bring to boil, scraping bottom of pot to loosen any browned bits. Cover, transfer to oven, and cook until meat is tender and chili is slightly thickened, 1½ to 2 hours, stirring occasionally to prevent sticking.

6. Remove chili from oven and let stand, uncovered, for 10 minutes. Stir in any fat that has risen to top of chili, then add vinegar and season with salt to taste. Serve, passing lime wedges, cilantro, and chopped red onion separately. (Chili can be made up to 3 days in advance.)

White Bean Dip

✓ WHY THIS RECIPE WORKS

Although we love beans, we've rarely been impressed by bean dips. Most are dense and gluey, with any bean flavor buried under over-zealous seasonings—the stuff you'd pass over at a party. To rescue this concept, our plan was twofold: Highlight the beans' earthy-sweet flavors and build on their natural starchiness to create a smooth, creamy texture.

ADD RESERVED LIQUID—AND YOGURT   Rather than spend hours soaking and simmering dried beans, we decided to go with canned and started with cannellini. We drained two 15-ounce cans—enough to make a party-size dip—rinsed the beans to remove excess starch, and pureed them with a few placeholder flavorings. No surprise: The result was thick and sticky enough to use as brick mortar. Thinning the dip with water would fix the problem, but not without washing out flavor. Olive oil wasn't ideal either, as it overwhelmed the beans' delicate richness; plus, some tasters thought it rendered the dip greasy.

Using some of the reserved bean liquid helped. But we needed something with body that wouldn't overpower the beans. We wondered if yogurt might do the trick. Indeed, ordinary yogurt worked fine, but thicker Greek-style yogurt was far better, enriching the dip without robbing it of flavor.

AND EDAMAME   When tasters complained that the dip was still slightly pasty, we realized that the culprit might be the beans themselves. Going for a more radical approach, we tried replacing half of the cannellini beans with edamame, which are lighter in texture. The results were encouraging. The edamame's fresh sweetness brightened the beans.

CANNELLINI BEAN AND EDAMAME DIP WITH TARRAGON
MAKES ABOUT 2 CUPS

We prefer this dip when made with whole Greek yogurt, but 2 percent or 0 percent varieties can be substituted. Serve with chips, crackers, or vegetables.

1   small garlic clove, minced
½   teaspoon grated lemon zest plus 2 tablespoons
    juice
1   cup frozen edamame, thawed and patted dry
1   (15-ounce) can cannellini beans, 2 tablespoons
    liquid reserved, beans rinsed
1   scallion, white and light-green parts cut into
    ½-inch pieces, green part sliced thin on bias
¼   cup fresh tarragon
    Salt
    Pinch cayenne pepper
⅓   cup plain Greek-style yogurt
    Extra-virgin olive oil, for drizzling

1. Combine garlic and lemon zest and juice in small bowl; set aside for at least 15 minutes. Set aside 2 tablespoons edamame for garnish.

2. Pulse cannellini beans, reserved liquid, scallion whites and light greens, tarragon, ¾ teaspoon salt, cayenne, lemon juice mixture, and remaining edamame in food processor until fully ground, 5 to 10 pulses. Scrape down bowl with rubber spatula. Continue to process until uniform paste forms, about 1 minute, scraping down bowl twice. Add yogurt and continue to process until smooth and homogeneous, about 15 seconds, scraping down bowl as needed. Transfer to serving bowl, cover, and let stand at room temperature for at least 30 minutes. (Dip can be refrigerated for up to 1 day. Let refrigerated dip stand at room temperature for 30 minutes before serving.)

3. Season with salt to taste. Sprinkle with reserved edamame and scallion greens. Drizzle with oil and serve.

PRACTICAL SCIENCE
SUBSTITUTING CANNED BEANS FOR DRIED

You can do it . . . in some instances.

Most recipes that call for dried beans are soups or stews that require the beans to cook slowly with the other ingredients so that they release their starches and thicken the dish. When you replace the dried beans with canned beans and shorten the cooking time (cooking canned beans for the same amount of time as dried beans would cause the beans to disintegrate), you sacrifice both the flavor and texture of the finished dish. On some occasions (such as for a salad or quick pasta dish), a recipe might call for dried beans to be cooked, drained, and then added. In these instances, you can safely substitute canned beans. A general rule of thumb is that 1 cup of dried beans equals 3 cups of canned beans.

CHAPTER 43

Lentils

These tiny legumes cook quickly—and, like lean meats, benefit from a brine.

HOW THE SCIENCE WORKS

Lentils, botanically named *Lens culinaris*, are members of the legume family of plants—or plants that produce edible seeds inside protective pods. Within the legume family lie the pulses, which are legumes harvested primarily for dried seeds, including lentils, kidney, pinto, and navy beans, peas, chickpeas, and a few others.

There are many different types of lentils, varying in color from yellow to red-orange, green, brown, and black. The most commonly grown varieties are the large green Laird lentils, the small green French *du Puy* lentils, and petite red lentils. Lentils may be sold with or without their thin seed coat, and either whole or split in half. Today Canada is the largest producer and exporter of lentils, followed by India and Turkey.

Lentils are an ancient food. Evidence shows that hunter-gatherers consumed wild forms of lentils as long as 13,000 years ago. With the dawn of agriculture 10,000 years ago in the region known as the Fertile Crescent, lentils, along with wheat and barley, were among the first crops domesticated for human consumption. Within the Franchthi Cave in southern Greece clear evidence exists that larger, domesticated lentils were consumed in this region as long as 8,500 years ago.

Dried lentils contain about 8 percent water, 26 percent protein, 1 percent fat, and 63 percent total carbohydrate. Starch accounts for 42 to 47 percent of their weight. They are good sources of potassium, magnesium, calcium, phosphorous, and zinc. Like other legumes, lentils are deficient in tryptophan, an essential amino acid, one of the ten our bodies need to function. They are, however, high in another essential amino acid called lysine. Cereal grains, on the other hand, are high in tryptophan and low in lysine. This is why the popular combination of legumes and cereal grains (read: rice and beans) provide protein containing all of the essential amino acids.

Despite the simplicity of dried lentils, a number of processing steps are involved before they reach the supermarket. Field-dried lentils are harvested, cleaned, separated, optionally split, further dried, polished, and sorted by color and grade before sending to storage. The USDA has established non-compulsory grading standards for lentils, which range from grade 1 to 3, plus sample grade, with grade 1 being the highest and sample grade the lowest. The grades are based on the number of defects, including excess moisture (above 14 percent), insect damage, foreign material, and heat damage (due to drying), as well as color and size.

> **There are 12 different types of lentils, varying in color from yellow to red-orange, green, brown, and black.**

Because of their small size and relatively high surface area-to-volume ratio, and thin seed coat, lentils absorb water very rapidly and cook in much less time than other pulses. Like other dried beans, their skin can still blow out during cooking without proper precautions, however. To counter this, we brine lentils, so that the sodium can help to weaken the pectin in the skins, allowing the lentils to stay intact, and not become mushy, during cooking. We brine our lentils (quickly, in hot water) for our lentil salad (page 352) and our lentil and chorizo soup (page 353), before cooking them with other bold flavors and ingredients. For our Spiced Red Lentils, or Dal (page 355), we use delicate little red lentils, and in fact want them to break down in order to achieve the perfect, puree-like texture of our final dish. And don't forget about Rice and Lentils with Crispy Onions, page 240.

TEST KITCHEN EXPERIMENT

We wanted to dig deeper into the science of lentils so we connected with lentil expert Natsuki Fujiwara of the Northern Crops Institute in North Dakota. While discussing differences among lentil types, Natsuki mentioned that red and yellow lentils are nothing more than common brown and green lentils, respectively, that have been hulled. Considering how differently red and brown (or green and yellow) lentils cook, we were skeptical. To find out for ourselves, we set up the following experiment.

EXPERIMENT

Using a paring knife, we painstakingly peeled the hulls from ¼ cup of both brown and green lentils to examine their interior. We compared their raw appearance to red and yellow lentils that we purchased from the supermarket. Next, we cooked our hand-hulled lentils next to the supermarket lentils, comparing both cooking time and final texture.

RESULTS

To our surprise, peeling brown lentils left us with a small pile of red lentils. And the peeled green lentils looked identical to the store-bought yellow lentils. What about after cooking? With just 15 minutes of simmering, all of the lentils turned soft and mushy, regardless of whether we'd done the hulling or purchased them hulled.

TAKEAWAY

The world of lentils is smaller than we'd previously thought. Cooking hulled lentils is about easy as it gets—we want them to break down to a mushy consistency for soups so it's just a matter of cooking them long enough. When the hull is still in place, however, we have to do a bit more work. We've found that brining lentils (as for our lentil salad recipe, page 352), helps to soften the skins, allowing the interior to hydrate and soften without the hull bursting.

HULLING LENTILS: BROWN TO RED

We were surprised to hear that red and yellow lentils are nothing more than the common brown and green lentils, hulled. We decided to see for ourselves. Here, we halfway hulled brown lentils, making half-and-half brown/red lentils.

Technique 101: Brining

To brine is to soak a food item in a saltwater solution before cooking. We do it with everything from turkeys to beans. And the salt in that water has an almost magical ability to change things—the proteins in meats, the composition of the skin of beans, to start. We use this to our advantage, in a number of ways.

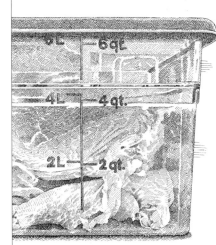

MEAT

We've found that soaking delicate, lean white meat, like pork, chicken, turkey, and even shrimp, in a salted water solution, or brine, before cooking results in moist, well-seasoned meat. But we don't brine beef. Why? In general, beef has a higher fat content than lean white meat, so it doesn't need the brine to remain juicy. Secondly, quick-cooking, tender beef cuts such as strip steaks or tenderloin roasts should ideally be cooked only to about 125 degrees (for medium-rare). In comparison, pork and chicken require a higher cooking temperature (145 for pork, 160 for white-meat poultry, and 170 for dark-meat poultry) and are, therefore, in greater danger of drying out. Tougher cuts of beef, such as chuck roast or brisket, are cooked to more than 200 degrees, but their extensive marbling of fat and collagen melts and acts as a natural moisturizer.

FISH

Though it may seem counterintuitive, brining fish can be beneficial. As it does with meat, brining fish serves two purposes: One, it helps season the flesh, which improves flavor; and two, by partially dissolving muscle fibers to form a water-retaining gel, it helps prevent the protein from drying out. And brining works a lot faster on fish because the structure of muscle in fish is different than that in meat: Instead of long, thin fibers (as long as 10 centimeters in meat), fish is constructed of very short (up to 10 times shorter) bundles of fibers.

We set up a series of tests using different brine concentrations (3, 6, and 9 percent salt-to-water solutions by weight) and types of fish (tuna, salmon, swordfish, and halibut). We found that, for up to six 1-inch-thick steaks or fillets, the optimum concentration was a 6 percent brine (5 tablespoons of salt dissolved in 2 quarts of water) and the ideal time was 15 minutes. It worked no matter the species, improving the texture of the fish without overseasoning.

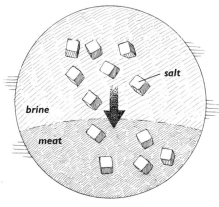

DIFFUSION

Salt will move from an area of greater salt concentration (the brine) to an area of lesser concentration (the meat).

CLOSE UP: SALT AND ANIMAL PROTEINS

In brining, salt travels from the area of greater concentration (the brine) into the less concentrated environment (the meat), via diffusion. But it's not simply the movement that makes brining helpful. The salt in the brine actually reshapes the protein molecules in the meat. How? Salt is made up of two ions, sodium and chloride, which are oppositely charged. Proteins, on the other hand, are larger, and contain many charges, positive and negative. When proteins encounter salt, they rearrange in order to accommodate the opposing charges. This creates gaps that then fill up with water. In addition, the salt dissolves some of the proteins, creating a gel that can hold on to even more water. And all of this together creates meat that is more tender and juicy when cooked.

BEANS

We frequently brine dried legumes, in order to help them cook up with tender skins. Why? When beans soak in a salt solution, the sodium ions replace some of the calcium and magnesium ions in the bean skin. Calcium and magnesium are responsible for keeping the pectin within strong and stable; the sodium helps weaken the pectin, and the skins, allowing the skins to expand.

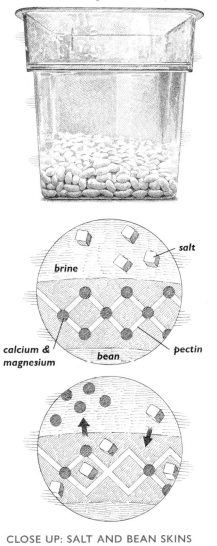

CLOSE UP: SALT AND BEAN SKINS

Before brining, the strong pectin molecules in the beans' skin are tightly bound by calcium and magnesium ions. When beans are brined, sodium replaces the calcium and magnesium ions, allowing the glue-like pectin network to more readily break down when heated, softening the skin and preventing exploding legumes.

Lentil Salad

✔ WHY THIS RECIPE WORKS

Lentils may not get points for glamour, but when properly cooked and dressed up in a salad with bright vinaigrette and herbs, nuts, and cheeses, the legumes' earthy, almost meaty depth and firm-tender bite make a satisfying side dish for almost any meal. The trouble is, perfectly cooked lentils are never a given. Too often, either their skins burst and their flesh disintegrates into starchy mush, or they don't cook through completely and retain chewy skin and a hard, crunchy core. Before we started adding accoutrements, we had to nail down a reliable way to produce tender, buttery lentils with soft, unbroken skins. And because the tiny, shape-retaining French green lentils we favor can be hard to come by, we were also determined to develop an approach that would yield perfect results with whatever lentil variety our supermarket had to offer.

BRINE THEM Fortunately, the test kitchen's previous work with bean cookery gave us a good idea of how to improve the skins. We've discovered that, odd as it may sound, brining beans overnight softens their outer shells and makes them less likely to burst. The explanation is twofold: As the beans soak, the sodium ions from the salt replace some of the calcium and magnesium ions in the skins. By replacing some of the mineral ions, the sodium ions weaken the pectin in the skins, allowing more water to penetrate and leading to a more pliable, forgiving texture. But with beans, brining requires an overnight rest to be most effective. Fortunately, due to the lentils' smaller, flatter shape, we found that just a few hours of brining dramatically cuts down on blowouts. And, since heat speeds up all chemical reactions, we managed to reduce that time to just an hour by using warm water in the salt solution.

COOK IN THE OVEN Another way to further reduce blowouts would be to cook the lentils as gently as possible. But we could see that even our stovetop's low setting still agitated the lentils too vigorously. We decided to try the oven, hoping that its indirect heat would get the job done more gently—and it did. And while the oven did increase the cooking time from less than 30 minutes to nearly an hour, the results were worth the wait: Virtually all of the lentil skins were tender yet intact.

COOK WITH SALT Despite the lentils' soft, perfect skins, their insides tended to be mushy, not creamy. It occurred to us that we could try another very simple trick with salt: adding it to the cooking water. Many bean recipes (including ours) shy away from adding salt during cooking because it produces firmer interiors that can be gritty. Here's why: While a brine's impact is mainly confined to the skin, heat (from cooking) affects the inside of the bean, causing sodium ions to move to the interior, where they slow the starches' ability to absorb water. But a firmed-up texture was exactly what our mushy lentils needed. Could a problem for beans prove to be the solution for lentils? Sure enough, when we added ½ teaspoon of salt to the cooking water, the lentils went from mushy to firm yet creamy.

LENTIL SALAD WITH OLIVES, MINT, AND FETA
SERVES 4 TO 6

French green lentils, or lentilles du Puy, are our preferred choice for this recipe, but it works with any type of lentil except red or yellow. Brining helps keep the lentils intact, but if you don't have time, they'll still taste good without it. The salad can be served warm or at room temperature.

1	cup lentils, picked over and rinsed
	Salt and pepper
4	cups warm water (110 degrees), plus 2 cups water
2	cups chicken broth
5	garlic cloves, lightly crushed and peeled
1	bay leaf
5	tablespoons extra-virgin olive oil
3	tablespoons white wine vinegar
½	cup pitted kalamata olives, chopped coarse
½	cup chopped fresh mint
1	large shallot, minced
1	ounce feta cheese, crumbled (¼ cup)

1. Place lentils and 1 teaspoon salt in bowl. Cover with 4 cups warm water and soak for 1 hour. Drain well. (Drained lentils can be refrigerated for up to 2 days before cooking.)

2. Adjust oven rack to middle position and heat oven to 325 degrees. Place drained lentils, remaining 2 cups water, broth, garlic, bay leaf, and ½ teaspoon salt in medium saucepan. Cover and bake until lentils are tender but remain intact, 40 minutes to 1 hour. Meanwhile, whisk oil and vinegar together in large bowl.

3. Drain lentils well; discard garlic and bay leaf. Add drained lentils, olives, mint, and shallot to dressing and toss to combine. Season with salt and pepper to taste. Transfer to serving dish, sprinkle with feta, and serve.

LENTIL SALAD WITH SPINACH, WALNUTS, AND PARMESAN CHEESE

Substitute sherry vinegar for white wine vinegar. Place 4 ounces baby spinach and 2 tablespoons water in bowl. Cover and microwave until spinach is wilted and volume is halved, 3 to 4 minutes. Remove bowl from microwave and keep covered for 1 minute. Transfer spinach to colander; gently press to release liquid. Transfer spinach to cutting board and chop coarse. Return to colander and press again. Substitute chopped spinach for olives and mint and ¾ cup coarsely grated Parmesan cheese for feta. Sprinkle with ⅓ cup walnuts, toasted and chopped coarse, before serving.

LENTIL SALAD WITH HAZELNUTS AND GOAT CHEESE

Substitute red wine vinegar for white wine vinegar and add 2 teaspoons Dijon mustard to dressing in step 2. Omit olives and substitute ½ cup chopped parsley for mint. Substitute ½ cup crumbled goat cheese for feta and sprinkle with ⅓ cup coarsely chopped toasted and skinned hazelnuts before serving.

LENTIL SALAD WITH CARROTS AND CILANTRO

Substitute lemon juice for white wine vinegar. Toss 2 carrots, peeled and cut into 2-inch-long matchsticks, with 1 teaspoon ground cumin, ½ teaspoon ground cinnamon, and ⅛ teaspoon cayenne pepper in bowl. Cover and microwave until carrots are tender but still crisp, 2 to 4 minutes. Substitute carrots for olives and ½ cup chopped cilantro for mint. Omit shallot and feta.

Hearty Spanish-Style Lentil and Chorizo Soup

✔ WHY THIS RECIPE WORKS

Spaniards have a long tradition of taking la comida, *their largest meal of the day, in the early afternoon. Hearty, sustaining soups and stews, many of which economically pair dried beans with some form of flavor-packed pork, such as ham, bacon, or sausage, are typically on the table. A particularly intriguing example is* sopa de lentejas con chorizo *(lentil and chorizo soup). It's a standout not just for its robust taste—provided by rich, garlicky chorizo, heady smoked paprika (pimentón), and the bright depth of sherry vinegar—but also for its unique texture: Neither entirely brothy nor creamy, the soup features whole lentils suspended in a thick broth. We set out to make our own version.*

PICK THE RIGHT LENTILS We started by evaluating different types of lentils. Spaniards are fond of *lentejas pardinas* (pardo means brownish or darkish) from Castilla y León. We mail-ordered a bag and found that they cooked up with a nutty, buttery flavor. But since pardinas are difficult to locate, we also simmered a few more-common varieties, finding that they were all similar though not without unique subtleties. French green *lentilles du Puy* were earthy; black beluga lentils, meaty; and standard brown lentils, vegetal. The du Puy type had the best tender-firm texture, so we went with them.

AND THEN BRINE THEM There was just one problem: keeping them intact. The "meat" of a lentil swells as it cooks, all too easily slipping out of its shell (which is called a blowout) and creating a mushy, split pea soup–like texture. Over the years, we have found two ways to address this issue. Both methods make use of salt to weaken the pectin and soften the shell, leading to fewer blowouts. The first approach involves cooking the lentils with salt and vinegar before adding liquid and fully cooking them; the second requires soaking the beans in a warm saltwater brine for an hour prior to cooking. We tried the salt and acid method first, sautéing some chopped onion in olive oil and then adding the lentils along with a bit of salt and sherry vinegar. We covered the pot and let the lentils cook for a few minutes before adding water, bay leaves, smoked paprika, and cloves and simmering until the beans were fully cooked. While the shape of these lentils was somewhat retained, many did still slip out of their skins and

We asked tasters to evaluate five kinds of lentils in our lentil soup, rating them in terms of taste, texture, and appearance. Here's what we found, with the lentils listed in order of preference.

LENTILLES DU PUY

These lentils are smaller than the more common brown and green varieties. While they take their name from the city of Puy in central France, they are also grown in North America and Italy. Dark olive green, almost black, in color, with mottling, these lentils were praised for their "rich, earthy, complex flavor" and "firm yet tender texture."

BLACK LENTILS

Like lentilles du Puy, black lentils are slightly smaller than the standard brown lentils. They have a deep black hue that tasters likened to the color of caviar. In fact, some markets refer to them as beluga lentils. Tasters liked their "robust, earthy flavor" and "ability to hold their shape while remaining tender." A few tasters found the color of the soup made with them "too dark and muddy."

BROWN LENTILS

These larger lentils are the most common choice in the market and are a uniform drab brown. Tasters commented on their "mild yet light and earthy flavor." Some found their texture "creamy," while others complained that they were "chalky." But everyone agreed that they held their shape and were tender inside.

GREEN LENTILS

Another larger lentil, this variety is the same size as the brown lentil and is greenish-brown in color. Although tasters accepted the "mild flavor" of these lentils and liked the way they "retain their shape while being tender," most complained that the soup made from them was "a bit anemic looking."

RED LENTILS

These small orange-red lentils "completely disintegrate when cooked." While they made our Hearty Spanish-Style Lentil and Chorizo Soup look "anemic," they worked perfectly in Indian dal, where smooth texture is desired.

form mush. We got much better results when we combined the approaches by brining the lentils (using boiling water cut the soaking time to 30 minutes) before sweating them with the salt and vinegar. Now each and every bean emerged fully intact and beautifully creamy.

SWEAT THE VEG Our first idea for creating depth was to swap chicken broth for some of the water, but that only seemed to cloud the soup's overall flavor. Next, we tried caramelizing the aromatics, but the profound sweetness that developed only obscured the smoky chorizo and tart vinegar. But all was not lost. The failed caramelized vegetable test got us thinking about an entirely different technique for enhancing the flavor of aromatics: sweating. This approach, used by cooks around the world, involves slowly cooking aromatics in a small amount of fat in a covered pot. The vegetables are kept just this side of browning, and during the process they develop a distinctive yet subtle flavor that is said to improve almost any dish. It was certainly worth a try. We prepared another batch of soup, first browning the chorizo and removing it from the pot and then slowly cooking the onion (plus carrots and parsley for a vegetal boost) in the rendered fat on low heat, all while the lentils brined. After 30 minutes, we dipped our spoons for a sample and discovered that a real transformation had occurred: The unbrowned vegetables boasted a clean, pure, sweet flavor that was altogether different from the sweet, roasted taste produced via caramelization. In the finished soup, the effect was equally impressive: The slow-cooked aromatics turned out to be an extremely well-balanced base that highlighted the main flavors of the dish.

MAKE A TARKA To finish the soup, we garnished it with an Indian preparation called a *tarka*, a mixture of spices and aromatics bloomed in oil. A tarka (also known as a *baghaar* or *chownk*) is a classic Indian preparation that involves blooming spices and sometimes garlic in hot ghee or oil to bring out their flavor and aroma. A tarka can be incorporated into a dish at the beginning of cooking or, more commonly, drizzled on at the end as a potent garnish. Since Indian cooks often use tarkas with lentils, we decided to adapt the technique for our soup. Our take calls for briefly sizzling sweet smoked paprika, ground black pepper, minced garlic, and grated onion in oil and incorporating the fragrant mixture into the soup when it is nearly finished cooking.

HEARTY SPANISH-STYLE LENTIL AND CHORIZO SOUP
SERVES 6 TO 8

We prefer French green lentils, or lentilles du Puy, for this recipe, but it will work with any type of lentil except red or yellow. Grate the onion on the large holes of a box grater. If Spanish-style chorizo is not available, kielbasa sausage can be substituted. Red wine vinegar can be substituted for the sherry vinegar. Smoked paprika comes in three varieties: sweet (dulce), bittersweet or medium hot (agridulce), and hot (picante). For this recipe, we prefer the sweet kind.

1	pound (2¼ cups) lentils, picked over and rinsed
	Salt and pepper
4	cups boiling water, plus 7 cups water
1	large onion
5	tablespoons extra-virgin olive oil
1½	pounds Spanish-style chorizo sausage, pricked with fork several times
3	carrots, peeled and cut into ¼-inch pieces
3	tablespoons minced fresh parsley
3	tablespoons sherry vinegar, plus extra for seasoning
2	bay leaves
⅛	teaspoon ground cloves
2	tablespoons sweet smoked paprika
3	garlic cloves, minced
1	tablespoon all-purpose flour

1. Place lentils and 2 teaspoons salt in heatproof container. Cover with 4 cups boiling water and let soak for 30 minutes. Drain well.

2. Meanwhile, finely chop three-quarters of onion (you should have about 1 cup) and grate remaining quarter (you should have about 3 tablespoons). Heat 2 tablespoons oil in Dutch oven over medium heat until shimmering. Add chorizo and cook until browned on all sides, 6 to 8 minutes. Transfer chorizo to large plate. Reduce heat to low and add carrots, 1 tablespoon parsley, chopped onion, and 1 teaspoon salt to now-empty pot. Cover and cook, stirring occasionally, until vegetables are very soft but not brown, 25 to 30 minutes. If vegetables begin to brown, add 1 tablespoon water to pot.

3. Add vinegar and lentils to vegetables; increase heat to medium-high; and cook, stirring frequently, until vinegar starts to evaporate, 3 to 4 minutes. Add remaining 7 cups water, bay leaves, cloves, and chorizo; bring to simmer. Reduce heat to low; cover; and cook until lentils are tender, about 30 minutes.

4. Heat remaining 3 tablespoons oil in small saucepan over medium heat until shimmering. Add paprika, garlic, grated onion, and ½ teaspoon pepper; cook, stirring constantly, until fragrant, about 2 minutes. Add flour and cook, stirring constantly, 1 minute longer. Remove chorizo and bay leaves from lentils and discard bay leaves. Stir paprika mixture into lentils and continue to cook until flavors have blended and soup has thickened, 10 to 15 minutes. When chorizo is cool enough to handle, cut in half lengthwise, then cut each half into ¼-inch-thick slices. Return chorizo to soup along with remaining 2 tablespoons parsley and heat through, about 1 minute. Season with salt, pepper, and up to 2 teaspoons sherry vinegar to taste, and serve. (Soup can be made up to 3 days in advance.)

Spiced Red Lentils

✓ WHY THIS RECIPE WORKS

Dals are heavily spiced lentil stews common throughout India. We wanted our dal to be simple yet still embody the complex flavors of Indian cuisine. To do this, we experimented with blooming the spices and adjusting the amount of water so that we could end up with a consistency that was porridge-like but needed no blender.

PICK RED Split red lentils gave the dish a mild, slightly nutty taste, and as the stew slowly simmered, they broke down to a smooth consistency.

BLOOM THE SPICES We created a balanced blend of warm spices with just a subtle layer of heat. Blooming the spices in oil until they were fragrant boosted and deepened their flavors. Onion, garlic, and ginger rounded out the aromatic flavor.

USE THE RIGHT AMOUNT OF WATER Authentic dal should have a porridge-like consistency, bordering on a puree (without the need for a blender). Getting this consistency required cooking the lentils with just the right amount of water: We finally settled on 4 cups water to 1¼ cups lentils for a dal that was smooth but not thin.

FINISH WELL Before serving, we added cilantro for color and freshness, diced raw tomato for sweetness and acidity, and some butter for richness.

SPICED RED LENTILS (MASOOR DAL)
SERVES 4

You cannot substitute other types of lentils for the red lentils here; they have a very different texture. Serve over rice.

1	tablespoon vegetable oil
½	teaspoon ground coriander
½	teaspoon ground cumin
½	teaspoon ground cinnamon
½	teaspoon ground turmeric
⅛	teaspoon ground cardamom
⅛	teaspoon red pepper flakes
1	onion, chopped fine
4	garlic cloves, minced
1½	teaspoons grated fresh ginger
4	cups water
8½	ounces (1¼ cups) red lentils, picked over and rinsed
1	pound plum tomatoes, cored, seeded, and chopped
½	cup minced fresh cilantro
2	tablespoons unsalted butter
	Salt and pepper
	Lemon wedges

1. Heat oil in large saucepan over medium-high heat until shimmering. Add coriander, cumin, cinnamon, turmeric, cardamom, and pepper flakes and cook until fragrant, about 10 seconds. Stir in onion and cook until softened, about 5 minutes. Stir in garlic and ginger and cook until fragrant, about 30 seconds.

2. Stir in water and lentils and bring to boil. Reduce heat to low and simmer, uncovered, until lentils are tender and resemble coarse puree, 20 to 25 minutes.

3. Stir in tomatoes, cilantro, and butter and season with salt and pepper to taste. Serve with lemon wedges.

PRACTICAL SCIENCE LENTILS AND NITROGEN

There is a reason lentils are a crop often rotated with grains.

Like other legumes, the roots of lentil plants are colonized by symbiotic bacteria known as *Rhizobium*, which have the ability to convert, or "fix," nitrogen in the air and soil into ammonia. Other common soil bacteria convert the ammonia to nitrate, which is the form absorbed by plants as their source of nitrogen. While most other crops remove nitrogen from the soil and require application of ammonia fertilizer, legumes, including lentils, restore nitrogen to the soil through their symbiotic relationship with *Rhizobium* bacteria. Farmers therefore rotate crops such as lentils and cereal grains such as corn and wheat in order to keep nitrogen in the soil and use less fertilizer.

CHAPTER 44

Olive Oil

We take care to preserve the earthy, fruity flavor of delicate extra-virgin olive oil.

HOW THE SCIENCE WORKS

Olive oil, which is simply juice pressed from olives, tastes great when it's fresh. The highest grade, called extra virgin, is lively, bright, and full-bodied, with flavors that range from peppery to buttery depending on the variety of olives used and how ripe they were when harvested. But olives are highly perishable, and their complex flavor degrades quickly, which makes producing—and handling—a top-notch oil time-sensitive, labor-intensive, and expensive.

The early history is not well established, but evidence suggests olive oil may have been produced from olives 8,000 years ago, making it one of the oldest known vegetable oils. Today Spain is the leading producer of olive oil, followed by Italy and Greece.

To qualify as extra virgin, the olive oil must be made from fresh olives and extracted from the fruit using only mechanical means. The fruit must be of high quality and, at least in Italy, processed within 24 hours of harvest. The temperature during processing cannot exceed 86 degrees and no solvents can be used. The oil must meet specific standards in over 20 laboratory tests, including free fatty acid level under 0.8 percent (an indication of breakdown) and peroxide value (an indication of oxidation) not to exceed 20 milliequivalents of oxygen. Most important: The oil must pass rigorous sensory tests specified by the International Olive Council (IOC). The taste tests identify specific defects, including lack of fruity flavor and the presence of musty, vinegary, and rancid flavors. In sum? To qualify for extra-virgin olive oil status, the oil must be free of all defects. Anything else is classified as a lower grade.

But the IOC standards are not enforced in the United States. And with no meaningful U.S. standards for olive oil, for a long time lower-quality oils found a ready market. In fact, a widely reported 2010 University of California, Davis, Olive Center study revealed that 69 percent of tested supermarket olive oils sold as "extra virgin" were actually lesser grades being passed off at premium prices.

Since then, the U.S. olive oil industry has taken steps to be more stringent. In 2010, the U.S. Department of Agriculture (USDA) adopted chemical and sensory standards for olive oil grades similar to those established by the IOC.

Olive oil is composed of hundreds of different chemical compounds, but predominantly ones called triglycerides. The triglycerides contribute very little to the flavor of olive oil. The fruity flavor comes from a combination of volatile aroma compounds, such as low molecular weight aldehydes, alcohols, and esters, while the bitter, pungent tastes are created primarily by the more abundant nonvolatile polyphenols. The aroma compounds are created by rapid enzyme reactions when the olives are crushed; the polyphenols are formed as olives ripen on the tree.

When it comes to cooking with olive oil, our goals are to keep as much of the fruity, earthy flavor of the oil as possible, while not making any of our dishes seem greasy. For our pasta with garlic and oil (page 360), we gently infuse extra-virgin olive oil with garlic and then cook the pasta in half the usual amount of water, so that the extra starch helps to reduce any oiliness. We poach fish in regular olive oil (page 361)—an act that may seem over the top, but in fact makes the lightest, most supple final dish, with the light flavor of olive oil. And finally, our Rosemary Focaccia (page 363) uses a technique called *autolyse* to create dense yet doughy loaves with bright extra-virgin olive oil flavor.

> **In 2010, 69 percent of supermarket extra-virgin olive oils did not qualify as extra virgin.**

TEST KITCHEN EXPERIMENT

We're pretty obsessed with temperature in the kitchen. And why not? Taking the temperature of a roasting chicken or a steak on the grill allows us to guarantee we don't overcook and ruin them. Oven temperature directly impacts how quickly cookies spread and brown. And knowing the difference in temperature between a simmer and a boil means we can turn out perfectly braised meat time and again. But what if temperature could also lie to us? Or to put it more accurately, what if temperature wasn't always the best indicator of how hot something was? To explore the difference between temperature and heat we set up the following experiments.

EXPERIMENT

We filled one 4-quart saucepan with 2 quarts of olive oil and a second 4-quart saucepan with 2 quarts of water. We heated both to 165 degrees, cracked a refrigerator-temperature egg into each, and cooked them for 6½ minutes. We then examined both of the eggs for doneness.

We also executed a second experiment where we heated oil and water, in separate pans, to 155 degrees and told test cooks to place a finger in each pot and hold them there until it felt too hot to do so any longer. We recorded which finger they pulled from the pot first.

RESULTS

Both experiments yielded consistent, and surprising, results. Even though they were maintained at the exact same temperature, the egg in the pot of water was clearly more cooked than the egg in the pot of oil. And as for the finger test? Though the test cooks were skeptical that there would be a difference, 100 percent of them pulled their finger immediately from the pot of water, but were able to leave their finger in the pot of oil for up to 30 seconds without discomfort.

TAKEAWAY

How can this be? Isn't temperature what determines speed of cooking? Well, yes and no. Given an identical cooking medium (such as two pots of water) temperature will tell us which one will cook food faster. But not all cooking mediums are the same. Every substance has its own specific heat.

Specific heat is the amount of energy required to raise the temperature of 1 gram of a substance 1 degree Celsius. For a substance with a higher specific heat it takes more energy to raise its temperature. As it happens, water's specific heat is more than twice that of olive oil, which means it requires more than twice the amount of energy to reach the same temperature as an equal volume of olive oil. So, those two pots in our experiment may have been at the same temperature, but the water contained far more energy. In the pot of oil that lower energy means the egg (or finger) heats more slowly and gently. We take advantage of oil's low specific heat to produce supermoist, tender fish in our poached fish recipe (page 361).

COOKING IN WATER VS. OIL

One of the niftiest things we learned from our poached fish fillets recipe is that the fish cooks more gently (and slowly) in oil than in water—even when both liquids are exactly the same temperature. This is true, it turns out, not just for fish but for any other food, including eggs (see photos below). But how can this be? Isn't temperature what determines speed of cooking?

As it happens, equally critical is the liquid's specific heat capacity, or how much energy is needed to change its temperature by 1 degree Celsius. Oil has roughly half the specific heat capacity of water, which means it requires half the amount of energy to reach the same temperature as an equal volume of water. This, in turn, means it has less energy to transfer to food and will cook it more slowly.

EGG IN WATER
After 6 minutes at 165 degrees, this egg is well on its way to being poached.

EGG IN OIL
After 6 minutes at the same temperature, this egg is still raw.

JOURNEY: EXTRA-VIRGIN OLIVE OIL PRODUCTION

Every stage of the process of making olive oil affects the quality of the oil. Let's take a closer look.

1 START WITH OLIVES

Producers must start with good fruit—that is, ripe olives that have been harvested carefully and aren't bruised or fermented—and get it to the mill as quickly as possible, before spoilage sets in. To produce extra-virgin olive oil the olives are harvested when they are midway between semiblack and completely black. At this stage, both the volatile aroma compounds and oil (23 to 27 percent by weight) are at their highest levels. In Italy the olives must be delivered to the processing facility within 24 hours to ensure freshness.

TYPES OF OLIVES

There are several thousand varieties of olives grown around the world, but 22 are most often used to produce olive oil. The most common olive varieties for producing extra-virgin olive oil are Arbequina and Picual from Spain, Koroneiki from Greece, and Coratina from Italy. Arbequina is noted for its ripe fruitiness, low bitterness, and pungency. Coratina is strongly green, herbaceous, bitter, and pungent. Koroneiki is strongly fruity and herbaceous, with mild bitterness, and pungency. Picual is very fruity with medium bitterness and pungency.

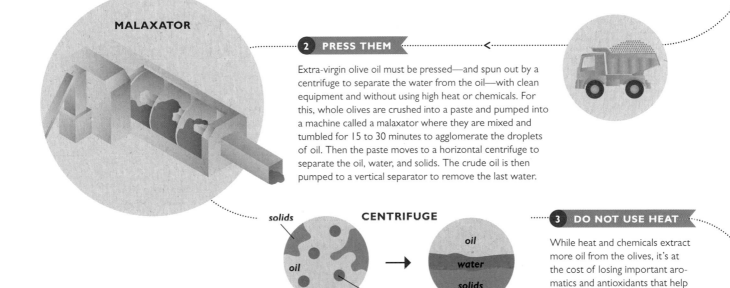

MALAXATOR

2 PRESS THEM

Extra-virgin olive oil must be pressed—and spun out by a centrifuge to separate the water from the oil—with clean equipment and without using high heat or chemicals. For this, whole olives are crushed into a paste and pumped into a machine called a malaxator where they are mixed and tumbled for 15 to 30 minutes to agglomerate the droplets of oil. Then the paste moves to a horizontal centrifuge to separate the oil, water, and solids. The crude oil is then pumped to a vertical separator to remove the last water.

CENTRIFUGE

solids

oil

water

BEFORE

oil

water

solids

AFTER

3 DO NOT USE HEAT

While heat and chemicals extract more oil from the olives, it's at the cost of losing important aromatics and antioxidants that help keep the oil fresh-tasting.

5 SENSORY TESTING

To meet sensory criteria, an oil must not just taste flawless—or have what experts call "zero defects"—but also possess good fruity flavor.

OTHER TYPES OF OILS

The lower grades of olive oils range in acidity from 1 percent to 2 percent (as opposed to 0.8 percent in extra-virgin) and exhibit a less-distinctive flavor and several identifiable defects. Regular olive oils are blends of chemically refined (neutralized) high-acid oil and higher quality or extra-virgin oils. "Light" olive oil means the amount of extra-virgin oil in the blend is low, rather than light in calories. It's only "light" in flavor.

4 TRANSPORT AND STORE

Producing high-quality oil is only half the challenge. Because olive oil begins to degrade as soon as it's exposed to air, heat, and light, producers must transport and store it carefully to preserve its freshness. In large operations the oil may be allowed to rest in big containers for up to several months before bottling. The oil may be bottled unfiltered or filtered to produce clear, transparent oil. Extra-virgin olive oil is produced by purely mechanical means, with no refining other than optional filtration, and therefore contains all of the natural constituents. Olive oil has a short shelf life—best consumed within 12 months of harvest date. Look for olive oils that are sold in dark-colored bottles. Those sold in clear glass or even plastic bottles expose the oil to more damaging light.

Garlicky Spaghetti with Olive Oil

✓ WHY THIS RECIPE WORKS

We like to maintain a revolving door–style kitchen pantry, rotating items in and out. It's how we pull off memorable dinners even when the fridge is nearly empty. While many ingredients come and go, there are three constants we make sure never to be without: spaghetti, garlic, and extra-virgin olive oil. Italians turn this trio into a quick pasta called aglio e olio, *an ultrasimple recipe that coaxes loads of flavor from the garlic. But there are also many variations in which the garlic is augmented by a few additional ingredients. To make our weeknight sauces even better, we set out to perfect the garlic, pasta, and olive oil components as a base to which we could add other ingredients we had on hand.*

INFUSE THE OIL As a first step, we needed to figure out how to infuse the oil with as much garlic flavor as possible. Many recipes call for sliced garlic, but we found that thinner slices turned dark brown (going from toasty-sweet to harshly acrid) by the time thicker slices became straw-colored. With a solution in mind, we put a pot of spaghetti on to boil and then pushed a few garlic cloves through a press to create identical bits. We cooked the minced garlic in ¼ cup of oil—enough to ensure that the bits were totally submerged—over low heat. After 10 minutes, the garlic was uniformly golden brown and the pasta was al dente. We set aside 1 cup of pasta cooking water, drained the noodles, and returned them to the pot. In went the garlic oil along with the starchy cooking liquid, which would help form a clingy sauce. For zing, we added ½ teaspoon of raw minced garlic at the last minute.

ADD STARCH Now the flavor was great, but the pasta was a bit oily. Doubling the starchy cooking liquid eliminated greasiness, but the spaghetti became bloated as it soaked up the excess water. That said, the extra starch did a great job of helping create a cohesive sauce. Our solution: Boil the pasta in 2 quarts of water instead of 4 quarts, effectively doubling the amount of starch in the cooking water. This way we could stick with adding just 1 cup of cooking water, ensuring that the dish was neither greasy nor soggy.

MAKE VARIATIONS Finally, we fiddled with supplementary ingredients. Incorporating toasted pine nuts, lemon juice and zest, Parmesan, and slivers of fresh basil made for a vibrant dish. Then, following the same template, we created a few more variations, all with oomph.

GARLICKY SPAGHETTI WITH LEMON AND PINE NUTS
SERVES 4

A garlic press makes quick work of uniformly mincing the garlic.

- ¼ cup extra-virgin olive oil
- 2 tablespoons plus ½ teaspoon minced garlic
- ¼ teaspoon red pepper flakes
- 1 pound spaghetti
  Salt and pepper
- 2 teaspoons grated lemon zest plus 2 tablespoons juice
- 1 cup chopped fresh basil
- 1 ounce Parmesan, grated (½ cup), plus extra for serving
- ½ cup pine nuts, toasted

1. Combine oil and 2 tablespoons garlic in 8-inch nonstick skillet. Cook over low heat, stirring occasionally, until garlic is pale golden brown, 9 to 12 minutes. Off heat, stir in pepper flakes; set aside.

2. Bring 2 quarts water to boil in large pot. Add pasta and 2 teaspoons salt and cook, stirring frequently, until al dente. Reserve 1 cup cooking water, then drain pasta and return it to pot. Add remaining ½ teaspoon garlic, lemon zest and juice, reserved garlic-oil mixture, and reserved cooking water to pasta in pot. Stir until pasta is well coated with oil and no water remains in bottom of pot. Add basil, Parmesan, and pine nuts and toss to combine. Season with salt and pepper to taste. Serve, passing extra Parmesan separately.

PRACTICAL SCIENCE LIGHT OLIVE OIL

Light olive oil is not lower in calories.

The label is misleading. Light olive oil contains the same number of calories as other olive oils; the "light" refers to flavor. After the first press for extra-virgin oil, European producers squeeze the olives again and sell this flavor-stripped, highly processed oil to American consumers who want the health benefits of olive oil in recipes—usually baking—where its characteristic strong flavor might be unwelcome. In these cases, light olive oil worked well: Tasters found it as undetectable as vegetable oil in yellow cake. However, in vinaigrette and roasted vegetables, testers preferred richer extra-virgin olive oil. The bottom line: If you're looking for a neutral oil for baking, light olive oil is an option. But in the test kitchen we'll stick with far cheaper vegetable oil for such applications.

GARLICKY SPAGHETTI WITH ARTICHOKES AND HAZELNUTS

Omit lemon zest and reduce lemon juice to 1 tablespoon. Stir in 1½ teaspoons fennel seeds, coarsely ground, with pepper flakes in step 1. Stir one 14-ounce can artichoke hearts, chopped, into pasta with lemon juice. Omit basil and substitute ½ cup hazelnuts, toasted, skinned, and chopped, for pine nuts.

GARLICKY SPAGHETTI WITH CAPERS AND CURRANTS

Omit lemon zest and reduce lemon juice to 1 tablespoon. Stir 3 tablespoons capers, rinsed and minced; 3 tablespoons currants, minced; and 2 anchovy fillets, rinsed, patted dry, and minced, into pasta with lemon juice. Omit basil and pine nuts.

Fish Poached in Olive Oil

✓ WHY THIS RECIPE WORKS

If your experience with poached fish is limited to the lean, bland preparation you might be served at a wedding or a weight-loss spa, a technique popular at high-end restaurants will permanently change your perception—and serve as a reminder as to why poaching became a classic approach to cooking fish in the first place. The key perk: Submerging fish in liquid and gently cooking it at below simmer temperatures—anywhere from 130 to 180 degrees— renders the delicate flesh silky and supple. In this case, however, there is one major amendment to the technique that elevates it above any poached fish we'd ever tasted: Rather than the usual lean bath of water, wine, broth, or some combination thereof, the poaching liquid is olive oil. We had to admit: On paper, cooking delicate fish fillets in a pot of fat sounds like a greasy recipe for disaster. But the results were stunning—lighter, moister, and more fragrant than any traditionally poached fish we'd ever tasted—and they explained why this technique has become so popular in top restaurants. (The modest amount of heat applied to the oil keeps its flavor intact—though note that we use regular olive oil, not extra virgin.) Another plus: The flavor-infused poaching oil can be whirred into a rich, glossy emulsion and drizzled over the fish as a sauce. The dish, we realized, would make elegant fare, provided we could get around one obvious challenge: the cost—and mess—of heating up a large amount of olive oil for just one meal. We would have to figure out how to scale the oil way back.

PICK COD Our first decision was to go with skinless fillets since the oil would never get hot enough to crisp the skin. We settled on cod for its firm, meaty flesh and clean flavor. As for the amount of oil, we reasoned that the smaller the surface area of the cooking vessel, the deeper the liquid would pool, so we reached past our trusty 12-inch nonstick skillet for its 10-inch sibling. Unfortunately, this setup still demanded about 1½ cups of oil to cover the four 6-ounce fillets. Our only other idea was to displace some of the oil by placing half an onion in the skillet and arranging the fillets around it—a trick that worked but got us down by only another ¼ cup. Clearly, we needed a more drastic solution.

USE LESS OIL That's when we started to wonder if completely immersing the fillets in oil was necessary. The alternative—pouring enough oil into the pan to come roughly halfway up the sides of the fish—would mean flipping the fish partway through poaching to ensure that it cooked through. We gave it a shot, basting the exposed half of each fillet with a few spoonfuls of oil, popping a lid on the pan, and placing the skillet over the lowest burner setting. The good news was that the method worked; the fillets were supremely moist and tender—considerably more so than any water-poached fish and not at all oily. The bad news was that it was fussy. With relatively little oil in the pan, the temperature spiked quickly and required that we constantly fiddle with the burner knob to keep the oil in our target range of 140 to 150 degrees, which would slowly bring the fish to an ideal internal temperature of 130 degrees, with little risk of going over. Placing a home-made heat diffuser fashioned from a ring of aluminum foil over the burner didn't reliably tame the flame. What we needed was a steadier, less-direct heat source, and for that we turned to the oven. We figured that we could simply bring the oil to 140 degrees on the stovetop, slip in the fish, and then transfer the skillet into a low oven.

AND THE OVEN But it wasn't quite that easy; the oil temperature immediately plummeted when we added the still-cold fillets, and the temperature recovery time in the oven was slow. But we had an idea: We'd heat the oil on the stovetop to well above our target temperature and then rely on the oven's more-even heat to keep it in the poaching sweet spot. After a slew of tests, we hit upon a winning combination: Heat the oil to 180 degrees, nestle in the fillets (each sprinkled with kosher salt), and set the pan in a 250-degree oven. The oil temperature recovered within 15 minutes, by which point the lower half of the fish was cooked. We flipped the fillets, replaced the lid, and returned them to the oven. This batch emerged incredibly moist and velvety, and thanks to our oven method, the process was now largely hands-off.

WHY OIL? Poaching in oil allows fish to retain more of its juices than poaching in wine or broth, leading to remarkably moist, velvety results. This is because cooking in oil is inherently more gentle than cooking in water (see Test Kitchen Experiment, page 358). And while you might expect that fish poached in fat would be greasy, it actually absorbs very little oil. Why? In order for oil to penetrate the fish, moisture must exit first. But because oil and water repel each other, it's very difficult for moisture inside the fish to readily enter the oil. Hence, more of the juices stay in the fish. In fact, in our tests, oil-poached fish lost just 14 percent of its weight during cooking, while water-poached fillets lost 24 percent.

SALT IT We often salt meat and allow it to rest before cooking, both to enhance juiciness and to bring seasoning deep into the interior. Why not try this with fish? For our next round of testing, we salted the fillets about 20 minutes before cooking. This technique worked beautifully: Moisture beaded on the surface of the fish, where it dissolved the salt and created a concentrated brine that was eventually absorbed back into the flesh to bolster flavor.

POACHED FISH FILLETS WITH ARTICHOKES AND SHERRY-TOMATO VINAIGRETTE
SERVES 4

Fillets of meaty white fish like cod, halibut, sea bass, or snapper work best in this recipe. Make sure the fillets are at least 1 inch thick. A neutral oil such as canola can be substituted for the pure olive oil. A 4-ounce porcelain ramekin can be used in place of the onion half in step 3.

FISH

4	(6-ounce) skinless white fish fillets, 1 inch thick
	Kosher salt
4	ounces frozen artichoke hearts, thawed, patted dry, and sliced in half lengthwise
1	tablespoon cornstarch
¾	cup olive oil
3	garlic cloves, minced
½	onion, peeled

VINAIGRETTE

4	ounces cherry tomatoes
½	small shallot, peeled
4	teaspoons sherry vinegar
	Kosher salt and pepper
1	tablespoon minced fresh parsley
2	ounces cherry tomatoes, cut into ⅛-inch-thick rounds

1. FOR THE FISH: Adjust oven racks to middle and lower-middle positions and heat oven to 250 degrees. Pat fish dry with paper towels and season each fillet with ¼ teaspoon salt. Let sit at room temperature for 20 minutes.

2. Meanwhile, toss artichokes with cornstarch in bowl to coat. Heat ½ cup oil in 10-inch nonstick ovensafe skillet over medium heat until shimmering. Shake excess cornstarch from artichokes and add to skillet; cook, stirring occasionally, until crisp and golden, 2 to 4 minutes. Add garlic and continue to cook until garlic is golden, 30 to 60 seconds. Strain oil through fine-mesh strainer into bowl. Transfer artichokes and garlic to ovensafe paper towel–lined plate and season with salt. Do not wash strainer.

3. Return strained oil to skillet and add remaining ¼ cup oil. Place onion half in center of pan. Let oil cool until it registers about 180 degrees, 5 to 8 minutes. Arrange fish fillets, skinned side up, around onion (oil should come roughly halfway up fillets). Spoon a little oil over each fillet, cover skillet, transfer to middle oven rack, and cook for 15 minutes.

4. Remove skillet from oven. Using 2 spatulas, carefully flip fillets. Cover skillet, return to middle rack, and place plate with artichokes and garlic on lower-middle rack. Continue to cook fish until it registers 130 to 135 degrees, 9 to 14 minutes longer. Gently transfer fish to serving platter, reserving ½ cup oil, and tent fish loosely with aluminum foil. Turn off oven, leaving plate of artichokes in oven.

5. FOR THE VINAIGRETTE: Process cherry tomatoes, shallot, vinegar, ¾ teaspoon salt, and ½ teaspoon pepper with reserved ½ cup fish cooking oil in blender until smooth, 1 to 2 minutes. Add any accumulated fish juices from platter, season with salt to taste, and blend for 10 seconds. Strain sauce through fine-mesh strainer; discard solids.

6. To serve, pour vinaigrette around fish. Garnish each fillet with warmed crisped artichokes and garlic, parsley, and tomato rounds. Serve immediately.

For fish, substitute 8 scallion whites, sliced ¼ inch thick, for artichoke hearts; omit garlic; and reduce amount of cornstarch to 2 teaspoons. For vinaigrette, process 6 scallion greens, 8 teaspoons lime juice, 2 tablespoons mirin, 4 teaspoons white miso paste, 2 teaspoons minced ginger, and ½ teaspoon sugar with ½ cup fish cooking oil as directed in step 5. Garnish fish with 2 thinly sliced scallion greens and 2 halved and thinly sliced radishes.

Rosemary Focaccia

✔ WHY THIS RECIPE WORKS

In the pantheon of artisan breads, focaccia has a looser history than most. Centuries ago, it began as a byproduct: When Italian bakers needed to gauge the heat of the wood-fired oven ("focaccia" stems from focolare, *meaning "fireplace") they would tear off a swatch of dough, flatten it, drizzle it with olive oil, and pop it into the hearth to bake as an edible oven thermometer. Because the technique was handy with just about any bread, there evolved countless variations on the theme. That said, it's the deep-dish Genovese interpretation that most Americans recognize: dimpled, chewy, and thick, with a smattering of herbs. We wanted to create a version that improved on the Genovese style, a bread with a crackly exterior, a more bubbly interior than the doughier Genovese focaccia, and just enough chew throughout.*

PRE-FERMENT To get great flavor, the biggest key here is fermentation—the process by which long chains of carbohydrates with little taste convert to sugars, alcohol, and carbon dioxide. And like many other organic processes, it's most effective over a long period of time. A slow ferment—usually several hours—not only allows the yeast to give the dough its lofty rise, but also produces a multitude of aromatic molecules that contribute to the flavor of the bread. To get the benefits of long fermentation with minimal effort, many bakers use a pre-ferment (also known as a sponge, starter, or *biga* in Italian): a mixture of flour, water, and a small amount of yeast that rests (often overnight) before being incorporated into a dough either in place of or along with more yeast. Time is the main factor here. That little bit of yeast in the biga grows as the hours go by, and the flavor that slowly develops is stronger and more complex than you would get by simply adding yeast to flour and water and kneading. We tried it and, after

baking, found loaves with already significant improvements: flavorful, golden-brown loaves perfumed—rather than saturated—with olive oil.

DON'T KNEAD We wanted a tender, airy interior. But our fast, powerful stand mixer was developing too much gluten, the strong, elastic network of cross-linked proteins that give bread its crumb structure. Hand kneading produced loaves that were even chewier. Figuring a gentler approach was warranted, we immediately recalled the most hands-off bread recipe we've published: Almost No-Knead Bread. This no-knead system relies on the ability of gluten to assemble into large networks on its own, given enough moisture in the dough and sufficient time. During the dough resting process called autolysis, enzymes that are present (known as proteases) snip the tiny nests of gluten into shorter strands, which quickly unravel and link together into the more organized sheets of gluten that exist in a well-developed dough. We also "turned" the dough while it proofed. Gently turning the dough over itself at regular intervals accomplishes three things: It brings the wheat proteins into closer proximity with one another, keeping the process going at maximum clip; it aerates the dough, replenishing the oxygen that the yeasts consume during fermentation; and it elongates and redistributes the bubbles.

HOLD THE SALT—FOR NOW The autolysis process worked well but took several hours. Could adjusting when we added salt to the dough help speed things along? To find out, we prepared two doughs. In the first, we combined the flour, water, yeast, and salt with the biga all at once before resting; in the second, we withheld the salt for 15 minutes. The results? Briefly omitting the salt hastened gluten development by an hour. After just 15 minutes, the unsalted dough was already pliant and smooth, while the salted dough was still gluey and stiff. So what does that all mean? Salt inhibits both the ability of flour to absorb water and the activity of the enzymes that break down proteins to begin the process of forming gluten. If allowed to rest without salt, the flour is able to get a jump on gluten development by absorbing as much water as it can and letting its enzymes work sooner to develop gluten networks.

USE CAKE PANS While our bread had just enough rich olive oil taste, the crust lacked the crunchy, almost fried bottom that most oiled-dough focaccia recipes produce. We moved our free-form breads into round cake pans, where a few tablespoons of oil coating the exterior would be contained. After swirling the bottom in the oil and some coarse salt, we flipped the dough, gently stretched it to the pan's edges, let it proof for just a few extra minutes, and scattered a healthy dose of chopped fresh rosemary over the top before sliding it onto the hot pizza stone. This focaccia was a revelation: crackly crisp on the bottom, deeply browned on top, with an interior that was open and airy.

ROSEMARY FOCACCIA
MAKES TWO 9-INCH ROUND LOAVES

If you don't have a baking stone, bake the bread on an overturned and preheated rimmed baking sheet.

SPONGE

½	cup (2½ ounces) all-purpose flour
⅓	cup warm water (110 degrees)
¼	teaspoon instant or rapid-rise yeast

DOUGH

2½	cups (12½ ounces) all-purpose flour, plus extra for shaping
1¼	cups warm water (110 degrees)
1	teaspoon instant or rapid-rise yeast
	Kosher salt
¼	cup extra-virgin olive oil
2	tablespoons chopped fresh rosemary

1. FOR THE SPONGE: Combine flour, water, and yeast in large bowl and stir with wooden spoon until uniform mass forms and no dry flour remains, about 1 minute. Cover bowl tightly with plastic wrap and let stand at room temperature at least 8 hours or up to 24 hours. Use immediately or store in refrigerator for up to 3 days (let stand at room temperature for 30 minutes before proceeding with recipe).

2. FOR THE DOUGH: Stir flour, water, and yeast into sponge with wooden spoon until uniform mass forms and no dry flour remains, about 1 minute. Cover with plastic and let rise at room temperature for 15 minutes.

3. Sprinkle 2 teaspoons salt over dough; stir into dough until thoroughly incorporated, about 1 minute. Cover with plastic and let rise at room temperature for 30 minutes. Spray rubber spatula or bowl scraper with vegetable oil spray. Fold partially risen dough over itself by gently lifting and folding edge of dough toward middle. Turn bowl 90 degrees; fold again. Turn bowl and fold dough 6 more times (for total of 8 folds). Cover with plastic and let rise for 30 minutes. Repeat folding, turning, and rising 2 more times, for total of three 30-minute rises.

4. One hour before baking, adjust oven rack to upper-middle position, place baking stone on rack, and heat oven to 500 degrees. Gently transfer dough to lightly floured counter. Lightly dust top of dough with flour and divide it in half. Shape each piece of dough into 5-inch round by gently tucking under edges. Coat two 9-inch round cake pans with 2 tablespoons oil each. Sprinkle each pan with ½ teaspoon salt. Place round of dough in 1 pan, top side down; slide dough around pan to coat bottom and sides with oil, then flip dough over. Repeat with second piece of dough. Cover pans with plastic and let rest for 5 minutes.

5. Using your fingertips, press dough out toward edges of pan, taking care not to tear it. (If dough resists stretching, let it relax for 5 to 10 minutes before trying to stretch it again.) Using dinner fork, poke entire surface of dough 25 to 30 times, popping any large bubbles. Sprinkle rosemary evenly over top of dough. Let dough rest in pans until slightly bubbly, 5 to 10 minutes.

6. Place pans on baking stone and lower oven temperature to 450 degrees. Bake until tops are golden brown, 25 to 28 minutes, rotating pans halfway through baking. Transfer pans to wire rack and let cool for 5 minutes. Remove loaves from pans and return to rack. Brush tops with any oil remaining in pans. Let cool for 30 minutes before serving. (Leftover bread can be wrapped in double layer of plastic wrap and stored at room temperature for 2 days. Wrapped with additional layer of aluminum foil, bread can be frozen for up to 1 month.)

FOCACCIA WITH KALAMATA OLIVES AND ANCHOVIES

Omit salt from pans in step 4. Substitute ½ cup coarsely chopped pitted kalamata olives, 4 minced anchovy fillets, and 1 teaspoon red pepper flakes for rosemary. Sprinkle each focaccia with ¼ cup finely grated Pecorino Romano as soon as it is removed from oven.

CHAPTER 45

Stock

Making great stock requires three steps: extraction, reduction, and filtration.

HOW THE SCIENCE WORKS

"The wonderful flavor of good French food is the result, more often than not, of the stock used for its cooking," wrote Julia Child in *Mastering the Art of French Cooking* (1961). The French term for stock, or *fond de cuisine*, she added, "literally means the foundation and working capital of the kitchen." It's the foundation of our kitchen, too.

The use of a stock to heighten the flavor of a dish goes back at least as far as 1651, when the French chef François Pierre de La Varenne published his influential book, *Le Cuisinier François*, which includes a recipe for a mushroom stock. In 1773, French chemist Antoine Baumé developed a process for making dried stocks from meat, in tablet form, for use during war; or, essentially the birth of the bouillon cube. In 1821, two more French chemists, Joseph-Louis Proust and Antoine-Augustin Parmentier, developed a method for making an "extract of meat" by soaking the meat in cold water followed by slowly warming the mixture, a process soon adopted by the great French chef Marie-Antoine Carême, the father of *grande cuisine*. It is still the basic method used today to prepare stock.

The preparation of stock involves three basic steps: extraction, reduction, and filtration, each playing a critical role in creating stock's intense flavor.

The traditional ingredients in a good stock are meat or fish, bones, and vegetables (typically onions, carrots, and celery). The first step extracts flavor molecules from the ingredients with water or wine. Starting the extraction step with cold water, and slowly warming it, allows the proteins to slowly coagulate and float to the top so these coagulated proteins (or scum) are easily removed by skimming the surface, as well as during filtration. (Starting with hot water

> **The French term for stock literally means the foundation and working capital of the kitchen.**

and boiling the liquid breaks the coagulated proteins down to small particles, which are hard to remove, and result in a cloudy stock.) In the slowly simmering water, the onions or leeks produce a sulfur-containing compound called 3-mercapto-2-methylpentan-1-ol (MMP), the strong meaty aroma of which is a potent contributor to the flavor.

The second step, reduction, evaporates some of the water to produce a concentrated, flavorful stock, as well as provides additional time for the creation of more flavor molecules. In addition to the creation of flavor, the steps that use heat (extraction and reduction) release gelatin from the collagen in the connective tissue of meat and bones (which, traditionally, were veal). Gelatin increases viscosity and provides a pleasing mouthfeel to the stock. And the final step? Filtration removes unwanted coagulated protein, fat, and insoluble ingredients to produce a clear stock.

For our own homemade stocks, we take a number of different routes to a finished product. First, the pressure cooker. This high-powered, steam-driven cooker makes a rich, flavorful stock in a short amount of time (page 368). Want to take it slow? No problem. We also made chicken stock in the slow cooker (page 369), gently cooking for 8 to 10 hours. Not everything is traditional: We use ground beef to create a quick and hearty beef broth for our earthy Vietnamese Beef Pho (page 369). Finally, not all stocks need meat. We take a totally different route for our Vegetable Broth Base (page 371), making a concentrated paste of vegetables, herbs, and salt that can be simply added to boiling water for a flavorful, easy stock. For a rich, yet simple, dish that includes broth as part of the cooking, look to our Simple Pot-au-Feu (in the Onion Chapter, page 237).

TEST KITCHEN EXPERIMENT

Modern pressure cookers are safe, quiet, and useful for turning out succulent braises and stews in record time. But is faster cooking time really the only difference between using a pressure cooker and regular pot on the stove? Or does a pressure cooker actually impact the flavor of the food as well? To find out, we set up the following experiment.

EXPERIMENT

We made a simple chicken stock by simmering 3 pounds of chicken wings in 3 quarts of water in a covered Dutch oven on the stovetop for 4 hours. We made an identical batch of stock in a pressure cooker, cooking it at high pressure (15 psi) for 1½ hours. We strained both stocks, skimmed off the fat, and tasted. We repeated the test two times.

RESULTS

To our surprise, both the color and the flavor of the stocks were noticeably different from each other. The pressure-cooked broth was darker, with a more complex, meaty flavor (despite having been cooked for less than half the time of the traditional broth), while the broth prepared in a Dutch oven had a cleaner, purer chicken taste.

TAKEAWAY

What gives? Pressure cookers work by trapping steam and creating pressure inside the pot. This raises the boiling point of water up to about 250 degrees at 15 psi. This high temperature does more than just shorten the cooking time. It also promotes more extraction of flavor compounds from the skin and bones while encouraging the breakdown of proteins into peptides, which produce rich meatiness (thanks to the Maillard reaction). Without these additional flavors, the broth cooked in a Dutch oven tasted more like chicken but was less meaty tasting overall. Do we have a favorite? Not exactly. When clean chicken flavor is the goal—as in a simple chicken soup—we might prefer the stock cooked in the Dutch oven. But for adding meaty richness to stews and braises, pressure-cooked chicken stock is an unmatched asset.

UNDER PRESSURE: CHICKEN STOCK

We made chicken stock in a Dutch oven, and in a pressure cooker, and got very different results. The pressure cooker stock was more complex and meaty, while the Dutch oven stock was cleaner and purer.

Technique 101: Pressure Cooking

Pressure cookers are powerful, steam-driven tools, used by chefs and home cooks to hasten cooking times for stocks, beans, braises, and stews.

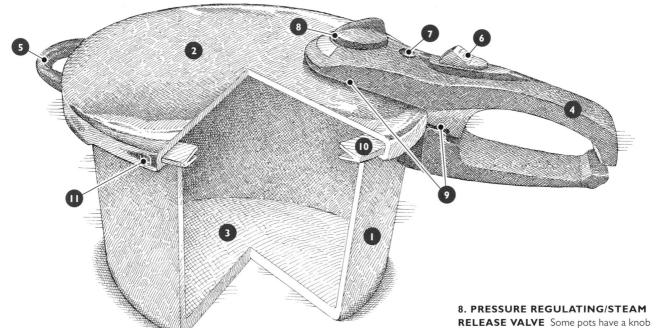

1. COOKING POT The main body of pressure cookers can be made from aluminum or stainless steel. They are made much like a standard-issue pot (which means you can also use them for other occasions when you need a large pot, like cooking pasta and deep frying). Though they're more expensive, we prefer the stainless pots since they're more durable.

2. LID This is no ordinary lid. Pressure-cooker lids are specially designed to create an airtight seal, with the help of the silicone gasket (10), when properly locked in place on the pot.

3. DISK BASE Typically made from aluminum, the disk base is a key feature because it retains and regulates heat. We found that the thicker the disk base, the more steady and hands-off the cooking is.

4. PRIMARY HANDLE Most pots have a long two-piece handle that also contains other components key to the functioning of the pressure cooker, including steam release valves, the pressure regulator (8), and the pressure indicator (7). The lid and bottom of the pot both have a handle piece; when the lid is properly locked in place the two parts line up.

5. SECONDARY HANDLE Opposite the primary handle, this grip is a useful secondary support when moving a full, heavy pot.

6. PRESSURE SAFETY LOCK/LOCKED LID INDICATOR Some pressure cookers have a button you have to slide into place to lock the pot once the lid has been properly closed; others simply have an indicator (for example, a window that displays red or green) to signify whether the lid is locked. The pot will not trap pressure unless the lid is properly locked in place. We found that the locks on some pots were more intuitive to use than others.

7. PRESSURE INDICATOR Every pressure cooker has a way to indicate that pressure has been reached—critical to know since this is when you turn down the heat to maintain the pressure level and start counting the cooking time. The pressure indicator is typically a pin or button that rises as pressure inside the pot increases. If the pot has a separate pressure-regulating valve (8), this pin/button will simply raise or drop. But if the pot does not allow you to specify high or low pressure, this pin/button typically has two rings indicating low and high, which will appear as the pressure in the pot rises.

The underside of the pressure indicator acts as a regulator and safety mechanism. If there is pressure in the pot, the rubber O-ring at the base of the indicator will seal off the opening and the cooker can't be opened. On some pots if the lid is not properly closed, or if there is too much pressure built up inside the pot, it will also act as a safety valve and allow excess pressure to escape.

8. PRESSURE REGULATING/STEAM RELEASE VALVE Some pots have a knob that you turn to low or high (called 1 and 2 or I and II on some pots), which allows you to indicate your target pressure level before you start to bring the pot up to pressure. The pressure indicator (7) will rise when that pressure level has been reached. This knob typically also acts as a valve to release excess pressure. On some of our favorite models, the steam released during a quick release is let out through this valve. On pots without this high/low setting feature, there is typically a simple steam release valve.

9. STEAM RELEASE POINTS Depending on the construction of the pot, various points built into the lid allow excess pressure to escape as needed. With some pots, as pressure builds, steam and/or liquid may also be released at these points until the pot is up to pressure.

10. SILICONE GASKET This rubber ring fits snugly in a channel around the perimeter of the underside of the lid. When the lid is in place correctly, the gasket allows an airtight seal to be created, which in turn allows pressure to build within the pot.

11. SAFETY VENTS These cutouts around the perimeter of the lid allow for release of steam in case of excess pressure. They are usually a backup safety feature that comes into play only if all of the safety valve(s) are blocked with food. In this case, the pressure will tear the gasket and steam will escape through these cutouts.

Pressure-Cooker Chicken Stock

✔ WHY THIS RECIPE WORKS

Preparing broths in the pressure cooker is not only faster than conventional methods, but the flavor is also significantly different. The intense heat promotes the extraction of flavor compounds from bones, skin, and vegetables, and in the case of chicken and beef broths, encourages the breakdown of proteins into peptides, which produces noticeably rich meatiness.

BROWN THE BIRD   A number of recipes recommend roasting the chicken parts first for both color and flavor. To mimic this effect without requiring the extra hours of work, we simply browned the chicken in the pot before browning the onion and adding the vegetables and water.

USE 3 QUARTS   We learned that getting the amount of water just right and nailing the cooking time were crucial elements. Using more than 3 quarts water creates a watery broth, but any less means a skimpy yield. As for the time, we found it takes a full hour and a half to extract all the flavor from the bones and meat.

STRAIN IT   Once the broth is finished, you need to strain off the solids. Be sure to press firmly on the solids in the strainer to extract as much liquid as possible. After you strain out the solids, you can strain the broth again to make it less cloudy if desired.

PRESSURE-COOKER CHICKEN STOCK
MAKES 3 QUARTS

I	tablespoon vegetable oil
3	pounds bone-in chicken pieces (leg quarters, backs, and/or wings), hacked with meat cleaver into 2-inch pieces
I	onion, chopped
3	garlic cloves, lightly crushed and peeled
3	quarts water
I	teaspoon salt
3	bay leaves

1. Heat oil in pressure-cooker pot over medium-high heat until smoking. Brown half of chicken on all sides, about 6 minutes; transfer to bowl. Repeat with remaining chicken; transfer to bowl.

2. Pour off all but 1 tablespoon fat left in pot, add onion, and cook over medium heat until softened and well browned, 8 to 10 minutes. Stir in garlic and cook until fragrant, about 30 seconds. Stir in 1 cup water and scrape up all browned bits from bottom of pot using wooden spoon. Stir in remaining 11 cups water, salt, bay leaves, and browned chicken with any accumulated juices.

3. Lock pressure-cooker lid in place and bring to high pressure over medium-high heat. As soon as pot reaches high pressure, reduce heat to medium-low and cook for 90 minutes, adjusting heat as needed to maintain high pressure.

4. Remove pot from heat. Quick release pressure, then carefully remove lid, allowing steam to escape away from you.

5. Strain broth through fine-mesh strainer into clean container, pressing on solids to extract as much liquid as possible; discard solids. Using large spoon, skim excess fat from surface of broth. (Broth can be refrigerated for up to 2 days, or frozen for several months.)

PRACTICAL SCIENCE
SALTED VS. UNSALTED CHICKEN BROTH

In the end, you can use either.

Our favorite chicken broth is Swanson Chicken Stock, which we appreciate for its "rich," "meaty" flavor. This broth stood out in our tasting because it's made with a relatively high percentage of meat-based protein compared with similar products and a moderate amount of sodium for the broth world—510 milligrams per 1-cup serving. Still, since many people monitor their sodium intake, we wondered how the "unsalted" version of this product would measure up.

Swanson Unsalted Chicken Stock has 130 milligrams of sodium, which is just under the USDA's 140-milligram ceiling for "low-sodium" products. (In fact, "unsalted" means only that no salt was added during processing, so some unsalted broths can contain much more sodium per serving.) When we compared ingredient lists, we found that the company didn't simply omit the sodium in the unsalted version but reformulated it from the ground up. While both products begin their ingredient lists with "chicken stock," the regular broth adds salt next, followed by vegetables and an herb. In the unsalted version, the vegetables disappear, replaced by more chicken-centric ingredients, including dehydrated chicken and chicken fat. Despite these differences, both contain 4 grams of protein per cup, identically low levels of sugars, and trace amounts of fat per 1-cup serving.

To compare flavor, we sampled the broths side by side plain, in vegetable soup, and in a simple Parmesan risotto, rating them on flavor, saltiness, off-flavors, if any, and overall appeal. We weren't that surprised to find that our tasters preferred the regular chicken broth in all three tastings, but the unsalted broth fared surprisingly well. When we need to restrict sodium, we won't hesitate to reach for Swanson Unsalted Chicken Stock.

Slow-Cooker Chicken Stock

✔ WHY THIS RECIPE WORKS

Homemade stock tastes so much better than even the best store-bought broth, but while it's not complicated to make, it does require a bit of attention—monitoring the temperature, skimming the foam that rises to the surface, standing at the stove. The last time we were standing in front of a simmering pot on the stovetop, we caught sight of our trusty slow cooker on the counter and wondered whether we could use it to make even these minor inconveniences disappear. It was worth a try, but we were adamant that the slow-cooker stock had to taste as good as the stovetop version.

USE LEFTOVER BONES One great thing about chicken stock is that it can be made with ingredients that you'd otherwise throw away: in this case, chicken bones. Whether they're bones left over from chickens you've roasted or from rotisserie chickens you've purchased, there's gold in them. We stockpiled 2½ pounds of bones (about three rotisserie chickens' worth) for each batch. (Later, for good measure, we tried this stock with meat-on chicken parts and chicken feet. They, too, will produce a lovely stock. But the value of using bones destined for the garbage bin makes this a remarkably thrifty endeavor.)

USE ENOUGH WATER The usual suspects for a basic stock (celery, carrot, and onion) joined the leftover chicken bones (broken up into smaller pieces to release more of their flavor and body-giving properties) in the slow cooker. Determining the amount of water to add took some trial and error. We had to have enough water to barely cover the bones but not so much that the stock would emerge from the slow cooker watery and pale. We found that 3 quarts of fresh, cold water did the trick, keeping the bones submerged—essential for a good stock and, as it turns out, actually easier to do in a slow cooker, where evaporation is a nonissue. (With stovetop stocks, you often have to add liquid to keep the bones submerged.)

SEASON AND LET COOK To season the stock, we added a bay leaf, whole black peppercorns, and salt. With the basic ingredients safely nestled in the slow cooker, time was the next piece of the puzzle to solve. After testing our stock at intervals from 4 hours to 12 hours, we found that we got the best, richest, most chicken-y flavor by setting our slow cooker to high and cooking for 8 to 10 hours.

SLOW-COOKER CHICKEN STOCK
MAKES ABOUT 3 QUARTS

You can freeze chicken carcasses one at a time until you have the 2½ pounds needed for this recipe; three to four rotisserie chicken carcasses or one 6-pound roaster carcass will weigh about 2½ pounds. This recipe was developed using bones from cooked chicken.

3	quarts water
2½	pounds roasted chicken bones
1	onion, chopped
2	carrots, peeled and cut into 1-inch chunks
2	celery ribs, chopped
1	teaspoon black peppercorns
1	teaspoon salt
1	bay leaf

1. Place all ingredients in slow cooker. Cover and cook on high for 8 to 10 hours.

2. Let stock cool slightly, then strain through fine-mesh strainer set over large bowl. Use immediately or let cool completely, then refrigerate until cold. (When cold, surface fat will solidify and can be easily removed with spoon.) Stock will keep, refrigerated, for up to 2 days, or frozen for several months.

Vietnamese Beef Pho

✔ WHY THIS RECIPE WORKS

The biggest selling point of pho, or Vietnamese beef and noodle soup, is its killer broth—a beefy, fragrant, faintly sweet concoction produced by simmering beef bones and water for hours with aromatics. Notably, those bones are often the only form of meat added to the cooking liquid; actual pieces of beef aren't introduced until serving, when the broth is strained and ladled onto very thin slices of raw steak (typically sirloin) and thin rice noodles in large individual serving bowls. Pouring hot broth over the contents cooks the meat just enough and softens the noodles and vegetables. Condiments such as hoisin, chili, and fish sauce and lime wedges are passed at the table for individual flavor tinkering. Those exotic yet approachable flavors are what fuel our frequent cravings for this dish. But who has the time to spend a day eking out a full-flavored beef stock? But if we could devise an equally intense, complex-tasting broth in less time, pho would surely become our ultimate beef and noodle soup to make at home.

MAKE BROTH WITH GROUND BEEF Ditching the bones was an obvious first move, but finding an equally beefy substitute wasn't so simple. It dawned on us that doing without beef bones didn't mean we had to do without beef altogether. Boiling ground beef (or, more traditionally, beef bones) for stock coaxes out great beef flavor—the ground meat releases its flavor quickly, and the connective tissue converts to gelatin. The only problem is that soluble proteins and melted fat render the liquid cloudy and leave a layer of scum on its surface. Frequently skimming away those impurities as the liquid cooks is one way to clear up the stock, but it's a tedious chore (especially when there are solids, like onions or spices, that you don't want to remove) and it never completely clarifies the stock. Blanching and rinsing the meat before adding it to the cooking liquid was a far more efficient method. The brief (2-minute) boil thoroughly agitated the meat so that its proteins and fat sloughed off, but didn't cook it long enough to wash away much flavor. A quick rinse rid the surface of any stubborn clingy bits.

CHOOSE STRIP STEAK Some pho shops throw tough cuts like brisket and tripe into their long-simmered broths and offer them as garnishing options, but thin slices of raw, relatively tender steak are the most common and would do fine for our purposes. The question was which cut exactly, so we tried all the options we could think of: tenderloin, rib eye, strip steak, tri-tip, blade steak, flank, and eye of round. Tenderloin was favored for its supple texture, and its uniform cylindrical shape made thin-slicing it a breeze. But its prohibitive price meant that it was ill-matched for this humble soup. Plus, it offered nothing in the way of beefy flavor. Strip steak, tri-tip, and blade steak all offered good beefiness and reasonable tenderness at a fraction of the price. We chose to work with strip since it is usually the easiest to find. To make the steak less challenging to slice thin, we employed the test kitchen's favorite trick for prepping stir-fry meat: briefly freezing the whole steak, which firms it up enough for the blade to make clean cuts. As a bonus, freezing also ensured that the steak didn't overcook when it came in contact with the hot broth.

ADD GARNISHES We pared down the list of table-side garnishes and condiments to the essentials. The must-haves—bean sprouts for crunch, basil (preferably Thai basil, though Italian basil will work), lime wedges, hoisin and chili sauces, and additional fish sauce—balanced the straightforward meatiness and mellow sweetness of the broth with heat, acidity, and freshness.

VIETNAMESE BEEF PHO
SERVES 4 TO 6

Our favorite store-bought beef broth is Better Than Bouillon Beef Base. Use a Dutch oven that holds 6 quarts or more. An equal weight of tri-tip steak or blade steak can be substituted for the strip steak; make sure to trim all connective tissue and excess fat. One 14- or 16-ounce package of rice noodles will serve four to six. Look for noodles that are about ⅛ inch wide; these are often labeled "small." Don't use Thai Kitchen Stir-Fry Rice Noodles since they are too thick and don't adequately soak up the broth.

1	pound 85 percent lean ground beef
2	onions, quartered through root end
12	cups low-sodium beef broth
¼	cup fish sauce, plus extra for seasoning
1	(4-inch) piece ginger, sliced into thin rounds
1	cinnamon stick
2	tablespoons sugar, plus extra for seasoning
6	star anise pods
6	whole cloves
	Salt
1	teaspoon black peppercorns
1	(1-pound) boneless strip steak, trimmed and halved
14–16	ounces (⅛-inch-wide) rice noodles
⅓	cup chopped fresh cilantro
3	scallions, sliced thin (optional)
	Bean sprouts
	Fresh Thai or Italian basil sprigs
	Lime wedges
	Hoisin sauce
	Sriracha sauce

1. Break ground beef into rough 1-inch chunks and drop in Dutch oven. Add water to cover by 1 inch. Bring mixture to boil over high heat. Boil for 2 minutes, stirring once or twice. Drain ground beef in colander and rinse well under running water. Wash out pot and return ground beef to pot.

2. Place 6 onion quarters in pot with ground beef. Slice remaining 2 onion quarters as thin as possible and set aside for garnish. Add broth, 2 cups water, fish sauce, ginger, cinnamon, sugar, star anise, cloves, 2 teaspoons salt, and peppercorns to pot and bring to boil over high heat. Reduce heat to medium-low and simmer, partially covered, for 45 minutes.

3. Pour broth through colander set in large bowl. Discard solids. Strain broth through fine-mesh strainer lined with triple thickness of cheesecloth; add water as needed to equal 11 cups. Return broth to pot and season with extra sugar and salt (broth should taste overseasoned). Cover and keep warm over low heat.

4. While broth simmers, place steak on large plate and freeze until very firm, 35 to 45 minutes. Once firm, cut against grain into ⅛-inch-thick slices. Return steak to plate and refrigerate until needed.

5. Place noodles in large container and cover with hot tap water. Soak until noodles are pliable, 10 to 15 minutes; drain noodles. Meanwhile, bring 4 quarts water to boil in large pot. Add drained noodles and cook until almost tender, 30 to 60 seconds. Drain immediately and divide noodles among individual bowls.

6. Bring broth to rolling boil over high heat. Divide steak among individual bowls, shingling slices on top of noodles. Pile reserved onion slices on top of steak slices and sprinkle with cilantro and scallions, if using. Ladle hot broth into each bowl. Serve immediately, passing bean sprouts, basil sprigs, lime wedges, hoisin, Sriracha, and extra fish sauce separately.

Vegetable Broth Base

✔ WHY THIS RECIPE WORKS

It's no surprise that most cooks opt for store-bought vegetable broth (or even water). But even the best of the commercial stuff is not ideal, which is a shame, since a good broth can be the difference between a ho-hum vegetarian dish and a flavorful one that satisfies all diners, vegetarian or otherwise. We wanted to make a broth that would boost our vegetarian meals the same way that chicken or beef stock boosts our meat-based cooking. But since vegetarian dishes can be more nuanced and subtle in their flavor, we would need a broth that wouldn't overpower the other ingredients or call too much attention to any one vegetable. If possible, we also wanted our recipe to generate minimal waste and be economical and simple to produce, so we could consider it a staple.

GROUND UP We started by trying a number of different techniques, including boiling vegetable scraps; cooking sous-vide with 10 different vegetables; using roasted vegetables; and a wild card, a raw puree whizzed in the blender like a vegetable smoothie and then strained through a fine-mesh sieve. None were great. But then we tried what was basically a recipe for a homemade bouillon cube—vegetables, herbs, and salt ground up in a food processor. We stirred a spoonful of this paste into boiling water to create a broth. It was easy to store in the freezer and use only what we needed at a time. We took that idea and ran.

PICK THE RIGHT VEG A *mirepoix*, a mixture of two parts chopped onion to one part each of carrots and celery, is the classic base for many broths, so we started there. But we found that celery added a bitterness and a slightly sour flavor. Our fix? Celery root. It turns out that celery root is not just milder than celery; it also has a more complex, creamy flavor. Both celery root and celery get their characteristic flavor from several phthalide compounds, but celery has more of one called sedanolide, which has a notably bitter flavor. And, onions have a high moisture content, making the base watery and more likely to solidify in the freezer. Leeks have less water, and possess the least amount of sugar of all the alliums. We decided to use them instead.

ADD PUNCH The onions had been a failure, but their diluting effect did give us an idea. What if we took the opposite tack and concentrated the vegetables' flavor? That way, we could use more of them. We sliced leeks, carrots, and celery root and dried them for hours in a low oven. Then we ground them up in the food processor and added parsley and salt. Despite starting with twice the amount of vegetables as in previous batches, the vegetable flavor was weaker. It turns out that water was not the only thing the vegetables lost in the oven; a lot of their volatile flavor compounds had evaporated, too. But this test was not a waste. It got us thinking about concentrated sources of flavor, which in turn led us to consider an option we've been quite snooty about in the past: those dried minced onions found in bottles in the spice aisle. Dried minced onions aren't simply dehydrated; they're freeze-dried. (Frozen food is placed in a vacuum-sealed chamber. In this vacuum, the ice transitions into vapor and is pulled out of the food. While the heat of a conventional oven pulls out flavor compounds along with the water, freeze-drying leaves many more of those compounds in place.) A little experimentation led us to the sweet spot: 5 ounces of leeks augmented with 3 tablespoons of dried minced onions.

AND UMAMI We wanted to add a little umami flavor to the mix. Canned and fresh tomatoes took the base back to a slurry, so next we tried tomato paste, which contributed an appealing savoriness. Shiitake mushrooms were too earthy, and miso paste was too subtle in small amounts and too identifiable in larger. Kombu, a dried seaweed, worked well, but we settled on a less exotic option: soy sauce. Three tablespoons gave the broth the muscle it had lacked. To compensate for the added sodium, we cut the salt.

NO NEED TO THAW Our recipe calls for 2 tablespoons of kosher salt (we use Diamond Crystal). That might seem like a lot, but once the base is diluted, it contains just 399 milligrams of sodium per 1-cup serving; commercial broth ranges from 240 to 1,050 milligrams per cup. Furthermore, because salt depresses water's freezing point, the concentrate will never freeze solid. This means that you can keep it in the freezer for months and scoop out exactly the amount you need without ever having to defrost it.

VEGETABLE BROTH BASE

MAKES ABOUT 1¾ CUPS BASE;
ENOUGH FOR 7 QUARTS BROTH

For the best balance of flavors, measure the prepped vegetables by weight. Kosher salt aids in grinding the vegetables. The broth base contains enough salt to keep it from freezing solid, making it easy to remove 1 tablespoon at a time. To make 1 cup of broth, stir 1 tablespoon of fresh or frozen broth base into 1 cup of boiling water. If particle-free broth is desired, let the broth steep for 5 minutes and then strain it through a fine-mesh strainer.

2	leeks, white and light green parts only, chopped and washed thoroughly (2½ cups or 5 ounces)
2	carrots, peeled and cut into ½-inch pieces (⅔ cup or 3 ounces)
½	small celery root, peeled and cut into ½-inch pieces (¾ cup or 3 ounces)
½	cup (½ ounce) parsley leaves and thin stems
3	tablespoons dried minced onions
2	tablespoons kosher salt
1½	tablespoons tomato paste
3	tablespoons soy sauce

Process leeks, carrots, celery root, parsley, minced onions, and salt in food processor, scraping down sides of bowl frequently, until paste is as fine as possible, 3 to 4 minutes. Add tomato paste and process for 1 minute, scraping down sides of bowl every 20 seconds. Add soy sauce and continue to process 1 minute longer. Transfer mixture to airtight container and tap firmly on counter to remove air bubbles. Press small piece of parchment paper flush against surface of mixture and cover. Freeze for up to 6 months.

CHAPTER 46

Red Wine

Red wine can add depth, complexity, and a welcome acidity to everything from beef stew to braised pork chops—as long as you treat it right.

HOW THE SCIENCE WORKS

Wine has been made for thousands of years, the first evidence of which was resin found in an Iranian pot dating around 6000 BCE. A greater understanding of the science of wine began with chemist Louis Pasteur, who analyzed the process of making wine, including the important role of oxygen, in the 1860s. "In my view," he wrote in *Études sur le vin*, "it is oxygen which makes wine."

Red wine can be produced from different varieties of grapes, but the most common by far is *Vitis vinifera*. Many factors affect the flavor of wine. Some come into play before the grapes are harvested, including climate, soil, and geomorphology (nearby landscape features like mountains or bodies of water). Other factors arise during processing: the method and length of fermentation, the vessel used, and whether the grape skins are included (red wines) or not (whites). And what about when it comes to cooking? Cooking with red wine can add depth, complexity, and a welcome acidity to everything from beef stew to braised pork chops.

First, the most basic question: When you have thousands of wines to choose from, what's the best type to use at the stove? To find out, we tested more than 30 bottles—from $5 jug wines to a $30 Bordeaux—using each to make a hearty tomato sauce, a quick-cooking pan sauce, and a slow-simmered beef stew, and divined a few guidelines.

Most important: Save the expensive wine for drinking. Wines that cost $10 are usually fine for cooking. Second, stick with blends like Côtes du Rhône or generically labeled "table" wines that use a combination of grapes to yield a balanced, fruity finish. If you prefer single grape varietals, choose medium-bodied wines, such as Pinot Noir and Merlot. Steer clear of oaky wines, like those made with Cabernet

> *"In my view," wrote Louis Pasteur, "it is oxygen which makes wine."*

Sauvignon, which turn bitter when cooked. Finally, whatever you do, avoid at all costs the generic "cooking wines" sold in supermarkets. These low-alcohol concoctions have little flavor, a high-pitched acidity, and enormous amounts of salt, all of which combine to produce inedible dishes.

When it comes to the act of cooking with wine, there are two things to keep in mind. First: There is a popular misconception that all of the alcohol in wine cooks off when heated. The truth is more complicated. When wine is mixed with broth or another water-based ingredient, as for a pan sauce or braising liquid, the two form a solution called an azeotrope, a mixture of two or more liquids that is not capable of being separated by simple distillation. This means that even though pure alcohol boils at a lower temperature than water, the vapor coming off of an ethanol-water mixture will always contain both ethanol and water, and is why we often reduce the wine in a pan sauce recipe alone before adding broth, like we do in our recipe for Red Wine Pan Sauce (page 377).

The second issue we face when cooking with wine is how to maintain wine's complex flavor, especially during long cooking times. Many of the fragrant aroma compounds in red wines are lost during cooking by evaporation. This means that the flavors of wine can be significantly muted in the act of cooking. In long-cooking dishes like our Tuscan-Style Beef Stew (page 376) and Modern Beef Burgundy (page 379), we often solve this by adding the wine in stages (see Test Kitchen Experiment, page 374). We use red wine in classic ways, long-cooking our Red Wine–Braised Pork Chops (page 378), and deglazing the pan in our Ragu alla Bolognese (page 380). Don't feel like cooking? Try The Best Sangria (page 381).

TEST KITCHEN EXPERIMENT

When we drink red wine we pay close attention to a huge array of characteristics including alcohol, acidity, tannins, sweetness, bitterness, and, of course, flavor. When adding red wine to a dish, cooks would be wise to consider these traits as well. For instance, highly tannic wines can turn unpleasantly bitter if concentrated in a reduction. But what about the aroma and flavor of the wine itself? Does that stay the same, or does it change when wine is cooked? To find out, we set up an experiment.

EXPERIMENT

We made two batches of a basic beef stew using a full 750-ml bottle of Chianti in each. For the first stew we added the entire contents of the bottle at the beginning of the recipe so that it cooked for a full 2½ hours. For the second stew we added the wine in three stages: 2 cups at the outset, 1 cup 15 minutes before finishing cooking, and the remaining ¼ cup at the very end.

RESULTS

Even though both batches contained the same amount of wine, tasters found the flavor of the stew where we added all of the wine at the beginning to be flat and lackluster, while the batch where wine was added in stages tasted deep and complex.

TAKEAWAY

The flavor compounds in wine can be classified by their behavior during cooking. Stable compounds don't change, but volatile compounds evaporate and unstable compounds break down. Over time, the result is a loss of flavor. In the batch where we added all of the wine at the start, the flavors remaining at the end of cooking were largely those of the stable compounds. By adding some of the wine 15 minutes before finishing cooking, and the remainder of wine at the end, we preserved more of the volatile and unstable compounds, capturing the most fleeting, bright, fresh flavors in the final dish. We use this to great effect in our recipe for Tuscan-Style Beef Stew (see page 376).

LAYERING THE FLAVOR OF WINE

We compared batches of stew in which we added all of the wine at the beginning, versus adding the same amount of wine in three stages. The results? The stew where we added all of the wine in the beginning tasted flat. The stew where wine was added in stages tasted complex. Why? During long cooking, the volatile compounds in wine evaporate, and the unstable compounds break down, resulting in an ultimate loss of flavor.

JOURNEY: RED WINE

All red wines begin, simply, with grapes. But the journey those grapes take is anything but simple. A long chain of actions and reactions transforms them into complex wines.

1 GROW GRAPES

Many factors influence the growing of grapes, from the varietal chosen to the climate conditions. The soil quality, water quantity, vineyard elevation, and orientation likewise influence the growth and ultimate quality of grapes.

2 HARVEST GRAPES

The process of producing wine starts with harvesting the grapes in the cool temperatures of the morning hours late in summer or early fall when the grapes have reached their peak of ripeness, and sugar content is high.

3 MACERATE GRAPES

For the production of red wine, the grapes are destemmed and crushed, and the juice, called "must," is allowed to remain in contact with the skins and seeds. At this stage, nonvolatile compounds called phenols are extracted from the skins and seeds, giving the must its red color and some of its astringent, tannic taste, in addition to the sweet and sour taste of sugars and acids in the juice.

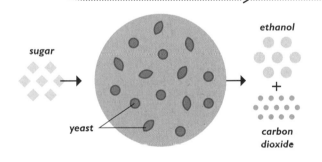

sugar

yeast

ethanol

+

carbon dioxide

4 FERMENTATION

Once the grapes are harvested and crushed, the must is fermented. This means the sugars (glucose and fructose) are converted to ethanol and carbon dioxide by different strains of yeast, which grow naturally on grape skins or are frequently added to enhance flavor development. The yeast produces many of the aromatic esters, such as isoamyl acetate, that create the true aroma of red wines. A mixture of compounds from the skins of grapes, called terpenes, give red wines their black currant flavor. Many different fruity, floral-smelling esters, alcohols, aldehydes, and ketones are formed by yeast during the fermentation step.

6 AGING

The first step toward aging new wine is called racking, in which the solid particles are allowed to settle, and the now-clearer liquid is removed. During aging, often in oak casks that contribute the flavor of vanilla, the wine is carefully exposed to very limited amounts of air, called micro-oxidation, creating the final aromatic flavor of red wine. Next, the wine is moved to glass bottles, which slows oxidation and allows further flavor to develop. During the aging step sulfur-containing amino acids such as cysteine and methionine are converted to very potent earthy, spicy-smelling sulfur-containing compounds.

5 MALOLACTIC FERMENTATION

After fermentation, the skins and seeds are removed. And most red wines are also subjected to a second fermentation by lactic acid bacteria in a step known as malolactic fermentation. During this step the bacteria convert the malic acid in grapes to lactic acid, which helps to mellow the flavor of the wine. This step also produces aromatic aldehydes and ketones, such as diacetyl, responsible for the characteristic aroma of butter.

Tuscan-Style Beef Stew

✔ WHY THIS RECIPE WORKS

Tuscan beef stew (peposo), a stew made by the tile makers of Florence's famous Santa Maria del Fiore Cathedral, or Duomo, is a simple stew of beef braised in wine, with loads of peppercorns and a head of garlic cloves. We wanted to create a version that hewed to its roots, but that also boasted balance and depth. To achieve that, we made use of additional ingredients beyond the basics—and some modern techniques.

GO BONELESS The tile makers would have likely used shin meat for this dish, which makes an excellent choice for stewing: As part of a very active set of muscles, it's got plenty of tough collagen-containing connective tissue, which breaks down into gelatin during a long braise. This gelatin thickens the cooking liquid, giving it a silky, unctuous texture, and lubricates the fibers of the meat, keeping them moist (long-braised meat that lacks gelatin is typically dry as a bone). However, shin isn't always readily available, so we used boneless short ribs, plus salt and powdered gelatin. Short ribs have less collagen than shin meat, but they are marbled with fat, which serves to keep the meat moist in a similar way. Salting them briefly helped them further retain moisture after long cooking, and adding powdered gelatin gave the sauce a silky texture in lieu of the collagen.

ADD MEATY FLAVOR To shore up the stew's underlying flavor, we seared half of the short ribs to give the sauce a bit more meaty complexity. A tablespoon of tomato paste lent depth without calling attention to itself. Similarly, we added a teaspoon of anchovy paste, a common test kitchen practice that boosts meatiness without adding any noticeable fishiness. For a little sweetness to help balance the wine's tartness, we added a few shallots and carrots, leaving both in large pieces so that they'd be easy to discard before finishing the sauce. Finally, bay leaves and fresh rosemary brought just the right herbal notes.

CHEAP WINE IS FINE Early recipes for peposo relied on inexpensive Chianti, while modern versions call for a mid-priced bottle (whether Chianti or a similar Tuscan wine such as Montepulciano or Brunello). We made batches using cheap ($5), mid-priced ($12), and pricey ($20) Chianti, along with other varieties we often use in the kitchen: Cabernet Sauvignon, Pinot Noir, and Côtes du Rhône. We were surprised that the stew made with the cheapest Chianti went over well with most tasters. While the mid-priced wine was agreeable to everyone, there was

no advantage to cooking with the expensive bottle. Highly oaked, tannic wines like Cabernet became harsh when cooked, but cheap bottles of fruitier Pinot and Côtes du Rhône made good stand-ins for the Chianti. (For more on the flavor of wine in this stew, see Test Kitchen Experiment, page 374.)

TUSCAN-STYLE BEEF STEW
SERVES 6 TO 8

We prefer boneless short ribs in this recipe because they require very little trimming. If you cannot find them, substitute a 5-pound chuck roast. Trim the roast of large pieces of fat and sinew, and cut it into 2-inch pieces. If Chianti is unavailable, a medium-bodied wine such as Côtes du Rhône or Pinot Noir makes a nice substitute. Serve with polenta or crusty bread.

- 4 pounds boneless beef short ribs, trimmed and cut into 2-inch pieces
  Salt
- 1 tablespoon vegetable oil
- 1 (750-ml) bottle Chianti
- 1 cup water
- 4 shallots, peeled and halved lengthwise
- 2 carrots, peeled and halved lengthwise
- 1 garlic head, cloves separated, unpeeled, and crushed
- 4 sprigs fresh rosemary
- 2 bay leaves
- 1 tablespoon cracked black peppercorns, plus extra for serving
- 1 tablespoon unflavored gelatin
- 1 tablespoon tomato paste
- 1 teaspoon anchovy paste
- 2 teaspoons ground black pepper
- 2 teaspoons cornstarch

1. Toss beef and 1½ teaspoons salt together in bowl and let stand at room temperature for 30 minutes. Adjust oven rack to lower-middle position and heat oven to 300 degrees.

2. Heat oil in large Dutch oven over medium-high heat until just smoking. Add half of beef in single layer and cook until well browned on all sides, about 8 minutes total, reducing heat if fond begins to burn. Stir in 2 cups wine, water, shallots, carrots, garlic, rosemary sprigs, bay leaves, cracked peppercorns, gelatin, tomato paste, anchovy paste, and remaining beef. Bring to simmer and cover tightly with sheet of heavy-duty aluminum foil, then lid. Transfer to oven and cook until beef is tender, 2 to 2¼ hours, stirring halfway through cooking time.

3. Using slotted spoon, transfer beef to bowl; cover tightly with foil and set aside. Strain sauce through fine-mesh strainer into fat separator. Wipe out pot with paper towels. Let liquid settle for 5 minutes, then return defatted liquid to pot.

4. Add 1 cup wine and ground black pepper and bring mixture to boil over medium-high heat. Simmer briskly, stirring occasionally, until sauce is thickened to consistency of heavy cream, 12 to 15 minutes.

5. Combine remaining wine and cornstarch in small bowl. Reduce heat to medium-low, return beef to pot, and stir in cornstarch-wine mixture. Cover and simmer until just heated through, 5 to 8 minutes. Season with salt to taste. Serve, passing extra cracked peppercorns separately. (Stew can be made up to 3 days in advance.)

PRACTICAL SCIENCE CORKS VS. SCREW CAPS

Screw caps prevent the presence of musty-smelling cork taint—and allow for proper aging.

Around 5 percent of natural wine corks contain traces of the compound responsible for "cork taint"—TCA, or 2,4,6-trichloroanisole—which imparts a musty, unpleasant taste in both red and white wines. As a result, screw caps have become a common replacement for corks. Yes, screw caps don't produce cork taint, but do they produce good wine?

Red wines are very susceptible to the effects of oxygen entering the bottle during the aging period. A trace of oxygen in the wine is essential for the full development of flavor, but too much oxygen produces unpleasant aromas. So how do screw caps and corks compare when it comes to high-quality red wines? Studies have shown that screw caps and corks allow about the same amount of oxygen to enter the bottle over time. Still, there are wine connoisseurs who believe that only corks should be used to enclose fine red wines destined for aging. Is this wine snobbery or is it based on fact?

In 2003 a test was conducted in France that involved 40 identical fine wines, with vintages dating back as far as 1980. All sets of wines were sealed with either natural corks or screw caps. Each set of identical wines was blind-tasted by 50 expert wine tasters, who were asked to identify which wine they preferred in each set. Surprisingly, a cork-sealed wine was preferred only once, while wines sealed with a screw cap were preferred 21 times, and the remainder were tied. Perhaps it is time to rethink the use of taint-free, easy-to-open-and-reseal screw caps as the best way to seal even the best wines.

Pan-Seared Steaks with Red Wine Pan Sauce

✔ WHY THIS RECIPE WORKS

A red wine pan sauce is a quick and easy way to make a normal seared steak or chop something special. One key is to incorporate the cooking juices and browned bits (called fond) left in the pan after searing; this will give the sauce a deep savory flavor.

REDUCE THE WINE SEPARATELY We reduced the wine separately from the broth when making this pan sauce. This is because, in experiments, we found that wine and broth reduced together had as much as eight times more alcohol than wine reduced on its own first. Less booziness allows more wine flavors to come to the fore: While the alcohol evaporates, the wine's nonvolatile flavor compounds concentrate, making it taste richer and more complex.

CHOOSE THE RIGHT WINE Wine choice is important, too: A medium-bodied fruity wine made from a blend of grapes, such as Côtes du Rhône, offers the most well-rounded flavor in the sauce.

PAN-SEARED STEAKS WITH RED WINE PAN SAUCE
SERVES 4

Serve the steaks with Red Wine Pan Sauce (recipe follows). Make the sauce while the meat rests.

1 tablespoon vegetable oil
4 (8- to 10-ounce) boneless strip steaks or rib-eye steaks, 1 to 1¼ inches thick
   Salt and pepper
1 recipe Red Wine Pan Sauce (page 378)

1. Heat oil in 12-inch skillet over medium-high heat until just smoking. Meanwhile, pat steaks dry with paper towels and season both sides with salt and pepper.

2. Lay steaks in pan, leaving ¼ inch between them. Cook, without moving steaks, until well browned, about 4 minutes. Using tongs, flip steaks and continue to cook until meat registers 115 to 120 degrees (for rare) or 120 to 125 degrees (for medium-rare), 3 to 7 minutes. Transfer steaks to serving platter and tent loosely with aluminum foil to rest or while preparing pan sauce, then serve.

RED WINE PAN SAUCE
MAKES ½ CUP

A medium-bodied fruity wine made from a blend of grapes, such as a Côtes du Rhône, offers the most well-rounded flavor.

1	large shallot, minced
½	cup red wine
¾	cup chicken broth
2	teaspoons packed brown sugar
3	tablespoons unsalted butter, cut into 3 pieces and chilled
1	teaspoon minced fresh rosemary
¼	teaspoon balsamic vinegar
	Salt and pepper

Pour off all but 2 teaspoons fat from pan used to cook meat. Add shallot to pan and cook over medium-high heat, stirring frequently, until softened, 1 to 2 minutes. Add wine and simmer rapidly, scraping up any browned bits, until liquid is reduced to glaze, about 30 seconds. Stir in broth and sugar and simmer until reduced to ⅓ cup, 4 to 6 minutes. Stir in any accumulated meat juices. Off heat, whisk in butter, 1 piece at a time, until melted and sauce is thickened and glossy. Stir in rosemary and vinegar. Season with salt and pepper to taste.

PRACTICAL SCIENCE AERATING WINE IN A FLASH

What if you want to pour a glass of wine and you haven't planned ahead? Use this trick to quickly aerate your bottle.

Red wines—especially young, undeveloped ones—often benefit from a breathing period after opening so that oxygen can react with tannins and sulfur compounds, softening harsh flavors. But merely uncorking a bottle and letting it sit for a bit is insufficient. In order to truly aerate wine, you must expose as much of its surface area as possible to oxygen. Typically, this so-called hard decanting is accomplished by pouring the wine into a wide, shallow vessel and letting it rest for up to several hours.

But what if you want to pour a glass and you didn't plan ahead? While specialized wine-aerating gadgets can speed things along (our favorite, the Nuance Wine Finer, costs $30), we'd also heard that immediate decanting can be done with just a blender or two pitchers. To investigate, we acquired several recent-vintage bottles of Cabernet and Sangiovese (both known for their punchy, highly tannic flavors) and held a blind taste test of samples poured straight from the bottle and samples poured from one pitcher to another 15 times or whizzed on high speed for 30 seconds (this seemingly harsh method is employed in some restaurants). The results were remarkable: The undecanted wines were predictably astringent and flat; the wines that had been decanted by pouring were bright and balanced, their tannins less prominent, with more complex aromas coming to the fore. The blender-decanted wines tasted more developed than the undecanted ones but not nearly as developed as the wines that were repeatedly poured. We'll be turning to this method the next time we need to let wine breathe in a hurry.

Red Wine–Braised Pork Chops

✓ WHY THIS RECIPE WORKS

When braising pork chops, it's important to avoid lean loin chops that have a tendency to dry out when even slightly overcooked. Instead, begin with a blade chop, which, like other braising cuts, has a larger amount of fat and connective tissue. Start with a solid pour of red wine and ruby port in the braising liquid, to temper the meatiness of the chops, and finish with a bit of red wine vinegar for some bright acidity.

TRIM THOSE CHOPS—AND SAVE THE SCRAPS The band of fatty connective tissue and shoulder meat along the outer edge of blade chops contributes body and flavor to the braise, but it also causes the chops to buckle. To cut out the structural issues without sacrificing flavor, we trim away the band, chop it up, and save the pieces for searing. When these trimmings are used for searing, they generate a substantial layer of fond—browning so impressive that we found we didn't even need to sear the chops themselves. To take full advantage of their flavor, we leave the trimmings in the pot during braising.

ELEVATE THE MEAT We balance the pork chops on the trimmings in the pot when they go in to braise. When the chops rest above the liquid line for cooking, they emerge noticeably juicier. Why? First, air conducts heat much less efficiently than liquid. Second, the secret to braising is ensuring that the temperature of the meat hovers for as long as possible in a particular sweet spot, that is, between 160 and 180 degrees. In that range, the meat's collagen converts steadily into gelatin, which holds on to the meat's juices. At lower temperatures, the meat retains moisture, but it takes a long time for collagen to convert to gelatin; too much heat, and the transformation is much faster, but you drive off a lot of the juice. The bottom line: the combination of air and liquid holds the less-submerged chops at a temperature that allows them to produce a good bit of gelatin and retain their moisture.

LET REST Resting the braised chops for 30 minutes before slicing into them gives the meat juices ample time to redistribute throughout the meat.

RED WINE–BRAISED PORK CHOPS
SERVES 4

Look for chops with a small eye and a large amount of marbling, as these are the most suited to braising. The pork scraps can be removed when straining the sauce in step 4 and served alongside the chops. (They taste great.)

	Salt and pepper
4	(10- to 12-ounce) bone-in pork blade chops, 1-inch-thick
2	teaspoons vegetable oil
2	onions, halved and thinly sliced
5	sprigs fresh thyme plus ¼ teaspoon minced
2	garlic cloves, peeled
2	bay leaves
1	(½-inch) piece ginger, peeled and crushed
⅛	teaspoon ground allspice
½	cup red wine
¼	cup ruby port
2	tablespoons plus ½ teaspoon red wine vinegar
1	cup low-sodium chicken broth
2	tablespoons unsalted butter
1	tablespoon minced fresh parsley

1. Dissolve 3 tablespoons salt in 1½ quarts cold water in large container. Submerge chops in brine, cover, and refrigerate for 1 hour.

2. Adjust oven rack to lower-middle position and heat oven to 275 degrees. Remove chops from brine and pat dry with paper towels. Trim off cartilage, meat cap, and fat opposite rib bones. Cut trimmings into 1-inch pieces. Heat oil in Dutch oven over medium-high heat until shimmering. Add trimmings and brown on all sides, 6 to 9 minutes.

3. Reduce heat to medium and add onions, thyme sprigs, garlic, bay leaves, ginger, and allspice. Cook, stirring occasionally, until onions are golden brown, 5 to 10 minutes. Stir in wine, port, and 2 tablespoons of vinegar, and cook until reduced to thin syrup, 5 to 7 minutes. Add chicken broth, spread onion and pork scraps into even layer, and bring to simmer. Arrange pork chops on top of pork scraps and onions.

4. Cover, transfer to oven, and cook until meat is tender, 1¼ to 1½ hours. Remove from oven and let chops rest in pot, covered, 30 minutes. Transfer chops to serving platter and tent with aluminum foil. Pour braising liquid through fine-mesh strainer set over large bowl; discard solids. Transfer braising liquid to fat separator and let stand 5 minutes.

5. Wipe out now-empty pot with wad of paper towels. Return defatted braising liquid to pot and cook over medium-high heat until reduced to 1 cup, 3 to 7 minutes. Off heat, whisk in butter, ¼ teaspoon minced thyme, and remaining ½ teaspoon vinegar. Season with salt and pepper to taste. Pour sauce over chops, sprinkle with parsley, and serve.

Modern Beef Burgundy

✔ WHY THIS RECIPE WORKS
We wanted our boeuf bourguignon recipe to have tender braised beef napped with a silky, rich sauce with bold red wine flavor but without all the work that the classic recipe requires.

BROWN AND BRAISE Much of the time-consuming hands-on work in traditional beef burgundy recipes comes from the time spent searing the salt pork and beef over the stove before the stew goes into the oven. We wanted to figure out a way to skip this initial 40 minutes of work. From previous recipes, we knew that we could brown and braise meat at the same time by not submerging the meat fully in the braising liquid. When we tried this trick, it worked like a charm. To further reduce hands-on time, we cranked the heat of the oven to brown the salt pork before adding the beef.

MAKE THE MOST OF YOUR OVEN Rather than taking out two more pans and spending an hour babysitting the mushrooms and onions, we spread them out on a baking sheet with some butter and let the even heat of the oven do the work. A little bit of sugar aided caramelization.

ADD THE WINE IN BATCHES To punch up the flavor of the wine, we opted to add part of the bottle at the beginning, saving some to add to the final reduction of the sauce at the end. This brightened the wine's flavor without having to open a second bottle.

MODERN BEEF BURGUNDY
SERVES 6 TO 8

If the pearl onions have a papery outer coating, remove it by rinsing them in warm water and squeezing the onions between your fingertips. Two minced anchovy fillets can be used in place of the anchovy paste. To save time, salt the meat and let it stand while you prep the remaining ingredients.

1 (4-pound) boneless beef chuck-eye roast, trimmed and cut into 1½- to 2-inch pieces, scraps reserved
   Salt and pepper

6 ounces salt pork, cut into ¼-inch pieces

3 tablespoons unsalted butter

1 pound cremini mushrooms, trimmed, halved if medium or quartered if large

1½ cups frozen pearl onions, thawed

1 tablespoon sugar

⅓ cup all-purpose flour

4 cups beef broth

1 (750-ml) bottle red Burgundy or Pinot Noir

5 teaspoons unflavored gelatin

1 tablespoon tomato paste

1 teaspoon anchovy paste

2 onions, chopped coarse

2 carrots, peeled and cut into 2-inch lengths

1 garlic head, cloves separated, unpeeled, and smashed

½ ounce dried porcini mushrooms, rinsed

10 sprigs fresh parsley, plus 3 tablespoons minced

6 sprigs fresh thyme

2 bay leaves

½ teaspoon black peppercorns

1. Toss beef and 1½ teaspoons salt together in bowl and let stand at room temperature for 30 minutes.

2. Adjust oven racks to lower-middle and lowest positions and heat oven to 500 degrees. Place salt pork, beef scraps, and 2 tablespoons butter in large roasting pan. Roast on upper rack until well browned and fat has rendered, 15 to 20 minutes.

3. While salt pork and beef scraps roast, toss cremini mushrooms, pearl onions, remaining 1 tablespoon butter, and sugar together on rimmed baking sheet. Roast on lower rack, stirring occasionally, until moisture released by mushrooms evaporates and vegetables are lightly glazed, 15 to 20 minutes. Transfer vegetables to large bowl, cover, and refrigerate.

4. Remove roasting pan from oven and reduce temperature to 325 degrees. Sprinkle flour over rendered fat and whisk until no dry flour remains. Whisk in broth, 2 cups wine, gelatin, tomato paste, and anchovy paste until combined. Add onions, carrots, garlic, porcini mushrooms, parsley sprigs, thyme sprigs, bay leaves, and peppercorns to pan. Arrange beef in single layer on top of vegetables. Add water as needed to come three-quarters up side of beef (beef should not be submerged). Return roasting pan to oven and cook until meat is tender, 3 to 3½ hours, stirring after 1½ hours and adding water to keep meat at least half-submerged.

5. Using slotted spoon, transfer beef to bowl with cremini mushrooms and pearl onions; cover and set aside. Strain braising liquid through fine-mesh strainer set over large bowl, pressing on solids to extract as much liquid as possible; discard solids. Stir in remaining wine and let cooking liquid settle, 10 minutes. Using wide, shallow spoon, skim fat from surface and discard.

6. Transfer liquid to Dutch oven and bring mixture to boil over medium-high heat. Simmer briskly, stirring occasionally, until sauce is thickened to consistency of heavy cream, 15 to 20 minutes. Reduce heat to medium-low, stir in beef and mushroom-onion mixture, cover, and cook until just heated through, 5 to 8 minutes. Season with salt and pepper to taste. Stir in minced parsley and serve. (Stew can be made up to 3 days in advance.)

Ragu alla Bolognese

✓ WHY THIS RECIPE WORKS

There are many different ways to interpret what "real" Bolognese sauce is. But no matter what the ingredients are, the sauce should be hearty and rich but not cloying, with a velvety texture that lightly clings to the noodles. For our version, the goal was for the richest, most savory interpretation of this famous slow-cooked meat sauce with a tinge of deep and earthy red wine.

USE (YES) SIX MEATS We were inspired for our Bolognese by that of Dante de Magistris, an Italian chef in Boston. He uses six different types of meat for this sauce—ground beef, pork, and veal; pancetta; mortadella (a bologna-like Italian deli meat); and chicken livers—and we followed suit. The beef, pork, and veal are traditional, and the pancetta, mortadella, and chicken livers bolster the sauce's complex, savory flavor. We added the meat to the pot before the *soffritto* (chopped carrot, celery, and onion) in order to get a better sear—and therefore flavor.

DEGLAZE WITH WINE We liked the unobtrusive texture of tomato paste in the sauce. After adding the paste to the mixture we let the fond take on a deep rust tone for optimal flavor. Then, to make sure those caramelized brown bits that are stuck to the bottom of the pot are incorporated into a flavorful sauce, we deglazed the hot pan with a likewise flavorful liquid—in this case, red wine—and scraped up the browned bits with a wooden spoon.

ADD GELATIN Chef Magistris's recipe calls for homemade *brodo* (or broth). Besides boosting the meaty flavor of the ragu, the bones used to make the broth give up lots of gelatin as they simmer, which renders the liquid glossy and viscous. We were not about to make homemade broth for this sauce, but we could add powdered gelatin. It's a trick we've used to lend suppleness to all-beef meatloaf and viscosity to beef stew—the two qualities we were looking for in our ragu. After testing a range of amounts, we found that 8 teaspoons did the trick.

LEAVE OUT THE DAIRY While many traditional recipes do contain dairy, when we tried adding 1 cup of milk to a batch, we found that the milk muted the meaty flavor of the sauce, and tasters preferred a nondairy version.

RAGU ALLA BOLOGNESE
MAKES 6 CUPS; ENOUGH FOR 2 POUNDS OF PASTA

Eight teaspoons of gelatin is equivalent to 1 ounce. If you can't find ground veal, use an additional 12 ounces of ground beef.

1	cup chicken broth
1	cup beef broth
8	teaspoons unflavored gelatin
1	onion, chopped coarse
1	large carrot, peeled and chopped coarse
1	celery rib, chopped coarse
4	ounces mortadella, chopped
4	ounces pancetta, chopped
6	ounces chicken livers, trimmed
3	tablespoons extra-virgin olive oil
12	ounces 85 percent lean ground beef
12	ounces ground pork
12	ounces ground veal
3	tablespoons minced fresh sage
1	(6-ounce) can tomato paste
2	cups dry red wine
	Salt and pepper
1	pound pappardelle or tagliatelle
	Grated Parmesan cheese

1. Combine chicken broth and beef broth in bowl; sprinkle gelatin over top and set aside. Pulse onion, carrot, and celery in food processor until finely chopped, about 10 pulses, scraping down bowl as needed; transfer to separate bowl. Pulse mortadella and pancetta in now-empty food processor until finely chopped, about 25 pulses, scraping down bowl as needed; transfer to second bowl. Process chicken livers in now-empty food processor until pureed, about 5 seconds; transfer to third bowl.

2. Heat oil in Dutch oven over medium-high heat until shimmering. Add beef, pork, and veal; cook, breaking up pieces with wooden spoon, until all liquid has evaporated and meat begins to sizzle, 10 to 15 minutes. Add pancetta mixture and sage; cook, stirring frequently, until pancetta is translucent, 5 to 7 minutes, adjusting heat as needed to keep fond from burning. Add chopped vegetables and cook, stirring frequently, until softened, 5 to 7 minutes. Add tomato paste and cook, stirring constantly, until rust-colored and fragrant, about 3 minutes.

3. Stir in wine, scraping up any browned bits. Simmer until sauce has thickened, about 5 minutes. Stir in broth mixture and return to simmer. Reduce heat to low and cook at bare simmer until thickened (wooden spoon should leave trail when dragged through sauce), about 1½ hours.

4. Stir in pureed chicken livers, bring to boil, and remove from heat. Season with salt and pepper to taste; cover and keep warm.

5. Bring 4 quarts water to boil in large pot. Add pasta and 1 tablespoon salt and cook, stirring often, until al dente. Reserve ¾ cup cooking water, then drain pasta and return it to pot. Add half of sauce and cooking water to pasta and toss to combine. Transfer to serving bowl and serve, passing Parmesan separately. (Leftover sauce may be refrigerated for up to 3 days or frozen for up to 1 month.)

The Best Sangria

✓ WHY THIS RECIPE WORKS

For a robust, sweet-tart sangria recipe, we experimented with untold varieties of both wine and fruit before concluding that simpler is better. We preferred a cheap wine and the straightforward tang of citrus in the form of oranges and lemons.

CHOOSE CHEAP WINE Across the board, bartenders, wine merchants, and Spanish restaurateurs all advised us to keep the wine choice cheap for sangria. The additional sugar and fruit throws off the balance of the wine, anyhow, so why spend a lot for something carefully crafted? After trying a number of wine varietals—from Beaujolais-Villages (too fruity and light) to Rioja (a bit flat and dull)—we settled on medium-bodied Merlot. The orange liqueur that is part of all sangria recipes gives added sweetness and fruitiness. After trying a range of expensive brands, we settled on triple sec for its bold, sweet flavor.

ADD FRUIT After tinkering with various combinations of fruit, we settled on two oranges and one lemon. Limes, we found, were too bitter. Mashing the fruit gently with sugar in the pitcher before adding liquids releases some juice from the fruit and oils from the zest—similar to what bartenders will do for a single cocktail (for example, mint and sugar for a mint julep) but on a larger scale.

LET IT REST Preparing sangria ahead of time and letting it rest in the refrigerator before serving is essential. After tasting an 8-hour-old sangria, a freshly made batch seemed harsh and edgy. We tasted batches that had rested 1 hour, 2 hours, and all the way up to 12 hours. We found that every batch up to 8 hours revealed a better blended, more mellow flavor, but did not find significant improvement over 8 hours. (Rest assured, though, if you can't stand the anticipation, 2 hours of refrigeration serves the purpose adequately.)

THE BEST SANGRIA
SERVES 4

The longer sangria sits before drinking, the more smooth and mellow it will taste. A full day is best, but if that's impossible, give it an absolute minimum of 2 hours to sit. Use large, heavy, juicy oranges and lemons for the best flavor. If you can't find superfine sugar, process an equal amount of granulated sugar in a food processor for 30 seconds. Doubling or tripling the recipe is fine, but you'll need a large punch bowl in place of the pitcher. An inexpensive Merlot is the best choice for this recipe.

2	oranges (1 sliced, 1 juiced to yield ½ cup)
1	lemon, sliced
¼	cup superfine sugar
1	(750-ml) bottle fruity red wine, chilled
¼	cup triple sec
6–8	ice cubes

1. Add sliced orange, lemon, and sugar to large pitcher. Mash fruit gently with wooden spoon until fruit releases some juice, but is not totally crushed, and sugar dissolves, about 1 minute. Stir in orange juice, wine, and triple sec; refrigerate for at least 2 hours or up to 8 hours.

2. Before serving, add 6 to 8 ice cubes and stir briskly to distribute settled fruit and pulp; serve immediately.

PRACTICAL SCIENCE FIGHTING CORK TAINT

Around 5 percent of natural, corked wines have "taint."

"Cork taint," or the musty unpleasant aromas found in both red and white wines due to a trace compound found on a small percentage of natural corks, has been recognized by the wine industry for more than 40 years. Cork taint is caused by compounds known as TCA (2,4,6-trichloroanisole) and TBA (2,4,6-tribromoanisole). These compounds, but predominantly TCA, create an aroma often described as smelling like wet cardboard—not exactly what you're looking for in a glass of wine! The presence of TCA also significantly reduces the fruity aromas of wines.

At one time the origin of TCA was thought to be the chlorinated bleach solutions used to wash the corks. But even untreated corks have been shown to exhibit cork taint, and today it's believed that fungi living in the small pores within cork (called lenticels) produce the compounds responsible.

The problem is made worse because the contaminating compounds can be detected at extremely low levels, as low as a few parts per trillion (ppt). Consider that one part per trillion is the same as one second in 32,000 years. But sensitivity to these compounds varies with the individual. Tests done with trained experts show that TCA can be recognized in wines at levels of 2.5 to 20 ppt.

A number of studies have been conducted to determine the percentages of corks and wines contaminated with cork taint. The best answer to date is that about 5 percent of all wines closed with natural corks show a recognizable level of cork taint. No wonder much of the wine industry has been moving to screw-on tops.

It never occurred to us that there might be a way to salvage the wine, but with a little digging, we actually found a quirky recommendation: Submerge a ball of plastic wrap in the wine and let it sit for a while. As odd as it sounds, the theory behind the suggestion makes sense: The polyethylene material attracts the TCA, effectively removing it from the wine.

With nothing to lose, we tracked down four corked bottles, poured half of each into a jar with a loose wad of plastic wrap, sealed the lids, and soaked them for 10 minutes, shaking each sample occasionally. When we sipped the treated wines, we found that the nasty "dirty-socks" odor and bitterness from the TCA were indeed greatly reduced. But we also noticed that the plastic had absorbed many of the desirable aromatic compounds, leaving the wines tasting flat and muted—and still unfit for drinking or cooking. Your best bet: Return the tainted wine for a refund.

CHAPTER 47

Honey

Because honey contains many small reducing sugars, we use it differently than other sweeteners.

HOW THE SCIENCE WORKS

Although honey is produced by a number of insects, such as the bumblebee and honey wasp, practically all of the honey consumed in the world today comes from the honeybee *Apis mellifera*, which originated in India.

Today, America has a sky-high demand for honey: According to the National Honey Board, we eat more than 400 million pounds of the stuff every year. To keep up with the demand, manufacturers source honey from all over the country and globe. Today, the average jar of honey on supermarket shelves is actually a mix of honeys from many hives that's been carefully blended and processed to engineer a preferred flavor and color.

Honeybees are social insects that live together in well-organized family groups. Each hive usually contains one queen, several hundred male drones, and tens of thousands of adult female worker bees. A honeybee gathers nectar by inserting its proboscis into the nectary of a flower, the contents of which it then deposits in its honey sac. The sac, as well as the bee's salivary glands, secrete enzymes that begin the process of converting nectar into honey even before the bee reaches the hive. Once in the hive, the contents are transferred to worker bees and then the honeycomb, where the process of converting nectar to honey is completed.

The final transformation takes place in a few stages. First, water evaporates from the nectar causing it to thicken. Next, enzymes convert sucrose to glucose and fructose. (This is important. Sugar, or sucrose, is a disaccharide, which means it contains two molecules bonded together. In the case of sucrose, this is glucose and fructose. But when sucrose is heated in a solution of strong acid, or treated with certain enzymes, it breaks down into individual glucose and fructose molecules. The mixture of glucose and fructose made from sucrose is called invert sugar, and is the form of sugar found in honey. Since fructose is 1.5 times sweeter than sucrose, and glucose is 0.75 times as sweet as sucrose, invert sugar—and therefore honey—is a little sweeter than pure sucrose.) Finally, aroma substances are formed, which are largely related to the source of the nectar. When the water content of the raw honey is reduced to between 16 and 19 percent, the bees close the honeycomb cells with a wax lid to allow further ripening. During this time, additional sucrose is converted to glucose and fructose along with the formation of small amounts of as many as 21 other sugars.

Invert sugar—and therefore honey—is a little sweeter than pure sucrose.

There are many types of honey; the differences are dependent on nectar source, ripening time, and heat treatment, among other things. Honey is often pasteurized, protecting it from the growth of unwanted yeasts.

We use honey in both cooking and baking for its sweetness and flavorful browning. Honey is an important part of the rub for our Easy Grilled Boneless Pork Chops (page 386)—honey's fructose content helps the chops to brown quickly on the grill. Honey also gives a nice balanced sweetness to our Honey Fried Chicken (page 388), for which we thin out some honey in the microwave to help make a dunkable glaze. We use only honey to sweeten our Honey Lemon Squares (page 387). Finally, our Honey Cake (page 389) is loaded with honey so that we can actually taste it—and is baked at a lower oven temperature to prevent the cake from browning too much.

TEST KITCHEN EXPERIMENT

We know well that different types of sugars (think granulated versus brown sugar) can impact not only the sweetness, but also the texture of baked goods. But the functional qualities of sweeteners go well beyond baking. We designed an experiment to demonstrate the impact that honey can have on ice cream.

EXPERIMENT

We churned two custard-based ice creams, keeping everything identical except for the sweetener. For both ice creams we began with a base that included 149 grams of granulated sugar. Then, for one batch we added additional granulated sugar and for the second we added honey. (An ice cream with all honey would not freeze into a solid.) To be exact, we used a refractometer to measure the sugar concentration in the honey, which clocked in at 80 percent. To keep the mass of sugars and water in our formulas identical, we added 64 grams of granulated sugar diluted with 16 grams of water in one batch to match the 80 grams of honey, which already contains water, in the other. After churning and then hardening the ice creams overnight, we placed a scoop of each in a mesh strainer over a measuring cup and tracked how quickly the ice creams melted back into a liquid. We also asked testers to scoop the ice creams and note firmness and then taste them side by side.

RESULTS

The ice cream made with a portion of honey was softer and easier to scoop straight from the freezer than that made with only granulated sugar. Tasters commented that, beyond the obvious difference in flavor, the honey ice cream was softer and melted more quickly in the mouth. Our melting test supported what we tasted. The scoop made with all sugar dripped melted ice cream at an average rate of 1.6 milliliters per minute, while the scoop that contained honey dripped at 1.9 milliliters per minute, or about 19 percent faster than the all-sugar batch.

TAKEAWAY

Sugar in an ice cream base influences its initial freezing point. A higher amount of sugar translates into a lower freezing point, and an ice cream that is both softer right out of the freezer and quicker to melt at room temperature. But because we adjusted for honey's water content, both ice creams contained an identical weight of sugar: 212.84 grams to be exact. So why the difference in melt rate? It all has to do with the types of sugar involved. Granulated sugar is 100 percent sucrose, a disaccharide made up of one molecule each of glucose and fructose. The sugar in honey is mostly fructose and glucose. This means that in a given weight of honey, there are roughly twice as many sugar molecules as in the same amount of granulated sugar. And more molecules means more impact on the freezing point. We use another good source of glucose and fructose to make our Frozen Yogurt (see page 159) soft and scoopable.

HOW SUGAR CHANGES ICE CREAM MELTABILITY
Ice cream made with honey (high in invert sugars) melted faster.

HONEY ICE CREAM: FAST MELTER
This ice cream dripped 1.9 milliliters/minute.

GRANULATED SUGAR ICE CREAM: SLOW DRIP
This ice cream dripped 1.6 milliliters/minute.

FOCUS ON: HONEY

Honeybees are fascinating insects, capable of communicating through dance and creating delicious honey. Here, we take a closer look at all of the elements that go into honey production.

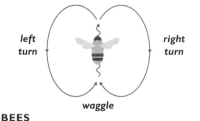

BEES

Bees communicate by secreting volatile chemical pheromones and by performing dances that communicate where nectar-bearing flowers have been located.

HONEYCOMB

Today, honey is produced in hives maintained by apiculturists (beekeepers, also known as apiarists) in backyards as well as large commercial operations. A backyard beehive can produce 30 to 100 pounds of honey per year, while a commercial hive can produce up to 200 pounds per year. In the U.S., backyard beekeeping and honey production have become a very popular hobby.

Bees generally forage within a one-mile radius of the hive.

HONEY

There are several different types of honey produced and sold for consumption. When we compared six samples of raw honey with traditional honey, we noticed that the texture of raw honey ranged widely, while the supermarket specimens were uniformly clear. The opaque appearance of raw honey is due to crystallization, with the size and shape of the crystals dependent on the balance of sugars in the honey. Raw honey is never heated, but traditional honey is heated to about 155 degrees in order to kill yeasts that might initiate fermentation, to make it easier to pass the honey through a very fine filter, and to dissolve every last crystal. Raw honey differs in flavor, a hyperlocal product that varies greatly and reflects its region of origin. Traditional honey is reliable and familiar.

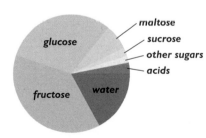

CLOSE UP ON HONEY

The typical composition of grade A honey is 17 percent water, 38 percent fructose, 31 percent glucose, 7 percent maltose, and about 2 percent sucrose. All other sugars amount to 1 to 2 percent, while total acids are present at about 3 percent. About 300 volatile compounds are present in the aroma of honey, with the chemical structure having been identified for more than 200 of these compounds.

SUGAR COMPOSITION OF HONEY

Sugar, or sucrose, is a disaccharide, which means it contains two molecules bonded together. In the case of sucrose, this is glucose and fructose. But when sucrose is heated in a solution of strong acid, or treated with an enzyme such as invertase, it breaks down into individual glucose and fructose molecules. The mixture of glucose and fructose made from sucrose is called invert sugar, and is the form of sugar found in honey. Since fructose is 1.5 times sweeter than sucrose, and glucose is 0.75 times as sweet as sucrose, invert sugar—and therefore honey—is a little sweeter than pure sucrose. Honey also contains two related enzymes from the bees called alpha- and beta-amylase, which convert starch in the nectar into smaller sugar molecules.

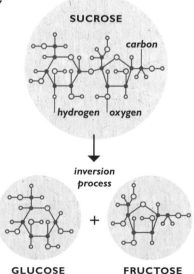

Easy Grilled Boneless Pork Chops

✔ WHY THIS RECIPE WORKS

Grab a pack of thin, boneless, center-cut pork chops from the supermarket, fire up the grill, and you're moments away from an inexpensive, simple, and satisfying supper. Or you would have been, half a century ago when American pork was still marbled and stayed juicy on the grill. Because today's pigs are bred for leanness rather than flavor, modern chops present a perennial challenge: How can you get a flavorful, browned crust without sapping the interior of its already meager juices? Most recipes for grilled pork chops tend to produce either beautifully charred slices of cardboard or juicy chops that are also pale and bland. Frustrated by these half measures, we wanted to develop a recipe that pays equal attention to juiciness and browning. At the same time, we aimed to retain the speed and ease that have always made grilled pork chops such an attractive weeknight dinner in the first place.

BRINE 'EM Luckily, we've done a lot of testing over the years to figure out how to keep meat juicy during cooking—even when exposed to high heat. Two of the most effective methods we've found are salting and brining. Both slightly alter muscle fibers so they remain tender and are better able to hold on to moisture. Salting is a dry process that first pulls moisture from the meat and then allows it to reabsorb, while brining actually increases the amount of moisture in the meat. We ran a quick side-by-side test, and the brined chops, with their added moisture, won hands down.

USE ANCHOVIES While we often talk of browning as a process of creation—one that develops flavor, color, and texture—it would be more accurate to describe it as a process of destruction. Heat breaks down large meat proteins into their amino-acid building blocks, while trace amounts of carbohydrates are split into simple sugars like fructose, glucose, and lactose. It's only after this destruction has taken place that the Maillard—or browning—reaction can begin. We always knew that cooking temperature had an impact on the speed of the reaction, but it turns out that both the amount and type of amino acids released, as well as the concentration of reducing sugars, play big roles as well. Meat browns relatively slowly because its proteins break down gradually in the presence of so much moisture and it doesn't contain very many carbohydrates to transform into reducing sugars. Could we coat the chop in something with a composition designed for speedy browning? We tried dried milk powder and flour, but neither worked too well. Then we tried anchovies. It turns out that

not only are anchovies a particularly concentrated source of muscle proteins but their protein has already been broken down through fermentation. We brined another batch of chops, patted them dry, and applied a superthin layer of anchovy paste to both sides. Back on the grill, these chops browned much faster than plain chops and emerged with a rich, meaty-tasting crust without a hint of fishiness, thanks to the flavor contributed by browning and the smoke from the grill.

AND HONEY Could we get the chops to brown even better and faster? After all, we now had plenty of amino acids but still little in the way of reducing sugars. But we had a ready source of fructose right in the pantry—honey. We mixed up the anchovy paste with some honey and a little vegetable oil and smeared the concoction over both sides of six chops. In just 4 minutes over the fire, the underside of the chops had turned a gorgeous burnished brown dotted with spots of real char. Another 4 to 6 minutes on the second side and they were ready to eat. Juicy? Check. Well browned? Check. Meaty? Check. Just as important, these chops can be prepped for the grill in about the time it takes to ready the charcoal.

EASY GRILLED BONELESS PORK CHOPS
SERVES 4 TO 6

If your pork is enhanced, do not brine it in step 1. Very finely mashed anchovy fillets (rinsed and dried before mashing) can be used instead of anchovy paste.

6	(6- to 8-ounce) boneless pork chops, ¾- to 1-inch-thick
3	tablespoons salt
1	tablespoon vegetable oil
1½	teaspoons honey
1	teaspoon anchovy paste
½	teaspoon pepper
1	recipe Onion, Olive, and Caper Relish (optional) (recipe follows)

1. Cut 2 slits about 1 inch apart through outer layer of fat and connective tissue on each chop to prevent buckling. Dissolve salt in 1½ quarts cold water in large container. Submerge chops in brine and let stand at room temperature for 30 minutes.

2. Whisk oil, honey, anchovy paste, and pepper to form smooth paste. Remove pork from brine and pat dry with

paper towels. Using spoon, spread half of oil mixture evenly over 1 side of each chop (about ¼ teaspoon per side).

3A. FOR A CHARCOAL GRILL: Open bottom vent completely. Light chimney starter filled with charcoal briquettes (6 quarts). When top coals are partially covered with ash, pour evenly over half of grill. Set cooking grate in place, cover, and open lid vent completely. Heat grill until hot, about 5 minutes.

3B. FOR A GAS GRILL: Turn all burners to high, cover, and heat grill until hot, about 15 minutes. Leave primary burner on high and turn off other burner(s).

4. Clean and oil cooking grate. Place chops, oiled side down, over hotter side of grill and cook, uncovered, until well browned on first side, 4 to 6 minutes. While chops are grilling, spread remaining oil mixture evenly over second side of chops. Flip chops and continue to cook until chops register 140 degrees, 4 to 6 minutes longer (if chops are well browned but register less than 140 degrees, move to cooler side of grill to finish cooking). Transfer chops to plate and let rest for 5 minutes. Serve with relish, if using.

ONION, OLIVE, AND CAPER RELISH
MAKES ABOUT 2 CUPS

¼	cup olive oil
2	onions, cut into ¼-inch pieces
6	garlic cloves, sliced thin
½	cup pitted kalamata olives, chopped coarse
¼	cup capers, rinsed
3	tablespoons balsamic vinegar
2	tablespoons minced fresh parsley
1	teaspoon minced fresh marjoram
1	teaspoon sugar
½	teaspoon anchovy paste
½	teaspoon pepper
¼	teaspoon salt

Heat 2 tablespoons oil in 10-inch nonstick skillet over medium heat until shimmering. Add onions and cook until softened, about 5 minutes. Stir in garlic and cook until fragrant, about 30 seconds. Transfer onion mixture to medium bowl; stir in remaining 2 tablespoons oil, olives, capers, vinegar, parsley, marjoram, sugar, anchovy paste, pepper, and salt. Serve warm or at room temperature.

Honey-Lemon Squares

✔ WHY THIS RECIPE WORKS

Lemon squares are a favorite in the American household, but they are so often ruined by soggy crusts and grainy, muddled curds. We wanted a lemon square with a mouthwateringly tart, lusciously smooth curd coupled with a sturdy, buttery crust. We chose honey to sweeten both components, both for its subtle flavor and its smooth texture that makes it perfect for liquid mixtures. Then we got to work.

PRESS IN THE CRUST For the crust, we chose a simple press-in crust. By mixing softened butter and flour to a sandy texture, we produced a crust with a texture between short and flaky. A small amount of honey provided sweetness, while a bit of water hydrated the dough just enough to make it workable.

START THE CURD ON THE STOVE For the curd, we started with traditional flour-thickened mixtures that were cooked in the oven. But these versions were consistently grainy, pale, and muted in lemon flavor. Without the aid of granulated sugar to disperse the flour in the mixture, clumps formed in the curd. Moreover, the curd's appearance was unreasonably sensitive to minute variations in baking time and temperature: If the curd was cooked 1 minute too long or the oven was running a bit too hot, the result was an unsightly cracked surface. We opted instead for the more foolproof method of starting the curd on the stovetop and then finishing it in the oven. Rather than rely on flour for thickening power, this method took advantage of the honey's viscosity to produce a smooth, velvety curd. A generous number of egg yolks gave a vibrant yellow color, richer flavor, and provided greater emulsifying power.

AMP UP THE LEMON To boost the lemon flavor, we introduced a hefty amount of lemon zest. Finishing the curd with a small amount of butter and cream gave the curd a silky consistency and greater dimension. Finally, straining the curd ensured an irresistibly smooth texture.

HONEY-LEMON SQUARES
MAKES 16 BARS

When cooking the curd, be sure the temperature reaches 165 degrees and cooks for at least 1 minute before removing it from the heat. To avoid air bubbles in the curd, stir in the cream with a spatula.

CRUST

- 1 cup (5 ounces) all-purpose flour
- ¼ teaspoon salt
- 6 tablespoons unsalted butter, cut into 6 pieces and softened
- 2 teaspoons water
- 1 teaspoon honey

LEMON CURD

- 2 large eggs plus 7 large yolks
- ½ cup honey
- ¼ cup grated lemon zest plus ⅔ cup juice (4 lemons)
- ⅛ teaspoon salt
- 4 tablespoons unsalted butter, cut into 4 pieces
- 3 tablespoons heavy cream

1. FOR THE CRUST: Adjust oven rack to middle position and heat oven to 350 degrees. Make foil sling for 8-inch square baking pan by folding 2 long sheets of aluminum foil so each is 8 inches wide. Lay sheets of foil in pan perpendicular to each other, with extra foil hanging over edges of pan. Push foil into corners and up sides of pan, smoothing foil flush to pan. Grease foil.

2. Using stand mixer fitted with paddle, mix flour and salt on low speed until combined, about 30 seconds. Add butter, 1 piece at a time, and mix until only pea-size pieces remain, about 1 minute. Add water and honey and continue to mix until mixture begins to clump and resembles wet sand, about 30 seconds.

3. Transfer mixture to prepared pan and press into even layer with bottom of dry measuring cup. Bake crust until golden brown, 20 to 25 minutes, rotating pan halfway through baking.

4. FOR THE LEMON CURD: Meanwhile, whisk eggs and yolks, honey, lemon zest and juice, and salt together in medium saucepan until smooth. Cook over medium-low heat, stirring constantly with rubber spatula, until mixture thickens slightly and registers 165 degrees, about 4 minutes. Continue to cook for 1 minute longer. Whisk in butter until melted. Immediately strain lemon curd through fine-mesh strainer into bowl, then gently stir in cream with rubber spatula.

5. Pour warm lemon curd over hot crust. Bake until filling is shiny and opaque and center jiggles slightly when shaken, 10 to 12 minutes, rotating pan halfway through baking. Let bars cool completely in pan, about 2 hours. Using foil overhang, lift bars from pan and transfer to cutting board. Cut into squares and serve.

> ### PRACTICAL SCIENCE
> #### IS PASTEURIZED HONEY SAFE FOR INFANTS?
>
> Consult your physician, but avoid it for babies under a year.
>
> While honey—raw or pasteurized—isn't the only cause of infant botulism, it is one that is easily avoided.
>
> The consumption of honey by infants has been linked to infant botulism, a paralyzing and sometimes deadly illness. The spores of the botulism bacteria (*Clostridium botulinum*) can be carried in soil, dust, and, sometimes, honey. While these spores lie dormant and are harmless when ingested by people over the age of 1, an infant's still-developing intestinal tract provides an amenable place for the spores to grow and ultimately release toxins.
>
> According to the Centers for Disease Control and Prevention, of the 145 or so cases of botulism reported each year, 65 percent of those are infant botulism—though in most of these cases the illness was contracted by swallowing microscopic dust particles rather than honey. Since the spores are heat-resistant, the pasteurization process that kills yeast strains in honey and prevents crystallization doesn't affect the spores, so pasteurized honey is no safer than raw honey when it comes to infant botulism.
>
> Consult your physician on this and all health matters related to diet; but in the meantime, do not feed honey to babies under the age of 12 months.

Honey Fried Chicken

✓ WHY THIS RECIPE WORKS

The concept of drizzling fried chicken with honey was popularized in the 1930s, but over the years, the pairing has mostly vanished. And no wonder—the recipes we found turned out dry, chalky chicken whose crispy coating had been made soggy with a heavy honey glaze. We set out to bring this traditional favorite back to life.

BRINE FIRST To keep the chicken moist and flavorful all the way through the cooking process, we brined it in the tried-and-true test kitchen combination of water, salt, and sugar.

FRY TWICE To solve the problem of the soggy coating, we turned to a popular method for Korean fried chicken: double frying. This method—in which the chicken is fried until just beginning to crisp, removed from the oil and rested, then returned to the oil again—is particularly effective at evaporating the moisture in chicken skin. Before frying, we dusted the chicken with cornstarch, which helped our simple cornstarch-water batter stick to the chicken.

HEAT YOUR HONEY   Straight out the jar, thick honey coated the chicken inconsistently. To thin it out, we heated it in the microwave until it was pourable. A couple of tablespoons of hot sauce balanced the sweetness and gave our glaze a kick. A quick dunk in the glaze and a drip-dry on a baking rack gave our chicken an irresistibly sticky, sweet-spicy coating.

HONEY FRIED CHICKEN
SERVES 4

You will need at least a 6-quart Dutch oven for this recipe.

BRINE

½   cup salt

½   cup sugar

3   pounds bone-in chicken pieces (split breasts cut in half, drumsticks, and/or thighs), trimmed

BATTER

1½   cups cornstarch

¾   cup water

2   teaspoons pepper

1   teaspoon salt

3   quarts peanut or vegetable oil

HONEY GLAZE

¾   cup honey

2   tablespoons hot sauce

1. FOR THE BRINE: Dissolve salt and sugar in 2 quarts cold water in large container. Submerge chicken in brine, cover, and refrigerate for 30 minutes to 1 hour.

2. FOR THE BATTER: Whisk 1 cup cornstarch, water, pepper, and salt in bowl until smooth. Refrigerate batter while chicken is brining.

3. Sift remaining ½ cup cornstarch into medium bowl. Remove chicken from brine and pat dry with paper towels. Working with 1 piece at a time, coat chicken thoroughly with cornstarch, shaking to remove excess; transfer to platter.

4. Set wire rack in rimmed baking sheet. Add oil to large Dutch oven until it measures about 2 inches deep and heat over medium-high heat to 350 degrees. Whisk batter to recombine. Transfer half of chicken to batter and turn to coat. Remove chicken from batter, allowing excess to drip back into bowl, and add chicken to hot oil. Adjust

burner, if necessary, to maintain oil temperature between 325 and 350 degrees. Fry chicken, stirring to prevent pieces from sticking together, until slightly golden and just beginning to crisp, 5 to 7 minutes. (Chicken will not be cooked through at this point.) Transfer parcooked chicken to platter. Return oil to 350 degrees and repeat with remaining raw chicken and batter. Let each batch of chicken rest for 5 to 7 minutes.

5. Return oil to 350 degrees. Return first batch of chicken to oil and fry until breasts register 160 degrees and thighs and drumsticks register 175 degrees, 5 to 7 minutes. Using tongs, transfer to prepared wire rack. Return oil to 350 degrees and repeat with remaining chicken.

6. FOR THE HONEY GLAZE: Combine honey and hot sauce in large bowl and microwave until hot, about 1½ minutes. Add chicken pieces one at a time to honey mixture and turn to coat; return to wire rack, skin side up, to drain. Serve

Honey Cake

✔ WHY THIS RECIPE WORKS

Honey cake, besides being a sweet treat as good for breakfast as it is for dessert, is a staple at dinners celebrating Rosh Hashanah, the Jewish New Year, as a symbol of a sweet new year. As we found in our research, traditions and recipes for this yearly treat vary from family to family—and cooks have very strong opinions about what makes a good one (or a bad one). We've tried many. But most cakes are not pleasant to eat, as they are by turns greasy, gummy, or dry. The biggest problem, though, is that even the ones with passable textures have dominant flavors of warm spices, citrus, or liquor—everything but honey. They all have honey in them, all right, but we just couldn't taste it.

USE LESS OIL   In keeping with Jewish dietary practices, this cake is traditionally made with vegetable oil rather than butter. First we backed off on the large amount of oil that most recipes call for and used a small amount—¼ cup combined with applesauce—for a moist cake without any greasiness.

ADD ORANGE JUICE   Adding orange juice (an acid) helped boost the leavening power of the baking soda and baking powder, keeping the cake light.

AND A LOT OF HONEY   All the recipes we tried early on called for at least some sugar in addition to the honey, but we were determined to use honey as the cake's sole source of sweetness. We baked through a slew of sticky tests where we slowly swapped out the sugar for honey ¼ cup at a time. We were pleased that the cake that traded all the sugar for honey turned out to be our favorite—it had a strong honey flavor. In order to be able to taste the mild, subtle flavor of the honey, we used a whopping 1¾ cups and lowered the oven temperature to prevent the cake from burning.

HONEY CAKE
SERVES 12

Make sure to use unsweetened applesauce in this cake. If you plan to make this cake ahead of time, hold off on glazing it until 30 minutes before serving. You'll need 20 ounces of honey for this recipe. This cake is sticky; baking spray with flour provides the cleanest release, but if you have only regular cooking spray, apply a heavy coat and then dust the inside of the pan with flour.

CAKE
2½   cups (12½ ounces) all-purpose flour
1¼   teaspoons salt
1   teaspoon baking powder
½   teaspoon baking soda
4   large eggs
½   cup water
¼   cup plus 2 tablespoons unsweetened applesauce
¼   cup vegetable oil
¼   cup orange juice
1   teaspoon vanilla extract
1¾   cups honey

GLAZE
1   cup (4 ounces) confectioners' sugar
4½   teaspoons water
1   teaspoon vanilla extract
    Pinch salt

1. FOR THE CAKE: Adjust oven rack to middle position and heat oven to 325 degrees. Heavily spray 12-cup nonstick Bundt pan with baking spray with flour. Whisk flour, salt, baking powder, and baking soda together in large bowl. Whisk eggs, water, applesauce, oil, orange juice, and vanilla in separate bowl until combined. Whisk honey into egg mixture until fully incorporated.

2. Whisk honey mixture into flour mixture until combined. Scrape batter into prepared pan. Bake until skewer inserted in middle of cake comes out clean, 45 to 55 minutes, rotating pan halfway through baking.

3. Let cake cool in pan on wire rack for 30 minutes. Using small spatula, loosen cake from sides of pan and invert onto rack. Let cool completely, about 2 hours. (Cooled cake can be wrapped with plastic wrap and stored at room temperature for up to 3 days.)

4. FOR THE GLAZE: Whisk together all ingredients. Drizzle glaze evenly over top of cake. Let sit until glaze is firm, about 30 minutes. Serve.

PRACTICAL SCIENCE DIFFERENT HONEYS

The different types of honey depend on different flowers.

Try different varieties of honey to determine what you like. Strongly flavored varieties like buckwheat honey can be too assertive for many recipes—save these honeys for your tea.

Supermarkets carry all kinds of honey (clover, buckwheat, tupelo, etc.). Some are quite expensive. What's the difference?

The raw material that bees use to produce honey is nectar, a sweet liquid created by plants for the purpose of attracting pollinating birds and insects. Most honeys are made from the nectar of many different flowers, but there are some "monofloral" varieties made in controlled environments from the nectar of a single type of flower. The flavor and chemical makeup of honey depend on the nectar that it's made from. Are the different kinds interchangeable in the kitchen?

To find out, we tasted four varieties of honey—three monoflorals (tupelo, orange blossom, and buckwheat) as well as wildflower honey—three different ways: plain, in tea, and baked into honey cake. In the plain and tea tastings, we found tupelo honey to be subtly floral and piney. Orange blossom was thicker and slightly less sweet, with a perfumed aroma and a flavor that one taster likened to an orange Popsicle. Wildflower honey bowled us over with its flowery flavor and aroma, which one taster compared to "fancy soaps," and buckwheat honey was dark, "malty," "robust," "barnyard-y," and "molasses-y," according to various tasters. As for the honey cake tasting, all honeys were fine, save one. Buckwheat honey has an uncommonly high protein content; the protein reacts with the sugar, producing the dark pigments, toasty aromas, and signature bold flavor. The flavor of buckwheat honey is so strong that some tasters didn't care for it in the honey cake.

CHAPTER 48

Balsamic Vinegar

Traditional balsamic vinegar takes at least 12 years to make—and it can keep salad dressing together for a surprising amount of time, too.

HOW THE SCIENCE WORKS

The use of vinegar as a seasoning dates back more than 10,000 years. In addition to its culinary uses, vinegar's high acidity lends it antibacterial properties; the ancient Greek physician Hippocrates relied on vinegar to treat wounds.

The production of vinegar is essentially a two-step process. First, yeast ferment a sugary solution, usually fruit juice, to produce alcohol. Second, acetic acid bacteria (AAB) oxidize the alcohol (ethanol) to acetic acid, the compound responsible for the acidity of vinegar. All balsamic vinegars are made from grape must, the pressed juice of whole grapes, including the grape skins and stems. The must is subject to either a traditional fermentation or a fast, industrial fermentation.

The process of making traditional balsamic vinegar (TBV), also known as *aceto balsamico tradizionale*, is regulated by the Italian *Denominazione di Origine Protetta* (DOP). To make the grade, balsamic vinegar must be produced according to the DOP guidelines, and must pass a certification taste test performed by a trained panel. TBV is produced only in the Emilia-Romagna region of northern Italy, where the white Trebbiano and red Lambrusco grapes are grown. The must from these grapes is concentrated by cooking and then treated with "seed vinegar," a starter culture that includes a mixture of yeast and AAB. The fermenting juice is placed in a large wooden barrel. After initial aging, a portion of the concentrated vinegar is transferred to a smaller barrel, where further concentration and fermentation take place. This process is repeated, with the aging vinegar moved to progressively smaller barrels, until the vinegar has aged a minimum of 12 years. (For more, see page 393.)

This long procedure is a study in concentration: Overall, 100 pounds of grapes are converted to about 1.5 cups

This long procedure is a study in concentration.

of vinegar. The thick, highly viscous nature of traditional balsamic vinegar arises from the massive loss of water that occurs over years of barrel aging. The complex flavors associated with the taste of aged balsamic come from products of the Maillard reaction. While the Maillard reaction occurs quite slowly at the temperature at which vinegar is aged, over the course of a decade or more, this reaction significantly impacts flavor development. Authentic traditional balsamic vinegar is divided into three grades: Orange, aged for at least 12 years; silver, aged for at least 18 years; and gold, aged for 25 or more years.

Not all balsamics are traditional. We also turn to vinegars called *aceto balsamico di Modena*, which are designated by *Indicazione Geografica Protetta* (IGP), or even industrially produced balsamic vinegars bearing no designation whatsoever. These differ from traditional balsamic in two ways. First, the fermentation process is often sped up. Second, supermarket vinegars are either aged for just a few months or not at all, resulting in much thinner brews. While many supermarket balsamic vinegars are perfectly acceptable, be wary of balsamic vinegars with 6 percent acid and higher, caramel coloring, and thickening agents.

We use balsamic vinegar in a range of ways in the kitchen. And it's not all about the flavor: Our Make-Ahead Vinaigrette (page 394) relies on the polymers called melanoidins, present in traditional balsamic, to help keep the vinaigrette emulsified for up to a week. The addition of balsamic vinegar at the end of cooking Italian Sausage with Grapes and Balsamic Vinegar (page 395) gives the easy one-pan dish a sweet-sour sauce. Finally, doctoring up supermarket balsamic with a bit of sugar and lemon makes a perfect topping for fresh strawberries (page 396).

TEST KITCHEN EXPERIMENT

There may be a rustic charm to dressing salad greens at the table with a splash of vinegar and a drizzle of olive oil, but for balanced flavor in every bite, you really need an emulsified dressing. Forming an emulsion between oil and vinegar isn't terribly challenging with a whisk and a little patience, but getting it to stay emulsified is another matter entirely. Over the years we've learned the value of adding emulsifiers like mustard and mayonnaise to help create a strong vinaigrette, but very recently we started exploring the potential of stabilizers in general, and aged balsamic vinegar in particular, to improve the longevity of vinaigrette emulsions.

EXPERIMENT

We prepared three batches of vinaigrette containing 3 parts oil and 1 part vinegar. The first contained just oil and vinegar, the second included small amounts of mustard and mayonnaise (both emulsifiers), and the third included mustard and mayonnaise as well as a tablespoon of syrupy 15-year-old balsamic vinegar. After whisking the vinaigrettes together we let them sit and tracked how long it took for each to start to separate back out into oil and vinegar.

RESULTS

The sample with just oil and vinegar began separating right off the bat and was completely separated by the 15-minute mark. The second sample, which contained mustard and mayonnaise, held together for 2 hours before breaking. The vinaigrette that contained aged balsamic in addition to mayonnaise and mustard remained emulsified for a full five days.

TAKEAWAY

What accounts for the massive increase in stability between the second and third samples? Aged balsamic is rich in compounds called melanoidins. These compounds are formed when sugars and proteins undergo the Maillard reaction, the chemical reaction that generates deep browning and flavor. Because the molecules of these compounds are extremely large, they increase the viscosity of emulsions so much that it becomes difficult for the oil droplets to move around and coalesce into larger droplets and eventually separate from the water; thus, the dressing is very slow to separate. (Melanoidins also happen to be responsible for the aged vinegar's inky color.) But considering that real aged balsamic is a pricey condiment often reserved for drizzling, we wanted to look around for other ingredients that contain a high quantity of melanoidins, and were pleased to find that molasses worked equally well, and can be used as a substitute in our Make-Ahead Vinaigrette (page 394).

THE SECRET TO LONG-LASTING VINAIGRETTE?

We tested three batches of vinaigrette. The one with aged balsamic lasted a full week.

JUST OIL & VINEGAR
This vinaigrette separated after 15 minutes.

OIL, VINEGAR, MUSTARD, & MAYO
This vinaigrette lasted 2 hours before breaking.

OIL, VINEGAR, MUSTARD, MAYO, & AGED BALSAMIC
This vinaigrette held together for a full 5 days.

JOURNEY: TRADITIONAL BALSAMIC VINEGAR

❶ GROW GRAPES

The most common grape used for the production of balsamic vinegar is Trebbiano di Castelvetro (a white grape), but the red Lambrusco Graspa Rossa and other grape varieties are also used. The grapes are picked when they're very ripe and thus have a high sugar content. The grapes, including the pulp, seeds, and skins, are crushed and pressed to provide what is called must.

❷ MAKE THE SAPA

The must is boiled to reduce the volume 30 to 50 percent. The resulting syrupy, reduced must is called sapa, and has a pH of is 2.3 to 3.2 This cooking stage achieves concentration of the must; Maillard and caramelization reactions also occur at this stage.

❸ INNOCULATE AND FERMENT

The concentrated must can be inoculated with the "seed vinegar" (also called the "mother of vinegar"), which is obtained from a previous batch of vinegar and contains a microbiologically undefined mixture of yeast and acetic acid bacteria. The initial fermentation takes place in a large wooden barrel called a *badessa*.

❹ USE A BARREL

This mixture is then transferred to the first barrel of the *batteria*, a collection of wooden barrels of progressively smaller sizes. The largest barrel holds around 50 to 75 L and the smallest holds around 10 to 16 L. There must be at least three sizes of barrels. The smallest barrel is called *prelivio*. Barrels are made of wood including oak, chestnut, ash, mulberry, juniper, locust, and cherry. The choice of wood(s) for the barrels imparts signature aroma and flavor to the vinegar.

❺ AGE IT

After the first year, and in each of the following years, the vinegar is transferred to smaller barrels, as evaporation of the water in the vinegar concentrates the brew. This process of transferring vinegars to smaller barrels is called "refilling." The *acetaio* (vinegar maker) assesses the vinegar as it progresses, and can top off the barrels with vinegar from "younger" barrels, or with fresh must.

❻ FINISH IT

When the acetaio judges the vinegar to be properly aged (and the vinegar has been aging for at least 12 years or longer), the mature vinegar will have taken on some notable characteristics. The volume will be greatly reduced. The fermentation will have remarkably slowed down, and there is no detectable microbiological activity in the vinegar in the last barrel (which is counterintuitively named "Number 1"). The final acidity of the product is 4.5 percent (pH around 2.5). Besides acetic acid, other acids present include tartaric acid (from the grapes), gluconic acid (from AAB), and succinic acid (yeast-derived). The Maillard reaction (taking place over the course of a decade or more) will have produced melanoidins (large brown-pigmented polymers that lend balsamic its color and contribute to its high viscosity) and flavor compounds.

Make-Ahead Vinaigrette

✓ WHY THIS RECIPE WORKS

We make a lot of salads, so we like to mix up a large batch of vinaigrette to last for several days. But no matter how carefully we whisk the oil into the other ingredients, it doesn't stay emulsified for long. Most vinaigrettes only hold together for a few hours. One option is to rewhisk the dressing in a bowl, but it never truly comes back together. But recently we stumbled on a potential solution in an unusual ingredient. Finding ourselves short on wine and sherry vinegars, we supplemented with some of the thick, syrupy aged balsamic vinegar that we would ordinarily drizzle on steak, good cheese, or berries. This vinaigrette had a thick, viscous consistency. Not only that but it had remarkable staying power; it remained fully emulsified for several days. It wasn't until the week was nearly over that a thin layer of vinegar sat at the bottom of the jar—and even then, a quick shake was all it took to restore a tight emulsion. This was a dressing we wanted to investigate further.

USE MELANOIDINS We needed to figure out what property of the aged balsamic gave the vinegar its remarkable hold on the emulsion. With a little research, and a lot of testing (see Test Kitchen Experiment, page 392), we hit upon the key component: melanoidins. These very large compounds, abundant in aged balsamic vinegar, are formed when sugars and proteins are heated and undergo the Maillard reaction. Because they are so large, melanoidins increase the viscosity of emulsions, making them very slow to separate. (Another ingredient containing melanoidins is molasses, which can be used in this dressing as well.)

USE EMULSIFIERS If the melanoidins created such a strong emulsion, did we need the emulsifying powers of the mustard and mayonnaise? Mustard and mayonnaise help the oil and vinegar combine into a unified sauce. Mustard contains a polysaccharide, and the egg yolks in mayonnaise contain lecithin; both of these agents attract oil and are compatible with water, so they hold the oil in small droplets dispersed within the vinegar. Balsamic vinegar's melanoidins increase the viscosity of the emulsion and make it difficult for the oil droplets to coalesce and separate from the water. We tried making the vinaigrette without the emulsifiers, but it separated within an hour. Turns out mustard and melanoidins work differently. While the mustard helps the emulsion form, the melanoidins prevent it from separating. It's basically the difference between emulsifiers and stabilizers.

TWO OILS ARE BETTER THAN ONE The only hitch to including the mayonnaise in the dressing was that the dressing needed to be refrigerated, and doing so caused the oil to solidify and the emulsion to break completely once it came to room temperature. But we had an idea. We knew that extra-virgin olive oil solidifies when its molecules form a lattice and crystallize, and we knew we could prevent crystallization by cutting it with another type of oil. Vegetable oil would be the easiest and most neutral addition, so we tried ratios ranging from 10:1 to 2:1 of olive oil to vegetable oil and eventually found that the 2:1 ratio kept the dressing smooth and pourable directly from the refrigerator while still allowing the distinct flavor of the olive oil to come through.

MAKE-AHEAD VINAIGRETTE
MAKES ABOUT 1 CUP

Regular or light mayonnaise can be used in this recipe. There are a few substitutes for traditional balsamic vinegar: In a small saucepan, reduce 1 cup of supermarket balsamic down to ¼ cup. Substitute 1 tablespoon of the reduced balsamic and reserve the rest for another use. Balsamic glaze can also be substituted for the traditional balsamic. Finally, molasses can also be substituted for traditional balsamic vinegar. (Do not use blackstrap molasses.) You can substitute toasted hazelnut or walnut oil for the extra-virgin olive oil. The dressing template is adaptable to a variety of oils and acids, as well as aromatics and fresh herbs.

1	tablespoon mayonnaise
1	tablespoon traditional balsamic vinegar
1	tablespoon Dijon mustard
½	teaspoon salt
¼	cup wine vinegar
½	cup extra-virgin olive oil
¼	cup vegetable oil

1. Combine mayonnaise, balsamic vinegar, mustard, and salt in 2-cup jar with tight-fitting lid. Stir with fork until mixture is milky in appearance and no lumps of mayonnaise or balsamic remain. Add wine vinegar, seal jar, and shake until smooth, about 10 seconds.

2. Add ¼ cup olive oil, seal jar, and shake vigorously until thoroughly combined, about 10 seconds. Repeat, adding remaining ¼ cup olive oil and vegetable oil in 2 additions, shaking vigorously until thoroughly combined after each addition. (After third addition, vinaigrette should be glossy and lightly thickened, with no pools of oil on its surface.) Refrigerate for up to 1 week. Shake briefly before using.

Italian Sausage with Grapes and Balsamic Vinegar

✓ WHY THIS RECIPE WORKS

We've always enjoyed the pairing of rich, salty pork and bright, sweet fruit—think pork chops and applesauce or prosciutto draped around cantaloupe. So naturally we were intrigued by the Italian combination of pork sausage links with grapes and balsamic vinegar, a humble dish that originated in Umbria as a quick meal for vineyard laborers. Rich, juicy, and well browned, the sausages are a great match for the tangy-sweet vinegar-based sauce with grapes that soften and caramelize in the pan. Take into account that this dish can be on the table in less than 30 minutes and it's no wonder it became an Italian classic. But like most preparations based on just a couple of simple components, the fewer the ingredients, the more important the technique. We tried recipes that failed at every turn, starting with bouncy, barely cooked grapes and vinegar that tasted harsh instead of in balance with the meat's richness. But the real problem was the sausage itself. Some recipes weren't explicit about how to cook the links—and as we discovered, you can't just throw them into a skillet and hope for the best.

COOK THE SAUSAGE Cooked over high—and even somewhat over medium—heat, the sausages tended to burn in spots before they had cooked all the way through, or their casings split, allowing their flavorful juices to leak into the pan and leaving their interiors dry and mealy. Borrowing the classic Chinese method for cooking potstickers, we cooked the sausages over medium heat and then added ¼ cup of water to the pan. We immediately covered the pan so that the links could steam gently; after about 10 minutes, they hit their target temperature of 160 to 165 degrees.

DON'T JUDGE BY COLOR While cooking the sausage, we kept running into a weird phenomenon: Sometimes sausages that were fully cooked to 160 degrees looked pink inside. We learned that persistent pinkness can be due to a variety of factors unrelated to the meat's doneness: the seasonings, the age of the pork when processed, and how it was stored. But according to Joseph Sebranek and Melvin Hunt, professors and meat experts at Iowa State University and Kansas State University, respectively, the most significant factor affecting the pigment is the pork's pH: The higher the pH, the more stable its pink pigment will be, even when the meat is fully cooked. We confirmed this effect by adding increasing amounts of alkaline baking soda to ground pork to raise its pH and then cooking all the samples via sous vide to exactly 160 degrees. Sure enough, the samples with the highest pH were noticeably pinker, proving that the color of the pork is not a good indication of its doneness. Instead, we trusted our instant-read thermometers.

ADD GRAPES AND VINEGAR All we had left to do was plug the grapes and a quick pan sauce into the equation. We wanted the fruit to break down a little, so we halved 1 pound of red grapes and added them to the skillet with the browned links just before adding the water. Once the sausages were cooked through, we removed them from the pan but continued to cook the grapes until they were caramelized and soft. We took them off the heat, stirred a couple of tablespoons of vinegar into the pan, and promptly spooned the glazy sauce over the sausages.

ITALIAN SAUSAGE WITH GRAPES AND BALSAMIC VINEGAR
SERVES 4 TO 6

Our favorite supermarket balsamic vinegar is Bertolli Balsamic Vinegar of Modena. Serve this dish with crusty bread and salad or over polenta for a heartier meal.

1	tablespoon vegetable oil
1½	pounds sweet Italian sausage
1	pound seedless red grapes, halved lengthwise (3 cups)
1	onion, halved and sliced thin
¼	cup water
¼	teaspoon pepper
⅛	teaspoon salt
¼	cup dry white wine
1	tablespoon chopped fresh oregano
2	teaspoons balsamic vinegar
2	tablespoons chopped fresh mint

1. Heat oil in 12-inch skillet over medium heat until shimmering. Arrange sausages in pan and cook, turning once, until browned on 2 sides, about 5 minutes. Tilt skillet and carefully remove excess fat with paper towel. Distribute grapes and onion over and around sausages. Add water and immediately cover. Cook, turning sausages once, until they register between 160 and 165 degrees and onions and grapes have softened, about 10 minutes.

2. Transfer sausages to paper towel–lined plate and tent with aluminum foil. Return skillet to medium-high heat and stir pepper and salt into grape-onion mixture. Spread

grape-onion mixture in even layer in skillet and cook without stirring until browned, 3 to 5 minutes. Stir and continue to cook, stirring frequently, until mixture is well browned and grapes are soft but still retain their shape, 3 to 5 minutes longer. Reduce heat to medium, stir in wine and oregano, and cook, scraping up any browned bits, until wine is reduced by half, 30 to 60 seconds. Remove pan from heat and stir in vinegar.

3. Arrange sausages on serving platter and spoon grape-onion mixture over top. Sprinkle with mint and serve.

Strawberries with Balsamic Vinegar

✓ WHY THIS RECIPE WORKS

While it may sound odd at first, strawberries splashed with balsamic vinegar is a classic Italian combo. The problem? Not everyone wants to invest in expensive traditional balsamic vinegar to get the viscous, sweet variety needed for this dish.

DOCTOR THE VINEGAR While searching for a way to improve the flavor and mellow the sharpness of supermarket-quality vinegar, we found that we could doctor inexpensive supermarket balsamic vinegar. We attempted to make an imitation by simmering supermarket balsamic until thick and reduced. While this worked to attain the right texture, the flavor was extremely sharp and harsh. We found that by adding a little sugar and a squeeze of lemon juice to the vinegar before reducing it, we were able to achieve a closer approximation.

MACERATE THE BERRIES We macerated the sliced strawberries with a little sugar to boost their flavor and draw out some of their juices. We tried all types of sweeteners with our sliced strawberries, and ultimately chose light brown sugar because its molasses notes echoed the flavor of the balsamic vinegar. An unexpected shot of ground black pepper accented the flavor of the berries.

STRAWBERRIES WITH BALSAMIC VINEGAR
SERVES 6

If you don't have light brown sugar on hand, sprinkle the strawberries with an equal amount of granulated sugar. Serve the strawberries and syrup as is or with a scoop of vanilla ice cream or a dollop of lightly sweetened mascarpone cheese.

⅓   cup balsamic vinegar
2   teaspoons granulated sugar
½   teaspoon lemon juice
1½   pounds strawberries, hulled and sliced ¼ inch thick or halved or quartered if small (5 cups)
¼   cup packed light brown sugar
      Pepper

1. Bring vinegar, granulated sugar, and lemon juice to simmer in small saucepan over medium heat. Simmer until syrup is reduced by half (to approximately 3 tablespoons), about 3 minutes. Transfer syrup to small bowl and let cool completely.

2. With spoon, lightly toss strawberries and brown sugar in large bowl. Let stand until sugar dissolves and strawberries exude some juice, 10 to 15 minutes. Pour syrup over strawberries, season with pepper to taste, and toss to combine. Divide strawberries among individual bowls or goblets and serve immediately.

PRACTICAL SCIENCE TRADITIONAL BALSAMIC VINEGAR VS. CHEAPER BALSAMIC VINEGAR

Science supports your splurge.

In an analysis of the flavor compounds in traditional balsamic vinegar (TBV) compared to those found in the cheaper balsamic vinegar of Modena (BV) published in the *Journal of Agricultural and Food Chemistry*, trained testers found that TBV's taste profile was characterized by a balance of intense sour and sweet, whereas the BV profile was dominated by a strong, one-note sourness. Quantitative analyses performed using chromatographic and mass spectrometry techniques revealed that wood-derived polyphenols, such as vescalagin, and its isomer castalagin, were clearly present in TBV, but were absent in BV. These polyphenols, which are also found in barrel-aged ferments like wine and whiskey, migrate from oak barrels into the vinegar during aging, and impart subtle wood-like notes to the flavor of the mature vinegar. Reflecting the results from the tasters' descriptions, BV had twice the concentration of acetic acid than did TBV, as well as a much lower concentration of the sweet-modulating compound 5-acetoxymethyl-2-furaldehyde, which is derived from dehydrated sugars and is close in structure to the key flavor compound HMF. Overall, these data support the notion that the careful and extended production of TBV results in a vinegar with complex, delicious flavor that is objectively superior to its industrially produced counterparts.

CHAPTER 49

Bittersweet Chocolate

This dark, high-cocoa chocolate needs attention to temperature in the kitchen.

HOW THE SCIENCE WORKS

In the past decade, Americans have gotten serious about dark chocolate. Rich, complex, and even bitter, its flavor transcends the mild, sugar-laden milk chocolate that many of us grew up with. As a result, ever-climbing cacao percentages are now printed prominently on packaging, and chocophiles have come to describe bars with the same level of detail that you might use for a fine Cabernet. "Bean to bar" is hot, as artisanal chocolatiers take control of every aspect of chocolate making, from sourcing to production. Single-origin bars are trendy, too, showcasing distinct regional characteristics such as the intensely floral flavor of beans from the mountains of Peru or the dried mint overtones of bars made from the beans from Trinidad.

Most chocolate has just three basic ingredients: cocoa butter, cocoa solids, and sugar. The "cacao percentage" you hear so much about in bar chocolate refers to the total amount of cocoa butter and cocoa solids contributed by ground-up cacao beans. Sugar accounts for the rest of the content, along with minute amounts (typically less than 2 percent) of emulsifiers, vanilla flavoring, salt, and sometimes milk fat. The FDA states that dark chocolate, whether labeled bittersweet, semisweet, or dark, must be at least 35 percent cacao. As a general rule, the higher the cacao percentage, the darker and more intense the chocolate.

Chocolate made for eating and baking comes in five different styles: unsweetened, bittersweet, semisweet, sweet, and milk chocolate. Bittersweet and semisweet are made for eating and baking, while sweet dark and milk chocolate are made primarily for eating. Other than unsweetened chocolate, all forms contain varying amounts of added sugar. Milk chocolate also contains added milk solids. (White chocolate is nothing more than cocoa butter, sugar, milk solids, and vanilla.)

The flavor of chocolate comes from the cocoa solids.

Here, we'll concentrate on bittersweet chocolate. It's important to note that the flavor of chocolate comes from the cocoa solids. Yes, bittersweet chocolate must contain at least 35 percent cocoa solids, but good-quality brands typically contain much higher levels. Higher levels of cocoa solids mean less sugar, resulting in a rich, intense, and fairly bitter chocolate flavor.

Still, good chocolate is not just about a high cacao percentage and plenty of cocoa butter. For complex flavor, a manufacturer must start with good-quality beans that have been grown and harvested under optimal conditions. The beans must be properly fermented and roasted (see page 399). Upscale chocolate makers claim that every detail is critical—and are loath to reveal their methods.

We use chocolate in the kitchen in many different ways. A custard filling (baked in a low oven) highlights the deep flavor of dark chocolate in our Rich Chocolate Tart (page 400), glazed with a glossy chocolate and corn syrup topping. For our Chocolate Truffles (page 402), we work hard to create a smooth and silky texture, which we achieve by adding butter and corn syrup, by mixing with methods that don't incorporate too much air, and by letting the truffles cool down slowly, a move that lets the unique structure of the chocolate crystallize in the right way. Crystallization is likewise important for the chocolate coating on our Florentine Lace Cookies (page 404)—so important that we devised a new way to "temper" the chocolate (see Test Kitchen Experiment, page 398). Finally, we use three types of chocolate for our Fudgy Triple-Chocolate Brownies (page 405), to get the deepest flavor possible. (Need more chocolate? Check out our Triple-Chocolate Mousse Cake, page 140.)

TEST KITCHEN EXPERIMENT

Good chocolate right out of the wrapper has been tempered, or melted and cooled to precise temperatures, lending it an attractive sheen and a satisfying snap when you bite into it. When cocoa butter solidifies, it can form any of six different types of crystals. Each of these has a different melting point, density, and level of stability. For the best sheen and texture you want as much of the cocoa butter as possible to form one particular type of crystal, called beta crystals. Beta crystals have a higher melting point than other, less stable crystals, which means the chocolate won't melt on your fingers. And you want the smallest possible beta crystals, because they will produce chocolate that sets up dense and shiny and snaps cleanly. We set up the following experiment to figure out the best way to temper chocolate at home.

EXPERIMENT

We softened bar chocolate three different ways for drizzling on cookies. For the first batch we simply microwaved the chocolate until it was completely liquid and registered 110 degrees. For the second batch we tempered the chocolate using the traditional method: After fully melting the chocolate (110 degrees), we cooled it quickly while stirring it constantly to form small crystals. Then we heated the chocolate up to 88 degrees to melt away all crystals except beta crystals and then cooled it rapidly back down again. For the third batch we microwaved three-quarters of the chocolate at 50 percent power until it was mostly (but not fully) melted. We then added the remaining chocolate, and stirred it until partially melted, returning it to the microwave for no more than 5 seconds at a time to continue the melting. We examined all of the cooled chocolate for sheen and snap.

RESULTS

The chocolate that was simply melted and then cooled never fully hardened at room temperature. It was flexible and easily melted onto our fingers. The second batch, which was tempered using the traditional method, hardened quickly into a shiny, snappy piece. The third batch displayed nearly all of the same characteristics as the traditionally tempered chocolate, though was slightly less shiny.

TAKEAWAY

Traditional tempering works. Unfortunately it's also time-consuming and fussy. Our simple method of partially microwaving a portion of chocolate and then adding the rest works nearly as well and requires a fraction of the effort. This method works for a few reasons. First, we don't let the chocolate get too hot during melting, which ensures that some of the desirable beta crystals remain. Second, we add more unmelted chocolate with plenty of intact beta crystals, which then act as seed crystals to encourage the formation of more beta crystals. Finally, our method keeps the chocolate close enough to 88 degrees to prevent less-stable crystals from forming.

A QUICK AND EASY NEW WAY TO TEMPER

IT'S A SNAP
Chocolate that's been properly tempered is glossy and breaks cleanly when snapped.

LOST ITS TEMPER
Chocolate that has melted and cooled without tempering looks dull and bends rather than breaking.

JOURNEY: FROM BEAN TO CHOCOLATE BAR

Chocolate is one of America's favorite foods. But not many people know how it's made.

1 HARVEST

The tropical cacao tree blooms all year round and each tree bears about 20 to 50 ripe fruits, or elongated pods. These pods are usually harvested twice each year. The hard-shelled pods contain a sweet, mucilaginous pulp, which surrounds 20 to 50 almond-shaped seeds.

2 FERMENT THE SEEDS

Following harvest, the pods are cut open and the seeds and pulp removed. The seeds are then naturally fermented with the pulp for two to eight days. At the end of the fermentation period the fermented seeds are dried; they're now called cocoa beans.

3 ROAST THEM

At the processor the beans are cleaned in a series of steps and separated by size in order to facilitate uniform roasting. Roasting oxidizes the tannic phenolic compounds and removes acetic acid and other undesirable aroma compounds. During this step more moisture is lost, the color deepens, the aroma is enhanced, and the beans harden and become more brittle. High-quality cocoa beans are heated to just under 265 degrees for around 30 minutes. At this point the beans are still covered by a brittle shell, which must be removed by a process that separates the shell from the inner bean, called the nib.

4 MILL THE NIBS

Following roasting, the cocoa nibs are milled to produce a homogeneous flowable paste called cocoa liquor. Alternatively, the cocoa nibs may be subjected to an alkalization process, which neutralizes the free acids, producing less astringency and a darker color. In either case, the cocoa liquor is still about 54 percent fat by weight.

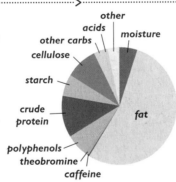

other
acids
other carbs
cellulose
starch
crude protein
polyphenols
theobromine
caffeine
moisture
fat

5 REFINE THE LIQUOR

Cocoa liquor is converted to chocolate in a final series of steps, starting by mixing it with other ingredients, including sugar, vanilla, and milk solids. It is then passed through heated rollers to form a very smooth-textured mass containing very fine particles, a process known as refining.

7 TEMPER

Finally, the chocolate is tempered to ensure that it has a smooth, glossy appearance and melts in the mouth. This is accomplished by a series of heating and cooling steps that cause the fat molecules in the cocoa butter to crystallize in a very specific crystal structure. Cocoa butter forms six different types of crystals, which melt over the range of 63 to 97 degrees. Only one type, called beta crystals, which melt around 93 degrees, have the desired melting point and appearance. Once tempered, the chocolate is molded and packaged.

6 CONCH IT

The next step, known as conching, creates the pleasant taste and aroma of chocolate by allowing the volatile acids to escape. The name originates from the shell-shaped vessel that was used for this step many years ago. During the conching process, the chocolate mass is mixed, ground, kneaded, and heated over many hours, which eliminates the harsh sour, acidic flavors, and improves mouthfeel.

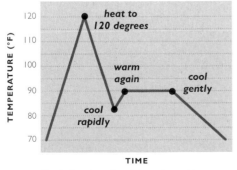

TEMPERING CHOCOLATE

TEMPERATURE (°F)

120 — *heat to 120 degrees*
warm again
cool gently
cool rapidly

TIME

Tempering gives chocolate a glossy appearance.

Rich Chocolate Tart

✔ WHY THIS RECIPE WORKS

Inflated descriptors like "unbelievably decadent" and "death by chocolate" are de rigueur when it comes to chocolate tarts. But for us, the real draw of the dessert is its pure, uncomplicated profile: The best versions boast a flawlessly smooth, truffle-like texture; unadulterated chocolate flavor; and a sophisticated polish. We decided to uncover what makes an exceptional chocolate tart so that we could serve it for the holidays or after any special dinner. We stocked up on high-quality bittersweet chocolate, heavy cream, eggs, and butter—the building blocks of just about every filling recipe we found—and started testing. While the filling ingredients were more or less identical for all the recipes we tried, the way in which those ingredients were treated separated the tarts into three unique styles: a baked, egg white-aerated dessert; a ganache-style tart; and a custard-style dessert. Our favorite? The custard. But we still had a long way to go.

USE A LOW OVEN   To nail down the basics, we tested varying ratios of chocolate to cream before landing on 9 ounces and 1¼ cups, respectively. With those amounts, the filling was intense but not cloying, and silky without turning runny. Two whole beaten eggs lent the filling just enough body without turning it rubbery. The trouble was, with eggs in the mix, the edges of the tart baked up ever so slightly curdled. It occurred to us that perhaps the 350-degree oven we'd been using was too hot for this custard-style filling—after all, eggs curdle when overcooked. So we prepared several more tarts and staggered their baking temperatures in 25-degree increments from 350 down to 250 degrees. The differences were astounding. The 350-degree tart was predictably stiff, but with each reduction in temperature the texture improved, and the 250-degree tart had the ethereal quality that we were after. It wasn't just curd-free; it was downright plush.

ADD BUTTER   If only the filling didn't taste—and look—so dull and one-dimensional. The ganache-style filling's buttery foundation may have been too rich, but dull it was not, which got us thinking: What if we strayed from the typical custard-style tart and added a moderate amount of butter? Using our working recipe, we compared fillings made with 8, 6, 4, and 2 tablespoons of butter and found that 4 tablespoons nicely rounded out the chocolate flavor without overdoing the richness. A touch of espresso powder, dissolved in the cream with a bit of salt, added an echo of bittersweetness that highlighted the chocolate.

GLAZE IT   As for looks, our tart needed a makeover—or at least some cover-up. In the heat of the oven, its surface formed tiny fissures and took on a matte finish. We wanted this holiday-caliber dessert to boast a glossy sheen and figured that a simple chocolate glaze would do the trick. We played with a few formulas and settled on a bittersweet chocolate ganache spiked with a little corn syrup for shine. Pouring the glaze over the baked and chilled tart created the polished look that we wanted.

MAKE A NUT CRUST   With the filling perfected at last, we test-drove pastry options for the crust, pitting a basic *pâte sucrée* (butter, flour, sugar, egg yolk, and heavy cream, all pulsed in the food processor) against versions dressed up with cocoa powder and toasted nuts. The cocoa pastry made for a dramatic-looking dessert (dark crust, dark filling), but a third chocolate component felt like overkill. Replacing ½ cup of the flour with ground toasted almonds turned out a rich-tasting, pleasantly nubby dough—an ideal match for the lush chocolate filling. (Not to mention: A dollop of lightly sweetened whipped cream plus either a sprinkle of coarse sea salt or a pile of chocolate curls produced a stunning presentation.)

RICH CHOCOLATE TART
SERVES 12

Toasted and skinned hazelnuts can be substituted for the almonds. Use good-quality dark chocolate containing a cacao percentage between 60 and 65 percent; our favorites are Ghirardelli 60 Percent Cacao Bittersweet Chocolate Premium Baking Bar and Callebaut Intense Dark Chocolate, L-60–40NV. Let tart sit at room temperature for 30 minutes before glazing in step 6 and then at least another hour after glazing. The tart can be garnished with chocolate curls or with a flaky coarse sea salt, such as Maldon. Serve with lightly sweetened whipped cream; if you like, flavor it with cognac or vanilla extract.

CRUST

1	large egg yolk
2	tablespoons heavy cream
½	cup sliced almonds, toasted
¼	cup (1¾ ounces) sugar
1	cup (5 ounces) all-purpose flour
¼	teaspoon salt
6	tablespoons unsalted butter, cut into ½-inch pieces

FILLING

- 1 ¼   cups heavy cream
- ½   teaspoon instant espresso powder
- ¼   teaspoon salt
- 9   ounces bittersweet chocolate, chopped fine
- 4   tablespoons unsalted butter, cut into thin slices and softened
- 2   large eggs, lightly beaten, room temperature

GLAZE

- 3   tablespoons heavy cream
- 1   tablespoon light corn syrup
- 2   ounces bittersweet chocolate, chopped fine
- 1   tablespoon hot water

1. FOR THE CRUST: Beat egg yolk and cream together in small bowl. Process almonds and sugar in food processor until nuts are finely ground, 15 to 20 seconds. Add flour and salt; pulse to combine, about 10 pulses. Scatter butter over flour mixture; pulse to cut butter into flour until mixture resembles coarse meal, about 15 pulses. With processor running, add egg yolk mixture and process until dough forms ball, about 10 seconds. Transfer dough to large sheet of plastic wrap and press into 6-inch disk; wrap dough in plastic and refrigerate until firm but malleable, about 30 minutes. (Dough can be refrigerated for up to 3 days; before using, let stand at room temperature until malleable but still cool.)

2. Roll out dough between 2 large sheets of plastic into 11-inch round about ⅜ inch thick. (If dough becomes too soft and sticky to work with, slip it onto baking sheet and refrigerate until workable.) Place dough round (still in plastic) on baking sheet and refrigerate until firm but pliable, about 15 minutes.

3. Adjust oven rack to middle position and heat oven to 375 degrees. Spray 9-inch tart pan with removable bottom with vegetable oil spray. Keeping dough on sheet, remove top layer of plastic. Invert tart pan (with bottom) on top of dough round. Press on tart pan to cut dough. Using 2 hands, pick up sheet and tart pan and carefully invert both, setting tart pan right side up. Remove sheet and peel off plastic; reserve plastic. Roll over edges of tart pan with rolling pin to cut dough. Gently ease and press dough into bottom of pan, reserving scraps. Roll dough scraps into ¾-inch-diameter rope (various lengths are OK). Line edge of tart pan with rope(s) and gently press into fluted sides. Line tart pan with reserved plastic and, using measuring cup, gently press and smooth dough to even thickness (sides should be about ¼ inch thick). Using paring knife, trim any excess dough above rim of tart; discard scraps. Freeze dough-lined pan until firm, 20 to 30 minutes.

4. Set dough-lined pan on baking sheet. Spray 12-inch square of aluminum foil with oil spray and press foil, sprayed side down, into pan; fill with 2 cups pie weights. Bake until dough is dry and light golden brown, about 25 minutes, rotating pan halfway through baking. Carefully remove foil and weights and continue to bake until pastry is rich golden brown and fragrant, 8 to 10 minutes longer. Let cool completely on sheet on wire rack.

5. FOR THE FILLING: Heat oven to 250 degrees. Bring cream, espresso powder, and salt to simmer in small saucepan over medium heat, stirring once or twice to dissolve espresso powder and salt. Meanwhile, place chocolate in large heatproof bowl. Pour simmering cream mixture over chocolate, cover, and let stand for 5 minutes to allow chocolate to soften. Using whisk, stir mixture slowly and gently (so as not to incorporate air) until homogeneous. Add butter and continue to whisk gently until fully incorporated. Pour eggs through fine-mesh strainer into chocolate mixture; whisk slowly until mixture is homogeneous and glossy. Pour filling into tart crust and shake gently from side to side to distribute and smooth surface; pop any large bubbles with toothpick or skewer. Bake tart, on baking sheet, until outer edge of filling is just set and very faint cracks appear on surface, 30 to 35 minutes; filling will still be very wobbly. Let cool completely on sheet on wire rack. Refrigerate, uncovered, until filling is chilled and set, at least 3 hours or up to 18 hours.

6. FOR THE GLAZE: Thirty minutes before glazing, remove tart from refrigerator. Bring cream and corn syrup to simmer in small saucepan over medium heat; stir once or twice to combine. Remove pan from heat, add chocolate, and cover. Let stand for 5 minutes to allow chocolate to soften. Whisk gently (so as not to incorporate air) until mixture is smooth, then whisk in hot water until glaze is homogeneous, shiny, and pourable. Working quickly, pour glaze onto center of tart. To distribute glaze, tilt tart and allow glaze to run to edge. (Spreading glaze with spatula will leave marks on surface.) Pop any large bubbles with toothpick or skewer. Let stand for at least 1 hour or up to 3 hours.

7. Remove outer ring from tart pan. Insert thin-bladed metal spatula between crust and pan bottom to loosen tart; slide tart onto serving platter. Cut into wedges and serve.

Chocolate Truffles

✔ WHY THIS RECIPE WORKS

Chocolate truffles are inherently simple confections. These rich, dense balls of ganache often contain nothing more than good-quality bar chocolate and heavy cream. Yet they're surprisingly difficult to get right. The chocolate-to-cream ratio must be spot-on; otherwise, the truffle will be either overly dense or too soft to hold its shape. Creating a smooth, shiny coating is even more finicky— and then you've got to contend with the mess of dipping the truffle into it. Finally, there's shaping. The pros use a pastry bag, but it takes practice to produce perfectly symmetrical pieces. Our goal was clear: come up with an approach that would produce flawless results for anyone, regardless of their candy-making experience. Ditching the tempered chocolate coating was one way we could abridge the process; we'd go for the more rustic approach of rolling the truffles in cocoa. Beyond that, we'd have to do some experimenting.

ADD BUTTER AND CORN SYRUP We threw together a basic ganache. Then we chilled the mixture, piped it into balls, firmed the pieces in the fridge, and rolled them in cocoa. What we wanted was fudgy, silky ganache. What we got, unfortunately, was dry and gritty. We needed a way to loosen up and smooth out the texture of the ganache without pushing it into the realm of chocolate sauce, so we tried an obvious quick fix: upping the cream. This made for a ganache that was creamier, but rolling the more-fluid mixture was nearly impossible. Paging through research recipes for ideas, we noticed that some called for adding butter to the ganache to make it more silky. Others also incorporated a little corn syrup, which makes the ganache feel smoother by reducing the size of the chocolate's sugar crystals; when they're too large, they can be detected as grainy. Adding a little of each helped, but even then the truffles weren't as satiny-textured as we wanted.

CLEAR THE AIR We'd taken the ingredient list as far as it could go, so we approached the graininess problem from another angle: the mixing method. The food processor, immersion blender, and stand mixer all produced truffles that weren't as smooth as we'd hoped. Mechanical intervention was not the way to go. The real problem? Air. Instead of smoothing out the ganache, the high-speed mixing was incorporating too much air, causing the emulsion to break. More specifically, the droplets of fat were coating the surface of the air bubbles instead of the cocoa particles; as a result, the cocoa particles absorbed water

and stuck together in larger clumps that we were detecting as graininess. That meant we needed to do everything we could to decrease the air in the ganache. We tried hand-whisking the chocolate and warm cream, but the method still required a good bit of stirring just to melt the chocolate. We were better off premelting the chocolate in the microwave until it was almost completely fluid. Then we stirred the corn syrup (plus vanilla extract and salt) into the cream and poured the liquid over the mostly melted chocolate. Instead of a whisk—specifically designed to incorporate air—we grabbed a wooden spoon, gradually working in the butter before piping and chilling the ganache. The improvement was startling. The grit wasn't gone, but it was markedly reduced.

COOL IT DOWN It was time to try a technique that we'd come across in our research: Instead of chilling the ganache immediately after mixing it, some chocolatiers allow it to sit at room temperature overnight, claiming that the gradual cooling makes for a creamier product. It was worth a shot. We mixed up another batch of ganache and

---

PRACTICAL SCIENCE
DUTCHED VS. NATURAL COCOA POWDER

> Both natural and Dutched cocoa will work in recipes; use whichever fits your preferences.

In the world of cocoa powder, there are two main categories: Dutched and natural. The natural product is made mainly of unsweetened cocoa solids that have had much of their fat removed and are then dried and ground to a powder. Dutching refers to the step of adding an alkali to neutralize the powder's acidity and to mellow its astringent notes (it also darkens the color).

While some recipes don't specify whether you should use Dutched or natural cocoa, others do and then go on to strongly caution against swapping one for the other. We wondered how interchangeable natural and Dutched cocoa are, so we tested a half-dozen recipes, including hot chocolate and chocolate crinkle cookies, side by side, using both types of cocoa in each recipe.

The biggest finding was that none of the recipes, even those with a high proportion of cocoa powder—and thus with the potential to be the most strongly affected—failed. But that didn't mean there weren't differences in appearance, texture, and flavor. Not surprisingly, Dutch-processed cocoa always produced cakes, cookies, and hot cocoa with a darker color than the versions made with natural cocoa. In terms of texture, natural cocoa produced slightly drier baked goods as well as cookies with less spread than did Dutch-processed. Finally, we found that baked goods and hot chocolate made with Dutch-processed cocoa displayed more of the fruity, bitter notes of dark chocolate, while natural cocoa delivered a more straightforward chocolate flavor.

---

let it cool on the counter for 8 hours before shaping the truffles. The change was astonishing—the texture of the ganache was silky-smooth, without a trace of grittiness. Why? When melted chocolate cools and resolidifies, the crystalline structure of its cocoa butter is reorganized. Chilling the ganache in the refrigerator produces a more stable crystalline structure that melts at higher than body temperature, leading to a perception of graininess. A slower cool-down leads to a different, more desirable set of crystals that literally melt in the mouth, for a sensation of ultrasmoothness. But did we really have to leave the ganache overnight? We wondered if we could get this same effect with a shorter rest at room temperature, to keep truffle making a same-day project. We found that a 2-hour cooldown produced the same marvelously creamy texture. The only issue was that without any refrigeration, the ganache was too soft to work with. We solved this by chilling the ganache for 2 hours after cooling it on the counter—a step that didn't add back any graininess.

CHOCOLATE TRUFFLES
MAKES 64 TRUFFLES

In step 5, running your knife under hot water and wiping it dry makes cutting the ganache easier. We recommend using Callebaut Intense Dark L-60–40NV or Ghirardelli Bittersweet Chocolate Baking Bar. If giving the truffles as a gift, set them in 1½-inch candy cup liners in a gift box and keep chilled.

GANACHE

2   cups (12 ounces) bittersweet chocolate, chopped coarse
½   cup heavy cream
2   tablespoons light corn syrup
½   teaspoon vanilla extract
    Pinch salt
1½   tablespoons unsalted butter, cut into 8 pieces and softened

COATING

1   cup (3 ounces) Dutch-processed cocoa
¼   cup (1 ounce) confectioners' sugar

1. FOR THE GANACHE: Lightly coat 8-inch baking dish with nonstick pan spray. Make parchment sling by folding 2 long sheets of parchment so that they are as wide as baking pan. Lay sheets of parchment in pan perpendicular to one another, with extra hanging over edges of pan. Push parchment into corners and up sides of pan, smoothing flush to pan.

2. Microwave chocolate in medium bowl at 50 percent power, stirring occasionally, until mostly melted and few small chocolate pieces remain, 2 to 3 minutes; set aside. Microwave cream in measuring cup until warm to touch, about 30 seconds. Stir corn syrup, vanilla, and salt into cream and pour mixture over chocolate. Cover bowl with plastic wrap, set aside for 3 minutes, then stir with wooden spoon to combine. Stir butter in, 1 piece at a time, until fully incorporated.

3. Using rubber spatula, transfer ganache to prepared pan and set aside at room temperature for 2 hours. Cover pan and transfer to refrigerator; chill for at least 2 hours. (Ganache can be stored, refrigerated, for up to 2 days.)

4. FOR THE COATING: Sift cocoa and sugar through fine-mesh strainer into large bowl. Sift again into large cake pan and set aside.

5. Gripping overhanging parchment, lift ganache from pan. Cut ganache into sixty-four 1-inch squares (8 rows by 8 rows). (If ganache cracks during slicing, let it sit at room temperature for 5 to 10 minutes and then proceed.) Dust your hands lightly with cocoa mixture to prevent ganache from sticking and roll each square into ball. Transfer balls to cake pan with cocoa mixture and roll to evenly coat. Lightly shake truffles in your hand over pan to remove excess coating. Transfer coated truffles to airtight container and repeat until all ganache squares are rolled and coated. Cover container and refrigerate for at least 2 hours or up to 1 week. Let truffles sit at room temperature for 5 to 10 minutes before serving.

HAZELNUT-MOCHA TRUFFLES

Substitute 2 tablespoons Frangelico (hazelnut-flavored liqueur) and 1 tablespoon espresso powder for vanilla. For coating, omit confectioners' sugar and use enough cocoa to coat you hands while shaping truffles. Roll shaped truffles in 1½ cups hazelnuts, toasted, skinned, and chopped fine.

Florentine Lace Cookies

✔ WHY THIS RECIPE WORKS

These wafer-thin almond cookies have a reputation for being fussy and unpredictable, but we ensured success by making just a few tweaks. Instead of temping the hot sugar mixture that forms the base of the dough, we removed it from the heat when it thickened and began to brown. We substituted orange marmalade for the usual candied orange peel and corn syrup combo, producing a more complex citrus flavor. These cookies are baked much darker than most cookies, which enhances their delicate crispiness, and a flourish of carefully melted chocolate completes the professional pastry shop effect.

MAKE THE CARAMEL Following a typical method, we melted butter with cream and sugar in a saucepan and cooked the mixture for 6 to 8 minutes, until it reached 238 degrees. We admit that we weren't keen on breaking out a thermometer for cookie making, so as the caramel mixture cooked, we kept our eyes out for visual indicators that might allow us to leave the device in its drawer. Happily, we noticed that the mixture turned a distinctive creamy beige color and started to catch on the bottom of the pan just as the temperature approached 238 degrees—exactly the kind of cue we had been hoping for. (No need for that thermometer after all.)

MAKE THE DOUGH Once the caramel was off the heat, we stirred in ground almonds, marmalade, flour, vanilla, orange zest, and salt. Why marmalade? Its concentrated flavor gave our Florentines the bright, citrusy, and faintly bitter taste that we wanted, and the jam provided a contrast to the rich, sweet caramel base.

PRACTICAL SCIENCE COCOA POWDER AND UNSWEETENED CHOCOLATE

You can substitute one for the other.

Cocoa powder is unsweetened chocolate from which 76 to 90 percent of the cocoa butter has been removed. It is generally called for when a big hit of chocolate flavor is desired without any additional fat, usually in recipes that already contain a lot of butter, such as cakes and cookies. Some cocoas are packaged with instructions indicating that 3 tablespoons of cocoa powder combined with 1 tablespoon of vegetable oil can be substituted for 1 ounce of unsweetened chocolate. To find out if this substitution works, we prepared batches of brownies made with the 6 ounces of unsweetened chocolate called for in the recipe and with the cocoa and oil substitution. To our surprise, tasters found no textural differences between the two batches.

"TEMPER" THE CHOCOLATE The classic Florentine has a thin, smooth coat of bittersweet chocolate on its underside, an elegant effect achieved by dipping the entire bottom surface of each cookie into a large container of melted chocolate. This approach presents two problems for the home cook: First, you wind up with loads of left-over chocolate; second, to ensure that the chocolate retains an attractive sheen, you have to either temper it (a painstaking process of melting and cooling the chocolate to ensure that it stays within the optimal temperature range) or get your hands on special coating chocolate, which contains a small amount of a highly saturated vegetable fat that extends the temperature range at which the chocolate can safely melt. We needed to come up with an easier, more practical alternative. After some trial and error, we devised a great faux-tempering method that involved melting part of the chocolate at 50 percent power in the microwave and then stirring in the remainder—a very gentle approach that kept the chocolate glossy when it resolidified (see Test Kitchen Experiment, page 398).

FLORENTINE LACE COOKIES
MAKES 24 COOKIES

It's important to cook the cream mixture in the saucepan until it is thick and starting to brown at the edges; undercooking will result in a dough that is too runny to portion. Do not be concerned if some butter separates from the dough while you're portioning the cookies. For the most uniform cookies, use the flattest baking sheets you have and make sure that your parchment paper lies flat. When melting the chocolate, pause the microwave and stir the chocolate often to ensure that it doesn't get much warmer than body temperature.

- 2 cups slivered almonds
- ¾ cup heavy cream
- ½ cup (3½ ounces) sugar
- 4 tablespoons unsalted butter, cut into 4 pieces
- ¼ cup orange marmalade
- 3 tablespoons all-purpose flour
- 1 teaspoon vanilla extract
- ¼ teaspoon grated orange zest
- ¼ teaspoon salt
- 4 ounces bittersweet chocolate, chopped fine

1. Adjust oven racks to upper-middle and lower-middle positions and heat oven to 350 degrees. Line 2 baking sheets with parchment paper. Process almonds in food processor until they resemble coarse sand, about 30 seconds.

2. Bring cream, sugar, and butter to boil in medium saucepan over medium-high heat. Cook, stirring frequently, until mixture begins to thicken, 5 to 6 minutes. Continue to cook, stirring constantly, until mixture begins to brown at edges and is thick enough to leave trail that doesn't immediately fill in when spatula is scraped along pan bottom, 1 to 2 minutes longer (it's OK if some darker speckles appear in mixture). Remove pan from heat and stir in almonds, marmalade, flour, vanilla, orange zest, and salt until combined.

3. Drop 6 level tablespoons dough at least 3½ inches apart on each prepared sheet. When cool enough to handle, use your damp fingers to press each portion into 2½-inch circle.

4. Bake until deep brown from edge to edge, 15 to 17 minutes, switching and rotating sheets halfway through baking. Transfer cookies, still on parchment, to wire racks and let cool. Let baking sheets cool for 10 minutes, line with fresh parchment, and repeat portioning and baking remaining dough.

PRACTICAL SCIENCE CHOCOLATE AND BLOOM

Temperature has everything to do with the unappealing white "bloom" on chocolate.

Chocolate requires careful storage to maintain its quality. It should be stored protected from light in a cool, relatively dry location. These conditions are important for maintaining the beta crystal structure of the chocolate fat. Improperly stored chocolate can form a "fat bloom," which looks like large white spots, and often happens when stored above 85 degrees. At these warm temperatures, the cocoa butter begins to melt and congeal into areas of concentrated cocoa butter. This happens most frequently with chocolate that has not been properly tempered to form beta crystals. Another form of bloom is called "sugar bloom," which appears as a grayish matte surface. Sugar bloom is caused by storing chocolate in moist conditions. The moist atmosphere causes tiny sugar particles on the surface of the chocolate to dissolve and then crystallize into larger sugar crystals that become more and more noticeable. Neither of these conditions make the chocolate unsafe to eat or significantly change its flavor, but they do alter the appearance and melting properties.

For bloom-free storage, milk and white chocolate will last six months, and darker chocolate will last as long as a year, when wrapped tightly in plastic wrap and stored at room temperature in a cool pantry.

---

5. Microwave 3 ounces chocolate in bowl at 50 percent power, stirring frequently, until about two-thirds melted, 1 to 2 minutes. Remove bowl from microwave, add remaining 1 ounce chocolate, and stir until melted, returning to microwave for no more than 5 seconds at a time to complete melting if necessary. Transfer chocolate to small zipper-lock bag and snip off corner, making hole no larger than ¹⁄₁₆ inch.

6. Transfer cooled cookies directly to wire racks. Pipe zigzag of chocolate over each cookie, distributing chocolate evenly among all cookies. Refrigerate until chocolate is set, about 30 minutes, before serving. (Cookies can be stored at cool room temperature for up to 4 days.)

Fudgy Triple-Chocolate Brownies

✓ WHY THIS RECIPE WORKS

We wanted a brownie that was distinctly fudgy—a moist, dark, luscious brownie with a firm, smooth, velvety texture. It had to pack an intense chocolate punch and have deep, resonant chocolate flavor.

USE THREE KINDS OF CHOCOLATE To develop a rich, deep chocolate flavor, we found it necessary to give our brownies a triple whammy of chocolate. Unsweetened chocolate laid a solid, intense foundation; bittersweet chocolate provided a mellow, even somewhat sweet flavor; and cocoa powder added further complexity.

BUILD A CHEWY TEXTURE Flour, a generous three eggs, and a full stick of butter made for a chewy, rich brownie base. We melted the butter instead of creaming it with the sugar and eggs; the melted butter produced a more dense and fudgy texture.

CUT SMALL We found it best to cut these dense, rich brownies into petite 1-inch squares.

FUDGY TRIPLE-CHOCOLATE BROWNIES
MAKES 64 SMALL BROWNIES

To melt the chocolates in a microwave, heat them at 50 percent power for 2 minutes. Stir the chocolate, add the butter, and continue heating until melted, stirring once every additional minute. Either Dutch-processed or natural cocoa powder works well in this recipe.

5	ounces bittersweet chocolate, chopped
2	ounces unsweetened chocolate, chopped
8	tablespoons unsalted butter, cut into 4 pieces
3	tablespoons unsweetened cocoa powder
1¼	cups (8¾ ounces) sugar
3	large eggs
2	teaspoons vanilla extract
½	teaspoon salt
1	cup (5 ounces) all-purpose flour

1. Adjust oven rack to lower-middle position and heat oven to 350 degrees. Make foil sling for 8-inch square baking pan by folding 2 long sheets of aluminum foil so each is 8 inches wide. Lay sheets of foil in pan perpendicular to one another, with extra foil hanging over edges of pan. Push foil into corners and up sides of pan, smoothing foil flush to pan. Grease foil and set pan aside.

2. Melt bittersweet chocolate, unsweetened chocolate, and butter in medium heatproof bowl set over saucepan filled with 1 inch barely simmering water, making sure that water does not touch bottom of bowl and stirring occasionally until smooth. Whisk in cocoa until smooth. Set aside to cool slightly.

3. Whisk sugar, eggs, vanilla, and salt in medium bowl until combined, about 15 seconds. Whisk warm chocolate mixture into egg mixture. Using rubber spatula, stir in flour until just combined. Transfer batter to prepared pan; spread batter into corners of pan and smooth surface. Bake until slightly puffed and toothpick inserted in center of brownies comes out with few moist crumbs attached, 35 to 40 minutes, rotating pan halfway through baking. Let brownies cool in pan on wire rack to room temperature, about 2 hours. Remove brownies from pan using foil, loosening sides with paring knife, if needed. Cut brownies into 1-inch squares and serve. (Do not cut brownies until ready to serve. Brownies can be wrapped in plastic wrap and refrigerated for up to 3 days.)

PRACTICAL SCIENCE MAGIC SHELL

Coconut oil makes homemade magic shells possible.

Chocolate sauce that instantly hardens into a shell when poured over ice cream is a classic treat, but could we engineer a better-tasting homemade version? Yes.

When we sampled Smucker's Magic Shell over ice cream, we were impressed by the way it hardened upon contact but were less bowled over by its cloyingly sweet, mild chocolate taste. We set out to engineer a better-tasting homemade version that would please children and adults alike.

A quick review of the Magic Shell ingredients revealed that the "magic" was the third ingredient listed: coconut oil. Coconut oil is extremely high in saturated fat, which makes it solid at room temperature and brittle at cooler temperatures. Combining melted coconut oil in a 2:3 ratio with melted chocolate produced a satiny mixture that solidified into a perfect, shatteringly thin shell over ice cream. To make your own: Microwave 4 tablespoons of refined coconut oil, 3 ounces of chopped bittersweet chocolate, and a pinch of salt at 50 percent power until smooth (2 to 4 minutes), stirring occasionally. Let cool to room temperature and spoon or pour over ice cream.

CHAPTER 50

Almonds

These versatile drupes can make everything from cake to soup to pizza dough.

HOW THE SCIENCE WORKS

Like a mini version of the coconut (page 285), almonds are not true nuts, but are drupes, or seeds surrounded by a shell, protected by an outer hull. Almonds come from the deciduous tree *Prunus amygdalus*, which grows best in a warm climate and is native to the Middle East and south Asia.

The almond tree is one of the earliest domesticated trees, first appearing in the early Bronze Age, about 4,000 to 5,000 years ago. The word almond comes from the early French word *almande*. The original wild variety of almond produces a bitter, toxic compound called amygdalin, which breaks down to hydrogen cyanide and fragrant benzaldehyde, the dominant component of almond extract. The more recent sweet variety, named *Prunus dulcis*, produces virtually no amygdalin, which is why it's the variety we eat.

Almonds consist of four parts: the outer hull, inner shell, seed coat or skin, and embryo, which is the kernel that we actually eat, usually with the brown skin attached. California is by far the world's largest producer of almonds, supplying 80 percent of the world's sweet almond crop.

The almond trees were first brought to California from Spain in the mid-1700s. By the early 1900s, almonds had become a major agricultural crop. The trees are dormant in the early winter, and in February and March produce blossoms, which are pollinated by (a huge number of) bees. The almonds mature in the spring; in the summer the hulls split open to expose the shells, which dry on the trees. Then the almonds are harvested, and allowed to dry. Following drying the almonds are processed with a roller machine that removes the hull and shell and then sorts the remaining skin-on kernels by size. From there they go into controlled storage. California grows more than 30 different varieties of almonds.

> ## Almond trees are pollinated by (a huge number of) bees.

Sweet almonds have earned the American Heart Association certified seal as a heart-healthy food. With skin attached, almonds contain approximately 22 percent by weight carbohydrates, of which 12 percent functions as dietary fiber, along with 21 percent protein, and about 50 percent fat. The fat is 10 percent saturated, 64 percent monounsaturated, and 26 percent polyunsaturated fatty acids. Dried almonds contain less than 6 percent moisture.

In 2007, with the urging of the Almond Board of California, the state of California required that all almonds must be pasteurized for safety following several incidents of contamination with Salmonella bacteria. Pasteurization is now the law in the United States, Canada, and Mexico, but not other countries where almonds are grown.

Almonds are available in forms including natural (shell removed with skin-on or without skin), sliced or slivered, roasted, and shell-on. They can be turned into a "milk," or ground to make almond butter or to produce almond flour.

Here, we grind almonds in a blender to give body to our cold White Gazpacho (page 410), and add just a drop of almond extract for the floral profile of bitter almonds. The addition of almond flour is key in our gluten-free pizza dough (page 411), giving the dough a bit of fat to aid in crispness and flavor development. Our Best Almond Cake (page 413) uses blanched almonds, ground up, for optimal almond flavor and a lighter texture than those cakes made with almond paste. Ground almonds likewise help with the texture of our Almond Biscotti (page 414), breaking up the strands of gluten to create cookies that are still dunkable in coffee or *vin santo*, but are in no danger of hurting your dental work. Finally, you can make your own Almond Milk (page 416)—it's simpler than you think.

TEST KITCHEN EXPERIMENT

Over the past few years almond milk has overtaken soy milk as the most popular dairy-free milk beverage in the United States. Part of the reason for this ascent is the almond's perceived health benefits. Almonds are high in protein, and their fat is composed mainly of monounsaturated and polyunsaturated fatty acids. But looking at the back of a carton of store-bought almond milk reveals that little of any of that actually makes it into the milk, while a host of thickeners and emulsifiers inevitably do. We were curious how homemade almond milk would stack up to store-bought, so we ran the following experiment.

EXPERIMENT

Over the course of a few weeks and over 30 tests, we settled on our ideal recipe for homemade almond milk. We combined and refrigerated 1 cup of skin-on almonds and 3 cups of water for at least 4 hours and up to 48 hours. We then blended the almonds and water on high speed for 2 minutes. Finally, we strained the mixture through three layers of cheesecloth or a clean dish towel (gathering the sides and squeezing gently to improve yield), reserving the milk and discarding the solids.

To compare our homemade almond milk to store-bought we did side-by-side taste tests plain, baked into white cake, and cooked into a custard. (We used Blue Diamond Almond Breeze and Silk Almond Milk brands for the store-bought tests.) We also sent samples of each to an independent lab to test for protein and fat content.

RESULTS

In side-by-side tastings, our homemade almond milk was preferred both plain and when cooked into custard, where it produced a rich, creamy product. The homemade version was much creamier, with a clean, round, nutty flavor. It didn't fare as well in white cake, where it created a dense, moist crumb, compared to the light, fluffy interior of the cake made with store-bought almond milk. The lab tests revealed some stark differences that helped explain these results. The average store-bought almond milk weighs in at 1.25 percent fat and 0.42 percent protein, while our recipe averaged 7.5 percent fat and 3.9 percent protein. Store-bought almond milk contains numerous thickeners and emulsifiers like guar gum, locust bean gum, and lecithin that provide the body and texture that higher fat and protein would provide.

It helps to compare these products to traditional dairy. Store-bought almond milk is comparable to 1% low-fat milk (though far lower in protein) while our recipe sits between whole milk and half-and-half in terms of fat (but is higher in protein than either). Our recipe's higher fat content was a boon for creating a supple, smooth custard, but was overkill in the already butter-rich cake. Going forward we'll look to homemade almond milk for protein-rich smoothies and recipes where a higher-fat dairy alternative is best.

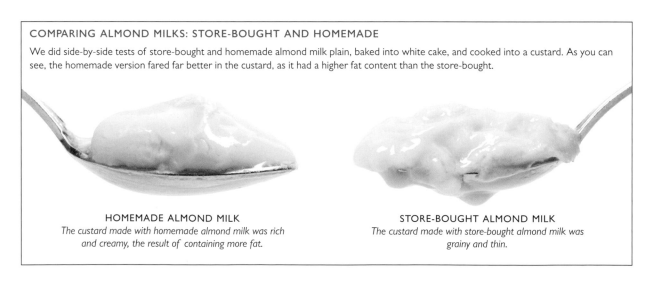

COMPARING ALMOND MILKS: STORE-BOUGHT AND HOMEMADE

We did side-by-side tests of store-bought and homemade almond milk plain, baked into white cake, and cooked into a custard. As you can see, the homemade version fared far better in the custard, as it had a higher fat content than the store-bought.

HOMEMADE ALMOND MILK
The custard made with homemade almond milk was rich and creamy, the result of containing more fat.

STORE-BOUGHT ALMOND MILK
The custard made with store-bought almond milk was grainy and thin.

FAMILY TREE: ALMOND PRODUCTS

Almonds are drupes, or seeds surrounded by a shell, like coconuts. We use almonds in many different forms. We eat them straight, toasted in their skins. We grind them into flour or meal or paste. We turn them into milk and into butter. The flavor of almond extract comes from the kernel of drupes.

ALMOND FLOUR

Almond flour is composed of ground-up almonds. If the almonds are blanched to remove their skins before grinding, the resulting coarse powder may be called almond flour. Almond meal is the same but may be made from nuts with or without their skins. Almond flour contains less starch and more fat than wheat flour, and it lacks the proteins glutenin and gliadin, which produce gluten, the stretchy network of proteins responsible for the structure that helps batters and doughs made with wheat flour hold air and stay together. But it does contain a lot of protein, which is why we like it in gluten-free baking.

ALMOND PASTE

This is a confection made with almond meal and sugar or honey, often used in baking.

ALMOND MILK

Almond milk is made by first soaking raw almonds in water to soften the nuts (anywhere from 4 to 48 hours). The nuts are then pulverized with the water they were soaked in to make a paste. The mixture is strained to remove any unground almond bits. Some commercial almond milks add sweeteners like evaporated cane juice to balance flavor, plus stabilizers and thickeners to adjust the texture and help keep the particles and proteins in suspension for a smoother and more homogenized liquid.

ALMOND EXTRACT

Pure almond extract is made from three primary ingredients: alcohol, water, and bitter almond oil. The last is extracted from almonds or (more frequently) from some of their drupe kin, which include peaches and apricots. The almond flavor comes from benzaldehyde, a substance in the kernels of drupes.

ALMOND BUTTER

A popular "alternative" nut butter, almond butter is made from ground-up almonds. We don't recommend substituting almond butter for peanut butter in baking applications. It turns out that almonds contain not only slightly more fat than peanuts and cashews (which share a similar fat percentage) but also a much higher proportion of unsaturated fat. Because unsaturated fat has a lower melting point than the saturated kind, cookies made with almond butter are more fluid, allowing the batter to spread before their structure is set.

White Gazpacho

✓ WHY THIS RECIPE WORKS

Our first introduction to Spanish white gazpacho, or ajo blanco, was a revelation. The silky soup arrived ice-cold in a small bowl, decorated with a delicate mosaic of almonds, sliced grapes, and vibrantly green olive oil. Its flavors were as intricate as its appearance: Some bites offered a nutty crunch, while others were sharply fruity and floral; in still others, peppery extra-virgin olive oil was at the fore. When we learned that the complexity had been coaxed from just a handful of ingredients, we were intrigued. A little research taught us that white gazpacho predates the familiar red version since tomatoes didn't reach Spain until after Columbus. The rock-bottom cheap ajo blanco was prepared by peasants with five ingredients at their disposal: stale bread, garlic, vinegar, oil, and salt. They pounded the bread and garlic with a mortar and pestle, added slugs of vinegar and oil with salt to taste, and either ate the gazpacho in that form or stirred in water to make it drinkable. When the dish migrated from the tables of laborers to those of aristocrats, upscale ingredients like almonds and grapes (or even fish or pickled vegetables) went into the mix, transforming a humble mush into a dish meant to impress.

USE A BLENDER   Although traditionalists rely on a mortar and pestle (and elbow grease), we planned on putting a kitchen appliance to work. We pulled out a blender and a food processor and loaded each with placeholder amounts of bread, almonds, garlic, vinegar, and water. We pureed the ingredients and then streamed oil into each machine. When we strained the soups, we could plainly see that the blender had done the better job of breaking down the solids, but the soup was still marred by tiny almond bits. We recalled that the recipes employing a mortar and pestle proceeded in a specific manner. First, the bread was soaked in water to facilitate grinding. Meanwhile, the almonds were finely crushed. The almonds and bread were then mixed into a paste and only then was liquid incorporated. We mimicked the process in a blender: We buzzed the almonds until they were powdery and then added the soaked bread, garlic, a splash of vinegar, and salt and pepper. Once these ingredients were pureed, we drizzled in the olive oil and finally thinned the soup with more water. This soup was thicker, creamier, and smoother than ever.

ADD ALMOND EXTRACT   Now that we had a foolproof procedure, we examined the ingredients. Stale bread never produced a soup that was significantly different from fresh, and plain old sandwich bread worked as well as (if not better than) fancy artisanal types. Sliced, blanched almonds were best since they didn't create brown flecks in the ivory soup. Brightened with sherry vinegar and a pinch of cayenne, our gazpacho was tasty, but we had yet to capture the fruity, floral flavors that had drawn us to this unique recipe in the first place. Switching from everyday extra-virgin olive oil to a premium brand added a fruity, peppery pop. We tried toasting the almonds but this darkened the soup and gave it a toasted flavor that was less than refreshing. Finally, we realized that the sharper, almost flowery profile of bitter almonds (found in almond extract) would be a better fit. We made another batch with just a drop of extract, and this hit the mark. However, even an extra drop of extract ruined the gazpacho. For foolproof measuring, we mixed ⅛ teaspoon of the extract into a tablespoon of soup and then stirred 1 teaspoon of the extract mixture into the soup.

SPANISH CHILLED ALMOND AND GARLIC SOUP (WHITE GAZPACHO)
SERVES 6 TO 8

This rich soup is best when served in small portions (about 6 ounces). Use a good-quality extra-virgin olive oil. Our favorite is Columela Extra Virgin Olive Oil. Too much almond extract can ruin the soup, hence the unusual mixing technique in step 4.

- 6   slices hearty white sandwich bread, crusts removed
- 4   cups water
- 2½   cups (8¾ ounces) plus ⅓ cup sliced blanched almonds
- 1   garlic clove, peeled
- 3   tablespoons sherry vinegar
  Kosher salt and pepper
  Pinch cayenne pepper
- ½   cup extra-virgin olive oil, plus extra for drizzling
- ⅛   teaspoon almond extract
- 2   teaspoons vegetable oil
- 6   ounces seedless green grapes, sliced thin (1 cup)

1. Combine bread and water in bowl and let soak for 5 minutes. Process 2½ cups almonds in blender until finely ground, about 30 seconds, scraping down sides of blender jar as needed.

2. Using your hands, remove bread from water, squeeze it lightly, and transfer to blender with almonds. Measure 3 cups soaking water and set aside; transfer remaining soaking water to blender.

3. Add garlic, vinegar, 1¼ teaspoons salt, and cayenne to blender and process until mixture has consistency of cake batter, 30 to 45 seconds. With blender running, add olive oil in thin, steady stream, about 30 seconds. Add reserved soaking water and process for 1 minute. Season with salt and pepper to taste. Strain soup through fine-mesh strainer set in bowl, pressing on solids to extract liquid. Discard solids.

4. Measure 1 tablespoon of soup into second bowl and stir in almond extract. Return 1 teaspoon of extract mixture to soup; discard remainder. Chill for at least 3 hours or up to 24 hours.

5. Heat vegetable oil in 8-inch skillet over medium-high heat until oil begins to shimmer. Add remaining ⅓ cup almonds and cook, stirring constantly, until golden brown, 3 to 4 minutes. Immediately transfer to bowl and stir in ¼ teaspoon salt.

6. Ladle soup into shallow bowls. Mound an equal amount of grapes in center of each bowl. Sprinkle cooled almonds over soup and drizzle with extra olive oil. Serve immediately.

The Best Gluten-Free Pizza

✔ WHY THIS RECIPE WORKS

Achieving a crispy crust and a tender interior on a gluten-free pizza is no easy feat. We've always embraced gluten as the magic ingredient in bread. It's the source of its structure and, as a result, much of its texture. So this was the bread baker's ultimate challenge: Develop a gluten-free pizza crust that everyone would want to eat, whether they were avoiding gluten or not.

MAKE A FLOUR BLEND   The first thing we needed was a substitute for the wheat flour. This isn't an easy swap since there isn't a single wheat-free flour that can supply the same characteristics as wheat flour's makeup of protein, starch, and fat. After much experimentation, we developed a gluten-free flour blend that mimicked many of the properties of wheat flour: white rice flour for starch, brown rice flour for wheaty flavor, potato starch for tenderness, tapioca starch for spring and stretch, and milk powder for browning and structure.

USE PSYLLIUM HUSK   We experimented with adding xanthan gum (made by fermenting simple sugars using the microorganism *Xanthomonas campestris*) and guar gum (produced by grinding the endosperm of Indian guar plant seeds) to help with the structural development of the pizza. The gluten-free flour blend's protein network is weak in comparison with the gluten network of wheat flour, and xanthan gum and guar gum behave like glue in many gluten-free baked goods, strengthening the weak network and improving elasticity. But neither worked. The dough didn't rise. And then we tried a small amount of ground psyllium husk. The psyllium husk was a definite improvement. One and a half tablespoons delivered a dough that rose visibly during proofing and a final crust that had a more open crumb. Why? Psyllium husk is far more effective at attracting and holding on to water molecules than the other gums are, which allows it to create a thick gel. This gel, combined with psyllium husk's soluble fiber and protein, was providing incredibly strong structural reinforcement for the dough's protein network, making it capable of trapping lots of gas during proofing as well as steam during baking.

AND HIGH HYDRATION   To create a tender, airy, open crumb, we first added a bit of baking powder. And then we significantly increased the water in the dough. The more water the dough contained the more it rose during proofing. As it happened, the dough seemed to benefit from the additional water far more than expected: The most tender crust and open crumb came when we'd added so much water that it went from being a dough to more of a thick batter. To deal with the excess water, we spread it out with a spatula, and then gently parbaked the crusts in order to drive off the excess moisture once it had served its purpose.

GROUND ALMONDS ARE KEY   Now that we had a pizza crust with a light and airy (but not gummy) interior, there was only one obstacle: The underside of the crust was more tough than crispy. No problem, we thought: Adding more oil to the dough would get it to fry up a bit. Alas, while this did help it crisp, it also left the pizza greasy. Gluten-free flours, we learned, don't absorb fats as readily as wheat flour does, and clearly we'd gone over the maximum. The solution turned out to be almond flour. Adding just 2½ ounces to the dough boosted the overall fat content and gave our crust the crispiness that it needed without causing any noticeable change in flavor. And because almonds (and nuts in general) don't shed all their oil when heated, the crust wasn't greasy.

THE BEST GLUTEN-FREE PIZZA
MAKES TWO 12-INCH PIZZAS

This recipe requires letting the dough rise for 1½ hours and pre-baking the crusts for about 45 minutes before topping and baking. If you don't have almond flour, you can process 2½ ounces of blanched almonds in a food processor until finely ground, about 30 seconds. Psyllium husk is available at health food stores. You can substitute 16 ounces (2⅔ cups plus ¼ cup) King Arthur Gluten-Free Multi-Purpose Flour or 16 ounces (2⅔ cups plus ½ cup) Bob's Red Mill GF All-Purpose Baking Flour for the America's Test Kitchen Gluten-Free Flour Blend. Note that pizza crust made with King Arthur will be slightly denser and not as chewy, and pizza crust made with Bob's Red Mill will be thicker and more airy and will have a distinct bean flavor.

CRUST

16	ounces (3⅓ cups plus ¼ cup) America's Test Kitchen Gluten-Free Flour Blend (recipe follows)
2½	ounces (½ cup plus 1 tablespoon) almond flour
1½	tablespoons powdered psyllium husk
2½	teaspoons baking powder
2	teaspoons salt
1	teaspoon instant or rapid-rise yeast
2½	cups warm water (100 degrees)
¼	cup vegetable oil
	Vegetable oil spray

SAUCE

1	(28-ounce) can whole peeled tomatoes, drained
1	tablespoon extra-virgin olive oil
1	teaspoon red wine vinegar
1	garlic clove, minced
1	teaspoon dried oregano
½	teaspoon salt
¼	teaspoon pepper
1	ounce Parmesan cheese, grated fine (½ cup)
8	ounces whole-milk mozzarella cheese, shredded (2 cups)

1. **FOR THE CRUST:** Using stand mixer fitted with paddle, mix flour blend, almond flour, psyllium, baking powder, salt, and yeast on low speed until combined. Slowly add warm water and oil in steady stream until incorporated. Increase speed to medium and beat until dough is sticky and uniform, about 6 minutes. (Dough will resemble thick batter.)

2. Remove bowl from mixer, cover with plastic wrap, and let stand until inside of dough is bubbly (use spoon to peer inside dough), about 1½ hours. (Dough will puff slightly but will not rise.)

3. Adjust oven racks to middle and lower positions. Line 2 rimmed baking sheets with parchment paper and spray liberally with oil spray. Transfer half of dough to center of 1 prepared sheet. Using oil-sprayed rubber spatula, spread dough into 8-inch circle. Spray top of dough with oil spray, cover with large sheet of plastic, and, using your hands, press out dough to 11½-inch round, about ¼ inch thick, leaving outer ¼ inch slightly thicker than center; discard plastic. Repeat with remaining dough and second prepared sheet.

4. Place prepared sheets in oven and heat oven to 325 degrees. Bake dough until firm to touch, golden brown on underside, and just beginning to brown on top, 45 to 50 minutes, switching and rotating sheets halfway through baking. Transfer crusts to wire rack and let cool.

5. **FOR THE SAUCE:** Process all ingredients in food processor until smooth, about 30 seconds. Transfer to bowl and refrigerate until ready to use.

6. One hour before baking pizza, adjust oven rack to upper-middle position, set baking stone on rack, and heat oven to 500 degrees.

7. Transfer 1 parbaked crust to pizza peel. Using back of spoon or ladle, spread ½ cup tomato sauce in thin layer over surface of crust, leaving ¼-inch border around edge. Sprinkle ¼ cup Parmesan evenly over sauce, followed by 1 cup mozzarella. Carefully slide crust onto stone and bake until crust is well browned and cheese is bubbly and beginning to brown, 10 to 12 minutes. Transfer pizza to wire rack and let cool for 5 minutes before slicing and serving. Repeat with second crust, ½ cup tomato sauce (you will have extra sauce), remaining ¼ cup Parmesan, and remaining 1 cup mozzarella.

TO MAKE AHEAD: Extra sauce can be refrigerated for up to 1 week or frozen for up to 1 month. Parbaked and cooled crusts can sit at room temperature for up to 4 hours. Completely cooled crusts can be wrapped with plastic wrap and then aluminum foil and frozen for up to 2 weeks. Frozen crusts can be topped and baked as directed without thawing.

GLUTEN-FREE FLOUR BLEND
MAKES 42 OUNCES (ABOUT 9⅓ CUPS)

Be sure to use potato starch, not potato flour, in this recipe. Tapioca starch is also sold as tapioca flour; they are interchangeable. We strongly recommend that you use Bob's Red Mill white and brown rice flours. We also recommend that you weigh your ingredients; if you measure by volume, spoon each ingredient into the measuring cup (do not pack or tap) and scrape off the excess.

24	ounces (4½ cups plus ⅓ cup)	white rice flour
7½	ounces (1⅔ cups)	brown rice flour
7	ounces (1⅓ cups)	potato starch
3	ounces (¾ cup)	tapioca starch
¾	ounce (¼ cup)	nonfat dry milk powder

Whisk all ingredients in large bowl until well combined. Transfer to airtight container and refrigerate for up to 3 months.

Best Almond Cake

✔ **WHY THIS RECIPE WORKS**

Almond cake is elegantly simple, consisting of a single layer so rich in flavor that it requires no frosting. That nearly every European country has a version of the cake—from Sweden's visiting cake to Italy's torta di mandorle *to Spain's* tarta de Santiago *(which harks back to the Middle Ages)—is a testament to its appeal. In addition to its great taste, a reason for the cake's popularity in Europe may be that it's almost impossible to screw up. Putting one together is a straightforward matter. First you cream almond paste or ground almonds with sugar and then butter. Eggs go into the bowl next, followed by a small amount of flour, a bit of salt, and perhaps some almond extract. The batter is poured into a prepared pan and baked, and the dessert is ready to eat as soon as it's cool. Since recipes for almond cake typically call for little flour and rarely include a leavening agent, the texture of the cake is usually quite dense—the opposite of a fluffy American yellow cake. And when almond paste is used instead of ground almonds, the cake becomes even more solid, bearing a particularly smooth, almost fudge-like consistency. While this is exactly what European cooks intend, we've always found this style a bit too heavy to nibble with tea or to enjoy after a rich dinner. We didn't want an ultra-fluffy crumb, but we did want a dessert that was more cake than confection—without sacrificing the trademark rich almond flavor and simplicity of the original.*

USE BLANCHED ALMONDS Our first decision was to nix the almond paste. Store-bought almond paste is usually made up of a 1:1 ratio of ground almonds to sugar, along with a binding agent, such as glucose syrup. But its high sugar content is at least partially responsible for the candy-like texture that we wanted to eliminate. That said, commercial almond paste does have one thing going for it: great nutty flavor. Could we replace the almond paste without losing that? We tried store-bought almond flour and toasted whole almonds ground in a food processor. Neither were ideal (bland and unsightly, respectively). But when we switched to blanched almonds, ground up, we were in business. This cake had the concentrated almond flavor of an almond-paste cake, and though it was still rather dense, the cake was now dotted with tiny nut particles that at least broke up the crumb a little.

USE THE PROCESSOR The goal when mixing most cake batters is to incorporate a lot of air into the eggs so that the cake will bake up light and tall, and a mixer is usually the best tool to get the job done. Here, however, we wanted a flat, level top; just a moderate rise; and a texture that was neither too fluffy nor too dense. Ditching the mixer in favor of a food processor did the trick. Here's why: When eggs and sugar are whipped in a mixer, the whisk gently unfolds the protein strands in the eggs while incorporating lots of air, producing a foam with a strong network that holds on to that air. The outcome? A tall, well-risen, domed cake. A food processor, with its high rpm and very sharp blade, similarly unravels the eggs' protein strands and incorporates air, but it also damages some strands along the way. The result is just what we were after: a flatter, slightly denser cake.

TOP WELL Finally, we wanted to create a crunchy, flavorful topping with a hint of citrus to play off of the great almond flavor. In keeping with the nearly effortless adornment of traditional almond cakes (usually just a dusting of confectioners' sugar), we decided on a sprinkling of sliced almonds and lemon-infused granulated sugar. To echo the lemony flavor of our topping, we also added some lemon zest to the cake batter itself. These easy additions produced a delicate crunch and a pop of citrus flavor. And for those who really want to dress up the dessert, we also developed an orange-spiked crème fraîche.

BEST ALMOND CAKE
SERVES 8 TO 10

If you can't find sliced blanched almonds, grind slivered almonds for the batter and use sliced unblanched almonds for the topping. Serve plain or with Orange Crème Fraîche.

1½	cups plus ⅓ cup sliced blanched almonds, toasted
¾	cup (3¾ ounces) all-purpose flour
¾	teaspoon salt
¼	teaspoon baking powder
⅛	teaspoon baking soda
4	large eggs
1¼	cups (8¾ ounces) plus 2 tablespoons sugar
1	tablespoon plus ½ teaspoon grated lemon zest (2 lemons)
¾	teaspoon almond extract
5	tablespoons unsalted butter, melted
⅓	cup vegetable oil

1. Adjust oven rack to middle position and heat oven to 300 degrees. Grease 9-inch round cake pan and line with parchment paper. Pulse 1½ cups almonds, flour, salt, baking powder, and baking soda in food processor until almonds are finely ground, 5 to 10 pulses. Transfer almond mixture to bowl.

2. Process eggs, 1¼ cups sugar, 1 tablespoon lemon zest, and almond extract in now-empty processor until very pale yellow, about 2 minutes. With processor running, add melted butter and oil in steady stream, until incorporated. Add almond mixture and pulse to combine, 4 to 5 pulses. Transfer batter to prepared pan.

3. Using your fingers, combine remaining 2 tablespoons sugar and remaining ½ teaspoon lemon zest in small bowl until fragrant, 5 to 10 seconds. Sprinkle top of cake evenly with remaining ⅓ cup almonds followed by sugar-zest mixture.

4. Bake until center of cake is set and bounces back when gently pressed and toothpick inserted in center comes out clean, 55 minutes to 1 hour 5 minutes, rotating pan after 40 minutes. Let cake cool in pan on wire rack for 15 minutes. Run paring knife around sides of pan. Invert cake onto greased wire rack, discard parchment, and reinvert cake onto second wire rack. Let cake cool, about 2 hours. Cut into wedges and serve. (Store cake in plastic wrap at room temperature for up to 3 days.)

ORANGE CRÈME FRAÎCHE
MAKES ABOUT 2 CUPS

2	oranges
1	cup crème fraîche
2	tablespoons sugar
⅛	teaspoon salt

Remove 1 teaspoon zest from 1 orange. Cut away peel and pith from oranges. Slice between membranes to release segments and cut segments into ¼-inch pieces. Combine orange pieces and zest, crème fraîche, sugar, and salt in bowl and mix well. Refrigerate for 1 hour.

Almond Biscotti

✓ WHY THIS RECIPE WORKS

Biscotti literally means "twice cooked." These classic Italian cookies are baked once as a single, oblong loaf. The loaf is then sliced into thin planks, which are returned to the oven to fully dry. The result: crunchy, nutty (almond is a popular flavor), finger-shaped cookies that are perfect alongside a cup of coffee—or, as in Italy, a glass of sweet vin santo. What separates one style from another mostly boils down to texture—specifically, just how crunchy or soft the cookies are. The most traditional biscotti, known as cantuccini, or biscotti di Prato, are extremely hard; they are meant to be dunked into a liquid to soften them before taking a bite (that's where the vin santo comes in). Then there are American biscotti—the big, buttery, much softer kind sold in coffeehouse chains, which are more like sugar cookies masquerading as biscotti. Both styles have their supporters, but for our own recipe, we wanted a hybrid: a cookie with big flavor and even bigger crunch but nothing so hard that it would jeopardize our dental work—a cookie that could be dipped into coffee but didn't need to be.

ADD EGGS FIRST A quick scan of several recipes suggested—and a subsequent biscotti bake-off confirmed—that the cookies' crunch or lack thereof corresponded with the amount of butter in the dough. Not surprisingly, batches made with little (or even no) fat were rock-hard, while doughs enriched with a full stick (8 tablespoons) of butter baked up much softer, thanks to the fat's tenderizing effect. Keeping that in mind, we began experimenting with a basic creaming formula—beat the butter and sugar; alternately fold in the dry ingredients (flour, baking powder, coarsely chopped almonds, salt, and spices) with the wet (eggs and vanilla or almond extract)—and varying the amount of butter in each batch. Half a stick turned out to be the ideal compromise; the dough was neither too hard nor too lean. The only problem was that a mere 4 tablespoons of butter (plus 1 cup of sugar) didn't give the stand mixer enough to work with. Instead of beating air into the butter to lighten it, all the mixer could do was soften the fat, and the resulting biscotti were dense and squat. It was time to brainstorm: What other elements of the dough could be aerated in the stand mixer? We scanned the ingredient list and landed on an ingredient so obvious we were surprised we hadn't thought of it sooner: eggs. Reversing the order of operations, we whipped two eggs until they were light in color and then added the sugar and continued to beat the mixture. Finally, we folded in the butter (melted and cooled), followed by the dry ingredients. The good news was that our unorthodox dough-mixing technique was a major breakthrough: The whipped eggs gave the dough the lightness and lift it had been lacking. But they were still too hard.

BREAK UP THE GLUTEN We wanted our biscotti to pack just as much crunch as the traditional Italian kind but also to break apart easily when we took a bite. Adding extra butter to the dough helped, but our ultimate solution was cutting the flour with finely ground nuts. While butter merely made the cookie more tender, ground nuts actually weakened its structure. Both ingredients influence the texture because of their effect on gluten, the web of flour proteins that gives baked goods structure. The fat in butter weakens the gluten network by surrounding individual strands and preventing them from linking up into larger networks. Ground nuts interfere with gluten formation in a slightly different way, getting in between pockets of gluten to create microscopic "fault lines" in the biscotti, which allow the hard cookie to break apart easily under the tooth.

LOAD UP ON SPICE AND EXTRACT While turning out batch after batch of biscotti, we noticed that many of the flavors we added to the dough—almond extract and aromatic herbs and spices—started off strong and fragrant but faded once the cookies had baked twice, since the successive exposure to heat drives off many volatile flavor compounds. To compensate, we loaded up on them, in some cases tripling the amount we started with.

ALMOND BISCOTTI
MAKES 30 COOKIES

The almonds will continue to toast while the biscotti bake, so toast the nuts only until they are just fragrant.

1¼	cups whole almonds, lightly toasted
1¾	cups (8¾ ounces) all-purpose flour
2	teaspoons baking powder
¼	teaspoon salt
2	large eggs, plus 1 large white beaten with pinch salt
1	cup (7 ounces) sugar
4	tablespoons unsalted butter, melted and cooled
1½	teaspoons almond extract
½	teaspoon vanilla extract
	Vegetable oil spray

1. Adjust oven rack to middle position and heat oven to 325 degrees. Using ruler and pencil, draw two 8 by 3-inch rectangles, spaced 4 inches apart, on piece of parchment paper. Grease baking sheet and place parchment on it, marked side down.

2. Pulse 1 cup almonds in food processor until coarsely chopped, 8 to 10 pulses; transfer to bowl and set aside. Process remaining ¼ cup almonds in now-empty food processor until finely ground, about 45 seconds. Add flour, baking powder, and salt; process to combine, about 15 seconds. Transfer flour mixture to second bowl. Process 2 eggs in now-empty food processor until lightened in color and almost doubled in volume, about 3 minutes. With processor running, slowly add sugar until thoroughly combined, about 15 seconds. Add melted butter, almond extract, and vanilla and process until combined, about 10 seconds. Transfer egg mixture to medium bowl. Sprinkle half of flour mixture over egg mixture and, using spatula, gently fold until just combined. Add remaining flour mixture and chopped almonds and gently fold until just combined.

3. Divide dough in half. Using your floured hands, form each half into 8 by 3-inch rectangle, using lines on parchment as guide. Spray each loaf lightly with oil spray. Using rubber spatula lightly coated with oil spray, smooth tops and sides of loaves. Gently brush tops of loaves with egg white beaten with salt. Bake until loaves are golden and just beginning to crack on top, 25 to 30 minutes, rotating sheet halfway through baking.

4. Let loaves cool on sheet for 30 minutes, then transfer to cutting board. Using serrated knife, slice each loaf on slight bias into ½-inch-thick slices. Set wire rack in rimmed baking sheet. Lay slices, cut side down, about ¼ inch apart on prepared rack. Bake until crisp and golden brown on both sides, about 35 minutes, flipping slices halfway through baking. Let cool completely before serving. (Biscotti can be stored at room temperature for up to 1 month.)

HAZELNUT-ORANGE BISCOTTI

Substitute lightly toasted and skinned hazelnuts for almonds. Add 2 tablespoons minced fresh rosemary to flour mixture in step 2. Substitute orange-flavored liqueur for almond extract and add 1 tablespoon grated orange zest to egg mixture with butter.

PISTACHIO-SPICE BISCOTTI

Substitute shelled pistachios for almonds. Add 1 teaspoon ground cardamom, ½ teaspoon ground ginger, ½ teaspoon pepper, ¼ teaspoon ground cinnamon, and ¼ teaspoon ground cloves to flour mixture in step 2. Substitute 1 teaspoon water for almond extract and increase vanilla extract to 1 teaspoon.

PRACTICAL SCIENCE WILD ALMONDS

Wild almonds are different than those you buy in the store—they can be lethal!

Amygdalin is produced as a protective compound by the wild varieties of almonds, but not the sweet varieties. Amygdalin is a type of compound called a glycoside (also called a glucoside), meaning it contains one or more glucose molecules attached to the parent molecule. In the case of amygdalin two molecules of glucose are attached. When the cells of the bitter (or wild) almond kernel are damaged by insect attack or chewing, an enzyme named emulsin is released that removes the two glucose molecules, which in turn destabilizes the parent molecule. The unstable parent molecule rapidly breaks down to the toxic gas hydrogen cyanide and the aromatic-smelling benzaldehyde, also known as almond oil. There is enough amygdalin present in wild almonds that the consumption of just a few almonds may result in death. (The removal of just one glucose molecule produces the compound known as laetrile. Many years ago laetrile was touted as an anticancer compound, but further study failed to show any convincing evidence that laetrile cures cancer.)

Almond Milk

✓ WHY THIS RECIPE WORKS

Almond milk is a refreshing dairy-free alternative to milk. Unfortunately, much of the almond milk available in stores is loaded with thickeners, stabilizers, and gums. We wanted a simple recipe for almond milk that tasted great. We set to work.

SOAK THE NUTS Before we could make the milk, we found it was essential to soak the nuts for at least 4 hours to soften them and ensure that our milk didn't turn out grainy. We tested several ratios of almonds to water to determine which produced both the best flavor and the best texture. We found that blending 1 cup of soaked almonds with 3 cups of water gave us the ideal flavor and consistency.

STRAIN IT We then poured the mixture through a cheesecloth-lined fine-mesh strainer to separate the almond milk from the pulp. Since the pulp still contained a great deal of milk, we squeezed the pulp in the cheesecloth until no liquid remained. To round out the flavor of the almond milk, we added a small amount of salt and some honey.

ALMOND MILK
MAKES ABOUT 3 CUPS

This recipe can be doubled.

1   cup whole blanched almonds
3   cups water
⅛   teaspoon kosher salt
2   teaspoons honey (optional)

1. Combine almonds and water in large bowl, cover, and refrigerate for at least 4 hours or up to 48 hours.

2. Line fine-mesh strainer with triple layer of cheesecloth that overhangs edges and set over large bowl. Process soaked almonds and soaking water in blender until almonds are finely ground, about 2 minutes. Transfer mixture to prepared strainer and press to extract as much liquid as possible. Gather sides of cheesecloth around almond pulp and gently squeeze remaining milk into bowl; discard spent pulp. Stir in salt and honey, if using, until dissolved. (Almond milk can be refrigerated for up to 2 weeks.)

Stocking Your Pantry

Using the best ingredients is one way to guarantee success in the kitchen. But how do you know what to buy? Shelves are filled with a dizzying array of choices—and price does not equal quality. Over the years, the test kitchen's blind tasting panels have evaluated thousands of ingredients, brand by brand, side by side, plain and in prepared applications, to determine which brands you can trust and which brands to avoid. In the chart that follows, we share the results, revealing our top-rated choices and the attributes that made them stand out among the competition. And because our test kitchen accepts no support from product manufacturers, you can trust our ratings. See AmericasTestKitchen.com for updates to these tastings.

TEST KITCHEN FAVORITE	WHY WE LIKE IT	RUNNERS-UP
ANCHOVIES **Ortiz Oil-Packed Spanish**	• Pleasantly fishy, salty flavor, not overwhelming or bland • Firm, meaty texture, not mushy • Already filleted and ready to use, unlike salt-packed variety	Flott Salt-Packed
APPLESAUCE **Musselman's Lite**	• Sweetened with sucralose, which doesn't overpower its fresh, bright apple flavor • Pinch of salt boosts flavor above weak, bland, and too-sweet competitors • Coarse, almost chunky texture, not slimy like applesauces sweetened with corn syrup	Musselman's Home Style
BACON, SUPERMARKET **Farmland Thick Sliced Smoked**	• Good balance of saltiness and sweetness • Smoky and full flavored, not one-dimensional • Very meaty, not too fatty or insubstantial • Crisp yet hearty texture, not tough or dry	Boar's Head Brand Naturally Smoked Sliced, Hormel Black Label Original
BARBECUE SAUCE **Bull's-Eye Original**	• Spicy, fresh tomato taste • Good balance of tanginess, smokiness, and sweetness • Robust flavor from molasses • Sweetened with sugar and molasses, not high-fructose corn syrup, which caramelizes and burns quickly	
BEANS, CANNED BAKED **B&M Vegetarian**	• Firm and pleasant texture with some bite • Sweetened with molasses for complexity and depth	Bush's Best Original, Van Camp's Original
BEANS, CANNED BLACK **Bush's Best**	• Clean, mild, and slightly earthy flavor • Firm, almost al dente texture, not mushy or pasty • Good amount of salt	Goya, Progresso
BEANS, CANNED CHICKPEAS **Pastene**	• Firm yet tender texture bests pasty and dry competitors • Clean chickpea flavor • Enough salt to enhance but not overwhelm the flavor	Goya
BEANS, CANNED RED KIDNEY **Goya**	• Sweet with strong bean flavor • Beautiful red, plump beans • Smooth, creamy texture, not mushy, chalky, or too firm • Flavor boost from added sugar and salt	S&W

TEST KITCHEN FAVORITE	WHY WE LIKE IT	RUNNERS-UP
BEANS, CANNED WHITE **Goya Cannellini**	• Clean, earthy flavor • Smooth, creamy interior with tender skins • Not full of broken beans like some competitors	Bush's Best Cannellini Beans White Kidney Beans
BREAD, MULTIGRAIN **Nature's Own Specialty 12 Grain**	• Substantial, chewy slices • Nutty, hearty seeds throughout and topped with rolled oats • Uses no white flour	Arnold 12 Grain, Pepperidge Farm 15 Grain
BREAD, WHITE SANDWICH **Arnold Country Classics**	• Subtle sweetness, not tasteless or sour • Perfect structure, not too dry or too soft	Pepperidge Farm Farmhouse Hearty White
BREAD, WHOLE-WHEAT SANDWICH **Pepperidge Farm 100% Whole Wheat**	• Whole-grain, nutty, earthy flavor • Dense, chewy texture, not gummy or too soft • Not too sweet, contains no corn syrup and has low sugar level (unlike competitors) NOTE: Available only east of the Mississippi River.	Rudi's Organic Bakery Honey Sweet Whole Wheat
BREAD CRUMBS, PANKO **Ian's Panko**	• Crisp, with a substantial crunch • Not too delicate, stale, sandy, or gritty • Oil-free and without seasonings or undesirable artificial flavors	
BROTH, BEEF **Better Than Bouillon Beef Base**	• Contains good amount of salt and multiple powerful flavor enhancers • Paste is economical, stores easily, and dissolves quickly in hot water	
BROTH, CHICKEN **Swanson Chicken Stock**	• Strong chicken flavor, not watery, beefy, or vegetal • Hearty and pleasant aroma • Roasted notes, not sour, rancid, or salty like some competitors • Flavor-boosting ingredients include carrots, celery, and onions	Better Than Bouillon Chicken Base
BROTH, VEGETARIAN **Orrington Farms Vegan Chicken Flavored Broth Base and Seasoning**	• Savory depth without off-tasting vegetable undertones • Easy to store • Yeast extract adds depth and richness	Swanson Certified Organic Vegetable Broth
BROWNIE MIX **Ghirardelli Chocolate Supreme**	• Rich, balanced chocolate flavor from both natural and Dutch-processed cocoa • Moist, chewy, and fudgy with perfect texture	
BUTTER, SALTED **Lurpak Slightly Salted**	• Made with cultured cream • Rich, creamy texture	Kate's Homemade, Plugrá European-Style, Land O'Lakes, Kerrygold Pure Irish, Challenge, Organic Valley
BUTTER, UNSALTED **Plugrá European-Style**	• Sweet and creamy • Complex tang and grassy flavor • Moderate amount of butterfat so that it's decadent and glossy but not so rich that baked goods are greasy	Land O'Lakes, Vermont Creamery European-Style

TEST KITCHEN FAVORITE	WHY WE LIKE IT	RUNNERS-UP
CHEESE, AMERICAN, PRESLICED **Boar's Head**	• Strong cheesy flavor, unlike some competitors • Higher content of cheese culture contributes to better flavor	Kraft Deli Deluxe
CHEESE, ASIAGO **BelGioioso**	• Sharp, tangy, and complex flavor, not mild • Firm and not too dry • Melts, shreds, and grates well	
CHEESE, BLUE For dressings and dips: **Stella**	• Sweet, balanced, and mild flavor, not too pungent • Wet and extremely crumbly texture similar to feta	Danish Blue
For eating out of hand: **Stilton**	• Balance of buttery, nutty, sweet, and salty flavors • Fairly firm with sliceable yet crumbly texture	Roquefort
CHEESE, CHEDDAR, EXTRA-SHARP **Cabot Private Stock**	• Balance of salty, creamy, and sweet flavors • Considerable but well-rounded sharpness, not overwhelming • Firm, crumbly texture, not moist, rubbery, or springy • Aged at least 12 months for complex flavor	Cabot Extra-Sharp, Grafton Village Cheese Company Premium, Cabot Sharp, Tillamook Special Reserve
CHEESE, CHEDDAR, PREMIUM **Milton Creamery Prairie Breeze**	• Earthy complexity with nutty, buttery, and fruity flavors • Dry and crumbly with crystalline crunch, not rubbery or overly moist • Aged no more than 12 months to prevent overly sharp flavor	Cabot Clothbound, Tillamook Vintage White Extra Sharp, Beecher's Flagship Reserve
CHEESE, CHEDDAR, PRESLICED **Tillamook Sharp**	• Slightly crumbly, not rubbery or processed, texture characteristic of block cheddar • Strong, tangy, and salty flavor, not bland or too mild	Cabot All Natural Sharp, Cracker Barrel Natural Sharp
CHEESE, CHEDDAR, REDUCED-FAT **Cracker Barrel Reduced Fat Sharp**	• Ample creaminess • Strong cheesy flavor • Good for cooking	Cabot 50% Light Sharp
CHEESE, CHEDDAR, SHARP **Cabot Vermont Sharp Cheddar**	• Buttery, creamy texture • Nutty, complex sharpness	Tillamook, Cracker Barrel, Kraft Natural, Kerrygold Aged, Sargento Tastings Aged Wisconsin
CHEESE, COTTAGE **Hood Country Style**	• Rich, well-seasoned, and buttery flavor • Velvety, creamy texture • Pillowy curds	Friendship 4% California Style, Breakstone's 4% Small Curd
CHEESE, CREAM **Philadelphia**	• Rich, tangy, and milky flavor • Thick, creamy texture, not pasty, waxy, or chalky	Organic Valley
CHEESE, FETA **Mt. Vikos Traditional**	• Strong tangy, salty flavor • Creamy, dense texture • Pleasing crumbly texture	Valbreso
CHEESE, FONTINA For eating out of hand: **Fontina Val d'Aosta**	• Strong, earthy aroma • Somewhat elastic texture with small irregular holes • Grassy, nutty flavor—but can be overpowering in cooked dishes	
For cooking: **BelGioioso Italian Fontina**	• Semisoft, super-creamy texture • Mildly tangy, nutty flavor • Melts well	

TEST KITCHEN FAVORITE	WHY WE LIKE IT	RUNNERS-UP
CHEESE, GOAT **Laura Chenel's Chèvre**	• Rich-tasting, grassy, tangy flavor • Smooth and creamy both unheated and baked • High salt content	Vermont Creamery, Chevrion, Cypress Grove
CHEESE, GRUYÈRE **Gruyère Reserve Wheel** **(Peney-Le-Jorat)**	• Grassy, salty flavor, not bland or pedestrian • Creamy yet dry texture, not plasticky like some competitors • Aged a minimum of 10 months for strong and complex flavor • Melts especially well	Gruyère Salé
CHEESE, MOZZARELLA **Galbani (formerly** **Sorrento) Whole Milk**	• Creamy and buttery with clean dairy flavor • Soft, not rubbery, chew	Kraft Low-Moisture Part Skim, Boar's Head Whole-Milk Low Moisture, Kraft Shredded Low-Moisture Part-Skim
CHEESE, PARMESAN **Boar's Head** **Parmigiano-Reggiano**	• Rich and complex flavor balances tanginess and nuttiness • Dry, crumbly texture yet creamy with a crystalline crunch, not rubbery or dense • Aged a minimum of 12 months for better flavor and texture	Il Villagio Parmigiano Reggiano, BelGioioso
CHEESE, PARMESAN **PRESHREDDED** **Sargento Artisan Blends**	• Mix of small and large shreds • Blend of 10- and 18-month-aged Parmesan • Rich, nutty flavor	Kraft Natural
CHEESE, PEPPER JACK **Boar's Head Monterey** **Jack Cheese with Jalapeño**	• Buttery, tangy cheese • Clean, balanced flavor with assertive spice	Tillamook Pepper Jack Cheese
CHEESE, PROVOLONE **Provolone Vernengo**	• Bold, nutty, and tangy flavor, not plasticky or bland • Firm, dry texture	
CHEESE, RICOTTA, **PART-SKIM** **Calabro**	• Clean, fresh flavor, not rancid or sour from addition of gums or stabilizers • Creamy texture with perfect curds, unlike chalky, grainy, and soggy competitors	Any freshly made ricotta cheese without gums or stabilizers
CHEESE, SWISS For cheese plate: **Edelweiss Creamery** **Emmenthaler**	• Subtle flavor with sweet, buttery, nutty, and fruity notes • Firm yet gently giving texture, not rubbery • Aged longer for better flavor, resulting in larger "eyes" • Mildly pungent yet balanced	Emmi Kaltbach
For cheese plate or cooking: **Emmi Emmenthaler** **Cheese AOC**	• Creamy texture • Salty mildness preferable for grilled cheese sandwiches	For cooking only: Boar's Head Gold Label Imported
CHICKEN, WHOLE **Mary's Free Range** **Air-Chilled**	• Great, savory chicken flavor • Very tender • Air-chilled for minimum water retention and cleaner flavor	
Bell & Evans **Air-Chilled Premium Fresh**	• Firm and tender texture • Full chicken flavor • Moist and juicy	

TEST KITCHEN FAVORITE	WHY WE LIKE IT	RUNNERS-UP
CHICKEN, BREASTS, BONELESS SKINLESS **Bell & Evans Air-Chilled**	• Juicy and tender with clean chicken flavor • Not salted or brined • Air-chilled • Aged on bone for at least 6 hours after slaughter for significantly more tender meat	Springer Mountain Farms, Eberly's Free Range Young Organic
CHILI POWDER **Morton & Bassett**	• Bold, full-flavored heat • Multidimensional flavor from a blend of cayenne and other chiles • Spices that complement but don't overwhelm the chiles	Penzeys Spices
CHOCOLATE, DARK **Ghirardelli 60% Cacao Bittersweet Chocolate Premium Baking Bar**	• Creamy texture, not grainy or chalky • Complex flavor with notes of cherry and wine with slight smokiness • Balance of sweetness and bitterness	Callebaut Intense Dark L-60-40NV (60% Cacao)
CHOCOLATE, MILK **Dove Silky Smooth**	• Intense, full, rich chocolate flavor • Supercreamy texture from abundant milk fat and cocoa butter • Not overwhelmingly sweet	Endangered Species All-Natural Smooth, Green & Black's Organic
CHOCOLATE, DARK, CHIPS **Ghirardelli 60% Cacao Bittersweet**	• Intense, complex flavor beats one-dimensional flavor of competitors • Low sugar content highlights chocolate flavor • High amount of cocoa butter ensures creamy, smooth texture, not gritty and grainy • Wider, flatter shape and high percentage of fat help chips melt better in cookies	Hershey's Special Dark Mildly Sweet
CHOCOLATE, MILK, CHIPS **Hershey's**	• Bold chocolate flavor outshines too-sweet, weak chocolate flavor of other chips • Complex with caramel and nutty notes • Higher fat content makes texture creamier than grainy, artificial competitors	
CHOCOLATE, UNSWEETENED **Hershey's Unsweetened Baking Bar**	• Well-rounded, complex flavor • Assertive chocolate flavor and deep notes of cocoa	Valrhona Cacao Pate Extra 100%, Scharffen Berger Unsweetened Dark
CHOCOLATE, WHITE, CHIPS **Guittard Choc-Au-Lait**	• Creamy texture, not waxy or crunchy • Silky-smooth meltability from high fat content • Complex flavor like high-quality real chocolate, no artificial or off-flavors	Ghirardelli Classic White
CIDER, HARD **Angry Orchard Crisp Apple**	• Crisp and refreshing • Strong apple sweetness • Juicy complexity	Strongbow Gold Apple, Woodchuck Amber
CINNAMON **Penzeys Extra Fancy Vietnamese Cassia**	• Warm, fragrant aroma with clove, fruity, and slightly smoky flavors • Mellow start with spicy finish • Strong yet not overpowering • Not harsh, bitter, dusty, or gritty NOTE: Available through mail order, Penzeys (800-741-7787, www.penzeys.com).	Smith and Truslow Freshly Ground Organic, Adams Ground

TEST KITCHEN FAVORITE	WHY WE LIKE IT	RUNNERS-UP
COCOA POWDER **Hershey's Natural Unsweetened**	• Full, strong chocolate flavor • Complex flavor with notes of coffee, cinnamon, orange, and spice	Droste
COCONUT MILK For savory recipes: **Chaokoh**	• Strong coconut flavor • Smooth and creamy texture superior to competitors • Not very sweet, ideal for savory recipes like soups and stir-fries	
For sweet recipes: **Ka-Me**	• Rich, velvety texture, not too thin or watery • Fruity and complex flavor, not mild or bland • Ideal sweetness for desserts	
COCONUT, SHREDDED **Now Real Food Organic Unsweetened**	• Nutty, tropical flavor • Fluffy, crisp texture	Woodstock Foods Organic
COFFEE, DECAF **Maxwell House Decaf Original Roast**	• Smooth, mellow flavor without being acidic or harsh • Complex, with a slightly nutty aftertaste • Made with only flavorful Arabica beans	Peet's Decaf House Blend Ground, Starbucks Coffee Decaf House Blend
COFFEE, WHOLE BEAN, SUPERMARKET, MEDIUM ROAST Brighter: **Millstone Colombian Supremo**	• Deep, complex, and balanced flavor without metallic, overly acidic, or otherwise unpleasant notes • Smoky and chocolaty with a bitter, not burnt, finish	Starbucks Coffee House Blend
Bolder: **Peet's Coffee Café Domingo**	• Extremely smooth but bold tasting with a strong finish • Rich chocolate and toast flavors • Few defective beans, low acidity, and optimal moisture	Millstone Breakfast Blend
CORNMEAL **Arrowhead Mills Whole Grain**	• Clean, pure corn flavor from using whole-grain kernels • Ideal texture resembling slightly damp, fine sand, not too fine or too coarse	
CREOLE SEASONING **Tony Chachere's Original**	• Strong garlic and red pepper notes • Vibrant and zesty with a punch of heat	McCormick Perfect Pinch Cajun Seasoning
CURRY POWDER **Penzeys Sweet**	• Balanced, neither too sweet nor too hot • Complex and vivid earthy flavor, not thin, bland, or one-dimensional NOTE: Available through mail order, Penzeys (800-741-7787, www.penzeys.com).	
DINNER ROLLS, FROZEN **Pepperidge Farm Stone Baked Artisan French Dinner Rolls**	• Tender on the inside with crispy crust • Has only seven ingredients • Tastes homemade, with a hint of salt	

TEST KITCHEN FAVORITE	WHY WE LIKE IT	RUNNERS-UP
EGG WHITES, PROCESSED Eggology 100% Egg Whites	• Work well in egg-white omelets • Pasteurized; safe for use in uncooked applications • Make satisfactory baked goods	
FISH SAUCE Red Boat 40° N Fish Sauce	• Intensely rich and flavorful • Not overly salty • Earthy, slightly "sweet" notes for a flavor that was "complex, not just fishy"	Thai Kitchen Premium Fish Sauce
FIVE-SPICE POWDER Frontier Natural Products Co-op	• Nice depth, not one-dimensional • Balanced heat and sweetness	Dynasty Chinese Five Spices, McCormick Gourmet Collection Chinese Five Spice, Dean & DeLuca Five Spice Blend, Morton & Bassett Chinese Five Spice
FLOUR, ALL-PURPOSE King Arthur Unbleached	• Fresh, toasty flavor • No metallic taste or other off-flavors • Consistent results across recipes • Makes tender, flaky pie crust, hearty biscuits, crisp cookies, and chewy, sturdy bread	Gold Medal Enriched Bleached Presifted, Gold Medal Unbleached, Heckers/Ceresota Unbleached Enriched Presifted
Pillsbury Unbleached Enriched	• Clean, toasty, and hearty flavor • No metallic or other off-flavors • Consistent results across recipes • Makes flaky pie crust, chewy cookies, and tender biscuits, muffins, and cakes	
FLOUR, WHOLE-WHEAT King Arthur Premium	• Finely ground for hearty but not overly coarse texture in bread and pancakes • Sweet, nutty flavor	Bob's Red Mill Organic
FRENCH FRIES, FROZEN Alexia Organic Yukon Select Fries	• Crispy exteriors with fluffy, creamy interiors • Earthy, potato-y flavor	Ore-Ida Golden Fries
GIARDINIERA Pastene	• Sharp, vinegary tang • Crunchy mix of vegetables • Mellow heat that's potent but not overpowering	Scala Hot
GNOCCHI Gia Russa Gnocchi with Potato	• Tender, pillow-like texture • Nice potato flavor • Slightly sour taste that disappears when paired with tomato sauce	De Cecco
GRITS Anson Mills	• Full, ripe, fresh corn flavor • Nice chew while still thick and creamy	Arrowhead Mills, Bob's Red Mill

	Test Kitchen Favorite	Why We Like It	Runners-Up
	HAM, BLACK FOREST DELI Dietz & Watson	• Good texture • Nice ham flavor	
	HAM, COUNTRY Harper's Grand Champion Whole Country Ham	• Aged three to six months • Porky and complex, with robust flavor and balanced salt levels • Available online or in some Southern supermarkets	Burgers' Smokehouse Ready to Cook Country Ham, Edwards Virginia Traditions Uncooked Virginia Ham
	HAM, SPIRAL-SLICED, HONEY-CURED Cook's Spiral Sliced Hickory Smoked Honey	• Good balance of smokiness, saltiness, and sweetness • Moist, tender yet firm texture, not dry or too wet • Clean, meaty ham flavor	
	HOISIN SAUCE Kikkoman	• Balance of sweet, salty, pungent, and spicy flavors • Initial burn mellows into harmonious and aromatic blend without bitterness	
	HONEY Nature Nate's 100% Pure Raw and Unfiltered	• Bold notes of citrus, clover, and anise • Mild sweetness and slight acidity	Aunt Sue's Raw-Wild Honey, Sue Bee Clover Honey
	HORSERADISH Boar's Head Pure	• No preservatives, just horseradish, vinegar, and salt (found in refrigerated section) • Natural flavor and hot without being overpowering	Ba-Tampte Prepared Horseradish
	HOT DOGS Nathan's Famous Beef Franks	• Meaty, robust, and hearty flavor, not sweet, sour, or too salty • Juicy but not greasy • Firm, craggy texture, not rubbery, mushy, or chewy	Hebrew National Beef Franks
	HOT FUDGE SAUCE Hershey's Hot Fudge Topping	• True fudge flavor, not weak or overly sweet • Thick, smooth, and buttery texture	
	HOT SAUCE Huy Fong Sriracha Hot Chili Sauce and Frank's RedHot Original	• Right combination of punchy heat, saltiness, sweetness, and garlic • Full, rich flavor • Mild heat that's not too hot	Original Louisiana, Tapatio Salsa Picante
	ICE CREAM, CHOCOLATE Ben & Jerry's	• Deep, concentrated chocolate flavor, not too light or sweet • Dense and creamy texture	Friendly's Rich & Creamy Classic
	ICE CREAM, VANILLA Ben & Jerry's	• Complex yet balanced vanilla flavor from real vanilla extract • Sweetness solely from sugar, rather than corn syrup • Creamy richness from both egg yolks and small amount of stabilizers	Häagen-Dazs Vanilla

TEST KITCHEN FAVORITE	WHY WE LIKE IT	RUNNERS-UP
ICE CREAM BARS **Dove Bar Vanilla Ice Cream** **with Milk Chocolate**	• Rich, prominent chocolate flavor • Thick, crunchy chocolate coating • Dense, creamy ice cream with pure vanilla flavor • Milk chocolate, not coconut oil, listed first in coating ingredients	Häagen-Dazs Vanilla Milk Chocolate All Natural, Blue Bunny Big Alaska, Good Humor Milk Chocolate
ICE CREAM CONES **Joy Classic Waffle Cones**	• Lightly sweet, with vanilla, toasty, and nutty flavors • Crunchy and crisp but not overly hard • Individual paper jackets keep things neat	Joy Sugar Cones, Keebler Waffle Cones, Keebler Sugar Cones, Comet (Nabisco) Sugar Cones
ICED TEA Loose leaf: **Tazo** **Iced Black Tea**	• Distinctive flavor with herbal notes • Balanced level of strength and astringency	Luzianne, Tetley Premium Blend
Bottled, with lemon: **Lipton PureLeaf**	• Bright, balanced, and natural tea and lemon flavors • Uses concentrated tea leaves to extract flavor	Gold Peak
JUICE, GRAPEFRUIT **Natalie's 100% Florida**	• Balanced and bright flavor, not too sweet • Clean and refreshing crispness	Florida's Natural Ruby Red
JUICE, ORANGE **Natalie's 100% Florida**	• Blend of Hamlin, Pineapple, and Valencia oranges • Fresh, sweet, and fruity flavor without overly acidic, sour, or from-concentrate taste • Gentler pasteurization helps retain fresh-squeezed flavor • Pleasant amount of light pulp	Tropicana Pure Premium 100% Pure and Natural with Some Pulp
JUICE, FROZEN ORANGE CONCENTRATE **Minute Maid Original Frozen Concentrated Orange Juice**	• Full-bodied orange flavor • Good texture, includes some pulp	Tropicana 100% Juice Frozen Concentrated Orange Juice
KETCHUP **Heinz Organic**	• Clean, pure sweetness from sugar, not high-fructose corn syrup • Bold, harmonious punch of saltiness, sweetness, tang, and tomato flavor	Hunt's and Simply Heinz
LEMONADE **Natalie's Natural**	• Natural-tasting lemon flavor from 20 percent real lemon juice, without artificial flavors or off-notes • Perfect balance of tartness and sweetness, unlike many overly sweet competitors	Simply Lemonade and Minute Maid Premium Frozen Concentrate
MACARONI AND CHEESE **Kraft Homestyle Classic Cheddar**	• Reinforces flavor with blue and cheddar cheeses • Uses creamy, clingy liquid cheese sauce • Dry noodles, rather than frozen, for substantial texture and bite • Crunchy, buttery bread-crumb topping	Kraft Velveeta Original

TEST KITCHEN FAVORITE	WHY WE LIKE IT	RUNNERS-UP
MAPLE SYRUP **Uncle Luke's Pure** **Maple Syrup, Grade A** **Dark Amber**	• Inexpensive • Dark, "molasses-y" color • Rich caramel flavor that tastes "pleasantly toasty" in pie	Highland Sugarworks, Coombs Family Farms, Anderson's, Maple Grove Farms, Maple Gold, Spring Tree, Camp Pure
MAYONNAISE **Blue Plate Real**	• Great balanced taste and texture • Tastes close to homemade NOTE: While it's one of the top-selling brands in the country, you'll have to mail-order it unless you live in the South or Southeast	Hellmann's Real Mayonnaise, Hellmann's Light Mayonnaise, Spectrum Organic Mayonnaise, Duke's Mayonnaise
MAYONNAISE, LIGHT **Hellmann's Light**	• Bright, balanced flavor close to full-fat counterpart, not overly sweet like other light mayos • Not as creamy as full-fat but passable texture NOTE: Hellmann's is known as Best Foods west of the Rockies.	Hellmann's Canola Cholesterol Free
MIRIN (JAPANESE RICE WINE) **Mitoku Organic** **Mikawa Mirin Sweet** **Rice Seasoning**	• Roasted flavor that is caramel-like and rich • Subtle salty-sweet and balanced flavor	Sushi Chef Mirin Sweetened Sake, Kikkoman Aji-Mirin Sweet Cooking Rice Seasoning
MOLASSES **Brer Rabbit All** **Natural Unsulphured** **Mild Flavor**	• Acidic yet balanced • Strong and straightforward raisin-y taste • Pleasantly bitter bite	Plantation Barbados Unsulphured, Grandma's Molasses Unsulphured Original
MUSTARD, BROWN **Gulden's Spicy**	• Complex flavor with both heat and gentle tang • Smooth, creamy texture that goes perfectly with hot dogs	French's Spicy Brown Mustard, Beaver Deli Mustard
MUSTARD, COARSE-GRAIN **Grey Poupon Harvest** **Coarse Ground**	• Spicy, tangy burst of mustard flavor • High salt content amplifies flavor • Contains no superfluous ingredients that mask mustard flavor • Big, round seeds add pleasant crunch • Just enough vinegar, not too sour or thin	Grey Poupon Country Dijon
MUSTARD, DIJON **Trois Petits Cochons** **Moutarde de Dijon**	• Potent, bold, and very hot, not weak or mild • Good balance of sweetness, tanginess, and sharpness • Not overly acidic, sweet, or one-dimensional like competitors	Maille Dijon Originale Traditional, Roland Extra Strong
MUSTARD, YELLOW **Annie's Naturals Organic**	• Lists mustard seeds second in the ingredients for rich mustard flavor • Good balance of heat and tang • Relatively low salt content	Gulden's, French's Classic, Westbrae Natural

	TEST KITCHEN FAVORITE	WHY WE LIKE IT	RUNNERS-UP
	OATS, ROLLED For hot cereal: **Bob's Red Mill Organic Extra Thick**	• Rich oat flavor with nutty, barley, and toasty notes • Creamy, cohesive texture • Plump grains with decent chew	
	Quick Oats: **Quaker Old-Fashioned**	• Plump, almost crunchy texture with a slight chew, not gluey or mushy • Hearty, oaty, and toasty flavor • Subtly sweet with a natural taste	
	OATS, STEEL-CUT **Bob's Red Mill Organic**	• Rich and complex oat flavor with buttery, earthy, nutty, and whole-grain notes • Creamy yet firm texture • Moist but not sticky NOTE: Not recommended for baking	Arrowhead Mills Organic Hot Cereal, Country Choice Organic, Hodgson's Mill Premium
	OLIVE OIL, EXTRA-VIRGIN, HIGH-END **Columela**	• Fruity, bold olive flavor and excellent balance • Medium-to-heavy texture	Nunez de Prado, Terra Medi
	OLIVE OIL, SUPERMARKET **California Olive Ranch Arbequina**	• Fruity, fragrant, and fresh with a complex finish • Flavor rivals winning high-end extra-virgin oil	Lucini Premium Select
	PANCAKE MIX **Hungry Jack Buttermilk Pancake and Waffle Mix**	• Flavorful balance of sweetness and tang, well seasoned with sugar and salt • Light, extra-fluffy texture • Requires vegetable oil (along with milk and egg) to reconstitute the batter	Aunt Jemima Original
	PAPRIKA **The Spice House Hungarian Sweet**	• Complex flavor with earthy, fruity notes • Bright and bold, not bland and boring • Rich, toasty aroma NOTE: Available only through mail order, The Spice House (312-274-0378, www.thespicehouse.com).	Penzeys Hungary Sweet (available through mail order, Penzeys, 800-741-7787, www.penzeys.com)
	PASTA, CHEESE RAVIOLI **Rosetto**	• Creamy, plush, and rich blend of ricotta, Romano, and Parmesan cheeses • Pasta with nice, springy bite • Perfect dough-to-filling ratio	Buitoni Four Cheese, Celentano
	PASTA, CHEESE TORTELLINI **Barilla Three Cheese**	• Robustly flavored filling from combination of ricotta, Emmentaler, and Grana Padano cheeses • Tender pasta that's sturdy enough to withstand boiling but not so thick that it becomes doughy	Seviroli, Buitoni Three Cheese

TEST KITCHEN FAVORITE	WHY WE LIKE IT	RUNNERS-UP
PASTA, EGG NOODLES Pennsylvania Dutch Wide	• Balanced, buttery flavor with no off-flavors • Light and fluffy texture, not gummy or starchy	De Cecco Egg Pappardelle; Light 'n Fluffy Egg Noodles, Wide
PASTA, ELBOW MACARONI Barilla	• Rich flavor from egg yolks • Firm, chewy bite • Wide corkscrew shape	Mueller's
PASTA, FRESH Buitoni Fettuccine	• Firm but yielding, slightly chewy texture, not too delicate, gummy, or heavy • Faint but discernible egg flavor with no chemical, plasticky, or otherwise unpleasant flavors • Rough, porous surface absorbs sauce better than dried pasta	
PASTA, LASAGNA NOODLES No-boil: **Barilla**	• Taste and texture of fresh pasta • Delicate, flat noodles	Ronzoni and Pasta DeFino
Whole-wheat: **Bionaturae Organic 100% Whole Wheat**	• Complex nutty, rich wheat flavor • Substantial chewy texture without any grittiness	DeLallo 100% Organic
PASTA, PENNE Mueller's Penne Rigate	• Hearty texture, not insubstantial or gummy • Wheaty, slightly sweet flavor, not bland	Benedetto Cavalieri Penne Rigate, De Cecco
PASTA, SPAGHETTI De Cecco Spaghetti No. 12	• Rich, nutty, wheaty flavor • Firm, ropy strands with good chew, not mushy, gummy, or mealy	Rustichella D'Abruzzo Pasta Abruzzese di Semola di Grano Duro, Garofalo, DeLallo Spaghetti No. 4
PASTA, SPAGHETTI, GLUTEN-FREE Jovial Gluten-Free Brown Rice Pasta	• High in fiber and protein with springy texture and clean taste • No gumminess or off-flavors as experienced with other brands	Andean Dream Gluten & Corn Free Quinoa Pasta
PASTA, SPAGHETTI, WHOLE-WHEAT Bionaturae 100% Whole Wheat	• Chewy and firm, not mushy or rubbery • Full and nutty wheat flavor	Barilla PLUS Multigrain
PASTA SAUCE Bertolli Tomato & Basil	• Fresh-cooked, balanced tomato flavor, not overly sweet • Pleasantly chunky, not too smooth or pasty • Not overseasoned with dry herbs like competitors	Francesco Rinaldi Traditional Marinara, Prego Marinara Italian, Barilla Marinara
PASTA SAUCE, PREMIUM Victoria Marinara Sauce	• Nice, bright acidity that speaks of real tomatoes • Robust flavor comparable to homemade	Classico Marinara with Plum Tomatoes and Olive Oil

TEST KITCHEN FAVORITE	WHY WE LIKE IT	RUNNERS-UP
PEANUT BUTTER, CREAMY Skippy	• Smooth, creamy, and spreadable • Good balance of sweet and salty flavors	Jif Natural, Reese's
PEPPERCORNS, BLACK Kalustyan's Indian Tellicherry	• Enticing and fragrant, not musty, aroma with flavor to back it up and moderate heat • Fresh, complex flavor at once sweet and spicy, earthy and smoky, fruity and floral NOTE: Available only by mail order, Kalustyan's (800-352-3451, www.kalustyans.com).	Morton & Bassett Organic Whole (widely available)
PEPPERONI, SLICED Margherita Italian Style	• Nice balance of meatiness and spice • Tangy, fresh flavor with hints of fruity licorice and peppery fennel • Thin slices with the right amount of chew	Boar's Head
PEPPERS, ROASTED RED Dunbars Sweet	• Balance of smokiness and sweetness • Mild, sweet, and earthy red pepper flavor • Firm texture, not slimy or mushy • Packed in simple yet strong brine of salt and water without distraction of other strongly flavored ingredients	Cento
PICKLES, BREAD-AND-BUTTER Bubbies	• Subtle, briny tang • All-natural solution that uses real sugar, not high-fructose corn syrup	
PICKLES, WHOLE KOSHER DILL Boar's Head	• Authentic, garlicky flavor and firm, snappy crunch • Balanced salty, sour, and garlic flavors • Fresh and refrigerated, not processed and shelf-stable	Claussen
PIE CRUST, READY-MADE Wholly Wholesome 9" Certified Organic Traditional Bake at Home Rolled Pie Dough	• Palm oil gives it a tender, flaky texture without artificial taste • Sold in sheets so you can use your own pie plate • Slightly sweet, rich flavor	
PIZZA, PEPPERONI, FROZEN Pizzeria! by DiGiorno Primo Pepperoni	• Thick, crisp, and airy crust with a browned and charred bottom • Herby, zesty sauce. Very meaty pepperoni	Freschetta Brick Oven Crust Pepperoni and Italian Style Cheese, Red Baron Fire Baked Pepperoni Pizza
PORK, PREMIUM Snake River Farms American Kurobuta (Berkshire) Pork	• Deep pink tint, which indicates higher pH level and more flavorful meat • Tender texture and juicy, intense pork flavor	D'Artagnan Berkshire Pork Chops (Milanese-Style Cut), Eden Farms French-Cut Kurobuta Pork

TEST KITCHEN FAVORITE	WHY WE LIKE IT	RUNNERS-UP
POTATO CHIPS **Lay's Kettle Cooked Original**	• Big potato flavor, no offensive off-flavors • Perfectly salted • Slightly thick chips that aren't too delicate or brittle • Not too greasy	Herr's Crisp 'N Tasty, Utz
POTATO CHIPS, REDUCED FAT **Cape Cod 40% Reduced Fat**	• Real potato flavor with excellent crunch and texture • Contain only potatoes, canola oil, and salt • Just the right balance of salt, with less sodium than many competitors	Lay's Kettle Cooked Reduced Fat Extra Crunchy
PRESERVES, PEACH **American Spoon Red Haven**	• Bold, ripe peach taste and balanced sweetness • Loose and spreadable texture, similar to homemade preserves	Bonne Maman, Smucker's
PRESERVES, RASPBERRY **Smucker's**	• Clean, strong raspberry flavor, not too tart or sweet • Not overly seedy • Ideal, spreadable texture, not too thick, artificial, or overprocessed	Trappist Red Raspberry Jam
PRESERVES, STRAWBERRY **Welch's**	• Big, distinct strawberry flavor • Natural-tasting and not overwhelmingly sweet • Thick and spreadable texture, not runny, slimy, or too smooth	Smucker's, Smucker's Simply Fruit Spreadable Fruit
RELISH, SWEET PICKLE **Cascadian Farm**	• Piquant, sweet flavor, lacks out-of-place flavors such as cinnamon and clove present in competitors • Fresh and natural taste, free of yellow dye #5 and high-fructose corn syrup • Good texture, not mushy like competitors	Heinz Premium
RICE, ARBORIO **RiceSelect**	• Creamier than competitors • Smooth grains • Characteristic good bite of Arborio rice in risotto where al dente is ideal	Riso Baricella, Rienzi
RICE, BASMATI **Tilda Pure**	• Very long grains expand greatly with cooking, a result of being aged for a minimum of one year, as required in India • Ideal, fluffy texture, not dry, gummy, or mushy • Nutty taste with no off-flavors • Sweet aroma	Kohinoor Super
RICE, BROWN **Lundberg Organic Long Grain**	• Firm yet tender grains • Bold, toasty, nutty flavor • Works with a range of cooking methods • Includes the best instructions	Riceland Extra Long Grain Natural, Carolina Whole Grain, Goya

TEST KITCHEN FAVORITE	WHY WE LIKE IT	RUNNERS-UP
RICE, LONG-GRAIN WHITE **Lundberg Organic**	• Nutty, buttery, and toasty flavor • Distinct, smooth grains that offer some chew without being overly chewy	Carolina Enriched Extra Long-Grain, Canilla Extra Long-Grain Enriched
RICE, READY **Minute Ready to Serve White Rice**	• Parboiled long-grain white rice that is ready in less than 2 minutes • Toasted, buttery flavor • Firm grains with al dente bite	
SALSA, HOT **Pace Hot Chunky**	• Good balance of bright tomato, chile, and vegetal flavors • Chunky, almost crunchy texture, not mushy or thin • Spicy and fiery but not overpowering	Newman's Own All Natural Chunky Hot, Herdez Hot Salsa Casera
SALSA, JARRED GREEN **Frontera Tomatillo Salsa**	• Sweet and nuanced flavor with a roasted, smoky taste from charred tomatillo skins • A good amount of heat • Has no preservatives or stabilizers	Ortega Salsa Verde Medium
SALSA, MEDIUM **Chi-Chi's Medium Thick and Chunky Salsa**	• Fresh, balanced flavor • Vegetables are firm and crunchy • Jalapeño chiles for medium-level heat	
SALT **Maldon Sea Salt**	• Light and airy texture • Delicately crunchy flakes • Not so coarse as to be overly crunchy or gritty nor so fine as to disappear	Fleur de Sel de Camargue, Morton Coarse Kosher, Diamond Crystal Kosher
SAUSAGE, BREAKFAST **Jimmy Dean Fully Cooked Original Pork Sausage Links**	• Big pork flavor, not bland or overly spiced • Good balance of saltiness and sweetness with pleasantly lingering spiciness • Tender, super juicy meat, not rubbery, spongy, or greasy	
SOUP, CANNED CHICKEN NOODLE **Muir Glen Organic**	• Organic chicken and vegetables and plenty of seasonings give it a fresh taste and spicy kick • Firm, not mushy, vegetables and noodles • No off-flavors	Progresso Traditional
SOUP, CANNED TOMATO **Progresso Vegetable Classics Hearty**	• Includes fresh, unprocessed tomatoes, not just tomato puree like some competitors • Tangy, slightly herbaceous flavor • Balanced seasoning and natural sweetness • Medium body and slightly chunky texture	Imagine Organic Vine Ripened
SOY SAUCE **Kikkoman Soy Sauce**	• Rich, well-balanced, and complex flavor • Notes of caramel, and a pleasant sherry-like aroma • A level of saltiness that is just right	Lee Yum Kee Table Top Premium Soy Sauce
STEAK SAUCE **Heinz 57 Sauce**	• Mellow, restrained flavor that doesn't overpower meat • Fruity, sweet, and tangy flavor with hints of heat and smoke • Smooth texture with enough body to cling to steak without being gluey	Lea & Perrins

TEST KITCHEN FAVORITE	WHY WE LIKE IT	RUNNERS-UP
SWEETENED CONDENSED MILK **Borden Eagle Brand Whole Milk**	• Made with whole milk; creamier in desserts and balances more assertive notes from other ingredients	Nestlé Carnation
TARTAR SAUCE **Legal Sea Foods**	• Creamy, nicely balanced sweet/tart base • Lots of vegetable chunks	McCormick Original
TEA, BLACK For plain tea: **Twinings English Breakfast**	• Bright, bold, and flavorful yet not too strong • Fruity, floral, and fragrant • Smooth, slightly astringent profile preferred for tea without milk	Lipton Black Tea
For tea with milk and sugar: **Tetley British Blend**	• Boasts caramel notes and full, deep, smoky flavors • Bold, fruity flavor	Celestial Seasonings English Breakfast Estate Tea
TERIYAKI SAUCE **Annie Chun's All Natural**	• Distinct teriyaki flavor without offensive or dominant flavors, unlike competitors • Smooth, rich texture, not too watery or gluey	
TOMATOES, CANNED CRUSHED **Tuttorosso in Thick Puree with Basil**	• Chunky texture, not pasty, mushy, or watery • Bright, fresh tomato taste • Balance of saltiness, sweetness, and acidity NOTE: Available only in New England, Mid-Atlantic region, and Florida.	Muir Glen Organic with Basil Hunt's Organic
TOMATOES, CANNED DICED **Hunt's**	• Bright, fresh tomato flavor that balances sweet and tart • Firm yet tender texture	Muir Glen Organic Diced Tomatoes
TOMATOES, CANNED PUREED **Muir Glen Organic Tomato Puree**	• Full tomato flavor without any bitter, sour, or tinny notes • Pleasantly thick, even consistency, not watery or thin	Hunt's, Progresso, Cento
TOMATOES, CANNED WHOLE **Muir Glen Organic**	• Pleasing balance of bold acidity and fruity sweetness • Firm yet tender texture, even after hours of simmering	Hunt's
TOMATO PASTE **Goya**	• Bright, robust tomato flavors • Balance of sweet and tart flavors	Pastene, Contadina
TORTILLA CHIPS **On the Border Café Style**	• Traditional, buttery sweetness and bright corn flavor • The perfect counterpart to salsa • Light, crisp exterior	Tostitos Original Restaurant Style, Santitas White Corn

TEST KITCHEN FAVORITE	WHY WE LIKE IT	RUNNERS-UP
TORTILLAS, CORN **Maria and Ricardo's Handmade Style Soft Corn Tortillas, Yellow**	• Soft and pliable, don't crack when rolled up • Light, corn-like sweetness with a hint of nuttiness • Wheat gluten added to dough makes tortilla more cohesive and elastic	Mission White Corn Tortillas, Restaurant Style; Guerrero White Corn Tortillas; La Banderita Corn Tortillas, White
TORTILLAS, FLOUR **Old El Paso 6-Inch**	• Thin and flaky texture, not doughy or stale • Made with plenty of fat and salt	Mission
TOSTADAS, CORN **Mission Tostadas Estilo Casero**	• Crisp, crunchy texture • Good corn flavor • Flavor and texture that are substantial enough to stand up to hearty toppings	Charras
TUNA, CANNED **Wild Planet Wild Albacore**	• Rich, fresh-tasting, and flavorful, but not fishy • Hearty, substantial chunks of tuna	American Tuna Pole Caught Wild Albacore, Starkist Selects Solid White Albacore
TUNA, CANNED PREMIUM **Nardin Bonito Del Norte Ventresca Fillets**	• Creamy, delicate meat and tender yet firm fillets • Full, rich tuna flavor	Tonnino Tuna Ventresca Yellowfin in Olive Oil
TURKEY, WHOLE **Empire Kosher**	• Moist and dense texture without being watery, chewy, or squishy • Meaty, full turkey flavor • Buttery white meat • Koshering process renders brining unnecessary	Good Shepherd Ranch Heritage (available through mail order, Good Shepherd Turkey Ranch Inc., 785-227-5149, www.reeseturkeys.net)
VANILLA BEANS **McCormick Madagascar**	• Moist, seed-filled pods • Complex, robust flavor with caramel notes	Spice Islands Bourbon
VANILLA EXTRACT **McCormick Pure**	• Strong, rich vanilla flavor where others are weak and sharp • Complex flavor with spicy, caramel notes and a sweet undertone	Rodelle Pure, Gold Medal Imitation by C.F. Sauer Co.
VEGETABLE OIL **Crisco Natural Blend Oil**	• Unobtrusive, mild flavor for stir-frying and sautéing and for use in baked goods and in uncooked applications such as mayonnaise and vinaigrette • Neutral taste and absence of fishy or metallic flavors when used for frying	Mazola Canola Oil
VINEGAR, APPLE CIDER **Spectrum Naturals Organic Unfiltered**	• Deep, warm profile with sweet, mellow, and smooth cider flavor • Balance of richness and tanginess • Complex with notes of honey and caramel with clear apple flavor	

TEST KITCHEN FAVORITE	WHY WE LIKE IT	RUNNERS-UP
VINEGAR, BALSAMIC **Bertolli Balsamic Vinegar of Modena**	• Tastes of dried fruit like figs, raisins, and prunes • Tastes pleasantly sweet once reduced or whisked into vinaigrette	Monari Federzoni of Modena, Colavita, Ortalli of Modena, Bellino, Lucini Aged
VINEGAR, RED WINE **Laurent du Clos**	• Crisp red wine flavor balanced by stronger than average acidity and subtle sweetness • Complex yet pleasing taste from multiple varieties of grapes	Pompeian Gourmet, Spectrum Naturals Organic
VINEGAR, SHERRY **Napa Valley Naturals Reserve Sherry Vinegar**	• Has just the right amount of tang • Contains flavors ranging from "lemony" to "smoky" • In gazpacho, adds nice depth that highlight fresh flavors	O Sherry Vinegar
VINEGAR, WHITE WINE For cooking: **Colavita Aged**	• Balance of tanginess and subtle sweetness, not overly acidic or weak • Fruity, bright, and perfumed	
For vinaigrettes: **Spectrum Naturals Organic**	• Rich, dark flavor tastes fermented and malty, not artificial or harsh • Fruity flavor with caramel, earthy, and nutty notes	
WORCESTERSHIRE SAUCE **Lea & Perrins Original Worcestershire Sauce**	• Contains balanced notes of vinegar, pepper, and tamarind • In a marinade, distinctively punchy and lends a bright tanginess	French's Worcestershire Sauce
YOGURT, GREEK WHOLE-MILK **Fage Total Classic**	• High in protein with no added stabilizers or thickeners • Rich, creamy, dense, faintly sweet flavor • Holds its own against garlicky sharpness of tzatziki sauce	Dannon Oikos Traditional, Wallaby Organic
YOGURT, WHOLE-MILK **Brown Cow Cream Top Plain**	• Rich, well-rounded flavor, not sour or bland • Especially creamy, smooth texture, not thin or watery • Higher fat content contributes to flavor and texture	Stonyfield Farm Organic Plain

Glossary

We use many scientific terms in this book. While we took care to define and explain the terms as they arose in each chapter, we also wanted to create a glossary where many of them could live together, a source for research or simple curiosity.

ACTIN	One of the two major proteins in muscle fibers, the other being myosin. See *Myosin*.
ADENOSINE TRIPHOSPHATE (ATP)	The universal energy molecule that fuels the cell.
AGGLOMERATION	A process in which small, individual particles, such as the casein micelles in milk, cluster into a mass of larger particles.
ALLIIN	The odorless precursor in garlic that is converted to the predominant aroma compound of garlic, allicin.
ALLIINASE	The enzyme in garlic responsible for converting alliin to the odor compound of garlic when cells are damaged. See *Alliin*.
ALLIUM	The genus containing onions, chives, garlic, shallots, and leeks.
AMPHOTERIC	Capable of acting as either an acid or an alkali (base).
AMYLOPECTIN	The very large branched-chain polymer that occurs in starch along with the linear molecule amylose. See *Amylose, Polymer*.
AMYLOSE	The smaller linear polymer that occurs in starch. See *Amylopectin, Polymer*.
ANTIOXIDANT	A compound that inhibits oxidation reactions such as those that occur when food browns or fats turn rancid in the presence of air.
ASTRINGENCY	The quality that produces the sensation of a dry, puckery feeling in the mouth.
AUXIN	A plant hormone that promotes the formation of new cells.
BOUND WATER	Water that is tightly bound within other substances, such as starch crystals, and is not able to act as a solvent.
BRIX SCALE	A scale to indicate the percentage of sugar in sugar solutions.
CARAMELIZATION	A process in which sugar is heated and the sugar molecules undergo an array of chemical reactions, such as dehydration and polymerization, to provide new flavorful and brown-colored compounds.
CAROTENOID	A yellow, orange, or red fat-soluble pigment found in plants.
CASEIN	The primary protein found in milk, which forms micelles containing calcium phosphate. See *Micelle*.
CATHEPSINS	A group of enzymes that can break down proteins and tenderize meat; active after the onset of rigor mortis.
CHEMESTHESIS	The sensation of pain, heat, or cooling in the mouth or on the skin.
CHITIN	A rigid polymer of aminoglucose (also called glucosamine) molecules that lends structural support to the cell walls of fungi and the exoskeleton of crustaceans and insects. See *Polymer*.
CHLOROPHYLL	The green pigment in plants that enables the harvesting of light in photosynthesis.
COAGULATION	The precipitation of a protein in a liquid, such as denatured proteins in acidified milk. See *Precipitate*.
COLLAGEN	The primary protein in connective tissue that supports muscle and prevents it from overstretching. See *Connective tissue*.

COLLOID	A substance in which small particles (0.001 to 1.0 micron in diameter, not visible to the human eye) are evenly dispersed in a continuous phase. See *Continuous phase*.
COMPLETE PROTEIN	A source of protein that contains all of the essential amino acids to support the human body's maintenance and growth.
COMPOUND	A molecular entity that contains atoms bonded together. See *Molecule*.
CONDUCTION	The transfer of heat through the collisions of adjacent molecules with one another.
CONNECTIVE TISSUE	A composite material composed of proteins that provide structure and adhesiveness to the surrounding tissues. See *Collagen*.
CONTINUOUS PHASE	The phase that surrounds the dispersed phase, such as the water surrounding fat in ice cream. See *Dispersed phase*, *Emulsion*.
CONVECTION	The transfer of heat by the circulation, or movement, of a gas or liquid.
CRYSTALLIZATION	The formation of a solid, in which the molecules are arranged in a highly organized lattice.
CURD	The coagulated portion of milk. See *Whey*.
DANGER ZONE	The range of temperatures (40 to 140 degrees Fahrenheit) at which food-contaminating bacteria thrive and can quickly replicate.
DENATURATION	An irreversible process in which a protein undergoes a structural change, usually the unfolding of its native form, that results in the loss of its function.
DENSITY	The mass of an object per unit volume.
DISPERSED PHASE	The phase dispersed within a continuous phase, such as the droplets of oil dispersed in water in an oil-in-water emulsion. See *Continuous phase*.
DRUPE	A fruit with seeds encased in a pit.
ELASTICITY	The ability of a substance to return to its initial form after deformation.
ELASTIN	A protein occurring in limited amounts within connective tissue. See *Connective tissue*.
EMULSIFIER	A compound that stabilizes emulsions, the chemical structure of which usually contains both hydrophilic (water-soluble) and hydrophobic (water-repulsing) properties. See *Emulsion*.
EMULSION	An inherently unstable mixture in which an immiscible (insoluble) liquid is dispersed as droplets in another liquid. See *Continuous phase*, *Dispersed phase*.
ENDOSPERM	The largest portion of a grain, containing all of the starch.
ENZYMATIC BROWNING	An enzyme-catalyzed oxidation of phenolic compounds that produces brown-colored pigments. See *Enzyme*.
ENZYME	A protein that catalyzes a chemical reaction without being altered or consumed by the process.
FATTY ACID	An organic acid attached to a hydrophobic tail that is between four and 24 carbon atoms in length.
FERMENTATION	The conversion of carbohydrates, often by bacteria or yeast, to an array of products, which usually include carbon dioxide and alcohol.
FIBROUS PROTEIN	Insoluble protein molecules with extended, elongated shapes that often provide structural support for cells, such as collagen. See *Collagen*.
FREE RADICAL	An unstable compound containing an unpaired electron that can react with cellular components, such as DNA.
GEL	A substance that is composed of a solid network or matrix with liquid trapped throughout, such as tofu and yogurt.
GELATINIZATION	A process in which particles absorb and trap water and undergo an increase in volume, such as when starch granules absorb a liquid and swell when heated in the liquid.

GLIADIN	A type of protein in wheat that is elliptical in shape and soluble in alcohol; it contributes to the plasticity of doughs. See *Gluten*.
GLUTEN	The protein that is formed when water is mixed with wheat flour and formed into dough. See *Gliadin, Glutenin*.
GLUTENIN	A type of protein in wheat that polymerizes into very large gluten molecules through the formation of disulphide bonds. See *Gluten*.
GRAM	A metric unit of weight that is equal to the weight of 1 cubic centimeter of water (also the same as 1 milliliter of water).
HEME	The red, iron-containing pigment that is found in the hemoglobin and myoglobin proteins responsible for oxygen transport in animal tissue.
HEMICELLULOSE	Carbohydrate polymers composed of various sugars and sugar acids that are a structural feature of plant cell walls.
HOMOGENIZATION	A mechanical process that breaks fat globules in a liquid, such as those in milk, into droplets so small that they do not easily separate from the liquid.
HUSK	The outermost covering of a cereal grain.
HYDROGEN BOND	A relatively weak, noncovalent chemical bond that can form between a partially positively charged hydrogen atom and a partially negatively charged atom, usually oxygen or nitrogen.
HYDROLYSIS	A chemical reaction, in which a molecule of water breaks a chemical bond within a molecule.
HYDROPHILIC	A term describing substances that are soluble, or miscible, with water, derived from the Greek for "water loving."
HYDROPHOBIC	A term describing substances that are insoluble, or immiscible, with water, derived from the Greek for "water fearing."
HYGROSCOPIC	Having the ability to attract and hold water.
INVERT SUGAR	An equal mixture of glucose and fructose produced by the hydrolysis of sucrose, often in the presence of acid.
INVERTASE	An enzyme that catalyzes the hydrolysis of sucrose to invert sugar, which is a mixture of glucose and fructose. See *Invert sugar*.
ISOELECTRIC POINT	The pH at which a protein has the same number of positive and negative charges, or no net charge, and is particularly susceptible to denaturation. See *Denaturation, pH Scale*.
LATENT HEAT	The amount of energy (measured in kilocalories) absorbed or released per gram of a substance as the substance changes phase—from a liquid to a gas, for instance—during which the temperature of the substance does not change.
LIGNIN	A nondigestible rigid structural component of plant cell walls and a major component of wood.
MAILLARD REACTION	The reaction of reducing sugars (such as glucose, fructose, and lactose) with amino acids and/or proteins to produce new, flavorful, brown-pigmented compounds.
MELTING POINT	The temperature, or temperature range, at which a solid becomes a liquid.
MICELLE	A spherical particle composed of many individual molecules, in which hydrophobic areas of the molecules are aligned and hydrophilic parts extend into the surrounding solution.
MOLECULE	Two or more atoms linked together by covalent bonds. See *Compound*.
MYOSIN	One of the two major proteins in muscle fibers, the other being actin. See *Actin*.
MYOTOMES	Layers of parallel short muscle fibers in fish muscle tissue.
NUCLEOTIDE	A small nitrogen-containing molecule that is the monomer that constitutes the important polymer of life, DNA, and is also found in the energy molecule ATP. See *Adenosine triphosphate, Umami*.

OSMOSIS	The movement of a liquid, usually water, across a semipermeable membrane from a dilute solution toward a more concentrated solution.
OSMOTIC PRESSURE	The pressure that develops when two solutions of different concentration are separated by a permeable membrane.
PASTEURIZATION	A method of preserving liquids, such as milk, by heating (often to 161 degrees for 15 seconds) to kill bacteria, yeast, and mold.
PECTIN	A polysaccharide primarily composed of a sugar acid called galacturonic acid; an important component of plant cell walls; the "glue" that holds cells together.
PEPTIDE	Two or more amino acids bonded together.
PEPTIDE BOND	The chemical bond linking two amino acids together in peptides and proteins, also known as an amide bond. See *Peptide*.
pH SCALE	A logarithmic scale measuring the acidity or alkalinity of a liquid, ranging from 0 to 14, with 7 being neutral. Below 7 is acidic and above is alkaline.
PLASTICITY	The ability of a substance to be shaped or molded.
POLYMER	A large molecule made up of many repeating subunits.
POLYPHENOL	An organic compound composed of multiple phenol rings, which are 6-membered aromatic rings containing one or more hydroxyl (OH) groups. See *Tannins*.
POLYSACCHARIDE	A general term for a carbohydrate polymer composed of many sugar molecules linked together. See *Polymer*.
PRECIPITATE	To separate out of a solution.
RANCID	The unpleasant odors and tastes associated with unsaturated fatty acids that have oxidized through a reaction with oxygen in the air.
RENNET	The commercial name for rennin. See *Rennin*.
RENNIN	An enzyme produced from the inner lining of calf's stomach used to produce cheese. See *Rennet*.
RESPIRATION	The oxidation of carbohydrates to produce carbon dioxide, water, and energy in the form of ATP. See *Adenosine triphosphate*.
RETROGRADATION	The formation of crystalline starch from gelatinized starch.
RIGOR MORTIS	The temporary state following death in which muscles stiffen.
RIPENING	The physical and chemical changes that occur when a fruit progresses from the mature stage to the ripe stage of development.
SARCOMERE	A unit of a muscle fiber, which consists of fibrils of actin and myosin and gives muscle its striated appearance when magnified.
SATURATED FATTY ACID	A fatty acid that is fully saturated with hydrogen atoms and lacks double bonds. See *Fatty acid*.
SMOKE POINT	The temperature at which a fat or an oil begins to smoke when heated.
SOLUBILITY	The degree to which one substance blends uniformly with another, usually in the form of a liquid.
SOLUTE	A solid, liquid, or gas dissolved in another substance, usually a liquid. See *Solution*.
SOLUTION	A completely homogeneous mixture of a solute dissolved in a solvent. See *Solute*.
SOLVENT	A substance, usually a liquid, in which another substance is dissolved. See *Solute. Solution*.
SPECIFIC HEAT	The amount of heat to raise the temperature of 1 gram of a substance by 1 degree centigrade.

STARCH	A complex carbohydrate consisting of two molecules, amylose and amylopectin, which are polymers of glucose. See *Amylose, Amylopectin.*
STARCH GRANULE	A solid mass of amylopectin and amylose molecules, which can swell in volume when mixed with water. See *Amylose, Amylopectin.*
STARTER	A culture, or population, of microorganisms used to produce fermented products, such as bread, cheese, and certain beverages.
STERILIZATION	The elimination of all microorganisms by heating at high temperatures well above the boiling point of water.
SUBSTRATE	A substance acted upon by an enzyme or chemical agent.
SURFACTANT	A surface-active agent, often containing both hydrophilic and hydrophobic components within its chemical structure, which reduces the surface tension of a liquid and stabilizes emulsions. See *Emulsifier.*
SUSPENSION	A mixture in which insoluble particles are suspended in a liquid.
SYNERESIS	The release of a liquid from a gel; for instance, the release of whey from yogurt during storage.
TANNINS	Polyphenols, many of which are reddish and brown-colored pigments. See *Polyphenol.*
TURGOR	The rigid firmness of a plant cell, resulting from being filled with water.
UMAMI	A savory taste sensation created by certain amino acids and peptides that is enhanced by the presence of nucleotides. See *Nucleotide.*
UNSATURATED FATTY ACID	A fatty acid that contains one or more carbon-carbon double bonds that is not fully saturated with hydrogen atoms. See *Fatty acid.*
VISCOSITY	The resistance of a fluid to flow, which arises from the presence of particles within the fluid.
VOLATILE	A property of a molecule that allows it to escape as a gas into the atmosphere at relatively low temperatures, a property associated with aroma compounds.
WATER ACTIVITY	A measure of the adsorbed and free water content of food, expressed as a dimensionless scale ranging from 0 to 1, in which pure water has a value of 1.
WATER HOLDING CAPACITY	The total amount of water a substance or material, such as muscle fibers, can hold within its network.
WHEY	The liquid portion of milk, consisting of water (about 93 percent), lactose, and whey proteins, which is removed from the curd when cheese is made. See *Curd.*

TAXONOMIC CLASSIFICATION LEVELS

The taxonomic classification of all living things was first developed by the Swedish scientist Carolus Linnaeus, who published the organization of all plants in 1753 and all animals in 1758.

There are five kingdoms of living things: plants, animals, fungi, bacteria, and single-celled protozoa. Linnaeus developed the two-name system of classifying specific organisms, with the genus name spelled with a capital letter and the species name with a lowercase letter. For example, the name for the species of sweet almond tree is *Prunus dulcis*. Almond trees belong to the genus *Prunus*, and the sweet variety of almond comes from the tree *Prunus dulcis*.

Below the level of the species of a plant lie the specific variety, and within the varieties are cultivars. Although variety and cultivar are often used interchangeably, a variety arises naturally in the plant kingdom from seed, while a cultivar, or "cultivated variety," arises from human intervention, such as from plant cuttings. The distinction is that the variety name is written within single quotation marks, such as the specific variety of red maple tree (*Acer rubrum*) 'Red Glory,' while the cultivar name is always written in lowercase letters in italics.

LINNAEUS'S SYSTEM OF CLASSIFICATION
Kingdom — Phylum — Class — Order — Family — Genus — Species

Selected Resources

The science in this book is based on the best available scientific literature, including scholarly textbooks, review articles, and original research papers published in peer-reviewed academic journals. The information in this book was gathered from approximately 300 scientific papers. A list of the key sources follows.　　　　— Guy Crosby, PhD

GENERAL REFERENCES

Belitz, H.-D., Grosch, W., & Schieberle, P. (2009). *Food Chemistry* (4th ed.). Berlin: Springer-Verlag.

Brown, A. (2011). *Understanding Food: Principles and Preparation* (4th ed.). Belmont, CA: Wadsworth.

Coultate, T. (2016). *Food: The Chemistry of Its Components* (6th ed.). Cambridge, UK: Royal Society of Chemistry.

McGee, H. (2004). *On Food and Cooking: The Science and Lore of the Kitchen.* New York: Scribner.

McWilliams, M. (2012). *Foods: Experimental Perspectives* (7th ed.). Upper Saddle River, NJ: Prentice Hall.

Reineccius, G. (2006). *Flavor Chemistry and Technology* (2nd ed.). Boca Raton, FL: CRC Press.

REFERENCES BY CHAPTER

1. SHORT LOIN
Jeremiah, L. E., Dugan, M. E. R., Aalhus, J. L., & Gibson, L. L. (2003). Assessment of the chemical and cooking properties of the major beef muscles and muscle groups. *Meat Science, 65*(3), 985–992.

Klont, R. E., Brocks, L., & Eikelenboom, G. (1998). Muscle fibre type and meat quality. *Meat Science, 49*(Suppl. 1), S219–S229.

2. FLANK
Astruc, T., Gatellier, P., Labas, R., Lhoutellier, V. S., & Marinova, P. (2010). Microstructural changes in *m. rectus abdominis* bovine muscle after heating. *Meat Science, 85*(4), 743–751.

Oury, M.-P., Dumont, R., Jurie, C., Hocquette, J.-F., & Picard, B. (2010). Specific fibre composition and metabolism of the *rectus abdominis* muscle of bovine Charolais cattle. *BMC Biochemistry, 11*, 12–24.

3. PORK LOIN
Van Laack, R. L. J. M., Stevens, S. G., & Stalder, K. J. (2001). The influence of ultimate pH and intramuscular fat content on pork tenderness and tenderization. *Journal of Animal Science, 79*(2), 392–397.

Wood, J. D., Nute, G. R., Fursey, G. A. J., & Cuthbertson, A. (1995). The effect of cooking conditions on the eating quality of pork. *Meat Science, 40*(2), 127–135.

4. PORK SHOULDER
Hambrecht, E., Eissen, J. J., Newman, D. J., Smits, C. H. M., Verstegen, M. W. A., & den Hartog, L. A. (2005). Preslaughter handling effects on pork quality and glycolytic potential in two muscles differing in fiber type composition. *Journal of Animal Science, 83*(4), 900–907.

Nold, R. A., Romans, J. R., Costello, W. J., & Libal, G. W. (1999). Characterization of muscles from boars, barrows, and gilts slaughtered at 100 or 110 kilograms: Differences in fat, moisture, color, water-holding capacity, and collagen. *Journal of Animal Science, 77*(7), 1746–1754.

5. PORK BELLY
Timón, M. L., Carrapiso, A. I., Jurado, Á., & Van De Lagemaat, J. (2004). A study of the aroma of fried bacon and fried pork loin. *Journal of the Science of Food and Agriculture, 84*(8), 825–831.

Trusell, K. A., Apple, J. K., Yancey, J. W. S., Johnson, T. M., Galloway, D. L., & Stackhouse, R. J. (2011). Compositional and instrumental firmness variations within fresh pork bellies. *Meat Science, 88*(3), 472–480.

6. CHICKEN BREASTS

Aliani, M., & Farmer, L. J. (2005). Precursors of chicken flavor II: Identification of key flavor precursors using sensory methods. *Journal of Agricultural and Food Chemistry, 53*(16), 6455–6462.

Petracci, M., Laghi, L., Rocculi, P., Rimini, S., Panarese, V., Cremonini, M. a., & Cavani, C. (2012). The use of sodium bicarbonate for marination of broiler breast meat. *Poultry Science, 91*(2), 526–534.

7. CHICKEN WINGS

Brent, A. E., & Tabin, C. J. (2004). White meat or dark? *Nature Genetics, 36*(1), 8–10.

Nakano, T., Ozimek, L., & Betti, M. (2012). Deboning broiler chicken legs and wings by dislocation of articular cartilage followed by stripping periosteum. *Poultry Science, 91*(11), 2938–2941.

8. LAMB

Duckett, S. K., & Kuber, P. S. (2001). Genetic and nutritional effects on lamb flavor. *Journal of Animal Science, 79*(E Suppl.), E249–E254.

Howes, N. L., Bekhit, A. E.-D. A., Burritt, D. J., & Campbell, A. W. (2015). Opportunities and implications of pasture-based lamb fattening to enhance the long-chain fatty acid composition in meat. *Comprehensive Reviews in Food Science and Food Safety, 14*(1), 22–36.

Young, O. A., & Braggins, T. J. (1993). Tenderness of ovine semimembranosus: Is collagen concentration or solubility the critical factor? *Meat Science, 35*(2), 213–222.

9. WHITE FISH

Johnston, I. A. (1981). Structure and function of fish muscles. *Symposia of the Zoological Society of London, 48,* 71–113.

Zimmerman, A. M., & Lowery, M. S. (1999). Hyperplastic development and hypertrophic growth of muscle fibers in the white seabass (*Atractoscion nobilis*). *Journal of Experimental Zoology, 284*(3), 299–308.

10. SALMON

Glover, K. A., Otterå, H., Olsen, R. E., Slinde, E., Taranger, G. L., & Skaala, Ø. (2009). A comparison of farmed, wild and hybrid Atlantic salmon (*Salmo salar* L.) reared under farming conditions. *Aquaculture, 286*(3–4), 203–210.

Johnston, I. A., Li, X., Vieira, V. L. A., Nickell, D., Dingwall, A., Alderson, R., Campbell, P., & Bickerdike, R. (2006). Muscle and flesh quality traits in wild and farmed Atlantic salmon. *Aquaculture, 256*(1–4), 323–336.

Johnston, I. A., Manthri, S., Alderson, R., Smart, A., Campbell, P., Nickell, D., Robertson, B., Paxton, C. G. M., & Burt, M. L. (2003). Freshwater environment affects growth rate and muscle fibre recruitment in seawater stages of Atlantic salmon (*Salmo salar* L.). *The Journal of Experimental Biology, 206*(Pt 8), 1337–1351.

11. SHRIMP

Boonsumrej, S., Chaiwanichsiri, S., Tantratian, S., Suzuki, T., & Takai, R. (2007). Effects of freezing and thawing on the quality changes of tiger shrimp (*Penaeus monodon*) frozen by air-blast and cryogenic freezing. *Journal of Food Engineering, 80*(1), 292–299.

Ravichandran, S., Rameshkumar, G., & Prince, A. R. (2009). Biochemical composition of shell and flesh of the Indian white shrimp *Penaeus indicus* (*H. milne* Edwards 1837). *American-Eurasian Journal of Scientific Research, 4*(3), 191–194.

Stephens, P. J., & Mellon, D. (1979). Modification of structure and synaptic physiology in transformed shrimp muscle. *Journal of Comparative Physiology A, 132*(2), 97–108.

12. SCALLOPS

Fisher, R. A., Kirkley, J. E., & DuPaul, W. D. (1990). Phosphate use in processing sea scallops, Placopecten magellanicus, in the mid-Atlantic region. *Fifteenth Annual Tropical and Subtropical Fisheries Technological Conference of the Americas.* SGR-105: 154–162.

Harris, B., & Stokesbury, K. (2006). Shell growth of sea scallops (*Placopecten magellanicus*) in the southern and northern Great South Channel, USA. *ICES Journal of Marine Science, 64*(5), 811–821.

Wongso, S., & Yamanaka, H. (1996). Changes in content of extractive components in the adductor muscle of noble scallop during storage. *Fisheries Science, 62*(5), 815–820.

13. LOBSTER

Miegel, A., Kobayashi, T., & Maéda, Y. (1992). Isolation, purification and partial characterization of tropomyosin and troponin subunits from the lobster tail muscle. *Journal of Muscle Research and Cell Motility, 13*(6), 608–618.

Mykles, D. L. (1985). Heterogeneity of myofibrillar proteins in lobster fast and slow muscles: Variants of troponin, paramyosin, and myosin light chains comprise four distinct protein assemblages. *The Journal of Experimental Zoology, 234*(1), 23–32.

14. TOFU

Chang, S. K. C. (2007). Soymilk and tofu manufacturing. In Y. H. Hui (Ed.), *Handbook of Food Products Manufacturing* (pp. 1063–1089). Hoboken, NJ: Wiley-Interscience.

Kao, F. J., Su, N. W., & Lee, M. H. (2003). Effect of calcium sulfate concentration in soymilk on the microstructure of firm tofu and the protein constitutions in tofu whey. *Journal of Agricultural and Food Chemistry, 51*(21), 6211–6216.

15. EGGS

Licciardello, F., Frisullo, P., Laverse, J., Muratore, G., & Del Nobile, M. A. (2012). Effect of sugar, citric acid and egg white type on the microstructural and mechanical properties of meringues. *Journal of Food Engineering, 108*(3), 453–462.

Sirvente, H., Beaumal, V., Gaillard, C., Bialek, L., Hamm, D., & Anton, M. (2007). Structuring and functionalization of dispersions containing egg yolk, plasma and granules induced by mechanical treatments. *Journal of Agricultural and Food Chemistry, 55*(23), 9537–9544.

16. CREAM

Bot, A., Kleinherenbrink, F. A. M., Mellema, M., & Magnani, C. K. (2007). Cream cheese as an acidified protein-stabilized emulsion gel. In Y. H. Hui (Ed.), *Handbook of Food Products Manufacturing* (pp. 651–672). Hoboken, NJ: Wiley-Interscience.

Lucey, J. A. (2002). Formation and physical properties of milk protein gels. *Journal of Dairy Science, 85*(2), 281–294.

17. BUTTER

Bendixen, H. A. (1940). Acid values and acid ratios as related to the keeping quality of salted butter. *Journal of Dairy Science, 23*(4), 275–284.

Kirkeby, P. G. (2007). Margarine and dairy spreads: Processing and technology. In Y. H. Hui (Ed.), *Handbook of Food Products and Manufacturing* (pp. 705–724). Hoboken, NJ: Wiley-Interscience.

18. YOGURT

Lee, W. J., & Lucey, J. A. (2010). Formation and physical properties of yogurt. *Asian-Australasian Journal of Animal Sciences, 23*(9), 1127–1136.

Lucey, J. A. (2002). Formation and physical properties of milk protein gels. *Journal of Dairy Science, 85*(2), 281–294.

Ott, A., Fay, L. B., & Chaintreau, A. (1997). Determination and origin of the aroma impact compounds of yogurt flavor. *Journal of Agricultural and Food Chemistry, 45*(3), 850–858.

19. GOAT CHEESE

Abu-Alruz, K., Mazahreh, A. S., Al-Shawabkeh, A. F., Al-Omari, A., & Quasem, J. M. (2009). Meltability and stretchability of white brined cheese: Effect of emulsifier salts. *American Journal of Applied Sciences, 6*(8), 1553–1559.

Attaie, R., & Richter, R. L. (2000). Size distribution of fat globules in goat milk. *Journal of Dairy Science, 83*(5), 940–944.

Carunchiawhetstine, M. E., Karagul-Yuceer, Y., Avsar, Y. K., & Drake, M. A. (2003). Identification and quantification of character aroma components in fresh chevre-style goat cheese. *Journal of Food Science, 68*(8), 2441–2447.

Clark, S., & Sherbon, J. W. (2000). Alpha s1-casein, milk composition and coagulation properties of goat milk. *Small Ruminant Research, 38*(2), 123–134.

Lucey, J. A., Johnson, M. E., & Horne, D. S. (2003). Invited review: Perspectives on the basis of the rheology and texture properties of cheese. *Journal of Dairy Science, 86*(9), 2725–2743.

Park, Y. W., Juárez, M., Ramos, M., & Haenlein, G. F. W. (2007). Physico-chemical characteristics of goat and sheep milk. *Small Ruminant Research, 68*(1), 88–113.

20. PARMESAN

de Angelis Curtis, S., Curini, R., Delni, M., Brosio, E., D'Ascenzo, F., Bocca, B. (2000). Amino acid profile in the ripening of Grana Padano cheese: a NMR study. *Food Chemistry 71*, 495–502.

Govindasamy-Lucey, S., Jaeggi, J. J., Bostley, A. L., Johnson, M. E., & Lucey, J. A. (2004). Standardization of milk using cold ultrafiltration retentates for the manufacture of parmesan cheese. *Journal of Dairy Science, 87*(9), 2789–2799.

Tansman, G. F., Kindstedt, P. S., & Hughes, J. M. (2015). Crystal fingerprinting: Elucidating the crystals of Cheddar, Parmigiano-Reggiano, Gouda, and soft washed-rind cheeses using powder x-ray diffractometry. *Dairy Science & Technology, 95*(5), 651–664.

21. GREEN BEANS

Baker, R. A. (1997). Reassessment of some fruit and vegetable pectin levels. *Journal of Food Science, 62*(2), 225–229.

Stolle-Smits, T., Beekhuizen, J. G., Kok, M. T., Pijnenburg, M., Recourt, K., Derksen, J., & Voragen, A. G. (1999). Changes in cell wall polysaccharides of green bean pods during development. *Plant Physiology, 121*(2), 363–372.

22. SWEET POTATOES

Buescher, R. W., & Balmoori, M. R. (1982). Mechanism of hardcore formation in chill-injured sweet potato (*Ipomoea batatas*) roots. *Journal of Food Biochemistry, 6*(1), 1–11.

Walter, W. M., Purcell, A. E., & Nelson, A. M. (1975). Effects of amylolytic enzymes on "moistness" and carbohydrate changes of baked sweet potato cultivars. *Journal of Food Science, 40*(4), 793–796.

23. CAULIFLOWER

Boriss, H., H. Brunke, & Kreith, M. (2006). *Commodity profile: Cauliflower*. Retrieved from http://aic.ucdavis.edu/profiles/Cauliflower-2006.pdf

Engel, E., Baty, C., le Corre, D., Souchon, I., & Martin, N. (2002). Flavor-active compounds potentially implicated in cooked cauliflower acceptance. *Journal of Agricultural and Food Chemistry, 50*(22), 6459–6467.

24. MUSHROOMS

Fischer, M. W. F., & Money, N. P. (2010). Why mushrooms form gills: Efficiency of the lamellate morphology. *Fungal Biology, 114*(1), 57–63.

Moore, D., & Holden, L. (2006). *Mushroom Structure: Teacher's Notes*. Retrieved from http://www.davidmoore.org.uk/Assets/fungi4schools/Documentation/WORKSHOP/mushroom_structure_teachers-notes.pdf

Zivanovic, S., Buescher, R., & Kim, S. K. (2003). Mushroom texture, cell wall composition, color, and ultrastructure as affected by pH and temperature. *Journal of Food Science, 68*(5), 1860–1865.

25. KALE

Drewnowski, A., & Gomez-Carneros, C. (2000). Bitter taste, phytonutrients, and the consumer: a review. *The American Journal of Clinical Nutrition, 72*(6), 1424–1435.

Hagen, S. F., Borge, G. I. A., Solhaug, K. A., & Bengtsson, G. B. (2009). Effect of cold storage and harvest date on bioactive compounds in curly kale (*Brassica oleracea* L. var. *acephala*). *Postharvest Biology and Technology, 51*(1), 36–42.

Kopsell, D. E., Kopsell, D. A., Randle, W. M., Coolong, T. W., Sams, C. E., & Curran-Celentano, J. (2003). Kale carotenoids remain stable while flavor compounds respond to changes in sulfur fertility. *Journal of Agricultural and Food Chemistry, 51*(18), 5319–5325.

26. CABBAGE

Scott, R., & Sullivan, W. C. (2008). Ecology of fermented foods. *Human Ecology Review, 15*(1), 25–31.

Yen, G.-C., & Wei, Q.-K. (1993). Myrosinase activity and total glucosinolate content of cruciferous vegetables, and some properties of cabbage myrosinase in Taiwan. *Journal of the Science of Food and Agriculture, 61*(4), 471–475.

27. TOMATOES

Baldwin, E. A., Scott, J. W., Shewmaker, C. K., & Schuch, W. (2000). Flavor trivia and tomato aroma: Biochemistry and possible mechanisms for control of important aroma components. *HortScience, 35*(6), 1013–1022.

Seymour, G. B., Colquhoun, I. J., Dupont, M. S., Parsley, K. R., & Selvendran, R. (1990). Composition and structural features of cell wall polysaccharides from tomato fruits. *Phytochemistry, 29*(3), 725–731.

Tandon, K. S., Jordan, M., Goodner, K., & Baldwin, E. A. (2001). Characterization of fresh tomato aroma volatiles using GC-olfactometry. *Proceedings of the Florida State Horticultural Society, 114*, 142–144.

28. GARLIC

Block, E. (2010). *Garlic and Other Alliums: The Lore and the Science*. Cambridge, UK: The Royal Society of Chemistry Publishing.

Jones, M.G., Collin, H. A., Tregova, A., Trueman, L., Brown, L., Costick, R., Hughes, J., Milne, J., Wilkinson, M. C., Tomsett, A. B., & Thomas, B. (2007). The biochemical and physiological genesis of alliin in garlic. *Medicinal and Aromatic Plant Science and Biotechnology, 1*(1), 21–24.

29. ONIONS

Granvogl, M., Christlbauer, M., & Schieberle, P. (2004). Quantitation of the intense aroma compound 3-mercapto-2-methylpentan-1-ol in raw and processed onions (*Allium cepa*) of different origins and in other *Allium* varieties using a stable isotope dilution assay. *Journal of Agricultural and Food Chemistry, 52*(10), 2797–2802.

Kopsell, D. E., & Randle, W. M. (2002). Incubation time, cultivar, and storage duration affect onion lachrymatory factor quantification. *HortScience, 37*(3), 567–570.

Randle, W. M., Kopsell, D. E., & Kopsell, D. A. (2002). Sequentially reducing sulfate fertility during onion growth and development affects bulb flavor at harvest. *HortScience, 37*(1), 118–121.

30. GINGER

Ali, B. H., Blunden, G., Tanira, M. O., & Nemmar, A. (2008). Some phytochemical, pharmacological and toxicological properties of ginger (*Zingiber officinale* Roscoe): A review of recent research. *Food and Chemical Toxicology, 46*(2), 409–420.

Ha, M., Bekhit, A. E. D. A., Carne, A., & Hopkins, D. L. (2012). Characterisation of commercial papain, bromelain, actinidin and zingibain protease preparations and their activities toward meat proteins. *Food Chemistry, 134*(1), 95–105.

Huang, X. W., Chen, L. J., Luo, Y. B., Guo, H. Y., & Ren, F. Z. (2011). Purification, characterization, and milk coagulating properties of ginger proteases. *Journal of Dairy Science, 94*(5), 2259–2269.

Nafi', A., Foo, H. L., Jamilah, B., & Ghazali, H. M. (2013). Properties of proteolytic enzyme from ginger (*Zingiber officinale* Roscoe). *International Food Research Journal, 20*(1), 363–368.

31. DRIED CHILES

Chuang, H., & Lin, S. (2009). Oxidative challenges sensitize the capsaicin receptor by covalent cysteine modification. *Proceedings of the National Academy of Sciences of the United States of America, 106*(47), 20097–20102.

Schweiggert, U., Carle, R., & Schieber, A. (2006). Characterization of major and minor capsaicinoids and related compounds in chili pods (*Capsicum frutescens* L.) by high-performance liquid chromatography/atmospheric pressure chemical ionization mass spectrometry. *Analytica Chimica Acta, 557*(1–2), 236–244.

32. APPLES

Costa, F., Cappellin, L., Longhi, S., Guerra, W., Magnago, P., Porro, D., Soukoulis, C., Salvi, S., Velasco, R., Biasioli, F., & Gasperi, F. (2011). Assessment of apple (*Malus x domestica* Borkh.) fruit texture by a combined acoustic-mechanical profiling strategy. *Postharvest Biology and Technology, 61*(1), 21–28.

DeEll, J. R., Khanizadeh, S., Saad, F., & Ferree, D. C. (2001). Factors affecting apple fruit firmness: A review. *Journal of the American Pomological Society, 55*(1), 8–27.

33. STRAWBERRIES

Baker, R. A. (1997). Reassessment of some fruit and vegetable pectin levels. *Journal of Food Science, 62*(2), 225–229.

Forney, C. F. (2001). Horticultural and other factors affecting aroma volatile composition of small fruit. *HortTechnology, 11*(4), 529–538.

34. ORANGES

Rouseff, R., & Perez-Cacho, P. R. (2007). Citrus Flavours. In G. Berger (Ed.), *Flavours and Fragrances: Chemistry, Bioprocessing and Sustainability* (pp. 117-134). Berlin: Springer-Verlag.

Song, K. J., Echeverria, E., & Lee, H. S. (1998). Distribution of sugars and related enzymes in the stem and blossom halves of 'Valencia' oranges. *Journal of the American Horticultural Society, 123*(3), 416–420.

35. COCONUT

Banzon, J. A., & Velasco, R. (1982). *Coconut: Production and Utilization*. Manila: Philippine Coconut Research and Development Foundation.

De Taffin, G. (1998). *Coconut*. Basingstoke, UK: Macmillan Education.

36. PASTA

Liu, C. Y., Shepherd, K. W., & Rathjen, A. J. (1996). Improvement of durum wheat pastamaking and breadmaking qualities. *Cereal Chemistry, 73*(2), 155–166.

Pagani, M. A., Lucisano, M., & Mariotti, M. (2007). Traditional Italian products from wheat and other starchy flours. In Y. H. Hui (Ed.), *Handbook of Food Products Manufacturing* (pp. 327–354). Hoboken, NJ: Wiley-Interscience.

Sung, W. C., & Stone, M. (2005). Microstructural studies of pasta and starch pasta. *Journal of Marine Science and Technology, 13*(2), 83–88.

37. WHOLE-WHEAT FLOUR

Doblado-Maldonado, A. F., Rose, D. J., Sweley, J. C., & Pike, O. A. (2012). Key issues and challenges in whole wheat flour milling and storage. *Journal of Cereal Science, 56*(2), 119–126.

Pomeranz, Y. (Ed.). (1990). *Wheat, Chemistry and Technology* (3rd ed.). St. Paul, MN: American Association of Cereal Chemists.

38. BROWN RICE

Cameron, D. K., & Wang, Y. J. (2005). A better understanding of factors that affect the hardness and stickiness of long-grain rice. *Cereal Chemistry, 82*(2), 113–119.

Lucisano, M., Mariotti, M., Pagani, M. A., Bottega, G., & Fongaro, L. (2009). Cooking and textural properties of some traditional and aromatic rice cultivars. *Cereal Chemistry, 86*(5), 542–548.

39. CORNMEAL

Gwirtz, J. A., & Garcia-Casal, M. N. (2014). Processing maize flour and corn meal food products. *Annals of the New York Academy of Sciences, 1312*(1), 66–75.

Pagani, M. A., Lucisano, M., & Mariotti, M. (2007). Conventional and typical Italian products from corn. In Y. H. Hui (Ed.), *Handbook of Food Products Manufacturing* (pp. 370-376). Hoboken, NJ: Wiley-Interscience.

40. OATS

Ganssman, W., & Vorwerch, K. (1995). Oat milling, processing and storage. In R. W. Welch (Ed.), *The Oat Crop: Production and Utilization* (pp. 369-408). London: Chapman and Hall.

Girardet, N., & Webster, F. H. (2011). Oat Milling: Specifications, storage and processing. *Oats: Chemistry and Technology* (2nd ed.) (pp. 301–319). St. Paul, MN: AACC International Press.

41. QUINOA

Abugoch James, L. E. (2009). Quinoa (*Chenopodium quinoa* Willd.): Composition, chemistry, nutritional, and functional properties. *Advances in Food and Nutrition Research, 58*, 1–31.

Zhu, N., Sheng, S., Sang, S., Jhoo, J. W., Bai, N., Karwe, M. V., Rosen, R. T., & Ho, C. T. (2002). Triterpene saponins from de-bittered quinoa (*Chenopodium quinoa*) seeds. *Journal of Agricultural and Food Chemistry, 50*(4), 865–867.

42. CANNELLINI BEANS

Kon, S. (1979). Effect of soaking temperature on cooking and nutritional quality of beans. *Journal of Food Science, 44*(5), 1329–1340.

Quintana, J. M., Harrison, H. C., Nienhuis, J., Palta, J. P., & Kmiecik, K. (1999). Differences in pod calcium concentration for eight snap bean and dry bean cultivars. *HortScience, 34*(5), 932–934.

43. LENTILS

Wang, N. & Daun, J. K. (2006). Effects of variety and crude protein content on nutrients and anti-nutrients in lentils (Lens culinaris). *Food Chemistry, 95*(3), 493–502.

Zhang, B., Deng, Z., Tang, Y., Chen, P. X., Liu, R., Ramdath, D. D., Liu, Q., Hernandez, M., & Tsao, R. (2014). Effect of domestic cooking on carotenoids, tocopherols, fatty acids, phenolics, and antioxidant activities of lentils (*Lens culinaris*). *Journal of Agricultural and Food Chemistry, 62*(52), 12585–12594.

44. OLIVE OIL

Vossen, P. (2007). *International Olive Oil Council (IOC) and California Trade Standards for Olive Oil.* Retrieved from http://cesonoma.ucanr.edu/files/27262.pdf

Vossen, P. (2007). Olive oil: History, production, and characteristics of the world's classic oils. *HortScience, 42*(5), 1093–1100.

45. STOCK

Christlbauer, M., & Schieberle, P. (2011). Evaluation of the key aroma compounds in beef and pork vegetable gravies a la chef by stable isotope dilution assays and aroma recombination experiments. *Journal of Agricultural and Food Chemistry, 59*(24), 13122–13130.

Snitkjaer, P., Frost, M. B., Skibsted, L. H., & Risbo, J. (2010). Flavour development during beef stock reduction. *Food Chemistry, 122*(3), 645–655.

46. RED WINE

Clarke, R. J., & Bakker, J. (2004). *Wine Flavour Chemistry.* Oxford, UK: Blackwell Publishing.

Goode, J. (2005). *The Science of Wine: From Vine to Glass.* Berkeley, CA: University of California Press.

van Leeuwen, C., & Seguin, G. (2006). The concept of terroir in viticulture. *Journal of Wine Research, 17*(1), 1–10.

47. HONEY

Berlitz, H.-D., Grosch, W., & Schieberle, P. (2009). Honey and artificial honey. *Food chemistry* (4th ed.) (pp. 883–891). Berlin: Springer-Verlag.

White, J. W. (1978). Honey. *Advances in Food Research, 24*(C), 287–374.

48. BALSAMIC VINEGAR

Antonelli, A., Chinnici, F., & Masino, F. (2004). Heat-induced chemical modification of grape must as related to its concentration during the production of traditional balsamic vinegar: A preliminary approach. *Food Chemistry, 88*(1), 63–68.

Budak, N. H., Aykin, E., Seydim, A. C., Greene, A. K., & Guzel-Seydim, Z. B. (2014). Functional properties of vinegar. *Journal of Food Science, 79*(5), R757–R764.

Chiarello, M., & Wisner, P. (1996). Balsamic vinegar. In *Flavored Vinegars: 50 Recipes for Cooking with Infused Vinegars* (pp. 46–59). San Francisco: Chronicle Books.

Giudici, P., Gullo, M., Solieri, L., & Falcone, P. M. (2009). Technological and microbiological aspects of traditional balsamic vinegar and their influence on quality and sensorial properties. *Advances in Food and Nutrition Research, 58*, 137–182.

Hillmann, H., Mattes, J., Brockhoff, A., Dunkel, A., Meyerhof, W., & Hofmann, T. (2012). Sensomics analysis of taste compounds in balsamic vinegar and discovery of 5-acetoxymethyl-2-furaldehyde as a novel sweet taste modulator. *Journal of Agricultural and Food Chemistry, 60*(40), 9974–9990.

Masino, F., Chinnici, F., Bendini, A., Montevecchi, G., & Antonelli, A. (2008). A study on relationships among chemical, physical, and qualitative assessment in traditional balsamic vinegar. *Food Chemistry, 106*(1), 90–95.

Riley, G. (2007). *The Oxford Companion to Italian Food.* New York: Oxford University Press.

49. BITTERSWEET CHOCOLATE

Counet, C., Callemien, D., Ouwerx, C., & Collin, S. (2002). Use of gas chromatography-olfactometry to identify key odorant compounds in dark chocolate: Comparison of samples before and after conching. *Journal of Agricultural and Food Chemistry, 50*(8), 2385–2391.

Hofberger, R. & Tanabe, N. A. (2007). Chocolate and cocoa. In Y. H. Hui (Ed.), *Handbook of Food Products Manufacturing* (pp. 675–691). Hoboken, NJ: Wiley-Interscience.

Smith, K. (2006). *Chocolate Tempering.* Retrieved from http://courses.ecolechocolat.com/lobjects/pdf/belgium_tempering.pdf

50. ALMONDS

Almond Board of California. (2010). *Technical Information Kit.* Retrieved from http://www.almonds.com/sites/default/files/content/Technical%20%20Information%20Kit.pdf

Civille, G. V., Lapsley, K., Huang, G., Yada, S., & Seltsam, J. (2010). Development of an almond lexicon to assess the sensory properties of almond varieties. *Journal of Sensory Studies, 25*(1), 146–162.

Fisklements, M., & Barrett, D. M. (2014). Kinetics of almond skin separation as a function of blanching time and temperature. *Journal of Food Engineering, 138*, 11–16.

Conversions and Equivalents

Some say cooking is a science and an art. We would say that geography has a hand in it, too. Flour milled in the United Kingdom and elsewhere will feel and taste different from flour milled in the United States. So we cannot promise that the loaf of bread you bake in Canada or England will taste the same as a loaf baked in the States, but we can offer guidelines for converting weights and measures. We also recommend that you rely on your instincts when making our recipes. Refer to the visual cues provided. If the bread dough hasn't "come together in a ball," as described, you may need to add more flour—even if the recipe doesn't tell you to. You be the judge.

The recipes in this book were developed using standard U.S. measures following U.S. government guidelines. The charts below offer equivalents for U.S. and metric measures. All conversions are approximate and have been rounded up or down to the nearest whole number. For example:

1 teaspoon = 4.9292 milliliters, rounded up to 5 milliliters
1 ounce = 28.3495 grams, rounded down to 28 grams

VOLUME CONVERSIONS

U.S.	METRIC
1 teaspoon	5 milliliters
2 teaspoons	10 milliliters
1 tablespoon	15 milliliters
2 tablespoons	30 milliliters
¼ cup	59 milliliters
⅓ cup	79 milliliters
½ cup	118 milliliters
¾ cup	177 milliliters
1 cup	237 milliliters
1¼ cups	296 milliliters
1½ cups	355 milliliters
2 cups (1 pint)	473 milliliters
2½ cups	591 milliliters
3 cups	710 milliliters
4 cups (1 quart)	0.946 liter
1.06 quarts	1 liter
4 quarts (1 gallon)	3.8 liters

WEIGHT CONVERSIONS

OUNCES	GRAMS
½	14
¾	21
1	28
1½	43
2	57
2½	71
3	85
3½	99
4	113
4½	128
5	142
6	170
7	198
8	227
9	255
10	283
12	340
16 (1 pound)	454

CONVERSIONS FOR INGREDIENTS COMMONLY USED IN BAKING

Baking is an exacting science. Because measuring by weight is far more accurate than measuring by volume, and thus more likely to achieve reliable results, in our recipes we provide ounce measures in addition to cup measures for many ingredients. Refer to the chart below to convert these measures into grams.

INGREDIENT	OUNCES	GRAMS
1 cup all-purpose flour*	5	142
1 cup whole-wheat flour	5½	156
1 cup granulated (white) sugar	7	198
1 cup packed brown sugar (light or dark)	7	198
1 cup confectioners' sugar	4	113
1 cup cocoa powder	3	85
4 tablespoons butter† (½ stick, or ¼ cup)	2	57
8 tablespoons butter† (1 stick, or ½ cup)	4	113
16 tablespoons butter† (2 sticks, or 1 cup)	8	227

* U.S. all-purpose flour, the most frequently used flour in this book, does not contain leaveners, as some European flours do. These leavened flours are called self-rising or self-raising. If you are using self-rising flour, take this into consideration before adding leavening to a recipe.

† In the United States, butter is sold both salted and unsalted. We generally recommend unsalted butter. If you are using salted butter, take this into consideration before adding salt to a recipe.

OVEN TEMPERATURES

FAHRENHEIT	CELSIUS	GAS MARK
225	105	¼
250	120	½
275	135	1
300	150	2
325	165	3
350	180	4
375	190	5
400	200	6
425	220	7
450	230	8
475	245	9

CONVERTING TEMPERATURES FROM AN INSTANT-READ THERMOMETER

We include doneness temperatures in many of the recipes in this book. We recommend an instant-read thermometer for the job. Refer to the above table to convert Fahrenheit degrees to Celsius. Or, for temperatures not represented in the chart, use this simple formula: Subtract 32 degrees from the Fahrenheit reading, then divide the result by 1.8 to find the Celsius reading.

Example: "Roast chicken until thighs register 175 degrees." To convert:

$$175°F - 32 = 143°$$
$$143° \div 1.8 = 79.44°C, \text{ rounded down to } 79°C$$

Index

A

Acetaio (vinegar maker), 393
Acetaldehyde, 14, 153
Acetic acid, 391, 393, 396
Aceto balsamico di Modena, 391
Aceto balsamico tradizionale, 391
Acidity, 6
   see also pH levels
Acid-set cheeses, about, 169
Actin, in muscle fibers, 25, 83, 107, 436
Adenosine triphosphate (ATP), defined, 436
Adipose cells, 25
Adsorbed water, 5, 300
Adsorption, 32, 60
Agaricaceae family, 197
Agglomeration, defined, 436
Aïoli, Garlic, 299
Albedo layer, on oranges, 279
Albumin, 129
Alcohol, cooking off, 373
Aldehyde, 84, 137, 192, 357, 375
Alkalinity, 6
   see also pH levels
Allicin, 14, 227, 229, 231
Alliin, 227, 228, 436
Alliinase, 227, 228, 229, 233, 436
Allium cepa, 233, 436
Alliums
   defined, 436
   types of, 227, 235
Almond(s), 407–416
   The Best Gluten-Free Pizza, 411–412
   Biscotti, 414–416
   butter, about, 409
   Cake, Best, 413–414
   Curried Cauliflower Rice, 196
   extract, about, 409
   Florentine Lace Cookies, 404–405
   flour, about, 409
   forms of, 407
   four parts of, 407

Almond(s) (cont.)
   and Garlic Soup, Spanish Chilled, 410–411
   Granola with Dried Fruit, 333
   harvesting of, 407
   Milk
      about, 409
      baking with, 286
      homemade versus store-bought, 408
      recipe, 416
   -Mint Relish, Sweet, Roast Rack of Lamb with, 78
   paste, about, 409
   pasteurization of, 407
   products made from, 409
   Rich Chocolate Tart, 400–401
   science of, 407
   Smoked, Radicchio, and Dates, Citrus Salad with, 283
   test kitchen experiment, 408
   wild, toxicity of, 416
Alpha- and beta-amylase, 385
Alpha-s1-casein, 162
Altitude, and canning temperature, 283
Aluminum, 11
American cheese
   Philly Cheesesteaks, 32
   taste tests on, 420
America's Test Kitchen process
   "five-recipe test" for magazine recipes, 2
   independent lab testing, 3
   quantitative instruments, 3
   scientific method, 2
Amino acids, 7, 8, 167
Amino group (-N-H), 5
Ammonia, 213
Ampeloprasum species, 232
Amphoteric, defined, 436
Amygdalin, 263, 264, 407, 416
Amylase, 183, 184
Amylopectin
   defined, 436
   description of, 9
   in high-starch potatoes, 185

Bacteria

for cabbage fermentation, 213, 214

in deceased lobster, 113

destroying, with boiling-water canning, 271

effect of pH on, 6

in fish skin, 88

high-moisture foods and, 5, 300

in honey, 388

for kimchi fermentation, 214

for natural fermentation, 215

preventing, in meat-curing process, 52

in raw chicken, 59, 64

in rice, 317

in unpasteurized almonds, 407

for yogurt fermentation, 153, 155

***Badessa*, 393**

Baked Brown Rice, 316

Baked Sweet Potatoes, 186

Baking soda, for chile burns, 252

Balsamic Vinegar, 391–396

and Grapes, Italian Sausage with, 395–396

how it is made, 391

Make-Ahead Vinaigrette, 394

of Modena (BV), taste profile, 396

of Modena (BV), taste tests on, 435

science of, 391

Strawberries with, 396

supermarket, about, 391

test kitchen experiment, 392

traditional (TBV), effect on vinaigrette emulsions, 392

traditional (TBV), grades of, 391

traditional (TBV), how it is made, 393

traditional (TBV), pH of, 393

traditional (TBV), regulation of, 391

traditional (TBV), taste profile, 396

Banh Mi, Tofu, 124–125

Barbecue Sauces

bottled, taste tests on, 418

Mustard, South Carolina, 48

Sweet and Tangy, 47–48

Vinegar, Lexington, 48

Barbecuing, compared with grilling, 45

Barrels, for aging vinegar, 393

Bars

Fudgy Triple-Chocolate Brownies, 405–406

Honey-Lemon Squares, 387–388

Bartoshuk, Linda, 14

Basil

Garlicky Spaghetti with Lemon and Pine Nuts, 360

Garlic Oil, and Three Cheeses, Thin-Crust Whole-Wheat Pizza with, 306–307

Grilled Portobello Burgers, 203–204

Pasta with Pesto, Potatoes, and Green Beans, 181

Pasta with Raw Tomato Sauce, 226

Thin-Crust Whole-Wheat Pizza with Pesto and Goat Cheese, 307

Vinaigrette, 110

***Batteria*, 393**

Baumé, Antoine, 365

Beans

Best Ground Beef Chili, 346–347

Black, and Cilantro, Hearty Baked Brown Rice with, 317

brining, 351

canned

baked, taste tests on, 418

black, taste tests on, 418

chickpeas, taste tests on, 418

red kidney, taste tests on, 418

substituting for dried, 348

Edamame, and Cannellini Bean Dip with Tarragon, 347–348

Refried, Simple, 31

soy, dried, average water content, 4

Ultimate Beef Chili, 259–260

Ultimate Vegetarian Chili, 257–259

wax, about, 182

see also Cannellini Bean(s); Green Beans

Beef

brining, note about, 351

brisket/plate, about, 17

broth, store-bought, ingredients in, 370

broth, store-bought, taste tests on, 370, 419

Chateaubriand, about, 15

Chili, Ultimate, 259–260

chuck (or shoulder), about, 17

Crispy Orange, 280–281

flank section, 23–32

about, 17

cuts from, 17

science of, 23

Flank Steaks

Bistro-Style, 26

collagen in, 23

cutting against the grain, 23, 24

flavor and texture, 23

Grilled Beef Satay, 28–29

Mexican-Style Grilled Steak (Carne Asada), 30–31

test kitchen experiment, 24

Thai Grilled Beef Salad, 26–27

and ginger-based marinades, notes about, 29, 244

grass-fed versus grain-fed, 20

Ground, Chili, Best, 346–347

hot dogs, taste tests on, 425

and Onion Ragu, Rigatoni with, 236–237

Philly Cheesesteaks, 32

Pho, Vietnamese, 369–371

primal cuts, 17

Ragu alla Bolognese, 380–381

rib section, cuts from, 17

round section, cuts from, 17

Satay, Grilled, 28–29

short loin section, 15–22

retail cuts from, 15, 17

science of, 15

C

Cabbage, 213–220
California Fish Tacos, 87–88
fermentation process, 213
fermented foods made with, 213, 215
French-Style Pork Stew, 50
Kimchi, 217–218
kimchi, about, 213
kimchi fermentation experiment, 214
Red, Braised, 219–220
red, color change after cooking, 220
red and green, swapping, 218
Sauerkraut, 216
sauerkraut, about, 213
Sautéed
   with Bacon and Caraway Seeds, 219
   with Chile and Peanuts, 219
   with Fennel and Garlic, 219
   with Parsley and Lemon, 218–219
science of, 213
taste and smell, 213
test kitchen experiment, 214
Tofu and Vegetable Salad, 122–123

Cacao nibs, 399

Cacao tree, 399

Cacio e Pepe (Spaghetti with Pecorino Romano and Black Pepper), 296–297

Caesar Salad, Kale, 212

Cakes
Almond, Best, 413–414
Apple, French, 264–265
Coconut Layer, 288–289
Gingerbread, Classic, 249–250
Honey, 389–390
Orange Bundt, 281–282
Pound, Cold-Oven, 147–148
Triple-Chocolate Mousse, 140–142

Calcium, 11, 351

Calcium chloride, 341, 342

Calcium disodium EDTA, 341

Calcium ions, 9

Calcium pectate, 341

Calcium sulfate, 119, 121

Caldo Verde, 210–211

California Fish Tacos, 87–88

Calpains, 33

Cannellini Bean(s), 341–348
canned, cooking with, 341
canned, taste tests on, 343, 419
canning process, 341, 343
cooked dried, calcium in, 342
cooked dried, taste tests on, 342
and Edamame Dip with Tarragon, 347–348
history of, 341

Cannellini Bean(s) (cont.)
Modern Succotash with Fennel and Scallions, 345
Pasta with Beans, Chard, and Rosemary, 344–345
science of, 341
test kitchen experiment, 342
texture and flavor, 341

Canning inserts, 271

Canning pots, 271

Canning temperature, and altitude, 283

Canthaxanthin, 89

Caper(s)
and Currants, Garlicky Spaghetti with, 361
Onion, and Olive Relish, 387
"Smoked Salmon Platter" Sauce, 93

Capsaicins, 243, 245, 251, 252, 253, 256

Capsicum genus, 251

Caramelization, defined, 436

Caramel Tofu, 123–124

Caraway Seeds and Bacon, Sautéed Cabbage with, 219

Carbohydrates, 8–9

Carbon dioxide, 127, 305, 375

Carême, Marie-Antoine, 365

Carne Asada (Mexican-Style Grilled Steak), 30–31

Carotene, 162

Carotenoids, 115, 191, 205, 277, 436

Carrot(s)
Best Chicken Stew, 72
and Cilantro, Lentil Salad with, 353
-Ginger Soup, 246–247
and Leeks, Cod Baked in Foil with, 85–86
Simple Pot-au-Feu, 237–238
Tofu Banh Mi, 124–125
Vegetable Broth Base, 371–372

Casalagin, 396

Casein
in cream, 42, 135
defined, 436
in goat's milk, 161, 162
in hard cheeses, 167
in milk, 37, 163, 169

Casein micelles, 163, 169

Cashews and Raisins, Indian-Spiced Mashed Sweet Potatoes with, 187

Cathepsins, defined, 436

Cauliflower, 191–196
colored, about, 191, 193
cooking, effect on flavor, 191, 192, 193
fiber in, 191
origins of, 191
Rice, 196
Rice, Curried, 196
Rice, Tex-Mex, 196
Roasted, 195
   with Bacon and Scallions, 195
   with Curry and Lime, 195–196
   with Paprika and Chorizo, 196

F

N

Naan (Indian Flatbread), 158–159
N-acetylglucasocamine, 197
Nectar, and honey flavors, 390
Neohesperidin, 277
Neral compounds, 243
New England Fish Chowder, 86
New England Lobster Roll, 117
Nigari-type coagulants, 119, 121
Nightshade family, 221, 251
Nitrites and nitrates, 52
Nitrogen, in soil, 356
Nixtamalization, 328
No-Knead Brioche, 150–151
Nontasters, 14
Noodles
  egg, taste tests on, 429
  lasagna, taste tests on, 429
  Vietnamese Beef Pho, 369–371
Nucleotides
  defined, 438
  in mushrooms, 197
  pairing with glutamates, 87, 277
  in shrimp cells, 97, 99
  in yeast extract, 370
Nut(s)
  Asian-Style Sweet Potato Salad, 190
  Best Baked Apples, 267–268
  Caramel Tofu, 123–124
  Citrus Salad with Watercress, Dried Cranberries, and Pecans, 282
  Indian-Spiced Mashed Sweet Potatoes with Raisins and
      Cashews, 187
  Oatmeal Muffins, 332–333
  Peanut Sauce, 29
  Pistachio-Spice Biscotti, 416
  Sautéed Cabbage with Chile and Peanuts, 219
  Thai Chicken Curry with Potatoes and Peanuts, 291–292
  Toasted, and Parsley Pesto, 231–232
  see also Almond(s); Hazelnut(s); Pine Nuts; Walnut(s)

O

Oat groats, about, 329, 331
Oatmeal
  Muffins, 332–333
  steel-cut, reducing cooking time for, 330
  Ten-Minute Steel-Cut, 334
Oats, 329–334
  Almond Granola with Dried Fruit, 333
  fat in, 329

Oats (cont.)
  FDA health claims and, 329
  health benefits, 329
  instant, about, 329, 331
  oat bran, about, 329
  Oatmeal Muffins, 332–333
  rolled, quick-cooking, about, 329, 331
  rolled, regular, about, 329, 331
  rolled, taste tests on, 428
  science of, 329
  steel-cut, about, 329, 331
  steel-cut, reducing cooking time for, 330
  steel-cut, taste tests on, 428
  stone-ground (Scottish), about, 331
  taste tests on, 428
  Ten-Minute Steel-Cut Oatmeal, 334
  test kitchen experiment, 330
  thickening soups with, 334
  three parts of, 329
Octalactone, 137
Oils
  rancidity of, 11
  smoke point, 11
  vegetable, taste tests on, 434
  see also Olive Oil
Oligosaccharides, 8–9
Olive Oil, 357–364
  extra-virgin, flavor loss after cooking, 58
  extra-virgin, processing method, 359
  extra-virgin, smoke point, 11
  extra-virgin, standards for, 357
  extra-virgin, taste tests on, 428
  flavor of, 357
  Focaccia with Kalamata Olives and Anchovies, 364
  Garlicky Spaghetti with Artichokes and Hazelnuts, 361
  Garlicky Spaghetti with Capers and Currants, 361
  Garlicky Spaghetti with Lemon and Pine Nuts, 360
  Garlic Oil, 306–307
  and Lemon, Grilled Tuscan Steaks with, 21–22
  light, about, 360
  lower grades of, 359
  Make-Ahead Vinaigrette, 394
  Poached Fish Fillets with Artichokes and Sherry-Tomato
      Vinaigrette, 361–362
  Poached Fish Fillets with Miso-Ginger Vinaigrette, 362
  Rosemary Focaccia, 363–364
  science of, 357
  specific heat capacity, 358
  supermarket, taste tests on, 428
  test kitchen experiment, 358
Olive(s)
  for extra-virgin olive oil, 359
  Greek Cherry Tomato Salad, 225–226
  Kalamata, and Anchovies, Focaccia with, 364
  Mint, and Feta, Lentil Salad with, 352–353

U

Ultimate Beef Chili, 259–260
Ultimate Vegetarian Chili, 257–259
Ultra-high temperature (UHT) pasteurization, 135
Umami flavor
  defined, 440
  discovery of, 12
  in mushrooms, 197
  in oranges, 277
  from pairing nucleotides and glutamates, 87, 99, 197, 277
  in scallops, 105
  in shrimp shells, 97, 98, 99
  in tomato jelly, 221, 223
Uncultured celery powder, 52
Unsaturated fat, 10
Unsaturated fatty acid, defined, 440
USDA grading standards for lentils, 349
USDA meat grading system, 28
USDA olive oil standards, 357

V

Vacuum-sealed bags, 61
Vanilla
  beans, taste tests on, 434
  extract, taste tests on, 434
  ice cream, taste tests on, 426
Varenne, François Pierre de La, 365
Veal
  Ragu alla Bolognese, 380–381
Vegetable oil, taste tests on, 434
Vegetable(s)
  brassica, about, 193
  Broth Base, 371–372
  cruciferous, about, 191, 193
  pH values, 271
  Spring, Pasta, 299–300
  and Tofu Salad, 122–123
  see also specific vegetables
Vegetarian broth, taste tests on, 419
Vents, in charcoal grill, 45
Vents, in smokers, 91
Vescalagin, 396
Video Imaging Analysis (VIA), 28
Vietnamese Beef Pho, 369–371
Vinaigrettes
  with aged balsamic, long-lasting emulsion of, 392
  Basil, 110
  Chile-Lime, 110
  Make-Ahead, 394

Vinaigrettes (cont.)
  Miso-Ginger, Poached Fish Fillets with, 362
  Orange-Lime, 109
  Sherry-Tomato, Poached Fish Fillets with, 361–362
  Tomato-Ginger, Warm, 62
  whisking, 128
Vinegar
  about, 215
  antibacterial properties, 391
  Barbecue Sauce, Lexington, 48
  culinary history, 391
  how it is made, 391
  Make-Ahead Vinaigrette, 394
  -Pepper Pan Sauce, Crispy-Skinned Chicken Breasts with, 65–66
  Sauce, 46–47
  taste tests on, 434–435
  see also Balsamic Vinegar
Violaxanthin, 277
Viscosity, defined, 440
Vitamin A, 11, 205
Vitamin B$_{12}$, 11
Vitamin C, 11, 205
Vitamin D2, 199
Vitis vinifera, 373
Volatile, defined, 440

W

Walnut(s)
  Apples, Dried Cherries, and Herbed Baked Goat Cheese, Salad with, 165
  Arugula, and Golden Raisins, Citrus Salad with, 283
  -Honey Yogurt Cheese, 156
  Spinach, and Parmesan Cheese, Lentil Salad with, 353
  Stuffed Mushrooms with Spinach and Goat Cheese, 201–202
  Ultimate Vegetarian Chili, 257–259
Warm Tomato-Ginger Vinaigrette, 62
Water, 4–6
  activity of food (Aw), 5, 300, 440
  adsorbed, 5, 300
  boiling point, 5
  bound, 5, 300, 436
  content, of common foods, 4
  free, 5, 300
  holding capacity, defined, 440
  molecular structure, 4–5
  in muscle fibers, 25
  pure, pH of, 6, 302
  role of, in pH of food, 6
  three forms, in food, 5
  why it forms into ice, 5

Y

Z